J2EE™ Applications and BEA WebLogic Server™

2nd Edition

J2EE™ Applications and BEA WebLogic Server™

2nd Edition

Angela Yochem
David Carlson
Tad Stephens

PRENTICE
HALL
PTR

Prentice Hall PTR, Upper Saddle River, NJ 07458
www.phptr.com

Library of Congress Cataloging-in-Publication Data

CIP date available.

Editorial/Production Supervision: *Mary Sudul*
Page Layout: *FASTpages*
Acquisitions Editor: *Gregory G. Doench*
Editorial Assistant: *Raquel Kaplan*
Manufacturing manager: *Alexis Heydt-Long*
Art Director: *Gail Cocker-Bogusz*
Interior Series Design: *Meg Van Arsdale*
Cover Design: *Design Source*
Cover Design Direction: *Jerry Votta*

© 2004 by Pearson Education Inc.
Publishing as Prentice Hall PTR
Upper Saddle River, NJ 07458

The first edition of J2EE Applications and BEA WebLogic Server by Michael Girdley, Rob Woollen, and Sandra L. Emerson was orginally published by Prentice-Hall, Inc. Copyright 2002.

Prentice Hall books are widely used by corporations and government agencies for training,

marketing, and resale.

The publisher offers discounts on this book when ordered in bulk quantities. For more information, contact Corporate Sales Department, phone: 800-382-3419; fax: 201-236-7141; email: corpsales@prenhall.com Or write Corporate Sales Department, Prentice Hall PTR, One Lake Street, Upper Saddle River, NJ 07458.

Product and company names mentioned herein are the trademarks or registered trademarks of their respective owners.

Printed in the United States of America

10 9 8 7 6 5 4 3 2 1

ISBN 0-13-101552-4

Pearson Education LTD.
Pearson Education Australia PTY, Limited
Pearson Education Singapore, Pte. Ltd.
Pearson Education North Asia Ltd.
Pearson Education Canada, Ltd.
Pearson Educación de Mexico, S.A. de C.V.
Pearson Education — Japan
Pearson Education Malaysia, Pte. Ltd.

Thanks to my wonderful family—Dan, Grace, Joy, Jo, Jerry, Karen, Dan R., and Eric. I am grateful for your love and support.
—*Angela Yochem*

For Madelyn, Sam, and Nicole.
—*David Carlson*

Thanks to Diane, Matt, Lew, and Jake for your patience and support. We have this treasure in earthen vessels to show that this power is from above and not of us.
—*Tad Stephens*

contents

Chapter 16   WebLogic Workshop 503

Chapter 17   Capacity Planning for the WebLogic Server 533

- WebLogic Server Overview
- How to Use This Book: Roadmap
- System Requirements and Conventions

What Is BEA WebLogic Server?

BEA WebLogic Server is the market-leading application server for enterprise-level, multitier, fully distributed applications. WebLogic Server's implementation of J2EE 1.3 technologies, Web services, and related standards make it the de facto industry standard for developing and deploying Java-based Web applications.

BEA WebLogic Server offers efficient use of system resources such as client and database connections. It can support commerce applications for millions of users and hundreds of thousands of requests per hour. It supports clustering of server instances for reliability, scalability, and high performance. It maintains and manages application logic and business rules for a variety of clients.

In this book, you will learn about BEA's implementation of Sun Microsystems' Java 2 Platform Enterprise Edition (J2EE). This preface and Chapter 1 introduce many acronyms that are part of the J2EE suite of technologies. The remaining chapters in the book cover many of these technologies in detail. No prior knowledge of J2EE technology is assumed, so if the J2EE terminology makes no sense at this point, don't worry. The remaining chapters provide an introduction to the J2EE specification and the WebLogic Server implementation.

WebLogic Server Overview

Figure 1 shows a typical multitier WebLogic Server configuration. Clients include Web browsers and application clients. The WebLogic Server tier is usually a *cluster* of cooperating WebLogic Servers.

The pentagon is the WebLogic Server container, a complex concept encompassing a wide variety of services and facilities.

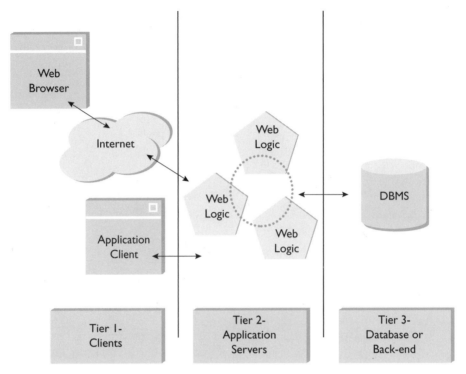

Figure 1
Typical BEA WebLogic Server configuration.

The Container-Component Model

The WebLogic Server platform (in Java parlance) can be thought of as a *container* that provides services to *components* of user applications. Components such as EJBs, JavaServer Pages (JSPs), and servlets reside in the WebLogic Server container and take advantage of the services provided by it.

In Figure 2, the WebLogic Server container (the large pentagon) encloses various J2EE services. Interconnections of services are depicted with lines and arrows. WebLogic Server management (via the WebLogic Management Framework) and security are shown as layers external to the container.

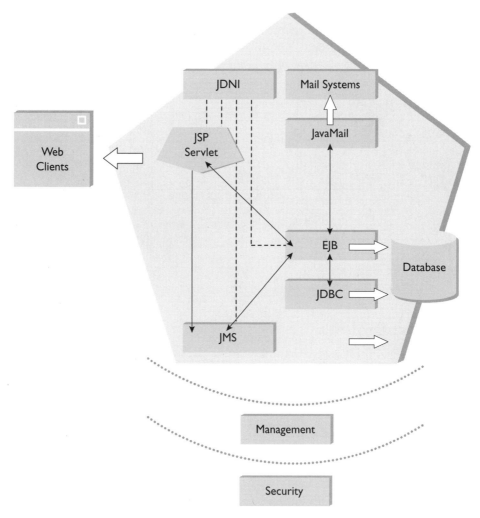

Figure 2
A Snapshot of the WebLogic Server container.

WebLogic Platform Overview

BEA's WebLogic Platform is a complete application infrastructure platform, enabling developers to build and integrate enterprise applications easily and rapidly. WebLogic Platform is designed to address end-to-end problems for the enterprise, providing standards-based frameworks to help you build, test, and deploy J2EE applications, business processes, workflows, messaging applications, enterprise portals, trading partner applications, and more.

WebLogic Platform consists of a suite of products, including WebLogic Server, WebLogic Integration Server, WebLogic Portal Server, WebLogic Workshop, and WebLogic JRocket JVM. These products share a common infrastructure and common tools, making WebLogic Platform an excellent choice for building and integrating enterprise applications.

Chapter 18 provides an overview of WebLogic Platform components and how they relate to one another.

How to Use This Book

J2EE *Applications and* BEA *WebLogic Server* contains 18 chapters, each of which covers a phase of developing Web-based applications using J2EE and WebLogic Server. Each chapter is organized around a particular Java Enterprise technology that you use to create a component of the *WebAuction* application, an online auction site that functions as the core example set for this book. The discussion of EJBs, which are the major players in J2EE application development, spans three chapters.

Each chapter notes where an application module fits in an overall application design; how to plan for efficient implementation; the specifics of the example implementation; and recommendations for best practices that can guide the implementation of a similar component at your site.

The Enterprise Java APIs and associated APIs that are part of the J2EE specification are discussed in this book in the approximate order in which a developer might use them. However, each technology is described and illustrated without dependencies on material covered in any other chapter.

Road Map

Whether you're an experienced Java developer or a novice, we assume that you're just getting started with developing applications for an application server. Because individual application development styles differ, each chapter is self-contained. You can read the chapters in the order that best suits your development style.

After getting a basic idea of the concepts and best practices for each technology, the developer can begin to design some of the major modules, such as the EJBs for the server-side logic, or the JSPs for the user interface.

In narrative form, the chapters follow this sequence: First, the developer can *prototype the user interface*, coding the server-side presentation logic in servlets (Chapters 2 and 3) and JSPs (Chapter 4). The Model-View-Controller (MVC) design pattern is explained in detail in these chapters.

When the basic outline of the application behavior is known, the developer can *plan for database connectivity* with JDBC and transactions (Chapter 5).

As application modules emerge, the developer sets up the central registry for object and method names, and the framework for Remote Method Invocation, or RMI (Chapter 6).

In order to ensure efficient performance when executing an application over a cluster of WebLogic Servers, the developer uses the JMS protocol to *set up the middleware-oriented messaging layer* to sequence and manage correct object behaviors (Chapter 7).

To ensure application component independence and to take maximum advantage of the WebLogic Server container's services, the developer *codes the* EJBs, which are at the heart of the application's functionality (Chapters 8, 9, and 10).

To include email functionality, the developer *connects the application to Internet mail* using the Java-Mail protocol (Chapter 11).

After unit testing, the developer *plans for deployment* of the completed application, surveying the hardware and software elements that need to interoperate when an application is deployed. WebLogic management and administration services allow applications to be deployed in production environments and allow those environments to be monitored for enterprise-quality availability and reliability. (Chapter 12). It is also necessary to implement and enforce appropriate levels of security (Chapter 13) based on the needs of the application and the business, which can be done with a combination of WebLogic Server features and J2EE security functions.

After the deployment design, methodology, and tools have been surveyed, the developer *compiles, tests, and deploys* the completed application (Chapter 14), following best practices and guidelines learned from years of experience.

An example application for review and deployment is outlined in Chapter 15 (the WebAuction application). BEA's unified development environment, WebLogic Workshop, offers an easy-to-use, intuitive suite of services for the J2EE and Web Services programmer. (Chapter 16). WebLogic Platform builds on the capabilities of WebLogic Server 8.1 by adding user presentation, business process management, data integration, and back-office system access in a complete, end-to-end application framework (Chapter 18).

An introduction to Web Services is found in Appendix A.

System Requirements

This book and accompanying CD-ROM can be used standalone as a learning tool.

Complete documentation for BEA WebLogic Server and other BEA products is available at *http://e-docs.bea.com*.

Supported Platforms

Supported platforms for BEA WebLogic Server include (among others) Windows 2000, Windows NT, and UNIX systems. For a complete list of supported platforms, refer to the BEA WebLogic Server data sheet at *www.bea.com/products/weblogic/server/datasheet.shtml*.

Software on the CD-ROM

The WebLogic Server and the other software necessary to develop the sample application are included on the CD-ROM that accompanies this book:

- WebLogic Server 8.1 evaluation copy
- WebLogic Server Administration Framework
- WebLogic Workshop
- Source code for the WebAuction application
- WebAuction application data, JSPs, EJBs, build scripts, and so forth

Developers can use the PointBase all-Java relational database (included as part of the WebLogic Server product suite), for prototyping. WebLogic Server supports many other commercial databases, including those from Oracle, Sybase, Informix, and IBM (DB2).

Versions Supported

Versions of BEA WebLogic Server tested for this book include

- WebLogic Server 8.1, Service Pack 2
- Check the BEA Web site at *www.bea.com* for news on the latest supported versions of J2EE technologies.

Conventions

This book uses the following typographic conventions:

Italics	Glossary terms
	Emphasis
	Names of files, scripts, directory paths, URLs
	Chapter names, book titles, and other proper names
	Web addresses
`Courier`	Names of Java programming elements, including object names, method names, classnames, variable names
	Code in general
Boldface	Default values
	Emphasis
Sidebars	Best Practice
	Note

acknowledgments

The authors would like to thank Bill Wentworth, M. Denise Cook, Jack Zheng, Matt Quinlan, Naveen Narula, Jame Holmes, Carl Sjogreen, and Samir Kothari for their gracious dedication of time and thoughtful reviews of the chapters in this book.

chapter 1

Overview

In This Chapter

- Overview of BEA WebLogic Server's support for the Sun Microsystems Java 2 Enterprise Edition (J2EE) platform
- Brief description of WebLogic Server's distributed deployment support
- The WebAuction sample application's use of J2EE technologies

WebLogic Server and J2EE

Sun Microsystems' J2EE framework was unveiled at the Java One conference in 1997. J2EE defines the standard for developing and deploying enterprise-level Web applications. With J2EE, the developer-friendly Java language and tools are extended for use in complex, multitier e-commerce and enterprise-level applications. J2EE provides broad support for the *component* model of development, providing tools and services for business logic in modular, reusable, platform-independent components.

J2EE Technologies Covered in This Book

J2EE Applications and BEA WebLogic Server covers the following J2EE technologies, all of which have been implemented in WebLogic Server according to the specifications certified by Sun. Table 1-1 is a brief summary of the J2EE technologies we cover in this book.

Table 1-1 J2EE Technologies

J2EE Service	Purpose
WebLogic Servlets	Presentation Logic
WebLogic JavaServer Pages (JSP)	Presentation Logic
WebLogic Java Database Connectivity (JDBC)	Access to Data Repositories
WebLogic Java Transaction API (JTA)	Transaction Management
WebLogic Java Naming and Directory Interface (JNDI)	Central Registry for Object Names

Table 1–1   J2EE Technologies *(continued)*

J2EE Service	Purpose
WebLogic Remote Method Invocation (RMI)	Distributed Execution of RMI Objects
WebLogic Enterprise JavaBeans (EJB)	Implementing Business Logic
WebLogic Java Message Service (JMS)	Coordinating Distributed Execution

Presentation Logic

Presentation logic is the server-side code in a WebLogic Server application that determines the client-side response to a specific request. For example, your presentation logic can be as simple as "report the time of day when a request is received." Coding server-side presentation logic can be done using Java servlets, JSPs, JavaBeans, and tag libraries.

Java Servlets

The Java servlet is a server-side technology that accepts HTTP requests from a Web browser and returns HTTP responses. Servlets can be multithreaded and offer signifcant performance advantages over mechanisms like Common Gateway Interface (CGI) for coding presentation logic. Because servlets are written in Java, they are portable from one platform to another. Servlets are an enterprise Java standard for the development of presentation logic.

WebLogic Server servlets act on the *request-response model*. Requests come into the servlet engine. The WebLogic Server servlet engine then executes the appropriate servlet, accesses the response object, and returns a response to the client. The servlet engine provides standard services to the servlet, including authentication, parallel execution, memory management, and the like.

The most commonly used servlet type is the HTTP servlet designed to fill HTTP (Web) requests. WebLogic Server supports *only* HTTP servlets.

HTTP servlets provide the following core features:

- `HttpServletRequest` objects capture request details from requests submitted via Web page forms, including data availability, protocol types, security levels, and so forth.
- `HttpSession` objects specific to each user handle user-session information in the server. The servlet developer can add and remove information about the user during execution of the servlet.
- `HttpServletResponse` objects capture response details. The servlet developer can output everything that is sent back to the client making the request. The servlet engine handles the rest.

Chapter 2 discusses how to integrate and build servlets for your application.

JavaServer Pages

The JSP technology gives developers a simple, HTML-like interface for creating servlets. JSPs can contain HTML code, Java code, and code modules called JavaBeans. JSPs reverse the structure of servlets. Rather than awkwardly embedding HTML markup in Java code, JSPs center around the markup. The JSP includes special tags and syntax to include Java code.

When a JSP page is requested for the first time, the application server compiles that page into a servlet. This servlet is then executed to serve further requests. In this way, the servlet engine and the JSP engine are intimately tied together, and JSPs can take advantage of the services provided by the servlet engine.

Chapter 4 describes and illustrates the technical details for using JSPs in a WebLogic Server application.

WebLogic Server JavaBeans and Tag Libraries

JavaBeans (which are different from EJBs) are Java components (classes) that developers use in WebLogic Server applications to encapsulate data either for display or for actions against the database. Developers create classfiles with a number of methods, which are typically used to get and set values.

JSP pages have special tags for including JavaBeans and automatically populating them with values. The JSP page calls methods on those JavaBeans to help create its HTML output.

Tag libraries supply custom HTML-like tags for use in JSP pages. Tag libraries abstract Java code into tags that can be easily manipulated by Web editors and designers. To build a tag library, a developer creates classfiles and a file called a Tag Library Descriptor that lists the available tags from the tag library.

JavaBeans and tag libraries manage the data and Java code that interacts with the data sources available via JDBC and EJB. As we cover in subsequent chapters, JavaBeans and tag libraries perform a valuable service by enabling Web application developers to keep explicit Java code out of JSP pages and servlets. This modularization minimizes the chance of accidental damage to the JSP page during an HTML editing session and permits presentation logic to be changed independent of the JSP page. Chapter 4 contains more information on the techniques and development of JavaBeans and tag libraries.

Database and Transaction Support

Database and transaction support is provided (behind the scenes) by JDBC and the JTA. The high-level interface to database use is provided by EJB.

Java Database Connectivity

JDBC is the Java standard for database connectivity. The JDBC specification provides everything needed to connect to databases from a standard set of Java APIs. Vendors supply JDBC "drivers" that map this standard set of Java APIs to the specifics of the underlying database.

WebLogic Server provides a number of JDBC drivers for different databases. You can, however, use almost any JDBC driver for a WebLogic Server–supported database, even drivers from vendors other than BEA Systems. WebLogic Server 8.1 supports JDBC drivers for Oracle, MS SQL Server, Sybase, Informix, DB2, and Pointbase.

Note that JDBC is the bridge that connects WebLogic Server with the database, from a programming standpoint. This functionality is transparent to the programmer: it's provided by EJB. The developer does not program JDBC directly except in special cases.

The typical WebLogic Server application relies on a database for key e-commerce application functionality such as transaction support, support for concurrent data access, and data integrity features. Relational databases support a common declarative language for access called Structured

Query Language (SQL). WebLogic Server's JDBC and SQL are covered in Chapter 5. Chapter 5 also discusses transactions and the JTA.

WebLogic Server JDBC provides the following functionality:

- APIs *for operations that modify the database.* These operations include SQL updates and administrative commands.
- APIs *for operations that read from the database by making SQL queries to the database.* These queries return ResultSet Java objects, which return results of JDBC database queries. These objects enable J2EE developers to programmatically access (via standard APIs) the values returned by a given SQL query.
- *Support for basic transactions.* JDBC provides an "automatic commit" of simple SQL statements. So, a simple single method call can pass a SQL statement directly to the database, and changes are automatically committed to the database.
- *Support for complex transactions.* WebLogic Server provides a service called JTA, which provides the capability to begin transactions and propagate them across multiple J2EE services and WebLogic Server.

Java Transaction API Support

JTA gives Web application developers access to the transaction functions in database systems or any legacy data store. Transactions coordinate single-database and multidatabase operations to ensure that all data resources remain accurate and consistent and that operations against the database are repeatable and durable. Transaction management is essential for enterprise-level e-commerce applications, which need to be Web-based and fault-tolerant.

JTA defines a high-level transaction management specification for resource managers for distributed applications. WebLogic Server 8.1 transaction services provide connectivity and support for database transaction functionality, most notably the two-phase commit (2PC) engine used to manage multidatabase transactions. Chapter 5 reviews the transactional capabilities of WebLogic Server 8.1 as well as the architectural approaches and the impact these can have on transactional solutions.

Object Registry and Remote Method Invocation

JNDI and RMI support naming services and remote method execution.

Java Naming and Directory Interface

JNDI is the Java standard for the "central registry" of naming and directory services. JNDI manages references to the core components needed to build distributed applications. When a developer builds an application that accesses a remote object, JNDI provides the application with a way to locate that object. The JNDI technology is the interface to naming and directory services and acts as a central registry for named application and data objects. The JNDI services help assure the proper level of uniqueness in the names of application components and help prevent, diagnose, and treat naming conflicts that might arise.

WebLogic Server implements JNDI as part of its platform. Application developers can store, modify, and remove references to Java components and resources in the WebLogic Server JNDI implementation. In the case of WebLogic Server clustering, JNDI is also used as the shared-naming service across the entire cluster.

The usage pattern of JNDI is relatively simple. Application developers do an initial lookup to find the object that they require in the WebLogic Server deployment. WebLogic Server services will return everything the application needs to access that object.

JNDI and the complete interfaces to build a WebLogic Server application that uses JNDI are covered in Chapter 6.

Remote Method Invocation

RMI is the Java standard that a Java application uses to make a method call on a remote Java object. RMI enables remote objects to "virtually" appear as if they are local to the application. RMI provides the framework for a distributed application and its remote clients to interact with remote methods and services. The remote host to allow calling by RMI exports the methods of remote objects. Objects can be located across the network or perhaps across your WebLogic Server cluster on another WebLogic Server implementation.

Chapter 6 covers the steps required to use RMI in your application.

Enterprise JavaBeans

EJB is the enterprise Java standard for building server-side business logic in Java. Whereas presentation logic automatically handles the type and format of information to be displayed to clients, business logic is used for operations such as funds transfers, product orders, and so forth. Developers build EJBs that take advantage of services provided by the WebLogic Server container.

This container provides services that include transaction support and security, and handles concurrency issues. All of these services are required for scalable, secure, and robust electronic commerce applications.

WebLogic Server's EJB container provides everything needed for developers to build business logic such as funds transfers, employee record management, and other functionalities.

There are four basic types of EJBs:

- Entity
- Message-driven
- Stateful session
- Stateless session

WebLogic Server Entity EJBs

Entity EJBs (*entity beans*) are the enterprise Java standard for representing data. They are standard Java language objects that reside in the WebLogic Server container.

In most cases, entity beans represent data from a database, although they also can represent data stored in other locations. In WebLogic Server deployments, beans represent data stored in a relational database, such as Oracle, IBM's DB2, and Informix.

Objects such as entity beans must be mapped to the relational structure of a relational database management system (DBMS). WebLogic Server includes *object-relational mapping technology* and also permits plug-ins that implement other mapping mechanisms.

The EJB specification defines an API for developers to create, deploy, and manage crossplatform, component-based enterprise applications. The EJB component model supports three types of components:

- Session beans, which capture business rules and methods that persist for the duration of a session
- Entity beans, which encapsulate specific data items from a database
- Message-driven beans, which integrate EJBs with the JMS

WebLogic Server makes activities such as managing transactions, concurrency issues, security, and other functionality automatic because the WebLogic Server container provides these services. When programming EJBs, developers do not have to worry about all of the low-level plumbing issues: the container takes care of that.

WebLogic Server Session EJBs

The enterprise Java standards specify two types of session beans: *stateless* and *stateful*. Stateless beans receive requests via RMI but do not keep any data associated with the client they are serving internally. Stateful beans, on the other hand, keep data specific to the client they are serving. From a developer's perspective, these two types of session beans are similar in construction. However, the way that the WebLogic Server container treats them is very different.

WebLogic Server session beans handle requests that arrive via RMI. Typically, they provide services to other Java objects. This is in contrast to servlets and JSPs, which are focused primarily on responding to requests from Web clients such as Web browsers (whose requests arrive via HTTP).

The objects that initiate requests to session beans can be any arbitrary object that is able to access the appropriate RMI client classes. In the case of WebLogic Server deployments, these Java objects are typically application clients. However, it is also possible for servlets and JSPs to be RMI clients to session beans. Use session beans to implement business logic on the server side for your application clients, servlets, or JSPs.

WebLogic Server Message-Driven Beans

With Version 2.0, the EJB specification added a completely new type of EJB and the option to use an entirely new execution paradigm in enterprise Java applications. In both entity beans and session beans, a synchronous programming model is used. Clients make requests to the EJB and wait for work to be completed on their behalf. Using message-driven beans (MDBs), the EJB is not attached to a client. Instead, it is attached to a message queue or topic defined in the JMS, as described later. When a message arrives, a method on the EJB is executed.

MDBs introduce an *asynchronous* processing paradigm to enterprise Java applications. Tasks can be queued and made available for processing when resources are available.

Use MDBs when your application requires asynchronous processing for tasks such as sending email responses or tabulating the winners of this month's lottery.

Java Message Service

The JMS specification provides developers with a standard Java API for enterprise messaging services such as reliable queuing, publish and subscribe communication, and various aspects of push/pull technologies. JMS is the enterprise Java standard for messaging. It enables applications and components in Java to send and receive messages. WebLogic Server provides a complete implementation of the JMS standard.

There are several paradigms for messaging in JMS, including:

- Queue model
- Topic-based, publish-subscribe system

The queue model enables JMS clients to push messages onto a JMS queue. Clients can then retrieve these messages. The topic-based model enables publishers to send messages to registered subscribers of the JMS topic.

WebLogic Server adds a number of features in its implementation of the JMS specification that are allowed by the specification but are not part of Sun's reference implementation:

- *Implementation of a guaranteed messaging service*. This messaging service uses the database or a file storage mechanism to make sure that messages are durable (able to persist when either the server or the client goes down).
- *Message filtering*. The WebLogic Server JMS implementation enables you to designate rules to filter the distribution of messages.

JavaMail

The JavaMail API provides classes that support a simple email and messaging service as well as connections to any standard email system. The JavaMail interface provides a standard, object-oriented protocol for connecting to many different types of email systems. Chapter 11 covers JavaMail.

Administration

New features in the WebLogic Server 8.1 release include broader, more enterprise-ready administration services. Long gone is the *weblogic.properties* file, replaced by an intuitive, easy-to-use, browser-based console, full-featured command-line interfaces, XML-based configuration files and deployment descriptors, and a wide range of wizards and utilities to guide both the novice and expert WebLogic administrator. The WebLogic Server 8.1 management framework is based on the Java Management eXtentions (JMX), a key JavaSoft standard for managing distributed Java components. JMX is used for WebLogic's own management environment and can easily be extended and integrated with third-party management tools and consoles as well as custom-developed solutions to meet specific needs. Chapter 12 introduces WebLogic Server's administration services, the technologies behind these services, and examples of deployment and management of a production environment.

Security

WebLogic Server supports a complete and comprehensive security solution based on the J2EE security services, leveraging the Java Authentication and Authorization Service (JAAS). This framework includes services for authentication, authorization, auditing, logging, and encryption and data privacy. In addition, WebLogic Server extends the J2EE security model in key ways, making it easier to manage and secure robust J2EE applications in production deployments. WebLogic Server 8.1 provides a pluggable security environment that can be easily adapted to existing and external security systems, such as authentication providers, authorization services, and credential and role-mapping providers. Chapter 13 reviews the complete security approach in WebLogic Server 8.1.

WebLogic Server's Distributed Deployment Support

In addition to J2EE technologies, WebLogic Server provides several important APIs and extensions to J2EE APIs that help provide reliable, scalable performance for a distributed application. The WebLogic Server clustering technology permits interconnection of several WebLogic Server instances (one per CPU) on a LAN so that the WebLogic Servers in a cluster can distribute workload and provide fault-tolerance as application demands increase.

Scenarios for distributed deployment are discussed througout the book, with specific emphasis in Chapter 15. Included there you will find an overview of WebLogic JRockit, BEA's high-performance server-side Java Virtual Machine (JVM), a review of the various deployment architectures, and a review of the mechanics of packaging, building, and deploying a moderately complex sample application called WebAuction.

WebLogic Platform 8.1

Throughout this book, the focus is on WebLogic Server and how the various J2EE technologies are implemented in the industry's leading application server. There are development recommendations, deployment best practices, and guidelines for securing a Web-based deployment. However, many problems in the enterprise require more than just APIs and scripts. As an infrastructure designed to be simplified, unified, and extensible, BEA released WebLogic Platform 8.1.

WebLogic Platform represents a comprehensive suite of components, including user presentation (WebLogic Portal), process management, data mapping and manipulation, and back-office integration (WebLogic Integration), and tools to enhance developer productivity and ease the burden on J2EE application deployment (WebLogic Workshop). All these services are delivered on and leverage the high-quality and rock-solid stability of WebLogic Server 8.1. Unique in the industry, WebLogic Platform offers a complete, end-to-end platform for developing comprehensive solutions, installed from one CD-ROM, with one set of installation and configuration tools and a common set of core services, such as transactions, security, naming, and communications, all based on J2EE. Chapter 18 provides a brief overview of WebLogic Platform and its services.

We now begin the first of the detailed chapters on J2EE technologies, with a discussion of servlets.

chapter 2

Presentation Logic

In This Chapter

- Building presentation logic

- The servlet lifecycle

- Building servlets in WebLogic Server

- Building Web applications

- Samples of servlets built for WebLogic Server

- Best practices for developing basic servlets on WebLogic Server

Presentation logic is the code that accepts user input, interprets user actions, and generates the resulting display elements and content. Combined with other Java 2 Enterprise Edition (J2EE) components, presentation logic gives users access to enterprise systems. For example, your presentation logic can be as simple as "report the time of day when a request is received." Or your presentation logic can trigger the appropriate business logic when a user orders a compact disc, then present a confirmation back to the user. Developers can code server-side presentation logic using Java servlets, JSPs, JavaBeans, and tag libraries.

Presentation Logic

Presentation logic represents a significant portion of any interactive application. The WebAuction application uses presentation logic to tie user actions to application logic and to dynamically generate pages displaying the results to the user. Some tasks handled by the presentation logic include:

- Determining if a visitor needs to register.
- Providing an interface for a new user to register.
- Displaying available auction items based on the user's query.
- Displaying a user's inventory of auction items.
- Calling business logic when a user places bids and displaying the result.

Model-View-Controller

The Model-View-Controller (MVC) design pattern is one approach for building interactive applications. The MVC pattern is important to this discussion because it defines a boundary between application and presentation logic. MVC developed within Smalltalk in the 1970s as a way to keep the internals of an application apart from the interfaces of the application. This approach leads to flexible systems and has become a powerful design tool in the J2EE community.

There are three components in the MVC design pattern:

- The model encapsulates the application data and the functional core of the application. In J2EE applications, the model is typically further decomposed and may use a variety of J2EE technologies, including Java classes, EJBs, and relational databases (using JDBC).
- The view component presents the interface to the user. Typically, J2EE applications implement the view component using JSPs. However, applications may use Swing classes to create a GUI.
- The controller handles user input and updates the model using this input. J2EE developers often choose to implement the controller component using servlets.

In practice, the distinctions between view and controller components are often blurred, and the view-controller components of an application define its presentation logic. J2EE defines two standards for presentation logic: servlets and Java Server Pages (JSPs). WebLogic Server supports both presentation logic technologies.

Chapters 2, 3, and 4 cover presentation logic. In this chapter, we cover servlet basics so that you'll understand the underlying mechanisms of dynamic HTTP generation. Chapter 3, "Advanced Servlet Techniques," adds advanced servlet techniques. Finally, Chapter 4, "Using WebLogic Server Java Server Pages," deals with JSPs, which complement servlets and simplify their use.

Introducing Servlets

Servlets are server-side Java code designed to handle user requests. Servlets listen for requests, and for each request, the servlet generates a response. In a typical scenario, a Web browser generates an HTTP (Hypertext Transfer Protocol) request. A servlet receives and processes the request and generates HTML as output. The browser presents this HTML code as text and images. While this typical scenario is most common, other clients, protocols, and output types are perfectly legal.

The J2EE family of standards includes servlets. Servlets written using these standards should run on any server that supports servlets. As with many standards, the servlet standard has evolved, and several versions of the standard exist. WebLogic Server 8.1 supports the Java Servlet Specification Version 2.3 (see *http://www.jcp.org/aboutJava/communityprocess/final/jsr053/*) and provides some extensions specific to WebLogic. This chapter covers both the servlet standard and the WebLogic extensions.

WebLogic Server and HTTP Requests

The WebLogic Server includes a servlet container. Servlet containers provide a framework for servlets that handles of many of the low-level functions common to all servlets.

After receiving an HTTP request, the WebLogic Server servlet container must determine which servlet should be executed. The servlet selection is typically determined by the request's Uniform Resource Locator (URL). The URL specifies the protocol used to access the resource and the location of the requested resource, including both the name of the server and the location of the resource on the server. For example, *http://www.learnweblogic.com/picture.gif* is a URL that specifies a resource using the HTTP protocol. The resource is located on the host (or the name of the machine) *www.learnweblogic.com* and is within the machine at the path */picture.gif.*

WebLogic Server identifies the appropriate servlet and then executes the servlet. In addition, WebLogic Server provides services to the servlet, including user authentication, parallel execution, memory management, access control, session management, and request forwarding.

Servlets take the form of a request handler. The container provides the servlet a request object. This object represents the details of the request. The servlet code uses the information contained in this request object to generate a response in a separate response object. The container then translates this response object into an HTTP response, which it returns to the requester.

Servlets and HttpServlets

The servlet specification defines servlets using Java inheritance. The `javax.servlet.Servlet` interface defines common methods required by all servlet classes. The abstract class `javax.servlet.GenericServlet` implements many methods required by the `Servlet` and the `ServletConfig` interfaces and leaves only the `service()` method to be implemented by concrete subclasses. The generic servlet provides a common framework for future protocols as they develop and does not specify any particular protocol.

Anatomy of a Servlet

WebLogic Server supports servlets using HTTP and which extend the class `javax.servlet.http.HttpServlet`. The `HttpServlet` class specializes the `GenericServlet` for the HTTP protocol. The `HttpServlet` class is defined as abstract; your servlet is a concrete subclass of the `HttpServlet`. The `HttpServlet` class is part of the standard Java extensions. For your convenience, these Java extensions are included as part of the WebLogic Server package.

The `HttpServlet` includes a number of methods called during the servlet's lifetime. Servlets may override these default methods and introduce any additional methods as needed. Otherwise, the source code looks just like any other Java class.

When you extend the `HttpServlet` class, your new class inherits implementations of several methods, including the `init()`, `destroy()`, and `service()` methods. WebLogic Server calls each of these methods.

When WebLogic Server brings a servlet into service, it calls the `init()` method of your servlet class. This method takes an instance of the `ServletConfig` class as a parameter, which contains information about the configuration of the servlet. The `init()` method allows your servlet to set variables, acquire resources, and prepare the servlet to handle requests.

To implement a servlet, override one of a number of different service methods defined in the default `HttpServlet` object. The focal method is called the `service()` method. It is called every time a request is made for your servlet.

There are two parameters accepted by the service method: an instance of the `HttpServletRequest` class and an instance of the `HttpServletResponse` class (both in the package `javax.servlet.http`). The container uses the `HttpServletRequest` object to pass the details of the HTTP request to your servlet. Your servlet uses the `HttpServletResponse` object to pass your response to the requester.

By default, the `service()` method dispatches calls to other, more specialized methods based on the request type (usually `doGet()` or `doPost()`). The specialized methods exist to handle different types of user input, such as Web forms. These more specialized methods for handling different request types are discussed later in this chapter.

Finally, when WebLogic Server removes your servlet from service, it calls the destroy() method in your servlet. This call allows the servlet to clean up and release resources.

A Basic Servlet

No programming book would be complete without at least one example that simply says hello. Here is a basic servlet that generates "Hello World!":

```
import javax.servlet.*;
import javax.servlet.http.*;
import java.io.*;

// Next, we define our class:
public class HelloServlet extends HttpServlet {

    // We define our service() method to handle HTTP
    // requests and generate responses
    public void service(HttpServletRequest req,
                HttpServletResponse res)
      throws IOException
    {
      // Now Set the Response Content Type
      resp.setContentType("text/html");
      // Now obtain a PrintWriter stream to write to.
      PrintWriter out = res.getWriter();

      // Now Print Out Our Text
      out.println("<html><head>" +
              "<title>Hello World!</title></head>" +
              "<h1>Hello World!</h1></body></html>");
    }
} // HelloServlet
```

Let's take a closer look at what went on in *HelloServlet.java*. First, we need to import the requisite classes into our servlet. For convenience, we grab everything in the javax.servlet, javax.servlet.http, and java.io packages into our servlet, which we are calling *HelloServlet.java*.

When you create a servlet, be sure to define it as a public class. Public access allows the WebLogic Server (or any other servlet container) to access your class. A servlet without the required access will cause lack-of-access errors, which can be difficult to diagnose.

The servlet implements the service() method, which takes a request and response object as parameters. The request object encapsulates all the details and parameters of the HTTP request. In the case of this example, the servlet is not interested in any information in the request object—the servlet only cares that the request was made. Later in this chapter, we examine how to read information within this object and how to handle the requests appropriately.

WebLogic Server creates a response object, used to send information to the requesting client, and passes both the request and response objects to the `service()` method. The response object represents the header and body of the HTTP response.

The `service()` method first sets the `ContentType` field within the HTTP response header. The browser uses the `ContentType` to determine how to display the information in the body of the response. HTTP uses the media type defined by another Internet standard to set the content type. For more information, refer to the Multimedia Mail Extension (MIME) standard for media types at *ftp://ftp.isi.edu/in-notes/rfc2046.txt*. In this case, the servlet sets the `ContentType` to text/html, telling the client that the response is HTML markup.

In order to create the body of the response, we call the `getWriter()` method of the `HttpResponse` object. This method returns a `PrintWriter` stream. The servlet can use standard `print()` methods to write text to this stream. WebLogic Server sends text written to this stream back to the client within the body of the HTTP response. Make sure that you call the `setContentType()` before calling `getWriter()`.

Readers familiar with Java output classes will notice that the sample does not perform common cleanup tasks. We did not `close()` the stream or call the stream's `flush()` method. WebLogic Server manages the output stream to optimize performance using a feature of HTTP 1.1 called Keep-Alive. The Keep-Alive feature allows WebLogic Server to reuse sockets and avoid the overhead of creating new connections wherever possible. See the "Best Practices for Servlets" section at the end of this chapter for additional ways to leverage the Keep-Alive feature.

The next step is to compile the servlet using your favorite Java compiler, package it up as a Web application, and then deploy it.

Deploying the Basic Servlet in WebLogic Server

In order to deploy the basic servlet, use an example deployment process that applies to every example in this chapter. The deployment process has four steps:

1. Set up a development environment.
2. Copy and unpack the example.
3. Build and deploy the example.
4. View the example.

First, find the example code for the basic servlet on the CD-ROM accompanying this book. It is located in the Web archive file named *HelloServlet.war*, which is located in the subdirectory */examples/ch2*.

Step 1: Set Up a Development Environment

Create a new, empty directory on your local hard disk. For this example, we use the directory *c:\dev*. You can do this either using the Windows Explorer or the DOS command-line shell. To access a command-line shell, click on *Run...* in the Windows Start menu and type the letters cmd into the resulting *Run* dialog box. Change to the new directory you just created using the cd command:

```
cd c:\dev
```

Next, set your environment variables to access the WebLogic Server Java services in WebLogic Server, such as the included Java compiler:

```
c:\bea\weblogic81\server\bin\setWLSEnv.cmd
```

The preceding path may differ if you have installed WebLogic Server on a different drive. In Figure 2–1, WebLogic Server is installed on the C: drive.

Figure 2–1
Setting the environment.

Step 2: Copy and Unpack the Example

You should now copy over the example code from the CD-ROM into this directory. If your CD-ROM drive is the E: drive, you might use the following command:

```
copy E:\examples\ch2\HelloServlet.war c:\dev
```

Generate a directory listing to double check that the file has arrived correctly using the `dir` command (see Figure 2–2).

Unpack the file using the `jar` utility that is included as part of WebLogic Server. This utility is used to package and unpackage application components. To extract all the components from the WAR file, type the following into the command line:

```
jar xvf *.war
```

You should see something like Figure 2–3.

The `jar` tool is quite powerful and used throughout J2EE applications. Virtually all the components of J2EE applications are packaged and unpackaged using `jar`. To see all the things `jar` can do and to display all the available options, type `jar` by itself into the command line.

The `jar` utility creates packages in the Zip file format. This means that you can use a standard utility, such as WinZip (*http://www.winzip.com*), to view the contents of any J2EE application package.

Figure 2–2
Checking that the Web archive has arrived.

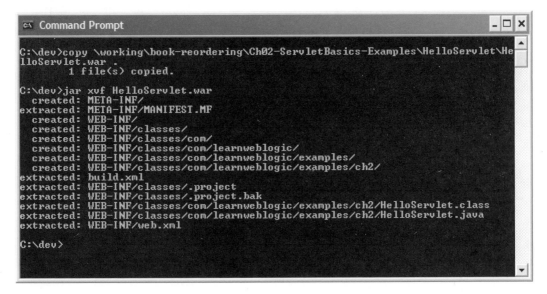

Figure 2–3
Unpacking the example package.

Step 3: Build and Deploy the Example

The sample archive includes an Ant *build.xml* script. The Ant build application, included with WebLogic Server, reads the *build.xml* file and performs build and deployment tasks. Ant runs on both UNIX and Windows platforms. As a result, the build script is crossplatform as well. Edit the build script to match your deployment configuration. Set the URL of the administration server and the user and password for the administration server in the property tags (`weblogic.adminurl`, `weblogic.user`, and `weblogic.password`).

Type `ant` and press Enter. The compilation, packaging, and deployment of the application should take place automatically (see Figure 2–4).

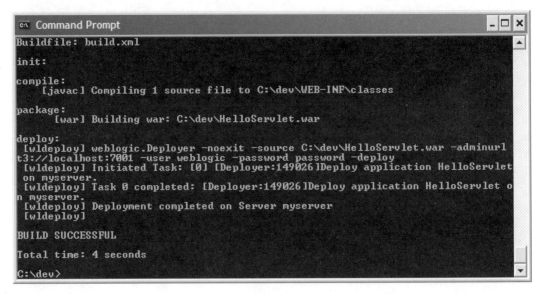

Figure 2–4
Compiling the servlet with the build script.

If the properties are properly set for your configuration, the build script compiles, packages, and deploys the *HelloServlet* Web application. You can review the list of deployed applications in the WebLogic Server console at *http://127.0.0.1:7001/console/* (see Figure 2–5).

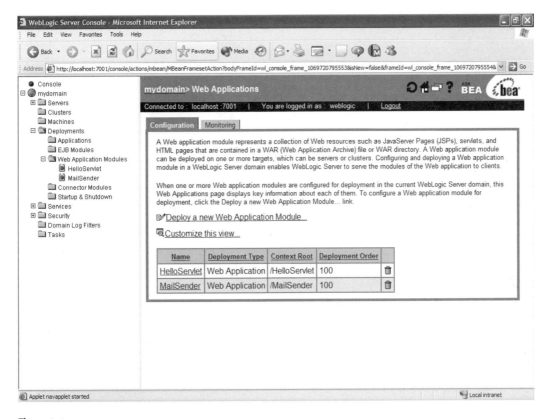

Figure 2–5
Viewing deployed applications in the WebLogic Server console.

Step 4: *View the Example*

To view the example, point a Web browser to *http://127.0.0.1:7001/HelloServlet*. You should see something like Figure 2–6.

If you do not see anything, be sure to check out the execution window for your Examples Server. The servlet in this example is designed to print out any problems to the console window for review.

If you receive an error that you cannot locate the server or the connection is refused, then you likely need to turn off your HTTP proxy settings inside the Web browser (see Figure 2–7).

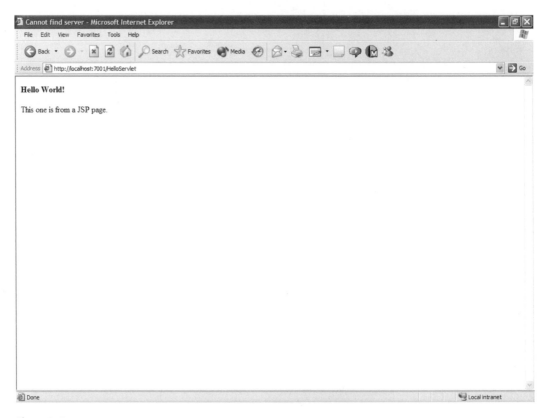

Figure 2–6
Output of the HelloWorld servlet.

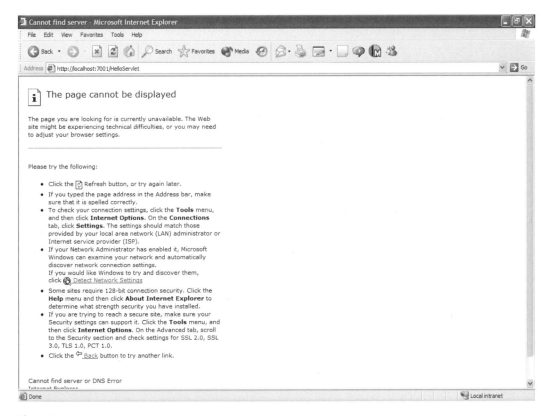

Figure 2–7
Connection failed error.

About the Packaging and Deployment Process

For more information, refer to the Ant documentation, available at *http://ant.apache.org/manual/index.html*. The *build.xml* script included with this example performs five steps. First, it defines a number of variables to be used throughout the script:

```
<project name="HelloServlet" default="deploy" basedir=".">
    <description>
        Build file to compile, package and deploy HelloServlet
    </description>

    <property name="servlet-name" value="HelloServlet"/>

    <property name="weblogic.user" value="weblogic"/>
    <property name="weblogic.password" value="password"/>
    <property name="weblogic.adminurl" value="t3://localhost:7001"/>
```

Next, the script creates a classes directory for the *HelloServlet.class* file. WebLogic Server looks to this directory for compiled Java classes.

```
<target name="init">
    <mkdir dir="WEB-INF/classes"/>
</target>
```

The script then calls the Java compiler, javac, to compile the Java files into the directory WEB-INF*classes*, where WebLogic Server will later find them.

```
<target name="compile" depends="init">
    <javac srcdir="." destdir="WEB-INF/classes"/>
</target>
```

This target is the equivalent of the command

```
javac -d WEB-INF\classes *.java
```

Next, the script uses the previously mentioned jar utility to create a new application package:

```
<target name="package" depends="compile">
    <war destfile="${servlet-name}.war" webxml="WEB-INF/web.xml">
        <fileset dir=".">
            <exclude name="${servlet-name}.war"/>
            <exclude name="WEB-INF/web.xml"/>
            <exclude name="META-INF/MANIFEST.MF"/>
        </fileset>
    </war>
</target>
```

In the Ant script, the destfile attribute specifies the name of the WAR file. The attribute webxml points to the web.xml deployment descriptor. And the fileset element defines the contents of the WAR file. In this case, the fileset element includes everything under the current directory except the current WAR file, the web.xml deployment descriptor, and the manifest file.

The following command line is equivalent to the Ant script:

```
jar cvf HelloServlet.war *
```

On the command line, the parameters cvf tell jar that we are creating an archive, with jar displaying verbose output, and that we are specifying the files to be included. The second parameter on the command line, HelloServlet.war, tells jar to output the file to a WAR file with the name *HelloServlet.war*. The third parameter, a wildcard specified by *, tells jar to include every file in the current directory and those below it into the package.

The resulting WAR file encapsulates the Web application. This WAR includes Java code, the compiled servlet, and a web.xml deployment descriptor. WAR files may also contain JSP pages, static HTML, supporting code, and configuration files necessary for the Web Application. Further, this WAR can be deployed on any servlet container that supports J2EE standards.

WebLogic provides the `weblogic.Deployer` utility to assist with deploying components. Conveniently, BEA includes the `wldeploy` Ant task using this deployment utility. The following lines of the build script deploy the WAR file:

```
<target name="deploy" depends="package">
    <wldeploy action="deploy"
      source="${servlet-name}.war"
      adminurl="${weblogic.adminurl}"
      user="${weblogic.user}" password="${weblogic.password}" />
  </target>
</project>
```

The `source` attribute references the WAR file. The `adminurl` attribute provides the address of the administration server. Finally, the `user` and `password` attributes authenticate the deployment command. Alternately, if your WebLogic Server instance is running in development mode, you can copy the WAR file to the applications directory of your WebLogic Server installation. WebLogic Server automatically recognizes and deploys the application. If that application component is already deployed, the new and updated version is distributed to all instances of WebLogic Server that have it deployed. Additional options for the `wldeploy` task are documented at *http://e-docs.bea.com/wls/docs81/deployment/tools.html*.

The Lifecycle of a Servlet

This section describes what happens during the birth, life, and death of every servlet. Although the servlet container handles much of the servlet's lifecycle automatically, understanding how servlets behave in the context of WebLogic Server helps you understand best practices for development.

Loading and Instantiation

WebLogic Server is responsible for loading and instantiating servlets. In this case, instantiating means that WebLogic Server creates one or more instances of a servlet object and stores the instance of the servlet object in memory for future use.

Initialization

After WebLogic Server creates an instance of a servlet, WebLogic Server calls the servlet's `init()` method. This method initializes the servlet to handle subsequent requests and may create database connections or initialize per-instance local variables.

Warning—you may initialize read-only instance variables, but read-write instance variables should be used with great caution. Servlet objects are reused, and typically the servlet object handles multiple requests concurrently. Unless you are prepared to manage instance variables in a multiuser and multithreaded environment, don't use modifiable instance variables. Don't worry about variables defined within your servlet's methods: these variables are safe. We address this issue in greater detail later in this chapter.

Request Handling

WebLogic Server encapsulates the details of an incoming request into an instance of the `HttpServletRequest` object. WebLogic Server then calls the `service()` method in the servlet to handle this request. Typically, the `service()` method calls a more specialized handler depending on the type of the request (e.g., GET or POST). The servlet determines how to respond to the request and updates the `HttpServletResponse` object.

End of Service

WebLogic Server occasionally releases a servlet object from memory, typically in response to a command from the WebLogic Server console or when the WebLogic Server is shut down. WebLogic first removes the servlet instance from active duty by calling the `destroy()` method.

End of service differs from when a servlet is undeployed. Undeployment occurs when the WebLogic Server administrator removes a servlet from the server altogether. The end of service portion of the servlet lifecycle may occur whenever WebLogic Server deems necessary.

Single-Threaded, Multithreaded

By default, WebLogic Server assumes that servlets are multithreaded. For multithreaded servlets, WebLogic Server creates a single instance of the servlet object and uses this single object to handle requests, even requests that occur at the same time. In order to handle concurrent requests, the servlet class must be thread-safe. Thread-safe classes are written so that multiple threads can execute within the class at the same time and still produce the expected results. Thread-safe classes should avoid class and instance variables that can be modified. Also, shared resources, like database connections, should be protected from concurrent access. Java synchronization, using the `synchronized` keyword, is an effective method for protecting code using shared resources.

If your servlet code is not thread-safe, modify your servlet class declaration to implement the `SingleThreadModel` interface. The WebLogic Server recognizes the servlet as single-threaded and asks it to handle only one request at a time. If a servlet is single-threaded, WebLogic Server creates a pool of servlet objects. By default, WebLogic Server populates this pool with five instances of the single-threaded servlet. Modify the number of threads WebLogic Server creates in the `weblogic.xml` deployment descriptor (later in this chapter). Single-threading limits scalability and is not appropriate for high-volume Web sites.

Servlet Methods

Your servlet inherits many methods from the `GenericServlet` and `HttpServlet` classes. Some methods, like `init()`, `destroy()`, and `do<request type>()`, are provided so your servlet can override them with custom behavior:

- `public void init()`—Override the `init()` method to perform initialization prior to servicing requests. Use this new version of the method rather than the previous `init(ServletConfig config)`. The older version requires that the overriding method call `super.init(config)`.
- `public void destroy()`—Override this method to clean up the servlet class during the end of service transition.
- `public void do<request type>(HttpServletRequest, HttpServletResponse)`—Override any of these methods to customize the behavior of your servlet. The servlet specification provides for `doGet()`, `doPost()`, `doDelete()`, and `doPut()`.

Other methods provide functions that may be useful to your servlets:

- `public String getInitParameter(String name)`—Developers and administrators may set initialization parameters for servlets. Use this method to retrieve the values of named parameters. For more information on setting servlet initialization parameters, see the section "Deployment Descriptors" later in this chapter.

- `public Enumeration getInitParameters()`—Returns an enumeration of all servlet initialization parameter names.
- `public ServletContext getServletContext()`—Returns a `ServletContext` object for the current Web application. See more about `ServletContext` later in this chapter.
- `public String getServletName()`—Returns the name of the servlet as set in the deployment descriptor.
- `public void service(HttpServletRequest req, HttpServletRequest res)`—Queries the request to determine which HTTP request type handler to call.

Handling Servlet Requests

The servlet container calls the servlet with both a request and response object. These objects encapsulate the user's request and the response generated by the servlet. In the generic case, the `service()` method of the servlet handles the request:

```
// The service() method to handle HTTP requests and responses
public void service(HttpServletRequest req,
                    HttpServletResponse rsp)
    throws IOException
{
    // use req and rsp to handle requests within this method.
    .
    .
    .
}
```

In this example, the `service()` method may contain arbitrary Java code used to process the request and to provide the appropriate response. Within the `service()` method, the servlet may use the variables `req` and `rsp`, which refer to the provided `HttpServletRequest` and `HttpServletResponse` objects (from the package `javax.servlet.http`).

In practice, you do not override the `service()` method. The `service()` method, as defined in the class `HttpServlet`, identifies the type of request and calls a more specific request handler. Typically, servlets should override methods like `doGet()` and `doPost()` and should leave the default implementation of the `service()` method. The following code shows how these handler methods follow the same pattern as `service()`:

```
// The doGet() method to handle HTTP requests and responses
public void doGet(HttpServletRequest req,
                  HttpServletResponse rsp)
    throws IOException
{
    // use req and rsp to handle requests within this method.
    .
    .
    .
}
```

Accessing Data in the Servlet Request

An HTTP request provides information to the servlet about the request. The servlet uses this information to generate an appropriate response. The `HttpServletRequest` class includes

- The requested URL
- An optional request body (for POST and PUT requests)
- Additional information known about the request

`HttpServletRequest` supports a number of methods for accessing data within the request. The following methods provide information regarding the requested URL:

- `public String getMethod()`—Returns the name of the HTTP method with which this request was made: for example, GET, POST, or PUT. Unless the Web browser is instructed otherwise, all requests are GETs of information.
- `public String getAuthType()`—Returns a string containing the name of the authentication scheme used to protect the servlet, for example, BASIC or SSL, or `null` if the servlet was not protected.
- `public String getRequestURL()`—Reconstructs the request's URL from the protocol name up to the query string in the first line of the HTTP request. For example, for the HTTP request of

      GET http://learnWeblogic.com/index.jsp?src=blah HTTP/1.0,

  this method returns

      http://learnWeblogic.com/index.jsp.

- `public String getRequestURI()`—Returns the part of this request's URL from the protocol name up to the query string in the first line of the HTTP request. For example, for the HTTP request of

      GET http://learnWeblogic.com/index.jsp?src=blah HTTP/1.0,

  this method returns

      /index.jsp.

- `public String getProtocol()`—Returns a string containing the name and version of the protocol the request uses in the form `protocol/majorVersion.minorVersion`; for example, `HTTP/1.1`.
- `public String getScheme()`—Returns the name of the scheme used to make this request; for example, http, https, or ftp.
- `public String getServletPath()`—Returns a string containing the part of this request's URL that specifies the servlet. This string includes either the servlet name or a path to the servlet, but does not include extra path information or a query string.
- `public String getPathInfo()`—Returns a string containing any extra path information associated with the URL the client sent when it made the request.
- `public String getPathTranslated()`—Returns a string representing the `PathInfo` (above) translated into a path on the server file system. Typically, WebLogic Server explodes WAR files (more on these later) into a directory on the local file system. The translated path references a resource relative to this directory.
- `public String getQueryString()`—Returns the query string that is contained in the request URL after the path. This method returns `null` if the URL does not contain a query string.

The following methods provide access to the body of the HTTP request:

- `public int getContentLength()`—Returns an integer representing the length, in bytes, of the request body in the input stream, or –1 if the length is not known. This is only useful when PUT or POST HTTP requests are made.
- `public String getContentType()`—Returns the MIME type of the body of the request, or null if the type is not known.
- `public ServletInputStream getInputStream()`—Returns an InputStream containing the body of the request. If no body is included in the request, the returned stream is valid, but empty. If you prefer a reader object, use the `getReader()` method. Warning: You may not use both methods.
- `public BufferedReader getReader()`—Returns a Reader class containing the body of the request. If no body is included in the request, the returned reader is valid, but empty. If you prefer an InputStream object, use the `getInputStream()` method. Warning: You may not use both methods.

The following methods provide access to additional information regarding the HTTP request:

- `public String getServerName()`—Returns the host name of the server that received the request.
- `public int getServerPort()`—Returns the port number on which this request was received. Typically, this is the port on which WebLogic Server is listening.
- `public String getRemoteAddr()`—Returns the Internet Protocol (IP) address of the client that sent the request.
- `public String getRemoteHost()`—Returns the fully qualified name of the client that sent the request, or the IP address of the client if the name cannot be determined.
- `public String getRemoteUser()`—Returns the login of the user making this request if the user has been authenticated, or null if the user has not been authenticated. Whether the user name is sent with each subsequent request depends on the browser and type of authentication.

Look to the javadoc for the `HttpServletRequest` object for a complete list of request methods. You can find this javadoc packaged with WebLogic Server or online at *http://java.sun.com/products/servlet/2.3/javadoc*.

The following code illustrates the process of using the `HttpServletRequest` object. The example uses multiple methods to determine information about the request and presents the results to the user. First, include common imports and define a servlet class:

```
import javax.servlet.*;
import javax.servlet.http.*;
import java.io.*;

public class ViewRequestServlet extends HttpServlet {
```

Unlike the `HelloServlet` example discussed earlier, this example does not override the `service()` method. Instead, this servlet defines both `doGet()` and `doPost()` methods. Each of these methods forwards the request to a `handleRequest()` method. The `handleRequest()` method demonstrates the use of the `HttpServletRequest` as described above.

```
/*
   Create a method to handle the
   GET request for your servlet:
 */
public void doGet(HttpServletRequest req, HttpServletResponse
res)
   throws ServletException, IOException {
      handleRequest(req, res);
   }

/*
   Create a method to handle the
   POST request for your servlet:
 */
public void doPost(HttpServletRequest req, HttpServletResponse
res)
   throws ServletException, IOException {
      handleRequest(req, res);
   }

/*
   Provide a common handler for GET and POST
 */
public void handleRequest(HttpServletRequest req,
HttpServletResponse res)
   throws ServletException, IOException {
```

As in the previous example, we set the content type, acquire a `PrintWriter` stream, and begin to compose the HTML page:

```
// set the response Content-Type
res.setContentType("text/html");
// obtain a PrintWriter stream to write to.
PrintWriter out = res.getWriter();

// print out our text
out.println("<html>");
out.println("<head><title>ViewRequest Servlet</title></
head>");
out.println("<body>");
```

We continue to compose the HTML page, inserting values read from the request object.

```
out.println("<h1>Requested URL:</h1>");
out.println("<pre>");
```

```
    out.println(req.getRequestURL().toString());     out.println("</
pre>");
```

Next, call a sampling of the available methods for the HttpServletRequest object and print out the results for each:

```
    out.println("<h1>HttpServletRequest information:</h1><pre>");
    // Returns the Request Method.  For Example, PUT or GET.
    out.println("<br>Request method " + req.getMethod());
    // Returns Request Scheme.  Likely "HTTP 1.1"
    out.println("<br>Request scheme " + req.getScheme());
    // The protocol type for the request.  Likely HTTP.
    out.println("<br>Request protocol " + req.getProtocol());
    // A subset of the complete URL.
    out.println("<br>Request URL " + req.getRequestURI());
    // Info on the path to the servlet.
    out.println("<br>Servlet path " + req.getServletPath());
    out.println("<br>Path info " + req.getPathInfo());
    out.println("<br>Path translated " + req.getPathTranslated());
    out.println("<br>Query string " + req.getQueryString());
    // Info on the Request Content
    out.println("<br>Content length " + req.getContentLength());
    out.println("<br>Content type " + req.getContentType());
    // Local Server Details.
    out.println("<br>Server name " + req.getServerName());
    out.println("<br>Server port " + req.getServerPort());

    // Remote Host and User Information
    out.println("<br>Remote user " + req.getRemoteUser());
    out.println("<br>Remote address " + req.getRemoteAddr());
    out.println("<br>Remote host " + req.getRemoteHost());
```

Finally, close off the HTML page, the handleRequest() method, and the class:

```
    out.println("</body></html>");
    } // handleRequest
} // ViewRequestServlet
```

The output from an execution of this servlet might look like Figure 2–8.

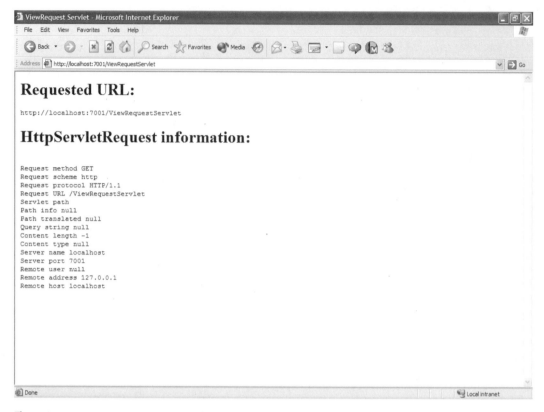

Figure 2–8
Output from servlet execution.

Deploying the ViewRequestServlet in WebLogic Server

The `ViewRequestServlet` is part of the `ViewRequestServlet.war` package, which can be found on the CD-ROM accompanying this book in the directory *examples\ch2*. It can be compiled, packaged, and deployed using the process previously described for the Hello World example. Be sure to create a separate directory for building and deploying each servlet.

Using the Servlet Response Object

As you have seen, the servlet uses an instance of the `HttpServletResponse` object passed into the `service()` method to create an HTTP response. This section describes the methods provided in the `HttpServletResponse` object.

Setting the Response Content Type

Typically, a servlet includes content in each HTTP response. The content may be HTML markup for a Web page, an image, or a sound file. Your servlet must use the `setContentType()` method with the appropriate MIME type to inform the client how to interpret the body of the HTTP response. In most cases, you'll use WebLogic Server to send HTML as in the following:

```
// set the response Content-Type
res.setContentType("text/html");
```

In the example above, the `HttpServletResponse` includes an HTTP header content type `"text/html"` to the client within the HTTP header. The content type may optionally specify the character set of the response. For example, the value `"text/html; charset=UTF-8"` instructs the client that the body of the response is HTML markup, and that the text of the body is encoded using Unicode. Alternatively, the servlet may call the `setLocale()` method described in the section "Other Useful Response Methods."

Getting an Output Stream

The sample servlet returns an HTML page. You may notice that the lines of code that generate HTML use standard Java I/O calls, or `println()` methods. The servlet gets an output stream from the `HttpServletResponse` object and then writes to the output stream. The servlet container includes this output in the body of the HTTP response. In this case, the servlet requests a `PrintWriter` object:

```
// obtain a PrintWriter stream to write to.
PrintWriter out = response.getWriter();
You can then print character data to the stream:
        // print html text
        out.println("<html>");
        out.println("<head><title>ViewRequest Servlet</title></head>");
        out.println("<body>");
        out.println("<h1>Requested URL:</h1>");
        out.println("<pre>");
        out.println(req.getRequestURL());
        out.println("</pre>");
        out.println("<h1>HttpServletRequest information:</h1><pre>");
```

Notice that we don't close or flush the output stream. This is intentional. As noted previously, WebLogic Server is efficient at buffering the responses that it sends back to clients and at managing server resources. Closing or flushing the output stream interferes with WebLogic Server's optimizations.

In the sample application, the `PrintWriter` object encodes the character data using the default character set: `ISO-8859-1`. If the `setContentType()` method or the `setLocale()` method has been used to override the default encoding, then the `HttpServletResponse` initializes the `PrintWriter` to use the specified character set. Note: You must set the character encoding prior to calling `getWriter()`.

In the preceding examples, the output was character data. If the response is an image or a sound file, your servlet must write binary data. To write binary rather than character data, use the method `getOutputStream()` to return a `ServletOutputStream`. The `ServletOutputStream` does not encode character data, but writes it directly. To write binary data, call `write(byte[] b)` on the `ServletOutputStream`.

Other Useful Response Methods

The `HttpServletResponse` provides a number of other useful methods:

- `public void setStatus(int status) throws IOException`—This method sets the response code for the HTTP response. The default status value is `200-HTTP_OK`. See the HTTP or servlet specification for a list of valid codes and their meanings. As a best practice, use the static final definitions defined in the `HttpServletResponse` class to set the status code.
- `public void sendRedirect(String location) throws IOException`— Instructs the client to request the resource from a different URL. To redirect the client to *http://www.learnweblogic.com*, include the following code in your servlet:

```
public void service(HttpServletRequest req, HttpServletResponse
res)
      throws ServletException, IOException
 {
   res.sendRedirect(http://www.learnweblogic.com/)
 }
```

Additional options for including and forwarding content are explored later in this chapter.

- `public void sendError(int status) throws IOException`
- `public void sendError(int status, String message) throws IOException`—These methods allow you to send an error message to the client. Look to the HTTP specification for response codes and their meanings. To send a status of 503 with the message "Backend systems unavailable," use the following code:

```
public void doGet(HttpServletRequest req, HttpServletResponse res)
    throws ServletException, IOException
 {
    .

    .

    res.sendError(res.SC_SERVICE_UNAVAILABLE,"Backend systems
unavailable");
 }
```

- `public void setContentLength(int len)`—Set the content length in the HTTP response header using this method. If the content length is not known, then don't call this method.

The following methods support internationalization by setting and getting the response locale and the character set used for encoding character output.

- `public void setLocale(java.util.Locale loc)`—Set the locale of the response using the `setLocale()` method. WebLogic Server uses the locale to set the character encoding in the response header and to set the encoding for character output. Call `setLocale()` prior to calling `getWriter()`.

- `public java.util.Locale getLocale()`—Get the locale setting of the response object.
- `public String getCharacterEncoding()`—Get the character encoding of the response. Set the character encoding using `setLocale()`.

The use the following methods to manage HTTP header fields:

- `public void setHeader(String headername, String value)`—Sets a response header with the given name and value. If the header has already been set, the new value overwrites the previous one. If the header value has already been committed, then this method and all other methods dealing with the header are ignored.
- `public void addHeader(String headername, String value)`—Adds a response header with the given name and value. This method allows response headers to have multiple values.
- `public boolean containsHeader(String name)`—Used to test for the presence of a header before setting its value.
- `public void setDateHeader(String headername, long date)`—This method provides a convenient way to set date fields. The date parameter is specified in terms of milliseconds since the epoch. This method converts the date parameter to the standard date format for dates. Otherwise, this method behaves like `setHeader()`.
- `public void addDateHeader(String headername, long date)`— This method provides a convenient way to set date fields. The date parameter is specified in terms of milliseconds since the epoch. This method converts the date parameter to the standard date format for dates. Otherwise, this method behaves like `addHeader()`.
- `public void setIntHeader(String headername, int value)`—Convenience method sets a response header with the given name and integer value. Otherwise, this method behaves like `setHeader()`.
- `public void addIntHeader(String headername, int value)`—Adds a response header with the given name and integer value. Otherwise, this method behaves like `addHeader()`.

A servlet typically returns both a header (status code and additional header fields) and a body in an HTTP response. WebLogic Server buffers the transmission of the response and may begin to send the response even before the servlet has completed writing the body. While this optimization improves response time and may reduce the memory required for each servlet, these benefits come at a price. Once WebLogic Server has sent, or committed, the HTTP status code and header fields, the servlet can no longer modify the HTTP response header. WebLogic Server will not begin to send the HTTP header until the servlet begins to write the HTTP response body. Therefore, servlets should finalize all header values prior to calling `getWriter()` or `getOutputStream()`. If a servlet must break this sequence, use the following methods to determine whether the servlet may safely modify status code or HTTP response header fields.

- `public boolean isCommitted()`—Determines whether the HTTP response status code or header fields have been transmitted to the client. Modification of either the status code or header fields will fail once the HTTP response has been committed.
- `public boolean reset()`—Clears the HTTP response status code, header fields, and body. If the response has been committed this method fails, throwing an `IllegalState-Exception`.

- `public boolean resetBuffer()`—Clears the HTTP response body, but leaves the status code and header fields intact. If the response has been committed, this method fails, throwing an `IllegalStateException`.

Additional methods help the servlet manage the WebLogic Server output buffer:

- `public int getBufferSize()`—Returns the size of the output buffer in bytes.
- `public void setBufferSize(int size)`—Sets the size of the output buffer in bytes. Call this method before calling `getWriter()` or `getOutputStream()`. If the servlet has written any content, this method fails, throwing an `IllegalStateException`.
- `public void flushBuffer()`—This method forces WebLogic Server to write the HTTP response header and any data currently in the output buffer. Calling this method guarantees that the response is committed.

GETs, POSTs, and Web Forms

In the `HelloServlet` example, we built a servlet that overrides the default `service()` method. The next example, `ViewRequestServlet`, did not override `service()`, but instead overrode `doGet()` and `doPost()` methods. If the `service()` method is not overwritten, the default implementation dispatches requests to more specialized handler methods, based on the request type.

For each request type, the `HttpServlet` class defines a default method. For example, the servlet specification defines a `doGet()` method to handle HTTP GET requests. These request type methods take the form of `do<request type>()`, where the type of HTTP request the method handles replaces `<request type>`.

Servlets most commonly deal with HTTP GET and POST requests by overriding the `doGet()` and `doPost()`, respectively. The next section discusses the mechanics behind Web forms and the use of these methods.

About GETs

A GET request instructs the Web server to return a given resource to the client. A sample GET might look like the following:

```
GET http://www.learnweblogic.com/pictures/nickd/index.html HTTP/1.1
```

The Web server receives this GET, parses it, and responds with the appropriate resource, using the protocol specified (version 1.1 of HTTP). The GET request may contain parameters (for example: `GET http://www.learnweblogic.com/pictures?id=nickd&idx=12 HTTP/1.1`), but the use of GET requests has several pitfalls where the client passes information to the servlet. For one, the parameter values are visible within the request URL. Also, due to practical factors, the length of the GET request and the amount of information included in the request may be severely limited.

About POSTs

A POST request can transfer additional data from a Web browser to the servlet. POSTs are most often used to transfer data (user name, password, bid amount, and so on) from Web forms for processing. The POST request starts much like a GET request and may begin with

```
POST http://www.learnweblogic.com/pictures/browse HTTP/1.1
```

Unlike the GET request, the POST request contains additional data in the body of the HTTP request. The above example demonstrates that this data is not visible in the URL.

As with GET, parameters to POSTs consist of name/value pairs. Each field in the form is given a name. When the user completes that field in the form, the name is set using the value the user entered. Once the request is completed (when the user presses the Submit button), the name/value pairs are encapsulated in the HTTP request sent to the Web server. WebLogic Server reads the POST body and hands off the name/value pairs to the servlet specified in the form.

While GET and POST are the most common request types, a number of other request types exist, including PUT and DELETE. For a more thorough discussion of HTTP request types, refer to the World Wide Web Consortium (W3C) (see *http://www.w3c.org*) and the HTTP protocol specification (see *ftp://ftp.isi.edu/in-notes/rfc2616.txt*).

For information regarding overriding the do<request-type>() methods, see the API documentation at *http://java.sun.com/products/servlet/2.3/javadoc*.

POSTs on the Form Side

We begin the *FormServlet* example with a static HTML page. The following is a basic Web form:

```
<html>
<body bgcolor=#FFFFFF>
<h1>
My Form!
</h1>

<p>
<font face="Helvetica">
<form method="POST" action="FormServlet">
<table border="0" bgcolor=#eeeeee align=center cellspacing=10>
    <tr>
      <td>Username:</td>
      <td>
        <input type="TEXT" name="username">
      </td>
    </tr>
    <tr>
      <td>Your age:</td>
      <td>
        <input type="TEXT" name="age">
      </td>
    </tr>
  </table>
  <p>
  <center>
    <input type="SUBMIT" name="submit" value="Submit">
  </center>
</form>
</font>
</body>
</html>
```

In a Web browser, this page might look like the Web input form in Figure 2–9.

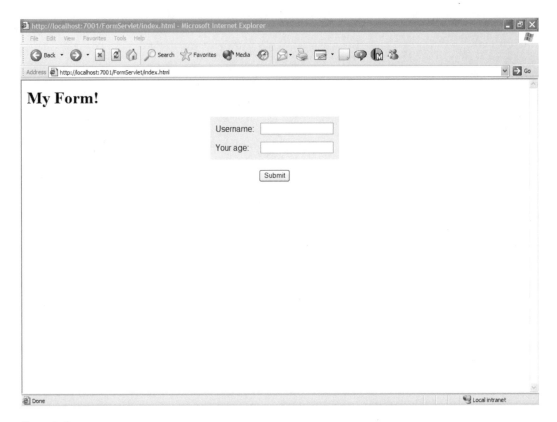

Figure 2–9
Web input form.

The form defines the request type (the form element defines the attribute method as POST) and has two fields, `Username` and `Your Age`. When the user completes the form and presses `Submit`, a POST request including the user's data is sent to WebLogic Server. WebLogic Server encapsulates that request in an instance of `HttpServletRequest`.

The next step is to write a method called `doPost()` into the servlet that handles the POST. As specified by the HTML form, the servlet that handles the POST is called `FormServlet`.

POSTs on the Servlet Side

When a POST is received, WebLogic Server calls the `doPost()` method in the servlet. The method signature looks like the following:

```
public void doPost(HttpServletRequest req, HttpServletResponse res)
        throws IOException, ServletException
```

This is similar to the `service()` method and is used in much the same way. The first step is to create an `Enumeration` of all the names of the parameters specified in the request using the `getParameterNames()` method available as part of the `HttpServletRequest` object:

```
Enumeration ParamNames = req.getParameterNames();
```

Then, the `Enumeration` can be traversed to evaluate each individual name/value pair:

```
while(ParamNames.hasMoreElements()){

    // Get the next name.
    String ParamString = (String)ParamNames.nextElement();

    // Print out the current name's value:
    pw.println("<b>" + ParamString + ":</b> " +
                req.getParameter(ParamString));
    pw.println("<P>");

    }
}
```

The `getParameter()` method returns the value of the parameter or `null` if the parameter does not exist.

All name/value pairs are encoded as strings. So, for example, if you are attempting to receive a dollar amount or a phone number, the return type out of the `getParameter()` method will always be a string, which you must be sure to parse appropriately.

Also, a parameter may have multiple values, so you should only use the `getParameter()` method when you are sure the parameter has only one value. If the parameter may have more than one value, you would use the method `getParameterValues(String name)`. The `getParameterValues()` method returns an array of string objects containing the values for the given request name, or `null` if the parameter does not exist.

A complete `doPost()` method for this form is included later in this section.

Note: Handling secure logins is slightly different from standard Web forms. Forms for secure logins are covered in Chapter 4.

Handling GETs and POSTs Together

Servlets can handle both GET and POST inside a single class. You can treat the `doGet()` and `doPost()` methods just as you treated the `service()` method in previous examples.

A simple servlet with a `doGet()` method might look like the following:

```
// Import Classes and Declare Servlet Class
import java.io.*;
import java.util.*;

import javax.servlet.*;
import javax.servlet.http.*;
```

```
public class FormServlet extends HttpServlet {

    // Define Method to Handle GETs
    public void doGet(HttpServletRequest req, HttpServletResponse res)
            throws ServletException, IOException
    {

        /* Set the appropriate return content type,
           and compose the HTML page: */
        res.setContentType("text/html");
        PrintWriterout = res.getWriter();

        out.println("<html>");
        out.println("<head><title>doGet Servlet</title></head>");
        out.println("<body></body></html>");
    }
}
```

The output of the servlet should be a simple HTML page with no content.

Extending the Servlet

We can now put together a single servlet to handle both an initial GET from the user and a subsequent POST. This single servlet handles each request separately by creating both the doGet() and doPost() methods:

```
package com.learnweblogic.examples.ch2;

import java.io.*;
import java.util.*;
import javax.servlet.*;
import javax.servlet.http.*;

public class FormServlet extends HttpServlet{

    /*  The doGet method handles the initial invocation of
        the servlet.  The default service() method recognizes
        that it has received a GET and calls this method
        appropriately. It responds with a form that uses
        the POST method to submit data.
    */
    public void doGet(HttpServletRequest req, HttpServletResponse res)
        throws IOException, ServletException
    {
        res.setContentType("text/html");
        res.setHeader("Pragma", "no-cache");
```

```
    PrintWriter    out = res.getWriter();

    out.println("<html>");
    out.println("<body bgcolor=#FFFFFF>");
    out.println("<h1>");
    out.println("My Form!");
    out.println("</h1>");
    out.println("<font face=Helvetica>");
    out.println("<form method=post action=FormServlet>");
    out.println("<table border=0 bgcolor=#eeeeee cellspacing=10>");
    out.println("<tr>");
    out.println("<td>Username:</td>");
    out.println("<td>");
    out.println("<input type=TEXT name=username>");
    out.println("</td>");
    out.println("</tr>");
    out.println("<tr>");
    out.println("<td>Your age:</td>");
    out.println("<td>");
    out.println("<input type=TEXT name=age>");
    out.println("</td>");
    out.println("</tr>");
    out.println("</table>");
    out.println("<p>");
    out.println("<center>");
    out.println("<input type=SUBMIT name=submit value=Submit>");
    out.println("</center>");
    out.println("</form>");
    out.println("</font>");
    out.println("</body>");
    out.println("</html>");
}

/* Finally, include a separate doPost() method to be called
   when the user responds by clicking on the submit button: */

/*
  Responds to the "POST" query from the
  original form supplied by the doGet() method.
*/
public void doPost(HttpServletRequest req, HttpServletResponse res)
  throws IOException, ServletException
{

  // Set the content type of the response.
```

```
   res.setContentType("text/html");
   res.setHeader("Pragma", "no-cache");

   PrintWriter pw = res.getWriter();

   pw.println("<HTML><HEAD><TITLE>Form Completed</TITLE></HEAD>");
   pw.println("<BODY>The information you have" +
     " submitted is as follows:");
   pw.println("<P>");

   // Loop through all the name/value pairs.
   Enumeration ParamNames = req.getParameterNames();

   // Loop through all the name/value pairs.
   while(ParamNames.hasMoreElements()) {

     // Get the next name.
     String ParamString = (String)ParamNames.nextElement();

     // Print out the current name's value:
     pw.println("<b>" + ParamString + ":</b> " +
       req.getParameterValues(ParamString)[0]);
     pw.println("<P>");
   }
   pw.println("</BODY></HTML>");
  }
}
```

Figure 2–10 shows what the first screen for the user might look like. The completed form after the POST is shown in Figure 2–11.

Can you explain the name/value pair submit: submit? The submit button itself is an input field. The value for the submit button supports pages with multiple submit buttons, each with a different name and value. Your servlet can look at the value of the submit parameter to see which button was pressed and handle the POST appropriately.

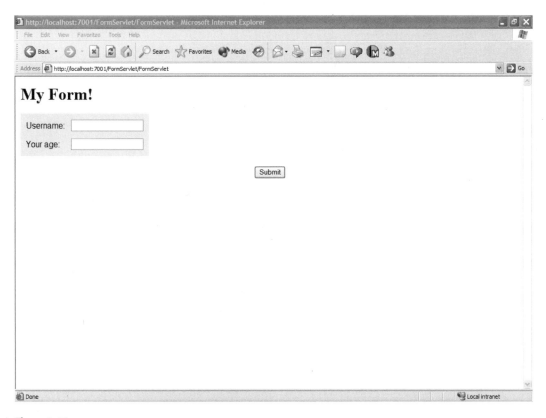

Figure 2–10
The user's first screen.

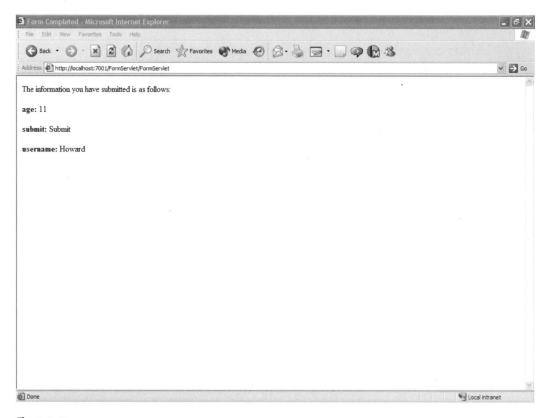

Figure 2–11
After the POST.

Deploying the Form Servlet in WebLogic Server

Use the code included on the CD-ROM accompanying this book to deploy the form servlet. The Web application archive is located in the file */examples/ch2/FormServlet.war*. Use the process described for the *HelloServlet* example as your guide.

The Web Application

So far, we've talked about servlets as distinct objects. As you might guess, it is desirable to organize servlets (and other Web resources) into a single package. We might want to group servlets so that we can share resources among servlets, host multiple applications on a single WebLogic Server, update a group of resources together, or easily refer to a group of resources under a single name.

About Web Applications

As of the servlet specification version 2.2, a new feature was added to J2EE: the Web application. A Web application is a collection of resources that can be bundled and run on servlet containers from multiple vendors.

A Web application is rooted to a specific path, called the *context-root*, within WebLogic Server. For example, a Web application could be located at *http://www.learnweblogic.com/mywebapp*. All requests that start with this prefix are handled by the Web application designated for that path. Web applications are typically bundled together to form a Web archive (WAR). WAR files are designated by a *.war* suffix on the filename.

A Web application can include

- Servlets
- JSPs
- Utility classes
- Static documents (HTML, images, sounds, etc.)
- Client-side applets, beans, and classes
- Descriptive meta-information that ties all the preceding elements together

Of these items, the last is the most important. Typically, the descriptive meta-information (documents that describe other documents in the Web application) resides in XML-encoded files. The XML files describe how the elements combine to make a single application.

In this section, we discuss how to build Web applications, including how to package WAR files and how do write deployment descriptors.

Web Archive Organization

Web archives have a hierarchical organization. The root of the archive maps to the WebLogic Server context-root—for example, *http://www.learnweblogic.com/mywebapp*. The WAR contains files in directories of the archive. To illustrate, let's say that we have the following components in our WAR:

```
/index.html
/howto.jsp
/feedback.jsp
/images/banner.gif
/images/jumping.gif
```

Top-level files such as *index.html* map to *http://www.learnweblogic.com/mywebapp/index.html*. The image jumping.gif maps to *http://www.learnweblogic.com/mywebapp/images/jumping.gif*.

Servlet classes, supporting classes, and descriptive metadocuments are included in the WEB-INF directory. In a typical Web application, the WEB-INF directory might contain the following:

```
/WEB-INF/web.xml → The main meta document
/WEB-INF/lib/jspbean.jar → Supporting classes for JSPs
/WEB-INF/classes/com/mycorp/servlets/MyServlet.class → Servlet
classes
/WEB-INF/classes/com/mycorp/util/MyUtils.class → Utility classes
```

The components stored in the /WEB-INF directory of the archive are protected. WebLogic Server hides this directory from the client and will never send files from this directory to the Web browser. Instead, these files are used by the Web application either to directly service clients or as infrastructure to service clients. The web.xml deployment descriptor ties all these components together. By default, WebLogic Server deploys Web applications with the name of the WAR file using the pattern

```
http://<server name>/<Web application archive name>/
```

A Web application archive named *foo.war* is automatically deployed at

```
URL: http://<server name>/foo/
```

So, if someone visits *http://127.0.0.1:7001/foo/*, WebLogic Server activates `HelloServlet`. See the section below on `weblogic.xml` to override this behavior.

Building a WAR File

The build scripts provided for each example create WAR files using Ant tasks. You can also build the same WAR by hand. Here are three steps to build a WAR using the items in the previous example.

Step 1: Creating a Directory Structure

Create a working directory for your Web application. This discussion uses the directory C:*dev*; however, you can use whatever directory you like. Open a command shell and change to that directory. Copy the *FormServlet* example code fragments from their location on the CD-ROM into your new directory. You should see something like Figure 2–12 after you have created your directory structure.

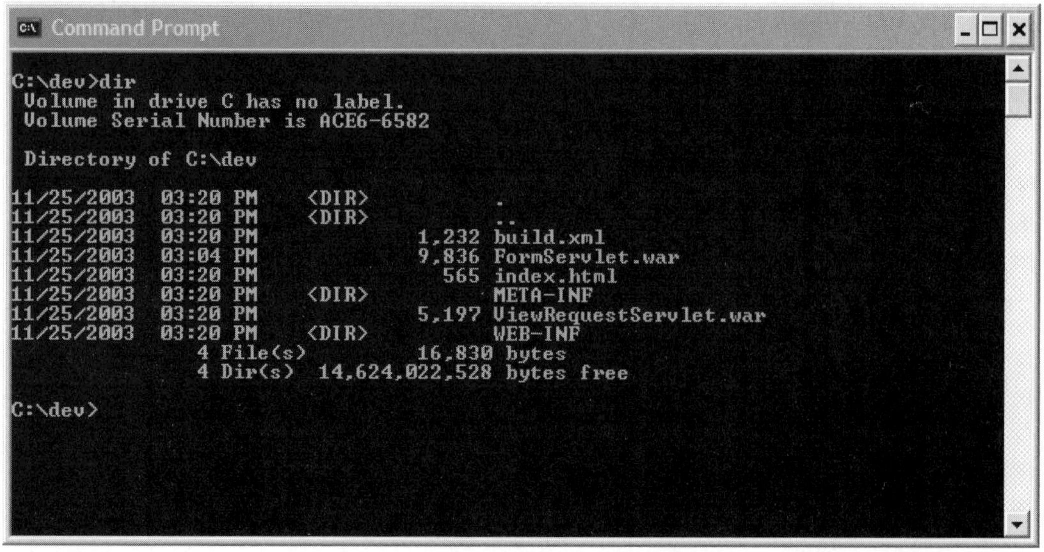

Figure 2–12
Directory listing for building the FormServlet package.

Step 2: Setting Your Environment

You can use the environment scripts included with WebLogic Server as we have in the previous examples. Using your WebLogic Server installation, run the **setWLSEnv.cmd** script, located in the WebLogic **bin** directory:

```
c:\bea\weblogic81\server\bin\setWLSEnv.cmd
```

You should see something like Figure 2–13.

Figure 2-13
Setting the environment.

Step 3: Running the Jar Utility

To run the *jar* utility, simply type jar at the command line with options to instruct the utility to create a new file:

```
jar cvf FormServlet.war *
```

The c option tells the jar utility to create a new file. The v option says that we would like for jar to work in a verbose mode, which means that it outputs details about everything that it does. The f option and the following entry tell jar that we are providing a name for the archive file and the name itself. In this case, use the file *FormServlet.war*. The fourth entry in the command line tells jar the name of the files to include. The asterisk (*) is a wildcard that instructs jar to include all the files in this directory and all subdirectories.

After typing the preceding into the command line, you should see something like Figure 2–14.

You now have a new WAR that can be deployed in WebLogic Server or any other application server with J2EE support. Note: If you look at the build script included with all the examples, this step is automatically done for you.

You can view the contents of the WAR file in any compression utility that supports the Zip file format. For example, the WAR file can be loaded into WinZip (*http://www.winzip.com*). See Figure 2–15.

The directory called META-INF is automatically created for you. It includes information about the package itself.

Note also that this Web archive includes both the build script and the source code in the application. In a real-world application, you probably would not want to make the source code to your application available to anyone visiting your site. For that reason, do not put files in your Web archive file unless you wish to make it available to users of your application.

Figure 2–14
Creating the archive.

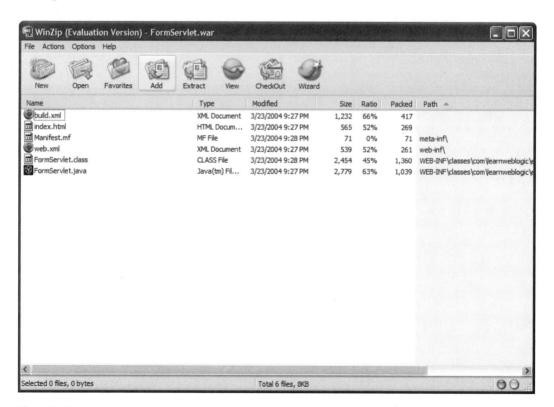

Figure 2–15
Looking at the WAR file with the WinZip utility.

Deployment Descriptors

WebLogic Server needs to know information about the Web application, such as what components are in the Web application, where they are located, what type they are, and so forth. The servlet standard defines the files containing this information about Web applications as deployment descriptors.

In the case of Web applications on WebLogic Server, there are two different deployment descriptors. The first, a file named *web.xml*, is defined by the servlet specification. The second file is a WebLogic-specific deployment descriptor called *weblogic.xml*. The *weblogic.xml* file configures WebLogic Server capabilities and controls beyond the servlet standards. Both the *web.xml* and *weblogic.xml* files are placed in the /WEB-INF/ directory in the Web application WAR.

In order to create deployment descriptor files and to understand how they work for Web applications, it is best to learn by example. In the next sections, we show examples of *web.xml* files. We also include a sample *weblogic.xml* file, but defer discussion of the WebLogic-specific deployment descriptor. The settings in the *weblogic.xml* file are best understood in the context of the functions they support.

web.xml

The *web.xml* file includes many settings necessary to define a Web application. Use the *web.xml* file to define servlets, map servlets to URLs, define configuration parameters (for individual servlets or the Web application as a whole), and configure how WebLogic Server should resolve requests for static resources. This section includes two sample *web.xml* files that are available on the CD-ROM accompanying this book.

Sample1-web.xml

This sample *web.xml* is simple. It is the deployment descriptor for the first example *HelloServlet*.

```
<!DOCTYPE web-app PUBLIC "-//Sun Microsystems, Inc.//DTD Web
Application 2.3//EN" "http://java.sun.com/dtd/web-app_2_3.dtd">
<web-app>

    <servlet>
        <servlet-name>HelloServlet</servlet-name>
        <servlet-class>book.ch2.HelloServlet</servlet-class>
    </servlet>

    <servlet-mapping>
        <servlet-name>HelloServlet</servlet-name>
        <url-pattern>/</url-pattern>
    </servlet-mapping>

</web-app>
```

If you are familiar with HTML, this format should look quite familiar. The first entry defines the document type to be an XML document and defines the Document Type Definition (DTD) of the file. The DTD tells WebLogic Server what format and version is being used for the deployment descriptor. Note that although this tag includes an external URL, WebLogic Server does not need a connection to the Internet to function. WebLogic Server does not use this external URL, but relies instead upon a local copy.

The root element, a <web-app> tag, defines a Web application. The first element names a Java class as a servlet within the Web application. The servlet-name element is used to refer to the servlet within the Web application, and the servlet-class element is the full path to a subclass of HttpServlet that you provide.

The last entry maps a URL pattern to the servlet named *HelloServlet*, which is defined above. In this case, we've specified that it should map to any URL pattern for the application. In a real-world application, you would specify a path within your Web application.

Sample2-web.xml

This sample deployment descriptor includes a number of other options. Comments about each component are included.

```
<!DOCTYPE web-app PUBLIC "-//Sun Microsystems, Inc.//DTD Web
Application 2.3//EN" "http://java.sun.com/dtd/web-app_2_3.dtd">

<web-app>
```

The <display-name> tag signifies the name used when the application is displayed in something like the WebLogic Server console:

```
<display-name>A Simple Application</display-name>
```

The <context-param> tag specifies a parameter to be included in the ServletContext and available to all servlets in the WAR. The ServletContext is covered in the next section. In this case, we define a parameter named Webmaster, with an e-mail address as the value:

```
<context-param>
    <param-name>Webmaster</param-name>
    <param-value>webmaster@mycorp.com</param-value>
</context-param>
```

The following specifies a servlet with the name catalog. It specifies the class to be used, com.mycorp.CatalogServlet and some initial parameters for the servlet. These are also located in the ServletContext for the servlet:

```
<servlet>
    <servlet-name>catalog</servlet-name>
    <servlet-class>com.mycorp.CatalogServlet</servlet-class>

    <init-param>
        <param-name>catalog</param-name>
        <param-value>Spring</param-value>
    </init-param>
</servlet>
```

The following maps the catalog servlet to a URL pattern. WebLogic Server receives requests for any URL beginning with *catalog/*.

```
<servlet-mapping>
    <servlet-name>catalog</servlet-name>
    <url-pattern>/catalog/*</url-pattern>
</servlet-mapping>
```

The following specifies the default timeout in seconds for HTTP session objects. More on sessions in Chapter 3.

```
<session-config>
    <session-timeout>30</session-timeout>
</session-config>
```

The following specifies a MIME type extension to be used. If a file with the .pdf suffix extension is sent, WebLogic Server affixes the MIME type as follows:

```
<mime-mapping>
    <extension>pdf</extension>
    <mime-type>application/pdf</mime-type>
</mime-mapping>
```

The next lines specify the file to be used as a welcome file for the Web application. If someone accesses the Web application without specifying a file (such as *http://www.learningweblogic.com/myApp/*), WebLogic Server attempts to display the welcome file. Note that the value has to be an actual file in the WAR file. If you want to direct the user to a servlet, use the default servlet mapping (see the *Sample3-web.xml* below). The files are chosen in the order listed, with highest precedent on the file listed first:

```
<welcome-file-list>
    <welcome-file>index.jsp</welcome-file>
    <welcome-file>index.html</welcome-file>
    <welcome-file>index.htm</welcome-file>
</welcome-file-list>
```

The following specifies the page to be used in the event of a 404 (File Not Found) HTTP error:

```
<error-page>
    <error-code>404</error-code>
    <location>/404.html</location>
</error-page>
```

The final line concludes the definition of the Web application:

```
</web-app>
```

Note that you can set the error page for any number of HTTP error codes. The complete list of all possible error codes is in the HTTP specification, available on the Internet at *ftp://ftp.isi.edu/in-notes/rfc2616.txt*.

You also can map an error page to an exception type. To do this, instead of listing an error code, list the fully qualified name of your Java exception type:

```
<error-page>
    <exception-type>
        com.learnweblogic.exceptiontype
    </exception-type>
    <location>/error.html</location>
</error-page>
```

The complete *Sample2-web.xml* listed here is located on the CD-ROM accompanying this book in the *code\ch2* directory:

```
<!DOCTYPE web-app PUBLIC "-//Sun Microsystems, Inc.//DTD Web
Application 2.3//EN" "http://java.sun.com/dtd/web-app_2_3.dtd">

<web-app>

  <display-name>A Simple Application</display-name>

  <context-param>
    <param-name>Webmaster</param-name>
    <param-value>webmaster@mycorp.com</param-value>
  </context-param>

  <servlet>
    <servlet-name>catalog</servlet-name>
    <servlet-class>com.mycorp.CatalogServlet</servlet-class>
    <init-param>
      <param-name>catalog</param-name>
      <param-value>Spring</param-value>
    </init-param>
  </servlet>

  <servlet-mapping>
    <servlet-name>catalog</servlet-name>
    <url-pattern>/catalog/*</url-pattern>
  </servlet-mapping>

  <session-config>
    <session-timeout>30</session-timeout>
  </session-config>
```

```
  <mime-mapping>
    <extension>pdf</extension>
    <mime-type>application/pdf</mime-type>
  </mime-mapping>

  <welcome-file-list>
    <welcome-file>index.jsp</welcome-file>
    <welcome-file>index.html</welcome-file>
    <welcome-file>index.htm</welcome-file>
  </welcome-file-list>

  <error-page>
    <error-code>404</error-code>
    <location>/404.html</location>
  </error-page>
</web-app>
```

Sample3-web.xml

This sample deployment descriptor demonstrates the use of url-patterns in servlet mapping:

```
<!DOCTYPE web-app PUBLIC "-//Sun Microsystems, Inc.//DTD Web
Application 2.3//EN" "http://java.sun.com/dtd/web-app_2_3.dtd">

<web-app>
  <servlet>
    <servlet-name>ViewRequestServlet</servlet-name>
    <servlet-
class>com.learnweblogic.examples.ch2.ViewRequestServlet</servlet-
class>
  </servlet>

  <servlet-mapping>
    <servlet-name>ViewRequestServlet</servlet-name>
    <url-pattern>/a</url-pattern>
  </servlet-mapping>

  <servlet-mapping>
    <servlet-name>ViewRequestServlet</servlet-name>
    <url-pattern>/b/*</url-pattern>
  </servlet-mapping>

  <servlet-mapping>
    <servlet-name>ViewRequestServlet</servlet-name>
    <url-pattern>*.c</url-pattern>
  </servlet-mapping>
```

```
<servlet-mapping>
  <servlet-name>ViewRequestServlet</servlet-name>
  <url-pattern>/</url-pattern>
</servlet-mapping>
</web-app>
```

The example provides an alternative web.xml deployment descriptor for the ViewRequest-Servlet and includes a number of servlet mappings. The mappings determine both how to map user requests to servlets and how to compute the values of ServletPath and PathInfo in the request object. Table 2–1 summarizes WebLogic Server's matching of URL patterns.

Table 2–1   WebLogic Server's Matching of URL Patterns

url-pattern	Request	Match?	ServletPath	PathInfo
Exact match	/	fails		
/a	/a	matches	/a	null
	/a/	fails		
	/a/b.c	fails		
Prefix match	/	fails		
/a/*	/a	matches	/a	null
	/a/	matches	/a	/
	/a/b.c	matches	/a	/b.c
Suffix match	/	fails		
*.c	/a	fails		
	/a/	fails		
	/a/b.c	matches	/a/b.c	null
Default servlet	/	Matches	/	null
/	/a	matches	/a	null
	/a/	matches	/a/	null
	/a/b.c	matches	/a/b.c	null

Multiple patterns may match a particular request URL, so WebLogic Server uses a priority scheme to select a pattern. WebLogic Server selects matches in the order of pattern types listed in Table 2–1. If multiple prefix patterns match the request URL, WebLogic Server selects the pattern with the longest matching prefix. Thus, a full pattern match takes priority over the default servlet.

Try replacing the original *web.xml* with the Sample3-web.xml for the ViewRequestServ-let. Deploy the servlet and request various URLs. The ViewRequestServlet will print the ServletPath and PathInfo variables.

Other web.xml Options

Many of the other options specifically support security, EJB, or JSP. We cover these other *web.xml* options in subsequent chapters. For your reference, here are some other important options that can be included in a *web.xml* file, with examples of each.

Icon Element

The `icon` element contains a `small-icon` and a `large-icon` element, which specify the location of a small and a large image used to represent the Web application in a GUI tool. At a minimum, tools must accept GIF and JPEG format images. The `small-icon` element contains the location of a file containing a small (16 × 16 pixel) icon image. The `large-icon` element contains the location of a file containing a large (32 × 32 pixel) icon image.

```
<icon>
<small-icon>filename</small-icon>
<large-icon>filename</large-icon>
</icon>
```

Display-Name Element

The `display-name` element contains a short name that is intended to be displayed by GUI tools.

```
<display-name>name</display-name>
```

Description Element

The `description` element provides descriptive text about the parent element.

```
<description>name</description>
```

weblogic.xml

WebLogic Server provides a number of features beyond the servlet specification, including:

- Setting WebLogic Server-specific values.
- Overriding default WebLogic Server behavior.
- Providing mappings of resources, including DataSources, EJBs, and virtual directories.
- Configuring custom security settings.

This sample `weblogic.xml` includes a sampling of available options. The `weblogic.xml` file begins with an open tag for the root element:

```
<weblogic-web-app>
```

The `description` element provides a free-text field to describe the Web application:

```
<description>Sample Web application</description>
```

Web applications may target a particular version of WebLogic Server. The `weblogic-version` element specifies the intended version of WebLogic Server. The element is only for informational purposes—WebLogic Server does not read the value. This line informs future readers of the `weblogic.xml` file that the author intends for this Web application to be run under WebLogic Server 8.1:

```
<weblogic-version>8.1</weblogic-version>
```

By default, the `context-root` of a Web application is based on the name of the WAR file deployed to WebLogic Server. To override this default, specify a `context-root` in the `weblogic.xml` file:

```
<context-root>mysample</context-root>
```

If the WAR is included within an enterprise archive file (EAR), the `context-root` specified in the EAR overrides the value in the `weblogic.xml` file.

Java Server Pages (JSP) is another presentation technology covered in more detail in Chapter 4. The following descriptor customizes WebLogic Server's handling of JSPs:

```
<jsp-descriptor>
    <jsp-param>
        <param-name>compileCommand</param-name>
        <param-value>/jdk130/bin/javac.exe</param-value>
    </jsp-param>
</jsp-descriptor>
```

Servlet sessions are a useful mechanism for storing a user's state between requests. Sessions are covered in greater detail in **Chapter 3.** The following lines customize how WebLogic Server manages sessions:

```
<session-descriptor>
    <session-param>
        <param-name>IDLength</param-name>
        <param-value>16</param-value>
    </session-param>
    <session-param>
        <param-name>CookiesEnabled</param-name>
        <param-value>false</param-value>
    </session-param>
    <session-param>
        <param-name>URLRewritingEnabled</param-name>
        <param-value>true</param-value>
    </session-param>
</session-descriptor>
```

The `container-descriptor` element includes multiple settings useful in configuring the WebLogic Server servlet container. This block overrides many default settings, including the number of instances WebLogic Server creates for a servlets implementing the `SingleThreadModel` interface (the default value is 5).

```
<container-descriptor>
    <single-threaded-servlet-pool-size>
        10
    </single-threaded-servlet-pool-size>
```

If your servlet fails to set a MIME type in the `HttpServletResponse` object, WebLogic Server returns `null`. To override this behavior, use the following directive:

```
<default-mime-type>text/html</default-mime-type>
```

When WebLogic redeploys an active Web application, it normally discards all active sessions. In order to save sessions during deployment, use the following line:

```
<save-sessions-enabled>true</save-sessions-enabled>
```

Finally, `weblogic.xml` can change the behavior of the WebLogic classloader. Normally, WebLogic Server selects classes found within the system `CLASSPATH` over those in the Web application. If you want to reverse this behavior, use the element `prefer-web-inf-classes`:

```
    <prefer-web-inf-classes>true</prefer-web-inf-classes>
  </container-descriptor>
</weblogic-web-app>
```

See *http://edocs.bea.com/wls/docs81/webapp/weblogic_xml.html* for additional configurations available in the `weblogic.xml` file.

The ServletContext

A Web application needs a way to tie all its components together programmatically. For example, as part of a Web application, a servlet can define elements that other servlets can use. Also, the deployment descriptor can to define parameters for the application as a whole. The `ServletContext` provides these capabilities.

The `ServletContext` is an object specific to a given Web application and represents the application to individual servlets. A `ServletContext` exists for each Web application on each WebLogic Server instance (or Java Virtual Machine). Some of the things that the servlet can do with the `ServletContext` include the following:

- Log events.
- Obtain URL references to resources such as images, multimedia, or a temporary working directory.
- Set and store attributes that other servlets in the context can use. Examples of these attributes include objects such as JavaBeans (covered in Chapter 4); cached results from database queries (covered in Chapter 5, "WebLogic Server JDBC and JTA"); and any other object that should be shared by all the servlet resources for any user who visits the application.

Getting the ServletContext

The process of acquiring the `ServletContext` is straightforward. The following simple servlet demonstrates this:

```
public void doGet(HttpServletRequest req, HttpServletResponse res)
    throws IOException
{

    // Locate Our Servlet Context
    ServletContext sc = getServletContext();

    // Use the Context here.
    .
    .
    .

}
}
```

Reading context-param from web.xml

The *web.xml* may contain attributes that apply to the Web application as a whole using the context-param element. The ServletContext class provides methods to read these parameters.

- public String getInitParameter(String name)—Returns the value of the named parameter as defined in the context-param of the web.xml file.
- public Enumeration getInitParameterNames()—This method returns the name of each context-param element defined in the Web application's *web.xml* file.

Setting and Getting Attributes

The ServletContext object offers you the ability to set and retrieve attributes. The attributes are named, and the value can be any Java objects. After attributes are set in the ServletContext, the attributes are available to any other servlet that is part of the same Web application. Attributes are useful any time you want to track a resource and share it among multiple servlets.

The following summarizes the methods that are available for attributes:

- public java.lang.Object getAttribute(String name)—Returns the servlet container attribute with the given name, or null if there is no attribute by that name.
- public java.util.Enumeration getAttributeNames()—Returns an enumeration containing the attribute names available within this servlet context.
- public void setAttribute(String name, java.lang.Object object)—Binds an object to a given attribute name in this servlet context.
- public void removeAttribute(String name)—Removes the attribute with the given name from the servlet context.

The following servlet shows how to acquire the ServletContext object, display context-param names and values, add and remove an attribute, retrieve an attribute, and retrieve an Enumeration of all the attributes available in the ServletContext:

```
import java.io.*;
import java.util.*;
import javax.servlet.*;
import javax.servlet.http.*;

public class ContextServlet extends HttpServlet {
    public void doGet(HttpServletRequest req, HttpServletResponse res)
    throws IOException {
        // set the response Content-Type
        res.setContentType("text/html");
        // obtain a PrintWriter stream to write to.
        PrintWriter out = res.getWriter();
        // print out our text
        out.println("<html>");
        out.println("<head><title>ContextServlet</title></head>");
        out.println("<body>");
        out.println("<pre>");
```

```java
// Locate Our Servlet Context
ServletContext sc = getServletContext();

/*
  Get an Enumeration of all the context-param
  elements defined in application web.xml.
 */
Enumeration myInitParams = sc.getInitParameterNames();

/*
  Cycle through each name in myInitParams and
  print both the name and the value.
 */
out.println("<h1>InitParameters</h1>");
while(myInitParams.hasMoreElements()) {
    String name = myInitParams.nextElement().toString();
    out.println(name + "=" + sc.getInitParameter(name) +
"<br>");
}

/*
  Set an attribute named "attrib1" that contains
  a value of "my value":
 */
sc.setAttribute("attrib1", "my value");
/*
  Get an Enumeration of all the attributes
  currently active in our ServletContext.
 */
Enumeration myAttributes = sc.getAttributeNames();

/*
  Cycle through each name in myAttributes and
  print both the name and the value.
 */
out.println("<h1>Attributes</h1>");
while(myAttributes.hasMoreElements()) {
    String name = myAttributes.nextElement().toString();
    out.println(name + "=" + sc.getAttribute(name) + "<br>");
}
/*
  Remove attribute named "attrib1".
 */
sc.removeAttribute("attrib1");
```

```
        out.println("</pre></body></html>");
    }
}
```

The above example employed a number of the methods available in `ServletContext`. The `doGet()` handler first reads the names of `context-param` entries using the `getInitParameterNames()` method, and then prints each name and corresponding value.

The handler then declares a new attribute named `"attrib1"` and sets its value equal to a string literal of `"my value"`. Note: The `setAttribute()` method is not limited to Strings; the method accepts any derivative of `java.lang.Object` (that is, any Java object) as an attribute. Also, if an attribute already exists, the `setAttribute()` method updates the value of that attribute.

After setting the first attribute, we call the `getAttributeNames()` method, which returns a `java.util.Enumeration` of all the names of the attributes available in the `ServletContext`, and prints each name and corresponding value. Also, this enumeration is useful if you need to locate an attribute but you're unsure of its exact name. Finally, we call the `removeAttribute()` method to remove the same attribute we added.

The `ServletContext` provides a mechanism for sharing data across multiple servlets within an instance of WebLogic Server. However, because these attributes exist locally to that WebLogic Server instance in which they are created, the `ServletContext` may not be used to communicate across multiple server instances. In later sections, we describe how to create a distributed shared-memory store.

Using Web Application Resources

Web applications can also include resources that are defined and contained in its package. These resources can be virtually any static content file, including text, images, or other multimedia. In order to access these components, you must include these resources in the Web application package.

The ability to access resources from your servlets can be quite useful. Some uses include

- Dynamically processing and filtering images for a given user. For example, you might want to overlay a user's name on top of a standard image to customize it.
- Simple queries of text resources or other data stored in the Web application. This is helpful for rapid prototyping.

Your application locates and accesses resources using the `ServletContext` object. Two methods are useful to locate and access resources:

- `public java.net.URL getResource(String path)`—Useful when you wish to understand the complete URL of a given Web application resource. You supply a relative path to the resource; you are returned the full URL.
- `public java.io.InputStream getResourceAsStream(String path)`—This method returns a reference to an `InputStream` whose source is the resource specified by the path.

In both of these methods, the parameter is a relative path to the resource from the root of the Web application. To illustrate, if you have a resource named *myimage.gif* contained in your Web application package in a subdirectory named */luke/images/*, then the relative path would be */luke/images/ myimage.gif*.

The following sample locates the full URL for this image and makes it available as an `Input-Stream`:

```
// Import classes, define servlet, etc. here.

public void doGet(HttpServletRequest req, HttpServletResponse res)
    throws IOException
{

    // Locate Our Servlet Context
    ServletContext sc = getServletConfig().getServletContext();

    // Get the Full URL to Our Image:
    java.net.URL myURL = sc.getResource("/luke/images/
myimage.gif");

    // Get Our Image As an InputStream:
    java.io.InputStream myIS =
    sc.getResourceAsStream("/luke/images/myimage.gif");
}
```

Note: Any resource accessed in this manner is treated as static content. As you'll see later, JSPs are stored as text files and compiled automatically. If you were to try to load a JSP using these methods for resources, you would see the text of the JSP page and not the output of the executed code. If you wish to include the output of another executable component of the Web application, such as a JSP or a servlet, you should use the `RequestDispatcher` discussed in the next section.

Forward and Include

The servlets in the previous examples receive requests and generate responses. In many cases, a Web application requires that a client be directed to another resource, whether a servlet, JSP, or static URL.

Earlier in this chapter, we discussed the `HttpServletResponse` and the method `sendRedirect()`. Servlets pass this method a URL to forward clients to another URL. This method sets the HTTP response code `TEMPORARY_REDIRECT` and includes the target URL. The client makes a second HTTP request to the indicated URL and displays these results.

To redirect the client to *http://www.learnweblogic.com*, include the following code in your servlet:

```
public void service(HttpServletRequest req, HttpServletResponse
res)
        throws ServletException, IOException
{
        res.sendRedirect(http://www.learnweblogic.com/)
}
```

The above example transfers the user to *www.learnwebblogic.com* but is inefficient because it requires the client to make two complete HTTP requests. If the target of the redirect is within the same WebLogic Server instance, the `RequestDispatcher` provides a better solution. Servlets may use the `RequestDispatcher` to handle requests using other Web resources on the server such as servlets, JSP, or HTML pages. The mechanism used by the `RequestDispatcher` is transparent to the client and requires only one HTTP request.

Using the RequestDispatcher

There are two ways to use the `RequestDispatcher` functionality. The servlet may forward a request to other resources, or the servlet may include the output of other resources within its own output.

Forwarding to Other Resources

Using the `RequestDispatcher` requires information stored in the `ServletContext` of the servlet. We can use the following to locate the `ServletContext` within our servlet class:

```
// Locate Our Servlet Context
ServletContext sc = getServletContext();
```
Next, you'll need to get a handle to the resource that you'll be forwarding to:
```
/*
  Specify the path of the resource we want to get using
  the Servlet context from above. Variations demonstrate
  the use of differing target types.
  */
RequestDispatcher rd = sc.getRequestDispatcher("/catalog/")
RequestDispatcher rd = sc.getRequestDispatcher("/login.jsp")
RequestDispatcher rd = sc.getRequestDispatcher("/target.html")
```

Alternately, you can look up a `RequestDispatcher` for a servlet using the servlet's name, as defined in the Web application's *web.xml* file.

```
RequestDispatcher rd = sc.getNamedDispatcher("catalog");
```
You can then use the `forward()` method to direct the request to the object of your choice:

```
/*
  Call forward on this request dispatcher using the
  parameters sent to our service method.
  */
rd.forward(myHttpServletRequest ,myHttpServletResponse );
```

The forward functionality of the `RequestDispatcher` may only be called if you have not sent any output to the client. If output does exist in the response buffer, you must reset the response if possible. See the following code as a demonstration:

```
if(!myHttpServletResponse.isCommitted()) {
    myHttpServletResponse.resetBuffer();
    rd.forward(myHttpServletRequest ,myHttpServletResponse );
    return;
} else {
    // The servlet is unable to forward the request.
    // The servlet may write an error message.
    .
    .
}
```

If a response has already been sent to the client and the servlet calls forward(), an IllegalStateException will be thrown at runtime.

Be sure to return from the request handler after the forward() call to the RequestDispatcher. This return causes the servlet container to stop processing your code.

Including Other Resources

You may also want to include the output of other resources within your response. For example, you may want to include a standard header, generated by either another servlet or a static HTML file, within your servlet output. Use the include functionality of the RequestDispatcher.

First, follow the process used above to locate the RequestDispatcher for the object that you want to include. Then, call the include method on that resource:

```
// Call Include on This Request Dispatcher Using the
// Parameters Send to Our Service Method
myRequestDispatcher.include (HttpServletRequest
myHttpServletRequest ,
HttpServletResponse myHttpServletResponse );
```

Web Application Events

The servlet specification provides for init() and destroy() methods within servlet classes to trigger servlet-specific code within the servlet lifecycle. In order to perform initialization and cleanup tasks for a Web application as a whole, create an instance of the ServletContextListener class.

At initialization and end of service, the WebLogic Server generates a ServletContextEvent object. The WebLogic Server passes this event to listener objects configured in the *web.xml* file. The servlet specification supports notification of Web application lifecycle events and changes to ServletContext attributes.

Web Application Lifecycle Events

Configure a Web application to handle lifecycle events by writing a class that implements the ServletContextListener interface and configuring the *web.xml* file to reference the new class.

The ServletContextListener interface defines the methods contextInitialized() and contextDestroyed():

- public void contextInitialized(ServletContextEvent event)—The servlet container calls this method during initialization of the Web application.

- `public void contextDestroyed(ServletContextEvent event)`—The servlet container calls this method during end of service of the Web application.

The `ServletContextEvent` object, provided to the `ServletContextListener`, provides only one method: `getServetContext()`.

Use the *web.xml* file to register `ServletContextListener` classes. WebLogic Server creates an instance of each registered class and calls the `contextInitialized()` method during servlet initialization. WebLogic Server calls the listener objects in the order they appear within the *web.xml* file. During a Web application's end of service, WebLogic calls `contextDestroyed()` on the listener objects in reverse order.

The following example includes two `ServletContextListener` classes. These classes should be included in the WAR, either in the /WEB-INF/ classes or a JAR file in /WEB-INF/*lib*. In the following *web.xml* sample, WebLogic Server creates an instance of `DatabaseConnectionManager` and `ModuleConfigurationManager`, and calls the `contextInitialized()` and `contextDestroyed()` methods during initialization and end of service phases.

```
<web-app>
  <display-name>Web application with Listeners</display-name>

  <listener>
    <listener-class>
      com.mycorp.DatabaseConnectionManager
    </listenerclass>
  </listener>
  <listener>
    <listener-class>
      com.mycorp.ModuleConfigurationManager
    </listener-class>
  </listener>
  <servlet>
    <servlet-name>catalog</servlet-name>
    <servlet-class>com.mycorp.CatalogServlet</servlet-class>
  </servlet>

  <servlet-mapping>
    <servlet-name>catalog</servlet-name>
    <url-pattern>/catalog/*</url-pattern>
  </servlet-mapping>

</web-app>
```

Attribute Change Events

In addition to the lifecycle events in the previous section, WebLogic Server generates events when attributes in the `ServletContext` change. Configure a Web application to accept attribute change events by writing a class which implements the `ServletContextAttributeListener` interface and configuring the *web.xml* file to reference the new class.

The `ServletContextAttributeListener` interface defines the methods `attributeAdded()`, `attributeRemoved()`, and `attributeReplaced()`:

- `public void attributeAdded(ServletContextAttributeEvent event)`— The servlet container calls this method when an attribute is added to the `ServletContext`.
- `public void attributeRemoved(ServletContextAttributeEvent event)`— The servlet container calls this method when an attribute value is removed from the `ServletContext`.

The `ServletContextAttributeEvent` provides `getName()` and `getValue()` methods that provide information regarding the modified attribute in the `ServletContext`.

- `public void attributeReplaced(ServletContextAttributeEvent event)`— The servlet container calls this method when an attribute value is replaced. The attribute is replaced rather than added when the method `setAttribute()` is called on the `ServletContext` using an existing attribute name.

Again, listener classes should be included in the WAR file and specified in the *web.xml* file. Configure the *web.xml* file using the same syntax as used above for lifecycle events. WebLogic Server determines how to direct events by checking which interface the target class implements.

Best Practices for Servlets

There are a number of best practices that can enable your servlet-based applications to be as successful as possible.

Define Public Servlet Classes

First, when you create a servlet, be sure to define the servlet class as `public`. WebLogic Server (or any other application server) requires this designation to access your class. Application servers can display lack-of-access errors that are very difficult to diagnose.

Use Defined Response Codes

The `HttpServletResponse` provides public, static, final definitions for all HTTP response codes. Use them rather than the numeric status code value to improve code readability and reduce the likelihood of mistakes. For example, rather than

```
res.sendError("503");
```

use

```
res.sendError(res.SC_SERVICE_UNAVAILABLE);
```

Use the No-Parameter init() Method

Override the `HttpServlet` method `init()` rather than `init(ServletConfig config)`. Before the 2.3 version of the servlet specification, the `init()` method needed to call `super.init(config)`. If a developer forgets to make this required call, the servlet may malfunction. The new `init()` method is safer because it does not require the developer to include any particular calls.

Use Web Application Lifecycle Events

Use the `ServletContextListener.contextInitialized()` callback to complete initialization tasks that have an effect beyond a single servlet. The `servlet.init()` method ties initialization tasks to a specific servlet and may limit future flexibility in configuring the Web application. The listener provides an initialization mechanism tied to the Web application as a whole.

Keep Scalability in Mind

Avoid doing things that inhibit scalability, such as using the single-thread model for your servlets. If you recall, this model allows only a single thread of execution at a time to execute your servlet. If possible, do not use this model.

Favor the RequestDispatcher

Don't use the `HttpResponse.sendRedirect()` for local URLs. When the request can be handled internally, the redirect creates unnecessary overhead. Use the `RequestDispather.forward()` method to redirect a user to another page (e.g., to a login page if that user's session is invalid).

include() to Reuse Common Components

Reuse common HTML components using the `RequestDispatcher.include()` method for programmatic server-side includes. For example, an application may include a listing of sports scores on every page. Write a single servlet that responds with a sports score and include this servlet on each generated page.

Optimize Keep-Alive

Keep-Alive is a key optimization in the HTTP 1.1 protocol. It helps Web servers be more efficient by minimizing the number of sockets created to service a client. Most Web pages contain multiple components, each downloaded separately and put together by the Web browser. In addition to the HTML page, components may include images, sounds, and other types of media. In the early days of the Web, the HTTP protocol required that the client and Web server each establish a socket for each of these requests. The Keep-Alive feature now allows a Web server to maintain a single socket to a client. Because the creation, removal, and establishment of sockets are expensive to a server, Keep-Alive enhances performance and scalability.

Keep-Alive will generally work if the servlet does not flush the output stream, WebLogic Server is able to determine the content length when it writes the response, and the Keep-Alive session does not time out.

Don't Close/Terminate the Response Stream

As mentioned previously, performance is enhanced when WebLogic Server is not required to create and destroy sockets many times to handle a single client session. In order to avoid breaking the

Keep-Alive optimization, do not `close()` or `flush()` streams that you send in your `service()` or `do<request type>()` methods.

Manage Content Length

The Keep-Alive feature in HTTP 1.1 requires that WebLogic Server set the content length in the response header. WebLogic Server can determine the content length for your servlet, but only if the servlet follows best practices. First, any content length set by your servlet takes precedence, so do not set the wrong content length. Also, WebLogic cannot determine the content length if the output exceeds the output buffer. If you know the content length, then set it. WebLogic Server will automatically adjust the buffer size. If the content length is unknown, set the buffer size to be larger than the anticipated output. Set content length or buffer size in the `HttpServletResponse`.

Tune Keep-Alive Configuration

WebLogic Server enables you to specify how long it maintains a Keep-Alive socket. The default value is 30 seconds. Use the WebLogic Server console to modify the socket timeout interval on a per-server basis. You should increase the timeout value if users download multiple resources per HTML page from WebLogic Server, if users spend a long time interacting with your Web application, or if users repeatedly make requests at very short intervals.

Exclude Source Code from Component Files

Several examples have created Web archives, including both the build script and the source code in the application. In a real-world application, you probably would not want to make the source code to your application available to anyone visiting your site. For that reason, do not put files in your Web archive file unless you wish to make them available to users of your application.

References

The working body that defines the HTTP standard is the World Wide Web Consortium, or W3C. The W3C homepage is at *http://www.w3c.org*.

The specification for HTTP is available as an RFC. HTTP 1.1 is available at *ftp://ftp.isi.edu/in-notes/rfc2616.txt*.

The Java Community Process page for JSR 000053 provides the final specification for the Servlet 2.3 specification: *http://www.jcp.org/aboutJava/communityprocess/final/jsr053*.

To read the javadoc for the Servlet classes, refer to *http://java.sun.com/products/servlet/2.3/javadoc*.

The content-types used by HTTP are defined in the RFC Multipurpose Internet Mail Extensions (MIME) Part Two: Media Types. This document is available at *ftp://ftp.isi.edu/in-notes/rfc2046.txt*.

The handy WinZip application is available online at *http://www.winzip.com*.

Full documentation of the deployment descriptor used to configure WebLogic Server (`weblogic.xml`) is available at *http://edocs.bea.com/wls/docs81/webapp/weblogic_xml.html*.

Ant documentation is available at *http://ant.apache.org/manual/index.html*.

The WebLogic deployment task is documented at *http://e-docs.bea.com/wls/docs81/deployment/tools.html*.

chapter 3

Advanced Servlet Techniques

In This Chapter

- Using sessions and storing state
- Using cookies for long-term storage
- Filtering HTTP requests
- Understanding WebLogic Server deployment issues
- Additional best practices for Web application development

Chapter 2 discusses the basics of handling HTTP requests and how to manage collections of Web resources. This chapter takes servlets a step further and discusses how to maintain information between HTTP requests, how to improve code reuse with filters, and how to plan Web application deployments on WebLogic to improve performance and reliability.

Servlets and Web Sessions

The Hypertext Transfer Protocol (HTTP) is, by design, a stateless protocol. However, many Web applications require information, previously gathered from the user, to process a request. With this information, a servlet can remember a user's name, items placed in a shopping cart, or a shipping address. The notion of saving information across multiple requests from a single client is typically called a Web session. Linking this information from one request to another is session tracking.

Store Information in a Session

In the early days of the Web, developers found many ways to maintain session information. Browsers and servlet containers provided different mechanisms to store, retrieve, and track information from one request to the next. Developers had to create their own session management schemes. Fortunately, the servlet standard defines a common mechanism to maintain sessions. This common mechanism, the servlet session, hides most of the technical complexities and allows developers to concentrate on writing Web applications. Servlets place information into a session and retrieve this information in subsequent requests. In this way, sessions add state information to the otherwise stateless HTTP protocol.

Sessions work by storing state information in a local object and creating a reference to that object. WebLogic Server passes this reference back to the browser to be returned in future requests. When the browser does make another request, it includes the reference. WebLogic Server matches the request to the appropriate session object using this reference and provides this session object to the Web application. This way, when a the servlet stores a user's account number in the session, the account number is still there when the user clicks the *Buy now* button.

The servlet session hides most, but not all, technical details. First, WebLogic Server must store the session object between requests. WebLogic Server offers a number of options to store this information, each with its own set of tradeoffs. The section on deployment considerations, later in this chapter, provides more options regarding session storage.

Second, WebLogic Server must pass the reference or session ID to the browser. Typically, WebLogic Server automatically selects between two mechanisms: URL rewriting and HTTP cookies. Again, each technique has tradeoffs. Developers can configure both the selection between these mechanisms and implementation details for either mechanism. In practice, the configuration of the client typically determines the selection between URL rewriting and cookies.

The class `javax.servlet.http.HttpSession` defines servlet sessions. You can access the `HttpSession` using the `getSession()` method of the `HttpServletRequest`. You can also set and get attributes on the `HttpSession` object. The `HttpSession` enables your application to maintain session information without dealing with all the details of tracking sessions.

What to Put in Your Session

There are a number of things you could store in a session object, including the following:

- Fields a user has entered that will be used to generate a subsequent page.
- Virtual shopping carts to hold the items that a user is currently interested in purchasing.
- A history of resources a user has viewed during the current session. For example, if you are building an e-commerce site, you'll want to see what pages the user has visited so you can decide what other pages might be of interest to him or her.

There also are things that you should not store in a session object. Do not store long-term data, such as a user record or account balance. Also, don't store transactional data in a session. Sessions can never provide the reliability necessary to record transactions. The session is a temporary object, so only store information that you can recover.

Session ID

WebLogic Server generates a long, randomly generated, and unique session identification number for each session. The servlet engine uses this number to track sessions across HTTP requests.

For each new browser session, WebLogic Server automatically creates a temporary HTTP cookie, a text object that can be placed on the client's machine and included in future requests to the server. WebLogic Server automatically assigns a session ID number, stores the session identification number in this temporary cookie, and attempts to place the cookie in the client browser. If successful, the browser sends this cookie back to the server along with each subsequent request. WebLogic Server automatically maps the session identifier to the `HttpSession` object it is tracking for that user. WebLogic Server locates the appropriate `HttpSession` and provides this session object to the servlet within the `HttpRequest` object.

Some clients do not support cookies, and users may consider cookies an invasion of privacy and reject them. If WebLogic Server fails to place a cookie on the client, it reverts to URL rewriting. URL rewriting works by adding the session ID to each URL in subsequent requests.

When storing session information, security is a concern. Even though the session information is maintained with the server, we are concerned with the session ID stored on the client. If the session ID is short, an attacker may be able to guess a valid session ID and masquerade as a valid user. The longer the session ID, the harder it is for an attacker to guess. By default, WebLogic Server generates a 52-digit session ID.

For most situations, the default session ID length is acceptable. In other cases, shorter session IDs are required. For example, some wireless devices (using WAP, or the Wireless Application Protocol) limit the entire URL to 128 characters. In this situation, use the `weblogic.xml` deployment descriptor to set the length of the session ID. The best practice is to use the longest session ID possible to ensure security.

Using Sessions

Accessing the Session Object

From one request to the next, the session object is available for the lifetime of the session. Access the `HttpSession` object from the `HttpServletRequest` object using the `getSession()` method, like this:

```
HttpSession session = request.getSession (false);
```

The method takes a `boolean` parameter to specify whether the method may create a new session. If the value is true, WebLogic creates a new session object if one does not already exist. If the value is false, the server does not create a new session object but instead returns `null`. For reasons that become apparent later, you typically want to set a value of false when you call this method.

Creating New Sessions

The `HttpSession` object provides an `isNew()` method—use it with caution. The best way to determine whether your user already has a session is to get the current session. If no session exists, you can force the user to log in and, only after a successful login, create a new session object. This sequence is a good practice because it prevents users from bypassing your security mechanisms.

Acquire the session object by calling the method `getSession(false)`. If the user does not already have a session, the method returns `null`. You can then force users to log in each time they begin a new session. In this case, redirect the client browser to the login page for your Web application when the `getSession(false)` returns `null`. If the session exists, or is not `null`, you can continue using the session:

```
HttpSession session = request.getSession (false);

if (session==null) {
    // We  Send a Redirect
    responseObj.sendRedirect("http://www.learnweblogic.com/login");
}
// continue processing
```

What NOT *to Do*

You might be tempted to do the following:

```
// An Example of What Not to Do:
HttpSession session = request.getSession (true);
// Check to See If the Session Is New
if (session.isNew()) {
    // We  Send a Redirect
    responseObj.sendRedirect("http://www.learnweblogic.com/login");
}
```

Don't do it.

In this code, we ask for the session object as usual. However, because we set the parameter value to `true` in the `getSession()` method, a new session is created if one does not already exist. While this code seems to do the right thing, it introduces a security problem. Someone can create a large number of session objects by repeatedly requesting the URL. These sessions accumulate as memory on your server for each request, so an attacker can tie up significant server resources. Ultimately, an attacker can destabilize the server.

> **Best Practice:** Use sessions to mark login status. Create a new session only on login and look for a session to confirm login status. When the user logs out, invalidate his or her session. Use filters to apply security checks consistently throughout your Web application.

Storing and Accessing Session Data

Session data is stored in the `HttpSession` object using name/value pairs. For each pair, a `String` name is used to reference a value `Object`. The value can be an instance of any Java class.

The servlet specification defines four methods that you can use to access the values in the `HttpSession` object:

- `public Object getAttribute (String name)`—Returns the object bound with the specified name in this session, or `null` if no object is bound under the name.
- `public void setAttribute (String name, Object attribute)`—Binds an object to this session using the name specified.
- `public Enumeration getAttributeNames ()`—Returns an Enumeration of string objects containing the names of all the objects bound to this session.
- `public void removeAttribute(String name)`—Removes the object bound with the specified name from this session.

> **Best Practice:** Keep your sessions small. Your servlet's performance can degrade if the session objects become too large. Keep your attributes small. When an attribute is changed, WebLogic Server must replicate the attribute. If your attributes are small, you minimize the required replication.

> **Best Practice:** Make sure all attribute objects implement the `Serializable` interface. WebLogic Server may serialize your session to move it to another instance.

URL Rewriting

WebLogic Server automatically generates temporary cookies to store the session ID, but what if a client does not accept cookies? URL rewriting provides a way to deal with these clients. URL rewriting works by modifying the HTML code sent to the client. WebLogic Server adds a session ID to the end of each URL on links back to your application. WebLogic Server can use this session ID in place of cookies to match the request to the right session.

URL rewriting requires that the servlet call an encoding method in the servlet response object for URLs in the generated HTML page. For URL rewriting to work reliably, all servlets in a Web application must use rewriting on all URLs. The methods to rewrite URLs take two forms:

- `public String encodeURL(String url)`—Includes the logic required to encode the session information in the returned URL. WebLogic Server automatically determines whether the session ID needs to be encoded in the URL. If the browser supports cookies, or if session tracking is turned off, URL encoding is unnecessary. To encode the URL, add the following code to your servlet:

  ```
  // Add the Session Information Via URL Encoding
  myHttpServletResponse.encodeURL(thisURL);
  ```

  So, if your original URL was

  ```
  <a href="foo.jsp">bar</a>
  ```

  you would use the `encodeURL()` method on that URL:

  ```
  out.println("<a href=\"" +
  response.encodeURL("<a href=\"foo.jsp\">") + "\">bar</a>");
  ```

- `public String encodeRedirectURL(String url)`—Performs the same task as the previous method, except it is specially geared to redirects in the response object. For redirection, you should have the following in your servlet:

  ```
  // Sending a Redirect with URL Encoded session ID
  myHttpServletResponse.sendRedirect
          (myHttpServletResponse.encodeRedirectUrl(anotherURL));
  ```

URL rewriting is also important when using Web frames and redirects. Depending on timing and the type of request, the browser may not send the cookie with every request. If you notice that your Web site mysteriously loses contact with the user sessions when frames are being used, you should force URL rewriting to solve the problem. See the section "Configure Sessions" in this chapter for specifics on forcing URL rewriting.

At the beginning of a session, WebLogic Server uses URL rewriting while it determines whether the client supports cookies. If the client browser does support cookies, then WebLogic Server stops rewriting URLs. If not, WebLogic Server continues to use URL rewriting.

By default, WebLogic uses both cookies and URL rewriting. To override this default behavior, set session parameters in the `weblogic.xml` deployment descriptor for the Web application. See the section "Configure Sessions" to set `CookiesEnabled` and `URLRewritingEnabled` session parameters.

Best Practice: Always rewrite URLs in your servlets and JSPs for links back to the Web application.

Testing URL Rewriting

Once you activate URL rewriting, the clients that you point at your server see a difference. In fact, you see something like this:

```
http://www.shinn.com/index.html;jsessionid=1234!a!b
```

The session ID number is encoded at the end of the URL for each page. You may notice that the session ID appears to be longer than specified. In the unrealistic example above, the session ID is four characters long. The values following this ID are used by WebLogic Server to support clustering.

Lifecycle of a Session

Servlets create new a new session object using `getSession(true)`. Following this call, WebLogic Server creates an HTTP session object and begins to pass the session ID to the browser. WebLogic Server passes this session ID to the Web browser as long as the session is active and WebLogic Server can match the request to the right session. The session remains active until it expires from lack of use or the servlet explicitly deactivates the session. To match the request to an active session, WebLogic Server requires the session ID. Under most circumstance, the browser continues to pass this ID until the browser is restarted.

Session Duration

If the client does not make any requests to the WebLogic Server for a specified period of time, WebLogic Server automatically invalidates and removes the HTTP session. By default, WebLogic Server times sessions out after one hour. You may set a timeout interval in the WebLogic Server configuration or in servlet code. If the user requests a page after WebLogic Server has closed the session, then the user has to log in again. After a session times out, any information you have stored in the HTTP session object is lost.

WebLogic Server discards timed-out session objects, but also the session is lost if the client loses its reference to the session. For instance, if the user shuts down the Web browser, the browser deletes the cookies storing the session ID. If the user restarts the browser, he must log in again. If URL rewriting is active and the user leaves the site, the HTML containing the session ID is lost. When a client loses its session ID, WebLogic Server cannot match the HTTP request with the `HttpSession` object. The user must log in, and the old session object on the server will eventually time out. As we see in the next section, the servlet may also explicitly end a session.

Finally, the `HttpSession` objects are managed by the WebLogic Server and should not be referenced outside the scope of an HTTP request (after the `service()` or `do<request type>()` method returns). Instead, reference the attribute objects stored in the session. If you must reference the `HttpSession` outside the scope of the request, then `clone()` the session first, and pass the copy.

Invalidating a Session

Under certain circumstances, such as logging out, you should explicitly invalidate a session. Use the `invalidate()` method of the `HttpSession` object, like this:

```
// Create the Session Object
HttpSession session = request.getSession (false);
// Invalidate the Session
session.invalidate();
```

WebLogic Server clears the HTTP session and invalidates it for further use. The next time the user visits your servlet, no session will be available. Your Web application may require the user to log in again and create a new session object.

Sessions, Inactivity, and Time

The `HttpSession` object supports other useful methods:

- `public long getCreationTime()`—Returns a long integer that represents when the session was created. To print the creation time of the object,

```
DateFormat df =
DateFormat.getDateTimeInstance(DateFormat.DEFAULT,DateFormat.FULL);
HttpSession session = request.getSession (true);
// Get the Creation Time and Print it in human-readable form
System.out.println(df.format(new Date(session.getCreationTime())));
```

- `public String getId()`—Returns a long integer of the ID number that WebLogic Server has associated with the session. To print the ID number of the servlet session,

```
HttpSession session = request.getSession (true);
// Get the Creation Time and Print it
system.out.println(session.getID());
```

- `public long getLastAccessedTime()`—Returns a long integer that represents the last time the session object was accessed. If the session is new, the last accessed time is the same as the creation time.
- `public int getMaxInactiveInterval()`—Returns an integer that represents the number of seconds that the session can be inactive before it is automatically removed by WebLogic Server.
- `public void setMaxInactiveInterval(int interval)`—Sets the number of seconds that the session can be inactive before the session is invalidated.

Configure Sessions

Use the Web application's deployment descriptor files to configure WebLogic Server management of sessions. The standard deployment descriptor, `web.xml`, provides a single configuration parameter: `session-timeout`. The following lines from a `web.xml` file specify a 5-minute timeout for sessions.

```
<session-config>
    <session-timeout>5</session-timeout>
</session-config>
```

Specify the `session-timeout` in minutes. A value of 0 or –1 means that the session never times out. Do not use this setting: over time, these permanent sessions will consume significant resources and overload the system. If you need information to persist beyond a user session, use cookies or use session lifecycle events to trigger permanent storage of the session information (both approaches are described later in this chapter). The value –2 instructs WebLogic Server to look to the *weblogic.xml* file for a timeout setting; this behavior is the default.

Use the WebLogic-specific deployment descriptor, `weblogic.xml`, to achieve greater control over session management. The `session-descriptor` element may contain several `session-param` elements; each `session-param` defines a parameter using a name/value pair. In the following example, the length of the session ID is shortened, `CookiesEnabled` is set to false, and `URLRewritingEnabled` is set to true. As a result, WebLogic Server generates a short session ID and uses only URL rewriting.

```
<session-descriptor>
    <session-param>
        <param-name>IDLength</param-name>
        <param-value>16</param-value>
    </session-param>
    <session-param>
        <param-name>CookiesEnabled</param-name>
        <param-value>false</param-value>
    </session-param>
    <session-param>
        <param-name>URLRewritingEnabled</param-name>
        <param-value>true</param-value>
    </session-param>
</session-descriptor>
```

Use the following parameters to configure session management for WebLogic Server:

- `TrackingEnabled`—Use this setting to turn on or off session tracking in WebLogic Server. If tracking is turned off, then WebLogic Server creates the session but does not save the session between requests. [`true`|`false`; default `true`].
- `TimeoutSecs`—This parameter specifies a default for how long a session remains active. WebLogic considers a session invalid if it remains inactive for the specified number of seconds. Your servlet code can override this value programmatically. If specified, the `session-timeout` parameter in `web.xml` takes precedence over this value. [1...`Integer.MAX_VALUE`; default 3600].
- `InvalidationIntervalSecs`—WebLogic Server checks for timed-out session objects on a regular basis, normally at least once a minute. This parameter tunes the frequency of the check. [1...604,800; default 60].
- `IDLength`—Tune the length of the session ID using this parameter. [8...`Integer.MAX_VALUE`; default 52].

- `URLRewritingEnabled`—Use this setting to enable or disable session tracking using URL rewriting. |`true`|`false`; default `true`|.
- `CookiesEnabled`—Use this setting to enable or disable session tracking using cookies. |`true`|`false`; default `true`|.
- `CookieMaxAgeSecs`—This parameter sets the timeout in seconds for the cookie used to track sessions on the client. After the specified time, the client deletes the cookie. Several values have special meaning. If set to –1, the client removes the cookie when the user exits the client. If set to 0, the cookie expires immediately. If set to `Integer.MAX_VALUE`, the cookie never expires. |–1, 0, 1…`Integer.MAX_VALUE`; default –1|.
- `CookieDomain`—Set the domain of the cookie used to track the session. By default, the value is set by the domain configuration of the WebLogic Server.
- `CookieName`, `CookieComment`, `CookiePath`—A number of parameters allow customization of the cookies used to track sessions. See WebLogic Server documentation for more details: *http://e-docs.bea.com/wls/docs81/webapp/weblogic_xml.html*.
- `ConsoleMainAttribute`—The WebLogic Server Admin console offers a session-tracking function. The console can use one of the session attributes as an identifier. Use this property to specify the identifying session attribute.

Additional attributes are described in the section "Configuration of Session Persistence" later in this chapter.

Best Practice: Be aggressive when setting session timeouts. Inactive sessions can be a drag on WebLogic Server performance.

Best Practice: Set the `CookieDomain` parameter. Some browsers will not send cookies received from HTTP responses with HTTPS requests because the two occur on different ports. Ensure the cookie is not lost by consistently setting the cookie's domain.

Session Example

You can easily add sessions to your servlets. As an example, let's build a servlet that counts the number of times you have visited a given page. To do this, create a session and insert a counter object into the session. Each time the user revisits the page, we increment the counter object.

The following listing demonstrates use of the servlet session:

```
package com.learnweblogic.examples.ch3;

import java.io.*;
import java.text.DateFormat;
import java.util.*;
import javax.servlet.*;
import javax.servlet.http.*;

public class SessionServlet extends HttpServlet {

    public void doGet(HttpServletRequest req, HttpServletResponse res)
```

```
throws ServletException, IOException {
        // Get the session object. Don't do this in real life.
        // Use getSession(false) and redirect the request to log in on
failure.
        HttpSession session = req.getSession(true);

        // set content type first, then obtain a PrintWriter
        res.setContentType("text/html");
        PrintWriter out = res.getWriter();

        // then write the data of the response
        out.println("<HEAD><TITLE>SessionServlet Output</TITLE></
HEAD><BODY>");
        out.println("<h1>SessionServlet Output</h1>");

        // Retrieve the count value from the session
        Counter cntr = (Counter)
        session.getAttribute("sessiontest.counter");

        // Increment the counter. If the counter is not
        // currently contained in the session, create it
        if (null!=cntr) {
            cntr.increment();
        } else {
            cntr = new Counter();
            session.setAttribute("sessiontest.counter", cntr);
        }

        // And print out number of times the user has hit this page:
        out.println("You have hit this page <b>" + cntr.toString() +
        "</b> times.<p>");
      out.println("Click <a href=" + res.encodeURL("/SessionServlet") +
        ">here</a>");
      out.println(" to ensure that session tracking is working even " +
        "if cookies aren't supported.<br>");
        out.println("<p>");

        // Finally, demonstrate some of the more common methods in the
        // HttpSession object surrounding sessions:
        out.println("<h3>Request and Session Data:</h3>");
        out.println("Session ID in Request: " +
        req.getRequestedSessionId());
        out.println("<br>Session ID in Request from Cookie: " +
        req.isRequestedSessionIdFromCookie());
        out.println("<br>Session ID in Request from URL: " +
        req.isRequestedSessionIdFromURL());
        out.println("<br>Valid Session ID: " +
```

```
        req.isRequestedSessionIdValid());
        out.println("<h3>Session Data:</h3>");
        out.println("New Session: " + session.isNew());
        out.println("<br>Session ID: " + session.getId());
        DateFormat df =
DateFormat.getDateTimeInstance(DateFormat.DEFAULT,DateFormat.FULL);
        out.println("<br>Creation Time: " +
        df.format(new Date(session.getCreationTime())));
        out.println("<br>Last Accessed Time: " +
        df.format(new Date(session.getLastAccessedTime())));
        out.println("</BODY>");
    }

    class Counter {
        private int counter;
        public Counter() {
            counter = 1;
        }

        public void increment() {
            counter++;
        }

        public String toString() {
            return String.valueOf(counter);
        }
    }
}
```

The output of this servlet looks something like Figure 3–1.

If you click refresh to visit this page multiple times, you'll see that the counter increments each time by incrementing the HTTP session object. If you restart the Web browser, the counter restarts at 1 because on restart, the browser lost its session ID. WebLogic Server recognizes the request as the beginning of a new session and starts over with a new session object and a new counter.

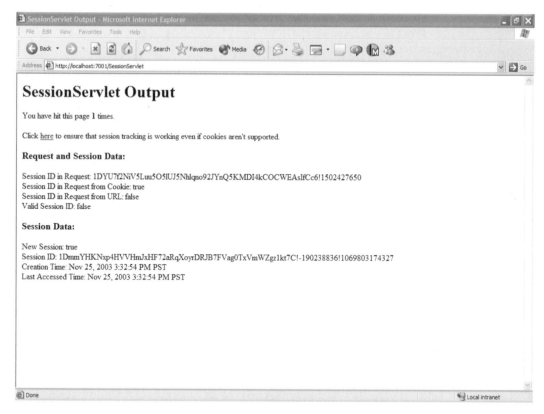

Figure 3-1
Servlet output.

Deploying the Session Servlet in WebLogic Server

In order to deploy the session servlet, you can use the code included on the CD-ROM accompanying this book. It is located in the file named *SessionServlet.war*, which is located in the subdirectory */examples/ch3*. It is deployed using the same process used for the `HelloServlet` example.

Session Events

Chapter 2 describes Web application events. These events can trigger code for various Web application events, like starting applications or binding attributes to the `ServletContext`. Similarly, developers can trigger code for session events. Developers can set triggers for similar session events, including session creation and attribute binding. These triggers are useful in initializing resources in session objects, releasing resources from session objects, or permanently storing session information for future reference.

Session Lifecycle Events

To configure code to handle session lifecycle events, write a class implementing either the `HttpSessionListener` or `HttpSessionActivationListener` and configure, and register the class in the `web.xml` deployment descriptor. The `HttpSessionListener` defines the following methods:

- `public void sessionCreated(HttpSessionEvent event)`—WebLogic Server calls this method in registered listener classes after a new session is created.
- `public void sessionDestroyed(HttpSessionEvent event)`—WebLogic Server calls this method in registered listener classes before an existing session is released. The session is released either because it has timed out or because it has been invalidated.

WebLogic Server may move a session from one server to another within a cluster. In order to move the session, WebLogic Server serializes the session object in a process called *passivation*. The target server then restores or activates the session. Some attributes of a session may not be serializable (e.g., a JDBC connection). The `HttpSessionActivationListener` provides handlers for both activation and passivation:

- `void sessionWillPassivate(HttpSessionEvent event)`—WebLogic Server calls this method before it serializes the session prior to migrating the session to another instance.
- `void sessionDidActivate(HttpSessionEvent event)`—WebLogic Server calls this method after it restores the session on the target server instance.

The `HttpSessionEvent` object, passed to all these methods, provides only one method: `getSession()`. This method returns a reference to the session that has just been created or is about to be destroyed.

Register `HttpSessionListener` classes using the same listener syntax used for Web applications event listeners. Assuming that the class `com.mycorp.SessionLifecycleListener` implements `HttpSessionListener`, add the following lines into the `web.xml` deployment descriptor to register the listener:

```
<listener>
  <listener-class>
    com.mycorp.SessionLifecycleListener
  </listenerclass>
</listener>
```

The listeners are called in the same order as they appear in the `web.xml` deployment descriptor. Again WebLogic Server checks the interfaces implemented by each listener in order to route events properly. As a result of this dynamic type-checking, a single listener may implement multiple interfaces. For each listener interface a class implements, WebLogic Server calls the appropriate event handlers. This behavior can come in handy in a number of scenarios. In the following example, a counter is initialized with Web application startup and updated with each session created or destroyed:

```
import javax.servlet.*;
import javax.servlet.http.*;

public class SessionCounter implements HttpSessionListener,
ServletContextListener {
```

```
    private static int totalSessionCount, activeSessionCount;
    /** Creates a new instance of SessionContextCounter */
    public SessionContextCounter() {
        totalSessionCount = activeSessionCount = 0;
    }

    public void contextInitialized(ServletContextEvent event) {
        ServletContext sc = servletContextEvent.getServletContext();
        sc.setAttribute("SessionContextCounter" ,new SessionCounter());
    }

    public void contextDestroyed(ServletContextEvent event) {}

    public void sessionCreated(HttpSessionEvent event) {
        totalSessionCount++;
        activeSessionCount++;
    }

    public void sessionDestroyed(HttpSessionEvent event) {
        activeSessionCount--;
    }
}
```

Session Binding Events

The HttpSessionAttributeListener interface works like the previous listener interfaces. Implement the interface and register the class in the web.xml deployment descriptor. WebLogic Server calls the event handlers of implementing classes when an attribute is added, removed, or modified in a session object:

- public void attributeAdded(HttpSessionBindingEvent event)— WebLogic Server calls this method when an attribute is added to the session.
- public void attributeRemoved(HttpSessionBindingEvent event)— WebLogic Server calls this method when an attribute value is removed from the session.
- public void attributeReplaced(HttpSessionBindingEvent event)— WebLogic Server calls this method when an attribute value is replaced. The attribute is replaced rather than added when the method setAttribute() is called on the session using an existing attribute name.

Each of these handlers takes an HttpSessionBindingEvent as a parameter. The event class encapsulates the attribute change using the following accessors:

- public String getName()—Returns the name of the modified attribute.
- public HttpSession getSession()—Returns a reference to the modified session.
- public Object getValue()—Returns the value of the modified value when the value is either added or replaced.

The HttpSessionAttributeListener monitors changes to session attributes. The servlet specification also provides the ability to monitor the objects that may be bound to sessions. Like the attribute listener, classes that implement the HttpSessionBindingListener interface receive notifications of binding events. Unlike the previous listeners, classes implementing the `HttpSessionBindingListener` are not registered in the `web.xml` deployment descriptor.

When application code calls the `setAttribute()` method on a session, the call includes both name and value parameters. If the value object implements `HttpSessionBindingListener`, WebLogic Server calls its `valueBound()` method. The `HttpSessionBindingListener` defines the following methods:

- `public void valueBound(HttpSessionBindingEvent event)`—WebLogic Server calls this method when the implementing value is bound to an `HttpSession`.
- `public void valueUnbound(HttpSessionBindingEvent event)`—WebLogic Server calls this method when an attribute value is unbound from an `HttpSession`. The value can be unbound if either the application calls the `removeAttribute()` method of the session or the session is destroyed (due to either an explicit call to `invalidate()` or a session timeout).

As discussed earlier, you should always configure sessions to time out. However, session event listeners, including the `HttpSessionListener` and the `HttpSessionBindingListener`, provide a way to persist session attributes. Persist the attribute using the `sessionDestroyed()` or `valueUnbound()` handler methods. When the user logs in again, restore the session using the data you saved from the previous session.

Baking Your Own Cookies

WebLogic Server uses cookies to track sessions, but developers may use cookies independent of HTTP sessions. Cookies provide a useful mechanism for storing long-term information about users. For example, you might want your application to recognize users when they return to your site. You might prepopulate the user's ID so that she does not have to enter it. Developers typically use cookies to implement handy features like this, common on many e-commerce sites.

In order to recognize users over longer periods of time, add a cookie into the HTTP response. If the user permits cookies, the browser stores the cookie on the user's machine and includes the cookie in future requests, even in future sessions. The application checks HTTP requests to see whether the cookie is included and uses the data found in the cookie. In the example above, this means that the user need only remember her password for authentication.

A cookie contains the following properties:

- A cookie name
- A single value
- Optional additional attributes such as a comment, a maximum age, a version number, and path and domain qualifiers

Cookies can store information for a long period of time, but this does not mean you should store all your data in cookies. As discussed in the previous section on sessions, browsers may not accept cookies. In addition, cookies are particularly bad places to store sensitive data: values can be intercepted, modified, or faked. For long-term storage of sensitive data, use another mechanism; the best practice is to use a database. See Chapter 5, "WebLogic Server JDBC and JTA," to use WebLogic Server to access a database using J2EE standards.

Cookies vs. Servlet Sessions

Servlet sessions are time-limited. Typically, servlet sessions last only as long as the lifetime of the browser session. Once the user exits the Web browser or the session times out, WebLogic Server automatically discards the `HttpSession` object. When you want your Web application to automatically recognize a user beyond the scope of a single session, use a cookie.

Here are some cases in which you should use servlet sessions:

- Track a user shopping cart.
- Cache data such as account balances that the user might look up more than once during a session.
- Store references or addresses of resources on which your application relies.

Problems best solved with a cookie might include these:

- Store convenience information such as a user's login ID.
- Store preference information such as the user's choice of language or color.
- Store an identifier used to track usage of your application.

Cookies have several characteristics: for one, you can use more than one cookie. Browsers impose limits on the use of browsers. The typical browser supports 20 cookies for each Web server, 300 cookies total, and may limit cookie size to 4KB each.

Making Cookies

Create a cookie using the `Cookie` constructor with two parameters: a name and a value. The value parameter represents the information that you want to store. This value may include the user's name or any arbitrary string value. To create a cookie, put the following in your servlet:

```
Cookie myCookie = new Cookie("Cookie name", "63");
```

Then, add your cookie to the HTTP response:

```
response.addCookie(myCookie);
```

The values stored in cookies can only be strings. Therefore, you should text-encode all data that you store in a cookie. Once you add a cookie to your response object, WebLogic Server automatically places it in the client browser. The client browser stores the cookie to the local computer disk for future requests.

Retrieving Cookies

When WebLogic Server invokes a servlet, the cookies sent by the browser are included in the `HttpServletRequest` object. These cookies are retrieved as an array of cookie objects using the following code:

```
Cookie[] cookies = request.getCookies();
```

Once you have the cookie objects, you can search for your specific cookie. You can use the `getName()` method to look at each cookie's name:

```
// Assign the Name of the First
// Cookie in The Array to String foo
```

```
String foo = Cookies[0].getName();
```

If the user's browser does not accept cookies it does not include cookies in subsequent requests. In this case, the result of `request.getCookies()` returns `null` (or an array without the cookie you added). In general, the servlet author has no way to determine in advance whether a particular client will accept cookies.

Useful Methods for Dealing with Cookies

There are a number of other methods that you can use with cookies:

- `public String getValue()` and `public void setValue(String newValue)`—Enable you to access the value stored in the cookie and set the value stored in the cookie respectively.
- `public void setMaxAge(int expiry)` and `public int getMaxAge()`—Set and get the number of seconds from the creation of a cookie to when the cookie expires (the cookie's age). The value 0 tells the browser to expire immediately. The value –1 means that the cookie expires when the Web browser exits—the default configuration. To make your cookies last indefinitely, set the value to the maximum possible integer:

  ```
  // Set the cookie myCookie to last indefinitely
  myCookie.setMaxAge(Integer.MAX_VALUE);
  ```

- `public void setDomain(String domain)`—Manually set the cookie's domain using this method. Browsers use the domain to select cookies to include in HTTP requests. The domain is typically the name of the server (e.g., `www.learnweblogic.com`). If the domain begins with a dot (`.`), the cookie should be returned with requests to any server in the specified DNS (Domain Name System) zone. For example, browsers will send a cookie with the domain `.learnweblogic.com` to a server named `www.learnweblogic.com`.

> **Best Practice:** Set cookie domains. Some browsers will not send cookies received from HTTP responses with HTTPS requests because the two occur on different ports. Ensure the cookie is not lost by consistently setting the cookie's domain.

- `public void setComment(String comment)` and `public String getComment()`—Can be used to set the comment field in your cookie and read the comment. This is very useful for occasions when individuals are browsing their cookie store on their Web browser. To set the comment field in a cookie named myCookie, place the following code in your servlet:

  ```
  // Set the Comment Field in Cookie myCookiemyCookie.setComment("gumby999");
  ```

- `public void setSecure(boolean)` and `public boolean getSecure()`—Enable you to set the security settings for the cookie. The following code requires that the cookie be sent only over a secure channel such as SSL:

  ```
  // Require That the Cookie myCookie
  ```

```
// Only Be Sent over Secure Channels
myCookie.setSecure(true);
Custom Cookies for Personalization
```

The first step in implementing a custom personalization cookie is to add the mechanism to set and look for the cookie in your pages. The following is a trivial doGet() method that indicates how to look for a cookie to prepopulate the login field:

```
public void doGet(HttpServletRequest req, HttpServletResponse res)
  throws IOException {
```

This example uses a session object to represent being logged in. We create and invalidate sessions to set the user's login status.

```
// Get the session if one exists
HttpSession session = req.getSession(false);
```

The local variables cookieFound and thisCookie represent the cookie named Login-Cookie. The for loop cycles through each of the cookies provided by the browser. If cookie-Found is true, the thisCookie variable will reference the cookie.

```
// Try to retrieve the cookie from the request.
boolean cookieFound = false;
Cookie thisCookie = null;
Cookie[] cookies = req.getCookies();
if(null != cookies) {
    // Look through all the cookies and see if the
    // cookie with the login info is there.
    for(int i=0; i < cookies.length; i++) {
        thisCookie = cookies[i];
        if (thisCookie.getName().equals("LoginCookie")) {
            cookieFound = true;
            break;
} } }
```

If the user has performed a logout action, invalidate the current session.

```
// Logout action removes session, but the cookie remains
if(null != req.getParameter("Logout")) {
    if(null != session) {
        session.invalidate();
        session = null;
} }
```

When the user is not logged in, check to see whether the user has provided login information. This code is for demonstration purposes only and will accept any login and password values.

```
    if(null == session) {        // If the user is not logged in
        String loginValue = req.getParameter("login");
        boolean isLoginAction = (null==loginValue)?false:true;
```

If no cookie exists, the code creates a new one with the login as its value. When the cookie exists, the servlet sets the changed value of the cookie. Note that we add the cookie again after we change the value of the cookie. This call informs WebLogic Server to send the cookie back to the client and updates the cookie's value.

```
    if(isLoginAction) {        // User is logging in
        if(cookieFound) {
            if(!loginValue.equals(thisCookie.getValue())) {
                thisCookie.setValue(loginValue);
                res.addCookie(thisCookie);
            }
        } else {
            // If the cookie does not exist, create it and set value
            thisCookie = new Cookie("LoginCookie",loginValue);
            res.addCookie(thisCookie);
        }
        // create a session to show that we are logged in
        session = req.getSession(true);
        displayLogoutPage(req, res);
```

In the case where we display the login page, use the value in the cookie to prepopulate the page's login field.

```
    } else {
        // Display the login page. If the cookie exists, set login
        if(cookieFound) {
            req.setAttribute("login", thisCookie.getValue());
        }
        displayLoginPage(req, res);
    }
```

Finally, logged in users are provided the opportunity to log out.

```
    } else {
        // If the user is logged in, display a logout page
        displayLogoutPage(req, res);
    }
}
```

Long-Term CookieServlet Example

In this example, we extend the preceding code to create a complete servlet. This servlet deviates only slightly from the preceding example. The `CookieServlet` example handles both GET and POST methods and extends the lifespan of the cookie to beyond the foreseeable future (roughly 65 years). Also, this version uses display methods to generate HTML pages.

```java
package com.learnweblogic.examples;

import java.io.*;
import javax.servlet.*;
import javax.servlet.http.*;

public class CookieServlet extends HttpServlet {

    public void doGet(HttpServletRequest req, HttpServletResponse res)
        throws IOException {
        handleRequest(req, res);
    }

    public void doPost(HttpServletRequest req, HttpServletResponse res)
        throws IOException {
        handleRequest(req, res);
    }

    public void handleRequest(HttpServletRequest req, HttpServletResponse res)
        throws IOException {
        // Get the session if one exists
        HttpSession session = req.getSession(false);

        // Try to retrieve the cookie from the request.
        boolean cookieFound = false;
        Cookie cookie = null;
        Cookie[] cookies = req.getCookies();
        if (null != cookies) {
            // Look through all the cookies and see if the
            // cookie with the login info is there.
            for (int i = 0; i < cookies.length; i++) {
                cookie = cookies[i];
                if (cookie.getName().equals("LoginCookie")) {
                    cookieFound = true;
                    break;
                }
            }
        }

        // Logout action removes session, but the cookie remains
        if (null != req.getParameter("Logout")) {
```

```
            if (null != session) {
                session.invalidate();
                session = null;
            }
        }

    if (null == session) { // If the user is not logged in
        String loginValue = req.getParameter("login");
        boolean isLoginAction = (null == loginValue) ? false : true;

        if (isLoginAction) { // User is logging in
            if (cookieFound) { // If the cookie exists update the
value only if changed
                if (!loginValue.equals(cookie.getValue())) {
                    cookie.setValue(loginValue);
                    res.addCookie(cookie);
                }
            } else {
                // If the cookie does not exist, create it and set value
                cookie = new Cookie("LoginCookie", loginValue);
                cookie.setMaxAge(Integer.MAX_VALUE);
                res.addCookie(cookie);
            }
            // create a session to show that we are logged in
            session = req.getSession(true);
            session.setAttribute("login",loginValue);
               req.setAttribute("login",loginValue);
            displayLogoutPage(req, res);
        } else {
            // Display the login page. If the cookie exists, set login
            if (cookieFound) {
                req.setAttribute("login", cookie.getValue());
            }
            displayLoginPage(req, res);
        }
    } else {
        // If the user is logged in, display a logout page
        String loginValue = session.getAttribute("login").toString();
         req.setAttribute("login",loginValue);
        displayLogoutPage(req, res);
    }
}

public void displayLoginPage(
    HttpServletRequest req,
    HttpServletResponse res)
    throws IOException {
```

```
        String login = (String) req.getAttribute("login");
        if (null == login) {
            login = "";
        }
        res.setContentType("text/html");
        PrintWriter out = res.getWriter();
        out.println("<html><body>");
        out.println(
            "<form method='POST' action='"
                + res.encodeURL(req.getRequestURI())
                + "'>");
        out.println(
            "login: <input type='text' name='login' value='" + login + "'>");
        out.println(
            "password: <input type='password' name='password' value=''>");
        out.println("<input type='submit' name='Submit' value='Submit'>");
        out.println("</form></body></html>");
    }


    public void displayLogoutPage(
        HttpServletRequest req,
        HttpServletResponse res)
        throws IOException {
        res.setContentType("text/html");
        PrintWriter out = res.getWriter();
        out.println("<html><body>");
        out.println("<p>Welcome " + req.getAttribute("login") + "</p>");
        out.println(
            "<form method='GET' action='"
                + res.encodeURL(req.getRequestURI())
                + "'>");
        out.println(
            "Click <a href='"
                + res.encodeURL(req.getRequestURI())
                + "'>here</a> to reload this page.<br>");
        out.println("<input type='submit' name='Logout'
value='Logout'>");
        out.println("</form></body></html>");
    }
}
```

In a real-world situation, you want your application to authenticate users using more secure methods. In Chapter 13, "Application Security with WebLogic Server 8.1," we further discuss how to have your application log in an existing user.

Deploying the CookieServlet in WebLogic Server

To deploy the `CookieServlet`, use the code included on the CD-ROM accompanying this book, in */code/ch3/cookieServlet.war*.

Step 0: Installing the CookieServlet Application

Follow the steps used in previous examples to build and deploy the application code. Be sure to create a new directory for your work.

Step 1: Modifying Browser Settings

To view the `CookieServlet`, modify your Web browser to enable you to see better what happens with cookies. If you are using Internet Explorer, use Tools → Internet Options... to delete. Choose the Advanced option in the left-hand panel. You see a screen such as the one in Figure 3–2.

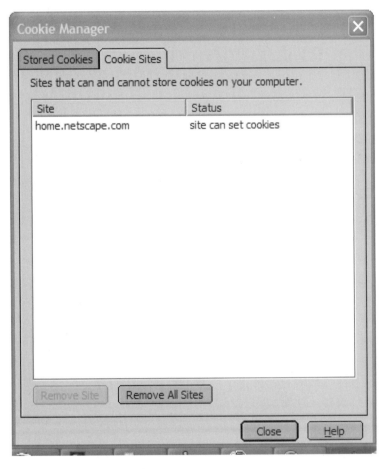

Figure 3–2
Netscape Navigator's preferences dialog.

Select the option to warn you before accepting cookies. This enables you to see any cookies that WebLogic Server intends to put into your browser. Microsoft Internet Explorer requires that you modify the settings and set your Internet security configuration for the browser. If you decide not to modify your browser settings, you won't see the details of the cookie placement—but the example still works.

Step 2: Visiting the CookieServlet

Visit the `CookieServlet` by pointing your Web browser at the deployment location for your WebLogic Server instance. If you have deployed on your local machine, at port 7001 (the default), you can view the example at *http://127.0.0.1:7001/CookieServlet*.

You should be immediately see the `CookieServlet` login screen (see Figure 3–3), which displays the following:

Fill in the User ID field (the servlet does not check the password) and press the submit button. You should see the cookie servlet display (see Figure 3–4).

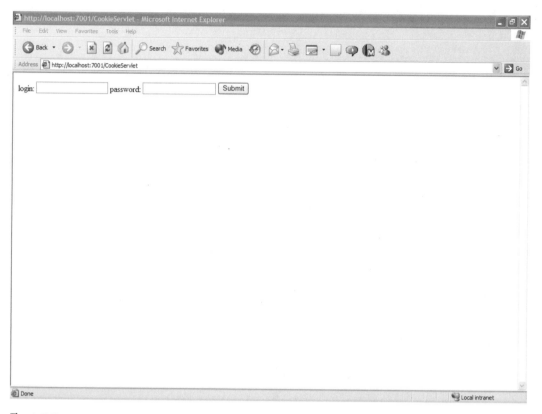

Figure 3–3
Initial response from CookieServlet.

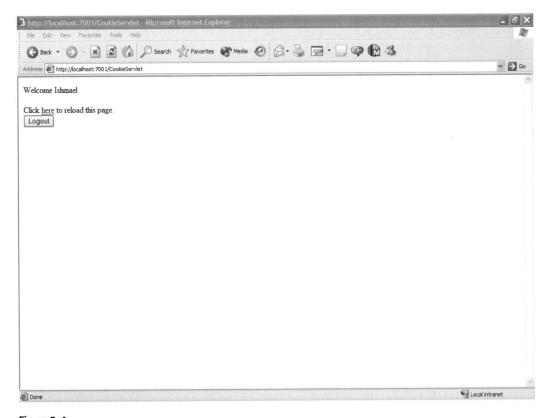

Figure 3–4
CookieServlet display after login.

Step 3: Revisiting the CookieServlet

Log out and visit the `CookieServlet` again, with the same Web browser, at *http://127.0.0.1:7001/CookieServlet*.

You should see the screen shown in Figure 3–5.

The `CookieServlet` recognizes the cookie in your Web browser and welcomes you with your previous ID.

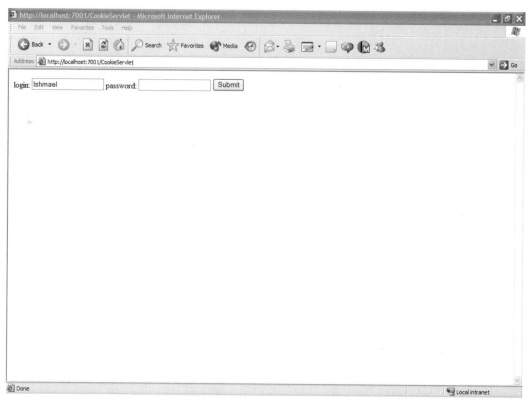

Figure 3–5
Revisiting the CookieServlet.

Filters

So far, we have discussed one way to handle HTTP events—Web browsers generate HTTP requests, and servlets process the requests. Filters augment the servlet request cycle. Filters intercept requests prior to servlet processing and responses after servlet processing. Filters can be used to perform functions across multiple servlets in a Web application, to add features to existing servlet code, and to create reusable functions for use in multiple Web applications.

For instance, a filter can be used to provide customized authentication. The filter intercepts requests prior to calling the servlet. The filter determines whether the user has sufficient privileges to access the requested servlet. Unauthorized users are rejected without the servlet ever knowing about the request. As a result, authentication code can be located in a single location, the filter, rather than scattered throughout the multiple servlets in the Web application.

Similarly, filters can log user actions, compress output streams, or even transform the servlet's output to meet the demands of a target browser. Filters can achieve this flexibility because they are not hardwired into servlets, but instead configured in the web.xml deployment descriptor to intercept requests.

Filter Interfaces

In addition to configuration similarities, filters and servlets share other characteristics. Both execute in a multithreaded environment. The same safeguards necessary to servlet development regarding careful use of class and instance variables apply equally to filters. Also, where servlets handle requests using the doGet() and doPost() methods, filters implement a doFilter() method.

Implement the Filter interface (javax.servlet.Filter) by writing init(), destroy(), and doFilter() methods:

- public void init(FilterConfig config) throws ServletException—WebLogic Server executes the init() method of registered filters during the initialization phase. Typically, the init() method stores the FilterConfig object for future use.
- public void destroy()—WebLogic Server executes the destroy() method of registered filters during the Web application's end of service phase.
- public void doFilter(ServletRequest request, ServletResponse response, FilterChain chain) throws IOException, ServletException—WebLogic Server calls the doFilter() method for selected filters. The Filter should handle the request or pass the request to the provided FilterChain.

The init() method takes a FilterConfig object. The FilterConfig provides the filter access to the ServletContext, and filter configuration parameters in the web.xml file. FilterConfig defines the following methods:

- public String getFilterName()—Use this method to access the name of the filter as set in the web.xml file.
- public String getInitParameter(String name)—Look up the value of an init parameter using this method and the name of the parameter. Parameters are defined in the web.xml file.
- public Enumeration getInitParameterNames()—Returns the names of all the parameters defined for the filter in an Enumeration.
- public ServletContext getServletContext()—Use the FilterConfig to access the Web application's ServletContext.

Also, the doFilter() method includes the familiar ServletRequest and ServletResponse objects and the new FilterChain object. The FilterChain interface defines only a doFilter() method but is at the center of filter flow control. In the following custom authentication example, a mean-spirited filter is used to limit access to logged-in users whose login name begins with the letter D. The filter itself intercepts the request prior to the servlet:

```
package com.learnweblogic.examples;

import javax.servlet.*;
import javax.servlet.http.*;

public class OnlyDsFilter implements Filter {

    FilterConfig config = null;

    public void doFilter(javax.servlet.ServletRequest req,
javax.servlet.ServletResponse res, javax.servlet.FilterChain chain)
```

```
throws java.io.IOException, javax.servlet.ServletException {
        if(req instanceof HttpServletRequest && res instanceof
HttpServletResponse) {
            HttpServletRequest httpReq = (HttpServletRequest)req;
            HttpServletResponse httpRes = (HttpServletResponse)res;
            String user = httpReq.getRemoteUser();
            if(null != user && !user.startsWith("D")) {
                httpRes.sendError(HttpServletResponse.SC_FORBIDDEN,
"Only D users allowed");
                return;
            }
        }
        chain.doFilter(req, res);
        return;
    }

    public void init(javax.servlet.FilterConfig filterConfig) throws
javax.servlet.ServletException {
        config = filterConfig;
    }

    public void destroy() {
    }
}
```

Configure Filters

Configure filters in the web.xml file. As with servlets, use the filter elements to define named filters, and filter-mapping elements to link this filter to specific requests. The filter element should contain a filter-name, and filter-class element. A bare-bones filter element looks like this:

```
<filter>
    <filter-name>OnlyDs</filter-name>
    <filter-class>com.learnweblogic.examples.OnlyDsFilter</filter-
class>
</filter>
```

The filter may also contain any number of init-params and the optional description element. The servlet specification also defines icon and display-name elements, but WebLogic Server ignores these. A more general version of the above filter might be configured as follows:

```
<filter>
    <filter-name>OnlyDs</filter-name>
    <description>OnlyDs limits access to resources by user name.</
description>
    <filter-class>com.learnweblogic.examples.AuthByName</filter-class>
```

```
        <init-param>
            <param-name>accept-pattern</param-name>
            <param-value>D.*</param-value>
        </init-param>
    </filter>
```

This configuration might be used with a more general authentication filter. The parameter `accept-param` provides a regular expression to define which names are allowed access. The modifications to the above filter, necessary to use this parameter, are left to the reader.

Map requests to filters using the `filter-mapping` element in the `web.xml` file. The mapping ties either a URL pattern or named servlet to a filter. The `filter-mapping` element contains a `filter-name` and either a `url-pattern` or a `servlet-name`. WebLogic Server selects filters by matching `url-patterns` against request URLs, and then selects the appropriate filter using the `filter-name`. WebLogic Server may select multiple filters, and it calls them in the order they appear in the `web.xml` file.

After matching URLs, WebLogic Server selects filters using servlet names. Rather than using the request URL, WebLogic Server matches the selected servlet `servlet-name` in the `filter-mapping` to the servlet it has selected to run. Again, these are selected in the same order as listed in the `web.xml` file.

```
<filter-mapping>
    <filter-name>OnlyDs</filter-name>
    <url-pattern>/D/*</url-pattern>
</filter-mapping>

<filter-mapping>
    <filter-name>OnlyDs</filter-name>
    <servlet-name>SpecialDServlet</servlet-name>
</filter-mapping>
```

Intercepting Servlet Output

The code example `OnlyDsFilter` intercepts requests prior to servlet processing. To intercept the response from the servlet, include code after the call to `doFilter()`:

```
    public void doFilter(javax.servlet.ServletRequest req,
javax.servlet.ServletResponse res, javax.servlet.FilterChain chain)
throws java.io.IOException, javax.servlet.ServletException {
        chain.doFilter(req, res);
        // do post-processing here...
        return;
    }
```

A single filter may include code both before and after it calls the servlet. In fact, to modify servlet output, create a stand-in `HttpServletResponse` before calling `doFilter()`, and modify the servlet output after the `doFilter()` call.

The classes `HttpServletRequestWrapper` and `HttpServletResponseWrapper` provide a starting point for creating these stand-in objects. The wrapper classes take request or response objects in their constructors. The wrappers provide methods that simply call each of the methods in the `HttpServletRequest` or `HttpServletResponse`. Override methods in these wrappers to customize the behavior of the class.

Filter Example

In the following example, a filter replaces special tokens in the body of the HTTP response. The filter works like the Ant task named `filter`. The deployer of the filter configures both a token and value. The filter looks for the token, preceded and followed by the @ sign, in the response body. The filter then replaces instances of the token and @ signs, adjusts the response `content-length`, and returns the modified response body.

```java
package com.learnweblogic.examples;

import java.io.*;
import javax.servlet.*;
import javax.servlet.http.*;

public class TokenReplacementFilter implements Filter {
    private String replToken, replValue;

    public void init(FilterConfig filterConfig)
    throws ServletException {
        replToken = filterConfig.getInitParameter("token.name");
        replValue = filterConfig.getInitParameter("token.value");
        if (null == replToken) {
            throw new ServletException("TokenReplacementFilter named " +
            filterConfig.getFilterName() +
            " missing token.name init parameter.");
        }
        if (null == replValue) {
            throw new ServletException("TokenReplacementFilter named " +
            filterConfig.getFilterName() +
            " missing token.value init parameter.");
        }
    }
    public void destroy() {}

    public void doFilter(ServletRequest request,
    ServletResponse response, FilterChain chain)
    throws IOException, ServletException {
        BufferedResponse resWrapper = new BufferedResponse(
        (HttpServletResponse)response);

        chain.doFilter(request, resWrapper);
```

```
        if (resWrapper.getOutputType() == BufferedResponse.OT_WRITER) {
            String resBody = new String(
          resWrapper.toByteArray(),resWrapper.getCharacterEncoding());
            if (resWrapper.getContentType().equals("text/html")) {
                resBody = resBody.replaceAll("@" + replToken + "@",
replValue);
                response.setContentLength(resBody.length());
            }
            PrintWriter writer = response.getWriter();
            writer.println(resBody);
        } else if (resWrapper.getOutputType() ==
BufferedResponse.OT_OUTPUT_STREAM) {
            ServletOutputStream out = response.getOutputStream();
            out.write(resWrapper.toByteArray());
        }
    }
```

The `init()` method reads `init-params` and sets the search and replace strings as instance variables within the filter. Notice that if either parameter is missing, the filter halts initialization of the Web application when it throws a `ServletException`. The `doFilter()` method creates a substitute `HttpServletResponse` and passes this object to the `FilterChain` for further processing. When the `FilterChain` returns, `doFilter()` extracts the body of the response, modifies the response body, and then writes this modified value to the original response object. Finally, the `doFilter()` method is careful to not replace strings if the servlet uses an `getOutputStream()` or if the `content-type` is not `text/html`.

The `BufferedResponse` class provides an `HttpServletResponse` to be used by a servlet. The response provides all the normal methods to the servlet but buffers servlet output for later processing by a filter.

```
    class BufferedResponse extends HttpServletResponseWrapper {

        public static final short OT_NONE = 0, OT_WRITER = 1,
OT_OUTPUT_STREAM = 2;

        private short outputType = OT_NONE;
        private PrintWriter writer = null;
        private BufServletOutputStream out = null;
        private String contentType;

        public BufferedResponse(HttpServletResponse response){
            super(response);
        }

        public ServletOutputStream getOutputStream() throws IOException {
            if (outputType == OT_WRITER) {
                throw new IllegalStateException();
            } else if (outputType == OT_OUTPUT_STREAM) {
```

```
            return out;
        } else {
            out = new BufServletOutputStream();
            outputType = OT_OUTPUT_STREAM;
            return (ServletOutputStream)out;
        }
    }

    public PrintWriter getWriter() throws IOException {
        if (outputType == OT_OUTPUT_STREAM) {
            throw new IllegalStateException();
        } else if (outputType == OT_WRITER) {
            return writer;
        } else {
            writer = new PrintWriter(
            new OutputStreamWriter(
            getOutputStream(),getCharacterEncoding()));
            outputType = OT_WRITER;
            return writer;
        }
    }

    public short getOutputType() {
        return outputType;
    }

    public String getContentType() {
        return contentType;
    }

    public void setContentType(String contentType) {
        this.contentType = contentType;
        super.setContentType(contentType);
    }

    public void flushBuffer() throws IOException {
        if (outputType == OT_WRITER) {
            writer.flush();
        } else if (outputType == OT_OUTPUT_STREAM) {
            out.flush();
        }
    }

    public void reset() {
        resetBuffer();
        outputType = OT_NONE;
        super.reset();
```

```
    }

    public void resetBuffer() {
        if(null != out) {
            out.reset();
        }
    }

    public byte[] toByteArray() {
        flushBuffer();
        if(null != out) {
            return(out.toByteArray());
        } else {
            return null;
        }
    }
}
}
```

The `BufferedResponse` extends the `HttpServletResponseWrapper`. The wrapper provides a default implementation for all of the methods in the `HttpServletResponse`, which passes the request to the wrapped response. The `BufferedResponse` overrides several of these methods.

First, we review the `getWriter()` and `getOutputStream()` methods. These methods create `PrintWriter` or `OutputStream` objects that write to a byte array rather than into the response. The servlet writes to this temporary store. The filter accesses the array using the `toByteArray()` method and processes the array before writing it to the real response object.

The servlet specification is very clear that servlets may call only one of these two methods. The `BufferedResponse` enforces this restriction by storing the first selected method in the instance variable, `outputType`, and by checking this variable before returning an `OutputStream` or `PrintWriter`.

Again, the default behavior of the `HttpServletResponseWrapper` is to call the wrapped response object. As a result, the default behavior of methods `flushBuffer()`, `reset-Buffer()`, and `reset()` is to update the original response object's output buffer. The `BufferedResponse` uses a temporary buffer, so method calls that update to the original buffer will have unexpected results. Instead, override these methods to update the local buffer. Chapter 2 includes the admonition to avoid flushing output streams in your servlet. Similarly, you should be careful to override these methods to ensure servlets do not prematurely flush the response output buffer.

Best Practice: Override `HttpResponseWrapper` methods `flushBuffer()`, `reset()`, and `resetBuffer()`.

This filter needs to know the `Content-Type` of the response. Normally, the response object does not provide a method to get this value. The `BufferedResponse` overrides the setter to mirror this value to a local variable and provides a getter for the same value.

The final piece of code is the `BufServletOutputStream`. The `getOutputStream()` method of `ServletResponse` returns a `ServletOutputStream`. The `ServletOutput-Stream` is declared abstract, so in order to create our own, we must provide a class implementing write(int i). In addition, we provide methods toByteArray() and reset() to gain access to and control over the underlying ByteArrayOutputStream:

```java
class BufServletOutputStream extends ServletOutputStream {
    ByteArrayOutputStream bufferedOut;

    public BufServletOutputStream() {
        bufferedOut = new ByteArrayOutputStream();
    }

    public void write(int i) throws IOException {
        bufferedOut.write(i);
    }

    public byte[] toByteArray() {
        return bufferedOut.toByteArray();
    }

    public void reset() {
        bufferedOut.reset();
    }
}
}
```

To finish out the example, here is a web.xml file that configures the filter to replace @version@ with 1.0 on all URLs in the servlet:

```xml
<!DOCTYPE web-app PUBLIC "-//Sun Microsystems, Inc.//DTD Web
Application 2.3//EN" "http://java.sun.com/j2ee/dtds/web-app_2_3.dtd">

<web-app>
  <filter>
    <filter-name>ReplaceVersion</filter-name>
    <filter-class>com.learnweblogic.examples.TokenReplacementFilter</
filter-class>
    <init-param>
      <param-name>token.name</param-name>
      <param-value>version</param-value>
    </init-param>
    <init-param>
      <param-name>token.value</param-name>
      <param-value>1.0</param-value>
    </init-param>
  </filter>

  <filter-mapping>
```

```
      <filter-name>ReplaceVersion</filter-name>
      <url-pattern>/*</url-pattern>
   </filter-mapping>
</web-app>
```

Deploying TokenReplacementFilter

In order to deploy the session servlet, you can use the code included on the CD-ROM accompanying this book. It is located in the file named *TokenReplacementFilter.war*, which is located in the subdirectory */examples/ch3*. It is deployed using the same process used for the `HelloServlet` example. Once deployed, access the servlet at *http://localhost:7001/TokenReplacementFilter*, and then at *http://localhost:7001/TokenReplacementFilter/replace*, to see the impact of the filter. See Figures 3–6 and 3–7 for the display of the servlet with and without the filter.

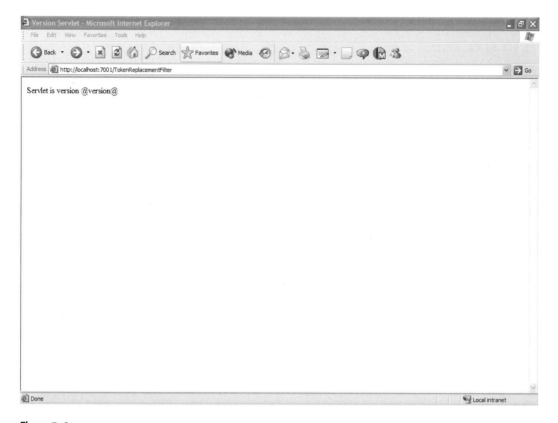

Figure 3–6
Version servlet display without filter.

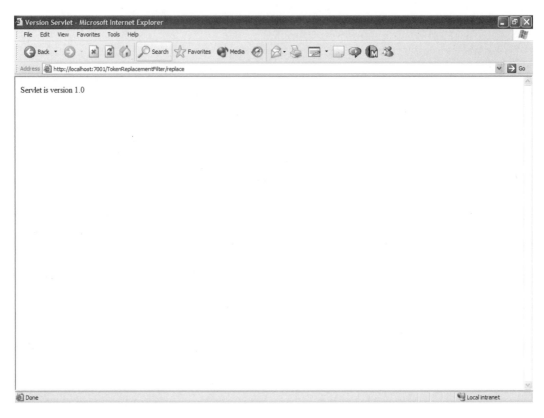

Figure 3–7
Version servlet display with filter.

Best Practice: Use filters to apply features to a Web application as a whole. Filters can reduce download times by compressing servlet output and can apply security policies to all resources in a Web application.

Using Servlets with WebLogic Server Clustering

Clustering, discussed in Chapter 12, is an important capability that provides redundancy and task balancing across multiple processes and/or machines. For WebLogic Server deployment, it is necessary to design your hardware environment to accommodate clustering. Similarly, you must design your servlets and Web applications to work well when clustered.

Persisting Session Information

When a Web application runs in a clustered environment, the cluster can recover from the failure of any one instance. When one instance fails, WebLogic Server directs client requests to one of the remaining instances. In many cases, redirecting the client request is sufficient. However, if the Web application uses sessions to store information between requests, you must take special precautions to make the session available on the target instance.

You have five options for storing session information in a WebLogic Server deployment:

- Do not protect your session information. In the event of a failure, all user sessions on the failed instance are lost. Sessions are lost because the sessions are only stored in that WebLogic Server instance.
- Protect your session information in a database. In the event of a failure, all session information is persisted in the database and readily available. WebLogic Server saves the data in the database after each request, and with each new request, WebLogic Server recovers the session data.
- Protect your session information with in-memory replication. In this model, a given session is always directed to the same server in a cluster, typically referred to as the primary for that session. The cluster automatically chooses another secondary server to act as a hot backup to the primary server. This node is updated across the network by the primary node after every change to the `HttpSession` object. In other words, every time you call `setAttribute()` or `removeAttribute()`, WebLogic Server automatically and synchronously updates the copy of the `HttpSession` on the secondary server. In the event of a failure to either the primary or secondary server, a different server in the cluster automatically takes its place to handle the session.
- Protect your session information in a temporary file. Using this option, WebLogic Server can recover sessions of a failed instance if it has access to the file. In environments using networked file systems, WebLogic Server can recover sessions across machines.
- Protect your session information in a cookie. In this model, WebLogic Server stores session information in an HTTP cookie. WebLogic Server instances take no special precaution to recover from instance failure because information is stored on the client. However, the use of cookies imposes a number of limitations. Many of these limits are discussed in the "Baking Your Own Cookies" section of this chapter. Among these are that some browsers do not accept cookies, and the data stored in cookies is subject to manipulation. In addition, when cookies are used to store sessions, you must store only string values in the session.

Session Protection Performance Implications

WebLogic Server greatly improves its ability to recover from failure when it stores session information in a database or on the filesystem. However, this additional reliability comes with a performance cost. Unprotected session storage provides the highest level of performance. The overhead required to store session information adds work and degrades performance to varying degrees. The right match of performance, reliability, and features depends on your needs, including your application's characteristics, hardware configuration, and the cost of failure.

In general, in-memory replication imposes the least overhead. File, cookie, and database persistence share similar performance characteristics and are much slower than in-memory replication. In one test, in-memory replication rated 5.5 times faster than database replication. However, generic benchmarks provide little guidance for your application.

The size of a session has a huge impact on performance. A larger session slows response times and magnifies the impact of session protection. Make sure you limit the data stored in sessions. Also, your specific configuration will impact performance greatly. Another test has shown that for database storage, moving the database from the same machine as WebLogic Server to a remote machine will slow session management by 68 percent.

Choosing the Right Level of Protection

The right amount of session protection for your application depends on your needs. To what extent is performance critical? What is the cost of losing a user session? If performance is most important, you may choose not to protect your session information. If the loss of session information is merely inconvenient, then you should consider leaving session data unprotected.

For rock-solid protection of session information, database or file persistence is the best choice. You are much less likely to lose your session information, because every change in the session is saved as a transaction against the database or saved to a file. WebLogic Server can recover sessions stored to a database or filesystem as long as the target system is still available. Unfortunately, the reliability of storing sessions in a database or filesystem comes at the cost of slower performance.

If your session storage needs are minimal, and you can be sure your users' browsers will accept cookies, then cookie storage is an option. Because session information is stored on the client rather than the server, cookies are a reliable option. Unfortunately, cookie storage has all the performance issues of file and database storage, is insecure, limits functionality, and is not universally supported by clients.

WebLogic Server provides the additional option of in-memory replication. In-memory replication is highly reliable and provides better performance than database or file persistence. WebLogic Server performs in-memory replication by storing the session in memory and copying the session on another instance. If the primary instance fails, the user is directed to the secondary instance. In-memory replication is highly reliable, because the likelihood is low that multiple servers go down simultaneously. Yet, the performance cost of replication is significantly lower than file or database storage. In-memory replication provides a high-performance reliable alternative.

> **Best Practice:** Begin with in-memory replication. For greater performance, stop protecting sessions. For greater reliability, store sessions to a database or the filesystem.

Configuration of Session Persistence

Configure the way WebLogic Server manages sessions using the `weblogic.xml` deployment descriptor. Use the following session parameters to customize WebLogic Server session management:

- `PersistentStoreType`—This parameter specifies where WebLogic Server stores session objects between user requests. For additional information regarding this setting, see the section "Using Servlets with WebLogic Server Clustering" in this chapter. Set the storage type to one of six values:
  - `memory`: Store session objects in memory.
  - `file`: Store session objects to files on the server. If specified, also set `PersistentStoreDir`.
  - `jdbc`: Uses a database to store persistent sessions. If specified, also set `PersistentStorePool`.
  - `replicated`: Same as memory, but session data is replicated across the clustered servers.
  - `cookie`: All session data is stored in a cookie in the user's browser. The use of cookies to store session data introduces additional limitations. See the discussion on deployment in this chapter.
  - `replicated_if_clustered`: If the Web application is deployed to clustered servers, use replicated. Otherwise, use memory. This value is the default.

- `PersistentStoreDir`—If the `PersistentStoreType` is `file`, this property specifies either an absolute path of the directory to use or a path relative to a WebLogic Server temporary directory. The system administrator must manually create the specified directory and set appropriate ownership and permissions for the directory.
- `PersistentStorePool`, `PersistentStoreTable`, `JDBCConnectionTimeoutSecs`—If the `PersistentStoreType` is `jdbc`, these properties specify the name of the JDBC Connection Pool, the name of the table in which to store sessions, and the time WebLogic Server waits to time out a JDBC connection. The pool has no default value and must be specified when using JDBC. By default, the table is named `wl_servlet_sessions`; use this property to override the default. The timeout defaults to 120 seconds.
- `CacheSize`—If the `PersistentStoreType` is `file` or `jdbc`, this parameter specifies how much memory to dedicate to cache session objects. WebLogic Server can access cached sessions much faster than if the server must read the session object from a file or database. However, under some circumstances, caching can degrade performance significantly (i.e., thrashing of virtual memory). If set to 0, caching is disabled. The default is 256 sessions cached. [0..`Integer.MAX_VALUE`; default 256].
- `PersistentStoreCookieName`—If the `PersistentStoreType` is cookie, this property names the cookie WebLogic Server uses to store session data.

Specify session parameters in the session descriptor as described in the section "Configure Sessions" earlier in this chapter.

Special Considerations for In-Memory Replication

There are a number of special considerations for using in-memory replication of session state:

- In a single server instance, nonserializable data placed into HTTP sessions works fine. Unfortunately, in-memory replication does not work with nonserializable data. You'll incur many debugging headaches, only to discover that a portion of the data is not being replicated.
- Large, complex objects bring down the server performance. There is a good amount of overhead for serializing/deserializing the data, in addition to the network costs.
- Don't put hash tables, vectors, and so forth in the session because WebLogic Server cannot detect changes to objects in them. WebLogic Server ends up replicating the whole object, even though you changed just one part.
- It is a good practice to make all custom objects implement the serializable interface.
- Data that doesn't change should be made static so that it is not replicated.

Best Practices for Servlets

A number of best practices enable your use of advanced servlet features to be as successful as possible.

Limit the Size of Sessions

If your application protects sessions, the size of the session becomes important to servlet performance. WebLogic Server takes much more time to save larger sessions, so take pains to limit the amount of information stored in sessions.

Be Smart About Session State

If you are using in-memory replication or any other mechanism to protect your session state, it is important to be smart about how you treat the session state objects. In order to maximize efficiency, you want to make sure that session information is updated only when needed. Minimizing the changes that are made to the session state minimizes the number of updates either to the database or to the other nodes in the cluster.

WebLogic Server is smart about what it needs to replicate for in-memory replication. WebLogic Server monitors the session object to see what objects are placed in it, so it is important to be smart about how you treat session state objects. In order to maximize efficiency, minimize the updates to the database or secondary server.

WebLogic Server only transmits updates to the database or secondary server. To take advantage of this, you should make session information stored in the session object as granular as possible. It is better to store many small objects than to store one large object, such as a hash table or vector. If you change the state of a complex object that is already in the session, you must use the `setAttribute` again to notify WebLogic Server of the change.

If cached information is stored in the user session, consider writing the cache object so that it does not serialize. WebLogic Server does not transmit objects that do not serialize to databases or secondary servers. Your application can cache expensive objects in sessions without imposing performance-sapping overhead. If a server instance fails, the application can recompute the cached values.

Finally, only include necessary information in sessions. If data does not change across user sessions or multiple accesses, put data in static variables. Static variables are not shared across cluster nodes.

Check Serializable Status of Session Objects

When WebLogic Server passivates sessions, it serializes session objects to transmit them to secondary servers or to a database. Check that all objects added to a session are serializable (unless you do not want the information persisted). Objects that are not serializable are lost during passivation. This loss results in disappearing data that can be difficult to trace.

Persist Important Information in a Database

Session objects are appropriate for transient data that is specific to a user session. This information may include navigation state and items in a shopping cart. You should not expect that session objects are available for very long periods of time. Instead, for information that you expect to store for long periods, your best strategy is to store information about the user in the database. A database is the best location for storing long-term data.

Set Session Timeouts Aggressively

Sessions consume resources in WebLogic Server. If the timeout is set too large, inactive sessions can become a drag on WebLogic Server performance. For that reason, set your inactive intervals to be as short as possible.

Activate URL Rewriting and Encode URLs

Many users configure Web browsers to refuse cookies. For this reason, you should always enable URL rewriting in your servlets. URL rewriting ensures that you maintain compatibility and the highest level of usability for all your users.

Servlet/JSP developers should always use the URL encoding methods when embedding URLs in their HTML. Careful encoding ensures that WebLogic Server can properly track user sessions using URL rewriting. However, encode only URLs referring back to the Web application. If you pass session data to external servers, you may make your session IDs vulnerable to attack.

Use In-Memory Replication for Protecting Sessions

WebLogic Server provides reliable and high-performance replication of user sessions. Start with in-memory replication and only switch to unprotected or to protection using a database or filesystem to meet specific needs.

Increase reliability even further using replication groups. Replication groups can be used ensure that primary and secondary server instances are not on the same machine or even in the same data center.

Use Sessions to Mark Login Status

Use sessions to mark whether a user is logged in. Create a new session only on login and use sessions as a marker to determine whether a user has logged in. When a user logs out, invalidate his session. Sessions help ensure that an attacker cannot work around security measures by not logging in.

Use filters to apply security checks and configure the application of the security filter in your `web.xml` deployment descriptor.

Set Cookie Domains

Some browsers do not send cookies received from HTTP responses with HTTPS requests, or vice versa, because HTTP and HTTPS services are hosted on separate ports. As a result, Web applications may lose cookies and sessions identified using cookies. To ensure that cookies work across HTTP and HTTPS requests, set the cookie domain.

Set the cookie domain for custom cookies using the `setDomain()` method. To ensure that WebLogic maintains sessions, set the `CookieDomain` session parameter:

```
<session-descriptor>
  <session-param>
    <param-name>CookieDomain</param-name>
    <param-value>mydomain.com</param-value>
  </session-param>
</session-descriptor>
```

Using Cookies to Track Users

You may want to use cookies to store user identification information and make it easier for users to log in. However, you should remember that cookies are not particularly secure or a reliable form of permanent storage. Use the following guidelines for tracking users with cookies:

- Do use cookies to make your application more convenient. Provide an option to prepopulate a user's login ID. Provide nonsensitive user-specific information even before login.
- Do not assume that the information in a cookie is correct. Multiple users may share a machine, or a single user may have multiple accounts. Always allow users to sign in as someone else.
- Do not assume that the user is on her own machine. A user may access your application from a shared machine. Ask the user whether your application should remember the user's ID.
- Always require passwords before providing sensitive information.

Use Filters to Improve Code Reuse

Filters encourage code reuse because a filter can add functionality to a servlet without modifying servlet code. This aspect is useful when the servlet code is difficult to modify. Filters are even more useful when functionality can be applied to multiple servlets or even across Web applications. Use filters to apply security policies, cache unchanged information, transform XML output for a specific target browser, or dynamically compress output.

Override HttpResponseWrapper Methods

Use filters with subclasses of the `HttpResponseWrapper` to postprocess servlet responses. If your subclass of `HttpResponseWrapper` overrides the output buffer, be sure to override all the methods that access the output buffer. In particular, override `flushBuffer()`, `reset()`, and `resetBuffer()` methods.

Resources

The working body that defines the HTTP standard is the World Wide Web Consortium or W3C. The W3C homepage is at *http://www.w3c.org*.

The specification for HTTP is available as an RFC. HTTP 1.1 is available at *ftp://ftp.isi.edu/in-notes/rfc2616.txt*.

The Java Community Process page for JSR 000053 provides the final specification for the Servlet 2.3 specification: *http://www.jcp.org/aboutJava/communityprocess/final/jsr053*.

To read the javadoc for the Servlet classes, refer to *http://java.sun.com/products/servlet/2.3/javadoc*.

Full documentation of the deployment descriptor used to configure WebLogic Server (weblogic.xml) is available at *http://edocs.bea.com/wls/docs81/webapp/weblogic_xml.html*.

The developers at Sun have created a number of example filters. Among these filters are a filter to transform XML using XSL-T and a filter to compress servlet output. See *http://java.sun.com/products/servlet/Filters.html*.

To achieve the highest degree of reliability with in-memory replication, use the BEA feature called *Replication Groups* to customize how WebLogic Server selects secondary servers for replication. Documentation is available at *http://edocs.bea.com/wls/docs81/cluster/failover.html*.

Putting It All Together

Most Web applications have a need to store information from one request to another. WebLogic Server provides support for servlet standards to provide session and cookie storage mechanisms to applications. WebLogic Server goes beyond the basics of the specification with support for clustering. Clustered instances of WebLogic Server can provide high-performance and highly reliable applications and maintain a positive user experience.

Also, tools that improve the organization of code can benefit programmer productivity software quality. Filters provide just this kind of tool. Using filters, developers can declaratively apply a feature to components of a Web application.

With the powerful tools of filters, cookies, reliable sessions, and the best practices in applying these elements, you should have the skills you need to write enterprise-strength servlets. Next, you will learn about the other major presentation technology, JavaServer Pages.

chapter 4

Using WebLogic Server JavaServer Pages

In This Chapter

- The details for building JSPs in WebLogic Server
- Samples of JSPs built for WebLogic Server
- Techniques for including Java code such as JavaBeans and custom tag libraries
- Best practices for developing and deploying WebLogic Server JSPs

In Chapter 2, we introduced two presentation technologies: servlets and JavaServer Pages (JSPs). Chapter 3 discusses the development of servlets in detail. In this chapter, we discuss JSP technology, including when to use JSP, how to use it, and how JSP and servlet technologies complement one another.

Why JSP

Servlet technology provides presentation technology, so why add JSP to J2EE? The Java community recognized that two distinct types of work contribute to Web application development: application logic programming and Web page design. The servlet specification provides little support for Web page design, so the Java community introduced the JSP standard. With servlets and JSP, Java provides development tools to support the development of both application logic and interactive Web pages. Programmers build the code that executes business and presentation logic to perform tasks such as credit card transactions and order processing. The Web page designers build the HTML pages, graphics, and other resources required to render pages in a user's Web browser. The tools, tasks, and even the people who perform these tasks often differ.

Servlets are written in a Java, a general programming language, and work well for defining application logic. But servlets do less well at generating HTML. Consider the following code from a simple example in Chapter 3:

```
out.println("<br />Servlet path " + req.getServletPath());
out.println("<br />Path info " + req.getPathInfo());
```

```
out.println("<br />Path translated " + req.getPathTranslated());
out.println("<br />Query string " + req.getQueryString());
```

You can see that this code represents functionality at two levels: Java and HTML. And the Java code is dominant. You can see that matching open and close tags might be difficult, and quotes are extremely difficult to use because you have to escape every one:

```
out.println("<image height=\"16\" width=\"16\" src=\"/selected_icon.gif\">"
```

Also, most HTML pages have a large amount of static markup, not modified by your application. In these cases, adding `out.println("");` around each one becomes a tedious and unproductive waste of time.

Note also that the developer of a Web page is not always a Java programmer. The tools, goals, and thought processes differ. An HTML author may use WYSIWYG (What You See Is What You Get) tools like Macromedia Dreamweaver. Page developers think not in terms of classes and methods, but in page elements. HTML authors need a language that does a better job of defining HTML (or XML or XHTML) output.

In one way, JSPs reverse the structure of servlets. Rather than awkwardly embedding HTML markup in Java code, JSPs center around the markup. The JSP includes special tags and syntax to include Java code. Compare the JSP version of the previous example to the servlet code:

```
<br />Servlet path <jsp:expression>request.getServletPath()</
jsp:expression>
<br />Path info <jsp:expression>request.getPathInfo()</jsp:expression>
<br />Path translated <jsp:expression>request.getPathTranslated()</
jsp:expression>
<br />Query string <jsp:expression>request.getQueryString()</
jsp:expression>
```

Even better, the designers of JSP provide a number of markup-based actions that do not require Java code at all. You may extend these markup-based actions using custom tag libraries to meet your specific needs. WebLogic Server includes a number of these extension tags to meet address common needs.

Because JSPs are a better fit for page development tasks, the use of JSPs can greatly accelerate the development process.

JSPs Are Like Servlets

Despite the difference in appearance, JSPs and servlets are very much alike. In fact, JSPs provide essentially the same services as servlets. WebLogic Server provides a JSP container, which instantiates, executes, and provides services to JSPs. When a client sends an HTTP request for a JSP page, WebLogic Server's JSP container executes the appropriate JSP page, provides services to that JSP page, and then sends the appropriate response back to the requester. The first time a client requests a JSP page, the WebLogic Server container converts the JSP page into Java code and compiles the code into a Java class that very much resembles a servlet.

You may have noticed in the example that, just like a servlet, the JSP page has access to the `HttpServletRequest` object. In fact, the JSP provides access to all the same functionality servlets have. JSPs can query request parameters, create sessions, and add cookies to the response. In short, JSP pages can do nearly anything servlets can do.

WebLogic Server converts JSP pages to compiled Java bytecode using a two-step process. First, WebLogic Server translates the JSP page into Java code. Second, WebLogic Server compiles the Java classes into executable code. Normally, this process is transparent, and WebLogic Server deletes the intermediate Java code. However, you can tell WebLogic Server to save the Java representation. In order to demonstrate the transition from JSP to Java, we include both a simple JSP page and the resulting Java code.

The JSP file `HelloJsp.jsp` is a simple JSP page:

```
<jsp:base>
  <html>
    <head>
      <title>Hello World</title>
    </head>
    <body>
      <jsp:scriptlet>
        out.print("<p><b>Hello World!</b>");
      </jsp:scriptlet>
    </body>
  </html>
</jsp:base>
```

As you might imagine, this example generates an HTML page with the words Hello World! During the first request for this JSP page, WebLogic Server converts the page into a class `__hellojsp.java`, listed below. We have edited the resulting page to simplify the code and improve readability.

```
/* compiled from JSP: /hello.jsp
 *
 * This code was automatically generated at 9:05:04 AM on Sep 23, 2003
 * by weblogic.servlet.jsp.Jsp2Java -- do not edit.
 *
 * Copyright (c) 2003 by BEA Systems, Inc. All Rights Reserved.
 */

package jsp_servlet;

import java.io.*;
import java.util.*;
import javax.servlet.*;
import javax.servlet.http.*;
import javax.servlet.jsp.*;
import javax.servlet.jsp.tagext.*;

// User imports

public final class __hello extends weblogic.servlet.jsp.JspBase {
```

```
// ...

  private final static String _wl_block0 = "<!doctype html public \"-//
w3c/dtd HTML 4.0//en\">\r\n<html>\r\n<head>\r\n<title>Hello World</
title>\r\n</head>\r\n<body>\r\n";
  private final static byte[] _wl_block0Bytes = _getBytes(_wl_block0);
  private final static String _wl_block1 = "\r\n</body>\r\n</html>\r\n";
  private final static byte[] _wl_block1Bytes = _getBytes(_wl_block1);

  public void _jspService(javax.servlet.http.HttpServletRequest
request, javax.servlet.http.HttpServletResponse response) throws
java.io.IOException, javax.servlet.ServletException {

    // declare and set well-known variables:
    javax.servlet.ServletConfig config = getServletConfig();
    javax.servlet.ServletContext application = config.getServletContext();
    javax.servlet.jsp.tagext.Tag _activeTag = null;
    // variables for Tag extension protocol

    Object page = this;
    javax.servlet.jsp.JspWriter out;
    javax.servlet.jsp.PageContext pageContext =

javax.servlet.jsp.JspFactory.getDefaultFactory().getPageContext(this,
request, response, null, true, 8192, true);

    out = pageContext.getOut();
    JspWriter _originalOut = out;

    javax.servlet.http.HttpSession session = request.getSession(true);

    try { // error page try block

      _writeText(response, out, _wl_block0, _wl_block0Bytes);
      //[ /hello.jsp; Line: 7]
      out.print("<p><b>Hello World!</b>"); //[ /hello.jsp; Line: 8]
      _writeText(response, out, _wl_block1, _wl_block1Bytes);
    } catch (Throwable __ee) {
      while (out != null && out != _originalOut) out = pageContext.popBody();

((weblogic.servlet.jsp.PageContextImpl)pageContext).handlePageExceptio
n((Throwable)__ee);
    }
    //before final close brace...
  }
}
```

Requests come in to the WebLogic Server. The server calls the `_jspservice()` method, which is analogous to the `service()` method of a servlet. Notice that WebLogic Server automatically creates the `_jspservice()` method. Unless you are debugging JSP code, you won't ever notice it exists.

The code within the try block labeled `// error page try block` generates the resulting HTML page. The two variables `_wl_block0` and `_wl_block1` contain the bulk of the JSP file, and the code calls the method `writeText()` to write this information to the output buffer. Also, WebLogic Server copies the Java code from the JSP scriptlet into the `_jspservice()` method.

Deploying HelloJsp

The files listed above are part of the `HelloJsp.war` package, which can be found on the CD-ROM accompanying this book, in the directory `examples\ch4`. It can be compiled, packaged, and deployed using the process previously described for the `HelloWorld` example.

Integrating Java Code and JSP Markup

JSPs include both Java code and HTML, but JSPs are not the full answer to Web application development. Consider the following:

- JSP code emphasizes markup text, not code. Extensive use of Java in JSP pages makes the Java and the JSP difficult to read and understand. Markup is easier to read in JSP; code is easier to read in Java files.
- Web designers can accidentally spoil your code with errant key presses or an overaggressive find/replace. An extra semicolon or bracket left in your JSP file is likely to have unexpected consequences.
- Because WebLogic Server creates an intermediate representation, developers often have difficulty tracking down errors in JSP files.

Rather than integrate Java code directly into JSP pages, JSP provides two different mechanisms for embedding the output of code and executing complicated logic within the JSP page. These mechanisms are JavaBeans and custom tag libraries.

JavaBeans used by JSP pages are not the same as Enterprise JavaBeans (EJBs), discussed later in this book. JavaBeans are basically special Java classes that you build to contain application data and business logic for methods called from a JSP page. To use JavaBeans, create a Java class with getter and setter methods (`getAttribute()` and `setAttribute()` methods). Within the JSP page, specify the JavaBean with the `useBean` element.

```
<jsp:useBean …>
```

Look for more details on using JavaBeans with JSPs later in this chapter.

Custom tag libraries are a second mechanism for specifying business and presentation logic in JSP pages. Introduced in Version 1.1 of the JSP specification, custom tag libraries enable you to define your own specific HTML-like tags that can be used by Web developers. We cover both custom tag libraries included with WebLogic Server and how to create your own custom tag libraries later in this chapter.

Again, the designers of JSP have provided two options. Select between them using the following guidelines. Use a JavaBean when

- You are primarily encapsulating data, or business logic.

- You want to modularize your Java code for reuse in something other than JSP.
- You want to minimize the chance of having the Web/HTML designers inadvertently modify your Java code.

Use custom tag libraries when

- You have application logic that only makes sense within the Web application.
- You want to remove presentation logic from the JSP. For example, your application may select between two components based on the user's login status. Use a tag library to select the appropriate component.
- You want to perform preprocessing and postprocessing of content for tasks such as personalization or content management. Personalization might include special tags that look up a user's information. Content management might enable you to create special tags to load data from your content repository.

In many cases, you could use either JavaBeans or custom tag libraries to accomplish your particular goals. In these cases, use the solution that works best for your particular situation.

JSP Basics

JSP Lifecycle

Like servlets, JSP resources go through a sequence of stages within their lifecycle. Because JSPs are compiled into classes similar to servlets, their behavior, controls, and lifecycle are nearly identical to servlets. The WebLogic Server JSP container handles the lifecycle automatically and transparently. In most cases, the JSP developer and the deployer never actually deal with compiled servlet code, but understanding how JSPs behave in the context of WebLogic Server helps you understand best practices for development.

Initialization

Before WebLogic Server can serve JSP pages, it must compile your JSPs into Java classes. For all practical purposes, JSPs are compiled into servlets. Technically speaking, the resulting components are not servlets, but are classes that extend JspBase. One difference between servlets and JSP classes is that the WebLogic Server JSP translator automatically includes initialization code in the JSP code.

Loading and Instantiation

WebLogic Server is responsible for loading and instantiating JSPs. During this phase, WebLogic Server uses the standard class-loading mechanism to load the classes generated from JSP pages. During this stage, WebLogic Server calls the JSP classes init() method.

Request Handling

The request-handling section of the JSP lifecycle is where real work gets done. WebLogic Server calls the _jspservice() method, analogous to the service() method of a servlet, to handle requests. Again, the JSP container automatically creates the _jspservice() method from the JSP page.

There are two options when building JSPs: multithreaded and single-threaded. Single-threaded JSPs, defined in a property that is specific to each application server or by setting the `isThread-Safe=false` attribute in the page directive (see the section on page directives later in this chapter). This directive means that your JSP can service only one request at a time by each instance of your JSP class. WebLogic Server, by default, automatically creates five instances of each JSP object that uses the single-threaded model. Because multiple threads of execution in WebLogic Server can execute only a single-threaded JSP one at a time, using single-threaded servlets limits scalability.

> **Best Practice:** Write thread-safe JSP pages. Pages that are not thread-safe severely limit the scalability of your Web application.

End of Service

As defined by the JSP specification, the JSP container can remove the JSP from active duty at any time. WebLogic Server commits an end of service for a JSP, only on receiving a command from the administration console or when WebLogic Server itself shuts down.

Most JSP containers, including WebLogic Server, allow you to configure how often your JSP page should be recompiled and reinitialized. The process of reinitialization forces the JSP into the end-of-service phase and then to start over with initialization. In WebLogic Server, this time is configurable through a parameter called `pageCheckSeconds`. Review your product documentation for more information.

Anatomy

A JSP file is a sequence of HTML interleaved with special JSP tags. The JSP tags define how to modify the HTML in response to user's requests. JSP provides three categories of tags:

- *Directives* define messages your page sends the JSP container.
- *Scripting elements* include variable declarations, Java code to be executed, and expressions.
- *Actions* use JSP tags as an alternative to embedding Java code in the JSP page.

The next sections discuss how to use each of the three different JSP page element types.

Scope

In Chapters 2 and 3, we discussed a number of objects where applications can store attributes. Developers can store information to the `ServletRequest`, the `ServletContext`, and, if a session is active, to an `HttpSession`. These storage facilities provide a mechanism for passing information from one part of a Web application to another. JSP refers to these various storage facilities using the concept of scope.

The JSP specification defines the following scopes:

- `page`—Attributes defined within the `page` scope are active only within the current page.
- `request`—The `request` scope remains active throughout the processing of the current request. Attributes placed in the `request` scope are available even following include or forward operations. The JSP container references the `ServletRequest` for the current request.
- `session`—If a session is active, attributes can be placed in the `session` scope. These attributes are available across requests while the session remains active.

- `application`—The `application` scope is shared by all JSPs and servlets within the Web application. Attributes stored in the `application` scope are available as long as the Web application is active. Note: The application scope is only available within the current Java Virtual Machine (JVM).

The `request`, `session`, and `application` scopes map to the `ServletRequest`, `Session`, and `ServletContext` objects in servlet development. The JSP specification adds the `page` scope.

A Word on Notation

In the original versions of JSP, designers used special sequences of characters to denote JSP tags. Back then, HTML and XML bore a family resemblance to one another, but only because they derived from the same origin (SGML). A new version of the HTML standard reformulated as XML has largely erased this difference. Now, XHTML 1.0 is fully compliant XML. Using XML for markup brings several advantages. XML authoring tools can properly parse the page, and XML tools like XSLT support XML generation.

The 1.2 version of the JSP specification introduced JSP documents, which use an XML version of JSP tags. Now, either the JSP-syntax or the XML-syntax is equally valid.

This book and the accompanying examples use the new XML syntax. The two styles are functionally equivalent, but the new syntax uses the JSP element names rather than the sequences of symbols used in JSP 1.0 and 1.1. Also, you may not mix tag styles within a page, but you can include or forward a JSP page using a different style. The XML tags and their JSP-style counterparts are summarized in Table 4-1 for your reference.

Table 4-1   Summary of XML and JSP Syntax

	XML syntax	JSP syntax
JSP root	<jsp:root>	N/A
Page directive	<jsp:directive.page property-attribs />	<%@ page property-attribs %>
Include directive	<jsp:directive.include file="filename"/>	<%@ include file="filename" %>
Tag Library directive	N/A – Tag libraries are defined in the root element.	<%@ taglib uri="uri" prefix="tagPrefix" %>
Declaration	<jsp:declaration>	…declarations here…
</jsp:declaration>	<%!	…declarations here…
%>	Scriptlet	<jsp:scriptlet>
…code here…	</jsp:scriptlet>	<%
…code here…	%>	Expression
<jsp:expression>	…expression here…	</jsp:expression>
<%=	…expression here…	%>
Include action	<jsp:include>	<jsp:include>
Forward action	<jsp:forward>	<jsp:forward>

Table 4-1 Summary of XML and JSP Syntax *(continued)*

	XML syntax	JSP syntax
Plugin action	<jsp:plugin>	<jsp:plugin>
Text action	<jsp:text>	N/A
Use bean action	<jsp:useBean>	<jsp:useBean>
Get bean property	<jsp:getProperty>	<jsp:getProperty>
Set bean property	<jsp:setProperty>	<jsp:setProperty>

Finally, the old syntax is not entirely gone. In some cases, you can set the attributes of JSP tags using an expression. Within the original JSP syntax, some attributes can be defined using the syntax:

```
<jsp:include page="<%= bean.getForward()%>">
```

The new XML syntax tweaks this syntax by removing the angle brackets:

```
<jsp:include page="%= bean.getForward()%>">
```

Directives

When you construct JSP pages, you can specify certain directives to the JSP container. For example, you can specify an error redirect for the current page. If there are problems with your JSP page, WebLogic Server catches the exception and forwards the request to the error page. Or, you can specify what Java classes you want to include during JSP execution. Specify these processing characteristics using a JSP directive.

Directives are specified with the <jsp:directive.directive-type attributes/> element (in JSP syntax, the sequence <%@ directive-type attributes%>). The following example directive instructs the JSP container to import all the classes in the java.util package:

```
<jsp:directive.page import="java.util.*"/>(XML syntax)
<%@ page import="java.util.*"%>(JSP syntax)
```

There are several types of directives for JSP:

- Page directives provide processing instructions for the current page.
- Include directives are used to include another file within a JSP.
- Tag library directives specify how to include and access custom tag libraries. Tag libraries enable developers to create custom tags for Web developers to use. We go into more detail on tag library directives in the section "Custom Tags" later in this chapter.

Each of these directives may have multiple attributes. Some attributes have default values if you don't include the attribute. For example, the default size of the output buffer is 8KB. In the following sections, we signify default values with **bold text**. The default values are convenient because developers don't have to specify every single directive explicitly.

Page Directives

Page directives take the form <jsp:directive.page attribute-settings/>, where the attributes describe settings meaningful to the JSP container . For example, the following tag is a page directive that tells the JSP container that your JSP page should be activated to work with sessions. As you would expect, sessions for JSP pages are similar to those for servlets.

```
<jsp:directive.page session="true"/>
```

You can include more than one page directive in a page element. For example,

```
<jsp:directive.page session="true" import="com.learnweblogic.beans"/>
```

Page directive attributes include

- `language="`**java**`|language name"`—Enables you to specify the programming language used in the JSP page. The default value for this directive is `java`. For applications built on WebLogic Server, this tag is only informational because WebLogic Server only supports JSP scripting using the Java language. In the future, the JSP standard may include other languages.
- `extends="class"`—Enables you to specify that your JSP page (and therefore the resulting Java class) extends another class. For example, if you want to have your JSP extend a base class called `com.learnweblogic.JspCommon`, include a page directive like this:

```
<jsp:directive.page extends=" com.learnweblogic.JspCommon " />
```

You also can create a public class that includes helper methods. Extend the helper class and use these methods in your JSP page. You could create this class like this:

```
public class JspCommon {

    public String myHelperMethod() {
        // Do work here...
    }
}
```

If your JSP page extends `JspCommon`, your JSP page could access the method `myHelperMethod()` from scriptlets in your JSP page. Note: You must either use the fully qualified class name or use the import tag to identify the class. If WebLogic Server cannot find the base class, it will generate a `ClassNotFoundException` exception.

- `import= " { package. class | package .* } , … "`—Enables you to specify that the container should import Java classes into your JSP page. Once the classes are imported, you can reference a class using just the class name. For example, if you want to use a cryptographic library in your JSP pages, include the following page directive:

```
<jsp:directive.page import="com.cryptographic-package.*"/>
```

The following would make utility classes, `java.util.Hashtable` and `java.util.Vector`, available in your JSP page:

```
<%@ page import="java.util.Hashtable,java.util.Vector"%>
```

Note: The following packages are implicitly imported, so you don't need to specify them with the import attribute:

```
java.lang.*
javax.servlet.*
```

```
javax.servlet.jsp.*
javax.servlet.http.*
```

- `session="`**`true`**`|false"`—Enables you to specify whether your JSP page requires an active HTTP session. When set to true, the JSP code defines the implicit object session using `request.getSession(true)`. When set to `false`, the JSP code does not define a session object. We discuss how to access session information later in this chapter.

> **Best Practice:** Always set the session page directive to `false` unless you expect to use information from the session within your JSP page. The `false` setting does not remove an existing session, but a `true` setting will create a session—perhaps unintentionally. See Chapter 4 for warnings regarding the use of `request.getSession(true)`. In order to avoid the security problems introduced by this call, make sure that you restrict use of JSP pages with the page directive `session="true"`. Direct requests only to these restricted pages after confirming a session does exist. You can limit access to JSPs by placing them in the WEB-INF directory of your Web application. You can include or forward resources in the WEB-INF directory, but external users cannot access these resources directly.

- `buffer=" none|` **`8KB`** `| size KB"`—Enables you to specify the minimum buffer size for the HTTP response that goes to the client. By default, the response is buffered in 8KB (kilobytes) chunks. You can change the buffer size to suit the needs of your application. If you are returning very large files to the client, you might want to increase the buffer size. In typical Web scenarios, leave the buffer size at the default value of 8KB. This setting allows the Web browser to begin displaying your page before it has been completely generated.
- `isThreadSafe="`**`true`**`|false"`—Specifies whether the JSP page is thread-safe. Setting this value to `true` means that multiple threads can execute the code in your JSP page at the same time. Setting this value to `false` means that only one thread can execute the code in your JSP page at a time. The default value of this directive is `true` if it is not explicitly set.

JSP pages that are not thread-safe limit scalability. When a JSP page is not thread-safe, only one thread of execution can run in the JSP page at any given time. For this reason, you should always design your JSP pages to be thread-safe.

> **Best Practice:** Write JSP pages to be thread-safe.

- `errorPage="relativeURL"`—Enables you to specify a relative path to a JSP error page. WebLogic Server directs requests to this error page when it catches exceptions thrown from the current page. For example, to specify that when a JSP page generates an exception, it should redirect requests to the page `error.jsp`, include this directive:

```
<jsp:directive.page errorPage="error.jsp" />
```

A good architecture for a JSP application includes one or more error-handling JSPs.

> **Best Practice:** Use the `errorPage` directive to specify an error page for each JSP.

- isErrorPage="true|**false**"—Enables you to specify that the given JSP page is an error-handling page. As mentioned previously, you should build JSP pages specifically to handle errors that arise during execution of your application. If set to true, this tag indicates that the JSP container should treat the current page differently. Later in this chapter, we cover how to access the error information to handle it appropriately.
- contentType="mimeType [; charset =characterSet]—Enables you to specify the MIME type and character set in HTTP headers returned by your JSP page. The default MIME type is text/html and the character set is charset=ISO-8859-1. Use this tag to define the character set for languages other than English. The following defines that the JSP should display a Kanji (Japanese) character set:

```
<%@ page contentType = "text/html"; charset="SJIS" %>
```

WebLogic Server inherits its support for internationalized text and content directly from the Java platform. Therefore, WebLogic Server also supports any character set that the underlying Java platform supports. Look for more information on locales and character sets supported by Java on the Java Web site at http://java.sun.com/j2se/1.3/docs/guide/intl/encoding.doc.html.

Authors can specify multiple page directives in a single element or across multiple elements. Each of the following examples is equivalent:

```
<!-- Individual page directives -->
<jsp:directive.page import="javax.naming.*,java.util.*,java.sql.*"/>
<jsp:directive.page errorPage="error.jsp"/>
<jsp:directive.page isThreadSafe="true"/>
<jsp:directive.page session="false"/>

<!-- Combined page directive -->
<jsp:directive.page
    import="javax.naming.*,java.util.*,java.sql.*"
    errorPage="error.jsp"
    isThreadSafe="true"
    session="false"/>
```

Include Directives

Use the include directive to insert arbitrary text or JSP page code within the current JSP. The syntax of the include directive is <jsp:directive.include file="relative-filename"/>. For example, if you want to instruct WebLogic Server to include the contents of a text file named todaysweather.txt in the output of your JSP, use the following code:

```
<jsp:directive.include file="todaysweather.txt"/>
```

The include directive refers to a file specified by a path relative to the location of the JSP page within the Web application. If the included JSP page were in a subdirectory named mysubdirectory and was named foo.txt, the relative path would be mysubdirectory/foo.txt.

The include directive can also be used to include entire JSP files. If the included file is a JSP, WebLogic Server includes the referenced JSP code in the current JSP page and includes the included code during compilation:

```
<jsp:directive.include file="response.jsp"/>
```

In either case, the include directive instructs WebLogic Server to compile the referenced resource into the current JSP page.

Why Include Directives?

Include directives are extremely powerful in the context of a J2EE Web application. They enable you to modularize your JSP pages, making development and maintenance much simpler. For example, to place a navigation bar into every JSP page, create a single page called `navigation.jsp`. The output of this JSP page would be the navigation bar that you show to every user.

However, JSP provides an additional mechanism to include resources within a page. The include action also embeds resources within the current page, using the syntax

```
<jsp:include page="foo.jsp">
```

For more information, see the section on "Actions" later in this chapter.

Given the choice between two options to include resources, how should a developer select between them? In order to make an informed decision, you must understand the technical differences between each option. Both the include directive and action insert an external resource into the current JSP file. WebLogic Server completes the include directive when it compiles the JSP page. The include action includes resources when WebLogic Server serves the page. In either case, changes to the included page are reflected to the user. WebLogic Server tests all included files to determine whether they have changed. If any of the included files have changed, WebLogic Server recompiles the including page.

Because the include directive occurs at compile time, the directive is faster than the action. The include action is slower, but provides additional functionality. You may include parameters in the include request or dynamically select the target of an include action. The include directive works on JSPs and static resources. The include action includes any resource, static or dynamic (including servlets). Lastly, the two mechanisms provide different supports for internationalization. Files included using the directive can not set `contentType:charset` independent of the including page. If you need to control encoding by module, you must use the include action.

> **Best Practice:** Use the appropriate include mechanism. Use the include directive to modularize your pages. If your site regularly reuses components, such as a navigation bar or a banner across the top of the Web site, consider placing the code to generate those components into separate JSP pages. Then, use the JSP include directive to include that code into each one of your pages. The include directive is an efficient operation. If you have special needs to dynamically select the included resource, or if you need advanced control over character encoding, use the include action.

Scripting Elements

While directives are special JSP tags that send commands to the WebLogic Server JSP container, scripting elements specify arbitrary Java code for the container to execute. One convenience of JSP scripting over servlet coding is that JSP contains many predefined implicit objects. This means that you do not need to write code to generate an output stream, look up the `ServletContext`, and so forth—the container does these things for you.

There are three types of scripting elements for use with JSP:

- Declarations enable you to declare methods, variables, and so forth in a JSP page.

- Scriptlets are Java code fragments executed when clients request your JSP page.
- Expressions are Java code expressions that is evaluated, converted to text, and then automatically written into the response.

Before discussing the three types of scripting elements in detail, we discuss the implicit objects created for the developer by WebLogic Server.

Implicit Objects

Implicit objects are objects automatically provided to JSPs by the JSP container. For example, WebLogic Server provides the user session object in a variable named `session`. Other objects are available for different tasks. In general, these objects match the objects available for servlet development.

The following is a summary of available objects.

Implicit Object: out

WebLogic Server provides an instance of the `JspWriter` class as the `out` object. The `JspWriter` provides print methods that pass output to the requester. Whenever you need to send the results of an operation back to the client browser, use the `out` object provided by the JSP container. You may simply call the `out.print()` or `out.println()` methods. The following code prints "I play basketball with Nick D." to the requesting client:

```
out.print("I play basketball with Nick D.");
```

The scope of the `out` object is the current page. That means that there is a single instance of the object for each JSP page. You can do everything with this `out` object that you did with the `PrintWriter` object you used in your servlets in Chapter 3.

Remember, the `out` object is buffered in 8KB chunks. But, you can change the value of this buffering using the page directive buffer (described earlier in this chapter). Regardless of the size of the buffer, at the end of the execution of your JSP, WebLogic Server flushes your output buffer and sends the remaining data in your response back to the client.

You can use a number of other methods on the `out` object:

- `public abstract void clear()` and `public abstract void clearBuffer()`—Enable you to clear the existing output buffer for the JSP page. Use the following code if you have data already buffered for output to the client, but decide that you want to clear that buffer. The difference between the two methods is that the `clear()` throws an exception if data has already been sent to the client. `clearBuffer()` does not throw an exception if data has already been sent, but clears the current buffer.
- `public abstract void flush()`—Clears the current output buffer and sends the data to the client. The JSP container automatically calls this method. In general, you should not call the `flush()` method unless you need to streamline the transfer of large files. Also, you may want to flush output following an exception.

Best Practice: When your application calls the `flush()` method, this call undermines WebLogic optimizations. Wherever possible, allow WebLogic Server to handle flushing buffers automatically. While JSP actions for forwarding to other resources can `flush()` the output buffer, WebLogic Server is optimized to work in those circumstances.

- `public int getBufferSize()`—Returns the size of the buffer in bytes. This is basically the value set using the `<jsp:directive.page buffer="buffer-size"/>` discussed earlier in this chapter.
- `public abstract int getRemaining()`—Returns the size of the remaining free space in the output buffer. The return value represents the number of bytes available.

Implicit Objects: request, response

WebLogic Server provides objects named `request` and `response` to JSP pages. These objects are instances of the classes `javax.servlet.HttpServletRequest` and `javax.servlet.HttpServletResponse`. You should use this `request` object to access the parameters and the respective values included in the request. Use the `response` object to send redirects, modify HTTP headers, and specify URL rewriting. To use the `response` object directly, use the same methods described in Chapter 3.

Implicit Object: session

Your JSP page has access to the implicit object `session`. This object is an instance of the `javax.servlet.http.HttpSession` class and represents the `session` object for the current user session. WebLogic Server provides the `session` object when the `session` page directive is `true` (the default value). If the directive is set to `false`, WebLogic Server does not provide the session object to the JSP. For additional information regarding sessions, refer to Chapter 3.

Implicit Objects: application, config

WebLogic Server provides the `ServletContext` and `ServletConfig` objects to JSP pages with the implicit objects `application` and `config`. Use the `application` object to communicate with the JSP container. For example, you can get initialization parameters from the `web.xml` deployment descriptor, access the `RequestDispatcher`, or share attributes within a Web application (limited to the current JVM). Use the `config` object as you would use the `ServletConfig` during servlet development (rarely necessary for JSP development). See Chapter 2 for additional information regarding both the `ServletContext` and `ServletConfig`.

Implicit Object: page

The implicit page object is a reference to the implementation class of the current JSP page. The page is of type `Object` because the JSP container has latitude in defining the implementation class. In the case of WebLogic Server, the object is an instance of `weblogic.servlet.jsp.JspBase`. You can use this object to call any of the servlet methods, but in practice, this is almost never necessary.

Implicit Object: pageContext

The `pageContext` object provides convenient access to scoped attributes, to all the other implicit objects, to forwarding and inclusion methods, and for error handling. The `pageContext` also provides support for nested output streams as used by custom tag Libraries. For the most part, the `pageContext` is used by the JSP container behind the scenes; however, several of its methods may be useful.

The `PageContext` provides a direct interface to the page scope. The simple forms of the `getAttribute()` and `setAttribute()` methods apply to the page.

- `public java.lang.Object getAttribute(String attributeName)`—Get the named attribute from the page scope.
- `public void setAttribute(String attributeName, Object attributeValue)`—Set a named object within the current page scope.

The `PageContext` object also provides unified access to attributes across all scopes. Use the following statically defined variables from the `PageContext` and the following methods to access attributes in the various scopes:

- `public static final int PAGE_SCOPE`
- `public static final int REQUEST_SCOPE`
- `public static final int SESSION_SCOPE`
- `public static final int APPLICATION_SCOPE`

Here are the methods:

- `public java.lang.Object getAttribute(String attributeName, int scope)`—Return the specified attribute from the specified scope.
- `public java.util.Enumeration getAttributeNamesInScope(int scope)`—Return an enumeration of all the named attributes within the specified scope. The enumeration contains the names of the attributes.
- `public void setAttribute(String attributeName, Object attributeValue, int scope)`—Set the attribute using the specified name and value within the specified scope.
- `public void removeAttribute(String attributeName, int Scope)`—Remove the attribute from the specified scope.

In addition to the above methods, the `PageContext` provides several convenience methods that automatically determine the appropriate scope. These methods search through the scopes in the order listed above and act on the first matching attribute.

- `public java.lang.Object findAttribute(String attributeName)`—Returns the value of the named attribute. The method looks in each of the scopes listed above in turn and returns the first matching attribute.
- `public int getAttributesScope(String attributeName)`—Returns the scope in which the named attribute was found.
- `public void removeAttribute(String attributeName)`—Removes the named attribute. The method looks in each of the scopes listed above in turn and removes the first matching attribute.

Implicit Object: exception

When you set the page directive `isErrorPage` to `true`, WebLogic Server provides an exception object to the JSP.

A JSP page may throw an exception while processing a request. If the page specifies an `errorPage`, WebLogic Server directs the request to an error-handling page. The `exception` object is an instance of `java.lang.Throwable` that encapsulates the error message. To access the error messages, you can use a number of available methods:

- `public String getMessage()` and `public String getLocalizedMessage()`—Returns the message contained in the `exception` object. The `getLocalizedMessage()` method is intended to provide messages in different languages, but in most cases, this method simply returns the same value as `getMessage()`. To print out the message of your exception to your user, you could use the following code in your JSP:

```
out.print("exception: " + exception.getMessage());
```

> **Best Practice:** Don't print exception messages to the user; these are useful for diagnosis and for debugging, but can be confusing and even threatening to users.

- `public void printStackTrace()` and `public void printStack-Trace(PrintWriter out)`—Prints out a complete stack trace of the error. This is helpful to see where the error originated and how it propagated through the system. By default, this method outputs the stack trace to the standard error output stream. To write the stack trace to the HTML page, include the `out` object as a parameter to `printStackTrace()`.

If you attempt to use these methods in a page that is not an error page, WebLogic Server will not be able to compile the page. Identify the page as an error page using the page directive `isErrorPage="true"`.

The following is a complete JSP error page similar to the one used in the WebAuction application. The error page accesses the implicit exception object and prints out a stack trace of the error:

```
<jsp:root>
  <jsp:directive.page session="false" isErrorPage="true"/>
  <html>
    <head>
      <title>WebLogic Server WebAuction Error</title>
    </head>
    <body text="#000000" bgcolor="#FFFFFF"
          link="#0000EE" vlink="#551A8B" alink="#FF0000">
      <p>An error occurred while processing your request.</p>
      <p>If this error persists, please contact the site administrator</p>
      <jsp:text><![CDATA[
<!--
]]></jsp:text>
      <jsp:scriptlet>
        java.io.PrintWriter pw = new java.io.PrintWriter(out);
        exception.printStackTrace(pw);
      </jsp:scriptlet>
      <jsp:text><![CDATA[-->]]></jsp:text>
    </body>
  </html>
</jsp:root>
```

Declarations

Declarations are scripting elements that declare methods and variables in a JSP page. You can use declared methods throughout the JSP page. Use the `declaration` element to identify declarations:

```
<jsp:declaration>
    // declarations here…
```

```
    int foo = 3;
</jsp:declaration>
```

The JSP style reads

```
<%!
    // declarations here…
    int foo = 3;
%>
```

The declared variable is available within the current page, or page scope. The variable is not available to other JSP pages. You can also declare methods in JSP declarations; for example, you can create a method named `inc` to increment the provided integer.

```
<jsp:declaration>
    private int inc(int x) {
        return x++;
    }
</jsp:declaration>
```

In general, avoid use of member variables in declared methods. JSPs can violate Java encapsulation and may make member variables available to other JSP pages, thus introducing issues of thread safety. Instead, craft your declared methods to use the call stack: pass all variables into methods as parameters. This design approach ensures that the method can be accessed in parallel.

Scriptlets

Scriptlets are essentially code fragments that exist in the JSP page. The JSP container executes these scriptlets while servicing client requests. Declare the programming language for the scriptlets on a page using the page directive language. In the current JSP specification, the only language that is available for scriptlets is Java. Scriptlets are designated as

```
<jsp:scriptlet>
    // scriptlet code here…
    foo = inc(foo);
    out.println(foo)
</jsp:scriptlet>
```

The JSP style is

```
<%
    // scriptlet code here…
    foo = inc(foo);
    out.println(foo)
%>
```

If you have the variable `foo` and the `inc()` declarations in your JSP page, you can reference them from within a scriptlet. As with declarations, scriptlets have a `page` scope.

Scriptlets are likely to use the implicit objects, like `out` or `pageContext`, available within JSP pages.

Expressions

Expressions are scripting elements that contain a Java expression. At execution time, the JSP container evaluates the expression, converts the result to a `String`, and writes this `String` to the implicit object, `out`. The expression can be any valid Java expression. To designate an expression in your JSP page, use the syntax

```
<jsp:expression>Java expression here…</jsp:expression>
```

The JSP style for expressions is

```
<%=Java expression here...%>
```

For example, to output the value of the variable `foo` as used in the previous sections on scriptlets and declarations, use the following code:

```
<tr>
  <td>The value of foo is</td>
  <td><jsp:expression>foo</jsp:expression></td>
</tr>
```

Actions

Actions are special JSP tags that provide operations to JSP developers. Use actions to forward requests to other pages or to include the output of another page in the current page. You could use scriptlets to perform any of the functionality provided by actions, but actions improve on scriptlets in several ways. Actions provide higher-level functions and are often easier to use than the underlying Java code. Also, actions help keep JSP pages free of Java code.

Two types of actions are available to developers:

- Standard actions are available by definition, in every container. These actions are available automatically.
- You may plug in custom actions using a JSP feature called custom tag libraries. WebLogic Server provides two tag libraries, for use in your JSP pages. Also, you may acquire tag libraries from third-party sources, or write your own. We include a more complete discussion of custom tag libraries later in this chapter.

Seven standard actions are provided by all compliant JSP 1.2 containers. This section discusses the first four of the standard actions:

- `<jsp:include>`
- `<jsp:forward>`
- `<jsp:plugin>`
- `<jsp:text>`

We defer discussion of the final three standard actions—`<jsp:useBean>`, `<jsp:set-Property>`, and `<jsp:getProperty>`—to the next section "Using JavaBeans with JSPs."

jsp:include

The jsp:include action includes static or dynamic resources into the current JSP page. The tag specifies the relative URL of the resource to be included in the following format:

```
<jsp:include page="copyright.html" />
```

Use the jsp:include element to reference any piece of content, including HTML pages, JSP pages, or servlets. The jsp:include action uses the RequestDispatcher described in Chapter 3. The JSP container includes the referenced resource in the output stream, and then resumes processing the JSP page.

Included pages have access only to the out object and cannot set headers. This means that if the included pages try to do things like call setCookie() on the response, the JSP container ignores these requests.

The JSP author may specify the flushing behavior of the jsp:include action. By default, the JSP will not automatically flush the output stream before including the referenced resource. To flush output, set the flush attribute of the jsp:include action to true.

Why two different mechanisms for including resources in JSP pages? Look back to section "Include Directives" earlier in this chapter for a more complete discussion of the differences. The jsp:include action provides some unique features. The jsp:include action can dynamically target the included resource using a Java expression. The JSP container evaluates the Java expression when the jsp:include action is called. See the following example using the variable dynamicRef:

```
<jsp:include page="%=dynamicRef%"/>
```

Also, the jsp:include action can parameterize the include request. Add jsp:param elements within the jsp:include action to set parameters on the request. The parameters are treated as if they were included in the URL and are accessed using the getParameter() method of ServletRequest. The value attribute can be either a String or a Java expression. The following example sets a request parameter using a Java expression:

```
<jsp:include page="/itemdetail.jsp">
    <jsp:param name="itemid" value="%=itemId%"/>
</jsp:include>
```

jsp:forward

The jsp:forward action allows a JSP to dispatch the current request to another resource. The tag specifies a resource using the page attribute. WebLogic Server forwards the request to the specified resource. Use the following syntax to call the jsp:forward action:

```
<jsp:forward page ="foo.jsp" />
```

The jsp:forward action is useful to redirect requests. For example, you might want to check that a user still has a valid account. If the user has no valid account, you can forward him to a page called invalidAccount.jsp, which displays his lapsed account information.

You should call the jsp:forward action before generating output. If the output buffer has been flushed, the forward action throws an IllegalStateException. If the buffer contains data but is not yet flushed, then the JSP container clears the buffer prior to forwarding the request.

Like the jsp:include action, the jsp:forward action can include parameters. WebLogic Server adds these parameters to the request. For example,

```
<jsp:forward page="/login.jsp">
    <jsp:param name="reason" value="invalid-acct"/>
</jsp:forward>
```

The `jsp:forward` action uses the `RequestDispatcher` and handles user requests in a single HTTP request. The `jsp:forward` differs from an HTTP redirect. See the section "Forward and Include" in Chapter 2 for details.

jsp:plugin

The `jsp:plugin` action instructs the client browser to execute Java code. The `jsp:plugin` action defines attributes of the Java runtime environment, and the browser may download a Java plug-in in order to provide the proper environment for Java execution. This action helps the application developer overcome compatibility and versioning issues caused by the wide variety of Web browsers. Using this tag, you can be sure your applet or JavaBean executes within the appropriate JVM. This action improves the reliability of Java executed on the client by avoiding compatibility problems.

Due to the wide variety of JVM and browser versions and vendors available in the market today, users often experience compatibility problems when running client-side Java. Use the `jsp:plugin` action get the client browser to download the Java plug-in version that you specify. This helps alleviate compatibility problems for clients.

The following example shows the `jsp:plugin` being used for an applet:

```
<jsp:plugin type="applet" code="Foo.class" codebase="/html" jreversion="1.3">
    <jsp:params>
        <jsp:param name="foo" value="bar"/>
    </jsp:params>
    <jsp:fallback>
        <p> Unable to load the plug-in. Error!</p>
    </jsp:fallback>
</jsp:plugin>
```

Use `jsp:param` elements (within `jsp:params`) to parameterize the applet or JavaBean.

The `jsp:fallback` element specifies what the JSP page should do in the case where the client can not run and will not download the plug-in required for the client-side Java.

The following is the complete syntax for the plug-in action:

```
<jsp:plugin type="bean| applet"
  code="className"
  codebase="codebase-uri"
  [ name="instanceName" ]
  [ archive="URIToArchive, ..." ]
  [ align="bottom|top|middle|left|right" ]
  [ height="displayPixels" ]
  [ width="displayPixels" ]
  [ hspace="leftRightPixels" ]
  [ vspace="topBottomPixels"]
```

```
[ jreversion="JREVersionNumber | 1.2" ]
[ nspluginurl="URLToPlugin" ]
[ iepluginurl="URLToPlugin"] >
  [ <jsp:params>
    [ <jsp:param name="parameterName" value=" parameterValue " /> ]+
  </jsp:params> ]
  [ <jsp:fallback> text message for user </jsp:fallback> ]
</jsp:plugin>
```

jsp:text

Use the `jsp:text` element to pass text data through to the response output. The JSP container does not accept text and JSP nodes within the same element. Use the `jsp:text` action to enclose the text. The `jsp:text` element has no attributes.

Bean Actions

The JSP specification enables you to use self-contained, reusable code called JavaBeans within your JSP. JavaBean components differ from the Enterprise JavaBeans discussed later in this book. Java-Beans have several characteristics:

- JavaBeans include properties that can be set at design time or at runtime.
- JavaBeans use a common design pattern to define access to properties. This common pattern means that other components can determine the properties of a JavaBean using introspection.
- JavaBeans allow you to leverage Java object serialization to store changes made to Java-Beans. Store design-time JavaBeans to a file to use at runtime. Store runtime changes and save user changes in the user's session.

You can use JavaBeans to represent data-heavy model components or to encapsulate business logic. You can reuse this style of JavaBean across multiple views and for multiple clients (e.g., browser and wireless). Imagine a Web application with a search function. The Web application could represent the various search parameters within a JavaBean.

You can also use JavaBeans to pass results to a presentation component, like a JSP page. These special-purpose JavaBeans are often tied to a specific implementation and provide fewer opportunities for reuse.

The JSP specification includes action tags for using JavaBeans without using Java code. These tags allow Web developers to easily integrate data from JavaBeans in JSP pages. By avoiding Java code, JavaBean tags help you to avoid many mistakes that result from accidentally corrupting the code. As a result, JavaBeans help you create more maintainable pages.

Integrate JavaBeans with JSP pages using three built-in JSP actions. Let's take a look at each of these tags and how to use them.

jsp:useBean

Use the `jsp:useBean` tag to define a JavaBean for use in the JSP page. The `useBean` tag tries to create a reference to a JavaBean, using the attributes of the `jsp:useBean` tag. Two of the attributes define how you reference the JavaBean within your JSP page. The `id` attribute represents the name you will use to reference the bean. The scope of the JavaBean is one of page, request, session, and application. See the section "Scope" earlier in this chapter for more information. The `scope` attribute defines where the JSP container should store the JavaBean.

The JSP container uses `jsp:useBean` attributes `class`, `type`, and `beanName` to define the bean itself. JSP authors must supply one of the following combinations:

- class only
- type only
- class and type
- type and `beanName`

The following is the complete syntax for this tag:

```
<jsp: useBean
id=" beanInstanceName "
scope=" page |request| session| application"
{ class=" package. class " |
  type=" package. class " |
  beanName=" { package. class | <%= expression %> } "
{/>| > …useBean body… </ jsp: useBean> }
```

There are a number of possible attributes for the `useBean` tag:

- `id`—Represents the bean's name as it should be referenced in your application. Use this name in other JavaBean tags and in Java code within the JSP page to access the JavaBean instance.
- `scope`—Specifies the scope of the JavaBean. There are four possible values:
  - `page`: The JavaBean is available within the current page. Your JavaBean is discarded upon completion of the page.
  - `request`: The JavaBean is available from the current `ServletRequest` object. Use the request scope when you forward or include another JSP page using the page directives described earlier in this chapter. You can use the `getAttribute(name)` method on the `ServletRequest` object to locate a reference to the JavaBean in the forward or included pages.
  - `session`: Use session to make the JavaBean available within the user session. If a session is available, store the JavaBean in the current page's `HttpSession` object.
  - `application`: JavaBeans in the application scope are available indefinitely and to all requests to the current Web application. The JavaBean is stored in the `ServletContext`. To access the JavaBean, use the `getAttribute(name)` method on the `ServletContext` object.
- `class`—Specifies the complete class name representing the JavaBean. For example, `com.learnweblogic.myapp.mybean`.
- `beanName`—The name of a JavaBean. The beanName takes the form `"com.learnweblogic.myBean"` as specified in the `instantiate()` method of `java.beans.Bean`. The `instantiate()` method uses the classloader to locate a JavaBean object in serialized form, ending in file extension `.ser`—in this case `com.learnweblogic.myBean.ser`. Failing this, the `initiate()` method tries to instantiate the class `com.learnweblogic.myBean`.
- `type`—Specifies the type used to reference the JavaBean. By itself, the `type` attribute acts like the `class` attribute in specifying the JavaBean. If combined with `class` or `beanName` attributes, the type of the JavaBean can differ from the actual class. However, the object must

be compatible with the type. If you cannot assign the referenced object to the specified type, the JSP throws a `ClassCastException`.

The following is a simple example of this tag:

```
<jsp:useBean id="mybean" class="com.myco.myapp.mybean" scope="page"/>
```

The `jsp:useBean` tag first looks for an instance of the JavaBean using the `id` and `scope` attributes. The JSP queries the `ServletRequest`, `HttpSession`, or `ServletContext` to identify a JavaBean stored using the `id` attribute. Failing this, the JSP creates a new JavaBean using the `class`, `type`, or `beanName` attributes in the `jsp:useBean` element. The JSP container makes the resulting JavaBean available to your page within the current JSP page, HTTP request, user session, or application, depending on the specified scope.

On creation of a JavaBean, the JSP executes the any instructions found within the body of the `jsp:useBean` action. The body of the `jsp:useBean` tag is a good place to initialize values of the JavaBean.

WebLogic Server automatically handles the disposal of JavaBeans.

Creating a JavaBean

Let's take the example of a search request from the previous section and expand upon it—first, we must specify the JavaBean. You must be aware of several issues when defining JavaBeans. We start with the package declaration:

```
package com.learnweblogic.ch4;
```

In order to use JavaBeans with JSP, you should always define your JavaBeans within a named package. If you assign the class to the default package, you will not be able to explicitly import the class into your page. If you fail to specify a package, the resulting errors are difficult to diagnose.

Define the JavaBean class as public to ensure that you can use the class. Also, we define the class as serializable. If we want to attach this JavaBean to a session in a distributed environment, we must be able to persist the object by serializing and deserializing the object. The easiest way to make a JavaBean persistent is to declare it `Serializable`. For additional information on the `Serializable` interface, see Chapter 6.

```
public class UserSearchBean implements java.io.Serializable {
```

The `jsp:useBean` tag requires that the JavaBean provide a default constructor with no parameters:

```
    // the default constructor
    public UserSearchBean() {}
```

For this particular JavaBean, we want to define a property called `keywords`. The application should be able to read and modify the value for this property. Name the methods for accessing Java-Bean properties using a standard pattern. For a property, name your methods `getProperty()` and `setProperty()`. The properties themselves can be of any type. Note: The pattern for methods that return a `boolean` value differs and should be `isProperty()`. The `jsp:useBean` action uses introspection to identify bean properties by looking for methods matching these patterns. Also, be aware that case is significant. Methods `getGumby()` and `setGumby()` access the variable gumby, not Gumby. Using the wrong case is a common mistake and can result in some strange errors.

```
    private String keywords;

    public String getKeywords() {
        return this.keywords;
    }

    public void setKeywords(String keywords) {
        this.keywords = keywords;
    }
}
```

Next, we define an HTML page, `search.html`, to request search parameters:

```
<html>
  <head>
    <title>Using Search Bean</title>
  </head>
  <body>
    <h1>Using Search Bean</h1>
    <form action="emptysearch1.jsp">
      <p>
        Search keywords:
        <input type="text" size="30" name="keywords"/>
      </p>
      <input type=submit value="Submit">
    </form>
  </body>
</html>
```

This example doesn't try too hard to do anything useful. It immediately directs the user to the page `emptysearch1.jsp`.

```
<jsp:root>
  <jsp:descriptor.page session="false"/>
  <jsp:useBean id="searchBean"
               scope="request"
               class="com.learnweblogic.ch4.UserSearchBean" >
    <jsp:scriptlet>
      searchBean.setKeywords(request.getParameter("keywords"));
    </jsp:scriptlet>
  </jsp:useBean>
  <html>
    <head>
      <title>Using Search Bean: no items found</title>
    </head>
    <body>
```

```
      <h1>No items found</h1>
      <form action="emptysearch.jsp">
        <p style="color: red;">
          <jsp:text>Your search for "</jsp:text>
          <jsp:expression>
            searchBean.getKeywords()
          </jsp:expression>
          <jsp:text>
            " returned no items. Try another search to find a match.
          </jsp:text>
        </p>
        <p>
          <jsp:scriptlet>
           out.print("<input type=text size=30 name=keywords value=\"");
             out.print(searchBean.getKeywords());
             out.print("\"/>");
          </jsp:scriptlet>
        </p>
        <input type=submit value="Submit">
      </form>
    </body>
  </html>
</jsp:root>
```

The emptysearch1.jsp page defines a JavaBean using the jsp:useBean tag. The page then sets the keywords property of the bean. Later in the page, the scriptlet writes a text form element with the keywords property of the bean. The target JSP page does little to reduce the use of scriptlet code, but does demonstrate how you can use the jsp:useBean tag. We further refine this example as we explore the remaining JavaBean actions.

jsp:getProperty

The jsp:getProperty action allows a JSP page to query a JavaBean for a given property. The jsp:getProperty action puts the value of the property in the JSP's out object for display back to the client. The jsp:getProperty tag takes the form

```
<jsp:getProperty name="beanID" property="propertyName"/>
```

We modify the emptysearch1.jsp example from the previous section to replace one section of Java code (the expression) with a jsp:getProperty action to get emptysearch2.jsp.

```
        <p style="color: red;">
          <jsp:text>Your search for "</jsp:text>
          <jsp:getProperty name="searchBean" property="keywords"/>
          <jsp:text>
            " returned no items. Try another search to find a match.
          </jsp:text>
        </p>
```

When you redisplay a form, you may want to prepopulate the value of input fields in your response page. The code below modifies the `emptysearch2.jsp` using the `jsp:getProperty` action:

```
<p>
  <jsp:text>Search keywords: </jsp:text>
  <jsp:text>
  <![CDATA[<input type="text" size="30" name="keywords" value="]]>
  </jsp:text>
  <jsp:getProperty name="searchBean" property="keywords"/>
  <jsp:text><![CDATA["/>]]></jsp:text>
</p>
```

Admittedly, this approach is messy. The input tag must be passed in CDATA sections and is split into two `jsp:text` elements. This situation represents one case in which the JSP syntax provides a cleaner solution:

```
<p>
  <jsp:text>Search keywords: </jsp:text>
  <input type="text" size="30" name="keywords"
value="<%=searchBean.getKeywords()%>"/>
  </p>
```

Still, this solution forces the author to use an expression to generate the necessary output. A custom tag project, the Apache project Taglibs (`http://jakarta.apache.org/taglibs/doc/input-doc/intro.html`), provides an even better solution in the `input:text` tag:

```
<p>
  <jsp:text>Search keywords: </jsp:text>
  <input:text name="keywords" bean="searchBean"
attributesText='size="30"'/>
  </p>
```

jsp:setProperty

Predictably, the mirror action to `jsp:getProperty` is `jsp:setProperty`. The `jsp:set-Property` tag has a similar format to `jsp:getProperty`:

```
<jsp:setProperty name="searchBean" property="keywords" value="Learning
Weblogic" />
```

In this simplistic form, the `jsp:setProperty` action can be used within the body of a `jsp:useBean` element to initialize properties of the bean.

One very convenient feature of JavaBeans in JSP is that the `jsp:setProperty` action can automatically populate properties of a JavaBean. When a Web form generates an HTTP request, it typically includes several request parameters in the form of name/value pairs. These parameters represent user input. The JSP specification allows you to automatically populate JavaBeans properties using these request parameters.

Use an alternative syntax for `jsp:setProperty` to configure your JSP for automatic population:

```
<jsp:setProperty name="searchBean" property="keywords" param="keywords"/>
```

By using the `param` attribute rather than the `value` attribute, you instruct the JSP to set the JavaBean property `keywords` using the `request` parameter named `keywords`. Often, the names of the `property` and `request` parameters are the same. When this is the case, the `param` attribute is optional. If neither `param` nor `value` is provided, the `jsp:setProperty` action tries to populate the JavaBean property with a `request` parameter of the same name:

```
<jsp:setProperty name="searchBean" property="keywords"/>
```

Further, a JavaBean may have multiple properties. If each of the `request` parameter names and JavaBean properties match, you can use the following shorthand notation:

```
<jsp:setProperty name="searchBean" property="*"/>
```

> **Best Practice:** Be careful regarding the wildcard population of JavaBeans. Malicious users could include properties you didn't intend to expose. To avoid taking this risk, specify each property you intend to prepopulate.

We modify the `emptysearch3.jsp` example from the previous section to replace the body of the `jsp:useBean` action with a `jsp:setProperty` action to get `emptysearch4.jsp`:

```
<jsp:useBean id="searchBean"
             scope="request"
             class="com.learnweblogic.ch4.UserSearchBean">
  <jsp:setProperty name="searchBean" property="keywords"/>
</jsp:useBean>
```

Passing Data

As mentioned in our discussion of the Model-View-Controller design pattern (Chapter 2), servlets and JSPs often work hand in hand. In the following example, we extend the search function listed above. We use a servlet to dispatch business logic, and we use JSP pages both to convert the request into a JavaBean and, for the view, to generate the HTML passed to the client.

In this example, we continue to use a static HTML search form as a point of entry. We route the request to a search action. The `web.xml` deployment descriptor maps the search request to a JSP page, `searchcontroller.jsp`. This JSP page prepopulates user input and calls the servlet `PerformSearch`. `PerformSearch` completes the search. In this case, it does not try very hard: updates the `ViewMappingBean`, and returns to the `searchcontroller.jsp` page. The `searchcontroller.jsp` forwards the request to the JSP specified by the `ViewMappingBean`. Here is the listing for the `searchcontroller.jsp`:

```
<jsp:root
  xmlns:jsp="http://java.sun.com/JSP/Page">
  <jsp:descriptor.page session="true"/>
  <jsp:useBean id="searchBean"
```

```
                 scope="request"
                 class="com.learnweblogic.ch4.UserSearchBean">
    <jsp:setProperty name="searchBean" property="keywords"/>
  </jsp:useBean>
  <jsp:useBean id="viewMapping"
                 scope="session"
                 class="com.learnweblogic.ch4.ViewMappingBean">
    <jsp:setProperty name="viewMapping" property="state"
value="search-mode"/>
  </jsp:useBean>
  <jsp:include page="/WEB-INF/performsearch"/>
  <jsp:forward page="%=viewMapping.getView()%"/>
</jsp:root>
```

The servlet `PerformSearch.java` is really just a shell:

```
package com.learnweblogic.ch4;

import javax.servlet.http.*;

public class PerformSearch extends HttpServlet {
    public void service(HttpServletRequest req, HttpServletResponse res) {
        HttpSession session = req.getSession(false);
        if (null != session) {
            ViewMappingBean viewMapping = (ViewMappingBean)
session.getAttribute("viewMapping");
            // Normally, you might call business logic, and update the
            // state of the ViewMappingBean.

            // Replace the UserSearchBean with safe presentation version
            UserSearchBean bean = (UserSearchBean)
req.getAttribute("searchBean");
            req.setAttribute("searchBean", new UserSearchHelper(bean));
        }
        return;
    }
}
```

And the full code listing for `emptysearch.jsp` follows:

```
<jsp:root
  xmlns:jsp="http://java.sun.com/JSP/Page">
  <jsp:descriptor.page session="false"/>
  <jsp:useBean id="searchBean"
                 scope="request"
                 class="com.learnweblogic.ch4.UserSearchBean"/>
```

```
  <html>
    <head>
      <title>Using Search Bean: no items found</title>
    </head>
    <body>
      <h1>No items found</h1>
      <form action="search">
        <p style="color: red">
          <jsp:text>Your search for "</jsp:text>
          <jsp:getProperty name="searchBean" property="keywords"/>
          <jsp:text>
            " returned no items. Try another search to find a match.
          </jsp:text>
        </p>
        <p>
          <jsp:text>Search keywords: </jsp:text>
          <jsp:text>
            <![CDATA[<input type="text" size="30" name="keywords"
value="]]>
          </jsp:text>
          <jsp:getProperty name="searchBean" property="keywords"/>
          <jsp:text><![CDATA["/>]]></jsp:text>
        </p>
        <input type=submit value="Submit">
      </form>
    </body>
  </html>
</jsp:root>
```

The `ViewMappingBean` demonstrates one approach to identifying the appropriate view. In this case, the `ViewMappingBean` returns a reference to the JSP page `emptysearch.jsp`. In a more complete application, the `ViewMappingBean` can act as a state machine. The bean identifies the appropriate view using the application's current state and the outcome of application business logic. The `ViewMappingBean` encapsulates the logic for screen flows throughout the application. The bean also provides a convenient method to forward the request to the appropriate view.

```
<jsp:forward page="%=viewMapping.getView()%"/>
```

The `ViewMappingBean` code follows:

```
package com.learnweblogic.ch4;

import java.io.Serializable;

public class ViewMappingBean implements Serializable {

    public ViewMappingBean() {}
```

```
    public void setState(String state) {}
    public void setAction(String action) {}
    public String getView() {
        return "/emptysearch.jsp";
    }
}
```

Finally, you may notice that the servlet performs some slight of hand with the `searchBean`. The `service()` method of the `PerformSearch` servlet gets the search bean and writes it back into the request within a wrapper object. The wrapper follows the pattern of a view helper. In this case, we use the view helper to improve security by processing the `keywords` field before returning it to the JSP page for rendering.

Avoid Cross Site Scripting

The Computer Emergency Response Team (CERT), an organization dedicated to improving Internet Security, released an advisory in 2000 regarding a practice called cross-site scripting. In essence, cross-site scripting occurs when a malicious user provides scripting instructions that you may display as part of your HTML output. Many Web applications accept user input and include this data within a response. If you are not careful about how this data is displayed, an attacker can include a script on your page.

CERT recommends (`http://www.cert.org/tech_tips/malicious_code_ mitigation.html`) that you check user input for special characters and replace them prior to display on HTML pages. In our case, the view helper wraps the `UserSearchBean` and performs the recommended substitution prior within the `getKeywords()` method. The following is the listing for `UserSearchHelper`:

```
package com.learnweblogic.ch4;

public class UserSearchHelper extends UserSearchBean {

    private UserSearchBean bean;

    public UserSearchHelper(UserSearchBean bean) {
        this.bean = bean;
    }

    public String getKeywords() {
        if (null != bean) {
            return replaceBadCharacters(bean.getKeywords());
        } else {
            return null;
        }
    }

    String replaceBadCharacters(String property) {
        if (null != property) {
```

```
          StringBuffer propBuffer = new StringBuffer(property);
          replaceInStringBuffer(propBuffer, "&", "&amp;");
          replaceInStringBuffer(propBuffer, "#", "&#35;");
          replaceInStringBuffer(propBuffer, "<", "&lt;");
          replaceInStringBuffer(propBuffer, ">", "&gt;");
          replaceInStringBuffer(propBuffer, "(", "&#40;");
          replaceInStringBuffer(propBuffer, ")", "&#41;");
          replaceInStringBuffer(propBuffer, "\"", "&quot;");
          replaceInStringBuffer(propBuffer, "'", "&#39;");
          property = propBuffer.toString();
      }
      return property;
  }

    void replaceInStringBuffer(StringBuffer propBuffer, String
search, String replace) {
        int idx = 0;
        while ((idx = propBuffer.indexOf(search, idx)) >= 0) {
            propBuffer.replace(idx, idx + search.length(), replace);
            idx += replace.length();
        }
    }
  }
}
```

Deploying the DataBean Web Application in WebLogic Server

The files listed above are part of the `DataBean.war` package, which can be found on the CD-ROM accompanying this book, in the directory `examples\ch4`. It can be compiled, packaged, and deployed using the process previously described for the `HelloWorld` example.

JSP Comments

Comments add value to any type of code. The comments help to communicate the author's intent to future readers of the code. In the XML syntax for JSP, use XML comments to document your code:

```
<!-- This is a comment -->
```

If you are using the JSP syntax, use the format

```
<%-- This is a comment --%>
```

The JSP will not include these comments in the generated output.

Deployment Descriptors

Just as with servlets, you can control WebLogic Server's handling of JSP resources using the Web application's deployment descriptors. Again, the `web.xml` descriptor provides standard configuration options, and the `weblogic.xml` descriptor provides additional control over WebLogic Server's JSP handling.

Use the web.xml deployment descriptor to define a JSP file as a named servlet. In most of the examples, the JSPs are not defined as named servlets, but are referenced directly. In some cases, you might want to direct a request to either a servlet or a JSP using a single name or URL. Or you might want to hide the name of a JSP that you link to directly.

```
<servlet>
  <servlet-name>servlet-name</servlet-name>
  <jsp-file>/jsp-page.jsp</jsp-file>
</servlet>
```

Once you define the JSP file as a servlet, you can use the servlet-mapping to map URLs to the JSP. And you can reference the JSP using the ServletContext method getNamedDispatcher().

The weblogic.xml deployment descriptor provides additional control over JSP handling. The jsp-descriptor element may contain several jsp-param elements; each jsp-param element defines a parameter using a name/value pair. In the following example, the jsp-descriptor instructs WebLogic Server to compile all JSP pages during deployment, to keep intermediate Java source, and to not check the pages to see whether they have changed and require recompilation.

```
<jsp-descriptor>
    <jsp-param>
        <param-name>precompile</param-name>
        <param-value>true</param-value>
    </jsp-param>
    <jsp-param>
        <param-name>keepgenerated</param-name>
        <param-value>true</param-value>
    </jsp-param>
    <jsp-param>
        <param-name>checkPageSeconds</param-name>
        <param-value>-1</param-value>
    </jsp-param>
</jsp-descriptor>
```

Use the following parameters to customize how WebLogic Server handles JSPs:

- compilerSupportsEncoding—Use this parameter to tell the WebLogic Server JSP compiler how to interpret the text of Web application JSPs. If set to true, the JSP compiler reads the JSP text using the character encoding specified in the page's page directive contentType attribute or the character set defined with the encoding attribute of the jsp-descriptor. When set to false, the JSP compiler uses the default encoding. [**true**|false]
- debug—Specify whether WebLogic Server should include line numbers in the compiled JSP class. Line numbers come in handy during debugging. [true|**false**]
- encoding—Specify the default character set for text in JSP pages within the Web application using the param-value of the encoding parameter. You can override this setting in

individual JSP pages using the page directive. If not set, this attribute defaults to the encoding for your platform. [Set parameter using standard Java character set names; see `http://java.sun.com/j2se/1.3/docs/guide/intl/encoding.doc.html`.]

- `exactMapping`—Use this parameter to specify how strictly WebLogic Server should match URLs to JSP files. Normally, WebLogic Server requires that the requested URL matches the JSP exactly. With exact mapping, WebLogic Server may also return extended path information. If set to `false`, the extended path information is not available. [**true**|false]

- `keepgenerated`—Use the `keepgenerated` parameter to save the intermediate Java files that WebLogic Server generates during the JSP compilation process. [true|**false**]

- `noTryBlocks`—Normally, WebLogic Server uses try blocks to catch exceptions that may arise in your application. Sometimes, these try blocks interfere with deeply nested JSP tags, and WebLogic Server generates a `java.lang.VerifyError` during compilation. Correct this problem by setting this parameter to `true`. [true|**false**]

- `packagePrefix`—Use this parameter to specify a package for the JSP pages within the Web application. [default: **jsp_servlet**]

- `pageCheckSeconds`—WebLogic Server can check JSP pages to see whether they have been modified since they were last compiled. When the Web application is distributed in a WAR file, JSPs are unlikely to change. But when a loose group of files define a Web application, you may modify a JSP without notifying WebLogic Server that the file has changed. Use this parameter to configure the minimum number of seconds between checking a JSP file. When a JSP page is requested and the minimum number of seconds has passed since the last check, WebLogic Server will check to determine whether the file has changed and should be recompiled. When set to 0, WebLogic Server checks pages on every request. When set to −1, WebLogic Server does not check JSP pages. [-1, 0, **1**...Integer.MAX_VALUE]

- `precompile`—Normally, WebLogic Server waits for a JSP to be requested before compiling the page. Set the `precompile` parameter to `true` to instruct WebLogic Server to compile modified JSPs when you deploy or redeploy the Web application. [true|**false**]

- `printNulls`—Occasionally, a JSP will try to write a null value. WebLogic Server catches this problem and normally writes "null" to output. This behavior avoids a `NullPointerException` and alerts the developer that a problem exists. However, in a production environment, you may not want to print "null" within an HTML page. Set `printNulls` to `false` to print an empty string instead. [**true**|false]

- `verbose`—Determine whether WebLogic Server should log debugging information to the WebLogic Server log file. [**true**|false]

- `workingDir`—Specify the directory where WebLogic Server saves generated Java classes. This directory is also the location of intermediate Java source files if you also specify `keepgenerated=true`. [The default path is to a directory generated by WebLogic Server.]

In addition, WebLogic Server uses a compiler to convert the intermediate Java representation into Java classes. You can configure how the WebLogic Server interacts with the Java compiler using the following `jsp-descriptor` parameters:

- `compilerclassName`—Use the class defined by `compilerclassName` to compile JSP code into Java classes. The value should reference the main class of a compiler written in Java. WebLogic Server runs the specified compiler within the same JVM as WebLogic Server.

- `compileCommand`—Specify the external Java compiler that WebLogic Server should use to compile JSP code into Java classes. Use the full path name of the Java compiler. The default value is the standard `javac` compiler or the compiler specified in the Admin console (`Server‡Configuration‡General‡Java   Compiler`). For faster performance, specify a faster compiler, like the IBM `jikes` or Symantec's `sj`. The `compilerclassName` parameter overrides this setting. For example, to use the standard Java compiler, specify its location on your system as shown below:

```
<jsp-param>
  <param-name>
    compileCommand
  </param-name>
  <param-value>
    /jdk130/bin/javac.exe
  </param-value>
</jsp-param>
```

- `compileFlags`—Use the `compileFlags` parameter to pass one or more command-line flags to the compiler. Enclose multiple flags in quotes, separated by a space. For example:

```
<jsp-param>
  <param-name>compileFlags</param-name>
  <param-value>"-g -v"</param-value>
</jsp-param>
```

Custom tags

Custom tag libraries enable developers to encapsulate complex functionality inside of HTML-like tags. The JSP actions earlier in this chapter are tags that take the form `<jsp:action-name/>` and use implicit objects, also described earlier in this chapter, to perform various functions. Custom tags let you write your own tags that work just like any other JSP tag.

Using Custom Tag Libraries in JSP

Custom tag libraries are designed to hide complexity. Behind simple tags, Java code handles formatting tasks, access to external resources, and various other processing activities. The following JSP code demonstrates just how simple custom tag libraries are to use:

```
<jsp:root
  xmlns:jsp="http://java.sun.com/JSP/Page"
  xmlns:stock="http://www.learnweblogic.com/taglibs/stock">
  <html>
    <body>
      <h1>Today's Stock Price</h1>
      <p> <stock:stockPrice tickerSymbol="PRAS" /> </p>
      <p> <stock:stockPrice tickerSymbol="GIRD" /> </p>
    </body>
  </html>
</jsp:root>
```

Figure 4–1 shows this page displayed in a Web browser.

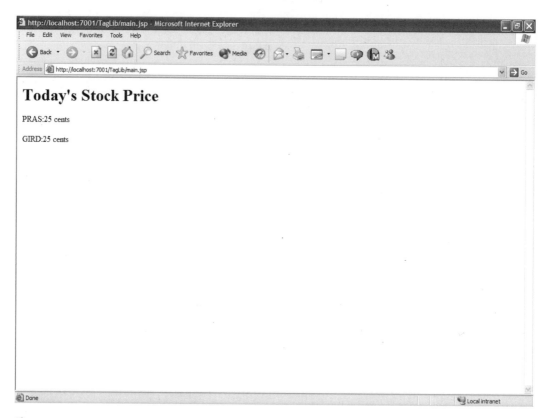

Figure 4–1
Output of a custom tag library.

In this page, we use a custom tag library to print out the stock price for some fictional companies. This is a standard JSP page that includes two special tags. The first is a directive that specifies tag library descriptor (TLD). This directive occurs within the `jsp:root` element and defines a namespace and a URI to identify a TLD. Within the above example, the descriptor looks like this:

```
<jsp:root
    xmlns:jsp="http://java.sun.com/JSP/Page"
    xmlns:stock="http://www.learnweblogic.com/tlds/stock">
```

Use the following directive syntax within JSP-style pages:

```
<%@taglib uri="http://www.learnweblogic.com/tlds/stock" prefix="stock"%>
```

The above directives specify that elements using the stock namespace reference custom tags defined by a stock tag library using the URI `http://www.learnweblogic.com/taglibs/stock`. WebLogic Server uses any number of methods to resolve this URI to a TLD file within the

Web application. WebLogic Server tries to match the specified URI to the published URI of a TLD in the `/WEB-INF` directory tree within the Web application. Typically, TLD files are placed in the directory `/WEB-INF/tlds`. WebLogic Server will also match the URI to a taglib mapping entry in the application's `web.xml` descriptor. This mapping ties a URI to the TLD file by explicitly listing the file location:

```
<taglib>
  <taglib-uri>http://www.learnweblogic.com/taglibs/stock</taglib-
uri>
  <taglib-location>/WEB-INF/tlds/stockPrice.tld</taglib-location>
</taglib>
```

Lastly, the URI may directly reference the TLD file. In this scenario, the taglib directive within the JSP might look like this:

```
<jsp:root
  xmlns:jsp="http://java.sun.com/JSP/Page"
  xmlns:stock="/WEB-INF/tlds/stockPrice.tld">
```

The TLD is an XML file containing mappings from tags to handler classes. These handler classes, also part of the tag library, implement the logic behind the tag. The handler uses tag attributes and elements within the body of the tag to generate the appropriate output.

From the JSP page, simply reference the custom tag and apply the appropriate parameters. For example, the action `<stock:stockPrice tickerSymbol="PRAS"/>` defines the `stockPrice` action within the stock tag library. When WebLogic Server executes this page, the `stockPrice` tag writes the stock symbol and price to the HTML page. The tag handler for the `stockPrice` tag uses the `tickerSymbol` attribute to look up the stock's current value and render this value into the HTML output.

Building a Basic Custom Tag Library

There are two steps to create a custom tag library. You must build a TLD file that matches tags to handlers within the tag library. And you must also build the handlers themselves—the Java classes that are executed by the JSP container when the tags are used in JSPs.

Tag Library Descriptor

The TLD is an XML-encoded file with the file extension *.tld*. The following listing demonstrates the format of the TLD file for the `stockPrice` tag library:

```
<!DOCTYPE taglib PUBLIC
"-//Sun Microsystems, Inc.//DTD JSP Tag Library 1.2//EN"
"http://java.sun.com/j2ee/dtds/web-jsptaglibrary_1_2.dtd">

<taglib>
  <tlib-version>1.0</tlib-version>
  <jsp-version>1.2</jsp-version>
  <short-name>stock</short-name>
```

```
<uri>http://www.learnweblogic.com/tlds/stock_1_0</uri>
<tag>
  <name>stockPrice</name>
  <tag-class>com.learnweblogic.examples.ch4.StockPriceHandler</tag-class>
  <body-content>JSP</body-content>
  <attribute>
    <name>tickerSymbol</name>
    <required>true</required>
    <rtexprvalue>true</rtexprvalue>
    <type>java.lang.String</type>
  </attribute>
</tag>
</taglib>
```

The first lines of the TLD file defines the current document as a tag library. The root element of the document, `taglib`, follows these lines. The elements within the `taglib` define the tag library. These elements include the following:

- `tlib-version`—The version of this tag library implementation. The value of this tag should be in the format *n.nnn*. The `tlib-version` is required.
- `jsp-version`—The `jsp-version` tag specifies the JSP version required for this tag library. Typically, you should use the value 1.2. This tag is required.
- `short-name`—Use this tag to specify a default namespace prefix for use in JSP pages. This value may be used by JSP authoring tools. The `short-name` tag is required.
- `uri`—Specify a unique URI to identify this implementation of the tag library. If WebLogic Server identifies a TLD file in a Web application and the TLD contains a URI, then WebLogic Server makes this taglib available to JSP pages in the application as if the tag library were defined in the `web.xml`. The `uri` tag is optional.
- `display-name`—JSP authoring tools may use this name to represent the tag library. WebLogic Server ignores this element.
- `small-icon`—Use the `small-icon` tag to reference an image to represent the tag library. JSP authoring tools may use this icon to represent the tag library. Use this optional tag to reference a 16 × 16 GIF image. WebLogic Server ignores this element.
- `large-icon`—Use the `large-icon` tag to reference an image to represent the tag library. JSP authoring tools may use this icon to represent the tag library. Use this optional tag to reference a 32 × 32 GIF image. WebLogic Server ignores this element.
- `description`—Use the `description` tag to describe the tag library. This tag is optional.
- `example`—Use the `example` tag to demonstrate use of the library. This tag is optional.
- `tag`—Use a `tag` element to define each of the tags available within the tag library. The JSP standard requires one or more instances of the `tag` element.

Additional tags are available to define validation and event handling. These additional elements are optional and are described later in this chapter.

Each tag element contains additional elements to define the specific tag. The `tag` element may contain the following:

- name—Use the namespace and the name of the action to reference a `tag` from your JSP page in the form `<namespace:name/>`. Define the name of the tag using this required field.
- `tag-class`—The `tag` class implements the handler for the tag. This class provides the logic behind the tag. The body of this required `tag-class` element should be a fully qualified class name.
- `body-content`—The `body-content` tag may contain one of three values: `empty`, `JSP`, or `tagdependent`. This tag tells the JSP compiler how to handle the body of a custom tag. If set to `empty`, this custom tag must always be empty. If the tag contains a body, the JSP compiler will fail during translation. If set to `JSP`, the compiler processes the body of the tag as JSP. If set to `tagdependent`, the JSP compiler passes along the contents of the tag body without further processing. Use this value if the body of the JSP tag represents a different language (e.g., SQL). The `body-content` tag is optional. By default, the JSP compiler treats the body of the tag as `JSP`.
- `attribute`—A tag may include attributes. The JSP page calls the `setAttribute()` method for each attribute included in the tag. Define each potential attribute within the tag element of the TLD. This element is required for each potential attribute. The body of the `attribute` tag is discussed further below.

In addition, a tag may include the following descriptive elements:

- `display-name`—JSP authoring tools may use this name to represent the tag. WebLogic Server ignores this element.
- `small-icon`—JSP authoring tools may use the `small-icon` to represent this tag. Use this optional tag to reference a 16 × 16 GIF image. WebLogic Server ignores this element.
- `large-icon`—JSP authoring tools may use this `large-icon` to represent the tag. Use this optional tag to reference a 32 × 32 GIF image. WebLogic Server ignores this element.
- `description`—Use the `description` tag to describe the tag. This tag is optional.
- `example`—Use the `example` tag to demonstrate use of the tag. This element is optional.

Additional tag elements allow you to set the `TagExtraInfo` class and apply validation rules to the tag. These options are covered later.

Finally, the `attribute` element should contain additional information regarding how the JSP page should handle attributes:

- name—Use this element to specify the name of the attribute. Required.
- `required`—Specify whether the JSP author must include this attribute within the current custom tag. [`true`|**`false`**|`yes`|`no`]
- `rtexprvalue`—Some attributes can be specified by a runtime expression using the syntax `%=expression%` or `<%=expression%>`. Specify whether this attribute must be static or will accept an expression as a value using the `rtexprvalue` element. [`true`|**`false`**|`yes`|`no`]
- `type`—If the attribute can accept a runtime expression (see `rtexprvalue` above), then you can optionally override the default attribute type. Select a type from the following options: `java.lang.String`, `boolean`, `byte`, `char`, `double`, `int`, `float`, `long`, `short`, `Object`, and `BeanProperty`. `BeanProperty` calls the bean `setAsText()` setter method. The default value is `java.lang.String`.
- `description`—Use the `description` tag to describe the attribute. This tag is optional.

Tag Handler

The `tag-class` elements, defined within the TLD file, reference a handler class. These handler classes define methods to process the tags as they appear in JSP pages. The handler classes implement one of three interfaces: `Tag`, `IterationTag`, or `BodyTag`. Typically, developers extend one of two classes, `TagSupport` or `BodyTagSupport`, and override default methods within these classes. The following list describes several methods defined in the `Tag` and `Iteration-Tag` interfaces that you are likely to override in your own custom tags:

- `public int doStartTag()`—The JSP page calls the `doStartTag()` method of a tag handler to process the start tag, or empty tag, of a custom tag found in a JSP. Override this method to specify behavior for your custom tag. The JSP page uses the return value of the `doStartTag()` method to determine how to complete further processing. Legal return values include `SKIP_BODY` to ignore any body within the tag. And, for handlers implementing `IterationTag`, `EVAL_BODY_INCLUDE` instructs the JSP to include content within the tag body.
- `public int doAfterBody()`—For handlers implementing the `IterationTag` interface, the JSP page calls the `doAfterBody()` method after processing the body of the custom tag but before the `doEndTag()`. Override this method to specify JSP processing of the tag body. Legal return values include `EVAL_BODY_AGAIN` to instruct the JSP to re-process the body and `SKIP_BODY` to move on and call the `doEndTag()` method.
- `public int doEndTag()`—The JSP page calls the `doEndTag()` method of a tag handler to process the end tag, or empty tag, of a custom tag found in a JSP. Override this method to specify behavior for your custom tag. The JSP page uses the return value of the `doEndTag()` method to determine how the JSP will continue processing the remainder of the JSP page. Legal values include `EVAL_PAGE` to continue processing the JSP page and `SKIP_PAGE` to terminate processing of the page.
- `public void release()`—WebLogic Server pools tag handler instances and reuses the handler objects. Override the `release()` method to free resources and reset variables within the tag handler instance.

The `TagSupport` class provides a default implementation of the `IterationTag` interface. Typically, you override methods from the `TagSupport` class, including `doStartTag()`, `doEndTag()`, `doAfterBody()`, and `release()` methods. The `TagSupport` class also defines the instance variable `pageContext`. Use this instance of `PageContext` (defined earlier in this chapter) to access implicit JSP objects.

The handler for the `stockPrice` tag is the Java class `StockPriceHandler`. This class extends `TagSupport` and overrides the methods `doStartTag()` and `release()`. Notice how the class provides a `setTickerSymbol()` method to accept the `tickerSymbol` attribute in the `stockPrice` tag. Also, the `doStartTag()` method accesses the `out` object and generates output directly using a `JspWriter`.

```
package com.learnweblogic.examples.ch4;

import javax.servlet.jsp.*;
import javax.servlet.jsp.tagext.*;

public class StockPriceHandler extends TagSupport {
```

```
private String myTickerSymbol;
private String price = "25 cents";

public String getTickerSymbol() {
    return myTickerSymbol;
}

public void setTickerSymbol(String ts) {
    myTickerSymbol = ts;
}

  public int doStartTag() throws JspException {
      /*
         You could place any work that you want to have done here.

        This method returns a status code.  There a number of different
        options for these codes, which are discussed later in this
        section.  This one instructs WebLogic not to evaluate any
        expressions inside of the body of the tag.

        At this point, you would insert code to go out and
        get the stock price from your source.  Take that value and
        put it into a string variable named 'price'.
      */

      String stockPrice = price;

      try {
          JspWriter out = pageContext.getOut();
          out.print(myTickerSymbol + ":" + price);
      } catch (Exception e) {
          e.printStackTrace();
          throw new JspException(e.getMessage());
      }
      return (SKIP_BODY);
  }

/*
   Called when the container wants to dispose of the current
   tag library.
*/
public void release() {
    myTickerSymbol = null;
    super.release();
}
}
```

Deploying the TagLib Web example

Look for the stock tag library on the CD-ROM in the directory \examples\ch4. The example includes the TLD file, the handler class, and a JSP page incorporating the stockPrice tag. The files listed above are part of the TagLib.war package. Compile, package, and deploy this application using the same process described in the HelloWorld example.

Tab Library Handler Lifecycle

The JSP instantiates handlers as needed within the JSP page. Once created, the JSP calls several methods within the handler. The following represents a typical call sequence:

- Instantiation—The JSP creates an instance of the requested handler class. The tag handler should provide a default constructor; utility classes TagSupport and TagBodySupport provide a default constructor.
- setPageContext()—The JSP initializes the tag handler by setting the PageContext of the tag handler using the PageContext of the JSP page.
- setParent()—The JSP passes the parent of the tag handler to the immediately enclosing custom tag. If the tag is not within another custom tag, the JSP passes a null value.
- setAttributeNames()—For each attribute in the JSP tag, the JSP page calls the setAttributeName() method within the tag handler object.
- doStartTag()—The JSP page calls the doStartTag() method at the opening of the custom tag.
- doAfterBody()—If the JSP processes the body of the tag, it will call the doAfterBody() method. Depending on the return value of this method, the JSP page may reprocess the tag body and call this method again.
- doEndTag()—The JSP page calls the doStartTag() method at the closing of the custom tag.
- release()—The JSP page calls the release method at the end of the JSP page.

In addition, the tag library can respond to Web application lifecycle events. Add a listener tag to the TLD to receive notification of lifecycle events. Use the following structure within the taglib element to register a listener. The servlet container treats this listener as if it were defined in the Web application's web.xml descriptor.

```
<listener>
    <listener-class>class-name</listener-class>
</listener>
```

Body Tag Handlers

We deferred discussion of tags that provide additional processing to the body of the tag. The TLD tag element body-content, the BodyTag interface, and the BodyTagSupport class all support the processing of tag bodies.

Use the body-content element to describe how the JSP page should handle the body of a tag. The tag accepts three different values: empty, JSP, and tagdependent. If the value is set to empty, the JSP translator generates an error during translation if the tag includes a body. If the value is tagdependent, the JSP processor provides no additional processing to the body of the tag. If the body-content field is omitted or set to JSP, the JSP page continues to interpret the body of the tag as JSP. In this case, the JSP container uses the output of the enclosed tags as the body of the custom tag.

In order to process the body of the tag, you should implement the interface BodyTag by subclassing the BodyTagSupport. The BodyTag interface extends the Tag and IterationTag interfaces in the following ways:

- public int doStartTag()—Within the BodyTag, the doStartTag() method may return SKIP_BODY, EVAL_BODY_INCLUDE, or EVAL_BODY_BUFFERED. The new return value allows the BodyTag class to process the body of the custom tag.
- public void doInitBody()—The JSP page calls the doInitBody() method prior to processing the tag's body.

Again, most developers extend the BodyTagSupport class and override methods as needed. BodyTagSupport adds a new instance variable named bodyContent. The JSP page initializes the bodyContent variable prior to calling doInitBody() so the bodyContent object is available throughout the rest of the tag lifecycle. The bodyContent variable provides access to the content of the tag's body.

When the JSP processes the body of your tag, the output does not go to the out object. Instead the JSP writes the output to the bodyContent object. Your handler may retrieve the content, process it, and optionally write the output to the out object. The bodyContent object is a subclass of JspWriter, so you may use the usual output methods with one caveat. Because the body-Content has no output stream behind it, the flush() method is illegal. If you call flush(), the bodyContent object will throw a java.io.IOException. Use these additional methods to interact with the bodyContent object:

- public void clearBody()—Clears the contents of the bodyContent object.
- public String getString()—Returns the current value of the bodyContent object as a String.
- public java.io.Reader getReader()—Provides a Reader with access to the content.
- public void writeOut(java.io.Writer out)—Causes the bodyContent object to write to the specified Writer.

Should you decide to write any content into the resulting page, use the getPreviousOut() method available from the BodyTagSupport class (which you are likely extending already). Use this method rather than access the out object within the PageContext because the output of this tag may, in fact, be the input to another tag.

The following doEndTag() method demonstrates processing of a tag body:

```
public int doEndTag() {
    String bodyText = bodyContent.getString();
        try {
            bodyContent.print("(body length = " + bodyText.length()
+ ")");
                getPreviousOut().print(bodyContent.getString());
        } catch (java.io.IOException e) {}
    return EVAL_PAGE;
}
```

Note: If using the XML syntax for JSP, the JSP will not recognize text directly within a custom tag body. Enclose text within another element or a `jsp:text` action.

Advanced Tag Concepts

Custom tags are powerful tools. The following sections provide an overview of advanced topics in custom tag development.

Tag Cooperation

You can develop tags that interact with one another. One tag can initialize resources for other tags, nested tags can refer to properties of enclosing tags, and the outer tags can postprocess the output of inner tags. By using multiple tags in conjunction, tag libraries can provide a rich set of features to JSP authors.

The previous section on `BodyTags` demonstrate how an outer tag can process the output of an inner tag. But tags can communicate in more direct ways. One tag can create a JavaBean and add the bean to the `PageContext`. Another tag can use values from the JavaBean. By convention, the defining object provides an `id` attribute. Referring tags use the `id` value in a `name` attribute:

```
<tag1 id="ref1" attrib="value"/>
<tag2 name="ref1"/>
```

The handler for `tag1` might store a resource using the line

```
pageContext.setAttribute(id, this);
```

The handler for `tag2` could use the following line to access the resource:

```
namedHandler = pageContext.getAttribute(idref);
```

Additionally, tags may rely on page structure to identify one another. A tag can identify its parent using the `getParent()` method, available in all tags. The `TagSupport` class also provides the handy method `findAncestorWithClass()`. If the class of the resulting tag is known, an enclosed tag can call methods on that tag directly. Consider the following JSP fragment:

```
<tag1>
    <tag2/>
</tag1>
```

Use the following methods within the `tag2` handler to identify the `tag1` handler object:

- `public Tag getParent()`—Returns the parent tag, or `null` if no custom tags enclose the current tag.
- `public static final Tag findAncestorWithClass(Tag from, java.lang.Class aClass)`—Starting from the specified tag (often `this`), this utility method follows the `getParent()` chain to return the first ancestor of the specified type, or if not found, `null`.

Customize Tag Translation

The JSP standard provides additional mechanisms to validate JSP tags at translation time and to integrate tag libraries into the JSP scripting environment. The TLD provides a declarative way to specify most validation and scripting requirements.

Specify a validation class in the `validator` element within the TLD `taglib` element. The JSP translator uses this class to check the validity of custom tags during translation. The `validator` class should extend the class `TagLibraryValidator`. The `TagLibraryValidator` tests the full content of the JSP as an XML fragment within an `InputStream` and returns error messages if there are problems, or nothing if the `validator` approves.

Additionally, you can define variable elements within the TLD tag element. Using the variable element, you can define new scripting variables available within your JSP.

If the `TagLibraryValidator` is too much, or the declarative mechanisms for specifying scripting variables are insufficient, you may provide your own class to support translation of the tags within the JSP. Specify a class to programmatically assist with JSP translation in the `tei-class` element of the TLD tag element. The specified class should implement the abstract class `TagExtraInfo`. Override the method `isValid()` to test tag attributes for validity. Override the `getVariableInfo()` method to specify scripting variables.

For more information on the validator element, variable declarations, and the `TagExtraInfo` class, refer to the JSP specification.

WebLogic Tags

WebLogic Server includes two custom tag libraries to support your development of JSPs. The first tag library provides conditional processing, iterative processing, and caching of JSP components. The second tag library provides declarative support for validating user input. BEA provides these tag libraries in the `jar` files `weblogic-tags.jar` and `weblogic-vtags.jar`.

To use these tag libraries, include the `jar` files in the `/WEB-INF/lib` directory of your Web application and the following lines in your `web.xml` deployment descriptor:

```
<taglib>
  <taglib-uri>weblogic-tags.tld</taglib-uri>
  <taglib-location>/WEB-INF/lib/weblogic-tags.jar</taglib-location>
</taglib>
<taglib>
  <taglib-uri>weblogic-vtags.tld</taglib-uri>
  <taglib-location>/WEB-INF/lib/weblogic-vtags.jar</taglib-location>
</taglib>
```

Add the taglib directives to your JSP page:

```
<jsp:root
  xmlns:jsp="http://java.sun.com/JSP/Page"
  xmlns:wl="weblogic-tags.tld"
  xmlns:vt="weblogic-vtags.tld"
>
```

or:

```
<%@ taglib uri="weblogic-tags.tld" prefix="wl" %>
<%@ taglib uri="weblogic-vtags.tld" prefix="vt" %>
```

The `weblogic-tags` TLD defines the following tags:

- `wl:process`—Use `wl:process` to conditionally include the body of the process tag. Parameterize the `wl:process` tag using the attributes `name`, `notname`, `value`, and `notvalue`. These attributes refer to either query parameter names or their values.
- `wl:repeat`—Use the `wl:repeat` tag to iterate over a set or a defined number of iterations. The set can be an `Array`, `Collection`, `Enumeration`, `Iterator`, `Vector`, or one of several other set types. Use the attribute `count` to refer to a static number of iterations. Use the attribute `set` to refer to the group, `id` to refer to the variable used to store the current element, and `type` to override the default type of `java.lang.String` for the members of the set.
- `wl:cache`—Use the `wl:cache` tag to optimize the serving of JSP pages. The `wl:cache` tag allows the JSP author to identify portions of the page to be cached by WebLogic Server rather than generated by the JSP page. The attributes and semantics of the `wl:cache` tag are too much for this chapter; refer to WebLogic Server documentation at `http://edocs.bea.com/wls/docs81/jsp` for more details.

The `weblogic-vtags` TLD defines a number of tags to validate user input. These tags allow the JSP author to add validation requirements to form elements within a JSP page. The JSP page uses these declarative tags to validate user input prior to processing by the form's target action. This tag library proves convenient because a significant portion of user input validation can be defined declaratively and is tightly linked to the input fields themselves. Again, refer to WebLogic Server for a full treatment of the form validation tags at `http://edocs.bea.com/wls/docs81/jsp`.

Best Practices

Debugging and developing JSPs for WebLogic Server is sometimes like performing microsurgery. The smallest details can cause much confusion during the development process. Of course, there are great benefits to success. This section includes best practices for debugging and developing JSPs and related technologies in WebLogic Server.

Keep in Mind that JSPs Are Just Specialized Servlets

Actually, JSPs are a simplification of the servlet paradigm. However, that does not mean that you should not follow the same best practices noted in Chapters 2 and 3. By applying these practices, you can ensure that the JSPs you build have the same characteristics of scalability, reliability, and maintainability as servlets.

Set Page Directives

Bullet-proof applications use page directives to override default values for `session` and `errorPage`. Always set the session page directive to `false` unless you expect to use information from the session within your JSP page. The `false` setting does not remove an existing session, but a `true` setting will create a session—perhaps unintentionally. See Chapter 3 for warnings regarding the use of `request.getSession(true)`. In order to avoid the security problems introduced by this call, make sure that you restrict use of JSP pages with the page directive `session="true"`. Only direct requests to these restricted pages after confirming a session does exist. You can limit access to JSPs by placing them in the WEB-INF directory of your Web application. You can include or forward resources in the WEB-INF directory, but external users cannot access these resources directly.

Further, you never know when your application might throw an exception. Use the `errorPage` page directive to redirect these failed requests to a user-friendly error page.

Base Your Development on Templates

There is no reason to write application components from scratch. Take an application that is close to the application you plan to develop, and modify it to meet your needs. The WebAuction application is designed to be used this way. Also, the J2EE Blueprints, published by Sun, provides an excellent starting point for application development.

Be Careful About Capitalization and Spacing

The advent of J2EE deployment descriptors that are XML-encoded means you need to be careful about capitalization and spacing. Hours can be spent trying to debug an application, only to realize that an errant space or bracket is causing failure. Tools are available to make this easier, including J2EE-specific development environments such as WebGain and J2EE modes for Emacs and other editors. A free set of JSP-editing modes for Emacs is available from the BEA Developer Center at *http://dev2dev.bea.com/resourcelibrary/utilitiestools/index.jsp*.

Use the Right Include Mechanism

Use the include directive to modularize your pages. If your site regularly reuses components, such as a navigation bar or a banner across the top of the Web site, consider placing the code to generate those components into separate JSP pages. Then, use the JSP include directive to include that code into each one of your pages. The include directive is an efficient operation. If you have special needs to dynamically select the included resource, or if you need advanced control over character encoding, use the include action.

Minimize Java in JSPs

Mixing JSP and Java code tends to obscure both. Take advantage of JavaBeans and custom tag libraries to minimize or, ideally, eliminate the use of Java code in JSP pages.

Put Business Logic in JavaBeans

One benefit of JSP design is the ability to avoid placing sensitive code in your Web pages. Business logic may apply to your application in Web applications, server operations, and Java client applications. You can use JavaBeans widely throughout the J2EE platform, so JavaBeans are a good place to define application business logic.

Presentation Logic in Tab Libraries

Custom tag libraries provide a way to replace presentation logic with JSP markup. However, tag library handler classes are closely tied to JSP and cannot be reused in other contexts. As such, custom tags are a good place to define presentation logic but a poor place to define business logic.

Use Existing Tag Libraries

Don't reinvent the wheel. Many general-purpose tag libraries exist. BEA includes a number of well-tested, highly functional tags you can use to remove Java code from JSP pages. In addition, the JSP community is standardizing around a set of common tags in the JSP Standard Tag Libraries (JSTL). Another source for tag libraries is the Jakarta Taglibs project. See the "References" section for links to these tag libraries.

Use WebLogic Cache Tags to Optimize Performance

BEA has gone to great effort to make JSP a high-performance tool. However, not running JSP code is always faster than running the JSP. As a result, use the WebLogic cache tags to improve your application's performance. The WebLogic tags identify portions of JSP pages that WebLogic can cache.

Precompile JSPs

WebLogic Server includes a JSP compiler, and WebLogic will automatically compile JSP pages as needed. But you also have the opportunity to precompile JSP pages. Precompiled pages include a number of advantages. First, by precompiling JSP pages, you can avoid the processing delay that otherwise occurs when WebLogic Server compiles the page following the first request for the page. Second, by precompiling you identify syntax errors immediately, even on infrequently visited pages.

You can instruct WebLogic Server to precompile pages on deployment, but you can precompile even earlier in the process. Manually precompile JSP pages prior to packaging the JSPs into a WAR file. Compiling earlier in the process allows you to avoid system slowdowns while WebLogic Server compiles the JSPs of an entire application. Place the resulting classes in the `WEB-INF/classes` directory. Compile JSPs using the class `weblogic.jspc`. For documentation on the JSP compiler, refer to the JSP compiler's documentation at `http://edocs.bea.com/wls/docs81/jsp/reference.html`.

References

Refer to the JSP 1.2 specification at *http://jcp.org/aboutJava/communityprocess/first/jsr053/index.html*.

BEA provides the documentation for programming JSPs. This documentation includes general JSP information, how to use the WebLogic JSP compiler, and WebLogic custom tags. See *http://edocs.bea.com/wls/docs81/jsp*.

BEA also provides a list of tools that are useful for creating JSP pages: *http://dev2dev.bea.com/resourcelibrary/utilitiestools/index.jsp*.

Sun has written a set of recommendations for J2EE applications called blueprints. See the blueprints document at *http://java.sun.com/blueprints/guidelines/designing_enterprise_applications/apmTOC.html*.

The JavaServer Pages Standard Tag Library (JSTL) provides a common set of tag libraries. The homepage for the JSTL project is at *http://java.sun.com/products/jsp/jstl*.

The Apache Jakarta group provides several custom tag libraries. The Taglibs subproject provides the reference implementation for JSTL as well as a number of other evolving projects. See the Taglibs subproject at *http://jakarta.apache.org/taglibs/index.html*.

Sun provides a tutorial for tag library development at *http://java.sun.com/products/jsp/tutorial/TagLibrariesTOC.html*.

chapter 5

WebLogic Server JDBC and JTA

One of the primary drivers—no pun intended—for many custom-developed applications is to extend relational database access to an extended group of users. In the past, client/server solutions provided a two-tier model for transactional data access, where the client's presentation and business logic are tightly intertwined. Although these systems are easy to build, changes to the business logic or presentation interfaces require the entire application to be rebuilt and redeployed. Services like security are heavily dependent on the database, and heterogeneous transactions to other databases are nearly impossible. In addition, the two-tier architecture will not scale beyond departmental needs. Three-tier architectures, with clean separation between presentation logic and business services and between business services and data access, offer a more manageable, more scalable, more secure alternative.

For the Java developer, the three-tier architecture is defined by the set of APIs available in the J2EE. Presentation logic is developed with JSPs and servlets, business logic is implemented on a component model using EJB, and *Java Database Connectivity* (JDBC) defines the data-access tier. In conjunction with data access, the ability to treat a business request as a transaction—a unit of work—is critical to enterprise applications. The J2EE standard for transactions is the *Java Transaction API* (JTA). This chapter is a presentation of WebLogic's implementations of JDBC and JTA. In this chapter you will find

- An introduction to the JDBC and JTA specifications.
- An explanation of how WebLogic Server implements the JDBC and JTA APIs.
- A presentation of database connectivity support in WebLogic Server applications.
- A presentation of transaction support in WebLogic Server applications.
- Examples of database and transaction applications.
- A review of best practices to be considered when using JDBC and JTA for access to data resources.

This chapter focuses on designing and coding access to databases in your applications, using WebLogic Server JDBC and JTA implementations. JDBC technology provides the basic APIs for connecting your client application to a database and submitting *Structured Query Language* (SQL) commands to select or modify data. JTA defines the concept of transactions, providing a structured environment for executing multistatement or multidatabase operations as a single *unit of work*.

157

Note: This chapter assumes a basic knowledge of relational databases, transactions, and SQL. Database design is critical to application performance.

If you need more information on these topics, it is best to consult an appropriate resource such as C. J. Date's An *Introduction to Database Systems, seventh edition* (Addison-Wesley, 2000).

WebLogic Server JDBC

JDBC is the J2EE standard for accessing your application's database resources. The JDBC standard specifies a Java API that enables you to write SQL statements that are then sent to your database. Let's take a look at the JDBC standard and how you can use it when developing and deploying WebLogic-based applications.

JDBC Overview

JDBC is one of the oldest and most widely used enterprise Java specifications. The earliest drafts date back to 1996. JDBC addresses the same challenge addressed be the Open Database Connectivity (ODBC) standard developed by Microsoft: to provide a universal set of APIs for accessing any database, using the database-specific driver. Without JDBC or ODBC, developers are forced to develop APIs proprietary to each database: one for Oracle, one for DB2, and so on. With JDBC or ODBC, a single set of APIs can access any database using the driver specific to that database. Developers are able to write applications to a single set of APIs and then plug and play different database drivers, depending upon what resource type they are accessing. With JDBC, it is possible to migrate an enterprise Java application from one database to another with a minimal impact on the application or its developers, because no database-specific APIs are used in the application itself.

JDBC Drivers

While SQL is generally portable across multiple databases, the actual protocols that those databases use to communicate (and some database-specific features) are not portable. For that reason, the JDBC specification supports products that map the calls in a JDBC-based application to the appropriate calls specific to the database. Such a product is called a JDBC *driver.*

There are JDBC drivers specific to commercial databases such as Oracle, Sybase, DB2, Microsoft SQL Server, and others. To access a database of a specific type, you need the JDBC database driver for that database. WebLogic Server 8.1 supports any JDBC driver that complies with the JDBC 2.0 specification. This means that you can use any JDBC 2.0 driver with WebLogic Server—including drivers that are available from other vendors—so long as the driver supports the JDBC standard. Even better, advanced features like WebLogic connection pooling are likewise available despite the source of the underlying driver.

JDBC Driver Types

There are four different types of JDBC drivers. However, most enterprise Java applications use only two of these types. The other two are mentioned here for completeness.

- *Type 1* is a JDBC driver that is commonly called a JDBC-ODBC *bridge*. This was the original implementation of JDBC provided by Sun to enable rapid adoption of the JDBC standard. Basically, calls are mapped from JDBC APIs to ODBC APIs. In this way, a Type 1 driver enabled developers to leverage the existing ODBC drivers on the marketplace when JDBC first became available. In today's practice, Type 1 drivers are rarely used.

- *Type 2* is a JDBC driver that maps JDBC APIs directly to the proprietary client APIs provided by the database vendor. The WebLogic Server includes a Type 2 driver for Oracle databases. A native code library exists for each of these drivers that includes the platform-specific access to the database-specific client APIs. For example, using the Oracle Type 2 driver, the native code is called the Oracle Client Interface (OCI) library. This type of driver is frequently used in enterprise Java applications.

- *Type 3* is a JDBC driver that supports three-tier JDBC access. In the early days of Java, when applets were quite popular, it was common to build an applet that directly accessed the database. However, the security model for applets prohibits applets from accessing data resources from more than one Web server. A Type 3 JDBC driver acts as a *proxy* for database access by the applet or another application. In practice, this type of driver is not often used.

- *Type 4* is a JDBC driver that is written completely in Java and speaks directly to the database instance. These drivers are intelligent enough to know which underlying protocol the database instance uses. Type 4 drivers are the future of database access in Java and are the drivers most commonly used in practice today. As the efficiency of Java code and Java Virtual Machines (JVMs) continues to improve, these drivers are markedly more attractive because of their simplicity and ease of use.

Note: The Type 1 JDBC-ODBC bridge available from Sun Microsystems is not thread-safe. It is not suitable for use in applications that require concurrent access to the database and database driver. Because of its inherent performance and scalability limitations, this Type 1 driver should not be used in enterprise-level applications. There are other vendor implementations (NEON Systems, IBM, etc.) of a JDBC-ODBC bridge that are thread-safe and can be used in an enterprise-level application.

For JDBC support, BEA offers WebLogic jDrivers—Type 4 JDBC drivers for Sybase and Microsoft SQL Server databases and Type 2 JDBC drivers for Oracle and SQL Server (deprecated). Other JDBC drivers are available free, packaged with a database management system, or for a nominal fee. A complete list of available JDBC drivers is on the Sun Web site at *http://industry.java.sun.com/products/jdbc/drivers*.

Choosing the Right JDBC Driver

In years past, the decision of what JDBC driver to use was more difficult than it is today. Before the advent of more advanced JVMs with performance equivalent to native code, developers usually chose Type 2 JDBC drivers because of the greater performance they delivered, even though Type 4 drivers offer other advantages for coding and maintenance. However, with newer, more efficient JVMs has come a narrowing of the performance gap between Type 2 and Type 4 JDBC drivers.

If you are developing an enterprise Java application today, the advent of faster JVMs and other platform-specific optimizations make Type 4 drivers an excellent alternative for enterprise class applications. Type 4 drivers remove a level of complexity in application development by bypassing the native code interfaces. Less complexity is better because there are fewer components that must work together. When there are fewer components, there is typically less room for conflict and error.

In fact, Type 4 drivers are often more reliable than Type 2 drivers. The presence of native code running outside the JVM in Type 2 drivers means it is much easier to crash your entire Java application. That is, a bug in the native code portion of the driver could cause the entire process to fail—

including your application and the instance of WebLogic Server itself. Type 4 drivers are written completely in Java, reside within the JVM boundaries, and do not rely on any native code. For these reasons, Type 4 drivers are attractive.

As you have seen, Type 4 JDBC drivers are a safe bet because they are simpler, provide comparable performance, and are supported on a wide range of platforms. However, Type 2 drivers do have the advantage of maturity and production-quality stability. Perhaps the best practice is to ask what driver your application server vendor recommends. In the case of BEA, viable Type 4 WebLogic jDrivers are available for Sybase and Microsoft SQL Server, and a Type 2 driver is available for Oracle. In addition, WebLogic Server 8.1 includes a copy of the Pointbase Java database for demonstration purposes. Database vendors also include JDBC drivers. For example, Oracle provides a Type 4 thin driver that can be downloaded, and IBM includes Type 4 JDBC drivers for DB2.

> **Best Practice:** Due to the problems that can be caused by executing native code within a JVM, it is a best practice to strongly consider a Type 4 JDBC driver for your deployment. The all-Java nature of Type 4 drivers provides a level of simplicity not seen in Type 2 drivers and overall performance between Type 2 and Type 4 JDBC drivers is comparable. It is also a good idea to consider the recommendations of your application server and database management system vendors.

Installing and Configuring Your JDBC Driver

A wide range of JDBC drivers are available. Configuring and installing your specific JDBC driver is beyond the scope of this book, since configuration and installation details depend on the JDBC driver that you are using. You should review the documentation for your specific driver in order to install and configure it correctly. BEA includes documentation on how to install and configure WebLogic jDrivers for Oracle, Sybase, and SQL Server as well as a number of popular third-party JDBC drivers. Refer to Chapter 5 of the *Programming WebLogic JDBC* documentation at *http://e-docs.bea.com/wls/docs81/index.html* for more information on configuring third-party JDBC drivers with WebLogic Server.

Database Connection Pooling

When WebLogic Server starts, you can create *connection pools* to the database resource. Connection pools contain multiple JDBC connections that are kept open to the database resource by the application server and shared across all the clients needing access. When your application needs to access the database, it grabs a connection from the connection pool and uses that connection object to communicate with the database. Once the work being done with the database for a given user is completed, the database connection is closed, releasing it back to the database connection pool.

> **Best Practice:** Always close a connection as soon as you are finished using it. While the server will eventually return the connection to the pool, it will hold the connection and prevent it from being used by other applications. Closing the connection allows the most efficient use of the database connection objects.

There are a number of reasons to pool connections to the database:

- Creating a new connection for every individual client that visits your site is quite expensive. Using connection pools is much more efficient than creating a new database connection for each client, each time.
- Explicitly coding details such as the database management system (DBMS) password in your application is brittle and inflexible. This is particularly beneficial in the case of J2EE services such as JavaServer Pages (JSPs), which typically store the source code with the application.
- The database management system can be modified or even replaced with minimal impact on your application code.
- Databases are most effective when the number of incoming connections is limited. With connection pooling, you can limit the number of connections to your DBMS.

JDBC connection pools are specified in the configuration of the server. Configuration parameters for connection pools include the following:

- Name of connection pool, used to identify which pool is being used by the application
- Number of connections to be made initially
- Maximum size of pool
- Minimum size of pool
- Location/URL for database
- Driver class name
- Driver-specific properties

> **Best Practice:** Although you may have access to a variety of connection pooling mechanisms, WebLogic Server provides efficient, standards-based connection pooling regardless of the vendor's JDBC driver. WebLogic Server tests the pooled connections and restarts any that are stale, grows and shrinks the pools based on usage demands, and ensures underlying data consistency through the JTA transaction service. It is a best practice to always use WebLogic Server connection pooling.

In WebLogic Server 8.1, database connection configuration can be completed using the configuration wizard when setting up the domain; in the WebLogic Server console, the `weblogic.Admin` command-line shell, using the JMX MBeans; or with a tool such as `WLShell`. Refer to Figure 5–1 for an example of connection pool configuration using the domain configuration wizard. The examples in this chapter use the Pointbase database, which is included in the WebLogic Server distribution.

The JDBC configuration wizard can be accessed from the domain configuration wizard by selecting the custom configuration option or from the Administrative Console by choosing the JDBC Connection Pool tab and selecting *Configure a new* JDBC *Connection Pool*. Figure 5–2 illustrates configuring the JDBC connection pools from the domain configuration wizard.

Setting up a connection pool configures a number of parameters, including the driver name, URL, filename of the driver code, pool capacity, and so forth. The connection pool JDBC URL is a locator for the database resource. All JDBC drivers follow this general pattern for the URL:

```
jdbc:driver:databasename
```

In this example, we configure a new JDBC connection pool using the Pointbase sample database delivered with WebLogic Server 8.1. This database is useful for demonstrations and examples but is not licensed for production applications. Please see the Pointbase license agreement

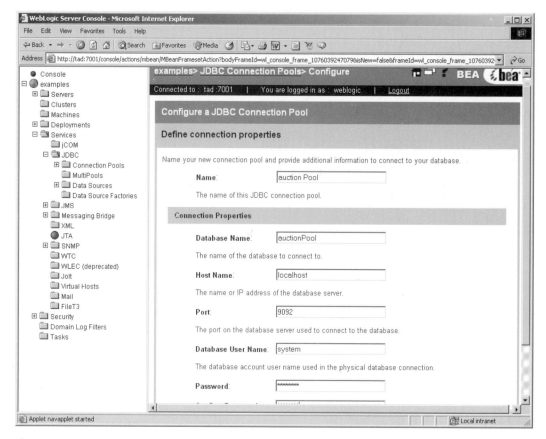

Figure 5-1
Using the WebLogic Server Administration Console to configure database connection pools.

included with WebLogic for additional information. The following steps are used to configure a JDBC connection pool:

1. Select *Configure a new JDBC Connection Pool* from the Administrator's Console main page.
2. From the pull-down list, select the database type and choose the database driver from the list of installed drivers. For our example, select the Pointbase database and the Pointbase Type 4 driver. You should use the non-XA driver for local transactions and the XA driver for global transactions. In our example, we use the non-XA driver. Click *Continue*.

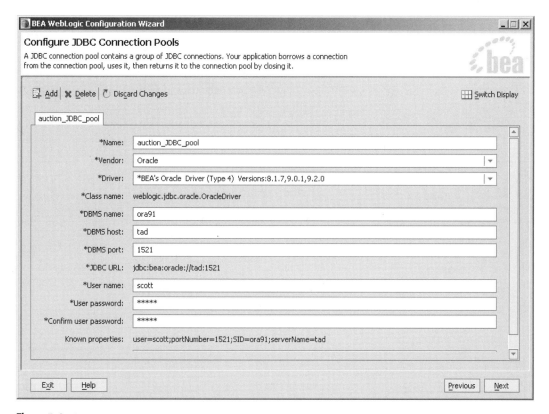

Figure 5–2
Using the domain configuration wizard to configure JDBC database connection pools.

3. Configure connection properties on this page, including the name of the database, the host name of the server and the port number the database is listening on, and the user name and password to use for the connection pool. For our example, the default user name for Point-base is *examples*, the local server name is *demo*, and the port is 9092, which is the default listen port for Pointbase database system. Figure 5–3 includes the JDBC connection pool configuration settings. Click *Continue*.

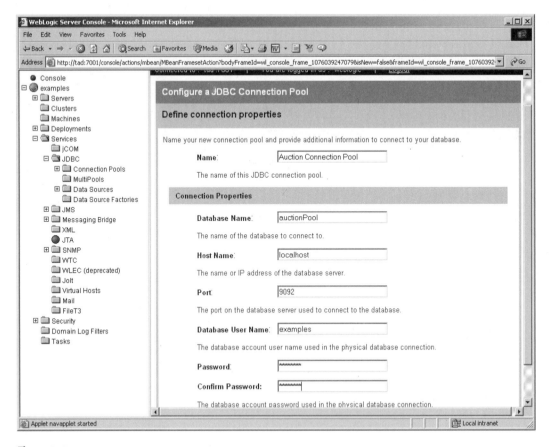

Figure 5–3
JDBC connection pool configuration.

4. This page allows you to test the configuration to make sure you have entered all the properties correctly. The driver classname is determined from the driver installation. You can also set additional properties for the pooled connections in the Properties Input box. Refer to Figure 5–4 for the example configuration. Select *Test Driver Configuration*. If your connection is correctly configured, you will see a message indicating a successful test connection was established.

5. Select *Create and Deploy* to create the connection pool you have created, and deploy the pool.

6. Once you have created a connection pool, you should select the *Connections* tab to set the pool parameters. You can determine the initial pool size, the maximum size, the capacity increment, the algorithm for statement caching, and the size of the statement cache. Refer to the section below for more information about how to leverage the prepare statement cache for performance.

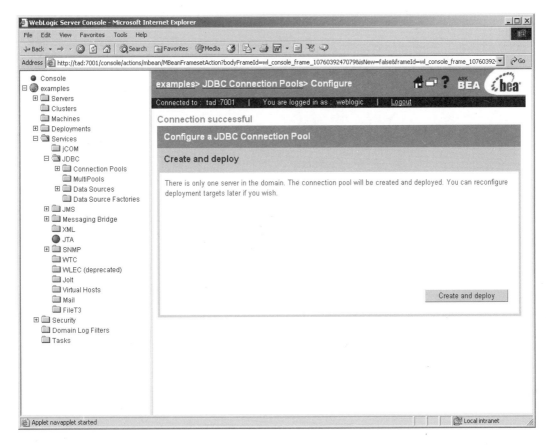

Figure 5–4
Testing the database connection pool configuration.

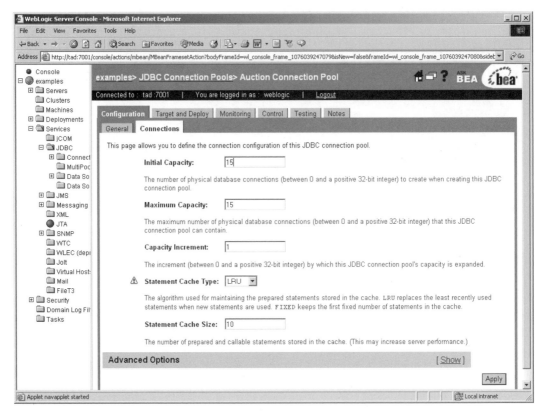

Figure 5–5
JDBC connection pool parameters.

Dynamic Connection Pool Growth and Shrinkage

Included in the connection pool are properties to define the initial number of connections in a pool, the maximum number of connections in a pool, the increment connections to be added when growing the pool, and how long to wait before harvesting connections from the pool. Although growing a connection pool is useful in certain circumstances, when a peak load of requests are issued to the server connection pool, growth can actually make a performance problem worse due to the latency involved in creating new connections.

For optimal performance, it is a best practice to determine the maximum number of connections required to satisfy the business requirements and set the initial pool size to the maximum pool size. There can be significant overhead added when the server tries to open a new connection—as happens when the connection pool grows. The additional latency can actually slow the overall server performance rather than improve it. By setting the initial capacity to the maximum capacity, you disable the growth of the pool but improve overall throughput and performance.

There are many more settings and parameters that can be applied to the connection pool. Consult your WebLogic Server 8.1 documentation at *http://e-docs.bea.com/wls/docs81/jdbc_drivers/index.html* for more details on connection pool settings.

> **Best Practice:** Opening database connections is an expensive process. At times of peak load, growing a connection pool by opening new connections to the database can create performance problems. Although growing a connection pool can be a useful feature, for applications where optimal performance is required, it is a best practice to set the initial connection pool size to the maximum connection pool size.

Statement Caching

For each connection in a connection pool, WebLogic Server creates a statement cache. If your application uses `PreparedStatement` objects, you may find significant performance benefits by caching these objects. You determine the size of the cache and the algorithm used for caching statements when you update your connection pool from the JDBC Connection Pools → Configuration → Connections tab of the Administration Console. Figure 5–6 illustrates an example of this page in the console.

The statement cache supports either a *least recently used* (LRU) algorithm to determine which statements should be held in cache or a *fixed* algorithm, where the first FIXED number of statements are cached. The cache size is used to determine the number of prepare and callable state-

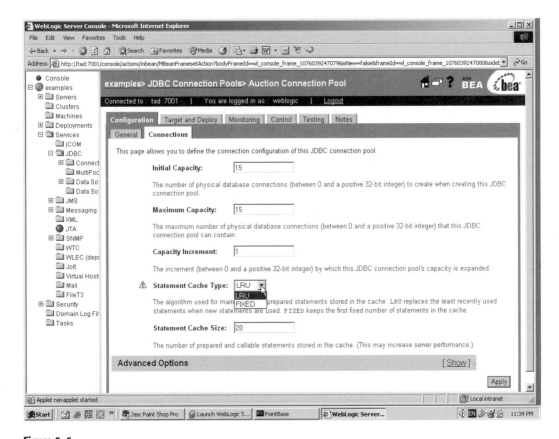

Figure 5–6

`PreparedStatement` configuration.

ments to be kept in the cache. Find further information about `PreparedStatement` objects in the section of this chapter on JTA.

Data Source Configuration

Once you have configured the connection pool, the next step is to configure a JDBC data source. To simplify the process of acquiring a connection to the database, the JDBC `DataSource` concept was introduced in the JDBC 2.0 specification and is a factory for JDBC `Connection` objects. To use a `DataSource`, you specify a connection pool to provide connections to the Java Naming and Directory Interface (JNDI) store, which is a registry of user and application variables and values described in detail in Chapter 6. Data sources allow either standard or transactional database connections that automatically use the JTA driver.

WebLogic Server 8.1 supports a single data source—the `DataSource` object. In past releases, there were `DataSource` objects used in local transactions for a single resource manager and `TxDataSource` objects for multiple resource managers needing support for distributed transactions. However, in the 8.1 release of WebLogic Server, these two types were consolidated into a single `DataSource` object, handling both local transactions and distributed transactions based on whether the data source honors global transactions.

You assign a `DataSource` object to a single connection pool or clustered multipool. You control the type of transactions supported by the data source through the `Honor Global Transactions` property. This property is set when creating a data source and must be `TRUE` any time you will be using the XA protocol to implement distributed transactions and two-phase commit (described in later sections). The `Honor Global Transactions` property must be enabled if your application

- Uses the JTA services detailed later in this chapter.
- Uses the EJB container to manage transactions.
- Uses distributed transactions, such as updates to multiple resource managers in the scope of a single transaction.

By default, `Honor Global Transactions` is set to `TRUE` when creating a new data source.

You should always use a JTA-aware `DataSource` to ensure transactional coordination and behavior when using EJB components or when using transactions that span multiple resource managers. Using the `DataSource` object ensures correct transactional semantics will be followed throughout the application. In addition, `DataSource` will trust critical yet hidden data access to JTA automatically, protecting consistency. You can find more information about configuring data sources at *http://edocs.bea.com/wls/docs81/ConsoleHelp/jdbc_datasources.html*.

Best Practice: You should always use a JTA-aware `DataSource` that honors global transactions with EJBs and when transactions span multiple databases or heterogeneous resource managers such as queuing systems. This property ensures that WebLogic Server protects the integrity of the transactions and the underlying database or resource manager.

To configure a data source in WebLogic Server using the Administrative Console, follow the steps outlined below.

1. After creating and deploying the connection pool, the next step is to create a data source or sources and associate them with the connection pool. From the main console page, select the link for Data Sources and then choose the link to *Configure a new JDBC Data Source*. Refer to Figure 5–7 for an example of this console page.

2. Provide a name for the data source and a JNDI name through which the data source will be bound. You should select *Honor Global Transactions* if the data source will participate in distributed transactions, if it will be used with EJBs, or if it uses JTA to manage global transactions. If the underlying JDBC driver does not support XA, you can choose to emulate XA behavior. For more information, refer to the sections on distributed transactions and JTA later in this chapter. Figure 5–8 details this configuration step. Click *Continue*.

3. Now, simply associate the data source with the JDBC Connection Pool name using the drop-down box. In our example, we select the Auction pool created earlier. Click *Continue*.

4. Finally, select the WebLogic Server instance within the domain you will deploy this data source to.

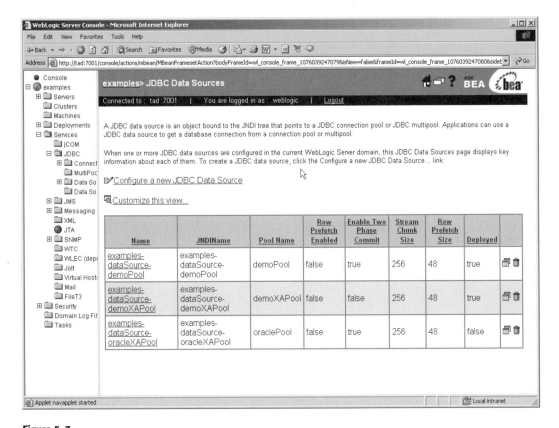

Figure 5–7
JDBC data source configuration.

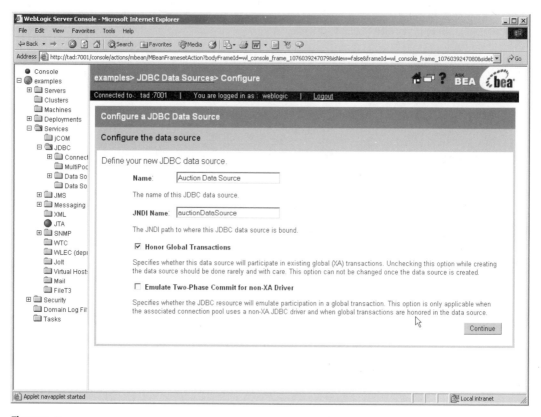

Figure 5–8
Data source settings.

JDBC Multipools

In WebLogic Server 8.1, you can now pool connection pools into *multipools*. A multipool is a pool of JDBC connection pools. All the connections in a connection pool share a common database instance and a common user to access the resource. With multipools, you can point to different database instances with different users for each connection pool. Multipools offer two algorithms based on your requirements:

- Load balancing—Connection pools can be load-balanced in a round-robin fashion based on the next connection pool in the list.

- High availability—In the event of a failure of a connection pool, WebLogic multipools allow you to failover to the next connection pool in the list.

Note that you can use multipools only with local transactions, since they do not support XA or distributed transactions. Refer to the section "WebLogic Server and Distributed Transactions" found later in this chapter. For more information on configuring multipools with WebLogic Server 8.1, refer to the BEA documentation at *http://edocs.bea.com/wls/docs81/ConsoleHelp/jdbc_multipools.html*.

Using JDBC to Read Data

We discuss two facets of JDBC access: using JDBC to read data stored in the database and using JDBC to update data in the database. While these two processes have many steps in common, there are some substantial differences. Let's look first at JDBC reads and then move on to updates.

Basic Steps for JDBC Reads

There are five basic operations for JDBC reads in your WebLogic Server application:

- Establishing a connection to the database
- Sending a query to the database
- Getting results
- Handling results
- Releasing the connection

Let's consider each step in more detail.

Connections to the database are represented by instances of the `java.sql.Connection` object. Each instance of this object represents an individual database connection. You establish a connection by calling factory methods on instances of the `javax.sql.DataSource` class.

To create a new connection to the database, you could use the following code block:

```
Connection myConn = null;

try {

Context ctx = new InitialContext();

javax.sql.DataSource ds
            = (javax.sql.DataSource)
                ctx.lookup ("examples-dataSource-auctionPool");

java.sql.Connection myConn = ds.getConnection();

} catch (SQLException sqle)
{
  // Handle the exception
}
```

The included code segment first locates the WebLogic Server JNDI naming service, which is discussed in detail in Chapter 6. The application uses the naming service to retrieve a context for the transactional `DataSource` of the requested database. Next, it creates a new instance of the `java.sql.Connection` class and assigns the object returned by `ds.getConnection()` to it. By calling `getConnection` with the appropriate `DataSource`, as defined in the WebLogic Server configuration, we can isolate our application from the database configuration.

Note that the method outlined here is the preferred method to establish a connection to the database. There are a number of antiquated methods that are not as efficient and should not be used. For example, you should avoid using `DriverManager`. Although this method is often used in JDBC tutorials, the problem is that it is a synchronized class, meaning that only one thread of execution can run at a single time. You should use the multithreaded `DataSource` technique instead.

```
Class.forName("WebLogic.jdbc.pool.Driver").newInstance();
/* Get a Connection from the Driver from the connection Pool named
demoPool.
*/
Connection myConn =
DriverManager.getConnection("jdbc:WebLogic:pool:demoPool", null);
```

> **Best Practice:** When establishing a connection with the database, you should use the multithreaded `DataSource` technique instead of older, antiquated methods such as the JDBC `DriverManager`.

The process of interacting with the database centers on the `java.sql.Statement` class. You first create an instance of this `Statement` class by calling a factory method, `createStatement()`, on the instance of the `Connection` class that was created. This typically looks like this:

```
Statement stmt = myConn.createStatement();
```

This code creates a new instance of the `Statement` object native to our connection.

You can then use your statement to execute SQL queries against the database. This is accomplished via the `execute()` method. For example, to return all rows from the table named EMPLOYEE, try the following:

```
stmt.execute("SELECT * FROM EMPLOYEE");
```

You can execute any valid SQL query using the `execute` method. (We cover statements that do not return results, such as the CREATE or UPDATE commands, later in the section, "Using JDBC to Update the Database.") The results of the query can be displayed with the `java.sql.ResultSet` datatype. The `Statement` class includes a method `getResultSetType()`, which returns query results as instances of the `java.sql.ResultSet` class. To get the result set for the previous query, use the following code:

```
ResultSet rs = stmt.getResultSet();
```

This creates an instance of the `ResultSet` class and returns the results of the query. A shortcut, single-line method is available for simple queries. This method is within the statement class `executeQuery(String SQLstring)`. For example,

```
ResultSet rs = stmt.executeQuery("SELECT * FROM EMPLOYEE ");
```

This executes the SQL and returns the resulting data in a single line of code. The `ResultSet(rs)` is a virtual table of data representing a database result set. For the statement

```
ResultSet rs = stmt.executeQuery(
"SELECT * FROM EMPLOYEE ");
```

the result set `rs` might display the following:

```
NAME                LOCATION            ID
Zornoza             Connecticut         1
Prasad              India               2
Shinn               Oregon              3
D'Attoma            New York            4
```

The next step is to access the results of your query. As mentioned previously, the data returned from the query using the `Statement` class is encapsulated in an instance of the `ResultSet` class. Call methods on the `ResultSet` to access the data. These methods follow the format of `get???`, where the `???`s are replaced by a Java type.

`ResultSet` is accessed very much like an `Enumeration`. A `ResultSet` object keeps a cursor pointing to its current row of data. Initially, the cursor is positioned before the first row. The `next()` method moves the cursor to the next row. Because it returns `false` when there are no more rows in the `ResultSet` object, it can be used in a `WHILE` loop to iterate through the result set. The following is an example:

```
while (rs.next()) {
    System.out.println(rs.getString("ID") + " - " +
                       rs.getString("NAME")   + " - " +
                       rs.getString("LOCATION"));
}
```

The output for this might be the following:

```
1-Zornoza-Connecticut
2-Prasad-India
3-Shinn-Oregon
4-D'Attoma-New York
```

`ResultSet` maps the data from the database to instances of Java objects. A relational-object mapping is required for object-oriented Java programs to be able to use relational data. Usually, results map directly from the SQL types that are defined by the database. Consult your database driver documentation to see how the types that are stored in the database map to Java objects.

Result Sets

There are many other important methods available in the `ResultSet` class. In fact, there are over 100 methods available to handle result sets. Here are some of the more important of these methods and examples of their use.

- `next()` moves the cursor down one row from its current position.
- `getString(int columnIndex)` gets the value of the designated column in the current row of this `ResultSet` object as a string. The following code gets the string in the second column at the row that is currently selected by the cursor and prints out its value:

```
System.out.println(rs.getString(2));
```

- `String getString(String columnName)` gets the value of the designated column in the current row of this `ResultSet` object as a string. The following code gets the string in the column named `"ID"` that is currently selected by the cursor and prints out its value:

```
System.out.println(rs.getString("ID"));
```

> **Note:** The `get<...>()` pattern is consistent for virtually every datatype available through JDBC. For example, you can implement `getDecimal()`, `get-ByteStream()`, and so forth. Please refer to the JavaDoc for your JDK for the complete list.

- `Void absolute(int row)` moves the cursor to the given row number in this `Result-Set` object. The following code accesses the third row in the result set and prints out the value

```
rs.absolute(3);
System.out.println(rs.getString("ID") + "-" +
                   rs.getString("NAME")  + "-" +
                   rs.getString("LOCATION"));
```

The output of this code would be

```
3-Shinn-Oregon
```

- `beforeFirst()` moves the cursor to the beginning of this `ResultSet` object, just before the first row. The following code puts the cursor at the beginning of the rows in the `ResultSet` object and begins a new Enumeration:

```
rs.beforeFirst();
while (rs.next()) {
     System.out.println(rs.getString("ID") + "-" +
                        rs.getString("NAME") + "-" +
                        rs.getString("LOCATION"));
     }
```

The output of this code would be

```
1-Zornoza-Connecticut
2-Prasad-India
3-Shinn-Oregon
4-D'Attoma-New York
```

- `boolean isAfterLast()` indicates whether the cursor is after the last row in this `ResultSet` object.
- `boolean isBeforeFirst()` indicates whether the cursor is before the first row in this `ResultSet` object.

- `boolean isFirst()` indicates whether the cursor is on the first row of this `ResultSet` object.
- `boolean isLast()` indicates whether the cursor is on the last row of this `ResultSet` object.
- `void refreshRow()` refreshes the current row with its most recent value in the database.

Releasing Connections

After you complete a query, you should release your statements and connections. This is done through the `close()` method available on both of those types of objects. For example, given these `Connection`, `ResultSet`, and `Statement` objects,

```
Connection myConn = null;

try {

    /* Create a connection to the WebLogic JNDI Naming Service:
    */
    Context ctx = new InitialContext();

    /* Create a new DataSource by Locating It in the Naming Service:
     */
javax.sql.DataSource ds
        = (javax.sql.DataSource)
            ctx.lookup ("examples-dataSource-demoPool");

    /* Get a new JDBC connection from the DataSource:
     */
myConn = ds.getConnection();

Statement stmt = myConn.createStatement();

ResultSet rs = stmt.executeQuery("SELECT * FROM EMPLOYEE ");
```

We can call the `close()` method on each of these objects to release the resources:

```
/* Release the ResultSet and Statement.
    */
    rs.close();
    stmt.close();

} catch (Exception E) {
    /*
        Handle exception here.
    */
    System.out.println("Service Error: " + E);
```

```
    } finally {
      if (rs != null) {
        try { rs.close(); } catch (Exception ignore) {};
      }
      if (stmt != null) {
        try { stmt.close(); } catch (Exception ignore) {};
      }
      if (myConn != null) {
        try { myConn.close(); } catch (Exception ignore) {};
      }
```

This closes the connection and releases the database and JDBC resources immediately instead of waiting for them to be closed automatically. It is important to close and release resources in the correct order, that is, the reverse of the order in which they were opened. First, close the instance of the `ResultSet` class. Next, close the `Statement`. This is accomplished, in both cases, by calling the `close()` method.

In each case, `close()` is called from within a `try/catch` block. If an exception is raised, it can be handled in the `catch{ }` statement. Note that the `finally{ }` block includes a single call to close the connection. Make sure that your connection objects are released as soon as possible in order to make the connection immediately available to serve other clients.

Best Practice: There are a number of best practices to remember when using JDBC. Make sure to release JDBC objects in the correct order and close your `Connection` object in the `finally` block of your JDBC access. Do not overload the `finally` block by placing more than one `close()` statement there. For example, if an attempt to close your `ResultSet` receives an exception, the rest of the `finally{ }` block is not executed, including the rest of the `close()` statements. If one of the `close()` statements is your `Connection` object, this unnecessarily ties up a database connection and limits the performance of your application.

Using JDBC to Update the Database

Using JDBC to update the database is actually *simpler* than using JDBC just to read information from the database. There are three basic operations for JDBC updates in your WebLogic Server application:

- Establishing connections to the database
- Executing statements
- Releasing connections

Establishing Connections to the Database

As with database reads, connections for database updates are represented by instances of the `java.sql.Connection` object. We can reuse the previous code for creating database connections:

```
/* Create a connection to the WebLogic Server JNDI Naming Service:
  */
```

```
Context ctx = new InitialContext();
/* Create a new DataSource by Locating It in the Naming
Service:
    */
javax.sql.DataSource ds = (javax.sql.DataSource) ctx.lookup
("examples-dataSource-demoPool");

/* Get a new JDBC connection from the DataSource:
    */

myConn = ds.getConnection();
```

This code behaves the same way as the JDBC Read example. Using the JDBC `DataSource`, a connection to the database is created.

Executing Statements

An instance of the Statement class is required to execute database updates. To get an instance for use, call the `createStatement()` method available in the `Connection` class. Here's the code:

```
Statement stmt = myConn.createStatement();
```

An instance of the `Statement` class is created for the specific connection to the database that you are using.

Three types of database updates are available in SQL:

- `INSERT`—To insert rows of data into tables
- `UPDATE`—To modify data in tables
- `DELETE`—To remove rows from tables

To use any of these statements via JDBC, insert the SQL string in an `executeUpdate()` method call on the instance of the `Statement` class. For example, the following inserts a new employee into the EMPLOYEE table:

```
stmt.executeUpdate ("INSERT INTO employee VALUES ('JOE',
'Louisiana'  ,5)");
```

If the original data in the database looked like the following,

```
NAME            LOCATION            ID
Zornoza         Connecticut         1
Prasad          India               2
Shinn           Oregon              3
D'Attoma        New York            4
```

the updated data in the table named EMPLOYEE would be

```
NAME            LOCATION           ID
Zornoza         Connecticut        1
Prasad          India              2
Shinn           Oregon             3
D'Attoma        New York           4
JOE             Louisiana          5
```

Releasing Connections

After updating the data in the database, release the connections and objects by running the close() method on each of these objects:

```
stmt.close();
myConn.close();
```

Adding and Dropping Tables

Data administration commands such as those for adding and dropping tables can be treated just like any other SQL update. The following demonstrates this operation. First, create a table named myTable with two columns, id and name. These columns contain values of INTEGER type, and a variable-length string (VARCHAR) of maximum length 25, respectively.

```
try {

    /* Load driver and create appropriate Connection here. */

            // Create the appropriate Statement object
        Statement crstmt = myConn.createStatement();

        // Execute SQL to create a new table named myTable
        crstmt.execute("create table myTable (id INTEGER, name
VARCHAR(25)");
        crstmt.close();
    }
```

To remove a table,

```
/* Load driver and create appropriate Connection here. */

    try {
        // Create the appropriate Statement object
    Statement crstmt2 = myConn.createStatement();
    crstmt2.execute("drop table myTable");
    crstmt2.close();
    }
```

Transactions and JTA

Transactions give us a way to guarantee that a series of operations against a database is executed completely. For example, the transaction framework ensures a correct result when you remove an item from inventory and simultaneously deduct money from the purchaser's account. In another scenario, you would use a transaction when your users want to place a bid on a given item available at auction. Transactions prevent multiple simultaneous users from winning the same auction or from placing identical bids on a given item. Transactions represent a *unit of work*, meaning the work within the transaction will either all complete or all be rolled back to a consistent state prior to the transaction starting. With a transaction, it is not possible to remove items from inventory without removing money from the purchaser's account.

The transaction is not complete unless all of its operations are successful. The application server and the database, working cooperatively, ensure that transactions have four essential properties known by the mnemonic ACID:

- *Atomicity*—The operations within a single transaction must either all complete successfully or all be completely rolled back to the state before the transaction was initiated.
- *Consistency*—A transaction must preserve its environment and any data it manipulates in a state that ensures integrity.
- *Isolation*—All the operations within a single transaction must execute independent of other transactions, and the results must reflect this independence.
- *Durability*—All results of the operations within a transaction must be recoverable and persistently stored. Typically, this information is maintained in a log stored on some type of disk.

Putting ACID into Practice

The ACID properties enable the application to ensure that the transaction will *commit* as a unit of work—either all operations complete or the entire transaction is rolled back. Let's consider how these properties are used in a simple banking transaction. If you want to transfer money from one account to another, you'll want atomicity to ensure that the transferred amount isn't "lost" between accounts due to some failure. If atomicity weren't enforced, an error might happen during the transfer—the money removed from one account may not be added to the second account, for example, and without atomicity, you would have no way to know what happened.

You also want your money transfers to be consistent. The removal of money from one account should not affect any other accounts in the system. Each transaction should execute as a unique operation, isolated from any other transactions. In addition, your transfer of funds operations, which simultaneously remove money from one account and give it to another, should produce the same results as if they were run sequentially. In the case of complex operations, isolation becomes very important.

Finally, you don't want your money transfer to be lost. Rather, it should be durable over time. Typically, this means that results are written to a recoverable resource such as a database with highly available offline storage media such as a Redundant Array of Inexpensive Disks (RAID). Computer memory (RAM) is not considered to be durable because a simple power supply problem could erase the entire bank record.

> **Best Practice:** A popular question is, When should I use transactions? This is important because the enforcement of the ACID properties is expensive from a performance perspective and adds complexity to the application. As a general rule, transactions prove useful in applications in which atomicity is important. A best practice is to use transactions when you want either *all* or *none* of the actions in an operation to complete.

Accessing Transactions Via SQL

The databases you use with WebLogic Server support ACID-compliant transaction management that can be accessed via SQL.

A transaction represents a span of control over one or more SQL statements. The SQL statements can affect multiple databases. The SQL standard's transaction language includes the following:

- BEGIN or START, which signifies to the database that transaction should begin. All subsequent operations to the database should be part of (within the scope of) that transaction.
- PREPARE, which signifies to the database that it should prepare to commit the transaction. This is only applicable to transactions that involve multiple resources or databases. Multidatabase transactions are discussed later in this chapter.
- COMMIT, which signifies to the database that it should commit the transaction. When a transaction is committed, it is written to the database disk and is final.

Local Transactions and WebLogic Server JDBC

You may not be aware of it, but transactions in some form have already been involved in the JDBC Read and Update examples. The transactions are implicit, applied automatically to each individual SQL statement. More complex transactions are typically done in the context of the JTA driver, described later in this chapter.

By definition, Connection objects are responsible for handling transactions. These transactions are automatically committed and enforce transactional properties. They are in *autocommit* mode. From a usability standpoint, autocommit for JDBC is a good thing. Developers do not have to worry about inserting begin, prepare, commit (and so forth) commands into their applications. Unfortunately, real-world transactions require more than single SQL statements to do their work. Even something as simple as transferring money between two accounts requires a number of SQL statements.

Transaction Options in WebLogic Server

There are two different options for implementing database transactions in WebLogic Server applications. The first uses the WebLogic Server JTA driver. This is a special "wrapper" on top of JDBC that enables a transaction to be associated with multiple J2EE services as the scope of the given user being served moves through different services. For example, a servlet could coordinate a Java Message Service (JMS) queue and an EJB in the scope of the same transaction. Another scenario would have multiple resources (databases) participating in a single transaction, typically constructed as a *two-phase commit* operation.

The other way to use transactions is to declare them explicitly on the JDBC connection or using the AutoCommit property. You, as the developer, explicitly use commands to tell the transaction to begin and commit. While explicitly declaring transactions is functionally easier to program, it is limited to simple applications and can limit performance and functionality.

In an enterprise J2EE application, such as when you rely on EJB and JMS services, you should never declare transactions explicitly on the JDBC connection. The only way that a JMS destination and EJBs can participate in a transaction is through JTA. For this reason, the JTA driver is used to implement transactions in the WebAuction application, which is discussed throughout this book. The JTA driver is enabled when the Honor Global Transactions property is set to TRUE when creating the JDBC data source. Although WebLogic Server supports explicit JDBC transactions, in the context of J2EE applications, it is a best practice to rely upon the JTA implementation in the WebLogic Server JTA driver.

> **Best Practice:** In an enterprise J2EE application that relies on EJB and JMS services, you should never declare transactions explicitly on the JDBC connection. It is easier and simpler to allow the JTA transaction driver to handle transaction demarcation. A development best practice is always to use the JTA transaction services in WebLogic Server. Always be sure to enable global transactions in the data source to allow JTA to manage the transaction.

Using the JTA Driver

The JTA driver enables multiple J2EE services in WebLogic Server to participate in the same transaction. These operations may involve services such as EJBs, JMS, direct SQL statements using standard JDBC calls. JTA is also useful when single services need transaction support, such as servlets that access the database directly. The JTA driver readily supports both transactions and connection pooling.

The JTA driver behaves differently depending on whether the transaction runs against a single database or against multiple databases. When the scope of the transaction is a single resource, WebLogic Server uses standard commands to the database to set or *demarcate* the beginning and ending of a transaction across a single database connection.

Once a transaction is begun, all of the database operations for a given user share that user's connection from the same connection pool. When the transaction is committed or rolled back, the connection is returned to the pool.

WebLogic Server Transaction Services: JTA, XA, and Two-Phase Commit

When WebLogic Server coordinates transactions across multiple resources, the more advanced features of transaction coordination in JTA come into play. For a transaction that spans multiple data resources, such as two relational databases or a relational database and a JMS queue, WebLogic Server uses a *two-phase commit*, or 2PC, engine.

Two-phase commit is a process whereby the transaction manager can enforce the ACID properties in a distributed environment, even across multiple, potentially heterogeneous, resource managers. In this model, a *transaction manager* is responsible for coordinating the transactions; each resource manager must be willing to submit to the transaction manager's instructions before committing a unit of work. When a transaction is completed, the transaction manager issues prepare statements to all the resource managers involved. These resource managers return a prepared state, implying they give up the right to abort the transaction. This is phase one. The transaction manager collects all the responses. If all the resources prepare, then the transaction manager issues a commit statement; however, if any of the resource managers cannot commit the transaction, then the transaction manager issues a rollback statement. This is the second phase.

Two-phase commit requires that all the resources involved in the transaction follow a transaction coordination specification, such as the TM-XA protocol. The protocol used between the transaction manager and the resource managers is the XA *protocol*. In this scenario, WebLogic Server JTA acts as the transaction manager, and the JDBC drivers implement XA for distributed transaction coordination. In practice, two-phase commit is transparent to the user.

You use the JTA driver in your application, acquire connections to multiple resources, specify operations on them, and so forth. As long as they are all XA-compliant resources, WebLogic Server takes care of the details of coordinating all the resources together into a single unit of work that either commits completely or is rolled back to the previous consistent state. Further details on multidatabase transactions are provided later in this chapter, in the section "WebLogic Server and Distributed Transactions."

> **Best Practice:** Transactions are costly. There is performance and networking overhead associated with coordinating transactions, especially when implementing two-phase commit. This overhead can have an impact on application performance and throughput. It is a best practice to use transactions only when they are required to fulfill a specific requirement of the business.

Using WebLogic Server JTA

There are seven basic steps for using WebLogic Server JTA in an application:

1. Establish the transaction.
2. Start the transaction.
3. Locate a `DataSource` with `Honors Global Transactions` enabled.
4. Establish a database connection.
5. Execute resource operations.
6. Close connections.
7. Complete the transaction.

Let's examine each step in detail. We now JTA-enable our JDBC examples from earlier in this chapter.

Establishing the Transaction

The first step in a WebLogic Server JTA implementation is to establish an instance of the `UserTransaction` class. The `UserTransaction` class controls the transaction on the current thread of execution. This transaction is associated with the current thread of execution for the user being served for all of the various services such as EJB, JMS, and JDBC. This class can be looked up in the JNDI. For now, we do not discuss the mechanics of JNDI, which is covered in detail in Chapter 6.

The following code is a lookup in JNDI for the `UserTransaction` object:

```
/* A Context which is used to store the user. */

Context ctx = null;
```

Locate a new initial context:

```
    ctx = new InitialContext();
```

Finally, create the `UserTransaction` object by locating it in the context object located in JNDI:

```
UserTransaction tx = (UserTransaction)
 ctx.lookup("javax.transaction.UserTransaction");
```

At this point, a `UserTransaction` object is available.

Starting the Transaction

Starting the transaction is simple. Simply call the `begin` method on the `UserTransaction` object:

```
tx.begin();
```

Now, any operations that use the database are within the scope of this transaction. This includes direct JDBC calls as well as other services that rely on JDBC, including EJB and JMS.

Locating a DataSource

The next step is to locate a transactional `DataSource`:

```
javax.sql.DataSource ds
          = (javax.sql.DataSource)
     ctx.lookup ("examples-dataSource-demoPool");
```

Establishing a Database Connection

Next, establish a database connection.

```
java.sql.Connection myConn = ds.getConnection();
```

This `Connection` object is now available for use.

Executing Resource Operations

At this point, things should look familiar to you. We have an instance of the `Connection` class that we can use to generate statements for the database. In contrast to the simpler examples from earlier in this chapter, it is now possible to execute multiple statements in the scope of a single transaction. All of the statements succeed and are committed in the database, or they all are rolled back, reverting the database to its original state.

For example, let's say that we want to have two different operations in a transaction. To continue our Employee Record example, we insert two new employees using multiple SQL INSERT statements after creating a new instance of the `Statement` object, named `stmt`:

```
/* Execute an Update to insert two new entries into the
         table named employee. */
     stmt.executeUpdate (
       "INSERT INTO employee VALUES ('Benjamin', 'FRANCE' ,55)");
     stmt.executeUpdate (
       "INSERT INTO employee VALUES ('ROB', 'Illinois' ,56)");
```

Close Connections

Just as in the simple Update example earlier this chapter, the connections to the resources you created should be closed and disposed. This is done by using the `close()` method on each object:

```
stmt.close();
myConn.close();
```

At this time, the `Connection` object is held in "limbo" and not returned to the connection pool until the transaction is either committed or rolled back. This greatly affects tuning. Even when the user closes the database connection, it is not returned to the pool until the transaction commits. For this reason, you need to be sure that you either commit or roll back your transactions as soon as possible. Letting a transaction stay open until it times out is not a good idea for a scalable site. Eventually, you could exhaust all of your database connections, causing severe performance problems.

> **Best Practice:** You need to be sure that you either commit or roll back your transactions as soon as possible. Letting a transaction stay open until it times out is not a good idea for a scalable site.

Completing the Transaction

The final step is to complete the transaction. Before a commit or rollback, you can execute further JDBC calls by creating a new `Connection` object from the same connection pool. The new connection is in the same transactional scope as those previously executed.

Once all work is completed, the final step is to either commit the transaction or roll it back. If we commit the transaction, we assert that no error has occurred and it is now appropriate to make those changes final in the database. If things have not gone smoothly and an exception was thrown within a unit of work, the appropriate thing to do is roll back the transaction.

It is customary to bracket all of the steps in a WebLogic Server JTA–enabled transaction with a `try/catch/finally` block to handle any exceptions. Most applications use a `catch` block for their `rollback()` call, which looks like this:

```
try {
    // Steps one through five here
          // Commit Transaction
          tx.commit();
stmt.close();
    } catch (Exception txe) {

      // Printout the Transaction Exception
      System.out.println("Servlet error: " + txe);

      // Roll Back Transaction
      try {

        tx.rollback();

      } catch (javax.transaction.SystemException se) {}
    } finally {

      /* Close Connections */
      try {
        if (conn != null)
          if (!conn.isClosed())
```

```
            conn.close();
    } catch (SQLException sqle) {; }
}
```

The JTA driver commits all the transactions on `Connection` objects in the current thread and returns the connection to the pool if the transactions were committed. However, in the event of an abort, then JTA rolls back all operations involved and releases all connections and resources used.

WebLogic Server and Distributed Transactions

Distributed transactions are those that span multiple resources such as an Oracle database, a Sybase database, and a message-oriented middleware (MOM) product such as IBM MQSeries. In these combinations, a single transaction should govern all of the operations on all of the resources. As with any other transaction, either all operations succeed or none of them do.

Distributed Transactions and Standards

A distributed transaction is one in which multiple, networked resources are involved in a single unit of work, protecting the ACID properties. Distributed transactions use the two-phase commit protocol, which follows standards from the X/Open Distributed Transaction consortium. The X/Open standards specify a model called X/Open Distributed Transaction Processing (DTP). As noted earlier, this model describes how all the different components in a distributed transaction work together. One important part of this standard is called XA, which is the standardized interface between a resource (such as a database) and the transaction manager (such as WebLogic Server's JTA implementation). Resources or databases that can work in distributed transactions are specified as XA-compliant resources.

Using XA-Compliant Resources and JTA

WebLogic Server can use any number of XA-compliant resources and coordinate transactions that span all resources. In practice, this works by creating *bridges* to multiple XA-compliant resources made available by using a JTA-aware `DataSource` object. *The JTA implementation handles enlisting the underlying resources in the JTA transaction.*

Within the scope of the JTA driver transaction, your application code can make SQL updates and reads to the database either directly using JDBC or indirectly by using higher level services such as EJB or JMS. Behind the scenes, the JTA driver handles all of the details to ensure that your operations either all succeed or all fail. From an application developer's point of view, all of this happens without your knowledge. To take advantage of distributed transactions, simply use the standard procedure for WebLogic Server JTA as described in this chapter, except extend your resource access to include more than one database or other resource.

You should understand that there is overhead for using two-phase commit: there are extra steps in committing transactions, extra latency as resources are coordinated, and the added complexity of getting multiple components to all agree on something. You can also have failure conditions called *heuristic damage*, where transactions are left in an inconsistent state. For example, if a transaction manager sends out a prepare statement to a database and queuing system, the transaction cannot be committed until all parties prepare. If there is a network problem in the middle of the transaction, the transaction manager will wait. However, while the transaction is waiting, there are locks held on the database, keeping the records from being accessed by others. At some point, a DBA may simply decide to abort these "hung" transactions, resulting in heuristic damage.

In the end, you should use two-phase commit only if it is required to satisfy some specific need of the business. Given a choice between using two-phase commit and doing a one-phase commit to a single resource, you should always follow the time-proven maxim—Keep It Simple, Sam. Use two-phase commit and distributed transactions only if you have multiple resources in a transaction, when transactions span heterogeneous resource managers, or when several operations must be completed synchronously as a unit of work.

Non-XA Resource Managers

What if a resource manager you are using doesn't support XA, or what if full two-phase commit processing is impractical? Obviously, one option is to limit transactions to a single resource manager; unfortunately, this may not be practical. A second option is to leverage asynchronous processing. For example, instead of updating two or three resource managers in a single, synchronous unit of work, you could update a resource and use a durable queuing system to deliver the update to the other resource manager(s). However, you will still need to wrap the messaging operations in transactions to ensure messages aren't lost. Also, you should be sure that the messaging or queuing system supports transactional interfaces.

WebLogic Server offers a third alternative—have the transaction act like a two-phase commit even when the resource managers do not support XA interfaces. In fact, the WebLogic Server's JTA implementation includes a *last commit* or *one-phase optimization*. Please note that this optimization does not mean a non-XA resource will act as an XA resource. Rather, it is a way to follow the two-phase commit process while protecting the transactional integrity of the non-XA resource. If only a single resource is enlisted, no two-phase commit is done; if multiple resource managers are involved, WebLogic places the non-XA resource at the end of the transaction. If all the XA resource managers prepare, then the transaction manager can commit the non-XA resource. If the non-XA resource commits, then the transaction manager sends out commit requests to all the XA resources; if not, then an abort message is issued. With this optimization, WebLogic Server enables you to enlist one non-XA resource in a two-phase commit transaction. You enable this option with the *Emulate Two-Phase Commit for non-XA Driver* option in the `Advanced  Options` section of the `DataSource` object's `Configuration` tab.

> **Note:** You can only include *one* non-XA resource manager in a distributed transaction that emulates two-phase commit processing. The other resource managers in this type of transaction must use XA.

Transaction Isolation Levels

Transaction isolation levels specify how the database handles the "I" in ACID. If you remember from previous discussions in this chapter, this is how the database handles concurrency issues, which are conflicts that arise when two or more simultaneous operations/transactions are operating on the same data. For example, one transaction might be in the process of obtaining data in the database while another process wants to update that same data. The setting of isolation levels enables you to specify how the database behaves in those situations.

Five levels of transaction isolation are defined by the JDBC specification. These five levels are database dependent, so you should review your driver and database documentation to see what works with your specific database. The five levels (going from least restrictive to most restrictive) are as follows:

- `TRANSACTION_NONE`—No attempt is made to isolate the transaction and participating data from other transactions.
- `TRANSACTION_READ_UNCOMMITTED`—Allows what are called "dirty" reads. A dirty read is a read of another transaction's uncommitted data. For instance, transaction-1 changes your account balance from $1,000 to $500. Before transaction-1 commits, transaction-2 reads the account balance as $500. This is a dirty read, since transaction-1's change has not yet been committed.
- `TRANSACTION_READ_COMMITTED`—Guarantees that all reads return committed data. This prevents dirty reads, but it does not guarantee repeatable reads (for instance, if transaction-1 reads the account balance as $1,000). Now, before transaction-1 commits, another transaction changes the account balance to $500 and commits the change. When transaction-1 reads the account balance again, it may now see the balance as $500. This is a nonrepeatable read because the same column was read twice within the transaction but different results were returned. Note that there was no dirty read because transaction-2 committed its account balance change before transaction-1 read the new value. `READ_COMMITTED` is the default isolation level for Oracle databases and is commonly used in practice.
- `TRANSACTION_REPEATABLE_READ`—Prevents dirty reads and nonrepeatable reads, but phantom reads are still possible. A phantom read occurs because a row has been added or deleted from a table, but this transaction still sees the side effects. For instance, consider a database schema with a Voters table listing citizens and their choice of candidate A or B. There is also an auxiliary table that lists the total vote count for each candidate. Transaction-1 reads in all of the rows in the Voters table and computes its own totals for candidates A and B. It then compares these totals against the vote totals in the auxiliary table and finds they do not match! The problem is that transaction-2 has inserted a new voter into the Voters table and updated the vote count. Transaction-1 has seen a phantom read. `REPEATABLE_READ` isolation is rarely used in practice because it is expensive to implement, and it does not provide true serializable transactions.
- `TRANSACTION_SERIALIZABLE`—Prevents dirty, nonrepeatable, and phantom reads. The `SERIALIZABLE` isolation level offers the highest level of protection, but it also gives the lowest performance.

> **Best Practice:** Choosing a transaction isolation level is a tradeoff between performance and correctness. You should use the lowest possible isolation level that guarantees correct semantics in your application. This delivers the maximum transaction processing performance while still ensuring the needs of the business are met.

Setting Isolation Levels

Developers can set the transaction isolation level for any or all transactions. The isolation level affects all JDBC access, because even the simplest accesses are treated as transactions by the database.

Setting transaction isolation levels is particularly important when data is shared between multiple clients. Many applications use the `READ_COMMITTED` isolation level because it enables readers to proceed without waiting for an update to commit. This is particularly important for Web-based applications, in which most users are browsing the data and not performing updates.

The mechanics of changing transaction isolation levels is simple. A method included in the `Connection` class called `setTransactionIsolation()` enables the transaction isolation level to be set for a given connection. The isolation level can be changed at any time for a given transaction on most databases, except during a transaction. The acceptable values are defined as constants in the `Connection` class:

- `Connection.TRANSACTION_NONE`
- `Connection.TRANSACTION_READ_UNCOMMITTED`
- `Connection.TRANSACTION_READ_COMMITTED`
- `Connection.TRANSACTION_REPEATABLE_READ`
- `Connection.TRANSACTION_SERIALIZABLE`

To set the transaction isolation level in a `Connection` myConn to `Connection.TRANSACTION_READ_COMMITTED`, you could use the following immediately after obtaining the database connection from the connection pool:

```
conn.setTransactionIsolation (Connection.TRANSACTION_READ_COMMITTED);
```

> **Best Practice:** The setting of isolation levels often brings out idiosyncrasies of different databases. For example, many databases do not support all isolation levels. In addition, it is important to realize that databases use different locking algorithms. In particular, Oracle databases use an optimistic scheme with multiple versions of data. An architectural best practice is to consult your database server's documentation when choosing an isolation level.

Prepared Statements

The JDBC specification supports language for executing the same statements repeatedly while changing only the parameters in the statements. Such operations use a `PreparedStatement` interface that extends the `Statement` interface.

To use prepared statements, first create an instance of the `PreparedStatement` object. You do this by calling the `prepareStatement()` method on your instance of the `Connection` object. This method takes a single parameter, a string of SQL with wildcards represented by question marks. Assuming that we have already acquired a `Connection` object, we can create the following `PreparedStatement`:

```
PreparedStatement pstmt = myConn.prepareStatement("INSERT INTO employee
VALUES (?,?,?)");
```

In the original Update example in this chapter, we used two different SQL statements to add users to our EMPLOYEE table:

```
/* Execute an Update to insert two new entries into the table named employee.  */
stmt.executeUpdate ("INSERT INTO employee VALUES ('JOE', 'Louisiana'  ,5)");
stmt.executeUpdate ("INSERT INTO employee VALUES ('SHANDELLE', 'Ohio'  ,6)");
```

For each of these statements, the database and JDBC driver must map our values to those understood by the underlying database. Performance can be greatly improved by removing this step. These two updates can be consolidated in a single `PreparedStatement`:

```
// Load DataSource Instance, Get Connection, etc. here

/* Create instance of the PreparedStatement
   class with SQL wildcards specified by ?'s */
PreparedStatement pstmt = myConn.prepareStatement(
"INSERT INTO employee VALUES (?,?,?)");

/* Execute an Update to insert two new entries
   into the table named employee using PreparedStatement.  */

/* Replace wildcards with values for each.  */
pstmt.setString(1, 'JOE');
pstmt.setString(2, 'Louisiana'
pstmt.setInt(3, 5));

/* Execute statement */
int opNum = pstmt.executeUpdate();

/* Replace wildcards with values for each.  */
pstmt.setString(1, 'SHANDELLE');
pstmt.setString(2, 'Ohio'
pstmt.setInt(3, 6));
pstmt.executeUpdate();

/* Execute statement and assign the returned integer
   to a holding variable.  Each time that the executeUpdate
   method is called the return value is either the row count for
INSERT, UPDATE or DELETE statements; or 0 for SQL statements that
return nothing. */
opNum = pstmt.executeUpdate();

.
.
.
```

The trick is to use methods in the PreparedStatement class to set values for the wildcards before executing the statement. Each setXXX method takes two different parameters. The first is the index of the wildcards they replace. These indexes begin with 1 and increment to the right. The second parameter is the values to be inserted. Specific setXXX methods exist for each type of Java object. A complete list of these methods can be found in the documentation or at the Java Web site at *http://java.sun.com/j2se/1.3/docs/api/index.html.*

All the methods that apply to standard Statement objects also apply to PreparedStatements. For example, prepared statements can return ResultSets when the executeQuery() method is called on them.

Where possible, use PreparedStatement as opposed to a standard statement. This enables the database to compile the SQL into a statement that can be used repeatedly with only the parameters changing. This increases speed of execution, because the database does not need to repeatedly recompile the SQL.

Error Handling and SQL Warnings

JDBC errors are thrown as exceptions. The specific class for representing these errors is `java.sql.SQLException`. As with any other exception, the appearance of a SQLException signifies that something has gone wrong and needs to be appropriately handled.

SQL warnings are represented by an instance of the `java.sql.SQLWarning` class that derives from the `java.sql.SQLException` class. It provides information on database access warnings. Unlike serious exceptions, SQL warnings are silently chained to the object whose method caused it to be reported.

Handling SQLException Errors

SQLExceptions store three pieces of information:

- A string describing the error.
- A SQLstate string, which follows the X/OPEN SQLstate conventions. The values of the SQLState string are described in the X/OPEN SQL specification.
- An integer error code that is specific to each vendor. Normally, this is the actual error code returned by the underlying database.

In the previous examples, a `try/catch` block bracketed the entire JDBC operation. In your `catch` block, you can handle the exception to suit the needs of your application.

```
try {
do JDBC work here
} catch (SQLException sqle) {

        // Print the summary message of the exception
        System.out.println("JDBC exception encountered: " + sqle);

        // Retrieve and print the SQLState for this SQLException object.
        System.out.println("SQL state string: " + sqle.getSQLState());

        // Print the database specific error code
        System.out.println("Database specific error code: " +
sqle.getErrorCode());
}
```

Handling SQL Warnings

SQL warnings arise when the DBMS wants to alert you about a possible unintended consequence of your executed SQL statements. For example, if you have received truncated data, SQLWarning returns a DataTruncation warning. SQL warnings are silently attached to the object that generates them. Any relevant JDBC class (including Connection, ResultSet, and Statement) can generate an SQL warning.

Accessing SQL warnings is relatively simple. Each relevant JDBC class includes a method called getWarnings(). Calling this method on any instance of those objects returns the last created SQL-Warning. You should always examine any SQL warnings before closing your Statement objects:

```
try {
/*do JDBC work here */

        /* Check for SQL Warnings */
        SQLWarning mySQLW = myStatement.getWarnings();

if (mySQLW != null) {

        // Print the summary message of the exception
        System.out.println("JDBC exception encountered: " + mySQLW);

        // Retrieve and print the SQLState for this SQLException object.
        System.out.println("SQL state string: " + mySQLW.getSQLState());

        // Print the database specific error code
        System.out.println("Database specific error code: " +
mySQLW.getErrorCode());
}
} catch (SQLException sqle) {

} finally {
        /* Close the Instance of Statement */
        myStatement.close();
}
```

Note that both SQL warnings and JDBC errors are "chained." Each exception might have other exceptions nested inside it, if it contains object references to those other exceptions. Nested exceptions can be accessed by calling the getNextWarning() method, which returns an instance of SQLException or SQLWarning, depending upon the exception from which it was called.

Metadata

Metadata is data about data. It provides information about how data is organized. In the case of JDBC, metadata includes information such as column names, number of columns, and so forth. Because you might not always know what type of information is returned by result sets, the JDBC standard includes features that let us look at the structure of the returned ResultSets. This is called ResultSetMetadata, or data about the organization of ResultSets.

> **Note:** JDBC keeps metadata about the database schema. A `DatabaseMetaData` object is available in most JDBC drivers. In the majority of WebLogic Server applications, the schema of the database is already known or not relevant. For this reason, `DatabaseMetaData` is not discussed in depth. The procedure to use `DatabaseMetaData` parallels that for using `ResultSetMetaData`.

Using Metadata

There are three basic steps for using metadata:

1. Generate a result set by executing a query.
2. Generate an instance of the metadata object by calling the appropriate method on the `ResultSet`.
3. Call the appropriate methods on the metadata object to derive the appropriate information.

The next section includes an example of using the steps based on the `EMPLOYEE` table from the previous sections of this chapter. As you might recall, you first generate a result set by executing a query on the database:

```
// Load DataSource, Get Connection, etc. here

/* Create an Instance of the java.sql.Statement class and
   use the factory method called createStatement() available
   on the Connection class to create a new statement. */
Statement stmt = myConn.createStatement();

/* Use the shortcut method the available in the Statement
   class to execute our query.  We are selecting all rows
   from the EMPLOYEE table. */
ResultSet rs = stmt.executeQuery("SELECT * FROM EMPLOYEE ");
```

Next, generate an instance of the `ResultSetMetaData` object by calling the appropriate method on the `ResultSet` object:

```
/* Use the factory method getMetaData to generate
   a ResultSetMetaData object for our result set 'rs'. */
ResultSetMetaData rsmd = rs.getMetaData();
```

Finally, call the appropriate methods on the metadata object to derive the appropriate information:

```
/* Find out how many columns are in the result set. */
System.out.println("Number of Columns: " +
rsmd.getColumnCount());

/* For each of those columns, print out information: */
for (int i = 1; i <= rsmd.getColumnCount(); i++) {
```

```
System.out.println("Column Name: " + rsmd.getColumnName(i));

System.out.println("Nullable: " + rsmd.isNullable(i));

System.out.println("Precision: " + rsmd.getPrecision(i));

System.out.println("Scale: " + rsmd.getScale(i));

System.out.println("Size: " + rsmd.getColumnDisplaySize(i));

    System.out.println("Column Type: " + rsmd.getColumnType(i));

    System.out.println("Column Type Name: " +
rsmd.getColumnTypeName(i));

}
```

This last section of code first displays the number of columns in the result set. Then, for each of those columns, it prints out data on different characteristics.

The methods illustrated here are only a subset of the methods available for metadata. A complete list can be found in the generated JavaDoc available with the standard JDK or via the Web at *http://java.sun.com/j2ee/1.3/docs/api/index.html.*

Advanced JDBC Features

This section covers some of the advanced features of JDBC:

- Binary Large Objects (BLOBs) and Character Large Objects (CLOBs), which make moving large objects to and from the database faster and easier.
- Dates and times, which are used to handle timestamps and so forth.
- Batch updates, which are used to improve the efficiency of making many updates to the database at a single time.

Let's look at each of these in detail.

BLOBs and CLOBs

BLOBs and CLOBs are SQL data types available for efficient storage and retrieval of large objects. BLOBs contain binary data, while CLOBs contain only characters.

BLOB and CLOB data types are created to store and retrieve very large objects such as a user's pictures or very large text files. BLOBs and CLOBs offer two benefits: First, they provide a convenient way to represent a large amount of data as a single database object. In other data types, such as integers, the amount of data that can be stored is limited. Second, DBMSs have been optimized to work with these data types, which means that reading and writing large objects is efficient, and certainly much faster than if you had to break them up into multiple smaller objects.

Using BLOBs and CLOBs

Both BLOBs and CLOBs are accessed via the `ResultSet` object returned as part of a SQL query. First, create instances of BLOBs and CLOBs:

```
java.sql.Blob myBlob = null;
java.sql.Clob myClob = null;
```

Next, get a `ResultSet` that contains a column named `"blobcolumn"` of BLOBs and a column named `"clobcolumn"` of CLOBs by doing a query:

```
/* query that returns ResultSet with BLOB and CLOB here */
myBlob = rs.getBlob("blobcolumn");
myClob = rs.getClob("clobcolumn");
```

Finally, display the BLOB using an `InputStream`:

```
java.io.InputStream readis = myReadBlob.getBinaryStream();
for (int i=0 ; i < STREAM_SIZE ; i++) {
    r[i] = (byte) readis.read();
    System.out.println("output [" + i + "] = " + r[i]);
}
```

Also, display the CLOB using another `InputStream`:

```
java.io.InputStream readClobis = myReadClob.getAsciiStream();
char[] c = new char[26];
for (int i=0 ; i < 26  ; i++) {
    c[i] = (char) readClobis.read();
    System.out.println("output [" + i + "] = " + c[i]);
}
```

Batch Updates

Batch updates enable you to combine a group of updates to the database into a single batch operation. All the updates can be sent inside of a single database call. So, if you have *n* updates, instead of doing *n* database calls, you only do one. This streamlines the process of doing multiple updates to the database. In single updates, the JDBC driver contains a lock on a given table and then releases it for every update. Batch updates enable updates to be optimized around a single lock and can only be used on a single table in a database.

If you remember from the earlier Update examples, multiple updates to the database are handled as follows:

```
// locate driver, create Connection Object, etc.

/* Execute an Update to insert two new entries into the
table named employee.   */
stmt.executeUpdate ("INSERT INTO employee VALUES ('JOE', 'Louisiana'  ,5)");
```

```
stmt.executeUpdate ("INSERT INTO employee VALUES ('SHANDELLE', 'Ohio'  ,6)");

// These statements could be combined into a single batch of // updates:
locate driver, create Connection Object, etc.

// create a Statement object
Statement stmt = myConn.createStatement();

// add SQL statements to the batch
stmt.addBatch("INSERT INTO employee VALUES ('JOE', 'Louisiana'  ,5)");
stmt.addBatch("INSERT INTO employee VALUES ('SHANDELLE', 'Ohio'  ,6)");

/* Send the statements using the executeBatch method
to the DBMS in a try/catch block to catch exceptions.  */
try {

        stmt.executeBatch();

} catch (Exception e) {
     System.out.println("Exception in batch:\n " + e);
}
```

Batch statements are executed in the order that they are received. Using batch updates with prepared statements is similar:

```
// Load Driver Instance, Get Connection, etc. here

/* Create instance of the PreparedStatement
   class with SQL  wildcards specified by ?'s
*/
PreparedStatement pstmt =
   myConn.prepareStatement("INSERT INTO employee VALUES (?,?,?)");

/* Execute an Update to insert two new entries
   into the table named employee using PreparedStatement.  */

// Replace wildcards with values for each.
pstmt.setString(1, 'JOE');
pstmt.setString(2, 'Louisiana');
pstmt.setInt(3, 5));

/* Instead of calling executeQuery() here, call addBatch
method to add the current batch parameter specified above.
*/
pstmt.addBatch();

/* Replace wildcards with values for each for the second
```

```
    values in the batch update. */
pstmt.setString(1, 'SHANDELLE');
pstmt.setString(2, 'Ohio'
pstmt.setInt(3, 6));

/* Instead of calling executeQuery() here, call a addBatch
   method to add the current batch parameter specified above.  */
pstmt.addBatch();

/* Call executeBatch to finish it off.  This method returns an array
of integers that specify the number of updated rows for each
statement in the batch. */
int[] updateCounts = pstmt.executeBatch();
```

.

.

Best Practices for JDBC

There are a number of best practices that enable your JDBC-based applications to be as successful as possible.

Make Your Queries as Smart as Possible

Learning to select only the data you really want at the server side is crucial. For many applications, poor performance is often due to poorly written SQL. Typical problems include returning too many rows, queries that are too general, and so forth. There are many tricks for SQL that are worth learning to optimize performance. Some are simple, some are complicated. While SQL joins and subqueries are beyond the scope of this book, there are simple things that you can do to improve your performance, such as using prepared statements and accessing stored procedures.

Tune the Database

Many databases enable you to specify which tables and objects should receive preferential treatment for being cached in memory. For applications that have a large working set but a small number of objects that are accessed repeatedly, an appropriate database-caching strategy can make a large difference. Examine your application's behavior and, for objects that are accessed regularly and repeatedly, be sure to designate those data sets to be cached in memory as much as possible. More broadly, you should have a DBA and use a tuned database with a tuned schema. The database is a part of the overall system that must be optimized for proper performance.

Put Initialization Code in init()

A common mistake is to cause your servlet to do more work than is necessary by placing too much in the `service()` method. Be certain to place code that is meant to be executed only once in a servlet if initialized inside of the `init()` method of your servlet. This ensures that the operations are only done once instead of every time the servlet is accessed.

Get Your JDBC Connection from a TxDataSource or the JTS Driver

To ensure the correct use of transactions, get your JDBC connection from a JTA-aware `DataSource` that honors global transactions. If the data source does not honor global transactions, it does not participate in the JTA transaction and you won't be able to include EJB or JMS services in the scope of the transaction. Always get your JDBC connection for JTA transactions from a JTA-aware `Data-Source`.

Use Batch Updates

Batch updates provide much improved performance for multiple updates. If you need to do many updates, it is not efficient to obtain a connection to the database for each update. Batch updates so that they can all be accomplished in the scope of a single command sent to the database.

Updates require the DBMS to obtain all the locks necessary on the various rows and tables; use them and release them. Each single-update lock blocks other clients from accessing this data and substantially degrades performance.

Do In-Place Updates Where Possible

It is more efficient to update a row in place than to remove a row and insert another. For this reason, architect your application to use updates rather than inserts, deletes and removes.

Use the Appropriate Method to Get a JDBC Connection Object

Use the `DataSource`-based technique, as described in this chapter. The older `DriverManager` technique for acquiring a JDBC connection is synchronized and prevents concurrent access. Because WebLogic Server is multithreaded internally, this presents scalability problems.

Release the JDBC Resources Appropriately

Release JDBC resources as quickly as possible and as efficiently as possible by placing the `close()` calls to each resource such as `Statements`, `Connections`, and `ResultSets` in the appropriate place in the `try/catch/finally` block. At the end of your `try  {}` block, you should release `ResultSets` and then release `Statements`. In the `finally{}` section, you should then release your `Connection`. By placing it in the `finally` section, you ensure that this connection is always released no matter what happens in the `try/catch` block.

Use Autocommit Appropriately

As noted in this chapter, it is possible to instruct the JDBC driver to commit on every statement or to require explicit committing of transactions. If possible, use explicit commits for your database operation. This requires much less overhead from the database and streamlined communication over the network to your database instance.

Don't Hang onto JDBC Connections

One common mistake in JDBC programming is to hold onto JDBC connections instead of immediately releasing those connections. For example, you may have a servlet that relies upon a JDBC connection. An inefficient application would store the JDBC connection persistently in the servlet and keep it open. This inhibits scalability: connections to the database are limited. If the number of simultaneous requests for the service is greater than the size of the JDBC pool, this could mean that requests must wait to acquire a new JDBC connection.

For the JDBC example for the WebAuction application, a JDBC connection is acquired for every method and released at the end of that method. This enables JDBC connections to be spread efficiently among incoming requests. To avoid this scalability trap, your application should acquire connections from the connection pool and release them as quickly as possible.

Work in the Database If You Can

If possible, find ways to execute work in the database, for instance, by using database triggers or stored procedures accessed through `CallableStatements`. This enables your application to avoid making unnecessary trips to the database, increasing performance.

Commit or Roll Back Your Transactions as Soon as Possible

You need to be sure that you either commit or roll back your transactions as soon as possible. Letting a transaction stay open until it times out is not a good idea for a scalable site.

Set Your Pool Size Appropriately

WebLogic Server enables variable pool sizes to be created for database connection pools. In general, there is no magic formula to determine how large these pools should be. However, a good rule of thumb is that the maximum size of the connection pool should be equal to the number of `ExecuteThreads` allocated for your WebLogic Server instance. This design assumes each thread uses one transaction to service a request and therefore needs one connection.

However, this value may need to be increased if a given thread uses more than one transaction in the scope of handling a user's request. For example, the WebAuction application generates ID numbers in a separate transaction from the other work being done in the database. For this reason, it could be helpful to specify a slightly larger connection pool in the WebAuction application or any that requires more than one transaction in the scope of a single user request.

Also, it is recommended that you set your minimum connection pool size equal to the maximum pool size. This minimizes the number of connections that are created to fill the connection pool to react to increased load on the server. This helps minimize response time and maximize performance by creating all of the database connections at server startup. Your server should not waste time creating connection pools when it is under load.

Do Not Have Your Transactions Span User Input

Transactions consume resources in the DBMS and WebLogic Server, and should be used judiciously. While a transaction is executing locks are held on these resources. For this reason you should avoid scenarios in which you unnecessarily rely on long-running transactions, particularly when involving user input. For example, if a transaction begins on the load of a browser page and only commits when the user clicks Submit, you could be asking for trouble. The open transaction retains locks on the resources in the database and in WebLogic Server. Sometimes it is necessary to break up a long transaction into several shorter transactions.

Note: WebLogic Server includes some good documentation on best practices for JDBC performance, available at *http://edocs.bea.com/wls/docs81/jdbc/performance.html*.

JDBC and Transactions in the WebAuction Application

JDBC is used substantially in the Auction application. However, it is not used explicitly during development. Instead, as in the context of a real application, the JDBC access is encapsulated in an EJB. The Auction application uses container-managed persistence (CMP), which automatically generates JDBC code to map the relational data in the database to an object form.

There is one instance in which explicit JDBC is used in the Auction application. It is necessary to use the database to keep a sequence for the WebAuction application to generate new ID numbers for auction items. An EJB is used to encapsulate this SQL.

Summing It Up

JDBC and transactions are two of the most important underlying services provided in WebLogic Server to the enterprise Java developer. They allow applications to leverage portability, ensure transactional integrity, and deliver robust, consistent applications. In this chapter, we reviewed the following topics:

- How to build database connectivity in WebLogic Server applications
- Sample database access using JDBC
- Best practices for using JDBC in WebLogic Server
- Using JDBC in transactions
- Sample JTA use
- Prepared statements, metadata, and batch database operations
- Coding database access in the Auction application

chapter 6

Remote Method Invocation and Distributed Naming

In This Chapter

- The RMI programming model
- Using the remote interface
- Automatic and hand-coded serialization
- Using JNDI
- Managing JNDI replication
- Best practices for using both RMI and JNDI in distributed applications

In the Internet age, networked applications are commonplace. Applications run on everything from Web browsers to handheld devices and communicate with distant servers. In this networked world, enterprise applications require communication and distribution facilities. Millions of users rely on standard protocols to access distributed programs. Protocols like Simple Mail Transfer Protocol (SMTP) for e-mail and Hypertext Transfer Protocol (HTTP) for Web traffic provide clients the means to access remote resources. Although bounced e-mails and slow Web sites sometimes undermine the illusion, these applications seem to provide access to the world's computers as if they were located under your desk.

Java applications also participate in this networked world and can access resources across the network. One foundation technology for distributed Java programming is Remote Method Invocation (RMI). RMI services allow Java code to make method calls to objects on a remote server, almost as if the object were local. Java 2 Enterprise Edition (J2EE) services such as Enterprise JavaBeans (EJB) are built on top of RMI. You may create RMI objects directly, but you more often use RMI indirectly by using higher level services like EJBs.

Naming services are another core component in distributed systems. Naming services are critical because they help applications find resources. With the explosion of the Internet, naming systems have become common and familiar. The most visible naming service is the Domain Name System (DNS). Most computers communicate with one another using an IP address, such as 198.137.241.43. However, people use names, like *www.learnweblogic.com*, to identify computers. The DNS system converts from the name to the address so that applications can identify the computer named by a user. Java defines a naming service called the Java Naming and Directory Interface (JNDI).

You might not code your own RMI objects or look up resources in the JNDI tree, but WebLogic Server uses these technologies to build higher level technologies. This chapter provides an introduction to RMI and JNDI and identifies issues that arise within distributed systems.

Remote Method Invocation

RMI is a Java-based model for distributed programming. Using RMI, Java code can call methods in remote objects. From the perspective of the caller, the RMI call is almost the same as a local call. WebLogic Server's RMI infrastructure handles the details of making the call work. The infrastructure passes requests to the remote object, executes the method call, and passes back the method's return value.

An RMI object consists of two components: a remote interface and an implementation class. The remote interface exposes methods in the RMI object that you can call remotely. Your interface should extend the `java.rmi.Remote` interface and define signatures for the methods you want to expose. The implementation class implements the remote interface and defines the methods you can execute remotely. By convention, if the remote object is named `Class`, the implementation class is named `ClassImpl`.

RMI clients call the remote object through the remote interface. WebLogic Server provides an object to the RMI client. This object acts as a stand-in for the remote object. This object, called a stub or proxy, implements the remote interface, and the RMI client calls the stub as if it were the implementation class. The methods of the stub don't process the request, but instead pack the request, including any parameters, into a message and send this message to the RMI server. The process of packing the request into a binary representation is called *marshaling*.

On the remote machine, WebLogic Server passes the request to another proxy or skeleton object. This proxy unpacks, or *unmarshals*, the binary representation of the request and calls the appropriate method of the implementation class. The implementation class executes the called method and passes any return value back to the proxy.

The return value takes the same path in reverse: from proxy-skeleton to RMI server, to proxy-stub, and finally back to the RMI client. See Figure 6–1 for an overview of the entire process.

The supports provided by RMI and by WebLogic Server make RMI easy to use. The client calls RMI methods like it would call a local method. WebLogic Server's RMI implementation handles transporting the method call from the client across the network and to the RMI object for processing. Finally, the RMI implementation returns values across the network to the client. Java programmers don't have to write the code to tie these components together, but provides only the remote interface and implementation object.

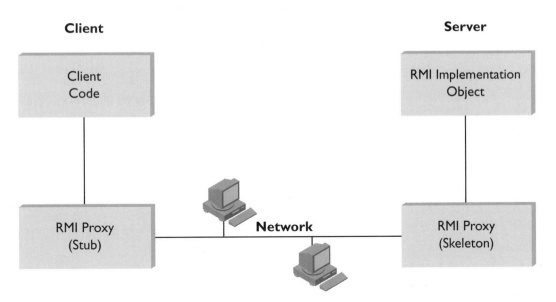

Figure 6-1
RMI call from client to remote server.

The RMI Programming Model

It is important to recognize that RMI is a programming model. The model does not designate the underlying mechanism used to pass data between the client and server. Actual RMI clients and implementation objects are independent of the wire format. The clients and implementation objects interface directly only with the RMI classes. The lower communication levels use the RMI wire format. This layered model is analogous to network programs communicating with TCP/IP. The applications interact with the TCP/IP network protocol, but the applications are concerned only with the TCP/IP layer. Like RMI clients, a TCP/IP client program does not care about the Ethernet card that actually transports the packets.

The WebLogic RMI implementation supports three different wire protocols: T3, T3/HTTP, and IIOP. T3 and its secure counterpart T3S are WebLogic's optimized protocols for transporting remote method calls over a network. T3/HTTP is the T3 protocol tunneled within HTTP packets. T3/HTTP can be used to make RMI calls across a firewall that only permits HTTP traffic. IIOP is the CORBA wire protocol. WebLogic's RMI/IIOP enables Java programs to communicate with legacy CORBA systems. Each of these protocols may also be encrypted with SSL for secure client-server communication.

Using the Remote Interface

Calls to RMI objects are similar to local calls, but there are important differences. To understand these differences, we must discuss the processes of marshaling and unmarshaling used to transmit and receive method calls and return values.

When client code acquires an RMI object, the client really has a proxy to a remote object. When the client calls a method on the local proxy, the proxy marshals the request or converts the request to a message it can send to the remote RMI object. When the remote object passes back a response message, the proxy unmarshals the message and returns it to the client.

Calls to RMI methods must be marshaled because the RMI proxy cannot merely write a native representation of the method call to the wire. For instance, a parameter to a method call is generally passed as a reference to an address in memory. This style of passing parameters is known as pass-by-reference. The RMI server runs in a different environment with different values in memory, so this address reference is meaningless. One marshaling strategy used by the proxy is to encode parameters into a byte stream. The proxy packages this stream into a message and sends the message to a remote RMI object. This encoding process is called *serialization*.

Alternately, parameters and return values can include references to remote objects. These objects must implement the `Remote` interface. The object passed or returned is again a proxy, just like other RMI objects.

In order to support the marshaling and unmarshaling processes, all the parameters and return values for methods in RMI objects must be either serializable or remote.

The Serializable Interface

Java's serialization process enables an object to be converted into a stream. When a Java program reads the stream and reconstitutes the object, the process is known as deserialization. Java applications can use serialization to save an object to a file or to pass a copy of an object to another application.

However, not every object can be serialized. In general, Java cannot serialize references to external resources. For instance, Java cannot serialize a database connection or a network socket. An object with a database connection normally releases the connection before serialization and reacquires the connection after deserialization.

A Java class indicates that it supports serialization by implementing the `java.io.Serializable` interface. The `java.io.Serializable` interface does not contain any methods; it merely acts as a marker to indicate that the class can be serialized. A serializable class must ensure that its member variables are serializable as well. If a member variable should not be serialized (such as a reference to a database connection), declare the variable `transient`. When Java serializes an object, it ignores all transient fields.

The author of a serializable class must also pay attention to the class's superclass. If the superclass is also serializable, then Java stores the class and the superclass in the output stream. If the superclass is not serializable, then serialization succeeds only if the superclass provides a default, no-argument constructor. During serialization, the superclass is not stored in the stream. During deserialization, Java instantiates the superclass using the no-argument constructor. If the superclass neither is serializable nor provides a default constructor, Java throws a `java.io.NotSerializableException` during the serialization process.

When an RMI method call includes a serializable object, the RMI proxy serializes the object and sends the byte stream to the RMI server. The server deserializes the bytes and creates a copy of the original object. Because this is only a copy of the RMI parameter, any changes made in the object are not visible to the client. This calling convention is known as pass-by-value.

Best Practice: Things to remember when passing serializable objects in RMI calls: RMI calls pass serializable objects using pass-by-value; classes marked as `Serializable` should ensure that all member variables are either serializable or marked as transient; and, parent classes of classes marked as `Serializable` should either be serializable or provide a default constructor.

Hand-Coding Serialization

In most cases, Java serialization is an automatic process. However, like most automatic procedures, there are cases when hand-coding the serialization process is advantageous. Java provides an alternative to the automatic serialization of `java.io.Serializable`. Instead, use the `java.io.Externalizable` interface to provide your own serialization and deserialization methods. Programmers generally implement the externalizable interface if they require precise control over their serialized representation or because the performance of Java's serialization is not sufficient. Remember that serializable classes must handle superclasses, so the externalizable class must also handle serialization of its superclasses. The `Externalizable` interface contains two methods:

- `writeExternal(java.io.ObjectOutput)`
- `readExternal(java.io.ObjectInput)`

An `externalizable` class writes its serialized representation in the `writeExternal()` method and reconstitutes itself in the `readExternal()` method. Implementing `externalizable` gives the programmer complete control over serialization; and the `readExternal()` and `writeExternal()` methods can run faster and generate smaller representations than Java's standard serialization process.

However, programmers need to be aware that writing `Externalizable` classes places the burden of serialization on the author of the class. A bug in serialization can lead to bugs that are difficult to find in a large application. Implementing `Externalizable` should be done with caution, but when used appropriately, it can improve the performance of marshaling and unmarshaling method calls.

> **Best Practice:** Use `Externalizable` to optimize marshaling performance only as needed.

Externalizable Example

The `ThreeIntegers` example below shows an example of a class that handles its own serialization. Notice that the class implements `java.io.Externalizable`, writes its fields in `writeExternal()`, and restores its values in `readExternal()`. Also, note that the member variables must be read and written in the same order. As you maintain an externalizable class, you have to be careful to read and write all important variables and, in each method, to handle each variable in the same sequence.

```
public final class ThreeIntegers implements java.io.Externalizable {
    private int a;
    private int b;
    private int c;

    public ThreeIntegers() {}

    public ThreeIntegers(int A, int B, int C) {
        a = A;
        b = B;
        c = C;
```

```
       }

       public void writeExternal(ObjectOutput out) throws IOException {
               out.writeInt(a);
               out.writeInt(b);
               out.writeInt(c);
       }

       public void readExternal(ObjectInput in) throws IOException,
ClassNotFoundException {
               a = in.readInt();
               b = in.readInt();
               c = in.readInt();
       }
}
```

The Remote Interface

All RMI interfaces must extend the `java.rmi.Remote` interface. Like the `Serializable` interface, `Remote` contains no methods but acts as a marker. Use the `Remote` interface to indicate that you can use the interface to access a remote RMI object. `Remote` interfaces can also be used to define parameters or return values for remote methods. For instance, an RMI service may act as a factory for creating other RMI objects. As we discuss in Chapter 9, the EJB home interfaces act as factories which return EJB objects. These EJB objects are examples of RMI objects.

Unlike serializable objects, remote interfaces are not stored by value in the stream. Instead, the proxy automatically replaces the remote interface with a stub during the unmarshaling process. A client can use this stub to call methods on the remote object. The client makes RMI calls through this proxy to the remote RMI object on the server.

Using RMI in Distributed Applications

By design, RMI objects closely resemble local Java objects. Programmers invoke a service on a distant networked server merely by making a method call. RMI's transparency is extremely valuable for programmer productivity because it makes distributing an application a relatively easy task. However, designing scalable, reliable, and high-performance distributed applications is never easy. Distributed programming introduces a whole new class of potential errors.

While RMI might provide the illusion of network transparency, it is important to disregard this illusion and design RMI applications as distributed programs. Distributed programming is a complicated task, and one chapter cannot discuss all the issues. However, we do discuss common mistakes that most programmers trip over at least once during their career.

Handling the Unreliable Network

While it seems obvious when stated in a book, many developers of distributed programs make a cardinal error by ignoring the unreliable and potentially insecure network between the client and server. Even though nearly every Web user has learned to expect Web site outages, it's all too easy to overlook these issues. It's not that programmers are careless, but in many cases, it is difficult to spot all the potential failure scenarios.

Consider an Internet banking application that allows customers to deposit money. Every programmer should see that the deposit needs to run as a transaction to ensure that the account update is atomic and durable. Customers will not accept balance mistakes or lost deposits. However, there are also new failure cases in a distributed application. The transaction infrastructure can automatically handle some of these failure cases. For instance, if the server machine or the database dies during a transaction, the transaction system rolls back partially completed operations. Of course, the client would see an undesirable error message, but customers can try their deposit again later.

Now consider the case where the deposit completes, the transaction commits, but the network fails during the communication with the client. In this case, the client again sees an error message, but in fact, the transaction has completed and the deposit is in the account. In this case, an unsuspecting customer might try the deposit again, not realizing that the previous transaction had in fact completed.

Programmers of distributed systems must consider the potential for failure during any point in the communication path. Sometimes, the only reasonable answer is to display a message to the user that the system is unavailable, and that he or she should contact a person to resolve the problem.

Distributed programs must consider the potential for failure at any point in the communication path.

Performance Implications of Cross-Network Method Calls

Another common distributed programming error is to neglect the impact of making method calls across the network on performance. Local method calls are a relatively cheap operation, but remote calls are usually at least 100 times slower.

There are two main problems with the performance of remote method calls: network bandwidth and latency.

RMI proxies must send method parameters and response values across a network connection, but networks limit how quickly the data is sent. As a result, the time to transmit data depends both on the speed of the network and the amount of data passed between the client and server. Local Java calls do not have this issue because in method calls, objects are passed by reference—Java passes only an address of the object to the method. RMI calls with large parameters might work fine on a local network, but on the Internet, network bandwidth becomes a real issue. Clients connecting from throughout the world across congested networks can see very poor performance, especially if large amounts of data must be transferred between the client and server.

In addition to minimizing the data sent across the network connection, distributed applications must also be concerned with the frequency of remote method calls. Local method calls are relatively inexpensive, and most Java programs can make thousands, if not millions, of method calls per second. Remote method calls across a network wire cannot achieve this level of performance. Programmers need to make this distinction and, where possible, minimize the number of round trips between the RMI client and server. One common pattern is to avoid calling fine-grained methods on a remote object. For instance, a customer might be a remote object. Instead of making individual remote calls to read the customer's name, address, and phone number, the distributed application should make a single remote call that returns all the required information in one network round trip.

Best Practice: Although RMI calls look like local calls, RMI calls can be much slower. Manage the impact of RMI calls on your application by minimizing the data sent over the network and by reducing the number of RMI calls.

WebLogic RMI Optimizations

In some cases, an RMI client and server are located on the same WebLogic Server. This situation is fairly common because EJBs use RMI to handle communication between EJB components. If a servlet needs to call an EJB, it makes an RMI call, although both components might run in the same WebLogic Server. Because this is a common case, the WebLogic Server includes optimizations to make these calls run nearly as fast as direct method calls. Obviously, there is no point in having the client and server communicate over a network connection, so the WebLogic RMI implementation recognizes that the client and server are collocated and no network communication is required.

The WebLogic Server also includes a collocation optimization in which client's call skips the RMI infrastructure and calls directly on the implementation object. This optimization makes the RMI call's performance comparable to a local method call. However, programmers should be aware that because the call is skipping marshaling and unmarshaling, the client and server are using pass-by-reference. While this optimization is a departure from RMI's parameter passing, the semantics should be familiar to programmers. In fact, pass-by-reference is the calling convention used by local Java method calls.

> **Best Practice:** Take advantage of WebLogic's RMI optimizations by collocating components.

Registration and Lookup of RMI Objects

We have discussed the mechanisms and design issues in making RMI calls. But, how do RMI objects make themselves available for access? How do Java applications acquire a remote RMI object? Registration and lookup of Java RMI objects are classic applications of naming services. Java's reference implementation of RMI provides a registry, available using the class `java.rmi.Naming`. In addition, WebLogic RMI can use the naming and lookup services of JNDI. We discuss JNDI, including its application to RMI, in the following section.

JNDI: Java's Naming Service

Naming services are integral to distributed systems. Distributed Java programs require a naming service to locate distributed objects. For example, naming services are used to find RMI objects. The Java specification includes JNDI. JNDI enables servers to host objects and to tag these objects with names. Remote clients acquire references to objects by looking up the object in the JNDI directory using the specified name.

The JNDI architecture consists of a common client interface and a number of JNDI providers that define the back-end naming systems. The Java specification defines a server provider interface (SPI) through which applications can plug JNDI providers into the JNDI system. WebLogic Server includes an implementation of JNDI. This section covers the WebLogic implementation of JNDI and how a user program makes use of the JNDI system.

Using JNDI

A JNDI client interacts with the JNDI system through the classes in the `javax.naming` package. The `javax.naming.Context` interface is the fundamental JNDI object. The `Context` interface provides clients with methods to add, remove, and look up objects in the naming service.

The `javax.naming.InitialContext` class implements the `Context` interface. Clients use this class to interact with the JNDI system. Create an `InitialContext` object with the following code snippet:

```
Context ctx = new InitialContext();
```

When an application creates an `InitialContext` within the WebLogic Server, the caller receives an `InitialContext` that references the JNDI service on the local server. Remote clients can also create `InitialContext` references, but the client must identify the WebLogic JNDI implementation and provide the JNDI client the location of the WebLogic Server. You can explicitly pass these parameters as a `Properties` object to the `InitialContext` constructor:

```
java.util.Properties p = new java.util.Properties();
p.put(Context.INITIAL_CONTEXT_FACTORY, "weblogic.jndi.WLInitialConte
xtFactory");
p.put(Context.PROVIDER_URL, "t3://revere:7001");
Context ctx = new InitialContext(p);
```

In this example, we create a `Properties` object and specify the WebLogic JNDI implementation and the address of the WebLogic Server JNDI provider. For example, in this case, we are creating a connection to the machine named `revere` on port 7001.

Your can use the default constructor even outside WebLogic Server, but you must pass the `InitialContext` factory and URL of the WebLogic server instance as properties. One option is to define the Java properties on the command line with

```
-Djava.naming.factory.initial=weblogic.jndi.WLInitialContextFactory
```

and

```
-Djava.naming.provider.url="t3://revere:7001"
```

Another option is to specify the factory and the URL in a `jndi.properties` file. This properties file is a Java resource file. For instance, our `jndi.properties` file would contain

```
java.naming.factory.initial=weblogic.jndi.WLInitialContextFactory
java.naming.provider.url="t3://revere:7001"
```

With the `InitialContext` object, the JNDI client can store objects in the naming system. Like RMI parameters, an object stored in JNDI must implement `java.io.Serializable`, `java.io.Externalizable`, or `java.rmi.Remote`. Use the bind method of the `InitialContext` object to establish a mapping from a name to an object in the JNDI tree. For instance, this example binds a `String` object to the name `Chapter7`.

```
Context ctx = new InitialContext();
String s = "Test String.";
ctx.bind("Chapter7", s);
```

The `bind()` method call establishes a mapping between the name `Chapter7` and our string. Clients can now use the name `Chapter7` in calls to the WebLogic Server's JNDI system to receive a copy of our `String`. If the bound object implemented `java.rmi.Remote`, the `bind()` method would make the local object available for use by RMI clients. Note that the bind call fails if an object named `Chapter7` already exists in this JNDI tree.

Use the `rebind()` call to reassign an already existing name. If there is no current mapping for the given name, `rebind()` behaves like `bind()`.

```
Context ctx = new InitialContext();
String s = "New Test String.";
ctx.rebind("Chapter7", s);
```

Delete mappings with the `unbind()` method. For instance, the following code fragment removes the object we just bound:

```
ctx.unbind("Chapter7");
```

A client uses the `InitialContext`'s lookup method to get a reference to an object in the naming service. For instance, after our call to bind, there is a mapping from the name `Chapter7` to our string. The client can get a reference to this object with

```
Context ctx = new InitialContext();
String s = (String) ctx.lookup("Chapter7");
```

Because `java.lang.String` is a `Serializable` object, the client receives a copy of the bound object. If the object implements the `java.rmi.Remote` interface, the client receives a stub object. Thus, use the `bind()` method to register RMI objects. Use the `lookup()` method to acquire an RMI stub.

> **Best Practice:** Whenever possible, use the `InitialContext` default constructor. Standalone clients should use the `jndi.properties` file to specify attributes. Clients within a WebLogic Server should set the `PROVIDER_URL` property only to access another WebLogic Server (or other JNDI provider). Clients within a WebLogic Server should not set the `PROVIDER_URL` property to acquire the `InitialContext` of the local server. If you do provide a URL, WebLogic Server will unnecessarily use a network connection. Further, startup classes run before WebLogic Server begins listening for network connections, and the `InitialContext` constructor will fail.

JNDI, Security, and Identity

In addition to providing an object naming service, JNDI can also establishes a client's identity within the server. By default, `InitialContext` objects are created by the guest user. When a client creates an `InitialContext`, the client can specify a user name and password. The WebLogic security system authenticates the user-password combination. If the password is invalid, the constructor throws a `javax.naming.NoPermissionException`. With a valid password, the `InitialContext` constructor establishes the client identity on the server.

Many resources in the WebLogic Server can be protected by Access Control Lists (ACLs). Use an ACL to grant access only to specified users. Then, create an `InitialContext` with a user name and password to specify a user with access rights. For instance, this example establishes the identity of `Paul` within the server:

```
Properties p = new Properties();      // Set WebLogic as the JNDI Provider
p.put(Context.INITIAL_CONTEXT_FACTORY,"weblogic.jndi.WLInitialContextFactory");

// Set the URL to machine named revere, port 7001
p.put(Context.PROVIDER_URL, "t3://revere:7001");

// Login as user Paul
p.put(Context.SECURITY_PRINCIPAL, "Paul");

// and the password
p.put(Context.SECURITY_CREDENTIALS, "Bee");

Context ctx = new InitialContext(p);
```

JNDI and Clustering

From the client's perspective, a WebLogic cluster should appear to be a single, high-performance, fault-tolerant server. This idea carries over to the WebLogic cluster's shared JNDI naming service. The naming service is fault-tolerant because the naming service survives server failures in the cluster. As new servers join the cluster, they automatically participate in the naming service. The multiple copies of the naming service improve performance because each server runs the naming service in parallel, and client requests can be processed on many servers simultaneously.

Replicated Naming Service

Each WebLogic Server maintains its own copy of the cluster's naming service. The advantage of this approach is performance. Each naming service is able to locally cache the cluster's naming tree and handle any naming request out of its own memory. This approach also provides transparency. To a client, a naming service is identical regardless of which clustered server is contacted. However, any distributed caching mechanism must keep the local cache data up to data. Whenever a change occurs in the JNDI tree, the other servers must be notified. For instance, when a new object is bound into the JNDI tree at a given name, every naming service must be made aware of the new mapping (see Figure 6–2).

WebLogic maintains a cluster-wide service through network updates. Each clustered WebLogic Server sends its JNDI updates over multicast messages to the other members of the cluster. IP multicast delivers a single message to a number of recipients. In this case, WebLogic Server addresses multicast messages to all the servers in the cluster. For tightly coupled clusters, multicast messages are much more efficient than multiple point-to-point connections because the WebLogic Server sends a single message rather than one for each cluster member.

When a clustered server receives a JNDI change from another server, it updates its local cached copy of the JNDI tree. It is possible for the update to conflict with another object in the cached copy of the JNDI tree. We discuss how this is possible and suggest solutions in a later section.

WebLogic Server's clustered naming service is designed for high performance and to minimize network traffic between servers. However, individual caches may return data that is invalid because it

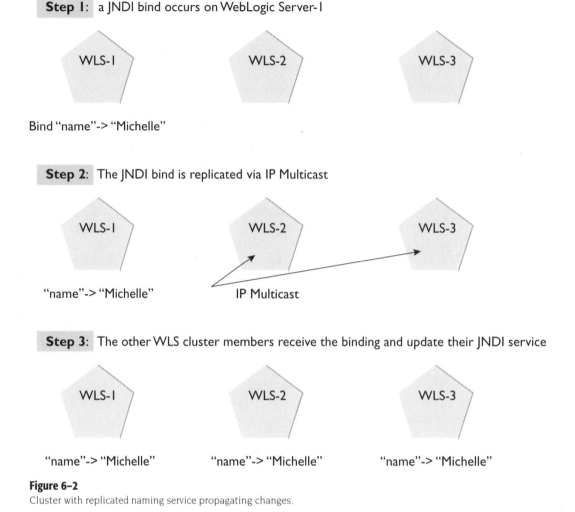

Step 1: a JNDI bind occurs on WebLogic Server-1

Bind "name"-> "Michelle"

Step 2: The JNDI bind is replicated via IP Multicast

"name"-> "Michelle"   IP Multicast

Step 3: The other WLS cluster members receive the binding and update their JNDI service

"name"-> "Michelle"   "name"-> "Michelle"   "name"-> "Michelle"

Figure 6–2
Cluster with replicated naming service propagating changes.

is slightly out of date. Updates may occur on one server, but may have not reached another server's cache. In general, this is not an issue. Because JNDI is a naming service, it is used to advertise services and objects residing on particular servers. JNDI updates are only sent when a JNDI bind, rebind, or unbind occurs within the cluster. These changes to the JNDI tree are relatively rare. Network traffic and coherency are generally not an issue with the WebLogic Server's JNDI implementation.

Understanding Conflicts in the JNDI tree

WebLogic provides a way to create local bindings. When binding an object to the WebLogic JNDI service, application code can specify whether this binding should be replicated to the other clustered servers. By default, bindings are replicated, and the WebLogic Server will send a multicast message to update the other cluster members. If you specify that the binding should not be replicated, the JNDI service only updates the local cache. Specify whether the WebLogic JNDI service should replicate bindings before you create the `InitialContext`.

```
java.util.Properties props = new Properties();
props.put(weblogic.jndi.WLContext.REPLICATE_BINDINGS, "true");
Context ctx = new InitialContext(props);
ctx.rebind("Chapter7", s);
```

Clustered JNDI with Replicated Bindings

By default, the WebLogic JNDI service replicates bindings to the other servers within the cluster. If the object you are binding is an RMI object, the semantics of replicated binding depends on whether or not the RMI object is marked as clustered.

If an RMI object is marked as clustered, the JNDI tree aggregates the clustered objects. When a clustered object is bound into the JNDI tree, its server is added to the list of servers offering that service. As long as every server binds in the same type, every server can offer a clustered object under a given name. This enables the WebLogic cluster to map a single JNDI name to a service offered by multiple cluster members.

Nonclustered RMI objects do not receive special treatment. When replicated bindings are used, a nonclustered object may not be bound to the same name on multiple servers. This condition is known as a conflict. On the second `bind()` call, WebLogic will detect this collision as an error. JNDI conflicts indicate that the WebLogic Servers have been misconfigured.

With replicated bindings, only a single server may bind a nonclustered object to a given name. JNDI conflicts are configuration errors and must be resolved manually by the WebLogic Server administrator.

> **Best Practice:** Normally, WebLogic Server compiles Java classes to create RMI proxies. The only time you need to use the compiler yourself is to mark RMI objects as clusterable. Run the WebLogic Server RMI compiler using the line

```
java weblogic.rmic –clusterable classname
```

This compiler creates a file called `classnameRTD.xml` to identify the class as clusterable to the RMI compiler at runtime. Note: Clusterable RMI objects cannot contain client state. Future requests may be directed to another WebLogic Server. See the RMI compiler documentation at *http://edocs.bea.com/wls/docs81/rmi/index.html*.

Clustered JNDI with Nonreplicated Bindings

When the JNDI context is created without replicated bindings, WebLogic Server does not send a multicast update when the JNDI bind occurs. Nonreplicated bindings can be useful to avoid JNDI conflicts. For instance, an application might read configuration details into a `Properties` object and bind the `Properties` object into the JNDI tree. Because this `Properties` object is not an RMI object, the JNDI system will identify a conflict if multiple servers attempt to `bind()` to a single name. With nonreplicated bindings, each server binds its own copy of the `Properties` object. Since the JNDI system does not replicate the bindings, there are no conflicts.

> **Best Practice:** Use nonreplicated bindings to store server-specific configuration information.

JNDI Best Practices

As with any distributed program, JNDI clients need to be concerned with performance and scalability. As with RMI calls, WebLogic Server optimizes JNDI lookups using local Java calls where possible. Therefore, a lookup within the WebLogic Server is an efficient operation. JNDI clients running within the server should not generally bother to minimize lookups using the naming service.

However, remote clients should consider minimizing the number of lookup calls. Each lookup requires a round trip between the client and server. Like any remote interaction, each lookup request must travel across the network connection between client and server. If lookups are performed repeatedly, repeated lookups can degrade application performance.

Local Caching

Where appropriate, you should consider caching the results of lookup. For instance, you might use JNDI to store a remote object containing runtime properties. Instead of accessing this object multiple times to read individual configuration properties, a client should perform a single lookup and read all the properties into a local object. Use the local object to read each runtime property. Use caching of JNDI lookups with care. If JNDI data is subject to frequent change, the local cache is likely to be out of date. On the other hand, if data is subject to frequent change, consider alternatives to JNDI. Consider local caching to avoid repeated JNDI lookups from remote clients.

Perform Lookups During Initialization

Perform as many JNDI lookups as possible during component initialization. For instance, it is better to look up a JDBC `DataSource` in a Servlet `init()` method and store it for future use than to look it up on every request.

Cache the InitialContext

While WebLogic Server optimizes JNDI lookups, requests to acquire an `InitialContext` can take some time. Again, use caching to improve application performance. Create the `InitialContext` once during component initialization and save it for future lookup requests. In a servlet or JSP, you can acquire the `InitialContext` within the `init()` method. For EJBs, use the `setSessionContext()`, `setEntityContext()`, or `setMessageDrivenContext()` method depending on the EJB type. You can store the `InitialContext` in a member variable or, for a servlet or JSP, in the `ServletContext`. Use the saved `InitialContext` to complete JNDI operations later in the application lifecycle.

In the previous chapter on servlets, we cautioned you regarding use of member variables. Servlets and JSPs typically run in a multithreaded environment, and multiple threads may access a servlet and member variables concurrently. Fortunately, the `InitialContext` object is thread-safe. Multiple threads can safely access an `InitialContext` at the same time. For lookups that cannot be performed during initialization, use an `InitialContext` in a member variable.

Minimizing Frequency of Updates

Remember that JNDI is merely a naming service. JNDI is not appropriate for every kind of data. In particular, JNDI is a poor place to store information that changes frequently. WebLogic Server's implementation of the JNDI service is optimized for read-mostly use. Each instance of WebLogic Server in a cluster maintains a copy of the entire JNDI tree. While this design makes lookup operations very fast, it adds overhead to update operations. WebLogic server must transmit updates to the JNDI tree to each of the other servers in the cluster. For instance, do not modify the JNDI tree with every RMI call. This approach does not scale, because the size of JNDI updates can grow quite large. Further, the update operation does not take place in real time. Clients performing `lookup()` operations may not retrieve the latest data.

Conclusion

RMI and JNDI are core services offered by the WebLogic Server to enable scalable, distributed applications. While RMI and JNDI make distributed programming much easier, it is important to understand the limitations and potential failure cases inherent in networked applications. As we see in the following chapters, core J2EE services such as EJB and Java Message Service (JMS) are built on top of RMI and JNDI.

References

WebLogic Documentation – Programming RMI: *http://edocs.bea.com/wls/docs81/rmi/index.html.*
WebLogic Documentation – Programming JNDI: *http://edocs.bea.com/wls/docs81/jndi/index.html.*

chapter 7

Enterprise Messaging with the Java Message Service (JMS)

In This Chapter

- The fundamentals of JMS, describing and illustrating both point-to-point and publish-and-subscribe messaging
- JMS queuing mechanisms for point-to-point messaging, with examples
- JMS topic creation for publish-and-subscribe messaging, with examples
- Configuring JMS messages
- JMS and transactions
- How JMS works in a WebLogic Server cluster
- JMS exception handling
- Best practices for using JMS in WebLogic Server applications

The Java Message Service (JMS) specification describes a standard enterprise messaging service for Java 2 Enterprise Edition (J2EE) applications. A JMS implementation acts as an intelligent switchboard for routing messages among application components and processes in a distributed application. JMS puts messages on queues and can deliver them asynchronously: messaging need not take place in real time, and messages can be sent and consumed at different times. JMS is an abstraction of the proprietary MOM (message-oriented middleware) protocols and models in use today. The benefit of JMS is that it is a standard by which you can access and manipulate messages on any JMS-compliant MOM implementation.

Benefits of JMS

There are a number of reasons to use a messaging system for interprocess communication instead of making direct method calls. A messaging system provides a clean way to connect disparate systems within an application or across applications. Messaging systems also help divide long-running work into multiple transactions for greater efficiency. When communication is asynchronous, the client need not wait for all of the processing to complete. Once the message has been successfully queued, the client can resume processing.

Messaging systems also provide reliability (or "guaranteed delivery"). JMS can optionally save a message to a persistent store. There is, however, a tradeoff between reliability and performance. The messaging system runs faster if messages are not persistent, but the application must tolerate lost messages in the event of a server crash. Messaging systems also enable clients to disconnect and reconnect to the server without losing work. JMS can be configured to save messages while the client is disconnected and deliver them once the client has reconnected. Unlike method calls on a single object, JMS allows sending a single message to many recipients.

Another benefit is the ability to take part in distributed transactions through transaction-processing (TP) monitors. For example, if you are parsing XML data from a JMS message and wish to write insert statements to move the data to the RDBMS, you could wrap the database transaction together with the JMS delivery so that if the message is unable to be parsed and inserted into the database, the delivery would fail as well.

Scalability is another benefit of JMS. For example, if your e-commerce Web site traffic jumps up to 50 times the normal rate, starting database-intensive transaction-processing threads to fulfill each order would introduce contention issues. Alternately, if you have a single thread able to pull these requests from a queue, your application will not be impacted by waiting on locked rows in the RDBMS.

Interprocess Communication

Most large systems are divided into several separate functional units. JMS provides reliable communication between these separate processes. For instance, an application might include a Web front end for customer order entry. A warehouse then receives the order, packages the appropriate items, and forwards the order to the shipping department. Finally, the shipping department sends the package and updates the customer's account records.

Note: JMS provides the communication backbone for workflow applications.

Point-to-Point Messaging

The order-fulfillment application uses JMS's point-to-point (PTP) messaging model to provide reliable communication within this multistage application. In PTP communication, a message is written to a queue and stored in order of delivery. The messages in the queue are processed by message consumers and are delivered in PTP order (assuming a single destination with the same JMS priority; otherwise, first in, first out [FIFO] ordering is not guaranteed). PTP delivers each message to a single message consumer. For instance, in the e-commerce application mentioned above, the Web front end sends a message including the new order information. The message is placed on a queue. A single warehouse receives the message and processes the order. The JMS provider guarantees that multiple warehouses do not fill the same order. This application may also use JMS's reliability guarantees. Because customer orders are important information that should be retained, the developer may request JMS to mark these messages as persistent. With persistent messages, JMS saves the message contents to a persistent store such as a database or file store. This guarantees that the message will survive a shutdown of the server supporting the queue. The message will remain in the queue until it is processed by a message consumer or its time-to-live (TTL) expires.

Publish-Subscribe Messaging

In addition to PTP communication, JMS provides a publish-and-subscribe messaging model. With publish-subscribe messaging (also known as pub/sub), a message is sent to a named *topic*. Multiple message consumers may subscribe to a single topic. The JMS subsystem delivers a copy of the message to each of the topic's subscribers. Messages can be marked as durable or nondurable. If a message is marked nondurable, it is removed from the topic once all connected subscribers have received the message. Otherwise, it is held in the topic until after all subscribers (connected or not) have processed the message or until its TTL expires. For instance, an e-commerce site might define a frequent-customer topic. When a customer makes several purchases, a message is sent to this topic. The site can then send "special deals" messages to a select group of listeners, the frequent customers. Because there might be several message listeners, each being offered a separate special deal, it is appropriate to use pub/sub instead of PTP communication.

JMS Fundamentals

The WebLogic Server's JMS implementation supports both PTP and pub/sub APIs as defined by the JMS specification. It also supports the fundamental objects defined by the JMS APIs in both PTP and pub/sub domains, as we will see later. It is important to understand that WebLogic JMS provides additional functionality not described by the JMS specification to facilitate the building of enterprise-class J2EE applications. Where appropriate, those distinctions are noted in this text. Before diving in to WebLogic-specific functionality, we look at the fundamental objects defined by the JMS APIs. Each object is separately defined in the PTP and pub/sub domains, but their function is nearly identical in both domains.

Connection Factories

Connection factories are created by the server administrator and bound into the Java Naming and Directory Interface (JNDI) tree at startup. A JMS client (your application) uses JNDI to look up the connection factory and then uses the connection factory to establish a JMS connection. Multiple connection factories can be created and assigned to each WebLogic Server instance or to a cluster of instances. WebLogic has two default connection factories: `weblogic.jms.ConnectionFactory` and `weblogic.jms.XAConnectionFactory`. These connection factories are enabled by default and support the deprecated PTP connection factory `javax.jms.QueueConnectionFactory` and the pub/sub domain factory `javax.jms.TopicConnectionFactory`.

It is possible to define additional connection factories with the WebLogic Server's administration console. An application uses a user-defined `ConnectionFactory` to impose additional security constraints on the connection factory, if needed.

In general, it's good practice to create connection factories specific to your application. This allows flexibility not available when using the default connection factories. A connection factory is created by the administrator using the WebLogic console. You can create the connection factory by accessing the *Connection Factories* folder in the navigation bar. Configuration settings include message delivery attributes like TTL, acknowledge strategy, distributed destination defaults for load balancing, and other characteristics of WebLogic JMS mentioned throughout this chapter.

Connections

A JMS connection represents the active connection between the JMS client and the WebLogic Server. The JMS client creates the JMS connection by calling the `createQueueConnection` or the `createTopicConnection` methods on the `ConnectionFactory`. A JMS connection is a relatively heavyweight object, and normally each client uses a single JMS connection. Each JMS connection can be associated with many JMS destinations. JMS connections are thread-safe, and more than one JMS connection to the messaging system is not required (although useful in some cases). The PTP connection is `javax.jms.QueueConnection`; the pub/sub connection is `javax.jms.TopicConnection`. These objects facilitate authentication, registering callbacks if necessary, sessioning, and the like. These connection objects can be created by calling the corresponding methods in the connection factories.

Sessions

A JMS session represents a client's conversational state with a JMS Server. As mentioned above, a session is created from the JMS connection, and it represents a single thread of conversation between a JMS client and server. This means that if your application expects a session to support multiple threads, it is up to you to build in support for that feature. Sessions define message ordering, and JMS uses sessions for transactional messaging. The PTP model uses `javax.jms.QueueSession`; the pub/sub model uses `javax.jms.TopicSession`. Transacted sessions and nontransacted sessions are discussed later in this chapter; these mechanisms allow the JMS consumer to inform the provider that it has finished processing the message.

Destinations

JMS destinations are the actual messaging resource for producers and consumers. PTP messaging defines `javax.jms.Queue`; pub/sub includes `javax.jms.Topic`. The server administrator uses the WebLogic console to create destinations with a specified JNDI name. The JMS client then performs a JNDI lookup to locate the JMS destination, and creates a corresponding producer or consumer. Temporary destinations for a particular JMS connection can be specified in the message header to indicate to the receiver where to respond to the message.

Table 7–1 compares the terminology for PTP and pub/sub APIs in the JMS specification (note that WebLogic 8.1 provides weblogic.jms.ConnectionFactory and deprecates javax.jms.Queue ConnectionFactory and javax.jms.TopicConnectionFactory).

Table 7–1 Comparing PTP and Pub/Sub APIs

	PTP	Pub/Sub
Connection Factory	QueueConnectionFactory	TopicConnectionFactory
Connection	QueueConnection	TopicConnection
Session	QueueSession	TopicSession
Destination	Queue	Topic

Sample JMS Queue Producer/Consumer

This section demonstrates simple JMS PTP and pub/sub message producers and consumers.

Configuring JMS

First, create a directory to use as a JMS file store in the filesystem. Create a directory called *jms_store* at the root level of your WebLogic Server installation.

Then, configure the JMS file store using the WebLogic Server administration console. Select JMS under the *Services* folder for your project, then select *Stores*. Figure 7–1 shows a JMS store named MyJMSFileStore that is mapped to the directory *jms_store*.

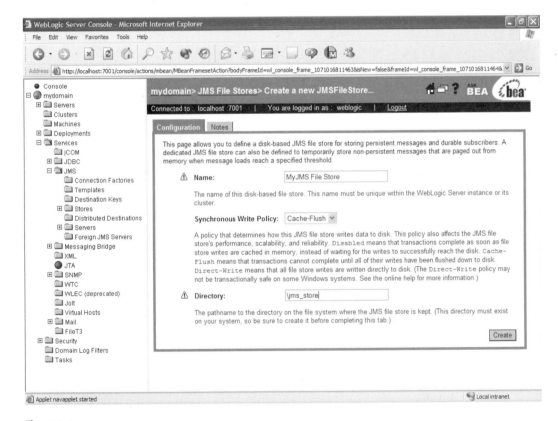

Figure 7–1
Creating the JMS Store.

Creating the JMS Server

Next, the WebLogic Server administrator configures a JMS Server with the administration console. All JMS-administered objects such as destinations or connection factories exist within a JMS Server. Each WebLogic Server instance can include multiple JMS Server instances. Because these examples use persistent messages, the server administrator has specified a message store, the file-based storage previously created (see Figure 7–2).

The server administrator can also create JMS connection factories at this time by going to the Connection Factories folder. Because these examples do not require any special configuration parameters, we can use the standard connection factories.

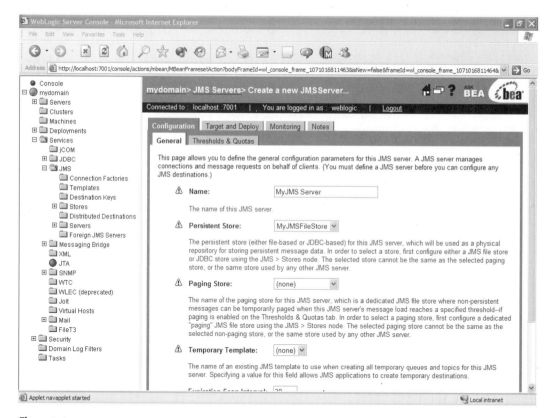

Figure 7–2a
Creating the JMS Server.

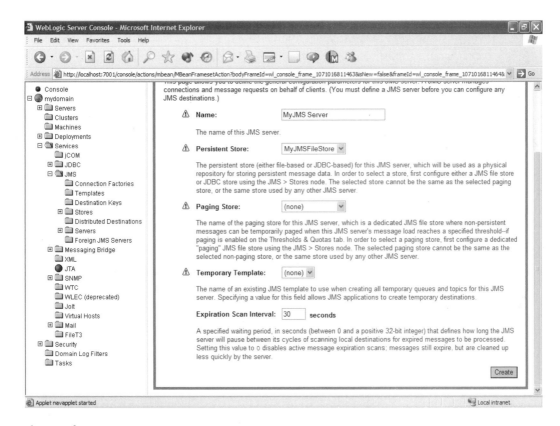

Figure 7–2b
Creating the JMS Server.

Administrator Creates JMS Destinations

After configuring the JMS Server, the server administrator creates the JMS destinations (access the Destinations folder under the Server folder). The application looks up the destination using JNDI (JNDI lookups are costly, so the application should cache the destination after a single lookup). These examples require a JMS queue named `MessageQueue` and a JMS topic named `Message-Topic` (see Figure 7–3).

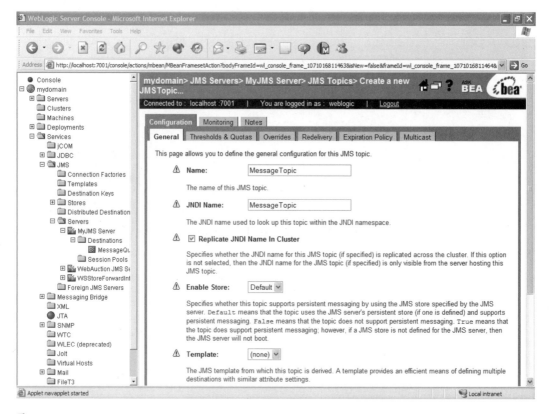

Figure 7–3a
Creating a JMS Queue.

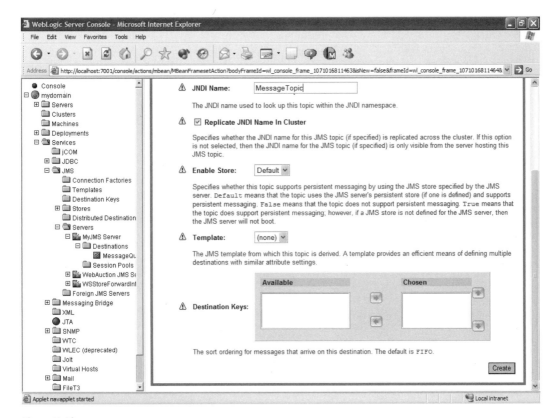

Figure 7–3b
Creating a JMS Queue.

Sample JMS Queue Producer/Consumer

This example demonstrates a message producer, a synchronous message consumer, and an asynchronous message consumer for a JMS queue.

Message Producer

The message producer begins by creating a JNDI InitialContext and looking up the JMS QueueConnectionFactory. Because our examples use the standard JMS connection factories, it looks up weblogic.jms.ConnectionFactory.

```
Context ctx = getInitialContext();
QueueConnectionFactory qConFactory =
     (QueueConnectionFactory)
     ctx.lookup("weblogic.jms.ConnectionFactory");
```

Now the `MessageProducer` looks up the JMS destination in JNDI. The server administrator created the JMS queue with the JNDI name `MessageQueue`. The WebLogic Server binds the queue into the JNDI tree, making it available to clients.

```
Queue messageQueue = (Queue) ctx.lookup("MessageQueue");
```

The message producer now creates the `QueueConnection` and a `QueueSession`. The parameters to the `createQueueSession` call specify that it is nontransacted and uses automatic message acknowledgment. Using transactions with JMS and message acknowledgment is covered later in this chapter.

```
QueueConnection qCon = qConFactory.createQueueConnection();

QueueSession session = qCon.createQueueSession(
    false, /* not a transacted session */
    Session.AUTO_ACKNOWLEDGE
);
```

Finally, the message producer creates a sender and a JMS message. This message is a `Text-Message` and includes only a string.

```
QueueSender sender = session.createSender(messageQueue);

TextMessage msg = session.createTextMessage();
```

The message producer is now prepared to send messages. The `TextMessage`'s `setText` method attaches our `Hello` string to the message. The `QueueSender`'s send method sends our message to the persistent queue. When the send call returns, the message producer may send another message.

```
msg.setText("Hello");
sender.send(msg);
```

Synchronous Message Consumer

The message consumer begins with an initialization code that is nearly identical to the message producer. The `QueueConnectionFactory` and queue are found in JNDI. Next, a `QueueConnection` and `QueueSession` are created.

```
Context ctx = getInitialContext();

QueueConnectionFactory qConFactory = (QueueConnectionFactory)
    ctx.lookup("weblogic.jms.ConnectionFactory");

Queue messageQueue = (Queue) ctx.lookup("MessageQueue");
```

```
QueueConnection qCon = qConFactory.createQueueConnection();

QueueSession session = qCon.createQueueSession(
  false, /* not a transacted session */
  Session.AUTO_ACKNOWLEDGE
);
```

The message consumer next creates a `QueueReceiver` from the `QueueSession`. Finally, the start method is called on the `QueueConnection`. Message delivery is inhibited until the start method is invoked. This allows a message consumer to finish initialization before messages become available.

```
QueueReceiver receiver = session.createReceiver(messageQueue);

qCon.start();
```

A synchronous message consumer uses the `receive()` method to ask JMS for the next message on this destination. The receive method blocks until a message is available on this destination. This client then uses the `TextMessage`'s `getText` method to retrieve the message string and prints it to the screen.

```
TextMessage msg = (TextMessage) receiver.receive();

System.err.println("Received: "+msg.getText());
```

Asynchronous Message Consumer

The asynchronous message consumer begins with the same set of initialization code as a synchronous message consumer.

```
Context ctx = getInitialContext();

    QueueConnectionFactory qConFactory = (QueueConnectionFactory)
      ctx.lookup("weblogic.jms.ConnectionFactory");

    Queue messageQueue = (Queue) ctx.lookup("MessageQueue");

    QueueConnection qCon = qConFactory.createQueueConnection();

    QueueSession session = qCon.createQueueSession(
      false, /* not a transacted session */
      Session.AUTO_ACKNOWLEDGE
    );

    receiver = session.createReceiver(messageQueue);
```

An asynchronous message consumer must use the receiver's `setMessageListener` method and pass an object that implements the `javax.jms.MessageListener` interface. Finally, the `QueueConnection`'s start method begins message delivery.

```
receiver.setMessageListener(this);

qCon.start();
```

Because this is an asynchronous consumer, the JMS implementation delivers messages by calling the `onMessage` method of the `MessageListener` object that was registered. This simple implementation just prints out the message's text and returns.

```
public void onMessage(Message m) {
    TextMessage msg = (TextMessage) m;

    System.err.println("Received: "+msg.getText());
}
```

Because message delivery is asynchronous, the client program is not blocked, waiting for messages to arrive. And, because our simple example program has no other work to perform, it exits before the messages can be delivered. To prevent this, we introduce an artificial wait to ensure that the program does not exit before the producer's messages are delivered.

Sample *JMS Topic Producer/Consumer*

The JMS topic example demonstrates publishing messages to a `MessageTopic` and synchronous and asynchronous message consumers. Because this is a topic, both consumers can run simultaneously and receive each message.

Message Producer

Like the JMS queue examples, the topic message producer begins by using JNDI to look up the ConnectionFactory and JMS destination. This example uses the standard JMS `ConnectionFactory`, so it looks up `weblogic.jms.ConnectionFactory`.

```
Context ctx = getInitialContext();

TopicConnectionFactory tConFactory = (TopicConnectionFactory)
    ctx.lookup("weblogic.jms.ConnectionFactory");

Topic messageTopic = (Topic) ctx.lookup("MessageTopic");

TopicConnection tCon = tConFactory.createTopicConnection();

TopicSession session = tCon.createTopicSession(
    false, /* not a transacted session */
    Session.AUTO_ACKNOWLEDGE
);
```

A topic message producer creates a `TopicPublisher` instead of a `QueueSender` and uses this object to publish messages to the topic.

```
    TopicPublisher publisher =
session.createPublisher(messageTopic);

    TextMessage msg = session.createTextMessage();

    msg.setText("Hello");
    publisher.publish(msg);
```

Synchronous Message Consumer

The topic's synchronous message consumer begins with the standard JMS initialization code.

```
Context ctx = getInitialContext();

 TopicConnectionFactory tConFactory = (TopicConnectionFactory)
     ctx.lookup("weblogic.jms.ConnectionFactory");

 Topic messageTopic = (Topic) ctx.lookup("MessageTopic");

  TopicConnection tCon = tConFactory.createTopicConnection();

  TopicSession session = tCon.createTopicSession(
     false, /* not a transacted session */
     Session.AUTO_ACKNOWLEDGE
   );
```

A topic consumer creates a `TopicSubscriber` object from the JMS session. The `TopicSubscriber` is then used to receive messages.

```
TopicSubscriber subscriber = session.createSubscriber(messageTopic);

tCon.start();

msg = (TextMessage) subscriber.receive();

System.err.println("Received: "+msg.getText());
```

Asynchronous Message Consumer

The asynchronous topic consumer begins with the standard JMS initialization code to find the ConnectionFactory and topic, and creates the `TopicSession` and `TopicSubscriber`. Because this is an asynchronous consumer, the client must call the subscriber's `setMessageListener` method.

```
Context ctx = getInitialContext();

    TopicConnectionFactory tConFactory = (TopicConnectionFactory)
        ctx.lookup("weblogic.jms.ConnectionFactory");

    Topic messageTopic = (Topic) ctx.lookup("MessageTopic");

    TopicConnection tCon = tConFactory.createTopicConnection();

    TopicSession session = tCon.createTopicSession(
        false, /* not a transacted session */
        Session.AUTO_ACKNOWLEDGE
    );

    subscriber = session.createSubscriber(messageTopic);

    subscriber.setMessageListener(this);

    tCon.start();
```

The JMS implementation delivers messages asynchronously by calling the onMessage method of the MessageListener object registered. This simple client prints out the text message and returns.

```
public void onMessage(Message m) {

    TextMessage msg = (TextMessage) m;

    System.err.println("Received: "+msg.getText());
}
```

JMS Messages

While our simple examples exchange only string messages, there are several possible JMS message types. Every JMS message type is a subclass of javax.jms.Message. The different message types merely dictate the type of the message contents. JMS message types include TextMessage, ObjectMessage, BytesMessage, StreamMessage, and MapMessage, to name a few. Available message types are outlined later in this chapter.

A JMS message consists of a header, a set of properties, and the message body.

JMS Header

The JMS header includes a standard set of fields defined in the JMS specification. The javax.jms.Message type includes a get and set method for each of the JMS header fields. The header fields are named metadata values used by the application to provide further information about the message.

Many JMS header fields contain basic information about the message, and these are commonly used to filter messages. This is done in JMS with selectors and is covered in detail later in this chapter.

JMS header fields also can be used by the application code. For instance, the `JMSReplyTo` can be used by the application programmer for a request/response application. The sender sets the `JMSReplyTo` header field to a response JMS destination. When the consumer processes the message, a response is sent to the `ReplyTo` destination (see Table 7–2).

Table 7–2 The JMS Header Fields

Name	Set by	Description
JMSDestination	Send Method	The `JMSDestination` includes the destination name to which the message was sent. The WebLogic Server sets it automatically after the `send()` method completes.
JMSDeliveryMode	Send Method	The `JMSDeliveryMode` specifies whether this is a persistent or nonpersistent message. A persistent message is stored on a message store such as a filesystem or database so that it survives a server crash.
JMSExpiration	Send Method	The `JMSExpiration` defines when the message has expired and will be removed from the system. This field depends on the (TTL specified when the message was sent. By default, messages have a TTL of 0 and a `JMSExpiration` of 0, which means they will never expire.
JMSPriority	Send Method	The `JMSPriority` specifies the priority (0–9) of the message. Message priorities from 0–4 indicate normal priority, while priorities from 5–9 are expedited priority. The default priority is 4.
JMSMessageID	Send Method	The `JMSMessageID` contains a string that uniquely identifies the message. The ID starts with `ID:` and is generated automatically by the WebLogic Server.
JMSTimestamp	Send Method	The `JMSTimestamp` is a long value that represents a timestamp of when the message was accepted for delivery by WebLogic's JMS system.
JMSCorrelationID	Application	The `JMSCorrelationID` is an arbitrary string that can be set by the application before sending the message. This can be used to correlate requests and responses by storing the `JMSMessageID` of the request in the `JMSCorrelationID` of the response. Another common use of this header field is linking several messages together in an application-specific manner. For instance, if an order consisted of multiple messages, the order number could be included in the `JMSCorrelationID` to allow the consumer to associate all of the messages together with a single order.

Table 7–2   The JMS Header Fields *(continued)*

Name	Set by	Description
JMSReplyTo	Application	The JMSReplyTo header is a JMS destination that the consumer can use to send a response. Note that this field only passes a destination to the consumer; it does not guarantee that the consumer will actually send a response to this destination. This is the responsibility of the application code.
JMSType	Application	The JMSType enables the application to associate this message with a message type. This message type is an arbitrary java.lang.String, and it may be used if applications want to distinguish messages based on an application-specific type.
JMSRedelivered	WebLogic Server	The JMSRedelivered flag is set when a JMS message is redelivered because the receiver failed to acknowledge the message or because the session is being recovered. Message acknowledgment is covered in detail later in this chapter.

Message Properties

JMS also provides message properties. A JMS message producer can set application-specific property values in the message. The properties are transmitted with the messages and may be read by JMS message consumers.

Properties are name/value pairs and are set with the setObjectProperty or the type-specific setProperty calls on javax.jms.Message. The valid property types are boolean, byte, double, float, int, long, short, and java.lang.String.

For instance, a message producer can set the property named "MyProperty" to the value 4 with

```
msg.setIntProperty("MyProperty", 4);
```

Properties are useful for associating application-specific metadata with a message. They are generally used for message filtering with JMS selectors. JMS selectors are covered in detail later in this chapter.

Message Types

There are five standard JMS message types, and the WebLogic JMS implementation defines an additional XML message type.

JMS Message Types

Table 7–3 lists the JMS message types.

Table 7-3   JMS Message Types

Message Type	Description
StreamMessage	This message type consists of a serialized stream of objects. The objects must be read from the stream in the order they were written. This type is typically used for the objects associated with Java primitives.
MapMessage	A message consisting of name/value pairs. Like a hash table, these are unordered, and each name must be unique within the map. Again, the values are typically the objects associated with Java primitives (java.lang.Integer, and so on).
TextMessage	A message type to hold a text string.
ObjectMessage	A message that holds a serialized object. Note: Java serialization relies on class version affinity between message sender and receiver, resulting in tight coupling.
BytesMessage	A raw stream of bytes. Clients who need complete control over the raw message format use this message type.
XMLMessage	The WebLogic JMS implementation extends the TextMessage type with the XMLMessage to provide optimized delivery and selection of XML messages (XPATH message selectors can be run on the message body).

Messages with XML payloads incur processing overhead not associated with other message types. The XMLMessage type should be used only where the advantages (interoperability, and so on) outweigh the cost of parsing XML-based messages. In every case, it is good practice to select the simplest message type that will meet your needs.

Reusing Message Objects

A JMS Message object can be reused for many messages. When a message is sent, the JMS provider copies the associated message data into an internal buffer before the send call returns control to the caller. Once the send call has returned, the sender can reuse the Message object. This enables the producer to avoid the cost of creating a Message object every time a message is sent.

The message consumer receives a Message object from the JMS Server. The JMS specification prohibits the message receiver from modifying the Message object. To the receiver, the Message object is read-only. This enables the WebLogic JMS implementation to be more efficient because it does not have to copy the message before it delivers it to the consumer.

JMS Delivery Modes

JMS allows messages to be either persistent or nonpersistent. When a persistent message is sent, the JMS implementation saves the message to the message store, such as a database or a file store, assigned to the destination JMS Server. The JMS Server ensures that the send does not complete until the message has been saved. Because this message is persistent (it's stored in \jms_store\MyJMSFileStoreXXX.dat), it can survive a system crash or a reboot. JMS also offers nonpersistent messages. Unlike persistent messages, JMS only keeps nonpersistent messages in memory. If a system crash or reboot occurs, all nonpersistent messages are lost.

The choice between persistent and nonpersistent messages is a tradeoff between reliability and performance. Nonpersistent messages offer higher performance because no disk writes or database updates are performed. However, nonpersistent messages can be lost in a system crash. Applications that require reliability and durable messages should use persistent messages.

> **Best Practice:** Choose nonpersistent messages when messages do not need to survive a server crash. Choose persistent messages when messages must be delivered at least once.

Be aware that both persistent and nonpersistent messages are stored in memory, and as the number of backlogged messages grows, so do the demands on the JVM's memory. If you enable paging and configure a paging store for your JMS server, WebLogic JMS will conserve memory by paging message bodies out of memory. There are other mechanisms available to you to limit the amount of consumed memory, including delivery overrides and destination quotas. These mechanisms are outside the scope of this chapter.

When the server administrator creates a `ConnectionFactory`, a default delivery mode may be specified. If no delivery mode is specified, the WebLogic JMS implementation defaults to persistent delivery. Any connection created from the `ConnectionFactory` will use the default delivery mode. The JMS client may override the default delivery mode when a message is sent by explicitly passing a delivery mode. For instance,

```
msg.setText("Override for this message");
sender.send(
  msg,
DeliveryMode.NON_PERSISTENT,
Message.DEFAULT_PRIORITY,
Message.DEFAULT_TIME_TO_LIVE
    );
```

Persistent messages require the WebLogic Server administrator to configure a message store. The WebLogic JMS implementation supports either Java Database Connectivity (JDBC) or file stores. If a persistent store is not configured, only nonpersistent messages may be used. Figure 7–1 illustrates creating a message store in the file system.

Synchronous Versus Asynchronous Consumers

JMS supports both synchronous and asynchronous message consumers. A synchronous consumer uses the `QueueReceiver`'s or `TopicReceiver`'s `receive()` method to retrieve the destination's next message. If a message is available, the JMS implementation returns it; otherwise, the client's call waits indefinitely for a message. JMS also offers two variants, `receiveNoWait()` and `receive(long timeout)`. The `receiveNoWait()` method returns a message if one is available; otherwise, it returns null. The `receive(long timeout)` method takes a timeout parameter to specify the maximum amount of time to wait for a message. If a message is available within the timeout, it is returned, but if the timeout expires, null is returned.

Asynchronous message consumers must implement the `javax.jms.MessageListener` interface, which contains the onMessage(Message) method.

```
public class AsyncMessageConsumer
  implements javax.jms.MessageListener
{

  ...

  public void onMessage(Message m)
    throws JMSException
  {

    // process message here
  }

}
```

The asynchronous receiver calls the `QueueReceiver`'s or `TopicReceiver`'s setMessageListener method to register itself with JMS.

```
receiver.setMessageListener(new AsyncMessageConsumer());
```

The JMS implementation delivers messages by calling the `MessageListener`'s onMessage method and passing it the new message. The JMS implementation will not deliver another message to this `MessageListener` instance until the onMessage method returns.

Most JMS applications should use asynchronous message consumers and avoid making synchronous receive calls. A receive call consumes a server thread while it is blocking, but an asynchronous receiver is dispatched to an available thread only when a message is received. Threads are valuable server resources, and blocking should be minimized or avoided. If a design requires a synchronous consumer, the `receiveNoWait` or `receive(long timeout)` method should be used instead of blocking, possibly indefinitely, in `receive()`. Providing a clean shutdown of this thread can be difficult; it is sometimes necessary to create a "shutdown thread" message so that this call will unblock and shut down with necessary housekeeping.

Best Practice: Use `receive(long timeout)` or `receiveNoWait` for synchronous consumers.

Including asynchronous message delivery in a JTA transaction is not supported by JMS. The JMS provider has no way of knowing to start a JTA transaction before delivering the message. This becomes an issue when you want to start delivering asynchronous messages to message-driven enterprise java beans (MDBs). WebLogic Server provides a mechanism by which a delivered, unacknowledged message can be associated with a JTA transaction, but this assumes that the EJB and JMS providers are from the same vendor.

Message Selectors

Many message consumers are only interested in a subset of all delivered messages. JMS provides a standard message selector facility to perform automatic message filtering for message consumers. The message filtering is performed by the JMS implementation before delivering the message to consumers, removing the need for remote clients to filter to avoid unwanted messages.

A JMS message consumer writes a JMS expression to perform message filtering. This expression is evaluated by the JMS implementation against the JMS message headers and properties. The message filtering never considers the message body. If the JMS expression evaluates to true, the message is delivered to this consumer. When the JMS expression evaluates to false on a queue, the message is skipped, but it still remains in the queue. On a topic, a false selector will ignore the message for this subscriber. If the topic includes multiple subscribers, then the message may be delivered to other subscribers who do not filter it out.

JMS message selectors are string expressions based on SQL-92. The expression must evaluate to a boolean value using a set of standard operators and the message's header and properties. Each message consumer may use a single selector, and the selector must be specified when the consumer is created.

For instance, this selector ensures that messages will only be delivered if the priority is greater than 5.

```
receiver = session.createReceiver(messageQueue,
    "JMSPriority > 5");
```

Most JMS filtering uses the message properties. This enables the producer to set application-specific values in the message, and then the message filtering can use these properties for filtering.

Durable JMS Subscriptions

In JMS's pub/sub domain, message consumers subscribe to topics. A given topic might have many subscribers. When a message arrives, it is delivered to all subscribers who do not filter the message. If the subscriber's process terminates or there is a network outage, the consumer misses messages delivered to the topic. These messages will not be redelivered when the client reconnects. This behavior is desirable for many pub/sub applications. For time-sensitive information, there is no reason to retain the message, and the JMS implementation has higher performance if it does not need to retain messages for lost clients. However, some applications might have identified clients that need to recover topic messages when they reconnect to the server. JMS provides durable topic subscriptions to allow this behavior. Note that durable subscriptions apply only to JMS topics. JMS queues cannot use durable subscriptions.

When durable topic subscriptions are used, the subscribing client must provide a unique identifier to mark the subscription. For instance, an application could use a user's login name. This enables the server to identify when a client is reconnecting to the JMS Server so that the JMS implementation can deliver any pending messages. The client can set the ID either by creating a connection factory with an associated ID or by calling the `setClientID` method on the `Connection` object. While the JMS specification recommends the `ConnectionFactory` approach, it requires the server administrator to create a `ConnectionFactory` for each durable client. This is impractical for large production systems. In reality, most applications should set the connection ID explicitly on the JMS connection. The `setClientID` method *must* be called immediately after the connection is obtained. Note that it is the client's responsibility to ensure that the client ID value is unique.

In a WebLogic cluster, the JMS implementation cannot always immediately determine that there are multiple clients with a given client ID.

This example code creates the `TopicConnection` from the JMS `ConnectionFactory` and then establishes a client ID of 1.

```
    TopicConnection connection =
connectionFactory.createTopicConnection();
    connection.setClientID("1");
```

The JMS consumer then uses the `createDurableSubscriber` method to create its subscriber object.

```
    TopicSubscriber subscriber = session.createDurableSubscriber(topic, "1");
```

The subscriber will now be attached to the JMS Server with a client ID of `"1"`. Any pending messages to this topic will be delivered to this client.

When any durable subscriber is not connected to the JMS Server, the JMS implementation must save any messages sent to the associated topic. This enables durable clients to return and receive their pending messages, but it also forces the JMS Server to maintain a copy of the message until all durable clients have received the message. If nonpersistent delivery applies to the buffered messages, the message are held in memory and subject to loss during outages. JMS provides the unsubscribe method for durable subscribers to delete their subscription. This prevents the server from retaining messages for clients that will never return.

```
    // unsubscribe the client named "1"
    session.unsubscribe("1");
```

Using Temporary Destinations

JMS destinations are administered objects created from the WebLogic Server's administration console. Destinations are named objects that survive server restarts and may be used by many clients. However, some messaging applications require a lightweight, dynamic destination that is created for temporary use and deleted when the client finishes. JMS includes temporary destinations to address this requirement.

A JMS client creates a temporary destination with QueueSession's `createTemporary-Queue()` method, or TopicSession's `createTemporaryTopic()` method.

```
    TemporaryQueue tempQueue = session.createTemporaryQueue();
```

The `TemporaryQueue` (and conversely `TemporaryTopic`) extend the Queue class and add only a `delete()` method. The `delete()` method destroys the temporary destination and frees any associated resources. This `TemporaryQueue` is a system-generated temporary queue. Temporary destinations do not survive server restarts, and clients may not create durable subscribers for temporary topics. Each temporary destination exists within a single JMS connection, and only the encompassing JMS connection creates message consumers for a temporary destination. Because temporary destinations never survive a server restart, there is no reason to persist messages. Any persistent message sent to a temporary destination will be remarked as NON_PERSISTENT by the WebLogic JMS implementation, and it will not survive a server restart.

One common use for temporary destinations is a reply queue. A JMS client sends messages to a JMS Server, setting the JMSReplyTo field to the temporary destination name. The message consumer then sends a response to the temporary destination.

Another use for temporary destinations is in creating a unified log file that collates log messages from multiple points in a distributed application.

> **Best Practice:** Temporary destinations enable JMS applications to dynamically create short-lived destinations. Because temporary destinations do not survive system failures, applications using temporary destinations must be prepared for lost messages.

JMS clients should always call the delete() method when they have finished with a temporary destination. Each temporary destination consumes resources within the WebLogic Server. These resources are reclaimed when the delete() method is called or through garbage collection.

Message Acknowledgment

The JMS Server retains each message until the consumer acknowledges the message. When messages are consumed within a transaction, the acknowledgment is made when the transaction commits. With nontransacted sessions, the receiver specifies an acknowledgment mode when the session is created. The JMS specification defines three standard acknowledgment modes, and the WebLogic JMS implementation adds two additional options.

Table 7–4 lists the JMS acknowledgment modes.

Table 7–4   JMS Acknowledgment Modes

Acknowledgment Mode	Description
AUTO_ACKNOWLEDGE	For synchronous receivers, the message will be automatically acknowledged when the consumer's receive method call returns without throwing an exception. With an asynchronous consumer, the message is acknowledged when the onMessage callback returns. In this mode, only a single message can be acknowledged at a time.
DUPS_OK_ACKNOWLEDGE	This acknowledgment mode enables JMS to lazily acknowledge message receipt. It is more efficient than AUTO_ACKNOWLEDGE because every message is not acknowledged immediately, but messages may be redelivered if a system crash or network outage occurs.
CLIENT_ACKNOWLEDGE	This acknowledgment mode requires the client to use the javax.jms.Message.acknowledge() method to explicitly acknowledge messages. It is not necessary for the client to acknowledge every message. Instead, a call to acknowledge() will acknowledge the current and any previous messages. This mode is useful for applications defining their own approach for acknowledgments.

Table 7–4 JMS Acknowledgment Modes *(continued)*

Name	Set by
`NO_ACKNOWLEDGE`	This is a WebLogic-specific JMS acknowledgment mode to indicate that no acknowledgment is required. The JMS implementation does not retain the message after delivering it to the consumer.
`MULTICAST_NO_ACKNOWLEDGE`	This is a WebLogic-specific JMS acknowledgment mode that delivers JMS messages via IP multicast to topic subscribers. Like `NO_ACKNOWLEDGE`, the JMS implementation does not retain the message after delivery.

Which Acknowledgment Mode Is Right for Your Application?

`NO_ACKNOWLEDGE` or `MULTICAST_NO_ACKNOWLEDGE` should be used by applications where performance outweighs any durability or recoverability requirements. In many applications, messages are created frequently to send out updates such as the latest stock quotes. Because this information is continually being generated, performance is paramount, and if a system crash occurs, there is no reason to recover any lost stock quotes, since the quote will be out of date by the time the system has recovered.

`AUTO_ACKNOWLEDGE` is a simple model because the container handles acknowledgment, but JMS programmers should be aware that messages can be redelivered. If there is a system outage between the time that the receive or `onMessage` call returns and the JMS Server acknowledges the message, the last message is redelivered when the system recovers. Consumers who need stronger messaging guarantees should use JMS's transaction facilities, which are discussed in the next section.

`DUPS_OK_ACKNOWLEDGE` allows higher performance than `AUTO_ACKNOWLEDGE` at the cost of more redelivered messages after a system failure. If consumers can detect or tolerate redelivered messages, its performance advantages make it preferable to `AUTO_ACKNOWLEDGE`.

`CLIENT_ACKNOWLEDGE` gives the receiver complete control over the message acknowledgment. It enables the client to acknowledge a batch of messages with a single operation.

All other things being equal, using `CLIENT_ACKNOWLEDGE` to acknowledge groups of messages in batch or using `DUPS_OK_ACKNOWLEDGE` are preferable for maximizing scalability and performance.

JMS and Transactions

The JMS acknowledgment modes provide varying levels of reliability for message consumers, but enterprise applications often require stronger, transactional guarantees. For instance, an application might need to dequeue a message, update some database tables, and enqueue the message on another JMS queue. If any of these operations fails or a system failure occurs, the entire operation should roll back to its original state. JMS offers two transactional options: transacted sessions and an integration with the WebLogic Server's JTA transaction service.

Using Transacted Sessions

Transacted sessions are used when transactional behavior is required within a single JMS session. Other resources such as database or EJB operations cannot participate in a transacted JMS session's transaction. Passing a boolean `true` argument when the session is created creates a transacted session. The acknowledgment mode is also specified, but it is ignored for transacted sessions.

```
Session txSession = qCon.createQueueSession(
    true, /* transacted session */
    Session.AUTO_ACKNOWLEDGE /* IGNORED for transacted session */
    );
```

Transacted sessions use the chained transaction model. A transaction is always open for each transacted session. When the transaction is committed, the JMS implementation automatically starts a new transaction. The `javax.jms.Session` object includes `commit()` and `rollback()` methods for the JMS client to explicitly commit or roll back the associated transaction.

Both message producers and message consumers may use transacted sessions. When a message producer uses a transacted session, sent messages are buffered until the transaction commits. No message consumers will receive these uncommitted messages. When the message producer calls the session's commit method, the messages are all enabled for delivery. If the transaction aborts, the JMS implementation will discard the buffered messages.

With message consumers, transacted sessions control message acknowledgment. The consumer can receive multiple messages just as with the `CLIENT_ACKNOWLEDGE` mode. When the associated transaction is committed, the JMS implementation acknowledges all messages received in the associated transaction. If the transaction aborts, the JMS implementation returns the messages to the associated queue or topic.

> **Best Practice:** Transacted sessions are used when transactional behavior is required within a single JMS session. Other resources, such as database, EJB operations, or JCA-accessible system operations, cannot participate in a transacted session's transaction.

Using JTA Transactions with JMS

Transacted sessions enable a JMS producer or consumer to group messages into a single, atomic send or receive. However, a transacted session is only used within JMS. Many applications need JMS and JDBC or EJB to participate in a single transaction. For instance, an application might dequeue a message containing a customer order and use the order information to update some inventory tables in the database. The order processing and the inventory update must be within the same transaction, so a transacted session is insufficient because it handles only JMS. One way to make your JMS session JTA-aware is to use an XA connection factory for all of your connections. This is the only way to specify that your application will use JTA user transactions.

> **Best Practice:** Make sure that if your connection factory is XA-enabled, the JDBC drivers used with any JMS message stores are not XA drivers. WebLogic's JMS implementation will provide the appropriate functionality for related transactions.

Best Practice: In order for you to use JTA `UserTransactions` with JMS, the server administrator must ensure that the `ConnectionFactory`'s XA Connection Factory Enabled checkbox is checked in the WebLogic Server's administration console under the Transactions Configuration tab for your JMS Connection Factory.

Best Practice: Unless your transactions include only JMS operations within a single session, JTA `UserTransactions` should be used instead of transacted sessions, since the transaction can enlist other resources such as JDBC or EJB access.

Clustering JMS

Many WebLogic Server deployments use WebLogic clustering to achieve scalability and reliability. When designing JMS applications, it is important to understand JMS clustering and its semantics within a WebLogic cluster.

JMS clustering offers functionality that provides JMS applications with one logical connection and one view to the messaging system and one logical destination regardless of the number of server instances in a cluster.

The concept of a JMS Server was introduced in WebLogic version 6. As mentioned earlier in this chapter, a JMS Server includes administered JMS objects such as connection factories, connections, and destinations. Each WebLogic Server instance may include multiple JMS Servers, but each JMS Server is deployed on a single WebLogic Server. Each JMS Server uses an associated message store. Deploying multiple JMS Servers within a single WebLogic Server allows multiple applications to each access a separate JMS instance (see Figure 7–4).

JMS destinations are assigned to a single JMS Server. Because JMS Servers exist on a single WebLogic Server instance, each JMS destination exists on a single WebLogic Server instance. Regardless, destination names must be unique across every JMS server on every server instance in the cluster. The server achieves scalability by distributing destinations to different WebLogic Server instances in the cluster. Because the destinations reside on different WebLogic Server instances, the JMS Server work is effectively load-balanced throughout the cluster.

Note: Although destinations exist on a single WebLogic Server instance, the message producers and consumers for a given destination can exist anywhere in the cluster or even in client applications.

When a WebLogic Server instance fails, all JMS destinations within the failed server become unavailable. All temporary destinations and nonpersistent messages are lost during a server failure. Note that only the failed server will be affected; destinations on other servers in the cluster continue to operate. When the failed WebLogic Server is restarted, the associated JMS destinations will again become available. All persistent messages and permanent destinations are again available.

The concept of distributed destinations was introduced as part of WebLogic JMS clustering to provide applications access to multiple JMS destinations via one logical destination. This allows applications to have a single view of a destination existing on multiple server instances in a cluster. WebLogic JMS handles the routing and load balancing under the covers on a per request basis. The factors influencing how this is handled by the underlying system are various.

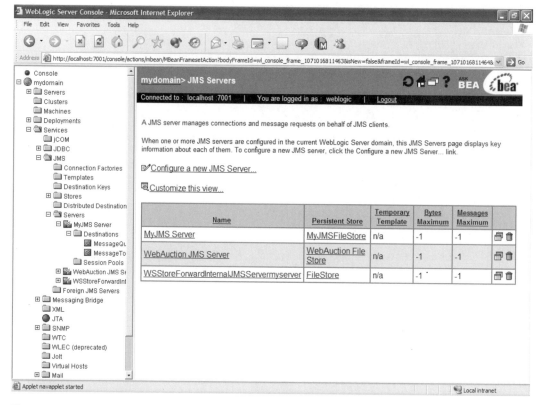

Figure 7–4
Multiple JMS Servers within a WebLogic Server instance.

You can create a distributed destination by mapping more than one JMS destination to a logical destination. It can then be treated like any JMS destination by your application. Controlling the underlying handling of the distributed destination by WebLogic JMS is possible, sometimes tricky, and outside the scope of this book.

If a JMS client is connected to a failed JMS Server, its connection `ExceptionListener` receives a `JMSException`. Any attempt to send or receive messages will also receive a `JMSException`. The client application must reconnect to an available JMS Server to restart JMS operations. If the connection is asynchronous and the destination server is separate from the connection server, you must register to receive a `JMSException` in the case where the destination server fails.

The concept of JMS server migration allows you to explicitly move destinations from one server to another in the same cluster in anticipation of a server outage. The WebLogic migration framework can be used for this purpose or for moving a JMS Server from one WebLogic instance in a cluster to another. The complexity of this task depends on how many resources are shared between server instances and how many must be migrated to the new instance.

Exception Listeners

Many messaging applications include consumers who receive messages and perform work but never send any JMS messages. Because these clients are only active when a message is delivered, there is no means to notify them when their JMS Server has failed. JMS provides the `ExceptionListener` facility to deliver these out-of-band exceptions to clients.

A JMS `ExceptionListener` asynchronously receives connection error exceptions. `ExceptionListener` only receives exceptions that cannot be thrown to a method call. For instance, a send call on a broken connection will receive a `JMSException`, but this exception will not be transmitted to the `ExceptionListener`.

`ExceptionListeners` implement `javax.jms.ExceptionListener` that contains the `onException(JMSException)` method. When an out-of-band exception occurs, the `ExceptionListener`'s `onException` method receives the raised exception. `ExceptionListeners` are not written to be thread-safe or reentrant. A new exception will not be delivered until the `ExceptionListener`'s `onException` method has returned.

```
public class MyExceptionListener
   implements javax.jms.ExceptionListener
{
   public void onException(javax.jms.JMSException e) {

      ... //handle exception
   }
}
```

A client registers an `ExceptionListener` on the JMS connection with the `setExceptionListener(ExceptionListener)` method.

```
qConnection.setExceptionListener(new MyExceptionListener());
```

WebLogic's JMS implementation also enables the `ExceptionListener` to be registered with the entire JMS session by using `WLSession`'s `setExceptionListener(ExceptionListener)` method.

```
import weblogic.jms.extensions.WLSession;

WLSession wlSession = (WLSession) session;

wlSession.setExceptionListener(new ExceptionListener());
```

Using Multicast JMS

A messaging system is commonly used as the application's communication backbone. Messages might travel to hundreds or thousands of subscribers. Appropriate message selectors can greatly limit the number of delivered messages, but systems with thousands of clients will still spend considerable system resources delivering messages.

> **Note:** WebLogic's JMS implementation provides a multicast option to efficiently deliver messages to a large number of subscribers.

The WebLogic JMS implementation optionally uses IP multicast to deliver a message to a potentially large set of subscribers. A message producer sends a JMS message to the WebLogic Server using a standard JMS connection. The WebLogic Server then sends a single message via IP multicast to the message consumers. This provides greater scalability than standard PTP connections because the server needs to send a single message to reach many clients instead of sending a message per client. This multicast option also greatly reduces the network traffic between JMS clients and the WebLogic Servers.

The multicast JMS option is only available for the pub/sub model, and durable subscriptions are not supported. Because a single message consumer receives each message from a JMS queue, it does not make sense to extend the multicast option to the JMS PTP model. The multicast JMS option also only supports asynchronous message listeners. Any attempt to synchronously receive messages with multicast JMS will cause a `JMSException` to be thrown.

Because IP multicast is based on UDP and therefore not a reliable protocol, message delivery is not guaranteed with the JMS multicast option. The messages are sequenced, and the WebLogic JMS implementation automatically indicates when a gap in the sequence has occurred. This gap indicates that a message has been lost or received out of order. The frequency of lost or misordered messages depends on the network topology and the message size. Small messages on a high-bandwidth LAN rarely (if ever) will be lost. Large messages across a congested network might frequently be lost or misordered. If a sequence gap is detected, a `weblogic.jms.extensions.SequenceGapException` is delivered to the session's `ExceptionListener`. It is important to balance the need for guaranteed delivery with the performance advantages of carrying just one copy of a message to numerous subscribers.

Not all network devices are configured to allow multicast traffic. Investigate your network security policy before designing an application with multicast JMS.

Message loss can be minimized if you select a multicast address and port for each topic. This allows you to better track message delivery and reduce the chances of message loss. If your WebLogic cluster is using IP multicast, make sure not to use the same address/port grouping for your topics.

Configuration Changes for Multicast JMS

The JMS destination is configured with the appropriate multicast address, port number, and TTL. Multicast addresses are in the range 224.0.0.0 to 239.255.255.255, and the port number should be an available port on the client machine. The TTL determines the Time To Live field in the IP multicast packet. Every time a multicast packet takes a network hop through a router, the TTL value in the packet is decreased. If the TTL value is 0, it is discarded. Thus, a TTL value of 1 will reach only hosts on the local network. A TTL value of 2 will reach all hosts on the local network and cross one router to reach an additional network (see Figure 7–5). If you are unsure how to set these values, please consult your network administrator for appropriate values.

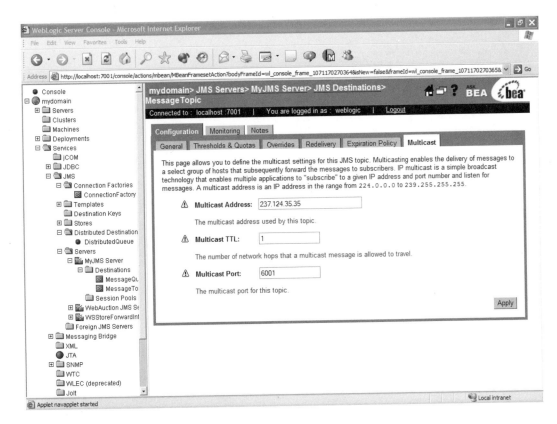

Figure 7–5
Configuring Multicast JMS.

Using Multicast JMS Sessions

A message consumer uses multicast delivery by creating a `TopicSession` with the `MULTICAST_NO_ACKNOWLEDGE` acknowledgment mode.

```
TopicSession multicastSession =
topicConnection.createTopicSession(
false, /* non-transacted session */
   WLSession.MULTICAST_NO_ACKNOWLEDGE
);
```

Because this is an asynchronous consumer, the `javax.jms.MessageListener` interface must be implemented.

```
public class MulticastMessageConsumer
   implements javax.jms.MessageListener
{
```

```
public void onMessage(Message m)
  throws JMSException
{
  // message consumer code
  ...
}
}
```

The message consumer must then register a `javax.jms.MessageListener` with the Top-
icSubscriber.

```
tsubscriber.setMessageListener(new MulticastMessageConsumer());
```

Once message delivery is enabled, the consumer will asynchronously receive multicasted JMS
messages.

JMS Best Practices

The following paragraphs describe some best practices for coding JMS applications.

Avoid Unneeded Features

JMS provides a powerful messaging facility with support for transactions, persistence, durable subscribers, and message selection and sorting. While these are important features of WebLogic's JMS
implementation, they do affect the messaging system's performance. Selecting the correct acknowledgment mode or using nonpersistent messages where appropriate can greatly increase the
throughput of a JMS application.

Best Practice: Avoid unnecessary features for maximum JMS performance.

Selection Performance Costs

JMS message selectors are a convenient and powerful means to filter messages from a queue or
topic, but care must be taken to ensure that selection does not negatively impact overall system
performance.

Every JMS message sent to a destination must be compared against the consumers' message
selectors. Message selectors that consider only message header fields run the fastest. A selector that
uses the message properties is slower, and a selector that examines the message body is even slower.

Message selection is well suited to JMS topics. The WebLogic JMS implementation can efficiently evaluate the selectors and deliver the messages to the appropriate consumers. If no topic
consumers select the message, it does not need to be retained.

Best Practice: Use selectors that examine only message header fields. A selector
that examines message properties is slower, and one that examines the message
body is the slowest.

However, message selection with queues can incur performance overheads if it is not used carefully. When a consumer does not select a message, it must be retained in the queue. Each selector must be compared against every undelivered message in the queue. If a message is never selected, it continues to consume resources.

> **Best Practice:** Message selectors are more efficient when used with topics than with queues.

Use Asynchronous Message Consumers Where Possible

JMS supports both synchronous and asynchronous message consumers. It is recommended that, where possible, asynchronous message consumers be used. Asynchronous message consumers provide better resource usage because threads are not blocked waiting for messages.

Synchronous message consumers always block a thread in the client. If the receive call is made from an external client, the WebLogic JMS implementation will not block a thread in the WebLogic Server. This is important for server scalability because the server cannot dedicate a blocking thread to each client. However, the thread in the client is blocked until the receive call returns.

If a synchronous receive call is made from within the WebLogic Server, a server thread must block until the receive call returns. Threads are valuable resources within a scalable server, and it is unacceptable to block these threads for long periods of time. Asynchronous consumers make better use of threads, especially within the server process.

> **Best Practice:** Use asynchronous message consumers.

Prefer JTA Transactions to Transacted Sessions

Many JMS applications require transactional messaging. Transacted sessions provide a convenient means to use transactions within JMS, but other components such as EJBs or JDBC access cannot participate in these transactions. The JTA `UserTransaction` interface enables nontransacted sessions to participate in a transaction that can encompass other components, including JDBC or EJB. However, JMS does not provide a method to include an asynchronous consumer's message receipt in a JTA transaction. The problem is that there is no way to explicitly start a `UserTransaction` before the `onMessage()` callback. In this case, transacted sessions could be used or, as we'll see in Chapter 10, EJB's message-driven beans are asynchronous message listeners whose message receipt may optionally participate in a JTA transaction.

> **Best Practice:** Use JTA `UserTransactions` rather than transacted sessions.

JMS Transactions and Error Handling

Large applications are often divided into multiple systems or separate processes, and JMS provides the communication between these subsystems. This workflow is PTP and is modeled with a queue. To ensure that messages are not lost, the JMS work is handled within a transaction. In production applications, it is possible that a message will contain application data that includes invalid data or errors. A transactional JMS client needs to be careful when handling invalid messages. If the transaction aborts, the message will be returned to the queue and delivered again to the consumer. Unless this error is transient, the second delivery will cause a transaction rollback, and the process continues.

One common solution is to introduce a separate error destination. When an invalid message is discovered, the message is sent to the error destination, and the JMS transaction commits. This ensures that the message is not redelivered. A message consumer on the error queue can handle the invalid messages appropriately. A simple solution is to use JavaMail to send an e-mail to the customer or system administrator informing them of the error condition.

Best Practice: Send invalid messages to a separate error destination.

Another common solution separates the message acknowledgment from the JDBC or EJB transaction. This is desirable if the JDBC or EJB layer will detect that the message is invalid and abort the transaction. The message consumer needs to ensure that the message is still acknowledged. The JMS consumer uses the CLIENT_ACKNOWLEDGE or AUTO_ACKNOWLEDGE modes. When a message is received, the transaction begins; the JDBC or EJB work is performed within the transaction; and the message consumer commits or aborts the transaction.

Then, the message consumer acknowledges the message. This opens the possibility that the transaction will commit, but the system will fail before the message is acknowledged. The application can often prepare for this case by making the message actions idempotent or by detecting this situation. For instance, an e-commerce application might send a JMS message that processes new customer accounts. If each message includes a customer ID number, the message consumer can determine whether this customer has already been processed.

Putting It All Together

JMS provides a standard enterprise messaging system for J2EE applications. The WebLogic Server provides a robust and high-performance version of JMS and includes a number of JMS extensions. JMS is often used in conjunction with other J2EE APIs to build a complete enterprise application. The EJB 2.1 specification includes message-driven EJBs and defines an integration between JMS and EJB.

References

The Java Message Service specification is available at *http://java.sun.com/products/jms/index.html*.
BEA's Programming WebLogic JMS documentation for WebLogic Server 8.1 can be found at *http://edocs.bea.com/wls/docs81/jms/index.html*.
Configuring JMS for WebLogic Server 8.1 is documented at *http://e-docs.bea.com/wls/docs81/ConsoleHelp/jms_config.html*.
Tuning JMS for WebLogic Server 8.1 is documented at *http://e-docs.bea.com/wls/docs81/ConsoleHelp/jms_tuning.html*.
Monitoring JMS for WebLogic Server 8.1 is documented at *http://e-docs.bea.com/wls/docs81/ConsoleHelp/jms_monitor.html*.

Using Session Enterprise JavaBeans

In This Chapter

- Basics of EJBs
- Programming stateless session EJBs
- Writing stateful session EJBs
- Using EJBs in transactions
- How to write secure EJBs
- Best practices for using session EJBs in WebLogic Server applications

Enterprise JavaBeans Overview

JavaSoft defined the Enterprise JavaBeans (EJB) specification to give Java developers a foundation for building distributed business components. EJBs are Java components that implement business logic and follow a contract designated in the EJB specification. EJBs live inside an EJB container, a program that provides a set of standard services, including transactions, persistence, security, resource pooling, and concurrency. This means that the application programmer is freed from developing these services from scratch. EJBs are invoked through RMI, RMI-IIOP, and in the case of message-driven beans (MDBs), JMS messages.

EJB also provides portability for its components. Any EJB that conforms to the EJB 2.0 specification works correctly in the WebLogic Server and other J2EE implementations. At this writing, the EJB 2.1 specification is in the proposed final draft stage and EJB 3.0 is under development.

Basics of EJBs

In EJB 2.0, there are four types of EJBs:

- Stateless session beans provide a service without storing a conversation state between method calls. The beginning and end of a transaction (transaction demarcation) can be either container-managed or bean-managed.

- Stateful session beans maintain state; each instance is associated with a particular client. The transaction demarcation can be either container-managed or bean-managed.
- Entity beans represent an object view of persistent data, usually rows in a database. Entity beans have a primary key as a unique identifier. There are two operational styles for entity beans: *container-managed persistence* (CMP) and *bean-managed persistence* (BMP). The transaction demarcation for entity beans is container-managed only.
- Message-driven beans were added in EJB 2.0. Message-driven EJBs, the integration between JMS and EJB, are used to perform asynchronous work between the server instance and the JMS source. The transaction demarcation for message-driven beans may be either bean-managed or container-managed.

Session Beans

Session beans (both stateful and stateless) represent a conversation with a client. Stateless session beans are generally used to provide a service. Because they are stateless, no conversation state is stored between method calls. For instance, you could model a bank teller as a stateless EJB with a method named withdraw. Each call to withdraw would have to include all of the information necessary to access the account.

> **Note:** The advantage of a stateless session bean is that a small number of instances can be used to satisfy a large number of customers. Each instance has no identity and is equivalent to any other instance.

The number of simultaneous tellers is the number of concurrent operations (similar to a real bank).

Stateful session beans also represent a conversation, but each instance is associated with a particular client. If the teller EJB were a stateful session bean, each client would create his or her own teller instance (perhaps passing the account number as a parameter). Now the teller stateful session bean is associated with a particular client and his or her account number.

> **Note:** In the stateful session bean example, the number of tellers is equal to the number of active customers. This can simplify the programming model.

Entity Beans

Entity beans represent an object view of persistent data, usually rows in a database. Entity beans have clients that use the entity bean for data access. These clients could be Web components or other bean types (session or message-driven). Entity beans have a primary key, which, like a database primary key, uniquely identifies the entity. There are two main divisions of entity beans: CMP and BMP. In a CMP entity bean, the EJB container automatically generates code to persist the entity bean to a database. In a BMP entity bean, the bean writer must write the data access code. Generally, this involves writing Java Database Connectivity (JDBC) code to insert, remove, and query the entity bean in the database.

The advantage of BMP is that it offers the bean writer complete flexibility about the entity bean's persistence. Because the bean writer is writing the data access code, almost any persistent store can be used. The main advantage of CMP is that it relieves the bean writer from having to write the data access code to persist the entity bean to a relational database. Instead of writing the tedious JDBC code, CMP automates this process. In addition, CMP offers standard mapping for relationships between entity beans. This enables the container automatically to manage the interactions between business objects. Because the container has more control over data access in CMP, the performance of CMP beans is usually better than with BMP entities.

The relationships that exist between entity beans typically mirror the relationships between the business entities that the beans model. These relationships are outlined in an object schema specified in the `ejb-jar.xml` deployment descriptor for the bean.

We cover entity beans in detail in Chapter 9.

Message-Driven Beans

Message-driven EJBs in EJB 2.0 were the integration between JMS and EJB. In EJB 2.1 (released with J2EE 1.4), the definition expanded to support messaging systems other than JMS. At this writing, the mainstream J2EE implementations (including WebLogic Server's) are still using JMS as the only exchange for MDBs. Unlike other EJBs, clients never directly call a message-driven EJB. Instead, the client posts a message to a JMS destination. When a message arrives at the JMS destination, a `MessageDrivenBean`'s `onMessage` method is called to process the message. A single MDB instance processes messages from multiple clients, but does not retain state for any client. It is not guaranteed that a particular MDB instance will handle all messages from a particular client; the EJB container is responsible for assigning messages to MDB instances. Message-driven EJBs generally are used to perform asynchronous work within the server.

Stateless Session EJB Example: HelloWorld

EJBs consist of three main pieces:

- *The local or remote interface*: This type of interface exposes business logic to clients and defines the methods clients can invoke. Local interfaces serve clients running as part of the same application, and bean and remote interfaces expose logic to remote clients running outside of the application.
- *The local home or remote home interface*: This type of interface, also called an EJB factory, provides methods that clients can use to find, create, or remove instances of the bean. The local home interface serves clients running as part of the same application as the bean, whereas the remote home interface serves clients running in a different application.
- *The bean class*: Business logic is implemented in the bean class.

To illustrate these components, we create a simple Hello World stateless session EJB with a remote interface and a remote home interface. The remote interface lists the business methods that are available to clients of this EJB. Because this is an interface, the EJB writer does not implement these methods. The EJB container is responsible for supplying the concrete implementation of the methods in the remote interface. The remote interface only stipulates the contract between the client and the EJB.

HelloWorld Remote Interface

We define the remote interface in a file called *HelloWorld.java*:

```
package com.learnweblogic.examples.ch8.helloworld;

import java.rmi.RemoteException;
import javax.ejb.EJBObject;
public interface HelloWorld extends EJBObject {
  public String helloWorld()
    throws RemoteException;

}
```

The EJB developer uses the remote interface to expose business logic to the client. In this case, the EJB offers a single helloWorld method. It is worth noting that this file will be generated for you if you use Workshop to develop your EJB. More on this later.

HelloWorldHome Interface

The home interface is the EJB's factory. Clients use the home interface to create, find, and remove instances of an EJB. Like the remote interface, the EJB writer defines only the signature for the methods in the home interface.

```
package com.learnweblogic.examples.ch8.helloworld;
import java.rmi.RemoteException;
import javax.ejb.CreateException;
import javax.ejb.EJBHome;

public class HelloWorldHome extends EJBHome {
  public HelloWorld create()
    throws CreateException, RemoteException;
  }
```

The HelloWorldHome interface contains a single create method. This create method is a factory that produces references to the HelloWorld EJB. Notice that the return type is the HelloWorld interface. The return type of create methods is always the EJB's remote interface. Workshop creates this file for you if you use Workshop to create your EJB.

HelloWorldBean EJB Class

The bean class implements the business logic that is exposed to the client through the remote interface. For instance, the bean class must implement the helloWorld business method:

```
package com.learnweblogic.examples.ch8.helloworld;

import javax.ejb.SessionBean;
import javax.ejb.SessionContext;

public class HelloWorldBean implements SessionBean {
```

```
  private SessionContext ctx;

  public void setSessionContext(SessionContext c) {
    ctx = c;
  }

  public String helloWorld() {
    return "Hello World.  Welcome to EJB!";
  }

  public void ejbCreate() {}
  public void ejbRemove() {}

  public void ejbActivate() {}
  public void ejbPassivate() {}
}
```

The remaining methods in the `HelloWorldBean` class (except for `ejbCreate()`) are inherited from the `javax.ejb.SessionBean` interface. We cover these methods in detail later in this chapter.

EJB Deployment Descriptors

Before clients can use the HelloWorld EJB, we must deploy it into the WebLogic Server. If you are using Workshop to build your EJB project, you can rely on Workshop to generate your deployment descriptors (although it is good practice to review them before deployment). If you are not using Workshop to building your EJB, you'll need to use the Java compiler to produce the classfiles, just like any other Java application. The next step then would be to create the deployment descriptors. When the EJB container deploys the EJB, it reads configuration parameters and metadata from the deployment descriptor. For instance, the container uses the deployment descriptor to determine what type of EJB is being deployed, the name of the home interface, and other vital information. There are three types of deployment descriptors supported by WebLogic Server 8.1: `ejb-jar.xml`, `weblogic-ejb-jar.xml`, and `weblogic-cmp-jar.xml`. The first deployment descriptor we examine is `ejb-jar.xml`.

The ejb-jar.xml Descriptor

The document type descriptor (DTD) for this XML document is defined by the EJB specification. This is a standard EJB 2.0 deployment descriptor that is used by all EJB vendors.

Here is the *ejb-jar.xml* file for the HelloWorld EJB:

```
<?xml version="1.0"?>
<!DOCTYPE ejb-jar PUBLIC
'-//Sun Microsystems, Inc.//DTD Enterprise JavaBeans 2.0//EN'
'http://java.sun.com/dtd/ejb-jar_2_0.dtd'>
```

```
<ejb-jar>
  <enterprise-beans>
    <session>
      <ejb-name>HelloWorld</ejb-name>
      <home>
        com.learnweblogic.examples.ch8.helloworld.HelloWorldHome
      </home>
      <remote>
        com.learnweblogic.examples.ch8.helloworld.HelloWorld
      </remote>
      <ejb-class>
        com.learnweblogic.examples.ch8.helloworld.HelloWorldBean
      </ejb-class>
      <session-type>Stateless</session-type>
      <transaction-type>Bean</transaction-type>
    </session>
  </enterprise-beans>
</ejb-jar>
```

The deployment descriptor begins by declaring its XML document type. EJB deployment descriptors are XML documents that must use the structure defined in the standard EJB DTD. The ejb-jar.xml descriptor gives the WebLogic EJB container the names of the home interface, remote interface, and the ejb (bean) class. The ejb-name parameter is a logical name for this EJB. It is used throughout the deployment descriptor to refer to this EJB (although the application code might use a different name to refer to the EJB). The ejb-jar.xml also includes a session-type parameter. This informs the container that this deployment is a stateless session EJB. Finally, we specify that we are using bean-managed transactions. We cover the EJB transaction options later in this chapter.

The weblogic-ejb-jar.xml Descriptor

In addition to the standard deployment descriptor, the WebLogic Server also requires a WebLogic-specific deployment descriptor. This deployment descriptor enables the EJB writer to configure parameters that are specific to the WebLogic implementation. This file is named weblogic-ejb-jar.xml. Here is the weblogic-ejb-jar.xml for the HelloWorld EJB.

```
<?xml version="1.0"?>
<!DOCTYPE weblogic-ejb-jar PUBLIC
"-//BEA Systems, Inc.//DTD WebLogic 8.1.0 EJB//EN" "http://
www.bea.com/servers/wls810/dtd/weblogic-ejb-jar.dtd"

<weblogic-ejb-jar>
  <weblogic-enterprise-bean>
    <ejb-name>HelloWorld</ejb-name>
    <jndi-name>HelloWorldEJB</jndi-name>
  </weblogic-enterprise-bean>
</weblogic-ejb-jar>
```

This simple WebLogic deployment descriptor contains only two pieces of information. First, it uses the `ejb-name` tag to specify that these parameters are for the HelloWorld EJB. This enables the container to associate these values with the parameters read from the `ejb-jar.xml` descriptor. The second tag is the Java Naming and Directory Interface (JNDI) name. When the HelloWorld EJB is deployed in the WebLogic Server, the EJB container binds the home interface into the JNDI tree using the `<jndi-name>` specified in the *weblogic-ejb-jar.xml*. Clients can then find the EJB by using JNDI to look up the name `"HelloWorldEJB"`.

Writing a Simple EJB Client

Once the HelloWorld EJB is built into an `ejb-jar` file and deployed to a server, it is ready to be used by clients. In the `weblogic-ejb-jar.xml`, the deployer specified a `jndi-name` where the HelloWorld EJB is bound in the JNDI tree. A client uses the EJB by first making a JNDI lookup for this name.

```
Context ctx = new InitialContext();
Object h = ctx.lookup("HelloWorldEJB");
HelloWorldHome home = (HelloWorld)
PortableRemoteObject.narrow(h, HelloWorldHome.class);
```

First, the client creates an `InitialContext` to access the server's JNDI service. Next, the client does a JNDI lookup to find the home interface. This JNDI name (`"HelloWorldEJB"`) is the JNDI name specified previously in the *weblogic-ejb-jar.xml* file. Finally, the client uses the `Portable-Remote-Object` to narrow the scope to the home interface. This is required by the EJB specification for portability reasons.

Next, the client can use the home as a factory to create an instance of the EJB.

```
HelloWorld hw = home.create();
```

The `create` method defined in the `HelloWorldHome` interface returns a new reference to the HelloWorld EJB.

The client can now call the `helloWorld` business method and print out the result.

```
String hello = hw.helloWorld();
System.out.println("My EJB said: "+hello);
```

The EJB Container

All EJBs exist inside the EJB container. The EJB container and other WebLogic Server subsystems provide the EJB writer with persistence, distributed objects, concurrency, security, and transactions. These services are available to an EJB at deploy time and at runtime. The container handles things like creating a session object after finding the home interface of a session bean, managing bean timeouts, and so on. Although it is not necessary to understand how the container works in order to take advantage of the services it provides, it is essential to understand the relationship between an EJB and its container.

Using JNDI to Look Up the EJB Home Interface

We now show the HelloWorld EJB example with comments on what is occurring in the EJB container underneath.

```
Context ctx = new InitialContext();
```

The client has created a standard JNDI context.

```
Object h = ctx.lookup("HelloWorldEJB");
HelloWorldHome home = (HelloWorldHome)
  PortableRemoteObject.narrow(h, HelloWorldHome.class);
```

When the EJB is deployed, the *weblogic-ejb-jar.xml* specifies Hello-WorldEJB as the JNDI name. At deployment time, the WebLogic Server binds an object that implements the HelloWorldHome interface at the name "HelloWorldEJB".

The client's lookup call travels across the network connection to the WebLogic Server. The server returns a Remote Method Interface (RMI) stub to the client.

The final step is to call PortableRemoteObject.narrow on the stub that is returned from the server. This step is necessary for portability reasons. Some EJB servers might not return a stub that implements the home interface. The narrow step takes the object returned from the server and produces an object that implements the home interface. The call to PortableRemoteObject.narrow is generally required on EJB servers that are CORBA-based.

Creating an EJB Instance

```
HelloWorld hw = home.create();
```

Because the home object is an RMI object, the create call travels across the network connection to the WebLogic Server. The EJB container is responsible for providing an object that implements the home interface. The create RMI call arrives on the WebLogic Server and calls the create method on the home object that the server has provided.

At this point, the EJB is using the EJB container. The implementation of the create method is part of the container's responsibility. The container's create method first performs security checks before proceeding (we cover the EJB security model in detail later in this chapter). You can specify which users are allowed to call EJB methods. In this case, the container must check that the current caller is allowed to call the create method.

The EJB container also provides a transaction service to EJB writers. For instance, the *ejb-jar.xml* file can specify that the container must automatically start a transaction before it calls any method on an EJB and must commit a transaction when the method completes. We cover EJB's transaction support later in this chapter. Depending on the deployment descriptor, the container might need to start a transaction at this point. It should be noted that the create method is not part of the client's transaction context, so if a client's transaction rolls back, the object is not destroyed.

The next portion of the container's create method depends on the type of EJB. We cover all four types of EJBs in detail in later chapters. For now, let's skip to the end of the container's create method. The container must return an object to the client that implements the EJB's remote interface. In the example, this is the `HelloWorld` interface. Because this is a remote object, the client receives an RMI stub.

Calling Business Methods

```
// call the business method
String hello = hw.helloWorld();
```

The client now has a stub to the `HelloWorld` interface. The `helloWorld` method call is an RMI call that travels to the WebLogic Server. Like the home interface, the EJB writer only supplies the interface for the `HelloWorld` interface. The EJB container provides an object that implements this interface.

Like the home interface, the container first checks security and then handles transactions for a business method call. The container's next responsibility is to get an instance of the bean class (in this case, `HelloWorldBean`) and call the `helloWorld` method on it. Remember that the EJB writer has implemented the business logic within the EJB bean class.

When the `helloWorld` method on the EJB bean class returns, the container again resumes control. Depending on the transaction settings, the EJB container might have to commit a transaction at this point.

The EJB container is also responsible for handling any exceptions that were thrown by the EJB's business logic. The exact behavior of exceptions is covered in a later chapter, but the EJB container might be required to roll back the transaction or even to destroy the EJB instance.

The EJB container takes the return value from the business method and returns it to the client. In this case, the `helloWorld` method returns a string across the wire to the client.

Obviously, the HelloWorld EJB is a simple EJB that makes little use of the services of an EJB container. While developing deployment descriptors and following the EJB specification's rules can be complicated, it is much easier to master these skills than to write a distributed, transactional, secure, and persistent component from scratch.

Stateless Session EJBs

In the previous sections, we developed, deployed, and used a simple stateless session EJB. In the following sections, we cover session EJBs in depth and explain how to take advantage of container services such as transactions and security.

Stateless session EJBs are generally considered the easiest to program. Their simplicity has a number of advantages for both the bean writer and the EJB server. As their name implies, stateless session beans follow a stateless programming model.

> **Note:** In a stateless programming model, the object cannot maintain any state on behalf of its caller.

For instance, imagine we are developing a bank account stateless EJB. We might develop a remote interface `Account.java` with these methods:

```
public double getBalance(int accountNumber)
    throws RemoteException;
```

```
public void deposit(int accountNumber, double amount)
     throws RemoteException;

public void withdraw(int accountNumber, double amount)
     throws RemoteException;
```

Because this is a stateless model, we do not store the `accountNumber` in the object. Each method takes the `accountNumber` as a parameter, performs the appropriate action, and then returns. Because the EJB does not contain any state, it is reasonable to use a database to store the account information. The `getBalance` method uses its account parameter to query the database and return the result.

Stateless Programming Model

The stateless programming model presents a number of advantages to the programmer. Because there is no state associated with the EJB instance, every instance of the bean class is essentially identical.

For instance, imagine the client calls the `getBalance` method on the remote interface. The container must then call the `getBalance` method on a bean class instance. Imagine that the container has two instances of the bean class in memory. Because the bean is stateless, the client does not care which of the two instances gets the `getBalance` method call. In this case, the account number is the necessary state, and it is passed as a parameter. If the EJB stored the account number (or any client-associated state) as a member variable, the stateless programming model would not be appropriate.

A stateless session bean must implement the `javax.ejb.SessionBean` interface. This interface contains a number of callbacks that the container makes to the stateless session bean class.

Stateless Session Bean Lifecycle

It is important to understand that the container determines the lifecycle of a stateless session bean. When a client calls `create` on the home interface, the container does not necessarily create an instance of the EJB. It merely needs to return an instance of the remote interface. When method calls are made against that remote interface, the container has to find or create an instance of the bean class. The container then calls the business method on this instance. Likewise, calling remove on a stateless session bean does not necessarily remove a bean instance.

Note: With stateless session EJBs, the container is allowed to create and destroy bean instances as it sees fit.

When the container creates a new instance, the bean class first receives a call to its default (no argument) constructor. The container then calls the `setSessionContext` method and passes in a `SessionContext` as a parameter. The `SessionContext` is an object that can be used by the EJB to communicate with the EJB container and perform a number of standard functions. We cover the `SessionContext` in a later section. Generally, the `setSessionContext` method stores this context in a member variable.

Finally, the EJB container calls the `ejbCreate()` method. A stateless session bean can have only a single, no-parameter `create` method. This restriction is necessary because `ejbCreate` is called at the discretion of the container. There is no mechanism for passing parameters. The `ejb-Create` method initializes member variables, and, depending on the EJB, may perform additional initialization. At this point, the EJB container can call business methods on this bean instance. If the EJB container ever decides that it no longer needs this instance, it calls `ejbRemove`.

About Stateless Session Bean Pooling

Within the EJB container, the WebLogic Server uses a technique called *instance pooling* to manage stateless session bean instances. An EJB server can comply with the EJB specification if it creates a new stateless bean instance every time a business method is called, but that would not perform well. Another option would be for the container to create a single instance of the bean and have method calls wait for this instance to be available. This saves the time to create an instance, but unless method calls are short, performance suffers.

The WebLogic Server implements a better approach that keeps around a pool of ready instances. When a stateless session bean method call enters the server, the EJB container grabs an instance from the pool. After the method call completes, the bean instance is returned to the pool. Thus, the EJB container saves the time required to create new instances and is able to concurrently service a large number of clients.

Configuring Pooling

There are two parameters in the *weblogic-ejb-jar.xml* file that control the pooling behavior. The `initial-beans-in-freepool` tag specifies an initial size for the instance pool. When the EJB is deployed, the container populates the instance pool with as many instances as specified by this tag. This enables the EJB container to immediately respond to requests without having to initialize bean instances.

The deployer also can specify a `max-beans-in-freepool` value in the *weblogic-ejb-jar.xml* file. This parameter is an upper limit on the number of instances of this stateless EJB that can be used concurrently. When the EJB container asks the pool for an instance and there are none available, it is allowed to create new instances until it reaches the `max-beans-in-freepool` limit. Once this limit is reached, the container waits until an instance becomes available. If the method's transaction times out before an instance enters the pool, the container aborts the current transaction and returns to the caller. With proper configuration, this should be a rare event.

Note: Most users should not tune the `max-beans-in-freepool` parameter.

The default configuration does not limit the number of bean instances in the pool. In reality, the maximum number of instances is limited by the number of execute threads in the WebLogic Server. The maximum parallelism is achieved when each thread is using an instance from the pool.

Stateless Session Bean Clustering

Remember that a bean instance is returned to the instance pool when the method call returns. This means that the WebLogic Server can use a small number of bean instances to service a large number of clients. For instance, imagine that there are 10,000 clients each using the account stateless session EJB. Perhaps at any given instant, there are only 30 users simultaneously accessing their balance. Because all instances are identical, the server can use only a relatively small pool of 30 instances to service a large client base. The stateless programming model provides another clear advantage with WebLogic clusters. Because all instances of a stateless session bean are equivalent, a WebLogic cluster cannot only choose from a pool of instances, but it also can consider multiple servers. For example, WebLogic can use load balancing to route stateless session bean method calls to different servers in a cluster. Stateless session beans also contribute to scalable architectures. Because WebLogic can automatically load-balance method calls on a stateless session bean, increasing capacity is as simple as adding more servers to the cluster. The clustered stateless session beans automatically use the new servers.

Handling Failure with Clustered Stateless Session EJBs

The behavior of stateless session beans during a WebLogic Server (or network) failure depends on the list of methods defined in the `idempotent-methods` element set in the *weblogic-ejb-jar.xml* descriptor at deploy time. If a method is listed in the `idempotent-methods` element, failures can be recovered if the EJB stub can find another server hosting the EJB.

> **Note:** A method is idempotent if it can be called many times and the results and effects are the same as if it were called only once.

Methods that merely do reads are usually idempotent. For instance, the `helloWorld` method on the `HelloWorldEJB` is idempotent. The caller always receives the same value, and it can be called many times without causing any side effects. On the other hand, a method that is incrementing a counter is clearly not idempotent because the client gets a new value on each call.

Idempotent Stateless Session EJBs

If the stateless session bean method is marked as idempotent, the "smart stub" always retries the call on another server in case one of the members in the cluster dies. For instance, imagine a WebLogic cluster of three servers named A, B, and C. When the client calls the idempotent stateless session bean, its business method is load-balanced and directed to one of the servers, to A for example. If A dies before the client receives a result from the stateless session bean call, the smart stub chooses between B and C and tries the call again. Because the methods are idempotent, it is always acceptable for the stub to automatically retry the method on another server.

Nonidempotent Stateless Session EJBs

Unfortunately, stateless session beans that are not idempotent cannot always automatically fail over. Consider the three-server cluster again, but now the client is invoking a deposit method. Clearly, the deposit method is not idempotent. Like the previous case, the smart stub load-balances the invocation and chooses a server in the cluster to call, B for example. If B fails, there are two possible scenarios: The first case is that B died before it started on the deposit method. In this case, the smart stub automatically fails over to another server. Because it knows that B has not done any of the work in the deposit method, there is no harm in automatically failing over. The second case is that B fails after it has already started on the deposit method call. The smart stub has no way to tell how far the call has proceeded before the server failed. It is even possible that the method call completed and the deposit was committed, but the server failed before it could respond to the client. If the smart stub were to automatically fail over, it is possible that two deposits would be committed instead of the expected one. While this situation might appeal to some bank customers, they would not be too happy if the example had a withdraw method. Now that server B is offline, the smart stub will not try server B until it reenters the cluster.

Using Member Variables with Stateless Session Beans

After understanding the stateless programming model, it is important to realize that stateless session beans can have member variables and even state! The important qualification is that the member variables cannot be associated with a particular client. For instance, a stateless session bean would not store an account number or a user name in its variable. This information is associated with a client, and it breaks when another instance is chosen to handle a method call.

However, stateless session beans can have member variables that are associated with the bean and not the client. For example, a common use of stateless session beans is to provide an object interface to a legacy system. Each instance of the stateless session bean can have a legacy system connection as a member variable. The caller does not care which connection it receives for the method call, so it is fine if subsequent method calls receive different instances and hence different connections.

Using Freepool Settings to Limit Resources

In fact, stateless session beans with connections (or other resources) as member variables is the reason that the container blocks if `max-beans-in-freepool` bean instances are already in use. For example, imagine that your legacy system allows 10 simultaneous connections and each stateless session bean instance has a connection as a member variable. If the EJB container continued to allocate bean instances when there were 11 simultaneous callers, the legacy system would not allow the 11th connection. This is why the WebLogic EJB container makes the `max-beans-in-free-pool` setting a hard limit. By setting `max-beans-in-freepool` to 10, the deployer is ensured that there will never be more than 10 stateless instances for the EJB concurrently in use.

Stateful Session EJBs

At first glance, stateful session beans seem quite similar to stateless session beans. In theory, there are no required code changes to convert a stateless session bean to become stateful. Both EJB types must implement the `javax.ejb.SessionBean` interface and have the same basic requirements on the home and remote interface. However, in practice, stateful session beans look quite different from their stateless counterparts. Most of this differentiation is due to their stateful programming model.

The Stateful Programming Model

In the stateful session bean programming model, a client calls a `create` method on the home interface to create a new instance. Unlike stateless session beans, this causes the container to allocate a new bean instance in the server and associate it with this client. The client often passes initial conversational state as a parameter to the `create` method. For example, the bank account number could be passed when we create the teller stateful session bean.

The client receives a reference to the stateful session bean's remote interface from the `create` method. When the client calls a business method on the remote interface, the container must dispatch the call to the instance that is associated with this particular client. Unlike stateless session beans, the container does not have a pool of instances to multiplex on client calls. Each client reference to a stateful session bean refers to a specific EJB instance (see Figure 8–1).

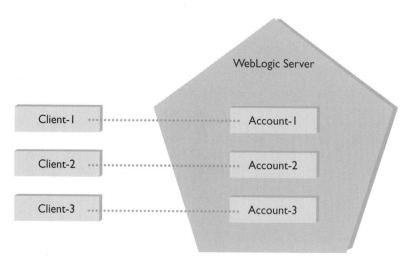

Figure 8–1
One stateful session EJB instance per client.

Most programmers are familiar and comfortable with the stateful programming model. For example, a Java program might create a list and add a string "WebLogic" to the list. If the program has not removed the value from the list, we assume that a search of the list finds the "WebLogic" string. Java uses the stateful programming model. If the list were implemented with a stateless session bean, a call could be routed to an instance that did not contain the "WebLogic" string.

Note: Coding stateful session beans is often easier than their stateless counterparts.

The stateful bank teller EJB could store the account number and other account metadata during the `create` call. Any subsequent business method call would have this information at its disposal, and it would not have to be passed as a parameter. This simplifies coding and can provide better encapsulation.

Stateful Session EJB Lifecycle

Because each instance of a stateful session bean has an implicit identity, its lifecycle is quite different from a stateless session bean. When a client calls a `create` method on the stateful session's home interface, the container allocates a new instance of the bean class. This calls the default (no parameter) constructor of the bean class. The container then calls `setSessionContext` with a `SessionContext` object. The `SessionContext` can be used to call back into the EJB container from the bean class. We cover the `SessionContext` in detail in a later section of this chapter. The container next calls the `ejbCreate` method in the stateful session bean class. The `ejbCreate` method is an opportunity to initialize the stateful session bean instance with parameters passed in the `create` method.

Creating Stateful Session EJBs

A stateful session bean can overload the `create` method in the home interface with many versions, each of which has different parameter types. Each `create` method in the home interface must have a corresponding `ejbCreate` method with the same parameters in the stateful session bean class. When a `create` method is called on the home interface, the container calls the corresponding `ejbCreate` method on the bean class.

After the `ejbCreate(...)` method has completed, the stateful session bean is in the ready state. If a business method is called on the stateful session's remote interface, the container can call the corresponding method on the bean class.

Removing Stateful Session EJBs

The `javax.ejb.EJBObject` interface defines a `remove()` method. Because all EJB remote interfaces must extend `EJBObject`, this method is available to clients of all EJBs. When a client makes a `remove` call on a stateful session bean instance, the container calls `ejbRemove` on the bean instance. This call removes the stateful session bean from the EJB container. After calling `remove`, the reference to the stateful session bean is dead. If a client attempts to call a business method after the bean has been removed, the EJB container throws a `java.rmi.NoSuchObjec-tException` to indicate that this stateful session bean instance no longer exists.

Passivation and Activation

The main advantage of the stateful programming model is that the object can store client-associated data within its member fields. For stateful session beans, this means that each client creates its own stateful session bean instance. For a large Internet site, however, the number of clients might be in the thousands, or even millions. It is not always feasible to store all of these instances in memory for the lifetime of a client.

In order to support large numbers of clients, the EJB container manages its working set of stateful session bean instances through mechanisms called passivation and activation.

Note: Just like a virtual memory system can swap memory pages to disk, the EJB container can swap out stateful session bean instances to free up memory and other resources.

Note: Swapping a bean out is called *passivation*. Before a passivated bean can be used for a method call, the container must activate the instance. This process is called *activation*.

Passivation

In the WebLogic EJB container, passivation is implemented with Java serialization. When a bean is passivated, it is serialized and stored on a backing store such as a disk. Before the bean can be passivated, the container must call the stateful session bean's `ejbPassivate`. This gives the bean writer a chance to clean up and release any nonserializable resources that the bean might hold in its member variables. For instance, if a stateful session bean held a database connection, it could release the database connection in the `ejbPassivate` method. The EJB specification requires that the container cannot passivate a stateful session bean while it is in use or is participating in a transaction. In EJB 2.1, you'll see that the field types that can be serialized and passivated (and not declared transient) are specified.

Activation

When a client calls a business method on a stateful session bean's remote interface, the EJB container needs to locate the corresponding bean class instance. If the bean is in memory, then the business method can be called, but if the bean has been passivated, the container must first activate the bean. This can involve reading the serialized bean from the disk and then deserializing the bean. The container then calls `ejbActivate()` on the bean, which gives the EJB a chance to reacquire any resources. For instance, the EJB could grab a database connection from a pool in the `ejbActivate` method.

Storing bean instances to disk and later reading them from disk is an expensive operation. In any modern computer, accessing memory is several orders of magnitude faster than reading from the disk. For this reason, the WebLogic EJB container uses a heavily optimized memory cache to store stateful session bean instances.

Configuring the EJB Cache

The WebLogic deployment descriptor contains a parameter `max-beans-in-cache`. This parameter represents the maximum number of stateful session bean instances that can be held in the in-memory cache. Most WebLogic deployments have sufficient memory, and it is not uncommon to see this parameter set to be tens of thousands of instances. In the common case, there is sufficient space in the EJB cache to store all active stateful session bean instances. The WebLogic EJB cache strives to add as little overhead to this case as possible. For example, a simple implementation might store all of the bean instances in a list ordered by the last time they were used. Whenever a new request comes in, the bean instance can be moved to the head of the list. While this is easy to implement, it does not scale well to a large server. For example, imagine a cache with a maximum size of 5,000 instances, but only 1,000 stateful session beans are currently being used. Clearly in this case, the EJB server can store all of the instances in memory. In the LRU (least recently used) implementation, the container must continually reorder the list as each method call is made. It's worse on a multiprocessor system because each CPU must contend for the list's lock.

In the WebLogic cache implementation, the container does nothing until the number of instances in the cache approaches a tunable percentage (usually 85 percent). At this point, the container begins to reorder its data structures. If the number of instances continues to grow, the WebLogic container passivates instances to disk to free up resources.

Stateful Session EJBs and Clustering

Clustering stateful session beans is a much more difficult proposition than clustering stateless session beans. Because all instances of a stateless session bean are equivalent, the container can route method calls to other servers. However, stateful session beans have an identity: Method calls are destined for a particular instance. One possible cluster implementation is to keep a copy of every stateful session bean in memory on every system in the cluster. Such an implementation quickly breaks down. In general, the problem is similar to cache coherency problems in multiprocessor machines.

First of all, the cluster must propagate any changes made to the stateful session bean to every member in the cluster. For a large cluster this might be very expensive, and it is problematic if a server fails or if the cluster becomes segmented. Another problem is that scalability is greatly affected. For instance, imagine that a single WebLogic instance can support n instances of a stateful session bean. Ideally, a 50-server cluster could support $50 \therefore n$ instances. However, if each server must store each instance in its cache, it is overwhelmed with recording all the updates on $50n$ instances. To overcome these problems, WebLogic uses an in-memory-replication cache based on process pairs.

By default, stateful session beans are not clustered. The `create` method on the home interface is load-balanced, and stateful session bean instances are created across the cluster. However, each instance will be tied to a particular server and lost if the server terminates. When the in-memory replication is selected in the WebLogic deployment descriptor, the container supports failover in a WebLogic cluster.

Stateful Session EJB Replication

In WebLogic in-memory replication, every stateful session bean instance is stored in memory on two servers. One server is designated as the primary, while the other is a secondary. The primary and secondary are determined per instance and are distributed throughout the cluster. For instance, consider a four-server cluster with servers A, B, C, and D. If a client creates a stateful session bean, the cluster might choose B to be the primary server and C to be the secondary for this instance. Another client might then create another stateful session bean instance. For this instance, the cluster chooses D as the primary and B as the secondary (see Figure 8–2).

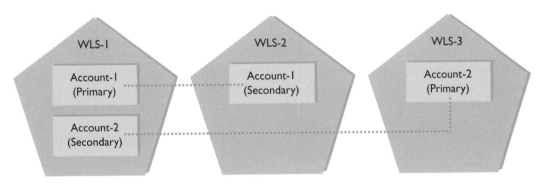

Figure 8–2
In-memory replication of stateful session EJBs.

Handling Failure with Clustered Stateful Session EJBs

Whenever a method call is made on the stateful session bean, it is routed to the primary server. If the primary server fails, the secondary server becomes the new primary, and the WebLogic cluster automatically chooses another available server as the secondary. If a secondary fails, the cluster automatically chooses a new secondary server. In the case where multiple WebLogic Servers are running on the same physical machine, the cluster attempts to locate the primary and secondary WebLogic Server instances on different machines, if possible.

Unlike a fully distributed cache, each instance is stored in memory in only two servers in the cluster. This makes updates much cheaper, and it greatly reduces the memory requirements of the WebLogic cluster. The stateful session bean instance is only lost if both the primary and secondary fail before the cluster is able to select new servers. This case is extremely rare in practice. Because stateful session beans are not persistent components, they do not contain mission-critical data such as account balances. For this reason, it is acceptable for an extremely rare occurrence to lose the instance. In practice, if the primary and secondary are both instantly lost, it indicates that there are probably major failures in the environment.

Managing State Updates

To implement failover correctly for stateful session beans, the WebLogic cluster must correctly propagate updates from the primary server to the secondary server. Because this update occurs across a network boundary, the bean instance must first be converted to a serialized form. The EJB specification requires that the bean writer receive an `ejbPassivate` callback before the bean is serialized. Because `ejbPassivate` can never be called while the EJB is participating in a transaction, the EJB container never sends an update to the secondary until the stateful session bean method call and its associated transaction have committed. After the transaction commits, the EJB container calls `ejbPassivate` on the bean and then sends the appropriate update across the wire to the secondary server.

There is a possibility that the primary server dies after the update has committed but before the secondary server has received the update. In this case, the client might see slightly stale data when the cluster fails over to the secondary. In general, this is acceptable with stateful session beans. Unlike entity beans (which we examine in depth in the following chapter), the state in a stateful session bean is not transactional.

Failover with Stateful Session EJBs

Like stateless session beans, a stateful session bean method call can automatically fail over to its secondary. However, this automatic failover can only occur if the method call is not started on the primary. If the method call does not connect to the primary, it automatically fails over to the secondary. If the primary starts processing the method call and then fails before returning to the client, the client has no idea of the data's state. It is possible that the transaction was rolled back, but it also is possible that the stateful session bean committed its transaction and the container died before it was able to return the value. In this case, the stub does not automatically fail over. Of course, any subsequent method calls use the new primary (see Figure 8–3).

Step 1: Client makes method calls to Primary

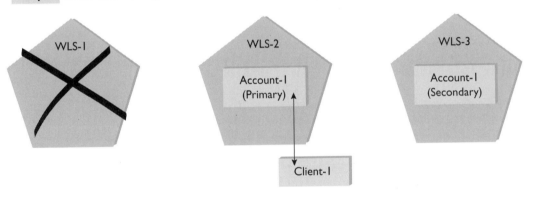

Step 2: Server fails, WebLogic Server moves Stateful Session EJB to new Server

Figure 8–3
Failover with in-memory stateful session EJBs.

Stateful Session Beans and Concurrency

It is important to remember that stateful session beans are designed for use by a single client. The EJB specification requires that only a single method call may be active on any single stateful session bean instance at a given time. If another call arrives on the EJB server for a given instance while the instance is already in a method call, the EJB server is required to throw a `RemoteException` to the second caller.

Best Practice: A multithreaded client should either serialize calls to a stateful session bean instance on the client or create a stateful session bean instance for each thread.

Using Stateful Session EJBs in Web Applications

Unfortunately, it can be difficult to use stateful session beans correctly from a servlet or Java Server-Pages (JSP) page. If a stateful session bean is used with the scope of a single request, then multiple threads do not use the instance. However, Web designers often store a reference to a stateful session bean in the servlet's session and attempt to use the stateful session bean with session scope. While this solution works for a while, it may fail if a session is ever used concurrently. This can happen, for instance, if a user clicks on Stop in a browser while a stateful session bean is processing a request. If the user then clicks on Reload, he or she enters the same session and attempts a concurrent call. If the previous call has not finished the previous invocation, the container throws a `RemoteException`.

There are two possible solutions for this scenario. One is to use stateful session beans only in the scope of a single request. While this is possible for requests that are very involved, it is a lot of overhead to create a new stateful session bean instance for every HTTP request. The other option is to enable a WebLogic-specific option `<allow-concurrent-calls>` in the `weblogic-ejb-jar.xml` deployment descriptor. When this option is enabled, the WebLogic Server blocks any concurrent callers until the previous method call has finished with the stateful session bean instance. Once the previous method call finishes, the concurrent call gains access to the stateful session bean instance.

Using Transactions with Session Beans

The EJB container provides support for transactions as one of its primary services. The WebLogic EJB container makes use of the WebLogic Server's JTA implementation.

In session EJBs, there are two transaction possibilities: bean-managed transactions and container-managed transactions. The `transaction-type` tag in the `ejb-jar.xml` selects the transaction type. For example, `<transaction-type>Bean</transaction-type>` would use bean-managed transactions.

Container-Managed Transactions

Container-managed transactions free the bean writer from explicitly coding calls to begin or commit a transaction. Instead, the EJB writer declares transaction attributes in the `ejb-jar.xml` deployment descriptor. The container reads these attributes and automatically starts and commits a transaction as required. This enables the EJB writer to concentrate on writing business logic. It also eliminates a class of bugs in which the EJB writer does not handle transaction demarcation correctly.

The container's behavior for each of these attributes also depends on whether the caller is participating in a transaction. This can occur if the caller is another EJB that is already participating in a transaction. It is also possible for clients to explicitly start a transaction with the `UserTransaction` interface. A client starts a transaction by looking up `"javax.transaction.UserTransaction"` in JNDI and calling `begin`. The transaction can be committed by the commit method on the `UserTransaction` interface.

For example,

```
// Use an InitialContext for JNDI lookup
Context ctx = new InitialContext();
```

```
// get a UserTransaction reference
UserTransaction tx = (UserTransaction)
  ctx.lookup("javax.transaction.UserTransaction");

// start the transaction
tx.begin();

// call an EJB
cart.addItem(new Car());

// commit the transaction
tx.commit();
```

There are six different keywords for container-managed transactions: `Never`, `NotSupported`, `Supports`, `Required`, `RequiresNew`, and `Mandatory`. These attributes determine how and when the container should start and stop transactions. See Table 8–1 for a list of keywords for container-managed transactions.

Table 8–1 Keywords for Container-Managed Transactions

Keyword	Definition
Never	This EJB call should not participate in a transaction. If the bean is called within a transaction, the EJB container throws a `RemoteException`.
NotSupported	The EJB call does not participate in a transaction regardless of whether the caller is transactional.
Supports	If the caller is participating in a transaction, the EJB call participates in that transaction. Otherwise, the EJB call does not participate in a transaction.
Mandatory	If the caller has a transaction, the EJB participates in that transaction. Otherwise, the container throws a `TransactionRequiredException`.
Required	If the caller has a transaction, the EJB participates in that transaction. Otherwise, the container starts a transaction before it calls the EJB method and commits the transaction when the method call completes.
RequiresNew	The container starts a new transaction before it calls the EJB's method. It commits the transaction when the method call returns.

The transaction attribute is assigned in the `ejb-jar.xml` deployment descriptor. It can be specified on a per-bean basis, on a method name, or on a particular method signature. The transaction attribute is set using the `container-transaction` tag.

> **Note:** If no transaction attribute is set, the WebLogic EJB container defaults to `Supports`.

Here is a snippet from the `ShoppingCart` stateful session bean where we define transaction attributes.

```
<container-transaction>
  <method>
    <ejb-name>ShoppingCartEJB</ejb-name>
    <method-name>*</method-name>
  </method>
  <trans-attribute>Required</trans-attribute>

</container-transaction>
```

Because the method-name is *, this declaration is specifying the default transaction attribute for the ShoppingCartEJB as Required. If no more specific transaction attribute is found for a method on this EJB, the container uses Required.

```
<container-transaction>
  <method>
    <ejb-name>ShoppingCartEJB</ejb-name>
    <method-name>getContents</method-name>
  </method>
  <trans-attribute>NotSupported</trans-attribute>
</container-transaction>
```

In this declaration, methods named getContents are assigned the transaction attribute of NotSupported. This overrides the previous declaration of Required.

```
<container-transaction>
  <method>
    <ejb-name>ShoppingCartEJB</ejb-name>
    <method-name>getContents</method-name>
    <method-params>
      <method-param>java.lang.Object</method-param>
    </method-params>
  </method>
  <trans-attribute>Supports</trans-attribute>
</container-transaction>
```

This declaration states that the method getContents(java.lang.Object) should get the transaction attribute of Supports. It overrides both of the previous declarations.

Using these declarations, we can see how the container assigns transaction attributes when methods are called on this EJB. For example, when the addItem business method is called, the container uses the transaction attribute Required because no rule other than the default applies. A call to getContents() is run as NotSupported because there is declaration for methods named get-Contents, but the signature does not match the getContents(java.lang.Object) declaration. Finally, a call to getContents(java.lang.Object) is run as Supports.

SessionSynchronization Interface

Stateful session beans with container-managed transactions can optionally implement the `javax.ejb.SessionSynchronization` interface. This interface contains three methods: `afterBegin()`, `beforeCompletion()`, and `afterCompletion(int)`. The container calls the `afterBegin` method when the stateful session bean enters a transaction. The `beforeCompletion` call occurs before the transaction is prepared to commit. The `afterCompletion` callback has a status `Boolean` as a parameter. If the container passes true to `afterCompletion`, the transaction was committed; a false value means there was a rollback.

> **Note:** The `beforeCompletion` callback is often used to write cached data to the database before the transaction commits. Because `afterCompletion` is called after the transaction has completed, it is inappropriate to do transactional work in this callback. Instead, `afterCompletion` is generally used to release locks on shared resources or to update statistics on transaction commits and aborts.

Bean-Managed Transactions

Session EJBs also support bean-managed transactions. In container-managed transactions, the EJB code never made an explicit reference to the `UserTransaction` interface. All transaction demarcation was done either in the client or automatically by the EJB container. In a session bean using bean-managed transactions, the bean writer explicitly codes transaction demarcation.

> **Note:** A session bean with bean-managed transactions cannot participate in the caller's transaction. If the caller is participating in a transaction and calls a session bean with bean-managed transactions, the container does not pass the caller's transaction to the bean-managed session bean.

The bean-managed transaction session bean gets a `UserTransaction` reference by calling the `getUserTransaction()` method on its `SessionContext`. Remember that the container calls the `setSessionContext` method before it calls `ejbCreate`. Generally, the `SessionContext` is then stored in a member variable and can be used throughout the bean's lifetime.

With the `UserTransaction` reference, the session bean can use the begin, commit, and rollback methods to demarcate transactions. Stateless session beans with bean-managed transactions must commit or roll back their transaction before returning from a method call. A stateful session bean is allowed to return from a method without finishing the transaction. When the stateful session bean instance is called again, the container reassociates the instance with the former transaction.

EJB Security

Security is an integral component of almost every enterprise application. A secure application must examine security policies and protect resources at every level. This section describes the standard security features in the EJB container. A secure EJB application makes use of the EJB container security services and integrates with an application security model.

The standard EJB security model is based on declarations in the EJB deployment descriptor as well as a simple programmatic security interface. EJB security relies on the concept of the security role. A security role is a logical group that represents an application role. For instance, a payroll application might define an administrator security role. The payroll application can specify that only the administrator role can modify the payroll schedule. The EJB deployer can define method permissions for EJB methods in the home and remote interfaces.

Method permissions define one or more security roles that may call the associated method. If the calling identity is a member of one of the listed roles, the EJB container permits the method call to proceed. Otherwise, the EJB container throws a `java.rmi.RemoteException`, and the method call is not permitted. It should be noted that the calling identity must only match one of the associated roles. Assigning multiple security roles to a method permission is a boolean OR, not a boolean AND.

Assigning Security Roles in the EJB Deployment Descriptors

EJB security roles are declared in the EJB deployment descriptor with the `security-role` tag. The security role includes an optional description and the name of the role. For instance, the following tag defines the administrator role:

```
<security-role>
  <description>
      Payroll Administrator. This role is permitted to change the
      payroll schedule and perform administrative functions.
  </description>
  <role-name>Administrator</role-name>
</security-role>
```

The EJB deployer also defines method access control lists in the EJB deployment descriptor with the `method-permission` tag. The `method-permission` tag contains a description, one or more role names, and one or more method declarations. The semantics of the tag are that any of the listed role names may access any one of the matching method declarations. The methods may be defined in three different ways. The first option is to specify the * wildcard, which applies to all methods within a given EJB. For instance, the following declaration requires that the caller be a member of either the payroll users group or the administrators group to access the payroll EJB.

```
<method-permission>
  <role-name>PayrollUser</role-name>
  <role-name>Administrator</role-name>
  <method>
    <ejb-name>PayrollEJB</ejb-name>
    <method-name>*</method-name>
  </method>
</method-permission>
```

The method tag also can specify that any overloaded method with a given name receives this method permission. For instance, this declaration requires that any method named `getSalary` can be called only by members of the management role.

```
<method-permission>
  <role-name>Management</role-name>
```

```
<method>
  <ejb-name>PayrollEJB</ejb-name>
  <method-name>getSalary</method-name>
</method>
</method-permission>
```

Finally, a method tag may specify an exact method signature, which receives the associated method permissions. For instance, this declaration restricts the `setSystemPassword(java.lang.String)` method to the administrator role.

```
<method-permission>
  <role-name>Administrator</role-name>
  <method>
    <ejb-name>PayrollEJB</ejb-name>
    <method-name>setSystemPassword</method-name>
    <method-params>
<method-param>java.lang.String</method-param>
    </method-params>
  </method>
</method-permission>
```

The EJB container always applies the most specific method permission declaration. Setting a method permission on the exact signature overrides any other settings. Likewise, setting the method permission on a named method would override the * setting.

At this point, the EJB deployer has defined a security model for the payroll EJB because only users in appropriate roles can access the sensitive portions of the `PayrollEJB`. However, the EJB deployer has not yet specified how to map actual system users (principals) to the application's security roles. This is accomplished with the `security-role-assignment` tag in the `weblogic-ejb-jar.xml` deployment descriptor. This tag includes the security role name and one or more principals that are members of the security role. The EJB deployer must map principals to all of the security roles defined in the EJB deployment descriptor. For instance, the following tag defines the users Bob and Jill in the administrator role:

```
<security-role-assignment>
  <role-name>Administrator</role-name>
  <principal-name>Bob</principal-name>
  <principal-name>Jill</principal-name>
</security-role-assignment>
```

Using declarative security has the advantage that the security policies are independent of the bean code. Security settings may be adjusted at deploy time to match the constraints of the runtime environment. However, not all security policies can be specified with declarative method permission tags. The EJB specification provides a simple programmatic interface for beans to write explicit security checks within the bean code.

Using Programmatic Security with EJBs

The EJB security API consists of only the `java.security.Principal getCallerPrinci-pal()` and `boolean isCallerInRole(String  roleName)` on the EJBContext. The `isCallerInRole(String)` method is a programmatic interface to the declarative security model. It merely tests whether the current user is a member of the passed role. The `getCaller-Principal` method returns the security principal of the method's caller. Generally, this method is used to perform explicit security checks against the principal (for instance, the payroll EJB that each user should be allowed to modify on his or her payroll account information). However, user A should not be able to access or modify user B's account information. This cannot be accomplished with EJB's declarative security because the allowed principals depend on the bean instance, and it would require a security role for each user. Instead, the security is contained within the bean code. For instance, the following code shows how the bean code might maintain that the caller of the `set-BillingAddress(String address)` function is a member of the users group and is also setting his or her own billing address.

```
// set in setSessionContext
private SessionContext ctx;

// user name of this Payroll account.  Set in ejbCreate.
private String userName;

public void setBillingAddress(String roleName) {

  if (! ctx.isCallerInRole("Users")) {

      throw new SecurityException("Caller is not a member of
Users");
  }

  if (! userName.equals(getCallerPrincipal().getName())) {
      throw new SecurityException("Caller cannot access this
account");
  }

  // business logic
  ...
}
```

When the EJB code uses the `isCallerInRole` method, it is referencing a logical role name that is local to the bean instance. This logical role name must be mapped to a concrete role name in the EJB deployment descriptor. This mapping can be accomplished with the `security-role-ref` tag. This tag contains an optional description as well as a concrete role being referenced. For instance, the following declaration maps the user's logical role to the payroll user's role already defined in the EJB deployment descriptor.

```
<security-role-ref>
  <description>A Payroll User</description>
  <role-name>PayrollUsers</role-name>
  <role-link>Users</role-link>
</security-role-ref>
```

EJB Environment

Almost every program requires a means for users to override configuration parameter values. Standalone Java programs typically use Java system properties, and these values can be changed by specifying -D options to the Java virtual machine. Likewise, EJB components can use the EJB environment to read configuration parameters whose values may be adjusted by the deployer. The EJB environment enables the bean code to refer to the configuration parameters with logical names that can then be assigned values during deployment. Because the EJB code only refers to the logical name, the values may be changed without touching the bean classes.

Declaring Environment Variables

EJB environment values are declared in the ejb-jar.xml deployment descriptor as name/value pairs. The values may be any of the Java wrapper types: string, character, integer, boolean, double, byte, short, long, or float. User-defined types may not be used as EJB environment values. The environment value is declared with an env-entry tag that consists of an optional description, the logical name, the type, and a value. For instance, an EJB might use a configuration parameter named maxWidgets. This can be declared as an EJB environment variable and assigned the value 100783 with the following entry in the ejb-jar.xml:

```
<env-entry>
  <description>
      Maximum number of widgets that our EJB accepts
  </description>
  <env-entry-name>maxWidgets</env-entry-name>
  <env-entry-type>java.lang.Integer</env-entry-type>
  <env-entry-value>100783</env-entry-value>
</env-entry>
```

The EJB environment values declared in the EJB deployment descriptor are made available through JNDI to the EJB code. When an EJB is deployed, the container creates a JNDI context at java:/comp/env that includes the EJB environment values. To obtain the value associated with a logical name, the bean writer makes a JNDI lookup for java:/comp/env/ followed by the env-entry-name declared in the EJB deployment descriptor. For instance, the writer of the widget bean could use the following code to find the value of maxWidgets at runtime:

```
Context ctx = new InitialContext();
Integer maxWidgets = (Integer)
  ctx.lookup("java:/comp/env/maxWidgets");
```

EJB environment variables are a convenient and standard method to store and retrieve configuration parameters from the bean class. It is important to note that these values are read-only. The bean code cannot use JNDI to bind in additional environment variables at runtime or modify the existing value for an environment entry. In addition, the bean writer should be aware that environment entries are local to the EJB deployment. They're not visible to other EJBs or components within the server. Also, there are no means for a client to look up these values. This is required, since every EJB uses the `java:/comp/env` context to read its environment variables. In the WebLogic Server, environment variables are implemented within the EJB server by attaching the bean's `java:/comp/env` context immediately before a method on the bean class is called and removing the `java:/comp/env` context when the bean method returns.

Note: Environment entries are read-only and local to the EJB.

EJB References

EJB components do not exist in a vacuum, and the business logic within EJBs often makes use of other EJBs deployed in the server. Normally, a client references another EJB by looking up the JNDI name where the EJB was deployed. It is undesirable to hardcode the JNDI name within the bean code because this limits the EJB's portability and reusability. One possible solution is to store the JNDI name as an EJB environment entry because this approach allows the names to be changed at deployment time without modifying the bean code. However, there is essentially no validation that can be performed on this JNDI name by the server's tools. For instance, the EJB server cannot validate that this JNDI name corresponds to an EJB of the appropriate type. The EJB specification includes EJB references as a portable way to safely reference another EJB within bean code. Unlike a simple JNDI name, an EJB reference gives the EJB server sufficient information to ensure that the EJB reference corresponds to a deployed EJB of the appropriate type.

Declaring EJB References

Like environment entries, EJB references are defined in the EJB deployment descriptor. The EJB deployer includes the `ejb-ref` tag to define an EJB reference. The `<ejb-ref>` tag consists of an optional description, the logical name, the type of the reference, the home interface class, and the remote interface class. The reference type is `Session` for all session EJBs and `Entity` for all entity EJBs. (Chapter 9 discusses entity beans in detail.) For example, the following XML tag provides an EJB reference named `ejb/WidgetEJB`.

```
<ejb-ref>
  <description>An EJB reference to the Widget EJB</description>
  <ejb-ref-name>ejb/WidgetEJB</ejb-ref-name>
  <ejb-ref-type>Session</ejb-ref-type>
  <home>chapter8.WidgetHome</home>
  <remote>chapter8.Widget</remote>
</ejb-ref>
```

Each EJB reference also requires an entry in the WebLogic deployment descriptor to map the `ejb-ref-name` to a concrete JNDI name in the server. The following example maps our `ejb-ref-name`, `ejb/WidgetEJB`, to the JNDI name `DeployedWidget`.

```
<ejb-reference-description>
  <ejb-ref-name>ejb/WidgetEJB</ejb-ref-name>
  <jndi-name>DeployedWidget</jndi-name>
</ejb-reference-description>
```

The bean class can now use this EJB reference to refer to the `WidgetEJB` without storing any concrete JNDI name. Like environment entries, EJB references are stored in JNDI under the `java:/comp/env` context. It is recommended that EJB references always be stored under the context `java:/comp/env/ejb`. As you can see in the preceding example, the EJB reference name begins with a leading `ejb/` in accordance with this recommendation. The bean code can reference the widget home interface by making a JNDI lookup to `java:/comp/env/ejb/WidgetEJB` as in the following code:

```
Context ctx = new InitialContext();
Object h = ctx.lookup("java:/comp/env/ejb/WidgetEJB");
WidgetHome home = (WidgetHome)
    PortableRemoteObject.narrow(h, WidgetHome.class);
```

The EJB container requires that EJB references specify the concrete JNDI name for each EJB reference in the WebLogic descriptor. This approach is flexible because the EJB reference might point to an EJB in another application that has not yet been deployed.

Resource Manager References

In addition to configuration parameters and EJB references, the EJB specification also provides a portable method to reference resource manager factories from the bean class. Like the other environment references, resource manager references are logical names that can be used to reference server resources. For instance, a resource manager reference might point to a JDBC `DataSource`. Instead of hardcoding the data source name and JDBC driver information, the bean code refers to a logical name. At deployment time, the EJB deployer maps the logical name to a concrete resource factory.

Declaring Resource Manager References

Like other environment references, resource manager references are defined in the EJB deployment descriptor. Resource references use the `resource-ref` tag, which contains a description of the reference, the logical name, the resource type, and an authorization setting. The resource type depends on the underlying resource factory that is being mapped. The authorization setting may be either `Container` or `Application`. When the `Container` setting is used, the appropriate security permissions should be set in the WebLogic Server before deploying the EJB. In this case, the bean code does not contain code to sign on or authenticate itself with the resource manager. When the authorization setting is `Application`, it is the bean code's responsibility to explicitly sign on to the resource manager. The container authorization setting is generally preferred because it defers security settings to deployment time. This enables the same bean code to be used in different environments where the security settings may not be identical. The following `resource-ref` example creates a logical name `jdbc/DBPool` that maps to a JDBC data source:

```
<resource-ref>
  <description>
      This DataSource is mapped to a connection where the Widget
      EJB  store inventory information.
  </description>
  <res-ref-name>jdbc/DBPool</res-ref-name>
  <res-type>javax.sql.DataSource</res-type>
  <res-auth>Container</res-auth>
</resource-ref>
```

Like EJB references, resource manager references also require an entry in the WebLogic deployment descriptor. The `resource-description` tag includes the corresponding `res-ref-name` of the `resource-ref` and maps it to a server-wide JNDI name of a resource. Table 8–2 shows the name of the resource type for each resource manager.

Table 8–2   Resource Manager Types

Resource Manager	Resource Type
JDBC DataSource	javax.sql.DataSource
JMS Connection Factories	javax.jms.QueueConnectionFactory
JavaMail Session	javax.mail.Session
URL Connection Factory	java.net.URL

For example, this entry in the *weblogic-ejb-jar.xml* maps `jdbc/DBPool` to the name `DBPool`.

```
<resource-description>
  <res-ref-name>jdbc/DBPool</res-ref-name>
  <jndi-name>DBPool</jndi-name>
</resource-description>
```

The final step in using a JDBC resource manager reference is mapping the serverwide JNDI name to an actual resource. For JDBC, this resource is a JDBC connection pool. The following `config.xml` entry maps the JNDI name `DBPool` to the connection pool named `DevelopmentPool`.

```
<JDBCTxDataSource
  Name="DBPool"
  Targets="myserver"
  JNDIName="DBPool"
  PoolName="DevelopmentPool"
/>
```

Resource Reference Advantages

At first glance, a lot of mapping and deployment descriptor elements are used to create a resource manager reference. However, this approach makes it easy for the deployer to reconfigure the application without changing the actual implementation classes. For instance, the development team might code and test the EJB in a private development environment. In this case, the JNDI name is mapped to the `DevelopmentPool` connecting to a development database. When the bean is deployed in the production system, the deployer can simply remap the `DBPool` JNDI name to the production database connection pool. No changes are required in the bean code or even the EJB deployment descriptors.

Like other environment references, the bean writer looks up resource manager references in the JNDI tree under the `java:/comp/env` context. By convention, JDBC `DataSources` are mapped under the JDBC subcontext; JMS connection factories typically use the JMS subcontext; JavaMail connection factories use mail; and URL connection factories use URL. The bean code can reference the `jdbc/DBPool` reference with the following code:

```
Context ctx = new InitialContext();
DataSource dataSource = (DataSource)
   ctx.lookup("java:/comp/env/jdbc/DBPool");
```

Handles

In some cases, an EJB client may wish to save its `EJBObject` reference to persistent storage for retrieval at a later date or more likely by another program. The EJB specification defined the concept of `Handles` as a serializable object that encapsulates sufficient information to reconstitute an `EJBObject` reference. `Handles` might be used to pass EJB references between two cooperating processes. The receiving process gets the `EJBObject` reference back again from the `Handle`. To get a `Handle`, the programmer calls the `getHandle()` method on the `EJBObject` interface. This returns to the programmer an instance of `javax.ejb.Handle`. To re-create the `EJBObject` reference, the `Handle` interface contains a `getEJBObject()` method. For instance,

```
// convert EJBObject into a Handle reference
HelloWorld hw = home.create();
javax.ejb.Handle handle = hw.getHandle();

// get the EJBObject reference back
HelloWorld backAgain = (HelloWorld)
   PortableRemoteObject.narrow(handle.getEJBObject(), HelloWorld.class);
```

HomeHandles

The EJB specification also defines the `javax.ejb.HomeHandle` interface. HomeHandles are similar to Handles but instead of applying to `EJBObject` references, they contain enough information to rebuild `EJBHome` references. To get a HomeHandle reference, the programmer calls the `getHomeHandle` method on the `EJBHome` reference. This method returns an instance of the `javax.ejb.HomeHandle` interface. The programmer can then regain the Home reference by calling HomeHandle's `getEJBHome` method. For instance,

```
// save to a HomeHandle reference
Context ctx = new InitialContext();
Object h = ctx.lookup("HelloWorldEJB");
HelloWorldHome home = (HelloWorldHome);
   PortableRemoteObject.narrow(h, HelloWorldHome.class);

HomeHandle homeHandle = home.getHomeHandle();

// rebuild the Home reference

Object nh = homeHandle.getEJBHome();

HelloWorldHome newHomeReference = (HelloWorldHome)
   PortableRemoteObject.narrow(nh, HelloWorldHome.class);
```

Advantages of Handles

The main advantage of HomeHandles and Handles is that they automatically store the information needed to rebuild the reference. For instance, a HomeHandle encapsulates the information necessary to create an InitialContext to the WebLogic Server and then looks up the correct Home object. A client that receives a HomeHandle can get the EJBHome reference without having to know the server's URL or the JNDI name of the EJBHome.

A common misconception is that HomeHandles are more efficient than explicitly building an InitialContext and performing a lookup on the JNDI name. In general, both cases perform identical steps. The HomeHandle merely stores the information that the programmer would have to provide.

It is also important to note that Handles do not store the current identity, and they may not be used as a security credential. For instance, consider a password EJB where only principals in the role of administrator may access the bean. An administrator may access the bean and store a Handle. Now, if another user receives the Handle and calls getEJBObject, the new user has a password reference. To call any restricted method on the password reference, the new user still needs to be authenticated as an administrator. The Handle does not automatically grant any permissions.

Development Tasks and WebLogic Workshop

Building an EJB involves several steps, although the process is simplified by WebLogic Workshop 8.1. For clarity, we include the steps here.

1. Create a directory structure for the files associated with your EJB (source files, deployment descriptors, and so on). Within an application in Workshop, you can select File, New, Project, then select EJB Project. Once you've created the project, you can right-click on the project name in the Application tab and select New, Folder, and name the folder according to the EJB package. Create subfolders as needed for your package address. The directories to hold the deployment descriptors will be created by Workshop.
2. Write the class code (java files) for your EJB. Right-click on the lowest directory of the EJB package and select New. Choose the EJB type and name it, then click Create. If you toggle over to the Source view, you'll see the EJB class is framed and ready for your code insertion.

3. Compile the source code (generating .class files). You can edit your build script by opening the *build.xml* file in the Applications tab. Once you have edited the script if necessary, you can select Build, Build Application, or go to the Ant view and double-click on Build.

4. Create deployment descriptors and container classes. One of the conveniences of using Workshop to build your EJB project is that it will create your deloyment descriptors for you, including `ejb-jar.xml` and `weblogic-ejb-jar.xml`. Workshop will also generate your container classes (classes for home and remote interfaces) and will package it up for you according to your build script.

5. Deploy to a managed server, such as WebLogic Server cluster. To check on deployment status, you can access your WebLogic Server Console, view Your Deployed Resources and choose EJB Modules. Then select BandsEJB and view the status of recent deployment activity.

Best Practices

The following are some best practices for coding stateful and stateless session EJBs.

Coding Business Interfaces

Many new EJB programmers are confused by the relationship between the remote interface and the EJB class. This arrangement is necessary for the container to intercept all method calls to the EJB. One confusing aspect is that the EJB class implements the methods defined in the remote interface, but the EJB class doesn't implement the remote interface itself. In fact, the EJB class should never implement the remote interface. While the EJB specification allows this practice, it can cause serious yet subtle bugs. The problem with having the EJB class implement the remote interface is that now the EJB class can be passed as a parameter to any method that expects the remote interface as a parameter.

Remember that the remote interface exists to allow the container to intercept method calls in order to provide necessary services such as transactions or security. If the bean class is used, the method calls arrive directly on the bean object—creating a dangerous situation in which the container cannot intercept method calls or intervene in case of error. If (as recommended) the EJB class does not implement the remote interface, this problem becomes apparent at compile time. The Java compiler will reject the attempt to pass the bean class as a parameter of the remote interface's type.

Best Practice: Never implement the remote interface in the EJB class.

The only advantage of implementing the remote interface in the bean class is that the Java compiler catches any method that is defined in the remote interface but not implemented in the bean class. However, this also means that the bean class has to provide dummy implementations of the remote interface's superclass (`javax.ejb.EJBObject`) to satisfy the Java compiler.

Clearly, implementing the remote interface in the bean class is not a good practice, but it is desirable to catch the bean writer's errors as early as possible. The WebLogic Server provides an EJB compliance checker to catch as many violations of the EJB specification as possible. The compliance checker analyzes an EJB and flags any specification violations with the related section in the EJB specification. The compliance checker can be run as `java weblogic.EJBComplianceChecker` on the command line or by using the graphical deployment tools. The compliance checker catches any methods that are defined in the remote interface but not implemented in the EJB class.

Another method for catching this class of errors is by using a pattern known as the business interface. In this pattern, all of the business methods are defined in a separate interface. The remote interface extends the business interface and the `javax.ejb.EJBObject` interface. The bean class can then implement the business interface. For instance,

```
public interface MyBusinessInterface {
  public void businessMethod()
    throws RemoteException;
}

public interface MyRemoteInterface
  extends MyBusinessInterface, EJBObject
{
  // empty
 }

public class MyBean
  implements SessionBean, MyBusinessInterface
{

public void businessMethod()
  throws RemoteException
{
  // provide implementation
}

// implement SessionBean methods here

}
```

By using the business interface, the compiler ensures that the bean class implements the methods in the business interface. The pattern is also safe because the bean class cannot be passed into a method expecting the remote interface. While both classes are assignable from the business interface, the remote interface is still a distinct type.

Tips for Transactions

Almost every EJB application uses transactions at some point. Transactions ensure correctness and reliability and are essential to e-commerce applications. However, misusing transactions can greatly affect performance and even produce incorrect results. It is important to understand that session beans themselves cannot be transactional.

A common misperception is that the member variables of the session bean will be rolled back when their transaction aborts. Instead, session beans merely propagate their transaction to any resource that they acquire. For instance, at the beginning of a transaction, a session bean has a member variable with a value of 0. During the transaction, the member variable is set to 2, and a row is inserted into the database. If the transaction rolls back, the member variable will not be reset to 0.

However, the row will no longer be in the database. Because a database is a transactional resource, it will participate in the session bean's transaction, and a rollback will abort any associated work.

> **Note:** Session bean state is not transactional.

Transactions can have a huge impact on performance. Because transactions provide durability, a transaction commit is a relatively expensive operation. Many EJB applications limit their performance by making their transactions too fine-grained. Operations that are closely related and occur in a series should usually be in the same transaction. For instance, our user page may read the associated user data and write the last accessed timestamp, all within the same transaction.

User Interactions and Transaction Performance

Transactions also can cause problems if they span too many operations. In particular, a transaction should never encompass user input or user think time. Regardless of the underlying concurrency model, transactions acquire locks and resources. If a user starts a transaction and then goes to lunch or even visits another Web site, the transaction is not committed. Instead, the transaction continues to hold valuable locks and resources within the server.

In general, all transaction demarcation should occur within the server. There are a number of well-known techniques to avoid keeping long-running transactions open. When you ask a user to submit a form, break the operation up into two transactions. The Web page should read the data in a single transaction along with a version stamp. This transaction is committed before the form is returned to the user. The user can now modify the data as he or she sees fit. The form update occurs in a new transaction.

But what if another transaction has modified the data and our user has updated a form with stale data? There are several methods to handle this case: the correct approach depends on the application. One option is to write back all the data in the user's form. In this case, our user can overwrite any modifications that occurred after we read the data.

A more common approach adds an additional time or version stamp to the associated database table. When the data is read, this version stamp is read as well. When the write occurs, the update statement is conditional and commits only if the versions match. This ensures that the data is only updated if another client has not modified the underlying data. If the update fails, the correct behavior in this scenario depends on the application. For instance, the user might be alerted to the situation and shown to the latest data. Another variant on this approach is to verify that only the modified fields are consistent with the read data.

> **Best Practice:** Transactions should never encompass user input or think time.

Container-Managed Versus Bean-Managed Transactions

The EJB specification allows a session bean to choose either container-managed or bean-managed transactions. In container-managed transactions, the bean writer declares transaction attributes in the deployment descriptor. The EJB container then automatically starts and commits transactions as requested. The bean writer does not have to write any code to manage transactions. In bean-managed transactions, the bean writer uses the `UserTransaction` interface to explicitly start and commit transactions. Container-managed transactions should always be the bean writer's first choice.

Transactions consume resources in both the application server and in databases, which means you should keep transactions as short as possible. Container-managed transactions encompass a set of method calls. When the outer method completes, the transaction is committed or rolled back by the container.

In bean-managed transactions, the bean writer must ensure that the transaction is committed or rolled back. While the WebLogic Server includes a transaction timeout, the bean writer should not rely on this feature, but instead release transaction resources as soon as possible. With bean-managed transactions, the bean writer needs to ensure that every exceptional path handles the transaction rollback or commit correctly. With container-managed transactions, this is handled automatically by the EJB container.

> **Best Practice:** Use container-managed instead of bean-managed transactions.

Transactions and Error Handling

When an EJB encounters an error, the bean writer often needs to force a transaction rollback. The EJB container automatically rolls back a container transaction if a system exception is thrown. For a bean writer, the easiest way to force transaction rollback is by calling the `EJBContext.setRollbackOnly` method. This makes the bean code easier to maintain because it is explicit that the transaction will be rolled back.

> **Best Practice:** Force transaction rollback with the `EJBContext`'s `setRollbackOnly` method.

Application Partitioning

Transactions should never span client input. As noted, a scalable application cannot start a transaction and wait for a user to complete a form or click Submit on a Web form. In fact, it is best to avoid handling transactions in the Web tier. JSPs and servlets should be concerned with presentation logic and use an interface to communicate with the business logic. Transactional business logic should be handled within the EJB layer.

Generally, a stateless session bean is a good interface between the Web tier and the EJB layer. The stateless session bean should be starting transactions, and committing or rolling back transactions, before returning to the Web tier. This ensures that transactions are short and only encompass the transactional logic.

> **Best Practice:** Don't expose transactions to the Web tier or presentation layer.

The EJB deployer selects the container-managed transaction demarcation by setting the transaction attribute to `Never`, `NotSupported`, `Supports`, `Required`, `RequiresNew`, or `Mandatory` in the EJB deployment descriptor. In general, `Supports` should not be used in an enterprise application. The danger of using the `Supports` setting is that the EJBs will run in a transaction only if the caller has started a transaction. If a business component must run in a transaction, use `Required`, `RequiresNew`, or `Mandatory`. If nontransactional behavior is needed, use `Never` or `NotSupported`.

> **Best Practice:** Avoid using the `Supports` transaction attribute.

When Not to Use Stateful Session Beans

Stateful session beans represent a stateful conversation between a single client and a bean instance. Stateful session beans cannot be shared between multiple users. You should not model a shared cache or any shared resource as a stateful session bean. If multiple clients need to access a single EJB instance, use an entity bean.

Note: Stateful session beans are not shared by multiple users.

Because each client requires its own stateful session bean instance, the number of bean instances and the associated resource requirements can grow quickly. If an application can tolerate the stateless programming model, stateless session beans are easier to scale than are stateful session beans.

Applications should always call `remove` after finishing with a stateful session bean instance. This enables the EJB container to release container resources as soon as possible. If the `remove` call is omitted, the EJB container will eventually passivate the bean, but this involves extra disk access.

Note: Stateless session beans are easier to scale than stateful session beans.

Stateful session bean writers must also be careful when integrating their stateful session beans with Web applications. Stateful session beans should not allow concurrent method calls. As mentioned earlier, it is possible for multiple requests to cause concurrent calls on a stateful session bean. Unfortunately, this error usually shows up under load, so it is often missed in testing. For this reason, use stateful session beans only within the scope of a request. Use entity beans or servlet sessions for applications that need to store data between requests.

Best Practices for EJB Security

EJB provides a declarative security support as well as a simple programmatic interface for explicit security checks within the bean code. In practice, EJB security settings need to be considered within the entire application's security model. It is common for Web-based applications to handle authentication within the Web tier. In this environment, the EJB tier may contain very few security constraints. This arrangement simplifies the EJB design, and because the security checks are localized to the presentation layer, the application may modify security policies without modifying the EJB tier.

Applications with standalone programmatic clients often directly access session beans. Because there is no intermediate tier, the security access control must be handled in the EJB tier.

Declarative security control is preferred for simple applications. Since the security constraints are declared in the deployment descriptor, the bean classes' business logic is not polluted with security checks. The declarative security model is based on security roles that are declared in the deployment descriptor. Declarative security works best when the number of roles is fixed and does not depend on the number of clients. For instance, an application might include a user role and an administrator role. Because there are only two access domains, it is feasible to declare these roles in the deployment descriptor.

However, declarative security should not be used when each user requires individual security constraints. Such applications require programmatic security checks within the EJB code. It is also common to combine both security models. For instance, an account bean might use declarative security to ensure only registered users access any methods. The bean code then includes additional constraints to ensure that each user only gains access to his or her account.

> **Best Practice:** Use declarative security checks when an application contains few roles. Choose programmatic security when each user needs individual security checks.

Putting It All Together

EJBs are server-side Java components that leverage the standard transaction, persistence, concurrency, and security services provided by the EJB container. This chapter described session beans, which represent conversations with clients. In Chapter 9, we discuss entity beans. Chapter 10 completes the coverage of EJBs with a discussion of message-driven EJBs.

References

The Enterprise JavaBeans 2.0 architecture specification page is available at *http://java.sun.com/products/ejb/2.0.html.*

BEA's Programming WebLogic Enterprise JavaBeans documentation for WebLogic Server 8.1 can be found at *http://edocs.bea.com/wls/docs81/ejb/.*

The Java Message Service specification is available at *http://java.sun.com/products/jms/index.html.*

Full documentation of generating and editing the deployment descriptors used to configure WebLogic Server EJBs (`weblogic-ejb-jar.xml` and `ejb-jar.xml`) is available at *http://e-docs.bea.com/wls/docs81/ejb/implementing.html.*

Ant documentation is available at *http://ant.apache.org/manual/index.html.*

The WebLogic deployment task is documented at *http://e-docs.bea.com/wls/docs81/deployment/tools.html.*

chapter 9

Entity EJBs

In This Chapter

- Entity beans and their lifecycle

- How to write container-managed persistence (CMP) and bean-managed persistence (BMP) entity beans

- Useful techniques, optimizations, and patterns for writing entity beans

- Best practices for developing and deploying entity beans

Entity Enterprise JavaBeans (EJBs) present an object view of persistent data. The fields in entity beans correspond to underlying data in a persistent store—usually, a relational database. An entity bean's state is transactional. When a client updates fields within a transaction, the updates are permanent only if the transaction commits. When a transaction rolls back, the entity bean's state returns to its last committed state. Later in this chapter, we discuss the contract between the EJB container and the entity bean that provides these guarantees.

Rationale for Entity EJBs

In a multitier e-commerce application, back-end persistence is provided by one or more databases. The Web engine uses HTML for static content and servlets and JSPs for dynamic presentation logic. EJBs provide the business logic between the Web tier and the database.

As described in Chapter 8, session beans can take advantage of container services such as transactions, security, and concurrency. Although session beans do not provide any direct persistence support, they often include Java Database Connectivity (JDBC) code that accesses persistent stores.

However, session beans cannot *directly* represent persistent data. Java is an object-oriented language, but databases store data relationally, as rows in tables. Session beans using JDBC cannot easily represent data as first-class objects. Moreover, session beans do not share some of the defining characteristics of persistent data: Multiple clients do not share them, and they do not generally survive server reboots or crashes.

The EJB specification provides *entity beans* as persistent, transactional, and shared components, so that business data can be simultaneously used by many clients and persistently stored until it has been explicitly deleted.

Entity Bean Basics

As a persistent object, an entity bean's state must be saved to the database. Entity beans have two operational styles: They use either BMP or CMP.

With BMP, the bean writer provides the code to load and persist the entity bean to the database. This usually requires JDBC code in the bean class to read and update the entity bean's fields to the database.

With CMP, the EJB container automatically provides code to persist the entity bean to the database. No JDBC code is required. The programming model for CMP changed drastically between EJB 1.1 and EJB 2.0. In this chapter, we discuss only the EJB 2.0 CMP model. The WebLogic Server 8.1 supports EJB 2.0 CMP entity beans. The emerging EJB 2.1 specification includes enhancements for entity beans, including an enhanced CMP model (support for container-managed relationships) and an augmented EJB-QL (Enterprise JavaBeans Query Language). The examples in this chapter focus on EJB 2.0, since the EJB 2.1 specification is not yet final. EJB 2.1 enhancements are mentioned for your consideration only.

Entity Bean Components

Entity beans consist of a home interface, the component interface (local and remote), bean class, primary key class, and deployment descriptors.

Home Interface

Home interfaces provide methods that allow local or remote clients to find, create, and remove instances of an entity bean. A local home interface extends the `javax.ejb.EJBLocalHome` interface and contains `create` methods, `remove` methods, `finder` methods, and home methods. Remote home interfaces extend `javax.ejb.EJBHome` and contain `create`, `remove`, and `finder` methods.

An entity bean's `create` method calls the corresponding `ejbCreate` method on the bean class. The responsibility of the `create` method is to create the persistent representation in the backing store. This is usually implemented as a database insert.

Note: An entity bean `create` is a database insert.

The entity bean's home interface must define a `remove` method that takes a primary key as a parameter. This method removes the entity bean instance with the corresponding primary key from the persistent store. Usually, this represents a database delete operation.

Note: An entity bean `remove` is a database delete.

Primary Keys and Identities

Like stateful session beans, entity beans have identities. A business method in the remote interface must be called against a specific entity bean instance. The entity bean client receives the entity bean reference by creating, finding, or using an EJB *handle.* A bean either has *identity* (it has a unique identifier such as a primary key) or it is *anonymous* (no primary key has been attached).

> **Note:** The primary key identifies an entity bean instance.

Each entity bean reference is associated with a particular primary key. When calls are made against that reference, they are dispatched to a bean instance with the same primary key.

Primary Key Classes

Unlike session beans, entity beans must include a primary key class. The primary key class identifies the entity bean instance: its value must be unique for the entity bean type. The primary key class can be either a Java primitive type such as `java.lang.String` or `java.lang.Integer`, or the user may write a custom primary key class. The primary key class maps to one or more fields in the entity bean. A primary key with multiple fields is known as a *compound primary key.*

Usually, the entity bean primary key fields are also its primary key fields in a database. The primary key class must provide suitable implementations of `public int hashCode()` and `public boolean equals (Object)`. Implementing `hashCode` and `equals` can be confusing. We discuss common techniques later in this chapter.

Finder Methods

Finder methods enable the client to make queries and receive references to an entity bean or collection of beans that satisfy query conditions. Every entity EJB must have a `findByPrimaryKey` method in its home interface. This special `finder` method returns an EJB reference that has the corresponding primary key. Bean writers may also define more complex `finders` that return many entity references that match the `finder`'s condition. For instance, a "U.S. citizen" entity bean might have a `finder` named `findBillionaires` that returns data on all citizens who are worth more than $1 billion.

Home Methods

The local home interface of an entity bean also can have home methods. Home methods are business methods that do not apply to a particular instance. Instead, the container merely chooses an available instance and calls the home method on it. This programming model is similar to stateless session beans. We discuss when to use entity beans instead of stateless session beans later in this chapter.

The Bean Class and Bean Context

The entity bean's component interface (local or remote) allows a client to invoke business methods, obtain an object's primary key (mapping to fields in a database), and a number of other operations. The client need only obtain a reference to the component interface. The types of component interfaces are local and remote. Local interfaces serve local clients running as part of the same enterprise application (EAR file), whereas remote interfaces are meant to be used by clients running as part of a different enterprise application. A remote interface extends the `javax.ejb.EJBObject` interface, while the local interface extends `javax.ejb.EJBLocalObject`. The component interface contains the signatures for business methods. The actual implementation of these methods is provided in the bean class.

The entity bean's implementation class implements the `javax.ejb.EntityBean` interface. Like the `javax.ejb.SessionBean` interface, the `EntityBean` interface contains the signatures for callbacks from the EJB container to the bean instance. The `setEntityContext` method is called immediately after the bean's constructor and passes the bean instance the `EntityContext`. The `EntityContext` is generally stored in a member variable and is used by the bean instance to make some standard calls into the EJB container. The `setEntityContext` method may be used to acquire some basic resources such as `DataSource` references that are not specific to a particular primary key.

When `setEntityContext` is called, the EJB container has not yet assigned a primary key to this bean instance. The entity bean interface also has a corresponding `unsetEntityContext` method that is called before the bean instance is destroyed. Generally, this method frees any resources acquired in `setEntityContext`.

Activation and Passivation

The entity bean interface also includes `ejbActivate` and `ejbPassivate` methods. Remember that in stateful session beans, `ejbActivate` and `ejbPassivate` are used to load and save the stateful session bean's state to a backing store, usually located in the file system. While the entity bean interface uses the same names, the `ejbActivate` and `ejbPassivate` methods have a different meaning.

> **Note:** In entity beans, `ejbActivate` is called when an entity bean instance is associated with a particular primary key. The `ejbPassivate` method is called when this association is removed and the entity bean instance no longer has a particular identity.

Home Methods and Business Methods

The entity bean's implementation class implements home methods and business methods from the remote interface. Home methods are called against an anonymous instance. A home method should not make use of or expect an associated primary key value.

Business methods are called on a specific instance having a primary key and identity. The remaining methods in the bean implementation class depend on whether the bean uses BMP or CMP.

CMP Entity Bean Example

Instead of writing cumbersome JDBC code, the CMP bean writer provides only the business logic and deployment descriptors. CMP can offer the developer faster development time and better performance than BMP entity beans. The CMP entity bean class is abstract. This enables the EJB container to implement persistence logic by generating a class that extends the bean class. Another advantage of CMP Entity Beans is that it can be used with any type of underlying resource manager; the developer uses the same EJB CMP methods regardless.

> **Note:** This section covers the EJB 2.0 CMP model. At the time of publication, the EJB 2.1 specification is not yet final. Please consult the EJB 2.1 specification for information about CMP-related enhancements in the specification.

Container-Managed Fields

Every container-managed entity bean has a set of container-managed fields, which are saved and loaded from the database. Generally, each container-managed field corresponds to a column in a relational database. For instance, in a Student entity bean, container-managed fields could be the name, the ssn (Social Security number or Student ID), and grade.

Writing getXXX and setXXX Methods

The bean provider cannot declare container-managed fields. Instead, the bean writer declares abstract get and set methods for each container-managed field. For instance, instead of declaring a private String name in the bean class, the bean provider uses public abstract void setName(String name); and public abstract String getName();. These get and set methods are public and abstract because the EJB container provides the actual implementation. While this requirement seems a bit strange at first, it allows the EJB container to detect when fields are read and written. This enables the EJB container to optimize the calls to the database. For instance, if no fields are updated within a transaction, the WebLogic Server EJB container does not write back to the database.

Declaring the Container-Managed Fields

Each container-managed field must be declared in the ejb-jar.xml deployment descriptor. This enables the container to match the container-managed fields with the setXXX and getXXX methods in the bean class. The bean provider then includes the database mapping in a separate CMP deployment descriptor named *weblogic-cmp-rdbms.xml*, which contains the database table name and a mapping between each container-managed field and its corresponding database column.

A CMP entity bean must set the values of the primary key fields in its ejbCreate method. Then the ejbCreate method always returns null.

The EJB container determines the primary key value by extracting the primary key fields after the ejbCreate has returned. The bean needs to set the primary key fields in ejbCreate because the container does the database insert after it calls ejbCreate.

The convention of returning null instead of void enables a BMP entity bean to extend a CMP entity bean (more about this later). The Java language specification does not allow you to overload a method while changing only the return type. Therefore, the bean writer could not have a BMP version in which ejbCreate returns the primary key type and extend that bean with a CMP version returning void.

Student CMP Example

Our first example demonstrates the simplicity of CMP. This is the StudentBean:

```
package com.learnweblogic.examples.ch9.cmp;

import java.util.Collection;

import javax.ejb.EntityContext;
import javax.ejb.EntityBean;

public abstract class StudentCMPBean implements EntityBean {

  private EntityContext ctx;

  // container-managed fields
  public abstract String getName();
  public abstract void setName(String n);

  public abstract Integer getSsn();
  public abstract void setSsn(Integer ssn);

  public abstract int getGrade();
  public abstract void setGrade(int gr);


  public void setEntityContext(EntityContext c) {
    ctx = c;
  }

  public void unsetEntityContext() {
    ctx = null;
  }


  public Integer ejbCreate(String name, int ssn, int grade)
  {
    setName(name);
    setSsn(new Integer(ssn));
    setGrade(grade);

    return null;

  }

  // This implementation requires no post-create initialization
  // so this required method is empty
  public void ejbPostCreate(String name, int ssn, int grade) {}
```

```
// These methods are required by the EntityBean interface but
// are not used in this implementation.

public void ejbRemove() {}

public void ejbLoad() {}

public void ejbStore() {}

public void ejbActivate() {}
public void ejbPassivate() {}

}
```

The bean class contains get and set methods for the bean's three container-managed fields: name, ssn, and grade.

ejb-jar.xml Deployment Descriptor

The ejb-jar.xml deployment descriptor specifies that our bean use CMP and the EJB 2.0 model. The <cmp-field> elements specify all the container-managed fields in this CMP entity bean. Note the EJB-QL query element for the findStudentsInGrade method.

```
<?xml version="1.0"?>

<!DOCTYPE ejb-jar PUBLIC
"-//Sun Microsystems, Inc.//DTD Enterprise JavaBeans 2.0//EN"
"http://java.sun.com/dtd/ejb-jar_2_0.dtd">


<ejb-jar>
  <enterprise-beans>
    <entity>
      <ejb-name>StudentCMPEJB</ejb-name>
      <home>com.learnweblogic.examples.ch9.cmp.StudentHome</home>
      <remote>com.learnweblogic.examples.ch9.cmp.Student</remote>
      <ejb-class>
        com.learnweblogic.examples.ch9.cmp.StudentCMPBean
      </ejb-class>
      <persistence-type>Container</persistence-type>
      <prim-key-class>java.lang.Integer</prim-key-class>
      <reentrant>False</reentrant>
      <cmp-version>2.x</cmp-version>
      <abstract-schema-name>StudentCMPBean</abstract-schema-name>
```

```
      <cmp-field>
        <field-name>name</field-name>
      </cmp-field>
      <cmp-field>
        <field-name>ssn</field-name>
      </cmp-field>
      <cmp-field>
        <field-name>grade</field-name>
      </cmp-field>

      <primkey-field>ssn</primkey-field>

      <query>
        <description>
            finds students in a given grade
        </description>
        <query-method>
          <method-name>findStudentsInGrade</method-name>
          <method-params>
            <method-param>int</method-param>
          </method-params>
        </query-method>
        <ejb-ql>
          <![CDATA[SELECT DISTINCT Object(s) FROM StudentCMPBean s
WHERE s.grade = ?1]]>
        </ejb-ql>
      </query>

    </entity>

  </enterprise-beans>


  <assembly-descriptor>
    <container-transaction>
      <method>
        <ejb-name>StudentCMPEJB</ejb-name>
        <method-name>*</method-name>
      </method>
      <trans-attribute>Required</trans-attribute>
    </container-transaction>

  </assembly-descriptor>
</ejb-jar>
```

weblogic-ejb-jar.xml Deployment Descriptor

The CMP EJB also requires a `weblogic-ejb-jar.xml` deployment descriptor that contains WebLogic Server-specific options and settings. The persistence stanza, required for CMP entity beans, specifies the persistence type and version (CMP version) and that the CMP deployment descriptor is located in META-INF/*weblogic-cmp-rdbms.xml*. This is required for WebLogic Server to support plug-in CMP engines from other vendors. The examples in this book assume the WebLogic Server CMP engine.

```xml
<?xml version="1.0"?>



<!DOCTYPE weblogic-ejb-jar PUBLIC
"-//BEA Systems, Inc.//DTD WebLogic 8.1.0 EJB//EN" "http://
www.bea.com/servers/wls810/dtd/weblogic-ejb-jar.dtd"

<weblogic-ejb-jar>
  <weblogic-enterprise-bean>
    <ejb-name>StudentCMPEJB</ejb-name>

    <entity-descriptor>
      <persistence>
        <persistence-use>
          <type-identifier>WebLogic_CMP_RDBMS</type-identifier>
          <type-version>2.0</type-version>
          <type-storage>
            META-INF/weblogic-cmp-rdbms.xml
          </type-storage>
        </persistence-use>
      </persistence>
    </entity-descriptor>

    <jndi-name>StudentCMPEJB</jndi-name>
  </weblogic-enterprise-bean>

</weblogic-ejb-jar>
```

weblogic-cmp-rdbms.xml Descriptor

The third required deployment descriptor is the CMP deployment descriptor *weblogic-cmp-rdbms-jar.xml*. The *weblogic-cmp-rdbms-jar.xml* includes the database information necessary to map the abstract persistence schema to the physical schema in the database. Each entity bean maps to a database table, and each container-managed field maps to a database column.

```xml
<?xml version="1.0"?>

<!DOCTYPE weblogic-rdbms-jar PUBLIC
```

'-// BEA Systems, Inc.//DTD WebLogic 8.1.0 EJB RDBMS Persistence//
EN' 'http://www.bea.com/servers/wls810/dtd/weblogic-rdbms20-
persistence-810.dtd'

```
<weblogic-rdbms-jar>
  <weblogic-rdbms-bean>

    <ejb-name>StudentCMPEJB</ejb-name>
    <data-source-name>DBPool</data-source-name>
    <table-map>
      <table-name>studentcmptable</table-name>

      <field-map>
        <cmp-field>ssn</cmp-field>
        <dbms-column>ssn</dbms-column>
      </field-map>
      <field-map>
        <cmp-field>name</cmp-field>
        <dbms-column>name</dbms-column>
      </field-map>
      <field-map>
        <cmp-field>grade</cmp-field>
        <dbms-column>grade</dbms-column>
      </field-map>
    </table-map>

  </weblogic-rdbms-bean>

</weblogic-rdbms-jar>
```

CMP

Entity beans that use CMP do not include JDBC code: The EJB container generates code that provides automatic persistence. The EJB container calls the ejbCreate methods before the bean has been inserted into a database. The ejbCreate method generally uses its parameters to initialize the entity bean's fields. The ejbCreate method must set primary key fields.

ejbCreate

After the ejbCreate method returns, the EJB container extracts the primary key fields from the bean instance and performs a database insert. The ejbCreate method always returns null in any CMP entity bean. While this looks strange at first, it is required to enable a BMP bean to extend a CMP bean. We discuss this requirement later in this chapter.

ejbRemove

A CMP entity bean's `ejbRemove` method is called before the EJB container deletes the entity bean from the database. The entity bean writer can include code in the `ejbRemove` method that is run immediately before the bean is deleted, but this is not a common practice.

ejbLoad

The EJB container calls the `ejbLoad` method of a CMP entity bean after loading the bean's state from the persistent store. The `ejbLoad` method can be used to postprocess any container-managed field loaded from the database. For instance, the `ejbLoad` method might decompress a container-managed field extracted from the database and store the value in a transient member variable. This, again, is not a common practice.

ejbStore

The `ejbStore` method is called before the entity bean's state is written to the database. You can add code to perform processing such as decompressing transient data, but this is not commonly done.

Finders

Unlike BMP entity beans, the CMP bean writer does not implement `finder` methods within the bean class. Instead, the bean writer provides a query for each `finder`. Queries are written in the EJB-QL language and are included in the deployment descriptor. EJB-QL, which resembles the SQL query language, is discussed in detail later in this chapter.

ejbPostCreate

Entity bean classes can contain an `ejbPostCreate` method for each `ejbCreate` method. The `ejbPostCreate` method has the same parameters as its corresponding `ejbCreate` method, but the `ejbPostCreate` method returns `void`. Generally, `ejbPostCreate` is used to initialize container-managed relationships (CMR).

Container-Managed Entity Bean Lifecycle

Entity beans exist in a persistent store until they are deleted by either the entity bean's `remove` method or a direct database delete. Therefore, the entity lifecycle must accommodate instances that exist before the EJB server is started and that continue to live after the EJB server is halted.

Entity bean instances exist in two states: *anonymous* and *identity*. An anonymous entity bean is similar to a stateless session bean. It has no associated identity: one anonymous instance is as good as any other. An identified bean has an associated primary key that uniquely identifies this instance. Through its lifetime, the entity bean transitions between these states in response to callbacks from the EJB container.

Anonymous Instances

When the EJB container creates a new bean instance, it first calls the bean's default constructor. Next, the EJB container calls the `setEntityContext` method, passing an `EntityContext` object to the newly created bean. Note that the bean is, at this point, anonymous. The `setEntityContext` method cannot use primary key fields, nor can it use the `EntityContext`'s `getPrimaryKey` method.

The WebLogic EJB container maintains a pool of anonymous instances so that it can quickly dispatch `finder`, home, and `business` methods. The container removes instances from the anonymous state by calling the `unset-EntityContext` method, which frees memory and other resources within the EJB server.

When a `finder` method is called on the home interface, the EJB container selects an anonymous instance and uses it to run the corresponding `finder` method. When a `finder` completes, the bean instance is returned to the pool. If the client calls a `create` method on the home interface, the container selects an anonymous instance and calls the corresponding `ejbCreate` and `ejbPostCreate` methods on the instance.

Identified Instances

At this point, the newly created instance transitions to the identity state. A `business` method invocation can also cause the bean to transition to the identity state. In this scenario, the EJB container selects an instance from the pool, assigns it a primary key, and then calls the `ejbActivate` method, which moves the bean to the identity state.

Entity beans in the identity state are ready to run `business` methods. The EJB container can preserve resources by returning an entity bean to the anonymous state by calling the `ejbPassivate` method. An `ejbRemove` callback also returns the bean to the anonymous state.

Reading and Writing the Database

Entity beans use the `ejbLoad` and `ejbStore` methods to synchronize their state with the database. Because entity beans are transactional components, these methods run within the `business` method's transaction. When `business` methods are called on an entity bean reference, the EJB container might need to load or store the bean's state to the database.

While there are many options to control when the EJB container calls `ejbLoad` or `ejbStore`, this section discusses the default behavior. Later in this chapter, we discuss techniques to optimize database access with `ejbLoad` and `ejbStore`. In the default behavior, the EJB container calls `ejbLoad` at the beginning of a transaction and runs any `business` methods within the transaction. When the transaction commits, the `ejbStore` method writes the bean's state back to a database. The bean then remains in the ready state until another business method appears or until the bean is passivated to the pool state.

Introduction to CMRs

Objects do not exist in a vacuum: Designs specify relationships between a system's objects. For instance, the `StudentBean` would naturally have a relationship with a `SchoolBean`. With the EJB 2.0 specification, there is standard support for relationships between entity beans. The container handles the persistence logic necessary to manage the relationship between CMP beans (see Figure 9–1).

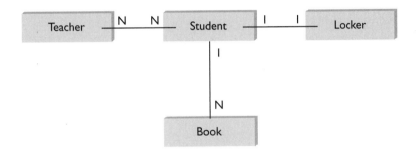

Figure 9–1
CMRs with the Student EJB.

Container-managed entity beans may use one-to-one (1:1), one-to-many (1:*N*), or many-to-many (*N*:*N*) relationships. A Student bean and a Locker bean might have a one-to-one relationship. Each Student has one corresponding Locker. Each Locker has one corresponding Student.

A Student bean and Book bean might have a one-to-many relationship. Each Student has many Books, but each Book is used by only a single Student.

A Student bean and a Teacher bean have a many-to-many relationship. Each Student has many Teachers, and each Teacher has many Students. Note that an entity bean can participate in several relationships, and each can be of a different cardinality.

Unidirectional and Bidirectional Relationships

CMRs can be either bidirectional () or unidirectional (). In a bidirectional relationship, either bean may navigate to its related bean. For instance, in our Student Locker example, the Student bean can get to the Locker bean, and vice versa. It is also possible to specify a unidirectional relationship, such as Student Locker. In this case, the Student bean can navigate to the Locker bean but not vice versa. There is no performance advantage to using unidirectional relationships; in general, bidirectional relationships should be preferred.

Like container-managed fields, CMRs are exposed via abstract `get` and `set` methods in the bean class. For single object relationships, the `get` and `set` methods take the remote interface of the target bean. For instance, in our preceding Student Locker example, the Student bean would contain a `public abstract Locker getLocker();` and `public abstract void setLocker(Locker l);` methods. If this relationship were bidirectional, the Locker bean would contain the corresponding methods to access the Student bean.

Many relationships have `get` and `set` methods that use a `java.util.Collection` or `java.util.Set` to contain the remote interface of the related beans. Unlike a `Collection`, using a `Set` guarantees there are no duplicates returned by the `get` method. For instance, in the Student-to-Book beans' 1:*N* relationship, the Student bean would include `public abstract Collection getBooks();` and `public abstract void setBooks(Collection books)` methods. Because this is a 1:*N* relationship, the Book bean would have `public abstract Student getStudent();` and `public abstract void setStudent();` methods.

CMR Example

Let's see how the Student CMP bean example can be modified to support CMRs. We have included a bidirectional 1:1 relationship with a Locker CMP bean, a bidirectional 1:N relationship with the Book CMP bean, and an N:N relationship with the Teacher CMP bean.

To keep things simple, we don't show all of the code here. Instead, we show the changes made to support relationships: We use ellipses in the code to show where code has been removed for brevity. We also omitted the home and remote interfaces of the related beans from the text.

```java
package com.learnweblogic.examples.ch9.cmp;

import java.util.Collection;

import javax.ejb.EntityContext;
import javax.ejb.EntityBean;

public abstract class StudentCMPBean implements EntityBean {

    private EntityContext ctx;

    public abstract String getName();
    public abstract void setName(String n);

    ...

    public abstract Locker getLocker();
    public abstract void setLocker(Locker l);

    public abstract Collection getBooks();
    public abstract void setBooks(Collection b);

    public abstract Collection getTeachers();
    public abstract void setTeachers(Collection t);

    ...

    public void assignLocker(Locker l) {
        setLocker(l);
    }

    public void assignBook(Book b) {
        Collection books = getBooks();
        books.add(b);
    }

    public void assignTeacher(Teacher t) {
```

```
      Collection teachers = getTeachers();
      teachers.add(t);
   }
}
```

> **Note:** Because the Locker bean is a 1:1 relationship, the getter returns the single Locker remote interface while the 1:N relationship with Books and *N:N* relationship with Teachers return `Collections`.

Note the code to add an element to a relationship. An empty-many relationship returns an empty `Collection` (not null), so it is always safe to call the getter and add an item. These relationships are bidirectional; there also are `get` and `set` methods included in the related classes.

Because the Locker bean is involved in a 1:1 relationship with Student, its getters and setters return the Student remote interface:

```
package com.learnweblogic.examples.ch9.cmp;

import javax.ejb.EntityBean;
import javax.ejb.EntityContext;

public abstract class LockerCMPBean implements EntityBean {

   private EntityContext ctx;

   public abstract Integer getNumber();
   public abstract void setNumber(Integer n);

   public abstract Student getStudent();
   public abstract void setStudent(Student s);

   ...
}
```

The Book bean is involved in a 1:*N* relationship with Student. Recall that Student's getBooks method returns a `Collection` of related Books, but because this is a 1:N relationship, the Book getters return only a single Student.

```
package com.learnweblogic.examples.ch9.cmp;

...

public abstract class BookCMPBean implements EntityBean {

   ...
```

```
public abstract Student getStudent();
public abstract void setStudent(Student s);


...
}
```

Finally, the Teacher bean is in an *N:N* relationship with Student. In the many-to-many case, both sides of the relationship use `Collection` or `Set` in their get/set methods.

```
package com.learnweblogic.examples.ch9.cmp;

...


public abstract class TeacherCMPBean implements EntityBean {

   ...


   public abstract Collection getStudents();
   public abstract void setStudents(Collection students);


   ...


}
```

Writing CMR Deployment Descriptors

All related beans are deployed in the same `ejb-jar.xml` deployment descriptor. This is a requirement for entity bean relations. Each relationship is described in the `ejb-jar.xml` deployment descriptor in the `<relationships>` element.

```
   <relationships>
```

This first stanza describes the 1:1 relationship from Student to Locker.

```
<!-- One to One Student - Locker -->
   <ejb-relation>
      <ejb-relation-name>Student-Locker</ejb-relation-name>
```

Because this is a bidirectional relationship, there are two `<relationship-role>` entries. The first, `student-has-locker`, describes the Student-Locker relationship. Note that the source is the Student bean, and the field is named Locker. The EJB container expects to find `getLocker` and `setLocker` methods in the Student bean class.

```
<ejb-relationship-role>
  <ejb-relationship-role-name>
    student-has-locker
```

```
  </ejb-relationship-role-name>
  <multiplicity>one</multiplicity>
  <relationship-role-source>
    <ejb-name>StudentCMPEJB</ejb-name>
  </relationship-role-source>
  <cmr-field>
    <cmr-field-name>locker</cmr-field-name>
  </cmr-field>
</ejb-relationship-role>
```

The second `ejb-relationship-role` describes the relationship from the Locker to the Student. This time, the Locker is the source and the `cmr` field is named `student`.

```
<ejb-relationship-role>
  <ejb-relationship-role-name>
    locker-has-student
  </ejb-relationship-role-name>
  <multiplicity>one</multiplicity>
  <relationship-role-source>
    <ejb-name>LockerCMPEJB</ejb-name>
  </relationship-role-source>
   <cmr-field>
     <cmr-field-name>student</cmr-field-name>
   </cmr-field>
 </ejb-relationship-role>
</ejb-relation>
```

The next stanza describes the bidirectional 1:N relationship from Student to Books.

```
<!-- One to Many Student - Books -->
   <ejb-relation>
     <ejb-relation-name>Student-Books</ejb-relation-name>
```

This describes the Student side of the relationship. Notice that the `<cmr-field-type>` indicates that the relationship uses the `Collection` type instead of a `Set`, which is required when the related role is many.

> **Best Practice:** The full package name, `java.util.Collection`, must be used. A common error is to just write "Collection." Unlike a Java program file, packages are not imported, so classes and interfaces should be specified with their full package names.

```
<ejb-relationship-role>
  <ejb-relationship-role-name>
      student-has-books
    </ejb-relationship-role-name>
```

```
        <multiplicity>one</multiplicity>
        <relationship-role-source>
            <ejb-name>StudentCMPEJB</ejb-name>
        </relationship-role-source>
        <cmr-field>
          <cmr-field-name>books</cmr-field-name>
          <cmr-field-type>java.util.Collection</cmr-field-type>
        </cmr-field>
        </ejb-relationship-role>
```

The second `ejb-relationship-role` is the Books-to-Student relationship. Notice that this relationship has a multiplicity of many. This indicates that many Books map into a Student.

```
  <ejb-relationship-role>
   <ejb-relationship-role-name>
     books-have-student
   </ejb-relationship-role-name>
   <multiplicity>many</multiplicity>
   <relationship-role-source>
     <ejb-name>BookCMPEJB</ejb-name>
   <relationship-/role-source>
   <cmr-field>
     <cmr-field-name>student</cmr-field-name>
   </cmr-field>
  </ejb-relationship-role>
</ejb-relation>
```

Finally, there is the *N:N* relationship between Students and Teachers. This is similar to the preceding 1:N relationship, except that now both sides are many, and both sides specify the `<cmr-field-type>`.

```
<!-- Many to Many Student - Teacher -->
   <ejb-relation>
      <ejb-relation-name>Student-Teacher</ejb-relation-name>
      <ejb-relationship-role>
        <ejb-relationship-role-name>
        students-have-teachers
      </ejb-relationship-role-name>
      <multiplicity>many</multiplicity>
      <relationship-role-source>
          <ejb-name>StudentCMPEJB</ejb-name>
      </relationship-role-source>
      <cmr-field>
        <cmr-field-name>teachers</cmr-field-name>
        <cmr-field-type>java.util.Collection</cmr-field-type>
      </cmr-field>
```

```
      </ejb-relationship-role>
      <ejb-relationship-role>
        <ejb-relationship-role-name>
        teachers-have-students
      </ejb-relationship-role-name>
      <multiplicity>many</multiplicity>
      <relationship-role-source>
          <ejb-name>TeacherCMPEJB</ejb-name>
      </relationship-role-source>
      <cmr-field>
        <cmr-field-name>students</cmr-field-name>
        <cmr-field-type>java.util.Collection</cmr-field-type>
      </cmr-field>
      </ejb-relationship-role>
    </ejb-relation>

  </relationships>
```

Like other EJBs, it is necessary to include a standard *weblogic-ejb-jar.xml* deployment descriptor. You need to make a few changes to the *weblogic-cmp-rdbms.xml* deployment descriptor for CMRs. Like CMP fields, CMRs must include their database mappings in the *weblogic-cmp-rdbms.xml* file.

The EJB container uses *foreign keys* to implement relationships in the database. A foreign key is a column in a database table that is a primary key of another table. For instance, the Student table's primary key is the Student's Social Security number. If the Locker table stored the Student's Social Security number as a foreign key, rows in the Locker table could be matched against the related rows in the Student table.

Creating the Database Tables

Before running the entity bean examples, the deployer must create database tables that support the entity beans. These database tables must include the required foreign key columns. A join table must be created for the N:N relationship.

Here, we show the data definition language (DDL) for the Student table and for the join table. The schemas for the other tables are similar to those cited for other examples.

```
create table studentcmptable (

  ssn integer primary key,
  name varchar(255),
  grade integer,
  lockerkey integer
);


create table StudentTeacherJoin (

  teacher_ssn integer,
  student_ssn integer
);
```

Note the `lockerkey` column in the `StudentCmpTable`. This is the foreign key column for the Student-Locker relationship. This database column must match the mappings given in *weblogic-cmp-rdbms.xml*.

Unlike 1:1 or 1:N relationships, N:N relationships cannot be implemented by storing a foreign key field in the bean's table. Instead, an auxiliary database table is used to store the sets of foreign keys. This extra table is often referred to as a *join table*.

The StudentTeacherJoin table is the join table for the *N:N* relationship between Students and Teachers. It stores the foreign keys described in the `weblogic-cmp-rdbms.xml` descriptor.

Mapping CMP Entity Beans to the Database

The physical mappings for CMRs depend on the cardinality of the relationship.

Mapping 1:1 Relationships

The WebLogic Server EJB container supports three different mappings for 1:1 relationships. There can be a foreign key on either side of the relationship, or foreign keys can be stored on both sides of the relationship. While it seems appealing at first to store foreign keys on both sides of the relationship, this mapping should usually be avoided. With twice as many foreign keys, there will be twice as many database updates when the relationship is changed.

Best Practice: Avoid storing foreign keys in both sides of a 1:1 relationship.

Here is the mapping information in the *weblogic-cmp-rdbms.xml* file for the Student-Locker example. In this mapping, we store a foreign key in the Student table. The database column named `lockerkey` maps to the number primary key field in the Locker bean.

```
<weblogic-rdbms-relation>
    <relation-name>Student-Locker</relation-name>
    <weblogic-relationship-role>
      <relationship-role-name>student-has-locker</relationship-role-name>
      <relationship-role-map>
        <column-map>
          <foreign-key-column>lockerkey</foreign-key-column>
          <key-column>number</key-column>
        </column-map>
      </relationship-role-map>
    </weblogic-relationship-role>
  </weblogic-rdbms-relation>
```

Mapping 1:N Relationships

The WebLogic Server EJB container supports a single physical mapping for 1:N relationships. Each bean on the many side of the relationship supports a foreign key pointing to the one bean on the other side.

In the Student Books relationship, the Books table stores a foreign key pointing back to the Student. The `studentkey` field points to the `ssn` primary key field of the `StudentCMPBean`.

```
<weblogic-rdbms-relation>
    <relation-name>Student-Books</relation-name>
    <weblogic-relationship-role>
      <relationship-role-name>student-has-books</relationship-role-name>
      <relationship-role-map>
        <column-map>
          <foreign-key-column>studentkey</foreign-key-column>
          <key-column>ssn</key-column>
        </column-map>
      </relationshiop-role-map>
    </weblogic-relationship-role>
  </weblogic-rdbms-relation>
```

Mapping N:N Relationships

Here is the Students Teachers mapping. The join table named `StudentTeacherJoin` includes foreign keys for both sides of the relationship. The `teacher_ssn` column is a foreign key to the `ssn` primary key field for Teachers, while the `student_ssn` field is a foreign key to the Student's `ssn` field.

```
<weblogic-rdbms-relation>
    <relation-name>Student-Teacher</relation-name>
    <table-name>StudentTeacherJoin</table-name>
    <weblogic-relationship-role>
      <relationship-role-name>students-have-teachers</relationship-role-name>
      <relationship-role-map>
        <column-map>
          <foreign-key-column>student_ssn</foreign-key-column>
          <key-column>ssn</key-column>
        </column-map>
      </relationship-role-map>
    </weblogic-relationship-role>

    <weblogic-relationship-role>
      <relationship-role-name>teachers-have-students</relationship-role-name>
      <relationship-role-map>
        <column-map>
          <foreign-key-column>teacher_ssn</foreign-key-column>
          <key-column>ssn</key-column>
        </column-map>
      </relationship-role-map>
    </weblogic-relationship-role>

  </weblogic-rdbms-relation>
```

Running the Example

Like any other entity bean, the client code calls the remote and remote home interfaces. We use the client code to update the relationships and view the changes in the database.

Again, we have simplified the client code and removed exception handling for brevity.

Before the client code executes, the database tables are empty:

```
select * from studentcmptable;
ssn | name | grade | lockerkey
-----+-------+-------+-----------
(0 rows)
```

Like other EJBs, the client does a Java Naming and Directory Interface (JNDI) lookup to find the StudentHome. It can then create the entity bean from the home interface.

```
StudentHome studentHome =
    (StudentHome) narrow(ctx.lookup("StudentCMPEJB"),
StudentHome.class);
```

In this example, several Students are created in a loop:

```
students[i] = studentHome.create(names[i], i, 10);
```

The database now includes the Students:

```
select * from studentcmptable;
 ssn |  name  | grade | lockerkey
-----+--------+-------+-----------
   0 | Andrew |    10 |
   1 | Evelyn |    10 |
   2 | Joe    |    10 |
   3 | Matt   |    10 |
   4 | Jim    |    10 |
(5 rows)
```

Notice that the lockerkey field is empty. This field is null until we call the setLocker method in the StudentBean to initialize the relationship.

The client now goes on to create some Locker entity beans:

```
Locker [] lockers = new Locker[N];
    for (int i=0; i<N; i++) {
      // create students in the 10th grade
      lockers[i] = lockerHome.create(new Integer(i));
    }
```

The Locker beans are very simple entity beans: only a single column is stored in the database.

```
select * from lockercmptable;
 number
--------
       0
       1
       2
       3
       4
(5 rows)
```

The client can now assign Students to Lockers. This updates the 1:1 relationship. The example client calls the `assignLocker` method on the Student remote interface. This method calls the `setLocker` method, which updates the relationship information.

```
// Assign each Student a Locker
    for (int i=0; i<students.length; i++) {
       students[i].assignLocker(lockers[i]);
    }
```

Now the database table includes the foreign key to indicate the relationship has been updated:

```
select * from studentcmptable;
 ssn |   name   | grade | lockerkey
-----+----------+-------+-----------
   0 | Andrew   |   10  |         0
   1 | Evelyn   |   10  |         1
   2 | Joe      |   10  |         2
   3 | Matt     |   10  |         3
   4 | Jim      |   10  |         4
(5 rows)
```

Using 1:N Relationships

The client also creates Book entity beans for the 1:N relationship. The bean creation code is identical to the other beans, so we do not show it again. The client can then call the `assignBook` method on the Student interface to add a Book to the 1:N relationship.

The Books array has a copy of each Book for every Student, so the client code iterates through all the Books, assigning each copy to a different Student.

```
// Assign the books out to the students
    for (int i=0; i<books.length; i++) {
       students[i % students.length].assignBook(books[i]);
    }
```

We can see the results of updating the 1:N relationship in the database by looking at the Book table. The foreign key points back to a Student.

```
select * from bookcmptable where studentkey=0;
 isbn | copynumber |     title     |   author    | studentkey
------+------------+---------------+-------------+------------
 0    |          0 | Hamlet        | Shakespeare |          0
 1    |          0 | Moby Dick     | Melville    |          0
 2    |          0 | The Stranger  | Camus       |          0
(3 rows)
```

This query shows that the Student with primary key 0 has a 1:N relationship with three books. The studentkey column is a foreign key into the Student table.

Using N:N Relationships

The client uses similar code to update the N:N relationship of Students and Teachers. In this case, the join table is updated.

```
// Assign students to teachers
   // Student 0 gets teacher 0
   // Student 1 gets teachers 0,1 etc.
   for (int i=0; i<teachers.length; i++) {
     for (int j=0; j<i; j++) {
       students[j].assignTeacher(teachers[i]);
     }
   }
```

The database contents of the join table show the updated *N:N* relationship:

```
select * from StudentTeacherJoin;
 teacher_ssn | student_ssn
-------------+-------------
           0 |           1
           0 |           2
           1 |           2
           0 |           3
           1 |           3
           2 |           3
(6 rows)
```

Writing EJB-QL for CMP Finders

The EJB-QL language is based on SQL-92 and should be familiar to database users. EJB-QL is used for finders and ejbSelect methods. Finder methods always return the entity bean's remote interface or a Collection containing remote interfaces.

Select methods are like finder methods, but they can return any of the container-managed fields. Select methods are not exposed in the remote interface and are called against an identified instance. Finders run against an anonymous instance. A select method is similar to a data access method on a stateless session bean. The advantage of using an `ejbSelect` method is that the query operates on the container-managed fields and relationships and is independent of the physical schema.

EJB 2.0 EJB-QL queries consist of three clauses: `SELECT`, `FROM`, and `WHERE`. EJB 2.1 will introduce an `ORDER BY` clause, but is not supported in WebLogic Server 8.1.

The EJB-QL query is specified with the `<query>` tag in the `ejb-jar.xml`. There is an optional description element, and the `finder` method must be specified. The EJB-QL query is then specified with the `<ejb-ql>` tag. Note that it is wrapped in a CDATA block. This instructs the XML parser not to attempt to interpret the query as anything but raw character data.

EJB-QL queries use the finder method's parameters. The first parameter is referred to as ?1. The second parameter is ?2 , and so on.

The Student CMP bean includes a `findStudentsInGrade(int grade)` in the home interface. This `finder` returns all the Students whose grade matches the parameter:

```
<query>
  <description>finds students in a given grade</description>
<query-method>
  <method-name>findStudentsInGrade</method-name>
    <method-params>
     <method-param>int</method-param>
    </method-params>
  </query-method>
  <ejb-ql>
   <![CDATA[SELECT DISTINCT Object(s) FROM StudentCMPBean s WHERE s.grade
=?1]]>
  </ejb-ql>
</query>
```

This query uses the `grade` container-managed field and compares it against the first parameter to the `finder`.

The client code accesses this code by calling the `findStudentsInGrade` method on the home interface. This method returns a `Collection` of Student remote interfaces. The client code must use `javax.rmi.PortableRemoteObject.narrow` to convert the Collection's contents into the remote interface. This is required by the EJB specification for compatibility with CORBA-based EJB servers.

```
Collection c = studentHome.findStudentsInGrade(10);

    if (c.isEmpty()) {
      System.err.println("No Students were found in grade 10.");
    } else {

    Iterator it = c.iterator();

    while (it.hasNext()) {
       Student s = (Student) narrow(it.next(), Student.class);

       System.err.println("Found student named: "+s.getName()+
```

```
                    " in grade 10.");
            }

            System.err.println("");
```

We can check the results of the finder by manually running the query against the database table.

```
select * from studentcmptable where grade=10;

ssn |   name   | grade | lockerkey
----+----------+-------+-----------
  0 | Andrew   |   10  |      0
  1 | Evelyn   |   10  |      1
  2 | Joe      |   10  |      2
  3 | Matt     |   10  |      3
  4 | Jim      |   10  |      4
(5 rows)
```

The finder query returns the expected results. Running queries manually in the database is a good way to check your EJB-QL statements.

```
Found student named: Andrew in grade 10.
Found student named: Evelyn in grade 10.
Found student named: Joe in grade 10.
Found student named: Matt in grade 10.
Found student named: Jim in grade 10.
```

Let's examine some other EJB-QL examples. We omit the XML descriptor format for readability.

```
findAllStudents:
find All of the Students
<ejb-ql>SELECT DISTINCT Object(s) FROM StudentCMPBean s</ejb-ql>

findSSNGreaterThan10:
find Students with a social security number > 10
<ejb-ql>SELECT DISTINCT Object(s) FROM StudentCMPBean s WHERE s.ssn
> 10</ejb-ql>

findStudentsBetweenGrades(int low, int high:
find Students whose grade is >= low and <= high

<ejb-ql>
SELECT DISTINCT Object(s) FROM StudentCMPBean s WHERE s.grade
BETWEEN ?1 AND ?2
</ejb-ql>
```

EJB-QL queries also can navigate CMRs. In our example beans, Student uses its Locker field to navigate the 1:1 relationship with its Locker.

`FindStudentsWithoutALocker`

```
<ejb-ql>
 SELECT DISTINCT Object(s) FROM StudentCMPBean s WHERE s.locker IS
NULL
</ejb-ql>
```

`findStudentsWithALocker`

```
<ejb-ql>SELECT DISTINCT Object(s) FROM StudentCMPBean s WHERE
s.locker IS NOT NULL</ejb-ql>
```

EJB-QL queries that are 1:N or N:N can use the `IN` operator to qualify each of the related beans. For instance, this query navigates the 1:N relationship from Student to Books. The b variable iterates over each book and compares its title to the passed parameter.

`findStudentsWithBooksTitled(String bookTitle)`

```
    <ejb-ql>
      SELECT DISTINCT Object(s) FROM StudentCMPBean s, b IN s.books
WHERE b.title = ?1
    </ejb-ql>
```

EJB-QL queries with 1:N and N:N relations can also use the `EMPTY` operator to determine if there are any related beans.

`    findStudentsWithNoBooks()`

```
    <ejb-ql>SELECT DISTINCT Object(s) FROM StudentCMPBean s WHERE
s.books IS EMPTY</ejb-ql>
```

These examples demonstrate many of the possible EJB-QL operators. The EJB 2.0 specification includes a complete grammar for EJB-QL and its operators.

CMR Programming Restrictions

The CMP 2.0 specification enables the EJB container to optimize the database accesses required to support relationships. These optimizations can greatly improve the application's performance, but there are also programming requirements that apply to CMRs but not to simple container-managed fields. In particular, a container-managed field can be assigned in the `ejbCreate` method, but a CMR cannot be set in the `ejbCreate` method.

> **Note:** The CMR must not be set until the `ejbPostCreate` method.

Another CMR restriction is that `getXXX` methods cannot be exposed in the remote interface. This rule exists because the EJB container might lazily load the relationship. If the `Collection` of remote interfaces were not materialized, it could not be serialized to an external client.

Materializing Collections

The WebLogic Server EJB container takes advantage of the CMP programming restrictions to auto-matically optimize database access with relationships. When a many relationship is accessed via a `getter` method, there is no database round trip. Instead, the container returns a `Collection` that includes enough information to materialize the `Collection`. The database is accessed only when the client actually attempts to iterate on the `Collection`.

The container also optimizes data access when an element is added to the `Collection`. For instance, it is a common pattern to call the CMR `get` method to return the `Collection` and add another element to the `Collection`. With a naive implementation, the EJB container would read all the related beans from the database into memory, add one element to the `Collection`, and write back all the elements to the database. Clearly, this would make adding beans to large collections quite expensive.

Instead, the WebLogic Server EJB container does not access the database on the `get` method. The `Collection` addition simply adds a single element to the memory cache. When the `Collection` is written back at the end of the transaction, only the single new element is written to the database. In the naive implementation, there are N beans read and $N + 1$ beans written to the database. In the WebLogic Server EJB container, there are 0 beans read and 1 bean written.

BMP Entity Beans

The EJB specification also supports entity beans with BMP. Unlike CMP entity beans that rely on the EJB container to provide the persistence logic, BMP entity beans must write explicit code to access the persistent store. For most users, this involves writing JDBC code to access a relational database.

Writing the Student BMP Entity EJB

The following sections demonstrate the process for creating an entity bean with BMP. In this example, we model a Student as an entity bean. This entity bean could be used to model Student records and make them available to Teachers and Parents.

First, create the remote interface, which extends `javax.ejb.EJBObject` and provides the signatures for business methods that the Student entity bean exposes to remote clients. Because this is an RMI interface, all methods must include `RemoteException` in their throws clause.

```
package com.learnweblogic.examples.ch9.bmp;
import java.rmi.RemoteException;
import javax.ejb.EJBObject;

  public interface Student extends EJBObject {
  public String getName() throws RemoteException;
```

```
public Integer getSsn() throws RemoteException;
public int getGrade() throws RemoteException;
public void setGrade(int grade) throws RemoteException;

}
```

The Student remote interface outlines a few basic methods that can retrieve and update fields in the entity bean.

Next, we define the remote home interface for the Student BMP EJB. This interface must extend `javax.ejb.EJBHome`, and it defines the `create` and `finder` methods for the Student BMP EJB.

```
package com.learnweblogic.examples.ch9.bmp;

import java.rmi.RemoteException;
import java.util.Collection;

import javax.ejb.CreateException;
import javax.ejb.FinderException;
import javax.ejb.EJBHome;

public interface StudentHome extends EJBHome {

  // create method

  public Student create(String name, int ssn, int grade)
    throws CreateException, RemoteException;

  // finders

  public Student findByPrimaryKey(Integer ssn)
    throws FinderException, RemoteException;

  public Collection findStudentsInGrade(int grade)
    throws FinderException, RemoteException;

}
```

Like the remote interface, the remote home interface is called through RMI: all methods must throw `RemoteException`. Additionally, all `create` methods must include `CreateException`, and all `finders` must include `FinderException`.

This remote home interface includes two `find` methods: `findByPrimaryKey` and `findStudentsInGrade`. The `findByPrimaryKey` (required) returns the Student with the matching Social Security number if that Student exists. If a matching Social Security number is not found, the bean writer throws a `FinderException`.

The `findStudentsInGrade` is an example of a multi-object finder. In this case, the container returns an `EJBObject` reference for each student whose grade matches the parameter.

Note that the container is returning a `Collection` of remote interfaces and not a `Collection` of beans. The actual bean class never travels to the client. As with session beans, the client always uses the entity bean by making calls on the home or remote interfaces.

> **Note:** Finders return `EJBObjects`, not the actual bean classes.

Writing the BMP Bean Class

The next step is to create the bean implementation class, which implements the `javax.ejb.EntityBean` interface and the business logic exposed in the remote interface. Because this is a bean-managed bean, the data-access code is also included in the implementation of the `create` method and the `finders`. The bean also implements the data-access code for `ejbLoad`, `ejbStore`, and `ejbRemove`.

```
package com.learnweblogic.examples.ch9.bmp;

import java.rmi.RemoteException;
import java.sql.Connection;
import java.sql.PreparedStatement;
import java.sql.ResultSet;
import java.sql.SQLException;
import java.util.ArrayList;
import java.util.Collection;

import javax.ejb.DuplicateKeyException;
import javax.ejb.EntityContext;
import javax.ejb.EntityBean;
import javax.ejb.EJBException;
import javax.ejb.NoSuchEntityException;
import javax.ejb.ObjectNotFoundException;
import javax.ejb.RemoveException;
import javax.naming.Context;
import javax.naming.InitialContext;
import javax.naming.NamingException;
import javax.sql.DataSource;
```

Note that this file uses explicit imports instead of importing a `package*`. While this is a matter of personal preference, using explicit imports allows the user to quickly scan the file and learn which package contains a class.

```
public class StudentBean implements EntityBean {
```

The next three variables are instance variables that are not tied to a particular identity/primary key. These variables are set in the `setEntityContext` method before the bean has an identity and are used for the lifetime of the bean instance.

```
private EntityContext ctx;
private DataSource dataSource;
private String tableName;
```

The name, ssn, and grade variables are the bean's fields. They are initialized in ejbCreate, loaded from the database in ejbLoad, and stored to the database in ejbStore.

```
private String name;
private Integer ssn; // primary key
private int grade;
```

setEntityContext/unsetEntityContext

The setEntityContext method stores the EntityContext reference in a member variable. It also uses the EJB's environment context to look up deployment-specific parameters. When the EJB is deployed, the deployer specifies appropriate values for the tableName and poolName parameters in the ejb-jar.xml. This prevents these values from being hardcoded into the bean. The setEntityContext method also gets a DataSource object from the environment, which gets database connections from the connection pool.

```
public void setEntityContext(EntityContext c) {

    ctx = c;

    try {
      Context envCtx =
         (Context) new InitialContext().lookup("java:/comp/env");

      tableName = (String) envCtx.lookup("tableName");

      String poolName = (String) envCtx.lookup("poolName");

      dataSource = (DataSource) envCtx.lookup("/jdbc/"+poolName);
    } catch (NamingException ne) {
      // EJB was not deployed properly
      throw new EJBException(ne);
    }

}

public void unsetEntityContext() {
   ctx = null;
}
```

ejbCreate

The ejbCreate method initializes the member variables from the passed parameters and inserts the new entity bean into the database. If the insert fails, a SQLException is thrown. The ejbCreate method then uses its ejbFindByPrimaryKey method to determine whether the key already exists in the table. If the insert failed because the key is already present in the table, ejbFindByPrimaryKey returns successfully, and the ejbCreate method throws the DuplicateKeyException to inform the caller. Otherwise, if it failed due to a SQLException, an EJBException is thrown with the SQLException.

```
public Integer ejbCreate(String name, int ssn, int grade) {

    this.name      = name;
    this.ssn       = new Integer(ssn);
    this.grade     = grade;

  Connection        con = null;
  PreparedStatement ps = null;

  try {
    con = dataSource.getConnection();

    ps = con.prepareStatement("insert into "+tableName+
       " (name, ssn, grade) values (?,?,?)");

    ps.setString(1, name);
    ps.setInt(2, ssn);
    ps.setInt(3, grade);

    ps.executeUpdate();

    return this.ssn;

  } catch (SQLException sqe) {
    try {
      ejbFindByPrimaryKey(this.ssn);

      throw new DuplicateKeyException("A student with social "+
        "security number: "+ssn+" already exists.");
    } catch (Exception Ignore) {}

    sqe.printStackTrace();

    throw new EJBException (sqe);

  } finally {
```

```
        try {
          if (ps != null) ps.close();
          if (con != null) con.close();
        } catch (Exception ignore) {}
    }

  }
```

ejbPostCreate

Since this implementation requires no post-create initialization, this required method is empty:

```
    public void ejbPostCreate(String name, int ssn, int grade) {}
```

ejbRemove

The ejbRemove method is responsible for deleting the instance from the database. This method uses a SQL delete to remove the instance.

```
public void ejbRemove()
    throws RemoveException
  {

    Connection con = null;
    PreparedStatement ps = null;

    try {
      con = dataSource.getConnection();
      ps  = con.prepareStatement("delete from "+tableName+
        " where ssn=?");
      ps.setInt(1, ssn.intValue());

      if (ps.executeUpdate() < 1) {
throw new RemoveException ("Error removing Student with"+
" ssn: "+ssn);
      }
    } catch (SQLException sqe) {
      throw new EJBException (sqe);
    } finally {
      try {
        if(ps != null) ps.close();
        if(con != null) con.close();
      } catch (Exception ignore) {}
    }
  }
```

ejbLoad

ejbLoad reads the entity bean's current state from the database and assigns the values to its member variables. The primary key is available from the EntityContext member variable. If the entity bean no longer exists, NoSuchEntityException is thrown. This might occur if the entity bean was deleted by another client or directly from the database.

```java
public void ejbLoad() {

    ssn = (Integer) ctx.getPrimaryKey();

    Connection con        = null;
    PreparedStatement ps  = null;
    ResultSet rs          = null;
    try {
        con = dataSource.getConnection();
        ps  = con.prepareStatement("select name, grade from "
            +tableName+ " where ssn=?");
        ps.setInt(1, ssn.intValue());
        ps.executeQuery();
        rs = ps.getResultSet();

        if (rs.next()) {
            name  = rs.getString(1);
            grade = rs.getInt(2);

        } else {
            throw new NoSuchEntityException("Student with social "+
                "security number: "+ssn+" no longer exists.");
        }

    } catch (SQLException sqe) {
        throw new EJBException(sqe);
    } finally {
        try {
            if (rs != null) rs.close();
            if (ps != null) ps.close();
            if (con != null) con.close();
        } catch (Exception ignore) {}
    }
}
```

ejbStore

The ejbStore method is called to write the entity bean's state back to the database. The primary key field is not written because primary keys cannot be changed. An optimized version of this bean also can skip writing the name field, if you assume that it is never updated.

```
public void ejbStore() {

    Connection con        = null;
    PreparedStatement ps = null;

    try {
      con = dataSource.getConnection();
      ps  = con.prepareStatement("update "+tableName+
        " SET name=?, grade=? " +
        " where ssn=?");

      ps.setString(1, name);
      ps.setInt(2, grade);
      ps.setInt(3, ssn.intValue());

      ps.executeUpdate();

    } catch (SQLException sqe) {
      throw new EJBException(sqe);
    } finally {
      try {
        if (ps != null) ps.close();
        if (con != null) con.close();
      } catch (Exception ignore) {}
    }
}
```

ejbActivate/ejbPassivate

The ejbActivate and ejbPassivate methods are required even though this bean does not use these callbacks.

```
public void ejbActivate() {}
public void ejbPassivate() {}
```

ejbFindByPrimaryKey

The ejbFindByPrimaryKey method tests whether the passed key exists in the database. If the select returns a row, then the primary key is returned. If the key does not exist, an ObjectNotFoundException is thrown.

```
public Integer ejbFindByPrimaryKey(Integer pk)
  throws ObjectNotFoundException
{

  Connection con = null;
  PreparedStatement ps = null;
```

```
   ResultSet rs = null;


   try {
     con = dataSource.getConnection();
     ps  = con.prepareStatement("select ssn from "+tableName+
       " where ssn=?");
     ps.setInt(1, pk.intValue());
     ps.executeQuery();

     rs = ps.getResultSet();

     if (rs.next()) {
       return pk;
     } else {
       throw new ObjectNotFoundException ("Student with social"+
         "security number: "+ssn+" no longer exists.");
     }
   } catch (SQLException sqe) {
     throw new EJBException (sqe);
   } finally {
     try {
       if (rs != null) rs.close();
       if(ps != null) ps.close();
       if(con != null) con.close();
     } catch (Exception ignore) {}
   }

}
```

Multi-Object Finders

The ejbFindStudentsInGrade method returns a Collection of students who match the query. The finder method returns a Collection of primary keys. The EJB container converts these into EJBObject references and returns them to the client. If no primary keys match the query, an empty Collection is returned.

```
public Collection ejbFindStudentsInGrade(int gradeValue) {

    Connection con = null;
    PreparedStatement ps = null;
    ResultSet rs = null;

    ArrayList keys = new ArrayList();

    try {
```

```
con = dataSource.getConnection();
ps  = con.prepareStatement("select ssn from "+tableName+
   " where grade=?");
ps.setInt(1, gradeValue);
ps.executeQuery();

rs = ps.getResultSet();


while (rs.next()) {
  keys.add(new Integer(rs.getInt(1)));
}

return keys;

} catch (SQLException sqe) {
  throw new EJBException (sqe);
} finally {
  try {
if (rs != null) rs.close();
    if(ps != null) ps.close();
    if(con != null) con.close();
  } catch (Exception ignore) {}
}
}
```

These methods implement the business methods defined in the Student remote interface.

```
public String getName() { return name; }
public Integer getSsn() { return ssn; }
public int getGrade() { return grade; }
public void setGrade(int grade) { this.grade = grade; }
}
```

The ejb-jar.xml Deployment Descriptor

Finally, the bean provider writes the deployment descriptors for the BMP entity bean. Like session beans, BMP entity beans use a standard ejb-jar.xml deployment descriptor and a WebLogic Server–specific weblogic-ejb-jar.xml descriptor. Here is the sample ejb-jar.xml:

```
<?xml version="1.0"?>

<!DOCTYPE ejb-jar PUBLIC
"-//Sun Microsystems, Inc.//DTD Enterprise JavaBeans 2.0//EN"
"http://java.sun.com/dtd/ejb-jar_2_0.dtd">
<ejb-jar>
```

```
<enterprise-beans>

  <entity>
    <ejb-name>StudentEJB</ejb-name>
    <home>com.learnweblogic.examples.ch9.bmp.StudentHome</home>
    <remote>com.learnweblogic.examples.ch9.bmp.Student</remote>
    <ejb-class>
       com.learnweblogic.examples.ch9.bmp.StudentBean
    </ejb-class>
    <persistence-type>Bean</persistence-type>
    <prim-key-class>java.lang.Integer</prim-key-class>
    <reentrant>False</reentrant>

    <primkey-field>ssn</primkey-field>

    <env-entry>
       <env-entry-name>tableName</env-entry-name>
       <env-entry-type>java.lang.String</env-entry-type>
       <env-entry-value>studenttable</env-entry-value>
    </env-entry>

    <env-entry>
       <env-entry-name>poolName</env-entry-name>
       <env-entry-type>java.lang.String</env-entry-type>
       <env-entry-value>dbpool</env-entry-value>
    </env-entry>

    <resource-ref>
       <res-ref-name>jdbc/dbpool</res-ref-name>
       <res-type>javax.sql.DataSource</res-type>
       <res-auth>Container</res-auth>
    </resource-ref>

  </entity>

</enterprise-beans>

<assembly-descriptor>
  <container-transaction>
    <method>
       <ejb-name>StudentEJB</ejb-name>
    <method-name>*</method-name>
    </method>

    <trans-attribute>Required</trans-attribute>
```

```
        </container-transaction>

    </assembly-descriptor>
</ejb-jar>
```

The `ejb-jar.xml` descriptor is similar to a session bean's descriptor. The main difference is that it uses the `<entity>` tag and defines a primary key class. The `<prim-key-class>` specifies the class being used as the primary key for this entity bean. If the primary key is a single field in the entity bean, the bean provider can use the field type as the primary key and specify the primary key field with the `<primkey-field>` tag. In this example, `java.lang.Integer` is the primary key class, and `ssn` is the primary key field.

It is also possible to have a compound primary key. This requires a user-defined primary key class. This class must have public data members whose names and types match the primary key fields in the bean class.

Note: With user-defined primary key classes, the bean provider specifies the user-defined class in the `<prim-key-class>` tag but must not specify a `<primkey-field>`.

The weblogic-ejb-jar.xml Deployment Descriptor

Here's the `weblogic-ejb-jar.xml` deployment descriptor:

```
<?xml version="1.0"?>

<!DOCTYPE weblogic-ejb-jar PUBLIC
'-//BEA Systems, Inc.//DTD WebLogic 8.1.0 EJB//EN' 'http://
www.bea.com/servers/wls810/dtd/weblogic-ejb-jar.dtd'>

<weblogic-ejb-jar>
  <weblogic-enterprise-bean>
    <ejb-name>StudentEJB</ejb-name>
    <reference-descriptor>

      <resource-description>
        <res-ref-name>jdbc/dbpool</res-ref-name>
        <jndi-name>
          DBPool
        </jndi-name>
      </resource-description>

    </reference-descriptor>

    <jndi-name>StudentEJB</jndi-name>
  </weblogic-enterprise-bean>

</weblogic-ejb-jar>
```

This deployment descriptor includes only the resource information for the JDBC `DataSource` and the entity bean's JNDI name.

Creating the Database Table

Before the entity bean can be deployed, the database tables must be created. The exact mapping of Java types to database types depends on the database vendor, but we show sample DDL here:

```
create table studenttable (
  name varchar(255),
  ssn integer primary key,
  grade integer
);
```

The database primary key field(s) must match the entity bean's primary key field(s). This enables the entity bean to use the database to prevent multiple entity beans from using the same primary key. Any attempt to create an entity bean with an existing primary key will be flagged as a constraint violation by the database.

Client Code

Like session beans, entity bean clients look up the home interface in JNDI. The entity bean can then be created via the home interface. Unlike a session bean, the entity bean `create` causes a database insert. You should check both the client code and the database contents as the client makes calls against the entity bean.

This client code is taken from the `StudentBMPClient.java` example. Before the client code runs, the database table is empty:

```
select * from studenttable;

 name | ssn | grade
------+-----+-------
(0 rows)
```

Then the client code executes:

```
StudentHome studentHome = (StudentHome)
narrow(getInitalContext().lookup("StudentEJB"), StudentHome.class);

Student s = studentHome.create("John Doe", 200, 10);
```

Now, let's look at the database contents after the `create`:

```
select * from studenttable;

   name   | ssn | grade
----------+-----+-------
 John Doe | 200 |    10
(1 row)
```

The `create` call has inserted a row into the database. The client code continues with a business method.

Now let's follow the execution of a business method: `setGrade(int)`. This business method starts a transaction. The EJB container calls the bean's `ejbLoad` method to refresh the state from the database. Next, the business method executes, and finally `ejbStore` is called to write the state back to the database.

The client calls a business method to change the `grade` field:

```
s.setGrade(4);
```

We can now see the updated database contents:

```
select * from studenttable;

   name    | ssn | grade
-----------+-----+-------
 John Doe  | 200 |     4
(1 row)
```

The `grade` column has been updated with the new value.

The client code then removes the bean. This causes the container to call `ejbRemove` on the bean, which deletes the row from the database.

```
s.remove();
```

Now the database table is empty once again:

```
select * from studenttable;
 name | ssn | grade
------+-----+-------
(0 rows)
```

Best Practices for BMP Entity EJBs

While BMP entity beans require a fair amount of JDBC code, almost every BMP bean uses similar code, and the code is not difficult to develop. However, you should make sure to include debugging code that prints out the SQL statements that are being executed. It is easy for typographic errors to result in cryptic database errors.

> **Best Practice:** Include debugging code to print out SQL statements.

Advanced Topics for Writing Entity EJBs

Having surveyed the basic process for developing and deploying container-managed and bean-managed entity beans, we now turn to some advanced topics that the entity bean developer needs to know. These advanced topics include how to develop a primary key class, entity beans and inheritance, locking strategies, and other details.

How to Write a Primary Key Class

The EJB primary key class serves as its unique identifier both in the persistent store and in the EJB container. Usually, the primary key class fields map directly to the primary key fields in a database. If the primary key is only a single entity bean field that is a Java primitive class (such as `java.lang.String`), the bean writer does not have to write a custom primary key class. Instead, in the deployment descriptor, the bean writer specifies the name of the class and the name of the primary key field.

If the primary key maps to a user-defined type or to multiple fields, the bean writer must write a custom primary key class. The primary key class must implement `java.io.Serializable` and contain the primary key fields. For CMP entity beans, the field names must match the corresponding primary key field names in the bean class. This enables the EJB container to assign the appropriate CMP fields to their corresponding fields in the primary key class.

For instance, we might define an employee's primary key as a compound key using the first name, last name, and office number. Our compound key would look like this:

```java
public final class EmployeePK implements java.io.Serializable {

    public String lastName;
    public String firstName;
    public int officeNumber;

    private int hash = -1;

    public EmployeePK() {}

    public int hashCode() {
        if (hash == -1) {
            hash = lastName.hashCode() ^ firstName.hashCode()
                ^ officeNumber;
        }
        return hash;
    }
    public boolean equals(Object o) {
        if (o == this) return true;

        if (o instanceof EmployeePK) {
            EmployeePK other = (EmployeePK) o;
            return other.hashCode() == hashCode() &&
                    other.officeNumber == officeNumber;
                    other.lastName.equals(lastName) &&
                    other.firstName.equals(firstName);
```

```
    } else {
      return false;
    }
  }
}
```

The primary key class consists of the primary key fields, which must be public, and a no-argument constructor. The primary key class must also implement the hashCode and equals methods. The EJB container uses a number of data structures internally, many of which are indexed by the primary key class. It is vital that hashCode and equals be implemented correctly and efficiently in the primary key class.

Implementing hashCode

The hashCode method is implemented by returning an integer using the primary key fields. The goal of this function is to produce an integer that can be used to index tables. The hashCode for a primary key should never change. Therefore, the hashCode should only be constructed from immutable values.

A common strategy is to XOR the hashCode of the primary key elements together. OR should never be used because ORing several values will generally have most or all bits set to 1. Similarly, AND should not be used because most or all bits will converge to 0.

The hashCode method must be implemented such that two equal objects have the same hashCode. However, two objects with the same hashCode are not necessarily equal. This hashCode implementation stores the hashCode in a member variable to avoid computing it every time hashCode is called.

Implementing equals

It can also be tricky to implement equals correctly. The first line of any equals method should check the passed reference against this. This optimization simply checks whether equals has been called against itself. While this sounds strange at first, it is a common operation when the container has a primary key object and is checking to see if it already exists in a data structure.

Next, the equals method should ensure that the passed parameter is its own type. If the primary key class is final, a simple instanceof check can be used. If the primary key class is not final, the passed parameter might be a subclass of our primary key class. In this case, the equals method must use getClass().equals to ensure that the class types exactly match. It is recommended that primary key classes be final because using instanceof is cheaper than comparing classes.

Best Practice: Primary key classes should be final.

Finally, the equals method compares all the values in the passed object. If all of the values are identical, the objects are equal. Notice that the hashCodes are compared first. If two objects are equal, then their hashCodes must be equal. Because our hashCode implementation precomputes the hashCode, and integer comparisons are relatively cheap, it is usually worthwhile to perform this comparison first.

Entity Bean Inheritance and Polymorphism

Inheritance is a key advantage of object-oriented systems. Objects in a hierarchy gain functionality from their parents or superclasses. Object-oriented systems also generally provide *polymorphism*, the capability to define common operations across distinct types. EJBs, especially entity beans, can take advantage of inheritance and polymorphism. An EJB programmer might define an employee entity bean with common methods such as getName and getSalary.

The programmer could then define a manager entity bean that extends the employee entity bean and adds manager-specific information. A method such as getSubordinates, for example, could return the manager's employees. The advantage of using inheritance is that a manager entity bean could also be treated as an employee. You could call a method getSalary, which prints the total salaries of all employees, on each employee bean in the list. Some of these beans might actually be manager beans, but to this routine, they would all be employees (see Figure 9–2).

Figure 9–2
Employee–manager inheritance.

Inheritance Restrictions

To design entity beans with inheritance, it is necessary to be cognizant of restrictions in the EJB specification. While the EJB specification allows component inheritance, there are some subtle rules that limit how inherited EJBs are designed. The EJB specification requires that the home interface's create method returns the remote interface type, not a subclass or a superclass. The ejbCreate method on an entity bean must return the primary key type, not a subclass or superclass. Similarly, the home interface's findByPrimaryKey method must take the primary key class as a parameter and return the remote interface. These requirements constrain how the bean writer may implement inheritance.

For instance, the employee home interface's create method returns the employee remote interface. If the programmer wants to make a management bean that extends the employee bean, a first approach might be to define a management home interface that extends the employee home interface and a management remote interface that extends the employee remote interface. However, this approach would violate the EJB specification because the management home interface would inherit the employee create method, which does not return the management entity bean's remote interface. In the next section, we cover a number of patterns that may be used within the guidelines of the EJB specification for entity bean inheritance and polymorphism.

Design Patterns for Inheritance and Polymorphism

When designing entity beans with inheritance and polymorphism, it is important to decide which attributes will be used generically. In our employee and manager example, the programmer wants to expose the employee business methods as generics for any employee. This can be accomplished by defining a separate interface that includes only the generic employee business methods. An interface such as `GenericEmployee` would include the `getName` and `getSalary` methods. Now the employee bean has a remote interface that extends `GenericEmployee`. The manager bean's remote interface also extends `GenericEmployee` (see Figure 9–3).

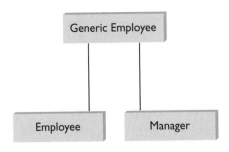

Figure 9–3
Remote interface.

Inheriting Interfaces

Because the EJBs use different remote interfaces and the `create` method must return the remote interface, our manager and employee beans must use different home interfaces. The employee home interface contains a `create` method that returns the employee remote interface. The manager home interface contains a `create` method that returns a manager remote interface. The `findByPrimaryKey` method is duplicated in each home interface. If the home interfaces contain generic methods such as home methods or `finders` returning `collection` types, these methods can be placed in a `GenericEmployeeHome` interface. In this case, the employee and manager home interfaces would extend `GenericEmployeeHome` (see Figure 9–4).

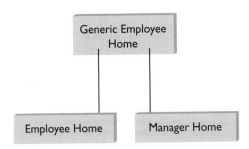

Figure 9–4
Home interface.

Inheritance can also be used when implementing the bean classes. A base class `GenericEm`-`ployeeBean` would implement the methods in `GenericEmployee` and `GenericEmployee`-`Home`. The employee EJB would have an employee bean class that extends the `GenericEmployeeBean` and implements the `create` and `find` methods. Likewise, the manager EJB would have a manager bean class that implements the `create` and `find` methods plus any manager-specific functionality.

The advantage of using the inheritance approach is that methods that treat employees polymorphically can use the `GenericEmployee` interface. In our total salary example, the method could take a `GenericEmployee` as its argument and call the `getSalary` method. Because both managers and employees implement this interface, the total salary method would work with either EJB. By using inheritance with the bean classes, the bean writer need only implement business methods once. Both beans then share this implementation.

Using Multiple Bean Implementations

Creating a base interface for the home and remote interface is not the only method for achieving polymorphism. Another common approach is to use identical home and remote interfaces, but implement them differently in the bean class. This approach is similar to using an interface that has several different implementations. The advantage is that the client does not know or care about which particular implementation is being used: the client just manipulates the interface.

For instance, an airline might model passengers as entity beans, using a remote interface with methods related to reserving seats on flights. Certain preferred or first-class seats would be available only to the airline's frequent customers. The entity bean writer could supply a different bean implementation of the passenger remote interface for frequent flyers. Ordinary customers would use a different implementation of the bean class. Any common methods could be implemented in a base class (see Figure 9–5).

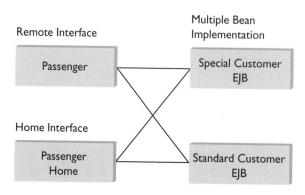

Figure 9–5
Passenger inheritance.

The advantage of this approach is that the back-end policies are independent of the client code. The bean writer could supply a new implementation of the bean class without changing any code in the client. If the airline established a new ultra customer whose benefits surpassed even the preferred customers, the bean writer would merely introduce a new bean class. The client code would be undisturbed.

Entity Beans and Locking

Entity beans are transactional, shared resources, simultaneously used by many clients. Clearly, to ensure that clients view consistent data, the EJB container and the database must enforce concurrency control. Entity EJBs are not written as re-entrant or thread-safe components. Each entity bean instance never has more than one thread of control in its object. This simplistic concurrency control is handled by the EJB container and mandated by the EJB specification. For this reason, methods in the entity bean class are not synchronized.

Database Concurrency

The database also provides concurrency control. The entity bean interacts with the database through its data-access code and transactions. Generally, the database knows nothing of entity beans: it sees only transactions and JDBC or SQL commands. The database uses a combination of locking and private per-transaction copies of the data to manage concurrency. The actual locking strategy used by the database depends on the database vendor and the transaction's isolation level. Any transaction that violates the database constraints is unable to commit, and a SQLException is thrown. For instance, a database using optimistic concurrency control might detect at commit time that the associated transaction cannot serialize correctly. Generally, this exception occurs as a result of the ejbStore call.

In addition to the database, the EJB container supports concurrency control for entity beans. Because the EJB specification mandates a single entity bean instance that must not be written as thread-safe, the EJB container must serialize all container callbacks and business methods. This means, for example, that the container cannot call ejbPassivate while the business method is running.

EJB Container Concurrency

Although the EJB specification does not require a specific implementation, there are two general strategies for implementing entity bean concurrency control within the EJB container.

One approach is to activate an entity bean instance for each transaction. In this scenario, if two clients in separate transactions each call the same entity bean, the EJB container activates two instances, one instance for each transaction. Each instance calls ejbLoad at the beginning of the transaction to read its state. To the database, it appears as two transactions accessing the same data. This is handled by the database locking: the specific behavior depends on the database vendor and the isolation level. In most cases, because both transactions have only requested read locks, the transactions can proceed concurrently.

Another strategy is to maintain a single entity bean instance per primary key. In this scenario, only one transaction accesses the entity bean at a time. Once the previous transaction commits or rolls back, another transaction is permitted to use the entity bean instance.

Choosing a Database Concurrency Strategy

There are two concurrency control strategies: database concurrency and exclusive concurrency.

Database Concurrency

The WebLogic Server enables the entity bean deployer to choose a concurrency control strategy. By default, the WebLogic Server activates an entity bean instance for each transaction. This approach is called the database concurrency strategy because it defers the locking to the database. The database concurrency model leverages the database's deadlock detection capabilities. When the database detects a deadlock, one of the deadlocked transactions is aborted. A SQLException is thrown to the victim, and the EJB container processes the transaction rollback.

Exclusive Concurrency

The WebLogic Server also offers an option to activate a single instance per primary key, per WebLogic Server instance. This scenario forces the bean writer to be even more vigilant in avoiding deadlocks and concurrency conflicts. Because there is only a single instance per primary key, the EJB container implements an exclusive lock. For entity beans that are used by many clients concurrently in read-only or read-mostly situations, the exclusive lock can greatly limit parallelism. On the other hand, the exclusive lock enables data to be cached between transactions. Note that the exclusive lock is a per-server lock. In a WebLogic cluster, there can be an active instance with the same primary key in every server. The concurrency between servers is managed by the database.

Generally, entity beans should use the default database concurrency option because it places much less burden on the programmer. EJB 2.0 CMP beans can employ more advanced concurrency options because the EJB container has greater control over when data is read and written to the database.

> **Best Practice:** Except in special cases, use the default database concurrency option.

Optimizing Data-Access Calls

Entity bean programmers concerned about performance try to minimize the number of round trips between the EJB container and the database. By default, the WebLogic Server calls the entity bean's ejbLoad method at the beginning of a transaction to read the current state from the database. When the transaction commits, the EJB container calls ejbStore to write the entity bean's contents to the database. Note that database access occurs on transaction boundaries, not on method-call boundaries.

Programmers writing their first entity beans can incur performance problems by making their transactions too fine-grained. For instance, a Web page might need to gather 10 attributes from an entity bean to populate a page. If each method call runs in its own transaction, there are 10 database reads (ejbLoad calls) and 10 database writes (ejbStore calls). If the 10 method calls are wrapped in a single transaction, there is only one database read and one database write. For an operation such as populating a Web page, the database write is actually unnecessary because this transaction is read-only. We discuss how the WebLogic Server EJB container eliminates unnecessary database writes in a later section.

Minimizing Database Round Trips

In addition to batching multiple operations in a single transaction, there are a number of optimizations to minimize database round trips. Note that there is little opportunity to optimize creates. As a database insert, a create must write the initial values passed to the ejbCreate method. Because creates are a relatively rare event, their database access generally does not limit performance.

The EJB writer should try to optimize database reads (`ejbLoad` calls), database writes (`ejb-Store` calls), and `finders` (database queries). BMP entity beans and CMP entity beans generally use different optimization strategies to minimize database round trips.

BMP Read Optimization

BMP entity beans that handle a great deal of data can optimize reads by writing `ejbLoad` so that it either reads a subset or, if appropriate, does nothing. In response to a `business` method call, the entity bean needs to determine whether the data has already been read in this transaction. You can achieve this by storing a bitmask in the entity bean that has one bit for each field. Then, `ejbLoad` sets a bit when its associated field is loaded. The remaining bits are cleared. The business method checks the bitmask to determine whether it needs to load its data.

The bitmask technique needs to be used with caution. If every attribute is brought in only on demand, the entity bean can exhibit extremely poor performance. The bitmask approach is best used when entity bean fields are very large, but seldom used. For example, an employee entity bean may have a picture stored as a binary image in the bean. Presumably, many users of the entity bean do not display the picture, so the bean limits the amount of data transferred from the database by only loading the picture when requested. If the remainder of the bean's fields are simple relational types or are frequently used, they should all be loaded in the `ejbLoad` call. The memory overhead of loading a few extra integers is minimal compared to the cost of extra trips to the database.

BMP Write Optimizations

There are two main write optimizations that can be performed with BMP entity beans: omitting database writes in read-only transactions and tuned writes. Read-only transactions are common in real-world applications because entity bean data is often used to populate Web pages. Tuned writes are used to write only modified fields, instead of every field in the entity bean. Both optimizations are implemented using the same technique and are generally combined.

The entity bean keeps a bitmask with one bit per field. The bitmask is cleared in the `ejbLoad` callback. As with EJB 2.0 CMP beans, the bean should access its fields through `get` and `set` methods. This simplifies porting EJBs to CMP. With BMP beans, the bean writer implements the `get` and `set` methods. The `get` method simply returns the associated field. The `set` method sets the bitmask field associated with the EJB field and then assigns the value. The `ejbStore` implementation first checks the bitmask. If the bitmask is all zeros, `ejbStore` returns immediately without writing to the database. The `ejbStore` method also can perform tuned writes because the bitmask shows which fields were modified in the transaction.

A common error when implementing this pattern is to clear the associated bit in the `get` method. This implementation does not work because the value may be read again after it has been written. If the bean writer clears the mask in the `get` method, the previous write is lost.

Optimizing Finder Methods

BMP entity beans also can optimize their `finder` methods, but the techniques apply only in certain situations. In general, BMP `finders` simply access the database and return the associated primary keys. As we see in the following section, CMP `finders` may be better optimized.

Implementing the `findByPrimaryKey` method is a special circumstance. The general contract for the `findByPrimaryKey` method is to ensure that the primary key exists and then return the primary key. Usually, the bean implementation selects the primary key from the database, and if a row is returned, the implementation knows that the key exists. In some application-specific situations, the entity bean may already be aware that this primary key exists, and findByPrimaryKey can skip the data access and simply return the primary key. This optimization only applies when the primary key exists in a known domain or verification is performed at another level.

Optimizing CMP Entity Beans

CMP entity beans also can minimize the number of database round trips, but because the EJB container controls the data-access code, optimizations are made in the deployment descriptor rather than in the bean code. By default, the WebLogic Server CMP implementation treats reads in the same way as standard BMP entity beans. At the beginning of the transaction, ejbLoad is called, and the bean's state is cleared. When the first getXXX method is called, the CMP engine reads the entire bean state from the database.

The standard behavior for finders is also identical to standard BMP behavior. Each finder selects the matching keys from the database. In the WebLogic Server CMP implementation, the container provides a feature called grouping to optimize finders and reads. The deployer must specify grouped fields in the CMP deployment descriptor. The bean writer can then assign finders or business methods to specific groups. When a finder or business method runs, it loads all the fields in its group.

For example, a U.S. citizen entity bean may have a Social Security number (as a primary key) and a name attribute. You could call findByPrimaryKey on a specific Social Security number, and then call a business method that reads the name attribute. By default, there would be one database access for the findByPrimaryKey call and another database access to load the name attribute. If the deployer specified a group containing the name and Social Security number fields, the findByPrimaryKey method and the getName method could use the same group. Then only one database access is required.

If the getName method is called again within the same transaction, it skips the data access and uses the cached name parameter. The grouping feature is effective because it does not require that every field be retrieved, which can be very expensive. Instead, the bean writer can create large entity beans that make small and efficient data-access calls. One of the limitations of the BMP programming model is that it cannot match the CMP container's cooperation between finders and subsequent business methods.

Using Read-Only Entity Beans

As we've seen throughout this chapter, entity beans provide an object view of persistent and transactional data. However, not all persistent data is truly transactional. Many Web applications are dominated by reads and can even tolerate slightly stale data. The WebLogic Server offers an option called *read-only entity beans* to provide greater performance for read-intensive applications.

The advantage of read-only entity beans is that their data can be cached in memory, in many servers in the cluster. Read-only entity beans do not use expensive logic to keep the distributed caches coherent. Instead, the deployer specifies a timeout value, and the entity bean's cached state is refreshed after the timeout has expired.

Like any entity bean, the bean state is refreshed with the ejbLoad method call. When a method call is made on a read-only entity bean, the EJB container checks whether the associated data is older than its timeout value. If the timeout period has elapsed, ejbLoad is called and the bean state is refreshed. Because read-only beans do not have updates, ejbStore is never called.

Read-only entity beans never participate in transactions, and they generally do not have create methods because creates should generally run in transactions.

Read-only entity beans are portable and follow the EJB specification. A WebLogic Server read-only entity bean is the same as a normal entity bean, except for some special deployment parameters in the WebLogic Server deployment descriptor and a different timing for calling ejbLoad and ejbStore.

Designing Read-Mostly Entity Beans

While there are many situations in which data is only read, most applications have some updates. Read-only entity beans can be very effective in environments where reads dominate, but there are occasional updates. For instance, a Web site displaying sports scores might use an entity bean to model the game score. The game entity bean could store the teams playing the game, the current score of the game, and the time remaining.

Most of the requests to this entity bean are from Web pages that are reading the associated data and displaying it to the user. The Web site also has software that receives the score updates; it can then call the game entity bean and update the page with the new score and the remaining time. Viewing a score is not a transactional operation. In general, it does not matter if a user misses an instantaneous score update. In fact, this deployment could increase its performance by writing the game bean as a read-only entity bean. Because sports scores change relatively rapidly, a timeout of 30 seconds might be reasonable. To perform the updates, you can write a game update entity bean that extends the game bean. The game update bean is a traditional transactional entity bean that includes the methods to update the entity bean's state. The technique of using a read-only bean and extending it with a traditional entity bean that adds the update methods is referred to as the read-mostly pattern. It greatly increases the performance of sites that are dominated by reads but also have some updates.

Read-Mostly Example

This example demonstrates the read-mostly pattern for a Web site that displays basketball game scores and receives updates from an external process. The BasketballScoreReader is a read-only entity bean deployed with a read-timeout of 30 seconds. The read-timeout parameter is set in the weblogic-ejb-jar.xml file. The methods exposed through the BasketballScore-Reader interface are read-only and return the cached copy of the data. The BasketballScore-Updater bean is a standard, read/write entity bean. Its interface extends the reader interface with update methods. The BasketballScoreReader bean reads the updated data every 30 seconds. Between updates, the BasketballScoreReader reads cached data.

```
public BasketballScoreReader extends EJBObject {

    public String getHomeTeamName() throws RemoteException;
    public String getAwayTeamName() throws RemoteException;

    public int getHomeScore() throws RemoteException;
    public int getAwayScore() throws RemoteException;

    public int getQuarter() throws RemoteException;
    public int getTimeRemaining() throws RemoteException;
```

```
}

public BasketballScoreUpdater extends BasketballScoreReader {

   public void setHomeScore(int s) throws RemoteException;
   public void setAwayScore(int s) throws RemoteException;

   public void setQuarter(int q) throws RemoteException;
   public void setTimeRemaining(int t) throws RemoteException;

}
```

Session Beans as a Wrapper for Entity Beans

One of the main advantages of modular software is *abstraction*. An abstract implementation's components communicate through well-defined interfaces so that any component could be replaced with an alternate module. Entity beans are not fully abstract: although they expose remote interfaces to clients, their structure is closely tied to the fields in a particular database.

As we have shown, the Web tier uses an EJB layer to interact with the database. If the Web tier manipulates the entity beans directly, encapsulation could be violated because the database schema is exposed through the entity beans to the Web tier. A better design is to place session beans in front of entity beans. In that case, the Web tier calls the session bean, which in turn calls one or more entity beans.

The advantage of this pattern is that the session bean exposes only a business interface to the Web tier. The actual persistence layer can be implemented with (your choice): straight JDBC, one or more entity beans, or even a persistent queue. Because the persistence layer is hidden behind a layer of abstraction, the Web tier is independent of the persistent implementation. The practice of wrapping entity beans with session beans is known as the *facade pattern*.

Transaction demarcation is another advantage of using stateless session beans to wrap entity beans. If the Web tier called entity beans directly using multiple calls in a transaction, the Web tier would have to use a `UserTransaction` and explicitly demarcate each transaction. In general, it is advisable to enclose transactions with the persistence logic and keep them out of the Web tier. The Web tier should be concerned with presentation logic, not systems-level programming.

> **Best Practice:** Transaction demarcation should be handled in the session bean facade. Transactions should not be exposed to the Web or presentation tier.

With a session bean facade, all of the transactions can be handled within the session bean. You can mark the session bean methods as `RequiresNew` and the entity bean methods as `Manda-tory`. In this scenario, the EJB container automatically begins a transaction before any method call on a session bean and commits the transaction when a session bean call returns. Any entity bean called from the session bean participates in its transaction. By marking the entity bean as mandatory, the bean writer asserts that the caller should be handling the transaction.

> **Best Practice:** Entity beans should never be exposed to the client or even to the Web tier.

Using Java Beans as Value Objects

Even when using the facade pattern, the EJB programmer must be careful to avoid exposing the entity beans directly to the client or Web tier. For example, a Web application displays a list of current orders for a given customer. The Web tier displays the information, and the EJB layer accesses the persistent store with an Order entity bean. With the facade pattern, the Web tier accesses a stateless session bean that finds the appropriate Order entity beans. The stateless session bean returns a `Collection` of Order entity objects to the Web tier. The Web tier can then call `getXXX` methods on the Order references and display the information to the user.

While this approach makes sense intuitively, it represents a poor use of entity beans and it does not perform well. Because entity beans are transactional components, the EJB container starts a transaction every time it calls `ejbLoad` and reads from the database. Because the Web tier should not be concerned with transactions, a single transaction cannot span the call to the stateless session bean and the presentation logic. The extra database round trips can greatly decrease performance.

A better approach is to never return the entity beans to the Web tier. Instead, the session bean can create Java bean *value objects* that encapsulate the information needed by the presentation logic. A collection of these value objects is returned to the Web tier. The presentation logic can make regular method calls to retrieve the order information from the `order` value object without returning to the database.

> **Best Practice:** Expose serializable value objects instead of entity beans to the Web or client tiers.

For example, here is an `OrderValueObject` that encapsulates the information in an Order entity bean. The client receives these objects and never directly touches an entity bean. This ensures a clean separation between the persistent tier and the presentation layer.

```
public final class OrderValueObject
    implements java.io.Serializable
{
    private double price;
    private int quantity;
    private int itemNumber;

    public void setPrice(double p) { price = p; }
    public double getPrice() { return price; }

    public void setQuantity(int q) { quantity = q; }
    public int getQuantity() { return quantity; }

    public void setItemNumber(int in) { itemNumber = in; }
```

```
    public int getItemNumber() { return itemNumber; }

}
```

BMP Versus CMP

An important design decision for entity bean developers is the choice between BMP and CMP.

> **Note:** The main advantage of BMP is its flexibility. Because the bean writer explicitly codes the data-access logic, he or she has complete control over the entity bean's persistence.

While most entity beans keep a persistent representation in a database, with BMP the bean writer has the flexibility to choose any type of persistent store. For instance, BMP might be used to persist an entity bean to a legacy system.

CMP Design Advantages

A clear advantage of CMP is simplicity. With CMP, the EJB container automatically generates the data-access code. This not only makes the bean simpler, but it also separates the bean code from its persistent representation. In a CMP bean, the database mappings occur at deployment time. The deployer can take a prepackaged CMP entity bean and map the persistent fields to arbitrary column and table names.

Another EJB 2.0 CMP advantage is the container's support for relationships between entity beans. In an EJB 2.0 CMP entity bean, EJB-QL and the EJB container automatically handle relationships. For a BMP bean to support relationships, the bean writer must explicitly manage foreign key relationships, join tables, and join queries.

CMP Performance Advantages

Many people believe that because BMP gives the bean writer control over the data-access logic, BMP should outperform container-generated code. However, this conclusion is generally not correct, especially with EJB 2.0 CMP beans. WebLogic Server's EJB 2.0 CMP container achieves high performance by minimizing the number of round trips between the EJB container and the database.

The most notable performance difference between BMP and CMP entity beans occurs with `finder` methods. In a BMP entity bean, `finder` methods return primary keys from the database. The EJB container creates a bean reference for each key and returns the references to the client. The key observation is that the BMP `finder` can return only the primary key. It is common for clients to find a set of beans and then call `business` methods on the returned references. Each `business` method triggers an `ejbLoad` call and a round trip to the database. If `business` methods are called on each reference, the BMP `finder` returns N references using $N + 1$ database round trips. Also, the `ejbLoad` call does not have any contextual information. For instance, the `ejbLoad` call does not know that it is immediately following the `finder`.

> **Note:** A BMP `finder` that returns N objects and then accesses each object makes $N + 1$ database round trips. A CMP `finder` can do a single `SELECT` that returns all of the necessary data.

The WebLogic Server EJB 2.0 CMP container enables the deployer to instruct the container how to optimize the situation by grouping attributes that should be loaded together. For instance, instead of loading only the primary key in the `finder`, the container could select the primary key plus attributes that are used in the following `business` method calls. In this case, there is only a single database access needed to run the `finder` and all the related `business` methods.

Another advantage of the WebLogic Server EJB 2.0 CMP implementation is that it does not require an all-or-nothing approach. The CMP implementation can load attributes in batches as they are required. For entity beans that represent a large amount of data, it is inefficient to load the entire bean from the database. The WebLogic Server EJB 2.0 CMP implementation enables the deployer to determine exactly how `finders` and methods bring data into the EJB container. The cooperation between `finders` and method invocations cannot be accomplished with a standard BMP entity bean.

Combining CMP and BMP

Choosing between CMP and BMP is not an absolute decision. In fact, it is possible to take a hybrid approach, using BMP and CMP within the same entity bean. When a CMP entity bean is deployed, the deployment descriptor specifies which of the bean's fields should be persisted by the EJB container. These are the container-managed fields. The entity bean may have other fields that are not in the container-managed list. In this case, the bean writer would explicitly manage the persistence of these fields. The BMP fields could be stored with the CMP fields, or they could be processed into a different table, a different database, or even a different persistent store.

Another option is to create both BMP and CMP versions of your entity beans. This approach is not as arduous as it sounds and does not require maintaining two completely separate code versions. First, write a CMP bean. The BMP version then extends the CMP bean class and provides the data-access code. For instance, the BMP version could implement `ejbLoad` by loading the appropriate data from the persistent store and then calling `super.ejbLoad()`. The BMP version must also provide implementations of the `get` and `set` methods for the container-managed fields and relationships.

Stateless Session Beans Versus Entity EJBs

How do entity beans compare to stateless session beans using explicit JDBC code? Stateless session beans with embedded data-access code give the developer direct access to the backing store. As with BMP entity beans, the developer has complete control over the data-access code. This is particularly useful when accessing a legacy or non-database system that does not support entity beans.

A stateless session bean also has complete control over the objects it returns from a query. Unlike `finder` methods, JDBC queries return raw objects, and the stateless session bean writer must handle the lifecycle and caching of these objects.

The CMP engine reads data from the database when the first container-managed field is accessed in a transaction. The bean writer then modifies state with `business` methods, and the EJB container calls `ejbStore` at the end of the transaction to write back the modified state. This read-modify-write model works well for a variety of applications, but there are exceptions that are better coded with session beans and SQL.

The usual example given is a *blind update*. If you run an election over the Web in which each candidate's vote count is stored in the database and an entity bean is used, each vote reads in the current vote total, increments it, and writes back the new total. This is a simple construction that results in terrible performance and risks database deadlocks. In this case, the database read is unnecessary. The operation simply needs to increment the current vote total, which can best be done using SQL in a session bean. As in the blind update UPDATE votes SET candidate_A_count = candidate_A_count + 1, this single JDBC statement performs much better than its entity bean counterpart and avoids database deadlock issues.

> **Note:** Entity EJBs use a read-modify-write model. When the read is unnecessary and only a modify and write are performed, JDBC outperforms the entity model.

CMP entity beans do possess a number of advantages over the stateless session bean with JDBC. In addition to freeing the programmer from having to write data-access code, CMP entity beans might outperform stateless session beans because CMP beans can maintain state and cache the results of queries.

CMP entity beans can also leverage the EJB container by writing an ejbHome method that uses an ejbSelect method to run the database query. Like stateless session beans, the EJB container selects a bean instance from the ready pool to run the ejbHome method. In using the ejbSelect method, the bean writer simply writes the EJB-QL query in the deployment descriptor, and the EJB container generates the required JDBC code. Using ejbSelect methods also allows the bean code to be separated from the database schema. The EJB-QL only accesses container-managed fields and relationships: it does not use physical database mapping names, which can be changed without updating the query.

Putting It All Together

Along with session beans, entity beans provide a powerful abstraction from Java objects to persistent, transactional business logic. CMP entity beans free the bean provider from writing tedious data-access code. Business logic can be rapidly developed while leaving the infrastructure to the EJB container. With the EJB 2.0 specification and WebLogic Server, the EJB container contains optimizations to make CMP entity beans' performance comparable to hand-coded SQL. As we've seen in this chapter, there are many cases in which the EJB container can optimize CMP entity beans to outperform BMP or hand-coded JDBC code.

References

The Enterprise JavaBeans 2.0 architecture specification page is available at *http://java.sun.com/products/ejb/2.0.html*.

BEA's Programming WebLogic Enterprise JavaBeans documentation for WebLogic Server 8.1 can be found at *http://edocs.bea.com/wls/docs81/ejb/*.

The Java Message Service specification is available at *http://java.sun.com/products/jms/index.html*.

Full documentation of generating and editing the deployment descriptors used to configure WebLogic Server EJBs (weblogic-ejb-jar.xml and ejb-jar.xml) is available at *http://e-docs.bea.com/wls/docs81/ejb/implementing.html*.

Ant documentation is available at *http://ant.apache.org/manual/index.html*.

The WebLogic deployment task is documented at *http://e-docs.bea.com/wls/docs81/deployment/tools.html*.

chapter 10

Using Message-Driven EJBs

In This Chapter

- Message-driven EJB lifecycle
- Writing deployment descriptors for message-driven beans
- Message-driven beans and concurrency
- Using transactions with message-driven beans
- Message-driven bean advantages

Session and entity beans use a well-defined interface for processing workflow from client requests. Enterprise JavaBeans (EJB) clients use the EJB component interfaces to make synchronous Remote Method Invocation (RMI) calls to the EJB server. The client thread making the EJB call blocks until the EJB server call returns. As discussed in Chapter 7, "Enterprise Messaging with the Java Message Service (JMS)," messaging allows an asynchronous model. Instead of waiting for the server's response, the client sends a message to a JMS destination and returns. In addition to scalability benefits, this model enables client programs to continue without waiting for server operations to complete.

In the EJB 2.0 specification, the message-driven EJB type was created to integrate EJB and JMS. Weblogic Server 8.1 implements the EJB 2.0 specification.

The emerging EJB 2.1 specification, defined as part of J2EE 1.4, describes the integration of EJB and generic messaging types. Support for APIs like JAXM (Java API for XML Messaging) facilitates the asynchronous delivery of XML documents using MDBs, and strengthens the EJB specification's support for Web services. Although not supported in WebLogic Server 8.1, keep this direction in mind as you design your applications, and look for the final EJB 2.1 specification.

In this chapter, our examples and discussion focus on the JMS message system.

Message-Driven EJB Basics

Like other EJB types, message-driven EJBs live within an EJB container and benefit from EJB container services such as transactions, security, and concurrency control. However, a message-driven EJB does not interact directly with clients. Its only responsibility is to process incoming messages. Message-driven EJBs are message listeners. They operate on messages from a message service provider. For example, a client publishes messages to a JMS destination. The JMS provider and the EJB container then cooperate to deliver the message to the message-driven EJB (see Figure 10–1).

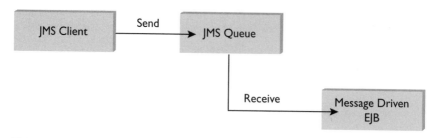

Figure 10–1
Message-driven EJBs.

Because message-driven EJBs do not have clients, they do not require home or remote interfaces. A message-driven EJB is a bean class that implements the `javax.ejb.MessageDrivenBean` interface and implements an `ejbCreate` method with no parameters (even though clients will not directly access the bean). The bean class must also implement an interface corresponding to the messaging system. In the case of JMS, that interface is `javax.jms.MessageListener`. The `MessageDrivenBean` interface includes two methods: `setMessageDrivenContext` and `ejbRemove`. The JMS `MessageListener` interface is even simpler: it contains only a single method, `onMessage`. The methods in the message listener interface contain the business logic to be executed when a message is received and are are invoked by the EJB container. The `ejbCreate` method can be used for JNDI lookups for things like JMS connections factories and destinations. The `ejbRemove` method would be used to close any resources obtained by the `ejbCreate` method. One of the best features of message-driven EJBs is their simplicity: This single bean class has only four methods.

Message-Driven EJB Lifecycle

The lifecycle of a message-driven EJB is similar to that of a stateless session bean. When the container creates a new message-driven EJB instance, it first calls the bean class's default (no-parameter) constructor. While EJBs may implement a constructor, it is preferable to place initialization code in the `setMessageDrivenContext` or `ejbCreate` methods. The container next calls the `setMessageDrivenContext` method and passes the EJB a `javax.ejb.MessageDrivenContext`. This context, like the `SessionContext` or `EntityContext`, is generally saved in a member variable and can later be used to make calls into the EJB container. Finally, the EJB container calls the `ejbCreate()` method.

Like stateless session beans, message-driven beans (MDBs) have only a single, no-argument `ejbCreate` method. Message-driven EJB instances do not have an associated identity and, like session beans, they are created at the container's discretion. Also, like stateless session beans, MDB instances should not keep any conversational state in the bean class.

When a message-driven EJB is deployed into the EJB container, the `ejb-jar.xml` specifies properties specific to the messaging system, such as a JMS queue or topic. Since JMS is the message system for EJB 2.0, the EJB container registers the MDB instance as a JMS listener. When a message arrives on the associated JMS destination, the EJB container retrieves a bean instance and calls the bean's `onMessage` method with the new message passed in as a parameter. Like stateless session beans, message-driven EJBs are pooled to minimize object creation. We discuss the WebLogic EJB container's pooling of message-driven EJBs later in this chapter.

Message-Driven EJB Example

Let's now develop a simple message-driven EJB to receive text messages from a JMS queue and print the messages to the server's `stderr`.

The `MessageDrivenBean` class includes the four required methods. The `onMessage` method receives the JMS message and prints the associated text. For this simple example, any error is simply printed to the server's `stderr`.

MessagePrinterBean Class

```
package com.learnweblogic.examples.ch10.textmessage;

import javax.ejb.MessageDrivenBean;
import javax.ejb.MessageDrivenContext;
import javax.jms.JMSException;
import javax.jms.Message;
import javax.jms.MessageListener;
import javax.jms.TextMessage;

public class MessagePrinterBean
   implements MessageDrivenBean, MessageListener
{
  private MessageDrivenContext ctx;

  public void setMessageDrivenContext(
MessageDrivenContext c)
  {
    ctx = c;
  }

  public void ejbCreate() {}
  public void ejbRemove() {}

  public void onMessage(Message m) {

    TextMessage msg = (TextMessage) m;

    try {
      System.err.println(
"Message-Driven EJB received message: "+
        msg.getText());
    } catch (JMSException e) {
      System.err.println(
"Exception receiving text from message: ");
      e.printStackTrace();
    }
  }
}
```

Writing Deployment Descriptors for Message-Driven EJBs

Like other EJBs, message-driven EJBs require an `ejb-jar.xml` deployment descriptor. This descriptor includes the name of the bean class, the transaction type, and other properties specific to the message system (i.e., the JMS destination). Like session beans, message-driven EJBs may use either bean or container transaction attributes. In the example below, we assume JMS is the messaging system. Transaction settings are discussed later in this chapter.

Sample ejb-jar.xml Descriptor

```
<!DOCTYPE ejb-jar PUBLIC
"-//Sun Microsystems, Inc.//DTD Enterprise JavaBeans 2.0//EN"
 "http://java.sun.com/dtd/ejb-jar_2_0.dtd">

<ejb-jar>
  <enterprise-beans>
    <message-driven>
      <ejb-name>MessagePrinterEJB</ejb-name>
      <ejb-class>
com.learnweblogic.examples.ch10.textmessage.MessagePrinterBean
        </ejb-class>
        <transaction-type>Container</transaction-type>
        <message-driven-destination>
          <destination-type>
            javax.jms.Queue
          </destination-type>
          </message-driven-destination>
        </message-driven>
      </enterprise-beans>
      </ejb-jar>
        .
```

Sample weblogic-ejb-jar.xml Descriptor

Message-driven EJBs also require a `weblogic-ejb-jar.xml` deployment descriptor. Like other EJBs, this deployment descriptor contains deployment information that is WebLogic-specific or simply not specified by the standard ejb-jar.xml deployment descriptor.

The only required element for a message-driven EJB is the `<destination-jndi-name>`. When the EJB container deploys the message-driven EJB, it uses this Java Naming and Directory Interface (JNDI) name to look up resource references like the JMS destination. Unlike other EJB types, a `<jndi-name>` for the EJB is not required because there is no direct client interaction.

```
<?xml version="1.0"?>

<!DOCTYPE weblogic-ejb-jar PUBLIC
"-//BEA Systems, Inc.//DTD WebLogic 8.1.0 EJB//EN" "http://
www.bea.com/servers/wls810/dtd/weblogic-ejb-jar.dtd"
```

```
<weblogic-ejb-jar>

  <weblogic-enterprise-bean>
    <ejb-name>MessagePrinterEJB</ejb-name>

    <message-driven-descriptor>
      <destination-jndi-name>
        MessageQueue
      </destination-jndi-name>
    </message-driven-descriptor>
  </weblogic-enterprise-bean>
</weblogic-ejb-jar>
```

Building and Deploying an MDB

The build and deployment process varies between organizations and might involve multiple staging steps, but on the simplest level, after compiling and building the client classes, the MDB class should be packaged along with the deployment descriptors in an `ejb-jar` file. Before deployment, the deployer must ensure that the associated JMS destination exists. In the example above, the server would have to have a JMS queue deployed with the JNDI name `MessageQueue`. Then, the `ejb-jar` can be deployed by copying the file into the server's applications directory.

An Example JMS Client

A client can now indirectly interact with the message-driven EJB by publishing JMS messages to the messages queue.

A message-driven EJB client uses standard JMS message producer code. The JMS client has no idea what consumers will receive the JMS messages—message-driven EJBs or other types of JMS consumers. For a more detailed explanation of JMS message producers, please see Chapter 7.

```
package com.learnweblogic.examples.ch10.textmessage;

public final class TextMessageSenderClient
  extends BaseClient {
  private QueueConnection queueConnection = null;
  private QueueSender queueSender       = null;
  private QueueSession queueSession     = null;
  private Queue queue                   = null;
  private TextMessage msg               = null;

  public TextMessageSenderClient(String [] argv)
    throws Exception
  {
    super(argv);
    try {
      Context ctx = getInitialContext();

      QueueConnectionFactory factory =
```

```
            (QueueConnectionFactory)
            ctx.lookup(JMS_CONN_FACTORY);

        queueConnection = factory.createQueueConnection();

        // Create a non-transacted JMS Session
        queueSession =
            queueConnection.createQueueSession(false,
                Session.AUTO_ACKNOWLEDGE);

        queue = (Queue) ctx.lookup(JMS_QUEUE);

        queueSender = queueSession.createSender(queue);

        msg = queueSession.createTextMessage();

        queueConnection.start();

    } catch (Exception e) {
      System.err.println("Error while attempting to "+
        "connect to the server and look up the JMS"+
          " QueueConnectionFactory.");
      System.err.println("Please make sure that you have"+
        " deployed the JMS Queue and specified the correct"+
        " server URL.");

      e.printStackTrace();

      throw e;
    }
}


public void send(String message)
      throws JMSException
{
  try {
    msg.setText(message);
    queueSender.send(msg);
  } catch (JMSException e) {
    System.err.println("Exception raised while sending"+
      "to queue: "+ JMS_QUEUE);
    e.printStackTrace();
    throw e;
  }
}
```

MDBs and Concurrency

Like other EJB components, the EJB container handles concurrency for MDB instances. Message-driven EJBs are not written with thread-safe code, and the EJB container never makes a re-entrant call into a bean instance. As with stateless session beans, MDB instances are pooled in memory by the container. The weblogic-ejb-jar.xml deployment descriptor contains two parameters to control the pool size: <initial-beans-in-freepool> and <max-beans-in-freepool>. When the EJB is deployed, the container preallocates as many instances as specified in the initial-beans-in-freepool parameter. As messages arrive, the server is able to immediately accept work without spending time creating bean instances. This parameter defaults to 0. The max-beans-in-freepool gives the upper bound on the number of bean instances created by the container.

> **Note:** The <max-beans-in-freepool> parameter determines the number of MDB instances that can concurrently process messages.

Parallel Message Dispatch

When a message arrives on the associated JMS destination, the EJB container asks the free pool for an available instance. If there is an instance in the pool, its onMessage method is called and the message is delivered.

If the free pool is empty and there are less than max-beans-in-freepool instances in use, the container allocates a new instance and uses it to deliver the message. If max-beans-in-freepool instances are already processing messages, the new message remains in the JMS destination until one of the MDB instances returns from its onMessage callback.

The EJB container will not wait for onMessage to finish processing before invoking another MDB instance to process another JMS message. Thus, parallel processing is supported.

Setting max-beans-in-freepool for Message-Driven EJBs

Most users should not need to tune the max-beans-in-freepool or initial-beans-in-freepool settings for message-driven EJBs. By default, the initial-beans-in-freepool parameter is 0, so beans will be created as needed. This ensures that instances are created only when needed.

The max-beans-in-freepool parameter is not limited by default. However, the number of concurrent instances is limited by the amount of execute threads in the server. The maximum parallelism is achieved when each thread is concurrently using a message-driven EJB instance to process a message.

> **Note:** The default max-beans-in-freepool setting gives the maximum parallelism.

Message Ordering

The message-driven EJB concurrency model enables the EJB container to process as many messages as possible in parallel. While this maximizes throughput, programmers should be aware that messages might be processed out of order. Because the container is processing the messages in parallel threads, it is possible for a later message to be processed before an earlier message.

> **Note:** Applications should not make assumptions about the order in which messages are delivered to MDBs.

Specifying a JMS Connection Factory

The WebLogic JMS server defines standard queue and topic connection factories, and additional user-defined connection factories may be created with the administration console. By default, message-driven EJBs use the standard JMS connection factories, but it is possible to override this and specify a user-defined connection factory with the `<connection-factory-jndi-name>` tag in the `weblogic-ejb-jar.xml`:

```
<connection-factory-jndi-name>
  MyConnectionFactory
</connection-factory-jndi-name>
```

Using Transactions with MDBs

Like other EJBs, MDBs make use of the EJB container's transaction service. Because MDBs never directly interact with clients, they never participate in the client's transaction.

Message-driven EJBs offer three different transaction options:

- `Required` transaction attribute
- `NotSupported`
- Bean-managed transactions

If container-managed transactions are used, then the only allowable transaction option is `Required`.

Required Transaction Attribute

If the `Required` attribute is specified, the EJB container automatically starts a transaction prior to invoking the MDB's `onMessage` method. The message receipt from the JMS queue or topic is included in this transaction. The MDB's `onMessage` method is then called in the transaction context. When the `onMessage` method returns, the EJB container commits the transaction. If the transaction aborts, the message remains in the destination and is delivered again to the message-driven EJB. The MDB does not share a transaction with the message sender. The scope of the transaction is from message delivery through subsequent transactional processing (like database access) by the bean.

> **Best Practice:** Use the `Required` transaction attribute to ensure receipt of the message and that the message receipt and `onMessage` callbacks participate in a Java Transaction API (JTA) transaction.

NotSupported Transaction Attribute

With the `NotSupported` transaction attribute, the EJB container does not start a transaction before calling the EJB's `onMessage` callback. The message-driven EJB acts as a standard consumer.

It relies on the messaging system's message acknowledgment semantics to confirm that the message was successfully received and processed. If subsequent transactions do not complete, the message is not redelivered, since it is considered received and processed. Chapter 7 provides details on JMS message acknowledgment facilities.

> **Best Practice:** Use the `NotSupported` attribute when message receipt is not transactional and JMS's acknowledgment modes are sufficient.

Bean-Managed Transactions

Finally, like session EJBs, message-driven EJBs may use bean-managed transactions. With bean-managed transactions, the bean code uses the `EJBContext.getUserTransaction()` callback to get a reference to a `UserTransaction` object. The bean code may then explicitly begin and commit transactions.

Because the transaction demarcation is within the `onMessage` callback, the message receipt does not participate in the transaction. If the `UserTransaction` aborts, the message does not automatically get redelivered.

> **Best Practice:** Use bean-managed transactions when message receipt is not transactional, but the `onMessage` callback uses Java Database Connectivity (JDBC), EJB, or other resources that need to participate in a transaction.

Error Handling with the Required Transaction Attribute

MDBs with the `Required` transaction attribute need to be careful when aborting transactions. A transaction aborts either because it was explicitly marked for rollback, or because a system exception was thrown. One potential issue is known as the poison message. In this scenario, a message-driven EJB receiving stock trade orders from an order queue might encounter a stock symbol that does not exist. When the message-driven EJB receives the error message, the underlying logic might be to abort the transaction because the symbol is invalid. When the messaging implementation delivers the message again in a new transaction, the process repeats. Clearly, this is not the desired behavior.

A good solution for this potential problem is to separate application errors from system errors. An application error, such as an invalid stock symbol, could be handled by sending an error message to a JMS error destination, for example. This enables the transaction to commit, and the poison message leaves the system. A system error might be that the back-end database has failed. In this case, our transaction should roll back so that this message is still on the queue when the database recovers.

> **Best Practice:** Use a separate JMS destination to handle application-level errors. This ensures that improper messages are not continually redelivered.

Message Acknowledgment

The EJB container automatically handles JMS message acknowledgment for message-driven EJBs. When a message-driven EJB is deployed with the `Required` transaction attribute, the container acknowledges the message when the transaction commits.

A message-driven EJB deployed as `NotSupported` or with bean-managed transactions uses `AUTO_ACKNOWLEDGE`. Like other asynchronous message consumers, the acknowledgment is performed when the `onMessage` method returns.

MDBs may also specify the `DUPS_OK_ACKNOWLEDGE` mode with the `<jms-acknowledge-mode>` tag in the `ejb-jar.xml` deployment descriptor. This acknowledgment mode enables the underlying JMS implementation to lazily acknowledge messages.

`DUPS_OK_ACKNOWLEDGE` performs better than `AUTO_ACKNOWLEDGE` because acknowledgments are less frequent, but the application must be able to tolerate duplicate messages in the case of failure.

Message-driven EJB writers should also be aware that even `AUTO_ACKNOWLEDGE` can cause a duplicate message to be delivered. This occurs if the JMS implementation fails after the `onMessage` method returns but before the acknowledgment completes. This case is covered in Chapter 7.

The WebLogic JMS implementation adds the `NO_ACKNOWLEDGE` and `MULTICAST_NO_ACKNOWLEDGE` modes that may also be selected for message-driven EJBs. `NO_ACKNOWLEDGE` provides the best performance but the worst reliability because messages leave the system as soon as they are delivered. `MULTICAST_NO_ACKNOWLEDGE` sends messages to a JMS topic over IP multicast.

Note: The acknowledgment mode is a tradeoff between performance and reliability. The strongest delivery guarantee is the `Required` transaction attribute, which ensures that the message receipt participates in JTA transaction. The `NO_ACKNOWLEDGE` and `MULTICAST_NO_ACKNOWLEDGE` modes provide the highest message throughput because messages are not retained after delivery.

New Customer Example

Let's now take a look at an example that combines message-driven EJBs with stateless session and entity beans. This example demonstrates the process of entering new customer records into a database. The customer information is sent to a JMS queue named `newCustomers`. A message-driven EJB listens on this queue, unpacks the message, and calls a stateless session bean to enter the new customer record.

```
public class NewCustomerReceiverBean
   implements MessageDrivenBean, MessageListener
{
   private static final int BAD_MESSAGE_TYPE = 1;
   private static final int CUSTOMER_ALREADY_EXISTS = 2;

   private MessageDrivenContext ctx;

   private NewCustomer newCustomer;
```

The `setMessageDrivenContext` creates a reference to the `NewCustomer` stateless session bean. This is stored in an instance variable and will be used in `onMessage` to enter new customers.

```
public void setMessageDrivenContext(
    MessageDrivenContext c)
{
  ctx = c;
  try {
    Context ic = new InitialContext();
    Object h =
     ic.lookup("java:/comp/env/ejb/NewCustomerHome");

    NewCustomerHome home = (NewCustomerHome)
      PortableRemoteObject.narrow(h,
          NewCustomerHome.class);

    newCustomer = home.create();

  } catch (Exception e) {
    e.printStackTrace();
    throw new EJBException(e);
  }

}

public void ejbCreate() {}
public void ejbRemove() {}
```

The onMessage method unpacks the information from the JMS message. Next, it calls the NewCustomer stateless session bean to enter the new customer record. This message-driven EJB is deployed with the Required transaction attribute, so the onMessage method runs in a transaction. A JMSException occurs if the message was incomplete. For instance, the sender might not have set one of the fields in the MapMessage. The InvalidCustomerException is thrown if the customer ID already exists. These two errors are considered application errors. The transaction still commits, but we publish an error message to allow the system administrator to correct this action. The RemoteException is considered a system exception. The message-driven EJB marks the transaction for rollback.

```
public void onMessage(Message m) {

  MapMessage msg = (MapMessage) m;

  try {
    int id             = msg.getInt("ID");
    String firstName    = msg.getString("FIRST_NAME");
    String lastName     = msg.getString("LAST_NAME");
    String emailAddress = msg.getString("EMAIL_ADDRESS");

    newCustomer.enterNewCustomer(id, firstName, lastName,
```

```
                    emailAddress);

      } catch (JMSException e) {
        // message was mal-formed

        publishError(BAD_MESSAGE_TYPE, e);

      } catch (InvalidCustomerException ice) {

        // customer id already exists

        publishError(CUSTOMER_ALREADY_EXISTS, ice);
      } catch (RemoteException re) {
        re.printStackTrace();
        ctx.setRollbackOnly();
      }
    }
  }
}
```

The NewCustomerBean is a stateless session bean that serves as a facade to the persistence layer. The setSessionContext looks up an EJB environment reference to find the Customer entity bean.

```
package com.learnweblogic.examples.ch10.customer;

public class NewCustomerBean implements SessionBean {

  private SessionContext ctx;

  private CustomerHome customerHome;

  public void setSessionContext(SessionContext c) {
    ctx = c;

    try {
      Context ic = new InitialContext();
      Object h =
            ic.lookup("java:/comp/env/ejb/CustomerHome");

      customerHome = (CustomerHome)
        PortableRemoteObject.narrow(h, CustomerHome.class);

    } catch (NamingException ne) {
      ne.printStackTrace();
      throw new EJBException(ne);
    }
```

```
}

public void ejbCreate() {}
public void ejbRemove() {}

public void ejbActivate() {}
public void ejbPassivate() {}
```

The enterNewCustomer method creates a new Customer entity bean with the passed customer information. An entity bean's create method throws a DuplicateKeyException if the ID already exists in the database. This exception is wrapped in an application exception and thrown back to the messaging layer.

```
public void enterNewCustomer(int id, String firstName,
   String lastName, String emailAddress)
   throws InvalidCustomerException
{
   try {
      customerHome.create(new Integer(id), firstName,
            lastName, emailAddress);

   } catch (DuplicateKeyException dke) {
      // customer already exists
      throw new InvalidCustomerException("Customer:" "+id
        + " already exists.");
   } catch (Exception e) {
      // unexpected error
      e.printStackTrace();
      throw new EJBException(e);
   }
}
```

Finally, the Customer entity bean models the actual persistent representation in the database. Because this is a CMP entity bean, the EJB container generates the required data access code. The CMP entity bean includes abstract get and set methods for each of the container-managed fields that are stored in the database.

```
package com.learnweblogic.examples.ch10.customer;

public abstract class CustomerBean implements EntityBean {

   // Container-managed fields

   // primary key field
   public abstract Integer getId();
   public abstract void setId(Integer id);
```

```
public abstract String getFirstName();
public abstract void setFirstName(String firstName);

public abstract String getLastName();
public abstract void setLastName(String lastName);

public abstract String getEmailAddress();
public abstract void setEmailAddress(String email);

private EntityContext ctx;

public void setEntityContext(EntityContext c) {
  ctx = c;
}

public void unsetEntityContext() {
  ctx = null;
}
public Integer ejbCreate(Integer id, String firstName,
  String lastName, String emailAddress)
{
  setId(id);
  setFirstName(firstName);
  setLastName(lastName);
  setEmailAddress(emailAddress);

  return null;
}

public void ejbPostCreate(Integer id, String firstName,
  String lastName, String emailAddress)
{
  // This bean does no ejbPostCreate initialization
}

public void ejbRemove() {}

public void ejbActivate() {}
public void ejbPassivate() {}

public void ejbLoad() {}
public void ejbStore() {}
}
```

Using JMS for Communication with Enterprise Systems

Just as MDBs are used to process messages from JMS and other messaging systems, MDBs can also send JMS messages to a messaging system.

Because sending a message is transactional, if the greater transaction is rolled back, the message will not be sent.

To send JMS messages, make sure that the JMS queue and connection factory are declared in the sender bean's JNDI environment (with the deployment descriptor). This allows the sender bean to access those objects with a JNDI lookup. Then, the bean can obtain a connection object from the connection factory, create a session object, a queue sender object, and finally send the message to the queue object.

Message-Driven EJB Advantages

Message-driven EJBs provide a number of advantages over standard JMS consumers, and they should be the default choice when writing message consumers. Some of these advantages include loosely coupled integration of applications and leveraging message delivery to trigger workflow events. Other advantages are outlined below.

Using JTA Transactions with an Asynchronous Consumer

The WebLogic JMS implementation provides a powerful integration with the JTA transaction manager. This allows JMS message producers and consumers to participate in JTA transactions and enlist other resources such as EJBs or JDBC code in these transactions.

A standard JMS consumer enlists a JTA transaction by explicitly using a `UserTransaction` reference to begin and commit transactions. The message consumer can begin a `UserTransaction` and then call its `receive` method to consume a JMS message within that transaction. This approach works fine for synchronous `receive` calls, but it is not possible with asynchronous message consumers.

There is no means in the JMS specification to register an asynchronous `MessageListener` (such as a message-driven EJB) and ask the JMS implementation to start a JTA transaction before delivering the message.

When message-driven EJBs use the `Required` transaction attribute, the EJB and WebLogic JMS implementations cooperate to start JTA transactions before the `onMessage` callback. This ensures that the message receipt is part of the transaction.

> **Note:** A message-driven EJB is the only way for an asynchronous consumer to include its message receipt in a JTA transaction. This is not possible with standard JMS consumers.

Parallel Message Processing

Many JMS applications need to maximize throughput by processing as many messages as possible in parallel. This can be accomplished with the JMS specification using the `ServerSessionPool` extensions, but it requires the application programmer to include additional logic to support parallel messaging processing.

Message-driven EJBs automatically support parallel message processing with the EJB container's deployment descriptors. The `weblogic-ejb-jar.xml` includes a `max-beans-in-freepool` parameter to configure the number of MDB instances that may be used in parallel. By default, the EJB container configures the message-driven EJB to process as many messages as possible in parallel.

> **Note:** The EJB and JMS containers automatically handle parallel message processing with message-driven EJBs.

Simple and Standards-Based

Message-driven EJBs require a single implementation class, which implements two small interfaces. They are simple to develop and portable to other Java 2 Enterprise Edition (J2EE) implementations.

> **Best Practice:** With their simplicity and standard J2EE architecture, message-driven EJBs should be the default choice for JMS consumers.

Putting It All Together

Message-driven EJBs provide an easy and effective means to integrate messaging into a J2EE application. They are commonly used to perform back-end work asynchronously. MDBs can take advantage of the EJB container's concurrency, security, and transaction support. This allows the bean writer to concentrate on writing the business logic without needing to develop the infrastructure code for a message listener.

References

The Enterprise JavaBeans 2.0 architecture specification page is available at *http://java.sun.com/products/ejb/2.0.html*.

BEA's Programming WebLogic Enterprise JavaBeans documentation for WebLogic Server 8.1 can be found at *http://edocs.bea.com/wls/docs81/ejb/*.

The Java Message Service specification is available at *http://java.sun.com/products/jms/index.html*.

Full documentation of generating and editing the deployment descriptors used to configure WebLogic Server EJBs (`weblogic-ejb-jar.xml` and `ejb-jar.xml`) is available at *http://e-docs.bea.com/wls/docs81/ejb/implementing.html*.

Ant documentation is available at *http://ant.apache.org/manual/index.html*.

The WebLogic deployment task is documented at *http://e-docs.bea.com/wls/docs81/deployment/tools.html*.

chapter 11

Interfacing with Internet Mail Using WebLogic Server JavaMail

In This Chapter

- The JavaMail API, which supports the `Session`, `Message`, and `Transport` classes
- Using Java to send simple e-mails
- Best practices for using JavaMail.

This chapter discusses Internet mail (e-mail) protocols, including the Simple Mail Transport Protocol (SMTP), the Post Office Protocol Version 3 (POP3), and Internet Mail Access Protocol (IMAP) mail retrieval protocols. JavaMail is the Java 2 Enterprise Edition (J2EE) implementation of a mail service.

Up to this point, user interactions with WebLogic Server applications have taken place either through a Web browser or through application clients. Web applications also typically interact with users through e-mail for operations such as confirming that a user's bid has been accepted or verifying a newly registered user's e-mail address. These connections to e-mail use WebLogic Server's implementation of the JavaMail functionality for integrating e-mail into Web applications.

About E-mail

E-mail is the Internet standard for exchanging messages between users or applications. E-mail messages can contain plain text or more complicated data types like spreadsheets or multimedia files. Every e-mail message includes an e-mail header, which includes information about the origination of the message, the address to which it is being sent, and other routing information.

About Simple Mail Transport Protocol (SMTP)

When a user sends an e-mail message, the message first visits what is called a mail server. This server receives the message transmitted by the sender using the SMTP. SMTP is the Internet standard for sending e-mail from client to server and also between mail servers. In most cases, mail servers are standard PC servers running one of the mail server application packages. Leading mail server packages include Sendmail and qmail on UNIX systems and Microsoft Exchange for the Windows platform.

359

Mail Retrieval Protocols (POP3, IMAP)

Clients use SMTP to deliver e-mail to a mailbox. Internet standards define two commonly used protocols for mail retrieval to access this mail from the mailbox. POP3 is the simpler of the mail retrieval mechanisms. Within the POP3 standard, the mail server stores a user's mail in a file. The user's mail client connects to the mail server and retrieves messages. In most cases, enterprises using POP3 expect users to download their messages and then delete them from the mail server.

In contrast, IMAP enables users to access their mail from the mail server, but without expectations that they immediately delete those messages. Using IMAP, the user's mail is stored on the mail server and is displayed by an IMAP e-mail client, such as Netscape Communicator or Microsoft Outlook. Further, IMAP allows users to create folders on the server and file messages within these folders. Because IMAP does not store messages on the user's local machine, individuals using IMAP can move from client machine to client machine with uninterrupted access to new and archived messages.

About JavaMail

JavaMail is the J2EE standard set of APIs for interfacing with e-mail systems. JavaMail specifies a plug-and-play architecture that supports various e-mail protocol implementations including POP3, IMAP, SMTP, and others. The WebLogic Server implementation of JavaMail includes implementations of SMTP and IMAP. WebLogic Server JavaMail is available as a standard part of the WebLogic Server environment.

WebLogic Server Version 6.0 does not include a native POP3 provider. To use JavaMail to access POP3 mail, download the POP3 provider available on the Java Web site at *http://java.sun.com/products/javamail/*.

The JavaMail API for WebLogic Server applications has several major components:

- JavaMail configuration
- The `Session` class
- The `InternetAddress` class
- The `Message` class
- The `Transport` class

We cover each in the following sections.

Configuring JavaMail

In order to use JavaMail, you must first configure a JavaMail session within the WebLogic Server console. WebLogic Server uses the properties defined in this `Session` to set properties within the `Session` objects you access within your application.

To create a new JavaMail session, navigate to *mydomain* → *Services* → *Mail* and click *Configure a new Mail Session*.... The resulting screen prompts you for three fields:

- `Name`—The name property is an internal identifier for the mail session. This property defines the display name used for the session within the WebLogic Server console.
- `JNDIName`—WebLogic Server registers the JavaMail session within the JNDI tree using this name. Your code uses this name to identify the session.
- `Properties`—Set properties for the JavaMail session in this field. Use `name = value` pairs to definethe behavior of the session.

You can set the following properties within the `Properties` field:

- `mail.host`—The host property defines the name of the mail host machine.
- `mail.user`—The user property identifies the name of the user to retrieve e-mail.
- `mail.store.protocol`—Set the default protocol for accessing e-mail in a message store. Protocols are typically POP3 or IMAP.
- `mail.transport.protocol`—Set the default transport mechanism for sending e-mails. The default `mail.transport.protocol` is SMTP.
- `mail.from`—The `mail.from` property defines the default **From:** field in e-mails sent using the session.
- `mail.protocol.host`—Override the host property for the specified protocol.
- `mail.protocol.user`—Override the user property for the specified protocol.
- `mail.debug`—Turn on mail debugging messages by setting this value to `true`.

The Session Class

The `Session` class defines the global and per-user mail-related properties that define how the clients and server interact. Applications locate an instance of the `Session` class and use this instance as the basis for creating new mail messages and for locating information about the remote mail server.

Configure JavaMail sessions with the WebLogic Server console. The WebLogic console registers the session in the JNDI tree. Applications use the JNDI lookup method to find the mail session; see the following code for an example:

```
Session mailSession;
String sessionJNDIName = "myMailSession";

try {
    Context ctx = new InitialContext();
    mailSession = (Session) ctx.lookup(sessionJNDIName);
} catch (NamingException ne) {}
```

Using this code, you can access a mail `Session`. In this case, the code looks up the `Session` registered as `myMailSession`.

The InternetAddress Class

JavaMail defines an abstract `Address` class to represent addresses for e-mail. JavaMail uses the `InternetAddress` class, representing addresses within the RFC 822 standard, to specify addresses for sending and receiving standard Internet e-mail. To create an instance of an `InternetAddress` from an e-mail address, use the following code:

```
// Create New Internet Address for Destination
InternetAddress dest = new InternetAddress("me@mine.com");
```

This line creates a new instance of an `InternetAddress` class called `dest`. This new address represents *me@mine.com*. Use this `InternetAddress` to direct a `Message` object to a particular mailbox. The following sets the destination address (that is, the **To:** field in the e-mail) to the address specified in the destination object `dest`:

```
msg.setRecipient(Message.RecipientType.TO, dest);
```

The Message Class

The `Message` class in the JavaMail package is an abstract class that represents a single e-mail. A `Message` object contains header attributes, including addressing information, and the contents of the e-mail. The standard implementation of the `Message` class is `MimeMessage`. MimeMessage may contain multiple parts and arbitrary media types.

The `Message` class defines a number of useful methods for working with e-mail header fields. See the methods below:

- `Address[] getFrom()`—Use the `getFrom()` method to get the **From:** field for the current message.
- `void setFrom()`—The `setFrom()` instructs WebLogic Server to use the default e-mail address for the current message. Define the default e-mail address in the `mail.user` property (or, if not set, the `user.name` property).
- `void setFrom(Address from)`—The `setFrom()` method to specify the **From:** field of the message.
- `Address[] getRecipients(Message.RecipientType type)`—Use `getRecipients()` to retrieve recipients of a given type. Recipient types include TO, CC, and BCC. The following code demonstrates how to call this method:

  ```
  InternetAddress[] toAddresses =
  (InternetAddress[])msg.getRecipients(Message.RecipientType.TO);
  ```

- `void addRecipient(Message.RecipientType type, Address recipient)`, `void addRecipients(Message.RecipientType type, Address recipient[])`, `void setRecipient(Message.RecipientType type, Address recipient)`, and `void setRecipients(Message.RecipientType type, Address recipient[])`—Use these methods to address Messages. With each call, you can add one or many recipients. The `set` methods overwrite any existing recipients.

- `Address[] getReplyTo()`, and `void setReplyTo(Address[] address)`— Get and set the **Reply-To:** field of the message. This field tells the e-mail recipient where to direct responses.
- `String getSubject()`, and `void setSubject(String subject)`—Use these get and set methods to access the **Subject:** field of the message.
- `void setSentDate(java.util.Date date)`—Set the **Date:** header field in the Message.
- `java.util.Date getReceivedDate()`—Get the date on which the message was received.

To get a new `Message`, call the constructor or the `reply()` method on an existing `Message`. Pass a `Session` object to the constructor. The `reply()` method takes a `boolean` argument to specify whether the new `Message` should *reply to all*. If set to `false`, the method addresses the

`Message` to the **Reply-To** addresses. If set to `true`, the method also includes the `Message`'s to TO and CC recipients.

```
Message msg = new MimeMessage(mailSession);
Message responseMsg = receivedMsg.reply(false);
```

The preceding code fragments create new `Message` objects that have the appropriate settings for use with the mail `Session`. To set message fields, use the methods defined above:

```
// Sets the subject of the message:
msg.setSubject("I missed you!");

// Set the recipient of the message in the TO: field:
msg.setRecipient(Message.RecipientType.TO,
    new InternetAddress("skywalker@someaddress.com"));

// Set the recipient of the message in the CC: field:
msg.setRecipient(Message.RecipientType.CC,
    new InternetAddress("me@mine.com"));
```

Finally, set the content of the e-mail using the `setContent()` method or the convenience method `setText()`. Advanced users can compose multipart e-mails and include alternative media types.

```
// Set the contents of the message to be "foo bar baz":
msg.setContent("foo bar baz", "text/plain");
// equivalent call
msg.setText("foo bar baz");
```

The Transport Class

Each implementation of a mail protocol such as POP3 and IMAP includes its own implementation of the `Transport` interface. These implementations define how to handle outbound e-mail. WebLogic Server applications generally use only a single static method defined within the `Transport` class:

```
Transport.send(msg);
```

The `send()` method takes an instance of the JavaMail `Message`. The `send()` method then routes the message appropriately, according to the settings in the `Message` object itself.

Using JavaMail to Send Simple E-mail

In this section, we use WebLogic Server JavaMail to construct a simple Web application. Within the application, users can enter an e-mail into a Web page. A Java ServerPage (JSP) Web page generates a form to get input from a user (see Figure 11–1).

Figure 11–1
Form for sending e-mail.

The user provides an e-mail address for both the recipient and the sender, and a message. The recipient of this message would see something like Figure 11–2.

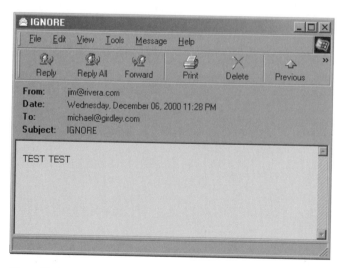

Figure 11–2
E-mail message received.

Note that the message subject is IGNORE. As you'll see, this is because our demonstration JSP sets it to that value.

To create a JSP page, we first import the necessary classes and declare the HTML page:

```
<jsp:root>
  <jsp:directive.page session="false"
      import="java.util.*,
              javax.mail.Message,
              javax.mail.Session,
              javax.mail.Transport,
              javax.mail.internet.MimeMessage,
              javax.mail.internet.InternetAddress,
              javax.naming.Context,
              javax.naming.InitialContext,
              javax.naming.NamingException" />

  <html>
    <head><title>Mail Sender JSP</title></head>
    <body>
```

Because this JSP page both displays the form and processes the results, we need to check what the request method is. If it is an HTTP POST, then the JSP page knows that it is to process a form submission:

```
    <jsp:scriptlet>
      if ("POST".equals(request.getMethod())) {
        try {
          String to = request.getParameterValues("to")[0];
          String from = request.getParameterValues("from")[0];
          String message = request.getParameterValues("message")[0];
```

Now that we have parsed the HTTP POST input that is part of the HTTP request, we can do the work with JavaMail:

```
          // Get the Naming context
          Context ctx = new InitialContext();

          // Lookup Mail Session
          Session mailSession = (Session) ctx.lookup("MailSession");

          // Create New Internet Message Object
          Message msg = new MimeMessage(mailSession);

          // Create New Internet Address for Destination
          InternetAddress dest = new InternetAddress(to);
```

```
      // Set Parameters for Message:
      msg.setFrom(new InternetAddress(from));
      msg.setSubject("IGNORE");
      msg.setRecipient(Message.RecipientType.TO, dest);
      msg.setContent(message, "text/plain");

      // Send the Message:
      Transport.send(msg);
      out.println("<h2>Your message to " + to + " was sent
successfully!</h2>");
        } catch (Exception e) {
        out.println(e);
        }
      } else {
    </jsp:scriptlet>
```

The rest of the JSP simply displays the HTML form:

```
    <p>In the rest of this JSP, we display the HTML form:</p>
    <h1>Send Email!</h1>
    <form method="post" name="mail" action="mailsender.jsp">
      <p>
        To: <input type="text" name="to" size="16"/><br/>

        From: <input type="text" name="from" size="16"/><br/>

        Message: <input type="text" name="message" size="16"/><br/>
      </p>
      <input type="submit" value="Submit" name="Command"/>
    </form>
    <jsp:scriptlet>
        }
    </jsp:scriptlet>
    </body>
  </html>
</jsp:root>
```

Note that this example is only for demonstration purposes and does not represent how you should write an application. In particular, we acquire the JNDI `InitialContext` within the body of the JSP page. This means that the context will be re-created for every request. You do not need to re-create the `InitialContext`, so you waste resources by creating the context for each request. Instead, you should create the context within the `init()` method of your servlet or JSP page.

Deploying MailSender.jsp

The complete source code for the MailSender JSP sample is included in the CD-ROM accompanying this book, in the directory *examples\ch11*.

Step 0: Configure WebLogic Server Mail Session

To deploy this JSP page, first configure a mail session inside of WebLogic Server. To do this, start your default server using the link from the WebLogic Server Start menu. In the WebLogic Server console, navigate to the *Mail* option in the left-hand navigation panel. Click on this option (see Figure 11–3).

Next, follow the steps to create a new mail session. You are prompted for a JNDI name and data about the server to be used to send mail (see Figure 11–4).

For the JNDIName, enter *MailSession*. This is the name that the JSP page uses to locate the mail session object. Finally, specify a mail server that accepts mail from you. Do not use the value *some-mailserver.com*. You need to set this value to be the name of the mail server or Internet service provider for your organization. This value is typically the same as the mail server configured for your e-mail client, such as Microsoft Outlook or Netscape Navigator.

Once you have entered the appropriate values, click the *Create* button. Then, manually deploy the mail session on your server instance. Click the *Targets* tab (see Figure 11–5).

Select the server *myserver* and move that into the *Chosen* panel using the Red Arrow button. Click to apply the changes.

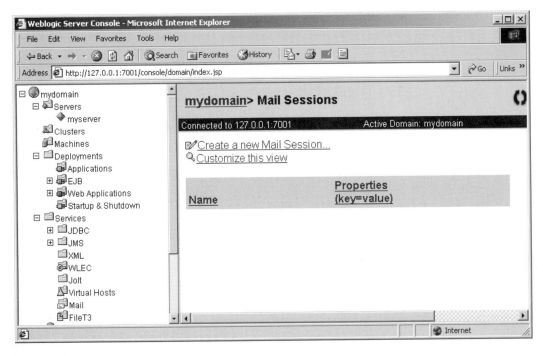

Figure 11–3
WebLogic Server console Mail option.

Figure 11–4
Creating a new mail session.

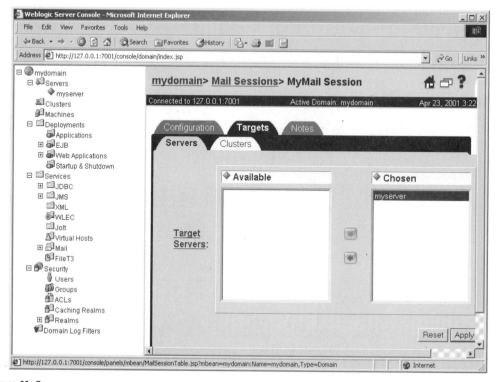

Figure 11–5
Selecting the target servers.

Step 1: *Deploy and Visit* JSP *Page*

Copy the *MailSender.jar* file from the CD-ROM into a working directory. Next, from within the working directory, set up your environment and extract the archive.

```
> \bea\weblogic81\server\bin\setWLSEnv.cmd
> jar xf MailSender.jar
```

To build and deploy the MailSender application, run the `ant` build script (*build.xml*). The build script takes advantage of the WebLogic Server deployment task.

```
> ant
```

Point your browser to *http://localhost:7001/MailSender* to visit the JSP. You should see a form; complete the form, and then click *Submit* (see Figure 11–6).

Note that problems with this sample are usually caused by the inability to reach a mail server that allows you to send messages through it. Unfortunately, because of the proliferation of unsolicited commercial e-mail (spam), most mail servers (including *somemailserver.com*) have restricted access to their mail services to registered users only. If you have questions, contact your mail system administrator.

Figure 11–6
Testing the MailSender JSP.

Where to Find More Information on JavaMail and Internet Mail

Note that WebLogic Server applications primarily make use of sending e-mail. For this reason, the details on how to receive e-mail messages through JavaMail are beyond the scope of this book. For more information on how to create a standalone Java application that is a consumer of e-mail messages, you can visit Sun Microsystems' JavaMail Web site at *http://java.sun.com/products/javamail/*.

In addition, this chapter has only introduced the concepts surrounding Internet Mail SMTP, POP3, and IMAP. For more information, consult the following links on the Internet:

- Internet Mail: *http://www.w3.org/Protocols/rfc822/*
- IMAP: *http://www.imap.org/*
- SMTP: *http://info.broker.isi.edu/in-notes/rfc/files/rfc821.txt*
- POP3: *http://info.broker.isi.edu/in-notes/rfc/files/rfc2449.txt*

JavaMail Best Practices

Here are some best practices you can follow when using JavaMail in your WebLogic Server applications.

Using JavaMail to Confirm E-mail Addresses

When a user registers for your site, your application probably asks for the user's correct e-mail address. Use JavaMail to send an e-mail from your system to validate the e-mail address. To have users confirm that they have correctly received the e-mail, have them revisit your site using a URL that you provide in the body of the mail.

The URL that the user clicks in the e-mail you send should be unique for that user. You can encapsulate a unique value into that URL by including it as an HTTP POST: `http://myhost.com/validate?token=someuniquevalue`. Use this unique value to link the HTTP request to the user. When you see this request, you can be comfortable that the user has received the e-mail, and as a result, the e-mail address must be functional.

chapter 12

Administering WebLogic Server 8.1

WebLogic Server provides a complete environment for developing, testing, and deploying distributed Java applications. Other chapters in this book address J2EE APIs, security, tools like WebLogic Workshop, and how to build applications with WebLogic Server. In this chapter, we detail the system administration tools provided with WebLogic Server 8.1. While not as dazzling as the latest caching capabilities for entity EJBs or as snazzy as WebLogic Workshop, the administration tools and utilities are no less key to delivering a rock-solid foundation for deploying, monitoring, and managing enterprise applications.

Over the most recent releases of WebLogic Server, there have been a number of enhancements made to the administration services provided by the application server. Long gone are the days of the clunky "it's slow but it's hard to use" administration console and the "everything but the kitchen sink" *weblogic.properties* file. WebLogic Server 8.1 includes an impressive list of management capabilities:

- A consistent management platform spanning the entire suite of products in WebLogic Platform 8.1.
- A complete browser-based administration utility that eases configuration, deployment, management, and monitoring.
- Wizards, utilities, and tools that ease the tasks accomplished by the administrator.
- Improved clustering configuration for availability, performance, and scalability.
- Complete support for Java Management eXtensions (JMX), a key Java standard for managing distributed Java components, and the basis for managing all WebLogic resources.
- Exposed APIs for integrating custom applications and third-party tools into the WebLogic administrative framework.
- A monitoring framework that communicates with collection and monitoring software running on WebLogic Server instances.
- Context-sensitive help to guide administrators through configuration tasks.

When finished with this chapter, you will have a much clearer understanding of the components that make up WebLogic Server's administrative framework. We review the JMX specification, how JMX is supported in WebLogic Server, and how developers can leverage JMX in their own applications. We describe the administrative tools delivered with the application server, including the console, command-line utilities, and some of the wizards and aids to ease deployment and configuration tasks. We also review clustering configuration in WebLogic Server 8.1. Lastly, we review the tasks required to support and maintain production J2EE applications and how WebLogic's administration services support aid in meeting these needs.

Java Management Extensions Overview

JMX is an emerging standard for administering and managing applications developed in Java. Evolved from the Sun Microsystems JMAPI specification, the standard defines

- A simple, lightweight mechanism for instrumenting Java objects
- A framework for plugging in and organizing the management objects
- An interface that can be used to integrate with external management tools
- A centralized management model for controlling and monitoring distributed resources

JMX does not specify the actual implementation; rather, it defines an infrastructure where self-describing components are retrieved over the network and dynamically plugged into the manager as needed. This lightweight, flexible model uniquely meets the needs of application developers, management tool vendors, system administrators, and users. With JMX, administrators are freed from reliance on specific products or technologies and can dynamically adapt tools and services to meet changing business needs.

The JMX architecture is divided into three tiers:

- Instrumentation—enables monitoring and control of Java objects via management wrappers called managed beans.
- Agents—relays core services to the managed resources within the centralized management container.
- Manager—provides a point-of-access for existing system management tools.

Figure 12–1 provides an overview of the JMX model. The following sections deal with each of these tiers in more detail. However, our primary focus in this book is on the instrumentation and agent tiers, since these are most applicable to the WebLogic management framework.

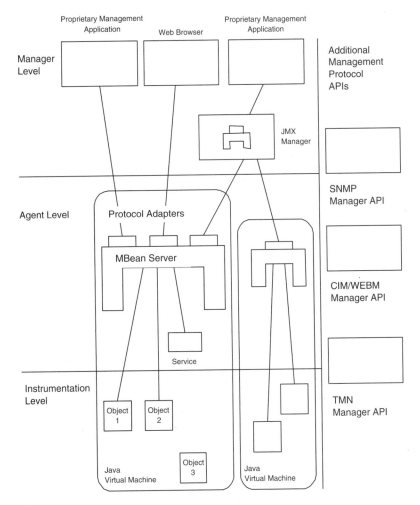

Manager Level

Agent Level

Instrumentation Level

Proprietary Management Application

Web Browser

Proprietary Management Application

Additional Management Protocol APIs

JMX Manager

SNMP Manager API

Protocol Adapters

MBean Server

CIM/WEBM Manager API

Service

TMN Manager API

Object 1

Object 2

Object 3

Java Virtual Machine

Java Virtual Machine

Figure 12–1
JMX management model.

JMX Instrumentation and Managed Resources

In the JMX model, each resource to be managed must provide a management interface, which consists of the attributes and operations used to monitor and manipulate the resource. A **JMX** *managed resource* is one that has been instrumented according to the patterns defined by the specification. These patterns specify that (1) the management interface must be a Java interface and have the same name as the resource, followed by "MBean," (2) the implementing class must include at least one public constructor, and (3) getters and setters for the interfaces attributes must follow strict naming conventions. A management interface adhering to these patterns is a *compliant* interface.

Each managed resource is instrumented to expose a set of attributes and operations. These attributes and operations are accessed via a special type of Java object called a *managed bean*

(MBean). The attributes and operations are used to control and monitor the resource from within the management container. *Attributes* are configuration parameters for the resource. For example, a JDBC connection pool MBean might include in its attributes the name of the connection pool, the name of the driver, and initial and maximum pool sizes. Managed resources may also expose additional administrative functions called *operations*; for instance, a Server MBean exposes operations for starting and stopping the server.

JMX Agents

The JMX model defines a management container made up of an MBean Server, a set of MBeans corresponding to the managed resources, agents for each of the MBeans, and at least one protocol adapter or connector for access by external management tools. The M*Bean Server* acts as a repository for the MBeans available in the container, aggregating the attributes and operations for each of the managed resources. The JMX *Agent* acts as the intermediary between the managed resources and the management container, registering its MBean with the MBean Server. Once registered by the agent, the MBean Server uses Java reflection to ensure adherence to the design patterns noted above, throwing an exception if there are any deviations.

JMX Manager

The JMX M*anager* represents access to the managed resources registered with the MBean Server by existing system management tools. Using the protocol adapters or connectors as communication channels, external management tools have the ability to monitor and control resources within the JMX environment. The JMX Manager flows information from the MBeans into the external management application for monitoring and allows the external tools to issue commands and control these components without requiring extensive, expensive, and often complex API-level coding.

Protocol adapters or connectors are the communications channels through which management applications can access an agent over the network and manipulate its MBeans. Protocols defined include HTTP or HTTPS, SNMP, WBEM (Web-Based Enterprise Management), or IIOP, enabling integrated as well as third-party management tools access to the managed resources. The variety of protocols supported allows administrators to leverage existing tools and expertise. For example, an administrator could write an automated script that uses an existing tool's command-line interface to remotely monitor and control WebLogic Server and custom-developed resources by accessing MBeans via HTTP or SNMP.

WebLogic Server Administration

WebLogic Server 8.1 implements the 1.0 version of the JMX specification. All WebLogic resources, such as JDBC connection pools, EJBs, and JMS servers, are controlled and monitored using supplied JMX agents and special MBeans. In this release, WebLogic Server makes available the interfaces necessary to register third-party and custom-developed applications with the WebLogic administrative framework. Before detailing the specifics of how WebLogic Server utilizes JMX for managing applications and subsystems, we need to review WebLogic's administration model. Refer to Figure 12–2 for an overview of the WebLogic administration architecture.

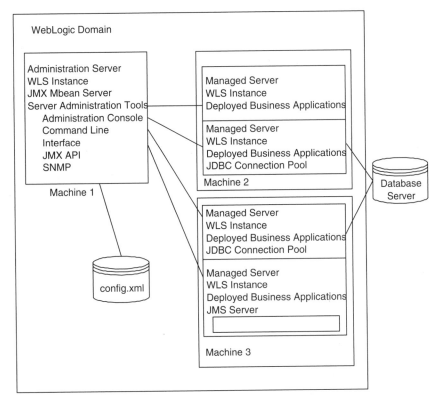

Figure 12–2
WebLogic administration model.

WebLogic Administration Overview

All WebLogic resources are grouped into a *domain*, defining the span of control for a deployment. Included in the domain is the *Administration Server*, a single instance of WebLogic Server acting as the central point of creation and control for all resources in the domain, including configuration and monitoring. The *domain configuration wizard* guides the administrator through creating the domain. This utility has both graphical and text-based interfaces. It guides you through the initial configuration for the domain. It also guides you through making changes to an existing domain; selecting from a con-figuration template; and setting the initial administrative user and password, the name of the domain, and the root directory for the administration server. In a Microsoft Windows environment, you access the Configuration Wizard from the BEA program group under the Windows Start menu. Refer to Figure 12–3 for an example of the initial screen presented in the Configuration Wizard.

Once a domain is configured, the Administration Server is used to configure one or more *managed servers*, instances of WebLogic Server where applications, EJBs, and other resources are deployed. The managed server instances are used for application processing while the Administration Server handles the management duties. Managed servers can be used to cluster applications for redundancy, can be added dynamically to the domain, and are monitored by the Administration Server. The Administra-

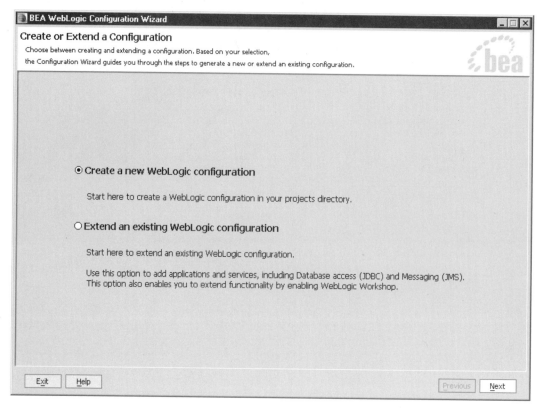

Figure 12–3
WebLogic domain configuration wizard.

tion Server retrieves *runtime* information from the managed server instances within the domain, while the managed servers retrieve *configuration* information from the Administration Server.

A valuable new feature of WebLogic Server 8.1 is the *managed-server independence* (MSI) mode, which minimizes the reliance on the Administration Server as a single point of failure. In prior versions, the Administration Server had to be running for the managed servers to start. With MSI mode (enabled by default), the managed server can start using a cached copy of its configuration information even if the Administration Server isn't running or accessible during managed server startup. When the Administration Server returns to the domain, the managed servers will automatically leave MSI mode and receive a fresh configuration for the domain.

> **Best Practice:** If there are problems with your application on a managed server and the WLS server instance itself is locked up, the only way the Administration Server can communicate with the locked instance is if the domain-wide administration port has been set and enabled. If the domain-wide administration port has not been set, then killing the managed server process may be the only way to free up the locked server instance. Please refer to the BEA documentation at *http://e-docs.bea.com/wls/docs81/ConsoleHelp/domain.html* if you are interested in configuring a domain-wide administration port.

The Administration Server maintains a list of the running managed servers it knows about in the file *running-managed-servers.xml*. Particularly when the Administration Server must be restarted, this file is used to restore the information about the managed servers running in a domain. By default, the discovery mode is enabled, allowing the Administration Server to discover and reconnect with running managed servers in the domain. Although this service can be disabled, it is recommended that the discovery mode be kept in the default state.

> **Best Practice:** You should always use the default discovery mode in the Administration Server to allow it to reconnect with running managed servers when it is restarted.

A key component of the WebLogic administration framework is the *node manager*, providing a "nanny" or "watchdog" function for remote managed servers. The node manager is a separate Java process to the WebLogic Server instance and provides remote management to remote managed server instances, including starting and stopping managed servers, killing managed server instances that have a health status of "failed," and automatically restarting managed server instances that have health status of failed. The Administration Server communicates with the node manager via SSL, using either the graphical console or the command-line interfaces, or using JMX programmatically. In WebLogic Server 8.1, the configuration for the node manager has been greatly simplified.

> **Best Practice:** Although its configuration is optional, the node manager is an important component of most enterprise deployments. Without the node manager, it is the responsibility of the administrator to ensure high availability and fault tolerance of WebLogic Server managed server instances within a domain. The node manager configuration is greatly simplified in WebLogic Server 8.1. It is an administrative best practice to configure the node manager in production deployments.

Getting back to how WebLogic uses JMX, the Administration Server is the central point to monitor and control the JMX-managed resources within the domain. The server provides both graphical and textual tools for administering, configuring, and monitoring the environment. Each instance of WebLogic Server in the domain—the Administration Server and the managed servers—includes an MBean Server subsystem. The MBean Server on each WLS instance registers and manipulates the MBeans deployed there.

To aid in configuration, WebLogic provides a special type of managed bean, called a *Configuration* MBean, which exposes the attributes and operations for configuring each of the managed resources. Configuration MBeans exist for all managed resources, on all server instances, within a defined domain. All the Configuration MBeans available in WebLogic Server can be accessed in the `weblogic.management.configuration` Java package. For a complete list of the WebLogic MBean configuration interfaces, refer to the `weblogic.management.configuration` package descriptions in the *WebLogic Server Javadoc* at *http://e-docs.bea.com/wls/docs81/javadocs/index.html*.

The Administration Server maintains all Configuration MBeans for the domain and stores the information about them in the *config.xml* file. The *config.xml* file is the repository for the domain's configuration. In it, you will find XML elements that correspond to the administration and managed servers, the defined clusters, and applications components and resources deployed. By default, the *config.xml* file is kept in the $BEA_HOME/*user_projects*/*<domain name>* directory, but an alternate directory can be specified on the command line when starting the Administration Server instance.

Best Practice: To ensure there are no problems if an Administration Server instance should hang or crash, you should always maintain a backup of the *config.xml* file as well as other domain configuration files. If an Administration Server should fail, you can copy these files to another server and restart a new instance of the Administration Server with the existing domain configuration. Best practice is to always shadow the directory structure of the Administration Server in a safe place, such as a shared filesystem.

As applications and resources are deployed to managed server instances, a copy of the Configuration MBean is propagated to the managed server. This copy is called the *Local Configuration* MBean. To change the configuration of a WebLogic Server resource, using either the Administration Console or provided command-line utilities, you modify the corresponding Administration MBean on the Administration Server. This propagates the modifications to the managed server via the Local Configuration MBean.

Once deployed, WebLogic has MBean objects for each managed server instance, internal resources, and application components (e.g., servlets and EJBs) under its control. The MBeans that provide information about the runtime state of a managed resource, such as performance metrics, application data, and operational control, are called *Runtime MBeans*. The Java package `weblogic.management.runtime` includes all of the Runtime MBeans for WebLogic Server. For a complete list of all WebLogic MBean runtime interfaces, refer to the *WebLogic Server Javadoc* for the *weblogic.management.runtime* package at *http://e-docs.bea.com/wls/docs81/javadocs/index.html*.

In addition to collecting runtime data, Runtime MBeans can also be used to modify runtime values or enable/disable services. For example, you can activate and deactivate a deployed module on a managed server using the `weblogic.management.runtime.DeployerRuntimeM-Bean` package.

There are a number of ways to manipulate the domain and access the underlying JMX services. The Administration Console in WebLogic Server 8.1 is a Web application that uses JMX to administer WebLogic Server resources. Almost all of the values accessed and viewed through the Administration Console represent attributes of Administration MBeans and Runtime MBeans. Likewise, the `weblogic.Admin command-line interfaces` provide a framework for building scripts that can be used to create, get and set values for, invoke operations on, and delete instances of Administration and Configuration MBeans, and to get values for and invoke operations on Runtime MBeans. The freely available open source tool WLShell offers another command-line tool for managing WebLogic resources via JMX. Finally, there is a JMX-based management API for managing custom-developed applications. More information about these utilities can be found in subsequent sections of this chapter.

Monitoring via MBeans

Now that you have the ability to track WebLogic resources and custom-developed components via the JMX MBeans, the next question is, What attributes are most important to monitor? All of the configuration and runtime information accessible via MBeans can be overwhelming. Narrowing the attributes monitored will allow the administrator to do a better job of tracking the health of a WebLogic deployment or cluster.

When monitoring the runtime usage of a WebLogic domain, the following Runtime MBeans provide general information about what is happening on each server instance: `Execute-QueueRuntime`, `JVMRuntime`, `ServerRuntime`, and `JDBCConnectionPoolRuntime`.

Each of these MBeans can be found in the `weblogic.management.runtime` Java package. Let's consider these in more detail:

- `ExecuteQueueRuntime`—This Runtime MBean includes a number of attributes measuring the number of execute threads in the server. Useful attributes include `ExecuteThread-CurrentIdleCount`, `PendingRequestCurrentCount`, `ServicedReqeust-TotalCount`, and `ExecuteThreads`.
- `JMVRuntime`—This Runtime MBean includes attributes reflecting the Java heap size. Useful attributes include `HeapFreeCurrent` and `HeapSizeCurrent`.
- `ServerRuntime`—This Runtime MBean presents a number of attributes for monitoring the server's runtime state, such as initialization, restarting, and running.
- `JDBCConnectionPoolRuntime`—This Runtime MBean details the runtime state of the requested JDBC Connection Pools. Important attributes are `ActiveConnectionCur-rentCount`, `ActiveConnectionsHighCount`, and `WaitingForConnection-HighCount`.

Figure 12–4 illustrates the type of information that can be provided about the server's health. These Runtime MBeans and attributes offer a good start when checking the health of the application

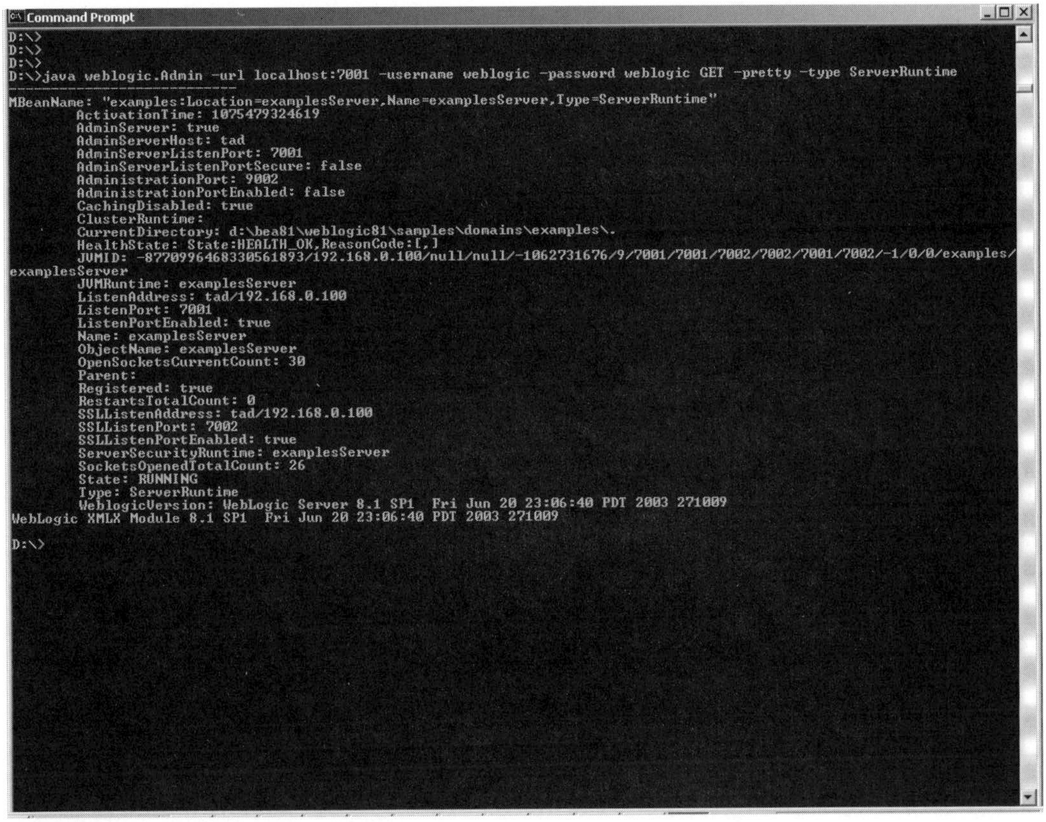

Figure 12–4
Runtime MBean server health information.

server instance. In addition, they can be incorporated into a monitoring script using `weblogic.Admin` or some other scripting tool. However, there are many additional Runtime MBeans and attributes available for monitoring. A reference for MBeans and attributes can be found in the BEA documentation at *http://e-docs.bea.com/wls/docs81/config_xml/index.html*.

WebLogic Administrative Tools

There are a number of tools and utilities included with WebLogic Server 8.1 that aid in performing administration of the WebLogic environment and J2EE applications deployed in the server. WebLogic includes a graphical, browser-based *Administration Console* for managing WebLogic resources, including initial setup and configuration, application deployment, undeployment, and redeployment, and runtime monitoring and manipulation. WebLogic also provides command-line interfaces that match what is offered by the graphical console. Included are a number of prebuilt scripts that can be used out-of-the-box or customized for your specific environment. For custom development, WebLogic Server 8.1 provides a JMX-based API for managing applications. In addition, a freeware utility called WL*Shell* offers an easy-to-use scripting tool for building management scripts around JMX. The following sections describe each of these services in more detail.

WebLogic Administration Console

WebLogic Server 8.1 provides an intuitive, easy-to-use graphical console. The *Administration Console* is a Web application hosted by the Administration Server. By entering the Administration Server's hostname and port number, authenticated users can access the console from any remote browser client. The Web application acts as a client to the Administration Server, issuing requests for information and commands and waiting for the response. All of the server's administration, configuration, and monitoring can be accomplished from the console without requiring any knowledge of JMX, MBeans, or script programming.

WebLogic Command-Line Scripts

Command-line scripting has always been an attractive approach to enterprise systems management. WebLogic Server 8.1 provides command-line interfaces for managing resources and deployed components. Typically, these interfaces are used when an administrator prefers to manage the domain with scripts, when there is no access to a browser, or for repetitive tasks that can be bundled into a script rather than being entered independently in the console. The console requires administrator interaction, whereas scripts can be written to handle mundane tasks without requiring an operator to be involved.

There are a number of command-line utilities provided with WebLogic Server 8.1. The `weblogic.Admin` utility is the command-line interface to administer, configure, and monitor WebLogic Server. The `weblogic.Deployer` utility is the command-line interface for deploying J2EE modules. Finally, WebLogic Server itself can be invoked via the command line by using the `weblogic.Server` Java class directly from a Java command. For more information, refer to the WebLogic Server Command Reference at *http://e-docs.bea.com/wls/docs81/admin_ref/index.html* in the BEA documentation.

Administrative APIs

In situations where more granular control is required than that provided by the Administration Console or command-line interfaces, WebLogic Server 8.1 also exposes the underlying JMX APIs for custom programming. For example, get or set operations can be made directly on the MBean attributes. This level of administrative programming requires extensive knowledge of the WebLogic Server MBean architecture. Refer to the BEA documentation for more information, including the "Commands for Managing WebLogic Server MBeans" at *http://e-docs.bea.com/wls/docs81/admin_ref/cli.html* and the *WebLogic Server Javadoc* at *http://e-docs.bea.com/wls/docs81/javadocs/index.html* for the Java management configuration and runtime packages.

WLShell Scripting Tool

WL*Shell* is an alternative command-line shell for managing WebLogic Server-based components and applications. WLShell is a freeware utility written by Paco Gomez, a BEA engineer, and downloadable from the BEA Dev2Dev developer site (*http://dev2dev.bea.com*) or from the WLShell Web site (*http://www.wlshell.com*). With the addition of JMX, WLShell offers access to the JMX MBeans bundled with WebLogic Server as well as custom-built MBeans that correspond to the deployed application components. WLShell has been tested with WebLogic Server 6.1, 7.0, and 8.1 versions.

WLShell supports both interactive and batch modes and offers the following services for WebLogic administration:

- Domain configuration
- Runtime configuration
- Application deployment (versions 7.0 and later)
- Server lifecycle control

Here are a few reasons you might consider using WLShell instead of `weblogic.Admin` for command-line scripting:

- `weblogic.Admin` uses the actual JMX MBean names, whereas WLShell uses a simplified notation that internally translates into the actual JMX MBean names. The WLShell notation is shorter, follows a pattern that is understood by the administrator, and is more intuitive.
- WLShell uses a telnet-like interface in which the administrator can "connect" to the WebLogic instance and navigate MBeans, create new ones, get and set attributes, and invoke operations. In addition, this connection can be shared, optimizing performance for batch operations.
- WLShell provides a scripting language with variables and flow-control statements.
- `weblogic.Admin` works only with WebLogic MBeans, whereas WLShell can be used with custom MBeans as well as WebLogic Mbeans.

There are a number of basic operations provided by WLShell. Through the MBean interfaces, you can navigate MBean types and names, get and set attributes, and invoke operations. The first step required is to connect to a running WebLogic Server instance, either locally or over the network, using the command syntax. This connection will remain open and allow multiple commands to be issued from the script. Opening a connection follows this format:

```
wlsh
```

```
connect <localhost or hostname>:<administration port> <username> <password>
```

WLShell implements a file-system style metaphor for access to MBeans. For example, JMX defines a server as

```
mydomain:Name=WebAuction,Type=Server
```

The corresponding syntax within the WLShell environment would be

```
mydomain:/Server/WebAuction
```

Following the filesystem metaphor, a fully qualified MBean attribute or operation would be identified as

```
Domain:/Type/Name/Attribute
```

In the following example, we obtain the maximum size of the connection pool for the WebAuction sample application. Initially, you find the JMX MBean syntax for this component, followed by the corresponding WLShell syntax.

```
webAuctionDomain:/Type=JDBCConnectionPool,Name=webauctionPool
```

```
webAuctionDomain:/JDBCConnectionPool/webauctionPool
```

```
connect localhost:7001 system weblogic
cd JDBCConnectionPool
cd webauctionPool
dir
get MaxCapacity
```

As you can see in the above example, MBean attributes can be retrieved using the shell command `get`. Likewise, attributes can be initialized using the shell command `set`. Finally, you can access MBean operations via the `invoke` command.

An additional feature of WLShell is the ability to configure a new domain, particularly useful when moving an existing pre-production environment to a production domain. In this scenario, we first create the Administration MBean for the service, then configure the service by setting the initial attributes. Once the service is configured, you can deploy the MBean to a server or cluster and save the domain's configuration in the *config.xml* file. The following example script can be used to configure the connection pool for the WebAuction example application.

```
connect localhost:7001 system weblogic
mkdir /JDBCConnectionPool
cd JDBCConnectionPool
mkdir webauctionPool
cd webauctionPool
set URL "jdbc:pointbase:server://localhost/WebAuction"
set DriverName "com.pointbase.jdbc.jdbcUniversalDriver"
```

```
set Properties "user=WebAuction"
set Password webauction
set MaxCapacity 10
invoke addTarget /Server/myserver

invoke $savedom $DOMAIN
invoke weblogic://Repository/Default/saveDomain
webAuctionDomain
```

WLShell offers an excellent option when considering command-line tools for managing and monitoring WebLogic Server deployments.

Application Deployment

Before an application can be used in production, you have to deploy it into the production domain. Of course, before you deploy the application, you have to build and package it. We covered building and packaging Web applications in Chapters 2, 3 and 4 and building and packaging EJBs in Chapters 8, 9 and 10. Basically, when you package the application, you associate the application files, XML deployment descriptors, Java classes, and other supporting files with the application. In this section, we review how to deploy and what happens when a Web or enterprise application is deployed.

When deploying a J2EE application, called a *deployment unit*, the WebLogic Administration Server controls the distribution of the files corresponding to the application itself to the managed server instances. You can deploy applications from an exploded directory, where all the application components, deployment descriptors, and supporting files are found in a standard directory structure, or as an archive, where all the files are collected into a special archive file.

The following types of applications can be deployed to a WebLogic Server instance:

- Web Applications—A *Web application* is made up of the JSPs, servlets, and their helper classes, and the `web.xml` and `weblogic.xml` deployment descriptors. Web applications are packaged into a special type of JAR file called a Web Archive (WAR) with a *.war* file extension. All the components within the WAR file share a common classloader.
- Enterprise Applications—An *enterprise application* is made up of Web applications, EJBs, and resource adaptors. Enterprise applications are packaged into a special JAR file called an Enterprise Archive (EAR) with an *.ear* file extension. Within an EAR, all the files share a common classloader. Included in the EAR file are the corresponding deployment descriptors for the various WARs and EJB JARs.
- Individual application components—Individual EJB and Web application components can also be deployed. These components are deployed as Web archives, Java archives for EJBs and other Java components, or J2CA resource adapters. Each component is loaded with a separate, unique application classloader, and any Web applications accessing the EJBs must use remote interfaces and pass `Serializable` objects.
- Client Applications—In addition to the types outlined above, J2EE also defines a way to associate a *client application* within an enterprise application. The client application includes all the deployment descriptors describing the components being called, such as EJBs, and the Java classes for the client itself. Client modules use the `application-client.xml` deployment descriptor.

> **Best Practice:** Deploying individual application components as separate applications is not recommended. Although this is a fairly simple deployment model, because each of these applications is unique common classes are not shared across components, Web applications must use the remote interfaces and `Serializable` objects to call EJBs and bypass performance optimizations, and the application becomes very difficult to manage. When deploying an enterprise application made up of Web applications and EJBs, use the Enterprise Application packaging and deployment model.

Deployment Models

Whether working with a Web application or an enterprise application, WebLogic Server provides three ways to deploy J2EE applications:

- Automatic deployment is enabled when starting WebLogic Server in development mode and deploying applications from the `<domain-name>/applications` directory.
- Utilities such as `weblogic.Deployer`, WLShell, and the Ant `wldeploy` task can be used for applications requiring manual redeployment.
- WebLogic Server Administration Console can be used to manually redeploy applications.

Each of these deployment options is useful in particular situations; likewise, there are situations when tasks might be better completed using one of the other methods. The primary factors affecting the deployment model are the mode the application server is being used and the location from which the application is deployed.

There are two modes used when starting WebLogic Server: *development* mode and *production* mode. While it may be obvious where each of these modes is used, the mode also defines how applications may be deployed, where files are deployed, and which options are appropriate. You define the WebLogic Server mode by setting the `PRODUCTION_MODE` variable when starting the server. Setting this variable to `true` starts the server in production mode and disables automatic deployment.

In addition, applications can be automatically redeployed only when initially deployed from the `<domain-name>/applications` directory. This directory exists in the domain's home directory. In development mode, the server checks the timestamp of application archives in this directory. If the server detects a change to the timestamp, it will automatically redeploy the application. For exploded applications, the `REDEPLOY` file will be updated when a change is made to any of the files in the application. The server will again detect this change and redeploy the application.

Table 12–1 illustrates how enabling or disabling the production mode and the location of the application affects application deployment.

Table 12–1   Production Mode and the Affect on Deployment and File Location

Production Mode Setting	Application Directory	Deployment Options
True	`applications` directory or alternate location	The server ignores timestamps, since automatic redeployment is disabled when the server is running in production mode. Modified applications must be redeployed manually.
False	`applications` directory	The server scans the timestamp of the archive file or the `REDEPLOY` file and automatically redeploys the application.
False	Alternate location	The server ignores timestamps. When an application changes it must be manually redeployed.

Let's review each of the deployment models in more detail.

Automatic Deployment

Automatic deployment is the simplest of the deployment methods for WebLogic Server. When using automatic deployment, WebLogic Server will periodically scan the `<domain-name>/applications` directory for new and updated applications. It automatically deploys any new applications and will undeploy and redeploy changes made to existing applications. Automatic deployment is most suitable for developing applications, since there are frequent updates and programmers don't like to be burdened with administrative operations like manually redeploying each time an application is updated or a change is made. By default, automatic deployment is used when deploying applications to the Administration Server instance.

Automatic deployment requires that the server be started with the `ProductionModeEnabled` flag set to `false`. When this flag is set to `false`, the server starts in *development* mode rather than *production* mode. Automatic deployment is not recommended for production environments because dynamically changing Web or enterprise applications on production WebLogic Server instances can cause instability in the environment. This flag can be set via the `PRODUCTION_MODE` variable in the `startWebLogic` command script or explicitly on the command line. For example, note the `ProductionModeEnabled` flag when starting WebLogic Server from the command line:

```
$ java -Dweblogic.Name=auctionServer \
-Dweblogic.ProductionModeEnabled=false weblogic.Server
```

weblogic.Deployer, WLShell, and wldeploy Ant task

WebLogic Server 8.1 comes with the `weblogic.Deployer` utility for deploying and managing applications. This utility replaces the `weblogic.deploy` utility in prior releases of WebLogic Server and provides a command-line alternative to the deployment functions in the Administration Console, including deploying, undeploying, and redeploying applications and specifying targets for an application. As noted above, `weblogic.Deployer` includes an upload service for moving files from the staging directory to the deployment directory. `Weblogic.Deployer` is often used to manage deployment in production environments.

WebLogic Server 8.1 also includes an Ant task for deployment, `wldeploy`. This task provides the same basic capabilities as the `weblogic.Deployer` command-line interface. A key advantage to `wldeploy` is that it can be combined with other Ant tasks in a single script, for example to automate building the application, creating a domain, starting the server, and deploying the application by combining `wlcompile`, `appc`, `wlserver`, `wlconfig`, and `wldeploy`. Refer to the BEA documentation at *http://e-docs.bea.com/wls/docs81/deployment/tools.html#1000506* for an example Ant build file for `wldeploy`.

With either of these utilities, the server must be started in production mode. As noted above, you can start the server in production mode by setting the `PRODUCTION_MODE` variable to `true` in the `startWebLogic` command script or directly on the command line with the option

```
-Dweblogic.ProductionModeEnabled=true
```

Changes to the application or archives will not be dynamically loaded using this mode; however, it allows the administrator to more consistently control the production environment. With either of these command-line services, deployment can be implemented without direct operator intervention, such as when bundling an existing deployment and moving it to a new production environment.

WebLogic Server Console

The third option for deployment is to use the WebLogic Server console. This option leverages the intuitive, easy-to-use graphical interface to deploy, undeploy, and redeploy applications as well as target the deployment to a single server or cluster of managed servers. To use the console for deployment the application server instance must be started with the production mode set to `true`. Please refer to the sections above on how to set the production mode for the server. In addition, the files to be deployed must be located in the staging directory.

Once the server is started in production mode and the files are located in the proper directory, you can use the console to deploy the application. The following two diagrams—Figures 12–5 and 12–6—illustrate deployment of the WebAuction example application using the WebLogic console.

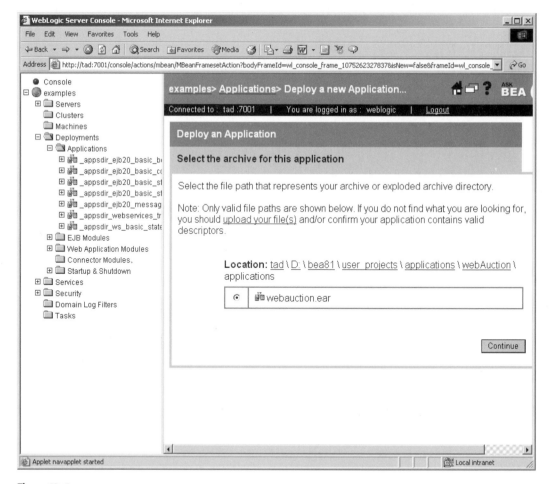

Figure 12–5

Selecting WebAuction with WebLogic console.

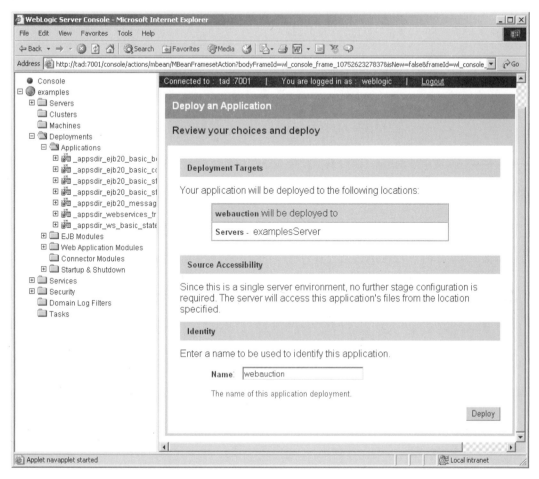

Figure 12–6
Deploying WebAuction application to a target.

During this deployment, the packaged *webAuction.jar* file is deployed from a location in the file system. Select the D*eployments* link and then select the A*pplications* link.

You will now see the Web applications currently deployed in your domain. Select the link to D*eploy a New Application* to deploy the *webAuction.ear* file.

Once an application is packaged, you deploy it to *deployment targets*, including the Administration Server, an individual managed server instance, or a cluster of WebLogic Server instances. Where the application is deployed affects how the application is deployed. The administrator copies the package files into a *staging directory* on the Administration Server, which acts as a repository for the application. You designate the staging directory using the Server tab on the Administration Console or setting the directory explicitly from the command line. However, the staging directory may or may not be the directory from where the application is actually deployed, which is called the *deployment directory*. When queried, the management MBean will return the deployment directory as the application's root directory. If configured to allow dynamic deployment, the server will scan the deployment directory for changes.

Staging Modes

Staging is the process of copying application files to the location from which they will be deployed. WebLogic Server uses the *staging mode* to determine this deployment behavior, including whether or not files will be copied, where, and by whom. WebLogic Server 8.1 supports three different staging modes: `no-stage`, `staging`, and `external-stage`.

1. `No-stage`—In the `no-stage` mode, the application files are not copied. A server in this mode will run applications directly from the source directory, and each managed server has its own copy of the application files. Changes to JSPs and servlets are detected automatically without redeployment. The application files are staged from a shared filesystem accessible to each managed server.

2. `Stage`—In the `stage` mode the application files are automatically copied to the staging directory on the server. Application files reside only on the Administration Server and are copied to a temp directory on each MSI where the application is targeted. The application is deployed on the managed server from the local temp directory. Application updates are made to the files on the Administration Server, which are then copied to the managed servers.

3. `External-stage`—In the `external-stage` mode, the user is responsible for copying the application files to the staging directory on the server. This mode is designed for environments that are managed by third-party tools, where an external tool is responsible for moving the application files or when a shared filesystem is not available for `no-stage` mode. A temp directory is created on each managed server; the application files are copied from the staging directory into the temp directory, and the application is deployed from the temp directory.

Table 12–2 presents a comparison of the three staging modes and when each is useful. More information about staging modes can be found in the BEA WebLogic Server documentation at *http://e-docs.bea.com/wls/docs81/deployment/overview.html* and at *http://e-docs.bea.com/wls/docs81/deployment/concepts.html*.

Table 12–2 Staging Modes

Deployment Staging Mode	When to Use
Stage	This mode is useful when deploying small or medium-sized applications to multiple managed servers or a small to medium-sized cluster of servers.
No-stage	This mode is useful when developing applications, when deploying to a single managed server or when deploying to a cluster of servers located on a multi-homed server.
External-stage	Use this mode when deploying third-party applications, when you won't be partially deploying unique application components, or when you need control over where the application files will reside.

Best Practice: Deploying an application with the *stage* mode requires the application files be copied from the Administration Server to each managed server. This is suitable for simple clusters and small to medium-sized applications. However, when deploying large applications or deploying an application across large clusters with many servers, an administration best practice is to use the *no-stage* mode and leverage a shared filesystem across the servers.

WebLogic Service Performance Monitor

You can monitor WebLogic Server resources and deployed applications using the Administration Console, command-line interfaces, and third-party tools using either JMX or SNMP. In addition, a new feature is available in WebLogic Server 8.1 as a separately downloadable extension to the Administration Console for collecting and monitoring information from the domain. Called the WebLogic Server Performance Monitor, this *monitoring dashboard* leverages the JMX infrastructure to allow the administrator to optimize production deployments and quickly isolate performance problems.

The monitoring service is implemented as a set of extensions to the WebLogic Administration Console that communicate with agents embedded within WebLogic Server instances. Since it is an extension to the existing console, it allows collection of runtime statistics without requiring tedious script programming. A key advantage is that it not only collects information about WebLogic Server but also can be extended to collect metrics about the end-user experience, external Web server farms, and response time from the database, providing an end-to-end analysis of application performance. This utility requires WLS 8.1 Service Pack 1 and can be downloaded from *http://commerce.bea.com/support/supportversions.jsp?file=/products/weblogicserver/support/support.html*.

WebLogic Clustering Configuration

One of the new features of WebLogic Server 8.1 administration is simplified cluster configuration. The goal is to make configuring and deploying a cluster much easier. We review the clustering architecture in WebLogic Server 8.1 in Chapter 14, "Designing the Production Deployment." In addition, the BEA documentation provides a complete review of clustering configuration at *http://e-docs.bea.com/wls/docs81/adminguide/createdomain.html*. The following section walks you through a clustered configuration for the WebAuction sample application.

Clustered WebLogic components are configured the same as nonclustered components. This has a particular benefit for the application developer, since whether the component is to be clustered or not does not affect the developer. For example, a stateless session EJB or stateful servlet that performs some business function is developed independently of how the component is deployed. This feature lowers the cost of developing and maintaining applications, and enhances component reuse.

It is important to note that you should not include the Administration Server as one of the instances within the cluster. The Administration Server cannot be clustered. We review the steps necessary to address what happens if the Administration Server fails in the section on Best Practices.

Best Practice: Do not add the Administration Server instance to a cluster.

There are a number of ways to configure a cluster with WebLogic. The easiest is new to WebLogic Server 8.1 and uses the domain configuration wizard. Here are the steps required to configure clustering in your domain.

1. Start the domain configuration wizard. From the first page, select *Create a new WebLogic configuration* and click *Next*.
2. On the Create a new WebLogic configuration page, select the *Basic WebLogic Server Domain template* and click *Next*.
3. On the Choose Express or Custom Configuration, choose *Custom* and click *Next*.

4. Configure the Administration Server as detailed earlier in this chapter, setting the Administration Server name and selecting the defaults. When finished, click Next.
5. On the Managed Servers page, select Yes and then click Next.
6. On the Configure Managed Servers page, click Add and fill in the fields of the Add Server row. The following parameters are listed:
    - Name—Enter a unique name for the server. Within the domain, each server, machine, cluster, and resource must have a unique name.
    - Listen Address—You can accept the default of All Local Addresses
    - Listen Port—You can accept the default here as well.
    - SSL Enabled—Click this box if you need this instance to have SSL enabled.
    - SSL Listen Port—You can accept the default here if you have chosen to enable SSL.
7. Refer to Figure 12–7 for an example.

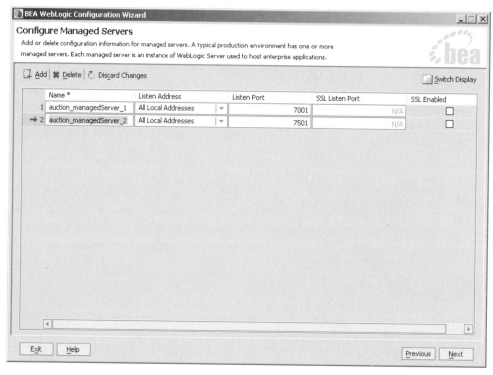

Figure 12–7
Example managed servers page.

8. Now, repeat this previous step for each server you wish to participate in the cluster. When finished, click Next to go to the Cluster Configuration page.
9. On the Configure Clusters page, define the cluster and how the managed servers will communicate. Click Add and fill in the fields for the Add Cluster row as follows:
    - Cluster Name—The name of your cluster. In our example, we use AuctionCluster as the name of our cluster.

- Multicast Address—This is the address the servers within the cluster will communicate with one another on.
- Multicast Port—This is the port the servers within the cluster will communicate with one another on.
- Cluster Address—This is an optional field that sets the host name portion of the URLs for requests directed to the cluster.

10.Refer to Figure 12–8 for the cluster configuration of our AuctionCluster.

11.Click *Next* to proceed to the Assign Servers page.

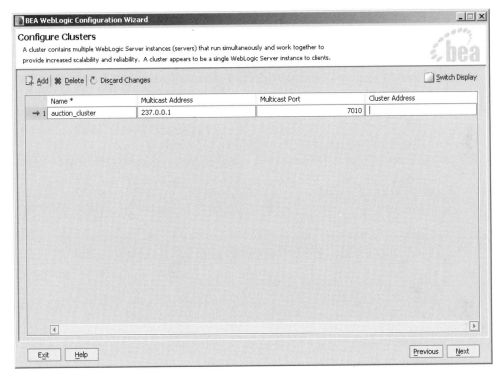

Figure 12–8
Example Cluster Configuration page.

12.On the Assign Servers page, we associate the managed servers with the cluster. In the Target list, select *AuctionCluster*. In the Source list, select *Managed Servers* and click the right arrow to assign managed servers to the cluster.

13.Refer to Figure 12–9 for the Assign Servers page for our Auction Cluster.

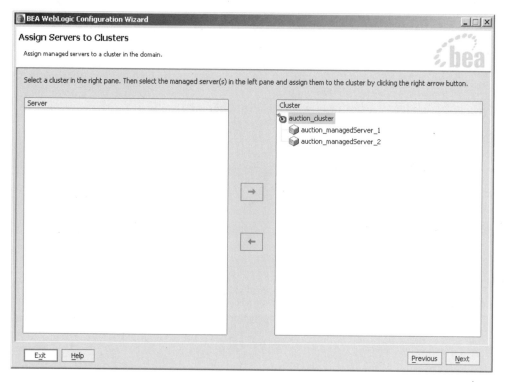

Figure 12-9
Assigning Servers to the AuctionCluster.

14. Click Next to proceed to the Configure Machines page.
15. On the Configure Machines page, we assign physical machines to our cluster. In the Name column, enter the name of the machine that will run a server Instance. If you plan to use the Node Manager, then enter the DNS name of the server in the Node Manager Listen Address field. Click Next to proceed to the Assign Servers to Machines step.
16. On the Assign Server to Machines page, select a machine you created from the target list, select a server from the source list, and associate the two by clicking the right arrow. Once you have finished associating machines and servers, click Next and proceed with the domain configuration. Refer to Figure 12–10 for a complete example of assigned servers and machines.

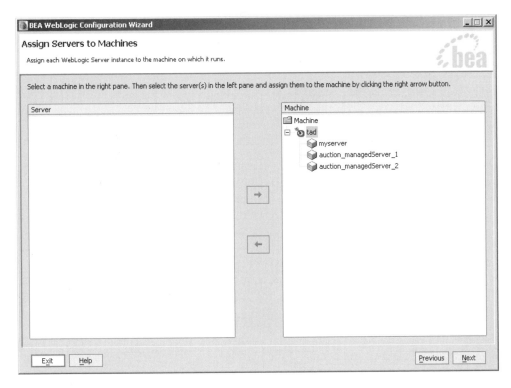

Figure 12-10
Assigned servers and machines in AuctionCluster.

At this point, you can continue with the domain configuration, creating JDBC data sources and connection pools, JMS components, defining the Java Virtual Machine you will use, and creating the domain. As you can see, with relatively few steps, you have created a cluster for the WebAuction example. You can also use the Administration Console to define your cluster.

When ready to deploy, you simply select the AuctionCluster as your deployment target from the Administration Console and WebLogic will deploy the WebAuction application onto the servers in the cluster defined in these steps..

Best Practice: A cluster cannot span multiple WebLogic domains. In addition, resources used within the cluster must also reside within the domain. For example, you cannot access a JDBC connection pool in one domain from a cluster deployed in a separate domain. An administrative best practice is to configure similar JDBC connection pools for each domain.

Administrative Best Practices

In this chapter, we reviewed the basic administrative services provided by WebLogic Server, how these services use JMX, and some of the tools and techniques used to manage and monitor WebLogic Server resources. Additional information on preparing for a production deployment can be found in Chapter 14.

However, there are a few best practices that we review here. These recommendations come from experience and work with existing customers, as well as BEA support, engineering, and product management. This is a dynamic list and will change as we learn more about WebLogic, as tools change, and as specifications adapt to meet additional customer requirements.

Handling Failures to the Administration Server

One of the first questions asked when determining administration best practices is how to protect the Administration Server instance. As detailed earlier in this chapter, the WebLogic Server domain model specifies a single Administration Server instance maintaining the configuration and managing the servers found there. Since there is only one instance of the Administration Server in the domain3 we need to determine a procedure for occasions when there is a problem with it.

The easiest response when the Administration Server fails is to simply restart it. Managed servers within the domain will continue to respond to client requests even if the Administration Server is unavailable, although until the Administration Server is restarted, no changes can be made to the domain. However, in certain situations, you may not be able to restart the Administration Server. In these cases, a second server must be started as the new Administration Server.

First, you must preserve the configuration files used by the Administration Server. The most important file is the *config.xml* file, holding the domain configuration information. However, other files related to the domain also must be preserved. The best practice is to shadow the directory structure of the administration server on a shared disk. If this is done, then the *config.xml* file and other files can be retrieved in the event the machine on which the Administration Server is running experiences a catastrophic failure.

Next, when starting the new Administration Server, you must be aware of the IP address of the failed Administration Server. If the `ListenAddress` is set, this information is stored in the *config.xml* file. The easiest way to migrate is to set the IP address of the new Administration Server to the IP address of the failed Administration Server and start the new server using the failed server's configuration files. However, if this is not possible, then the *config.xml* file must be updated with the IP address of the new Administration Server.

One additional point should be made on the topic of what happens when the Administration Server is unavailable. Normally, a managed server cannot start if the Administration Server is not available. However, if the managed servers are running with MSI enabled, then they can use a cached copy of the *config.xml* file rather than receiving one from the Administration Server. When started under MSI mode, the configuration files must be accessible locally on the managed server. This can be done with a shared filesystem, or the managed servers also have the option of receiving periodic configuration updates from the Administration Server using MSI *file replication*. You can enable MSI File Replication when configuring managed server through the WebLogic console by selecting the *Advanced Options* tab, clicking the *Show* link, then selecting the *Tuning Configuration* tab and clicking the MSI *File Replication* check box. Refer to the WebLogic Server 8.1 Administration Guide for more information about MSI mode and file replication at *http://e-docs.bea.com/wls/docs81/adminguide/overview.html*.

Implement One Site per Cluster Versus Multiple Sites

Although there are no settings within WebLogic Server that will prevent it, we do not recommend deploying WebLogic clusters across multiple sites. Although WebLogic Server can support a single domain crossing multiple sites, such as data centers in different locations, we don't recommend it. The networking overhead associated with clustering will cause reliability and networking performance problems unless the network bandwidth between the sites is significant. For most environments, it is a best practice to limit clusters to within a single site. For failover across sites, consider external load balancing and data replication services to ensure consistent behavior when failing across sites.

Protecting the Administration Server

Since the Administration Server is the central point for configuration within a domain, there can be security vulnerabilities unless this instance is properly protected. Exposing the Administration Server in the DMZ or an unprotected area can result in denial of service attacks or simple password cracking attempts. A best practice is to always keep the Administration Server behind a firewall, protecting it from external environments.

However, statistics show that many security breaches result from attacks within the network. Leveraging SSL communication for access to the Administration Server adds a level of protection to internal attacks as well as external. This can be accomplished by enabling the domain-wide administration port. In addition, you can configure the Administration Server to accept requests only from well-known machine addresses within the domain.

Log File Rotation for Deployment

Many operations within WebLogic Server generate log information. WebLogic Server maintains *log files* for each server in the domain as well as a standard HTTP access log. You configure the server's log file location using the *Server Logging* tab on the administration console when configuring each server in the domain. The Administration Server maintains a *domain log file*, recording changes made to the domain; managed servers' log files include *stdout* output for that server's applications. You can control how verbose the managed server's output will be.

A best practice for production systems is to always enable log file rotation for the Administration Server and managed servers, which allows the server to rotate to a new log file without requiring a server restart. Other log file settings can be configured, such as the frequency of log file rotation, when log files should be rotated, and how long to retain old log files. You can find more information about WebLogic Server logging at *http://e-docs.bea.com/wls/docs81/logging/index.html.*

Putting It All Together

In this chapter we introduced you to WebLogic administration. We learned about the JMX standard and how it can be used to manage J2EE applications. In addition, we learned how WebLogic Server leverages JMX for its own administrative functions. We reviewed the administrative framework within WebLogic Server and how to interface with it using the WebLogic Console, command-line interfaces, and administrative APIs. We detailed how to configure a WebLogic cluster and finished with a list of administrative best practices.

With this information, you can now understand the various components of WebLogic administration. The goal was to provide a broad survey of how the environment is organized and what services are available. Much more information on these topics can be found in the BEA documentation.

chapter 13

Application Security with WebLogic Server 8.1

Securing J2EE applications is one of the many services provided by WebLogic Server 8.1. A key advantage of the BEA strategy is that the security infrastructure offered by the server is leveraged across the entire suite of products in WebLogic Platform 8.1, yielding a consistent, modular mechanism for securing these packages as well as custom and third-party applications. WebLogic Server 8.1 features a number of security capabilities to deliver a comprehensive distributed security infrastructure, including the following:

- A security framework based on the Java Authentication and Authorization Service (JAAS), the Java 2 security model.
- A more flexible, more easily adaptable environment that leverages roles and policies to identify users and groups authorized to access resources controlled by WebLogic Server.
- Support for a variety of authentication models, including username/password, digital certificates, third-party services, and others.
- A "pluggable" architecture where third-party and external security systems can be fully utilized within the WebLogic security framework.
- A new approach in which the administrator is responsible for configuring security rather than relying on the developer to code security into the application.
- A security implementation for Web services based on emerging industry standards for protection and interoperability.

In this chapter, we review the relevant technologies for securing Java 2 and J2EE applications. We outline the WebLogic security environment and describe how BEA implements JAAS and other standards for securing applications. We introduce the graphical administrative features for security in WebLogic Server 8.1, and we finish by detailing many of the best practices for securing WebLogic-based deployments.

Security Technology Overview

There are several primary services necessary to secure any computing environment, particularly one based on distributed components and services. These basic services include authentication, authorization, auditing, logging, encryption, and data privacy. WebLogic Server 8.1 implements these services within the context of a J2EE application server, providing a complete security solution for the enterprise Java environment. The following sections describe each of these security technologies and note the corresponding industry standards. Once we have reviewed basic security, we address how WebLogic Server leverages JAAS to meet these security requirements.

Users and Groups

Before jumping into more complex topics like authentication and authorization, we need to review the basics. A *user* is the application end user's account name. The security system represents each user with a username or ID, such as "jamesdean" or "webuser1271," and some information (sometimes called *proof material*) for verifying the user's identity during the login process. The verification information is usually a password, but other authentication methods, such as tokens or digital certificates, may be used to validate the user's identity.

A *group* is a named collection of zero or more users. Typically, a group represents a set of application users who have similar permissions to access system resources. Groups are often mapped onto organizational structures. For example, you could have an employees group that contains every user in the company. A separate group, the managers group, could be a subset of the employees group that has greater access to privileged information, such as employees' salaries. In this context, the job of the security system is to verify that only members of the managers group can access sensitive salary data.

Authentication

Authentication is the process of identifying the requester of a service, in effect answering the question, Who are you? In addition, the requester can have assurance that the requested service is also identified: Are you who you say you are? The entire process begins with the notion of *identity* and *trust*—for example, a procedure that allows the application to trust the client's identity and the client to trust the server's. When a user answers some challenge for identity, there is a trusted mechanism to verify that identity.

There are many ways to identify the requestor, ranging from a username and password credentials to stronger forms of authentication, such as digital certificates and tokens. The security system should provide a flexible environment allowing the administrator to match the authentication scheme with the needs of the organization. Factors that affect this decision include the level of protection for exposed resources, the overall costs associated, and the anticipated modes of attack. Any system can be broken; the key is to make the effort required to break the system greater than the value to be gained from access to the protected information.

Authorization

Once you've answered the question, Who am I? the next step is to determine, What services do I have access to? Authorization is the control of access to resources. Either as a program or as a user, you must be granted permission before you can access a service or resource, load a servlet, invoke methods on an EJB, initiate a business process, or access a JDBC connection pool. A security administrator specifies the roles allowed to access a particular resource or component and the policies that define the scope of access. Authorization enables the administrator to ensure integrity, confidentiality, and availability.

Roles and Policies

A *role* is an abstract, logical grouping of users. Roles refer to groups of users or specific users who share permissions to access resources; roles are the mechanism used to restrict access to those resources. Roles are mapped at runtime onto security identities such as principals. For example, if you define a role for all users and call it *auction_user*, then every visitor to the site with a valid username is a member of the *auction_user* role. At runtime, the application server will authenticate each user and then include the user in the *auction_user* role. The *auction_user* role is used by the security system to control access to the resources and applications within the environment.

Roles are often confused with groups. The key to understanding the difference is that roles are used by the security system to restrict access to services, whereas groups are simply used to organize and manage users, such as by job description or organization. Roles are used to determine whether the requester is entitled access to the desired resource or service; at deployment time, the roles are mapped to the authorized users/groups. Using roles allows the security settings to be changed without altering the application code.

Policies are used to answer the question, What services does a specific role have access to? In the Java security model, the application server provides the authorization, using roles and policies, for requesters to access resources. The security role is a privilege granted to users or groups based on specific conditions. A *policy* is created when an administrator defines a relationship between a managed resource, such as a Web page, portal, EJB, or business process, and one or more security roles. For example, an administrator defines a policy that specifies the conditions required to access a particular resource or component, such as allowing members of the customer service role to access Web applications between the hours of 8:00 a.m. and 5:00 p.m.

Auditing and Logging

A key aspect of distributed security is the ability to go back later and review what you and other users in the environment have done. Auditing and logging is the process of collecting, storing, and distributing information about security events—requests and their outcomes—throughout the system. With auditing and logging, you have an electronic trail that can be used to verify who issued a transaction, if the transaction was successful, and whether the transaction can be considered binding (i.e., nonrepudiation). Not only is auditing and logging important for review of activities, it can also aid in detection and investigation of potential breaches in the application environment.

Firewalls

Generically, firewalls are used to separate or isolate danger. For example, a firewall in a car is designed to separate the engine compartment (and the danger of a fire) from the passenger compartment. Buildings have firewalls made of brick dividing areas within a building. In a networking security context, *firewalls* are powerful tools in the arsenal of the network security administrator. Firewalls are used to isolate or segregate network traffic between domains over the network. They can be a combination of hardware and/or software, including routers and dedicated gateways. Filtering firewalls block network traffic based on a variety of factors, such as protocols, source or destination network addresses, or even the service requested. Proxy firewalls actually make the network connections for you, acting as the intermediary between you and the network.

Refer to Chapter 14, "Designing the Production Deployment," for more information on how to leverage firewalls to secure WebLogic deployments.

Data Privacy and Secure Sockets Layer (SSL)

Along with proving who a user is and what services he or she may access, the security system must ensure the privacy of information traveling over the network. *Secure Sockets Layer* (SSL) is a broadly accepted protocol that ensures privacy of data by encrypting it before transmission over the network. *Transport Layer Security* (TLS) is a more recent data privacy standard that is gaining acceptance. Although there are subtle differences, for the purposes of this book we combine these technologies under the term SSL. SSL combines several encryption technologies, including digital certificates, standard encryption, and public key encryption. These technologies are described in the following sections.

The SSL model defines two levels of authentication: one-way and two-way. Using one-way authentication, SSL can provide an application-level means of authenticating programs, validating that a client is talking to the desired server. An added level of protection can be offered using two-way or mutual authentication, where the client validates the server and the server also ensures it is receiving a request from a valid client. Browsers utilize SSL through the HTTPS (Secure HTTP) protocol, and programmatic Java clients can leverage SSL through a process called *tunneling*. The SSL service is based on a technology called cryptography. This technology encrypts human-readable plaintext into ciphertext, which cannot be easily decoded.

Implementations of SSL follow the Internet standard for security between two hosts connected on an insecure network. You should use SSL whenever you want to protect data or the privacy of information traveling over the wire. The SSL protocol uses *public key encryption*. Public key encryption is a more secure form of standard encryption, also known as *symmetric key encryption*.

Symmetric Key Encryption

Most people are familiar with standard encryption in which there is a *shared secret* between two parties. For example, Patrick and Mary could share a secret, called a *key*, which would then be used as part of the algorithm for encrypting their messages to each other. With a shared secret, the notion of trust can be established.

Standard encryption uses a number of different algorithms. Some are secure and use industry- and government-standard encryption algorithms. Some are not secure, such as the key to a secret decoder ring that comes in the bottom of a cereal box. However, all standard encryption schemes share the concept that both sides know the same secret. As you can imagine, the distribution of the encryption keys can be a problem. How does Patrick secretly get a message to Mary before they have shared the secret key? What if Patrick and Mary are in separate countries? Will they need to meet in person before they can exchange encrypted messages? Even worse, would Patrick need a different secret key for each person he needs to secretly communicate with? Public key encryption provides an additional level of protection above symmetric key encryption and addresses these needs.

Public Key Encryption

Public key encryption technology was developed in the late 1970s by (among other scientists) MIT professors Rivest, Shamir, and Adleman, who gave their names to the RSA *algorithm*. Over time, the RSA algorithm has become a widely used and respected encryption algorithm. The RSA public key encryption algorithm enables anyone to encrypt a message for Patrick, but only Patrick can decode it.

To use public key encryption, Patrick has two keys: a public key and a private key. Patrick provides his public key to anyone and everyone. Anyone who wants to send a message to Patrick uses this public key to encrypt the message. Once encrypted, the private key is required to decrypt it. As long as Patrick keeps his private key to himself, security is ensured.

RSA encryption works in both directions. If Patrick encrypts something with his private key, then anyone can use his public key to decrypt that message. This process is called a *digital signature*, because only Patrick can encrypt a message that can be decrypted by his public key. However, how do you know if the public key you have for Patrick is really Patrick's public key? In practice, this problem is solved by a technology called *digital certificates*.

Digital Certificates

Digital certificates contain information that enables people to associate a given public key with a given user. If you receive Patrick's public key, you can use his digital certificate to prove that it is really Patrick's public key and not an impersonator's. A digital certificate typically contains the following information, at a minimum:

- Information regarding the keyholder's identity, such as name, organization, and so forth
- The keyholder's public key
- A digital signature on the information contained in the digital certificate, issued by an entity called a *certificate authority*

Certificate Authorities

A certificate authority certifies that a given public key corresponds to a given user. For example, a certificate authority might grant a digital certificate to a user who receives mail at a given e-mail address. The certificate authority verifies that the user definitely owns that e-mail address through a series of e-mail exchanges with the user. Certificate authorities sometimes require stronger proof material, such as a valid driver's license number.

Certificate authorities provide a number of well-known public keys that match highly protected private keys maintained by the certificate authority. These public keys also are included in digital certificates that can be found in all commercially available Web browsers.

A certificate authority uses its private key to sign certificates for the users that it validates. In a sense, it is vouching for every single one of those user's identities. Because the public keys of the certificate authorities are both well known and embedded in many applications, you can use them to verify the signature on the digital certificate.

This level of verification is required for sensitive online transactions, when customers want to do things like

- Manage their bank accounts
- Make credit card purchases
- Manage their 401K program

Digital certificates help give customers peace of mind, allowing users to *trust* their application infrastructure.

Commercial Certificate Authorities

Vendors such as VeriSign and Entrust are commercial certificate authorities. These vendors provide certificate authorities designed specifically for commercial applications. For convenience and use in development, most application servers such as WebLogic Server 8.1 provide a demonstration digital certificate. However, for a public deployment, such as an Internet e-commerce site, you must obtain a commercial digital certificate for each application server instance. BEA's documentation includes details on how to acquire digital certificates for your WebLogic Server deployment.

Notes on SSL Encryption

The SSL protocol aggregates several encryption technologies, including digital certificates, standard symmetric encryption, and public key encryption. For example, an SSL-protected data transfer connection uses all three technologies, as follows:

- The client requests the server's public key from the server's digital certificate.
- The client then uses that public key to encrypt a message for the server. The message contains the client information and bootstrap information for the SSL connection.
- Ultimately, the server and the client use each other's public keys to agree on a *symmetric key*, which they subsequently use to encrypt all the data they share.

SSL uses symmetric encryption once a secure connection has been verified because it is more efficient from a computational standpoint. However, public key encryption is expensive in terms of CPU utilization and can have a significant impact on application performance and throughput. If you were to implement "bulletproof" security using public key encryption exclusively, then without significant hardware resources, your systems would probably grind to a halt while maintaining a few simultaneous connections due to the overhead caused on the server's processors.

WebLogic Security and JAAS

Now that we understand the basics, let's take a closer look at the security architecture in WebLogic Server 8.1. The security framework provides a rich environment in which applications can be configured and deployed while protecting valuable corporate assets. WebLogic Server provides services for authentication, authorization, auditing and logging, and data privacy support. WebLogic Server implements the Java security model with adaptations for the unique challenges of a distributed J2EE environment. Refer to Figure 13–1 for an overview of the WebLogic security framework. The following sections describe the WebLogic Server 8.1 security architecture.

It should be noted that this section is intended to introduce you to the security framework in WebLogic Server. There are more than a few details that cannot be sufficiently explained in a single chapter. For more information, refer to the BEA documentation on WebLogic security at *http://e-docs.bea.com/wls/docs81/security.html* and the BEA Dev2Dev Web site at *http://dev2dev.bea.com*.

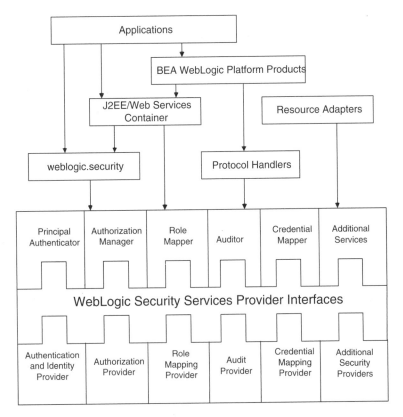

Figure 13-1
WebLogic Server 8.1 security architecture.

JAAS and WebLogic Server

WebLogic Server 8.1 uses the *Java Authentication and Authorization Service* (JAAS) for authenticating users, clients, and components. WebLogic Server's JAAS authentication determines who is currently executing Java code in WebLogic Server. These components may include servlets, fat clients, Enterprise JavaBeans, and all kinds of users.

WebLogic Server JAAS is built on top of the standard Java platform security available in the Java 2 Standard Edition (J2SE). The JAAS authentication framework is, in turn, built on pluggable authentication modules (PAMs), which defines a standard interface for plugging in external or third-party security solutions. It enables system administrators to plug in and configure the appropriate authentication service(s) to meet their specific security requirements without requiring component modification. More information on PAMs can be found at *http://java.sun.com/security/jaas/doc/pam.html*.

It is important to note that JAAS is a J2SE service and, in its current form, not originally designed for use with J2EE. The primary limitation is that JAAS does not propagate authentication information outside the boundaries of the Java Virtual Machine. For example, if a Java client authenticates using JAAS and calls a remote EJB, the specification does not define a way to propagate the user's identity. WebLogic Server uses JAAS for authentication within a virtual machine and has adapted JAAS to propagate credentials across distributed system calls.

Principals and Subjects

When a user authenticates (i.e., proves his or her identity), the WebLogic security service associates a *principal*, or multiple principals, with that user. A principal is an identity created as a result of successful authentication. Once a principal is created, the security service determines access to resources according to the security attributes associated with that principal. A given user can be mapped to multiple principals depending upon the security context and resources being accessed. For example, a user may have one principal that identifies the user to the WebLogic environment and have separate usernames and passwords for databases and existing legacy systems called by applications deployed in WebLogic Server.

JAAS provides the basis for the WebLogic Server 8.1 security framework. JAAS requires that principals be stored for each user as part of a *subject*. Subjects are objects defined by the JAAS authentication model as security containers and define an aggregation point for a user and their corresponding principals. Refer to Figure 13–2 for the relationships between users, groups, subjects, and principals.

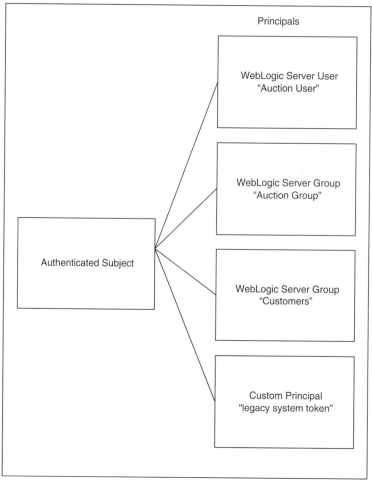

Figure 13–2
Relationship between users, groups, subjects, and principals.

WebLogic Roles

As noted in a prior section, a role is a privilege granted to a group of users or specific users based on conditions or circumstances. In the WebLogic security framework, roles are defined and evaluated at runtime using the role mapping provider. For example, once a new user has been created and added to the appropriate groups, she can begin accessing resources based on the roles that have already been mapped to the groups she belongs to.

WebLogic supports two types of roles: global roles and scoped roles. *Global roles* apply to all resources deployed throughout the WebLogic domain, whereas *scoped roles* are specific to individual applications and resources. You may specify custom roles to meet your needs, but WebLogic also defines a series of *default roles*. Table 13–1 lists these roles and their privileges.

Table 13–1   Default Global Roles and Their Privileges

Global Role	Privilege
Admin	Read and update the entire server's configuration. Start, stop, and restart servers; deploy, undeploy, and redeploy enterprise applications, Web applications, startup and shutdown classes, and Web Services.
Anonymous	All users, whether authenticated or not, are included in this role.
Deployer	Read the server's configuration but do not update. Deploy, undeploy, and redeploy enterprise applications, Web applications, startup and shutdown classes, and Web Services.
Operator	Read the server configuration but do not update. Start, stop, and restart servers.
Monitor	Read the server configuration but do not update. Effectively, this role provides read-only access to the WebLogic Server Administration Console, the `weblogic.Admin` command-line utility, and the MBean APIs.

JAAS Modules

JAAS modules are the components that map the JAAS API to the security store. During the authentication process, JAAS modules evaluate subjects. For example, a module might map a JAAS login to the Windows NT security domain. When you log in to a client application, the module provided by the vendor handles that subject's login. Modules exist for all the security stores that WebLogic Server supports, including the following:

- LDAP directories, including the embedded LDAP store
- Native WebLogic Server file realm
- Windows NT domain security
- RDBMS security realm

In addition, you can also create custom JAAS login modules to access other security stores.

JAAS LoginContext

The key component of JAAS authentication is the `LoginModule`, which creates the subject and aggregates corresponding principals into a security context when the user logs in. All authentication requests are routed through this interface. The `LoginModule` class is similar to the JNDI Initial Context that was used in prior releases of WebLogic Server to control access to EJBs. The `LoginContext` class includes the basic methods used to authenticate subjects and provides a way to develop an application independent of the underlying authentication technology. Your application server configuration specifies what modules are used to authenticate subjects. For example, WebLogic Server ships with a `LoginModule` for username/password authentication, the `UsernamePasswordLoginModule.class`.

JAAS Callback

To generate an initial `LoginContext`, you define a class to receive method calls from the JAAS module handling the authentication. These method calls implement the `CallbackHandler` interface. `CallbackHandler` enables the JAAS module to interact with the application to retrieve specific authentication data, such as usernames and passwords, or to display error and warning messages.

Method invocations on the `CallbackHandler` include implementations of the `Callback` class. These implementations provide the means to pass requests or messages to applications, and for applications, if appropriate, to return requested information to the underlying security services.

WebLogic Security Service Providers

Each service within the WebLogic Server 8.1 security architecture has a corresponding *service provider*. Each service provider communicates with the security framework via a *security service provider interface*, or SSPI. The SSPI model is what makes the WebLogic security framework so adaptable to meet the specific needs of your business. Underlying components of the security architecture can be changed without impacting the remainder of the environment.

Most deployments of WebLogic Server use most, if not all, of the default service providers; however, if you have special requirements or need to integrate with third-party packages, you can use the SSPI to write a custom service provider or plug a third-party service provider into your framework. For example, when integrating with a third-party single sign-on (SSO) solution, you need custom authentication and identity assertion providers; usually the SSO vendor provides these. The BEA Dev2Dev site includes sample auditing, authentication, identity assertion, authorization, and role mapping providers if you are interested in building a custom provider or would like more information about how security providers work. Refer to *http://dev2dev.bea.com/codelibrary/code/security_prov81.jsp* for the sample security providers.

The security providers in the WebLogic security framework include

- Authentication
- Identity assertion
- Authorization
- Auditing
- Principal validation
- Role mapping
- Credential mapping
- Adjudication
- Keystore
- Realm adapter

The following sections explain each of these service-provider interfaces.

Authentication

The *authentication* provider completes the validation of the user's identity via the provided credentials. The default provider supports username/password authentication and stores the user and group information in the embedded LDAP server. In addition, this provider includes administrative support for managing users and groups.

In WebLogic Server 8.1, *authentication* providers serve the purpose of identifying users, storing information associated with those users, and transporting security information to other applications requesting it. Using the JAAS LoginModule interface described above, the authentication provider uses the *principal validation* provider to validate the user's credentials, determine group membership, and assign the corresponding subject and principals for that user. The subject is used to pass the principals for the user or program identity to other components of the system, including tokens or credentials for external resources, using the *identity assertion* provider.

Authorization

The *authorization* provider controls access to system resources, deciding if a particular user is granted access to a resource based on the specified requirements as defined by security policies. Included with this provider are the services to deploy and undeploy security policies within the WebLogic environment.

When a resource is requested, a check is made to verify the role associated with the requester meets the defined constraints. When requested, the *authorization* provider in the WebLogic Server 8.1 security framework decides whether to grant or deny access to the resource. In past releases of WebLogic Server, authorization was defined using access control lists (ACLs). In WebLogic Server 8.1 security roles and policies replace ACLs and permissions.

Auditing

The *auditing* provider faithfully logs information concerning security operations within the WebLogic environment. These operations include other service provider requests coordinated through the security framework. The auditing provider is invoked any time a provider of any kind executes a function and logs all information associated with the request, including the provider, event data, and the resulting outcome. The audit SSPI also supports multiple auditors, making it easy to integrate with external logging and reporting systems.

Identity Assertion

The *identity assertion* provider offers a way for systems external to the WebLogic security framework to participate in the authentication process. For example, when using a third-party single sign-on solution such as Netegrity, Oblix, or Securant, the identity assertion provider allows authentication to be deferred to the external solution. The included provider supports X.509 certificates and CORBA IIOP CSIv2 tokens. You can easily support new types of external systems by simply adding a provider for that new system.

Role Mapping

The *role mapping* provider "maps" or assigns roles to a user for a specific request. Using the same policy engine as the authorization provider, the role mapper examines the user's subject and then updates the corresponding roles for access to WebLogic resources. The role mapping provider also functions to deploy and undeploy roles within the WebLogic environment.

Credential Mapping

Likewise, the *credential mapping* provider "maps" the WebLogic user's principals to credentials that correspond to external resources. For example, this provider might be used to map a username and password to a corresponding login identity in a database or existing legacy system. One key use of this provider is when implementing a single sign-on throughout the WebLogic environment and back-office applications like databases, transaction systems, and legacy systems not written in Java.

Adjudication

The *adjudication* provider handles conflicts that may arise when you are using multiple authentication providers. When making a decision, the adjudication provider waits until all of the authentication providers have returned their decisions; at that point, the adjudication provider decides whether or not access will be granted based on potentially conflicting results. The default adjudication provider uses two rules to evaluate these conflicts: all must grant or none can deny.

Realm Adapters

WebLogic Server also includes a series of *realm adapter* providers. These providers offer backward compatibility with 6.x WebLogic security realms. The WebLogic realm adapter providers map the realm API from the 6.x realm (`weblogic.security.acl`) to the APIs used in WebLogic Server 7.0 and later releases. Included are providers for authentication and identity assertion, authorization, auditing, and adjudication. These providers are intended to ease the migration from WebLogic 6.x environments to WebLogic 7.0, are deprecated, and should be used only while upgrading to the latest security architecture.

Embedded LDAP Server

A security realm is an administrative domain of control for securing users, groups, applications, and WebLogic resources. Each security realm consists of a collection of security providers, users, groups, roles, and policies. The information associated with a particular security realm is housed in some security provider database. A new feature WebLogic Server 8.1 is the inclusion of a complete LDAP directory server that acts as the default security provider database.

LDAP stands for *Lightweight Directory Access Protocol* and is an efficient way to store and share large amounts of information, such as security data. Each instance of WebLogic Server within the domain has its own LDAP server. The Administration Server maintains the master LDAP server, and each managed server maintains its own replica or copy of the data housed in the master server.

The LDAP server is used by the authentication, authorization, credential mapping, and role mapping providers and is the repository for the domain's security information, including users, groups, roles, policies, and credential map information. Using the graphical administration console, you can access information about the LDAP server by expanding the *Domain* tab, then selecting *Security*, and finally the *Embedded* LDAP tab.

Since this directory serves as the primary repository for your domain's security information, it is a good practice to regularly back up this information. Using the console, you can specify the hour and minute when the backup should be taken as well as how many copies of the backup should be maintained. When a backup is initiated, the Administration Server suspends writes to the LDAP directory, backs up the files into a ZIP archive, and resumes updates to the LDAP directory. The backup copies are kept in the *ldap/backup* directory.

> **Best Practice:** It is always recommended that periodic backups of the embedded LDAP directory are taken and that multiple copies are retained in the event the security information for the domain must be restored.

Securing WebLogic Resources

WebLogic Server provides a broad range of security services, as described throughout this chapter. Once you define the users, groups, roles, and policies, the next step is to apply them to secure the applications you build. There are three primary ways to secure application resources within the WebLogic security framework:

- J2EE deployment descriptors
- WebLogic Administration Console
- A combination of both

Let's consider each of these options in more detail.

> **Best Practice:** WebLogic Server 8.1 provides multiple models for securing Web and EJB applications. To ease the burden on the security administrator, rather than using multiple models, you should select one and use it throughout your environment.

J2EE Deployment Descriptors

Declarative security is one of the security programming models defined by J2EE. The declarative security model expresses an application's security structure, including roles, access control, and authentication requirements, in a form that can be changed without changing the application. J2EE standardizes Web application and EJB security in *deployment descriptor* files. The external security configuration is stored in XML, including *web.xml* and *weblogic.xml* for Web applications and *ejb-jar.xml* and *weblogic-ejb-jar.xml* for EJB components.

At deployment time, WebLogic Server reads the J2EE deployment descriptor for roles and policy information and uses the information throughout the lifecycle of the application. Before deployment, you must create the users and groups using the Administration Console. Then, the deployment descriptor is simply used to map user and group information to the roles required for the application. At runtime, you make environment changes to the users and groups rather than changing the underlying application's deployment descriptor.

WebLogic Console

WebLogic Server 8.1 also supports using the Administration Console to specify the roles and policies for your J2EE Web and EJB applications. You've already defined users and groups using the console, and now you can also define the security roles and policies there as well. The console provides a consistent graphical interface for the security configuration required throughout the WebLogic environment.

When using the console only, you must also take care to not allow security information from an application's deployment descriptor to override the security settings you've defined. (The next section reviews using the console and deployment descriptors together) To ensure deployment descriptor information does not override settings in the console, you need to set the default behavior for the realm. For example, in the webAuction realm, using the console, select the *Security‡Realms‡AuctionRealm* tab. Here you will find the security information for this realm. Under the *Check Roles and Policies for* attribute, you should check the *All Web applications and EJBs* option. Also, under the *On Future Redeployments* attribute, you should check the *ignore roles and policies from* DD option. These settings prevent deployment descriptors from inadvertently overriding settings in the console. You can also set security policies for any WebLogic resource. These policies represent a correlation between the resource and one or more users, groups, and roles. You can define these policies using the Administration Console. In the left pane of the console, right-click on the server resource—JDBC connection pools, for example—and select *Define a Security Policy*. Refer to Figure 13–3 for an example of these settings.

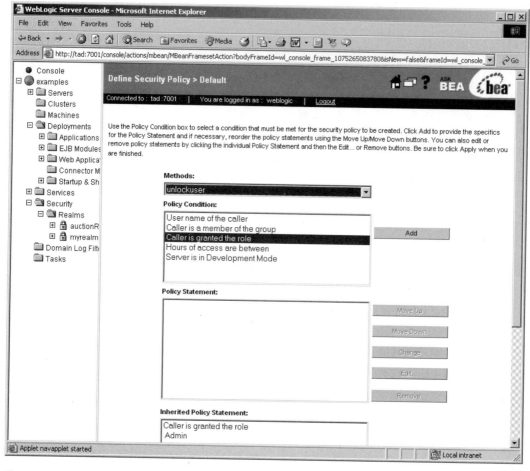

Figure 13–3

Setting access policies from the console.

Combining WebLogic Console and Deployment Descriptors

A third model for securing Web and EJB applications is to use a combination of both the WebLogic console and the corresponding deployment descriptors. In this model, the information from the deployment descriptors is used to deploy applications, and then the console manages the security after deployment. This method utilizes the standard J2EE model for securing Web and EJB applications while also leveraging the graphical console for management.

However, this model can also be more difficult for the security administrator to manage. When using both the console and deployment descriptors for security, the danger is that changes made in the console may be unknowingly overwritten by settings in the deployment descriptor the next time the application is deployed. From the console, make sure to set the *Check Roles and Policies for* attribute to the *All Web applications and* EJBs option. You should also set the *On Future Redeployments* attribute to initialize roles and policies from DD before deployment and then reset this attribute to ignore roles

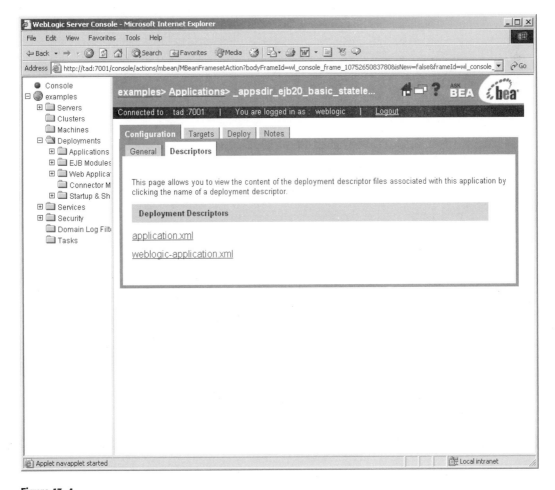

Figure 13–4

Combining the console with deployment descriptors.

and policies from DD after deployment. If you do not reset this value, then the security information will be reinitialized every time the application is redeployed. Refer to Figure 13–4 for an example of these settings.

> **Best Practice:** Since combining deployment descriptors and the console for securing Web and EJB applications can result in a complex and confusing deployment environment, it is a best practice to only use deployment descriptors or only use the console when securing your applications.

Use of the fullyDelegateAuthorization flag

It is important to note that before you can use either of the above console-based options, you must set the `fullyDelegateAuthorization` flag to `true`. If this flag is set to `false`—which is the default—then the WebLogic Security Service will ignore settings from the console and only use settings defined in the deployment descriptors.

The `fullyDelegateAuthorization` flag can be set one of three ways:

- Set the parameter explicitly on the `weblogic.Server` command line with the option

  `-Dweblogic.security.fullyDelegateAuthorization=true`

- Modify the startup script for WebLogic in the *<weblogic-home>/server/bin* directory to include the option on the server command:

  `-Dweblogic.security.fullyDelegateAuthorization=true`

- Modify the startup script to include *<weblogic-home>/user_projects/domains/auctionDomain* directory, where auctionDomain is the domain for our webAuction example application, to include the following setting:

  ```
  set JAVA_OPTIONS=... -
  Dweblogic.security.fullyDelegateAuthorization=true
  ```

Note that option 2 applies the `fullyDelegateAuthorization` flag to all servers within the domain, whereas option 3 allows you to select the servers to apply the setting to. To avoid confusion and unnecessary security complexity, set the `fullyDelegateAuthorization` flag on all servers in a domain.

WebLogic Server 8.1 and SSL

WebLogic Server uses SSL in three ways:

1. To protect communication with browser clients who are accessing Web resources such as JSP pages, servlets, or any other component in a Web application.
2. To secure communication with Java clients that are using SSL and making RMI calls.
3. To secure communication with the WebLogic Server administration infrastructure, which uses SSL to protect the RMI calls it uses to access the WebLogic Server management APIs.

To use SSL with WebLogic Server, you need a private key, a digital certificate containing the matching public key, and a certificate signed by at least one trusted certificate authority. The SSL protocol relies on digital certificates for authenticating clients and servers. Because each digital certificate maps to only one private key, each WebLogic Server instance has its own digital certificate. Clients connecting to WebLogic Server securely over the SSL protocol need to verify that they are connecting to the correct host. The host name entered on the digital certificate enables clients to verify that they are connecting to the intended server machine.

> **Best Practice:** WebLogic Server administrators and developers should take the time to understand how digital certificates work in the context of a secure application deployment. It is not a good idea to deploy your production application using the demonstration digital certificates that are provided for development purposes. The sample certificates are not secure enough for production deployments. Do not use the demonstration digital certificates included with the WebLogic Server in your production deployments.

By default, WebLogic Server supports one-way SSL authentication. In this model, the client can remain anonymous while the server is authenticated. Most Internet applications are deployed using one-way authentication, since the broad distribution of digital certificates can be impractical. In one-way SSL authentication, the Web browser embeds a digital certificate from a certificate authority such as VeriSign. Via the Administration Console, you can also configure WebLogic to enforce two-way authentication.

> **Note:** In most real world Web applications, only password-based authentication is used for the servers to authenticate a given user's identity. On the other hand, consumers want to be assured they are sending their credit card and personal information to a secure site. Digital certificates are used to authenticate servers to users when servers are handling sensitive information.

WebLogic Server 8.1 Security and Web Services

Many of the new features of WebLogic Server 8.1 involve support for Web Services. Included in these features is the ability to secure Web Services applications. There are three mechanisms for securing Web Services applications: transport security, role-based security, and message security. The transport level of security addresses the HTTP connection itself, used by Web Services SOAP messages for communication. Transport security is implemented using basic authentication, such as username and password, and data privacy using one-way or two-way SSL. Securing the application involves defining specific roles and policies via the roles-required, roles-referenced, and run-as modes.

The third level for Web Services security involves securing the messages and XML payloads. This release of WebLogic Server includes an implementation of the draft WS-Security specification. The Oasis Security Technical Committee is responsible for defining the WS-Security specification, which leverages existing security technology to deliver an interoperable, flexible security model for Web Services applications. WS-Security is at this time still a draft specification, but the specification provides a basic framework to begin building secure Web Services applications. This specification leverages secure tokens for authentication and authorization, and enforces message confidentiality via XML encryption and message integrity using XML Signature. We cover the topic of securing Web Services in more detail in Appendix A, "*Web Services.*"

In addition, WebLogic Server 8.1 also supports other mechanisms for securing Web Services applications. *Security Access Markup Language* (SAML) is an XML framework for exchanging authentication and authorization information across Web services applications. A key advantage to SAML is interoperability: you can share security information across otherwise disparate technologies. By default, WebLogic Server supports only two token types: username and X.509. Although SAML is not currently one of the token types supported in WebLogic Server 8.1, a custom identity assertion provider can be developed to support additional token types, such as SAML or Kerberos. As noted above, more information on securing Web Services can be found in Appendix A.

Web Application Security

Authentication is the process of validating the identity of the user or service making a request. Most Web applications enforce a simple username and password model to prove the identity of the browser's user. You can represent the security architecture for a Web application using either **declarative security**, where the information is specified in deployment descriptors, or **programmatic security**, where the security information is embedded within the application itself. When using declarative security, there are three primary ways to implement user authentication:

- Form-based authentication, which uses Web forms to collect the authentication information and pass it to WebLogic Server.
- Client-certificate authentication, which uses two-way or mutual authentication to verify the identity of the client using a client-side certificate.
- Browser-based authentication, which incorporates HTTP authentication methods to log users into the WebLogic Server environment.

The remainder of this section focuses on the declarative security model for securing Web applications.

Declarative Security

The declarative security model leverages deployment descriptors (*web.xml* and *weblogic.xml*) to express an application's security structure, including roles, access control, and authentication requirements. The information in the deployment descriptors maps the application's logical security requirements to its runtime representation. At runtime, the servlet container uses the security policy to enforce authentication.

The following deployment descriptor fragments define and map the role `web-users` in a Web application to the principal (group or username) that is stored in WebLogic Server. The following is part of a *web.xml* deployment descriptor:

```
<security-role>
     <role-name>web-users</role-name>
</security-role>

<security-constraint>
     <web-resource-collection>
          <web-resource-name>Success</web-resource-name>
          <url-pattern>/welcome.jsp</web-resource-name>
```

```
        <http-method>GET</http-method>
        <http-method>PUT</http-method>
    </web-resource-collection>
    <auth-constraint>
        <role-name>web-users</role-name>
    </auth-constraint>
</security-constraint>
```

The next section of the deployment descriptor sets a constraint on a resource in the Web application. In this case, a restriction on two types of HTTP access methods, GET and POST, is placed on the Java Server Page (JSP) page *welcome.jsp*, which is located at the root of the Web application.

This security role is mapped to a corresponding role in WebLogic Server. A principal can be mapped to either a WebLogic Server user or a WebLogic Server group in the declarative security entry in the deployment descriptor.

Declarative Security Scenarios

There are two possible scenarios for what happens in a Web application when a user attempts to access a restricted resource. Remember, the server handles the login and security checking automatically. The following processes happen behind the scenes:

- Group match—If you have mapped a security role in your Web application to a WebLogic Server group, WebLogic Server checks the group of the calling principal. If the principal's group matches the group in the security role, the principal is allowed access.
- Principal match—If you have mapped a security role in your Web application to a single user in WebLogic Server, the username of the calling principal is checked. If there is a match with the username in the security role, the calling principal is allowed access.

HTTP Authentication Types

When configuring a Web application with declarative security, the first decision is whether the resources are to be protected. If not, there is no reason to define any security constraints. However, for Web access to most applications, user validation is necessary and required. The next decision is then to decide the HTTP authentication method. There are three different types of authentication supported: **Basic or Password**, **Form**, and **Client-Cert**. The following examines each approach:

- **Basic**—The simplest form of HTTP authentication, the Basic or Password model designates the client GUI application to prompt for the user's name and password. In the case of a browser client, the HTTP authentication dialog box is displayed. Once the user enters the name and password, this information is checked against the WebLogic Server security service and the user is allowed access to the protected servlet or JSP.
- **Form**—Form-based authentication is a refinement on the Web browser login mechanism. A customized Web form is presented to the user, prompting for a username and password. The collected information is submitted via an HTTP POST to WebLogic Server. If the information is correct and the user is authorized, the Web container automatically redirects the browser to the requested servlet or JSP. If the authentication fails, the user is directed to a specified error page.
- **Client-Cert**—If you are using two-way SSL, you can rely on the server's validation of the client identity for authentication. This model requires that both the client and server present

valid certificates as well as an identity asserter that maps the client's certificate to the corresponding username in WebLogic Server.

When using declarative security, the type of HTTP authentication is determined by setting the auth-method element within the login-config element of the *web.xml* file. In the following example, we define Form-based authentication and specify the form's login page and error page. There is more information about the Form-based authentication model in the next section.

```
<login-config>
    <auth-method>FORM</auth-method>
    <form-login-config>
        <form-login-page>/login.jsp</form-login-page>
        <form-error-page>/error.jsp</form-error-page>
    </form-login-config>
    <realm-name>auctionRealm</realm-name>
</login-config>
```

In the *web.xml* file, the difference between the Form authentication and the Basic or Client-Cert approaches is that we do not include the form-login-config element. You simply replace FORM with BASIC or CLIENT-CERT in the auth-method element.

Form-based Authentication

In Form-based authentication, the username and password are collected via a custom JSP and are automatically logged into WebLogic Server security environment. For example, if the user's name is Skip, then all subsequent calls to resources in the WebLogic Server environment are done using the principal Skip. Consequently, if the servlet that Skip invokes calls an EJB, that access is done with the user and group permissions associated with Skip.

Internally, WebLogic Server manages security by associating a security context with a given thread of execution inside the server. As this thread executes—for example, beginning with a servlet, invoking JavaBeans, calling an EJB—every piece of code is executed on behalf of the user. This allows the security context to flow with a user and security checks to be made at each step in serving the request. With Form-based authentication, this allows a single point of login for all of the WebLogic Server services that execute on behalf of a user.

It is important to note that the J2EE servlet specification defines specific form elements and actions when using the Form-based authentication model. Your form must reference the j_username and j_password form element names to identify the username and password to the Web container, and the action must be represented using the j_security_check attribute. Here is an example form element:

```
<form method="POST" action="j_security_check">
    <input type="text" name="j_username">
    <input type="text" name="j_password">
    <input type="submit" name="Login">
</form>
```

Using SSL with Web Applications

Using SSL with Web applications requires only a change to the deployment descriptor *web.xml*. Add a new element `transport-guarantee` inside the `<security constraint>` element, which defines security properties for individual Web resources. For example,

```
<user-data-constraint>
<transport-guarantee>
CONFIDENTIAL
</transport-guarantee>
</user-data-constraint>
```

The keyword `CONFIDENTIAL` specifies to WebLogic Server that the SSL protocol needs to be used. There are three options:

- `NONE` means that the application does not require any transport guarantees.
- `INTEGRAL` means that the application requires that the data sent between the client and server be sent in such a way that it can't be changed in transit.
- `CONFIDENTIAL` means that the application requires that the data be transmitted in a fashion that ensures privacy by preventing other entities from observing the contents of the transmission.

In the case of WebLogic Server, the presence of the `INTEGRAL` or `CONFIDENTIAL` flag indicates that the use of SSL is required.

SSL Security Example

To illustrate how to use SSL security, we use a simple Web application with a single servlet. WebLogic Server 8.1 includes example servlets that are fine for our purposes. We protect the servlet by defining some security constraints. The following *web.xml* file has been modified with the `transport-guarantee` element set to `CONFIDENTIAL` to show how access to the servlet can take place only when using a secure connection to the server.

```
<!DOCTYPE web-app PUBLIC "-//Sun Microsystems, Inc.//DTD Web
Application 2.3//EN" "http://java.sun.com/dtd/web-app_2_3.dtd">
<web-app>

  <display-name>SnoopServlet Web Application</display-name>
  <servlet>
    <servlet-name>SnoopServlet</servlet-name>
    <servlet-class>examples.servlets.SnoopServlet</servlet-class>
  </servlet>
  <servlet-mapping>
    <servlet-name>SnoopServlet</servlet-name>
    <url-pattern>/SnoopServlet/*</url-pattern>
  </servlet-mapping>
  <security-role>
      <role-name>web-user</role-name>
  </security-role>
```

```
<security-constraint>
    <web-resource-collection>
        <web-resource-name>Success</web-resource-name>
        <url-pattern>/SnoopServlet/*</url-pattern>
        <http-method>GET</http-method>
        <http-method>PUT</http-method>
    </web-resource-collection>
    <auth-constraint>
        <role-name>web-user</role-name>
    </auth-constraint>
    <user-data-constraint>
        <transport-guarantee>
            CONFIDENTIAL
        </transport-guarantee>
    </user-data-constraint>
</security-constraint>

</web-app>
```

Note that this *web.xml* is virtually identical to a nonsecured *web.xml* with the exception of the CONFIDENTIAL transport guarantee. Also, the above security constraints apply only to the path /SnoopServlet in the Web application. All other URL requests are handled without SSL required.

To test the example, load the following URL in your browser: *http://localhost:7001/examplesWebApp/SnoopServlet*. You can view the servlet output on the screen. However, remember that only the *https://localhost:7002/examplesWebApp/SnoopServlet* path is protected by SSL. When you try to access this resource, you will receive an error message indicating you need an SSL connection to access this resource.

WebLogic Server listens for responses to SSL requests on a different port from incoming requests, typically 7002. To view a response, you must use the SSL port number and the protocol *https*. Type the following URL to view the SSL response: *https://localhost:7002/examplesWebApp/SnoopServlet*.

You will now be prompted to accept a new site certificate. Figure 13–5 illustrates this prompt. Remember, your Web browser needs to have the certificate authority information in order to validate a certificate. The demonstration certificates included with WebLogic Server are not signed by a certificate authority, which means they are not recognized by the browser. For development purposes, this is acceptable. However, for production applications, you should acquire an enterprise digital certificate from a certificate authority such as VeriSign.

You should be able to click to a browser-based security window in which you can enter a username and password to log in and view the servlet. The username and password must be previously defined and granted permission to access the servlet in the Administration Console. Once you have entered a known username and password, you will see the output of the SnoopServlet example application. See Figure 13–6 for the output from the SnoopServlet servlet.

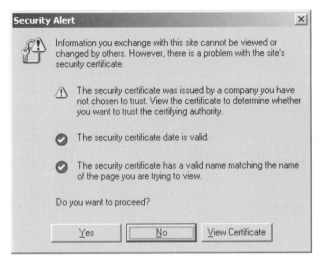

Figure 13–5
Prompt to accept the new site certificate.

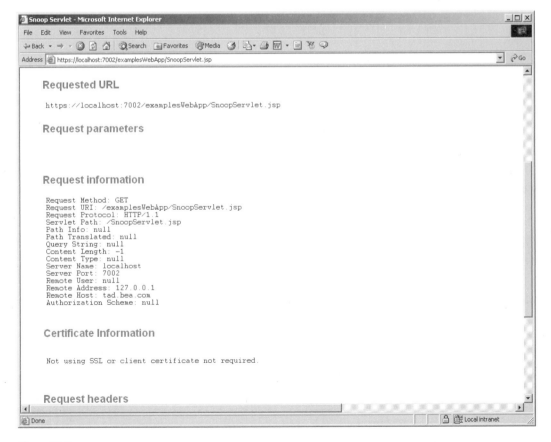

Figure 13–6
Output from the SnoopServlet servlet.

Administering WebLogic Server 8.1 Security

A key advantage of the security architecture within WebLogic Server 8.1 is that it shifts the responsibility of enforcing security from the application developer to the administrator. Past releases of WebLogic Server required the application developer to program security directly in the application itself. For example, restricting customer service representatives to only access an application between the hours of 8:00 a.m. and 5:00 p.m. requires extensive coding within the application itself. Beginning in WebLogic Server 7.0, the new security architecture removes this burden from the developer and places it on the administrator. Shifting this responsibility delivers a number of key advantages:

- Finer-grained control over access to all WebLogic and custom-developed resources.
- Increased reuse of application components in a variety of scenarios without coding changes.
- Security interfaces within the Administrative Console allow changes to be made dynamically without requiring expensive code maintenance.
- Flexible integration with third-party security service providers.
- Lower costs of system configuration and management.

The following sections describe how to secure various WebLogic resources; create users, groups, security roles, and policies; and customize the default security realm.

Configuring Security in WebLogic Server 8.1

WebLogic Server 8.1 includes a default security configuration, including a default security realm, authentication, authorization, identity assertion, role mapping, and credential mapping providers. To get started, you simply need to create users, groups, and security roles for the realm and create policies to protect the WebLogic resources in the domain. These steps can be implemented by updating the corresponding deployment descriptors for each of the resources (for example, for EJBs you would update the `ejb-jar.xml` and the `weblogic-ejb-jar.xml` descriptor files) or by using the realm node of the WebLogic Administrative Console.

Start the Administrative Console and select the *Realms* node.

Select *Create a new Realm*, or select *myRealm*, to modify the default realm. In this example, select *Create* and enter the realm name *auctionRealm*. See Figure 13–7.

For a new realm, you can select *None* or decide whether to control authorization explicitly (select *All Web applications and* EJBs in the dropdown) or control it by deferring to the corresponding deployment descriptors (select *Web Applications and* EJBs *protected in* DD). In this example, we explicitly set authorization.

Click *Create* to save the Auction Realm.

You can now manage the user, groups, and roles that will be part of your newly created realm. Before you begin adding users, you must associate an authentication provider for your newly created realm.

Select the *Providers* pane, then the *Authentication* pane, and then select the *Configure a new Default Authenticator...* node. See Figure 13–8.

Here you can change the behavior of the default authenticator, including the name and minimum password length, as well as set a control flag from the pull-down list. The options for the control flag are `Required`, `Requisite`, `Sufficient`, or `Optional`, which control how the results of the authentication request affect the overall authentication process. Higher levels, such as `Required` or `Requisite`, are appropriate for production systems but may be too restrictive for development environments. Set the name of the realm's authenticator to auctionAuthenticator.

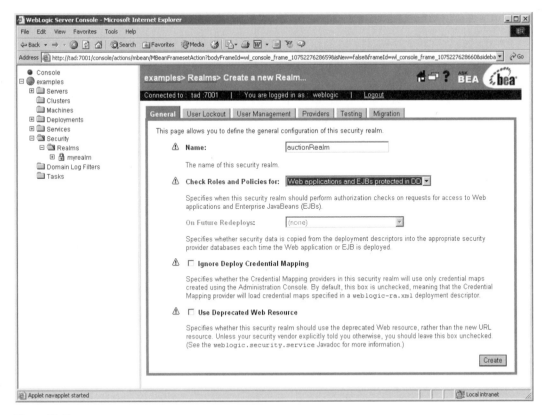

Figure 13–7
Create the auctionRealm.

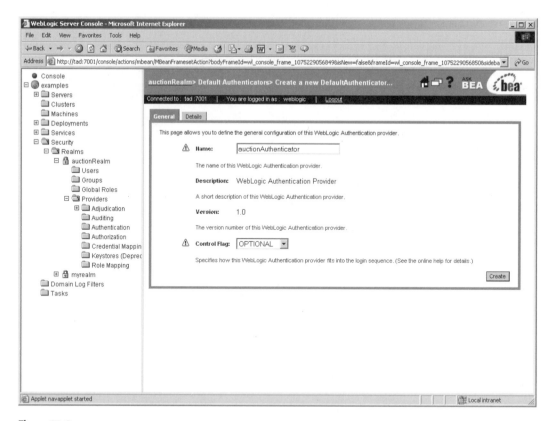

Figure 13–8
Configure a new default authenticator.

There are similar steps required to specify a Role Mapper, Authorizer, and Credential Mapper. Follow the default settings, using the auction name, to create each of these components for the auctionRealm. (If you decided to simply use the default realm instead of creating a new realm, these steps are already completed for you). Figures 13–9 through 13–11 illustrate each of these steps.

Now, select the *User Management* pane and select the *Manage Users within this Security Realm* node. The list of known users will be found here. In our example, the only current user known is weblogic. Select the node *Configure a new User....*

You can now enter the user's ID, a short description, and the initial password setting. Refer to Figure 13–12 for an example. Let's create a few users for access to the WebAuction application.

The next screen allows you to assign the new user to a group or set of groups. Remember to click *Apply* to make sure changes to the user's account are archived in the user store (by default, this repository is the embedded LDAP store).

Now you can create roles for your newly created security realm or reuse the default roles by associating the users or groups to whom you grant access to the service. In the WebAuction example, we create a role, *auction_user*, that all created users will belong to.

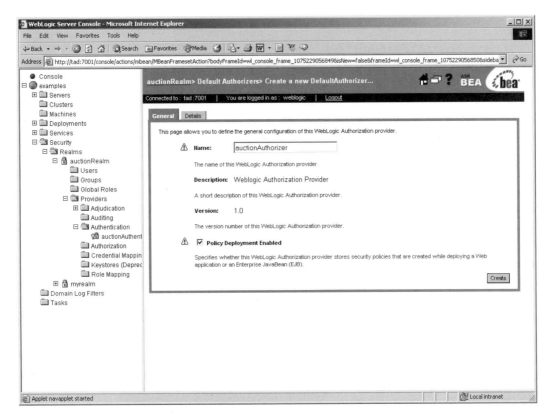

Figure 13–9
Configure a default role mapper.

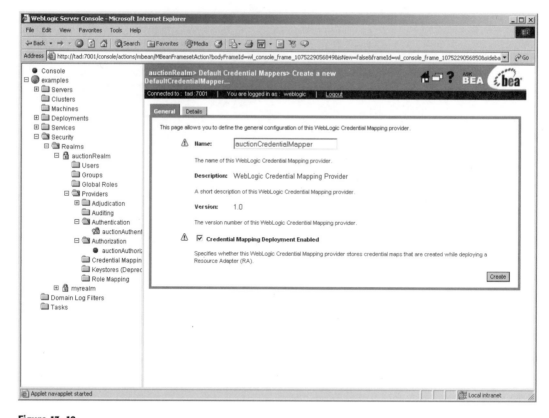

Figure 13–10
Configure a default authorizer.

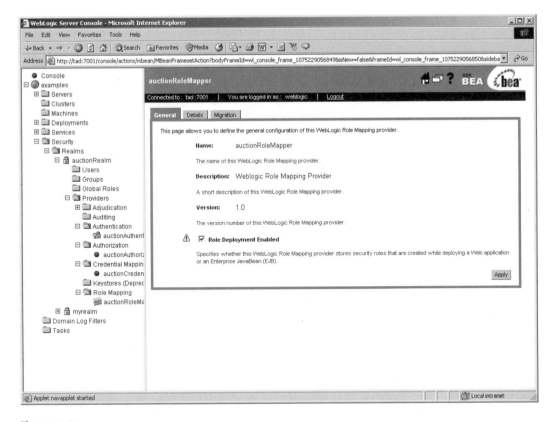

Figure 13–11
Configure a default credential mapper.

Figure 13–12
Create a new auction user.

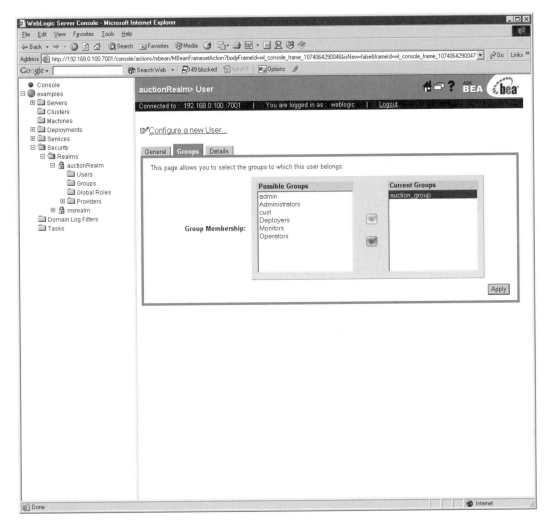

Figure 13–13
Associate users with groups for access to the Auction application.

Once you have created a role for our auction users, it is time to protect that resource via a security policy. The policy associates the WebLogic resource with a user, group, or security role and defines who has access to that resource. In our case, we define a policy indicating that the auction_user role, which applies to all users, has access to the WebAuction application resource. Figures 13–14 and 13–15 illustrate associating the user with a role and the security policy wizard. Refer to the BEA documentation at *http://edocs.bea.com/wls/docs81/secwlres/sec_poly.html* for more information about configuring security policies.

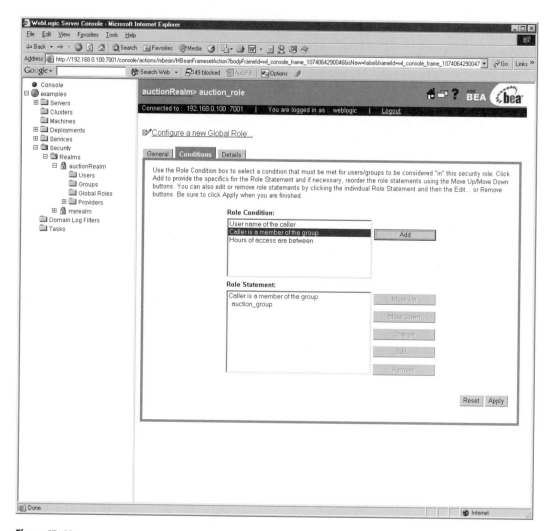

Figure 13–14
Configuring security policies.

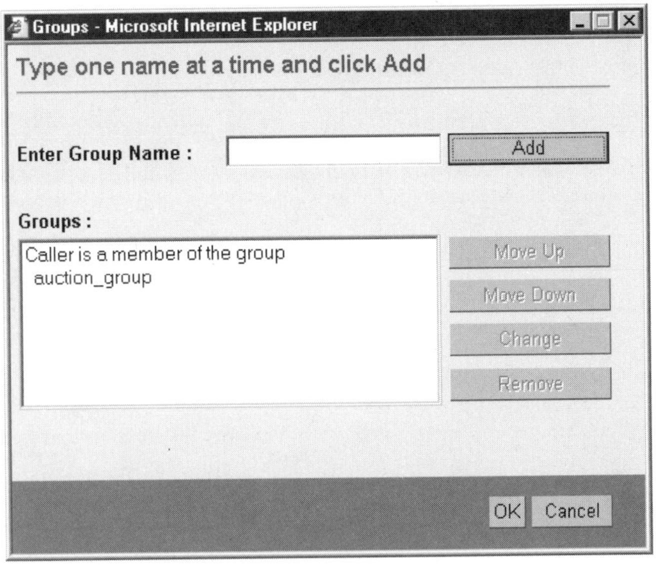

Figure 13–15
Role creation wizard.

At this point, we have configured users and groups, created a role for them, and created a security policy controlling who has access to our WebAuction application. To validate the realm's configuration, you can select the *Test Realm Configuration* tab. If everything is configured correctly, you will see a screen similar to that shown in Figure 13–16. Although this example has been fairly simplistic, the intention is to show you the console's GUI configuration support. For more information on the powerful security configuration support, refer to the online administration console help in the BEA documentation at *http://edocs.bea.com/wls/docs81/ConsoleHelp/security_7x.html*.

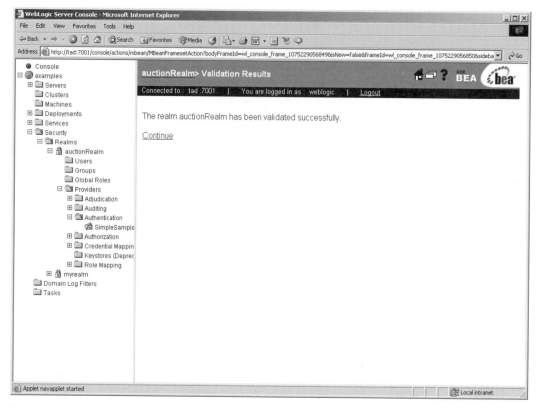

Figure 13–16
Testing the new auction realm.

WebLogic Server Security Best Practices

A number of key actions are required to ensure that a production application is properly secured. Follow these best practices to ensure a successful deployment of your security configuration and application.

Review the Documentation

The WebLogic Server 8.1 product documentation includes a section entitled "Securing Your WebLogic Server Deployment." This helpful document steps through all of the considerations for creating a secure deployment of WebLogic Server. The best practice is to consult this document and follow the instructions outlined there before deploying your applications into production.

Have Your Deployment and Code Reviewed

It is very helpful to have reviews of both the deployment architecture and application code for security holes. For large enterprises, it might be beneficial to engage an outside firm to do a security audit of both your deployment and application design. For institutions that do not have as many resources, peer reviews can be helpful as well. In these reviews, another developer reviews the application code and deployment configuration for possible security vulnerabilities.

Study Encryption and Digital Certificates

Administrators and developers of WebLogic Server applications should take the time to understand how digital certificates work in the context of a secure WebLogic Server deployment. For example, one of the greatest mistakes made is using the demonstration digital certificates that are provided with WebLogic Server. These certificates are used only for development and do not provide sufficient security for production deployments. A best practice is to not use the demonstration digital certificates included with WebLogic Server in your production deployment.

Determine Points of Risk

Securing distributed applications is a matter of determining where the risks are and providing appropriate levels of security in these areas. The analogy often used is to consider distributed system security like layers of an onion. Each layer of security must be peeled back to access the underlying parts of the application. The key is to make the level of difficulty to peel back a layer greater than the gain to be achieved.

For applications exposed to the Internet, you must use firewalls, routers, encryption, and application authentication and authorization to prevent hackers from accessing underlying areas of the application. For some applications, this may mean segregating the servlets and JSPs onto a separate tier of WebLogic Server instances from the cluster of instances hosting EJBs and JMS and providing access to existing systems. Between these tiers there may also be a separate firewall. There may be a small cost to pay in overall application performance due to the extra network latency, but the security benefits outweigh these costs.

Putting It All Together

In a typical WebLogic Server application, all of the following security technologies will be utilized in some fashion to create a secure deployment:

- Usernames, passwords, digital certificates, and other forms of authentication are stored in the embedded LDAP store and validated using the authentication provider.
- Once an identity has been authenticated, roles and policies are consulted to determine if the identity is authorized to access the requested resource.
- Single sign-on solutions are implemented using the additional information included in the authenticated principal, leveraging the identity assertion provider.
- Changes to the configuration can be made using the Security settings tab of the Administrative Console.

Additional information about securing deployed applications can be found in Chapter 14, *"Designing the Production Deployment."*

chapter 14

Designing the Production Deployment

This chapter details sample configurations and best practices for properly designing a WebLogic deployment for an e-commerce application such as our WebAuction example. You will find a review of the various deployment scenarios most often confronted in enterprises today, sample configurations for these deployments, and a review of WebLogic JRockit, a highly scalable Java Virtual Machine (JVM). This chapter describes and illustrates the following:

- WebLogic JRockit—We review the optimized, server-side JVM packaged with WebLogic Server 8.1 and WebLogic Platform 8.1. JRockit provides a scalable, reliable JVM for Intel-based machines.
- A variety of WebLogic deployment scenarios.
- A sample WebLogic deployment configuration for each deployment scenario.
- A review of the WebLogic clustering architecture.
- Best practices for deploying WebLogic Server applications.

As you move from development and testing of a new WebLogic Server application to production deployment on one or more WebLogic Servers, you create a *design for deployment*. WebLogic Server applications can be deployed in a variety of environments. The WebLogic Server product suite runs on many different platforms and supports many types of clients: Web browsers, Web Services, C++ applications, and Java applications. For each type of client, the WebLogic Server container provides a complete set of standard services such as messaging, transactions, and dynamic Web page generation. Both front-end and back-end components can be clustered to help assure performance, scalability, and reliability.

Using WebLogic Server's Java 2 Enterprise Edition (J2EE) implementation and extensions, WebLogic Server developers can build customized solutions for their unique mix of platforms and clients. However, WebLogic Server's support of mix-and-match platform and client deployments adds to the challenge of designing a scalable and robust deployment. This means that developers must follow good design principles.

Rather than detailing the specific "how to's" for deploying the WebAuction application (we do that in Chapter 15), this chapter gives the developer a general picture of how to plan for a successful WebLogic Server deployment and illustrates standard deployments with case studies.

Designing for Deployment

The successful deployment of an application should be one of the first design considerations, not the last. Once you know the basic functionality of an application, you should create a separate architecture sketch for the application as deployed into your customer base.

Deployment architecture specification details should include the following:

- Types of clients
- Types of server hardware and OS platforms
- Types of JVMs
- Available database management systems (DBMSs)
- Network configuration
- Expected number of users
- Expected volume of transactions
- Security requirements

Planning for deployment is not an idle exercise. Before your application "goes live" before a worldwide audience of thousands, you need to know that your application will continue to perform well as loads increase. You may code, configure, and test a prototype in a single-user, high-performance, development environment; however, you should also consider the real-world requirements of the deployed application. Without a reproducible cycle of development, testing, staging, and deployment, complete with repeatable processes, you risk destabilizing a production environment.

Now that we've reviewed the stages of deployment, from development to production, let's consider a few deployment scenarios.

WebLogic JRockit

The vision behind Java is to provide platform independence for applications. It allows you to write the application once and deploy it on other hardware platforms without requiring costly code modifications. In its infancy, this platform neutrality came at a price in raw execution speed. However, with time this price has grown smaller and smaller. Products like WebLogic JRockit 8.1 provide a scalable, reliable, high-performing execution engine for deploying enterprise scale applications.

WebLogic JRockit is a JVM optimized for server-side applications and for interprocess scalability. BEA designed JRockit specifically for Intel environments running Windows and Linux operating systems. It supports both 32-bit and 64-bit Intel architectures, fully utilizing the additional address space available. Java applications are reliant on the underlying virtual machine and perform based on how well the JVM handles code generation, garbage collection, memory and thread management, and native methods. Originally designed in 1998, WebLogic JRockit delivers an optimized virtual machine designed to exploit the available hardware resources, using adaptive code generation, advanced garbage collection, optimized code execution, and a robust management framework for profiling and tuning.

Compilation Options

JRockit provides two means for optimizing the compiled Java code into native execution. The first mechanism is a just-in-time (JIT) compiler that compiles during server startup. Server-side applications rely on fast execution; however, most JVMs are designed for faster startup and only interpret the Java bytecode, waiting to compile into native code until they are requested. JRockit precompiles every class as it loads via the JIT compiler. Although start times are somewhat longer, this cost is amortized over time and the overall result is much faster execution times.

The second area where JRockit provides superior performance is in the optimizing compiler. While compiling all classes with all available optimizations would take too long during server startup, WebLogic JRockit identifies the frequently used methods and runs these through a second, optimizing compiler. By fully optimizing only those functions that will deliver maximum application performance, JRockit provides optimal application performance while still maintaining acceptable server startup times.

How does JRockit recognize what functions warrant the optimized compilation? There is a sampling thread that periodically "wakes up" and checks the status of the various threads executing within the application. The information is recorded and, based on internal heuristics, JRockit determines which threads or functions should be earmarked for optimization. Many functions are never optimized for the life of the server. Typically, these optimizations are done shortly after the server starts, with fewer and fewer optimizations taking place the longer the server runs.

Garbage Collection

A second area of optimization for WebLogic JRockit is in garbage collection. Java applications allocate memory on a heap, and when the heap is full, it must be harvested, freeing up stale objects and other memory no longer in use. The process of harvesting the heap is known as *garbage collection*. While a server is garbage collecting, the application performance is impacted, since the virtual machine cannot dedicate itself to execution only. You can increase the size of the heap, allowing more objects to be allocated and garbage collection to occur less frequently, but the price you pay is in longer garbage collection times. A tuned garbage collection model allows optimal heap usage while minimizing the impact of the garbage collection on application performance. Lastly, the application design has a significant impact on the most optimal garbage collection scheme; garbage collection that performs well for one application may negatively affect performance in another.

To address these needs, WebLogic JRockit supports four different garbage collectors:

- Generational copying—In this model, the memory is separated into two or more areas called *generations*. Instead of allocating all objects into a single space and garbage collecting it all at once, objects are allocated into the new generation called the *nursery*. This model is best suited to small heap sizes on single CPU machines.
- Single-spaced concurrent—This collector uses the entire heap and removes pauses completely by executing concurrently with application processing. While the application is executing, a background thread is harvesting the heap. This model is best suited for garbage collection without disrupting server execution; however, there is a risk if the garbage collection thread cannot harvest the heap as fast as the application places new objects on it.
- Generational concurrent—This collector combines the approaches of the first two. New objects are allocated to the new generation, which is garbage collected by "stopping the world" and pausing execution. Active objects in the new generation are moved to a separate generation called the *old generation*. Garbage collection of the old generation follows the con-

current model, with a background thread harvesting concurrently with execution and not causing execution pauses.

- Parallel—In this model, all garbage collection is performed in "stop the world" mode, pausing all execution while garbage collection takes place. Multiple threads are used for the harvesting, and although there are execution pauses, this model maximizes throughput and memory utilization.

By default, JRockit uses the generational concurrent collection model. The garbage collection model right for your application depends on a number of variables. The ideal model is to minimize the impact of garbage collection, determined by the number of times garbage collection is run and the duration of each run. However, if the application has constraints around response time and cannot tolerate execution pauses, one of the concurrent models may the best choice.

Configuring the garbage collector is done by setting the `-Xgc <collector type>` parameter when starting the JVM. Valid collector types are `gencopy`, `singlecon`, `gencon`, and `parallel`. In addition, you can set the initial and maximum heap sizes using the flags `-Xms <heap size>` and `-Xmx <heap size>` parameters. When using the generational models, you can also control the size of the new generation using the `-Xns <heap size>` parameter. For example, to start JRockit using the generational concurrent collector with an initial and maximum heap size of 512MB and a new generation size of 256MB, you would use the following command:

```
java -jrockit -Xgc:gencon -Xms512m -Xmx512m -Xns256m …
```

Tuning the garbage collection with WebLogic JRockit can deliver optimal performance for your application. However, it is a good idea to consult BEA's documentation before making changes to any of the JVM parameters, as these changes can also result in penalizing your application performance as well. Refer to *http://e-docs.bea.com/wljrockit/docs81/tuning/index.html* for more information on tuning JRockit.

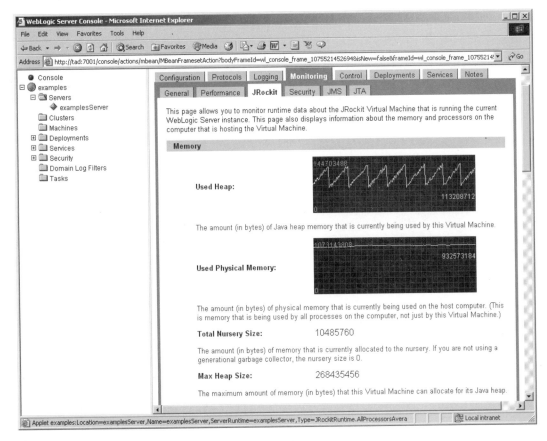

Figure 14–1
JRockit management console and memory utilization.

JVM Management and Monitoring

A key capability in tuning your application for optimal performance is identifying the behavior occurring in the underlying JVM. WebLogic JRockit includes useful tools for profiling and tuning the JVM performance. JRockit includes a management console for observing real-time information about server and resource utilization. This console can be run standalone or accessed using the WebLogic Server Administration Console. Through information presented in the console, you can identify bottlenecks to performance and change operating and environment variables to deliver maximum performance. Figures 14–1, 14–2, and 14–3 illustrate all the information the JRockit graphical console presents to the administrator.

JRockit 8.1 also supports the JVM Profiling Interface (JVMPI) and the JVM Debugging Interface (JVMDI), allowing Java applications to interact with the JVM and assist in profiling and debugging activities. This is particularly useful when using third-party tools designed to comply with these standard interfaces.

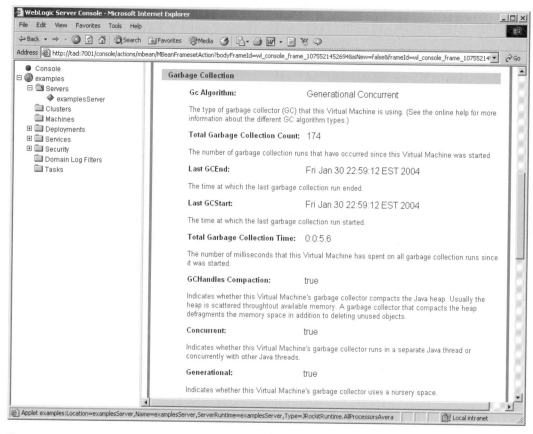

Figure 14–2
JRockit console and garbage collection settings.

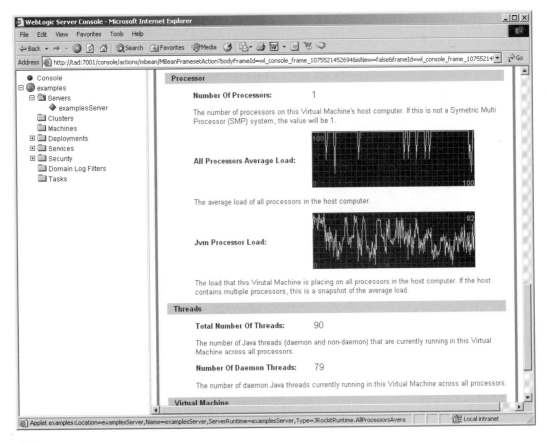

Figure 14–3
JRockit console and processor utilization.

WebLogic Deployment Scenarios: Case Studies

WebLogic deployment architectures can be differentiated according to the following:

- The types of client software that connect to WebLogic Server
- The degree of clustering required for WebLogic Server instances
- The use of servlets and Java Server Pages (JSPs) with Enterprise JavaBeans (EJBs) in the same cluster
- The use of ervlets and JSPs with EJBs in separate clusters
- Deployment of WebLogic Server's native Web server as the front-end to the Internet
- Deployment of a third-party Web server such as SunOne/iPlanet, Apache, or Microsoft Internet Information Server (IIS) in front of WebLogic Server

We discuss these deployment possibilities in the following sections.

Types of Client Software

Clients in a WebLogic Server deployment can be

- Web deployments (clients are Web browsers)
- Application deployments (clients are applications)
- Mixed deployments (clients are both Web browsers and applications)

Web deployments and mixed deployments are the most common scenarios for production systems. The WebAuction application is a mixed deployment.

Web Deployments: A Standard Configuration

A Web deployment of WebLogic Server is one in which the client software accesses WebLogic Server on the Internet using the protocols (such as HTTP and HTTPS) of the World Wide Web. In most cases, a Web browser is used for the presentation of HTML-encoded information on the end user's machine.

Web deployments are the preferred deployment style when you do not have control over the client hardware accessing the application. The beauty of the Web is that the ubiquitous Web browser enables you to build systems that do not require client code on every machine that accesses your site. Yet, you can still have rich presentation in user interfaces using an open Internet standard such as HTML.

The basic Web deployment architecture begins with the connection to the Internet. In most cases, this is a direct feed from an Internet service provider (ISP). This connection typically terminates to a router that has Ethernet capability. Client connections (typically, HTTP requests) are routed through this hardware to servers at your location.

You have a deployment decision to make: whether to use a commercial Web server or WebLogic Server as the Web server.

Web Deployment Scenario 1: Commercial Web Server

WebLogic Server provides customers with the option to integrate with standard Internet Web servers such as Apache, SunOne Enterprise Server, or Microsoft IIS. WebLogic Server is distributed with modules that can plug in to these different Web servers. In this scenario, you configure the *proxy plug-in* to recognize HTTP requests with a relative path that includes a WebLogic Server object in the URL and forward those requests to a remote WebLogic Server instance. The remote server instance is configured in the proxy plug-in itself via the appropriate means. The plug-ins can also work by file extension or content type. For example, you can set the plug-in to forward all JSPs to WebLogic Server while the third-party Web server handles everything else.

The WebLogic Server HTTP Server plug-ins fully support the proxy capability in the `Http-ClusterServlet` described later in the section "Using WebLogic Server Clustering in a Mixed Deployment." Figure 14-4 shows a cluster of WebLogic Servers residing behind a Web server containing the HTTP server plug-in.

Requests made to the Web server are forwarded to WebLogic Server if appropriate. Other requests can be handled directly by the Web server.

No matter what components you choose for your deployment configuration, WebLogic Server provides a means of integration. In the case of SunOne/iPlanet, WebLogic Server can share the same store of users and groups in a Lightweight Directory Access Protocol (LDAP) repository. WebLogic Server also can integrate with Active Directory domains, ensuring security information is not duplicated in multiple stores (see Figure 14-5).

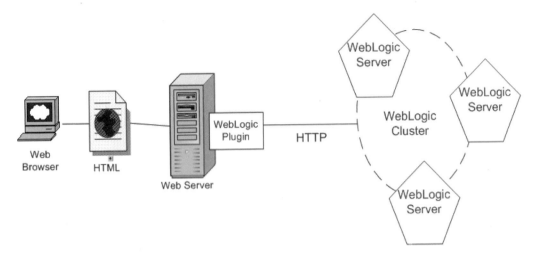

Figure 14-4
A cluster of WebLogic Servers residing behind a Web server.

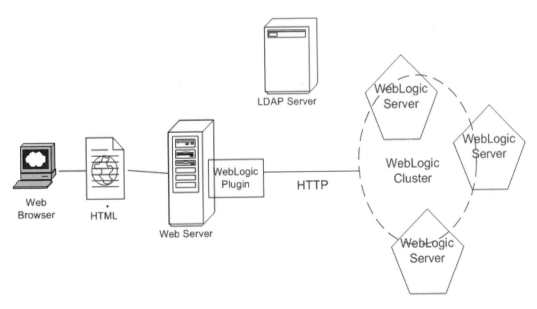

Figure 14-5
WebLogic Server residing behind a Web server with a shared security store.

Scenario 2: Using WebLogic Server as the Web Server

Although BEA WebLogic Server integrates well with commercial Web servers, you also can use WebLogic Server itself as the HTTP server for enterprise deployments. Features of WebLogic Server that support this include the following:

- *Native code acceleration for static file serving.* Version 8.1 of WebLogic Server takes full advantage of native operating system calls to optimize file serving. In virtually all cases, WebLogic Server is equivalent to a commercial Web server in static file-serving performance for a single user. WebLogic Server also is generally more scalable because it takes advantage of Java's threading architecture.
- *Advanced Web server virtual hosting.* Virtual hosting is the ability to host multiple domains on a single instance of a Web server. Therefore, a single Web server can host *www.domain2.com* and *www.domain1.com* without having to have a separate Web server for each domain name.
- *Advanced Web server LDAP integration and cryptography.* WebLogic Server 8.1 also includes an embedded LDAP server to ease integration with external LDAP environments and cryptographic acceleration for Secure Sockets Layer (SSL) communication.
- *Integration with a number of the Web routers used in enterprise-scale Web deployments.* It is possible to deploy a cluster of WebLogic Servers and take advantage of all advanced functionality without needing to use one of the WebLogic Server proxy plug-ins.

> **Best Practice:** Integrating with a third-party Web server should be considered when a legacy Web server deployment already exists in an enterprise. Otherwise, you should consider using WebLogic Server as the Web server, since it allows for a simple, easy-to-maintain deployment.

Using a DMZ and Firewalls in a Web Deployment

Most secure Web deployments involve the use of a demilitarized zone (DMZ) for greater security. A DMZ is a protected network that is isolated from the internal corporate network.

A Web architecture utilizing a DMZ is the preferred structure for a Web deployment of WebLogic Server. Figure 14–6 shows the components of this architecture.

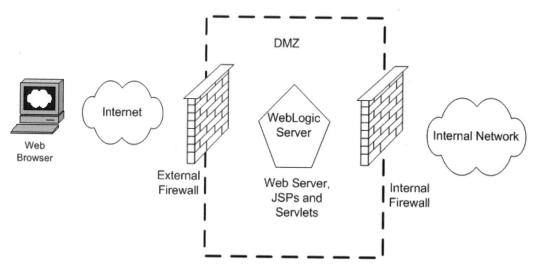

Figure 14–6
A DMZ deployment of WebLogic Server.

Client requests arrive from the Internet and are routed through firewall 1. This firewall is configured to support only HTTP connections originating from the Internet. WebLogic Server receives requests, processes them, and then responds directly. All of these components are connected via a standard LAN.

Best Practice: A DMZ should be considered for secure production WebLogic Server deployments.

Although an architecture that includes a DMZ is suitable for basic e-commerce deployments of WebLogic Server, a more complex architecture using WebLogic Server clustering, firewalls, and other features may be required for deployments that need greater scalability and reliability. There are a variety of approaches when leveraging the additional capabilities. Refer to "Hardware Specifics for Clustering" later in this chapter more other tools that can be leveraged.

Firewalls

A firewall helps guarantee Internet security. Much like a firewall in a car, firewalls on the network isolate areas of danger. Firewall products exist that address the needs of enterprise deployments; they include products by companies such as Cisco and Checkpoint down to personal firewalls from companies like Zone Labs. If you are not familiar with the mechanisms by which a firewall protects Internet resources, you should visit the Web sites of some of the leading vendors of firewall software and hardware, including Checkpoint, Symantec Axent, and Cisco.

Firewalls can be used to protect *both* the DMZ and your internal network. The DMZ is protected against non-HTTP traffic such as Telnet or other Internet protocols. In addition, a firewall can be used to segregate traffic within the DMZ from your internal network. Figure 14–7 shows how firewalls fit into the typical WebLogic Server security picture.

Best Practice: Firewalls should be as restrictive as possible. Be sure to disallow access for any protocol type or client type that is not required for your application. For example, firewalls can allow HTTP but disallow SMTP, FTP, and other Internet protocols.

Internet traffic crosses the DMZ firewall to access a WebLogic Server residing in the DMZ. The corporate network is protected by another firewall.

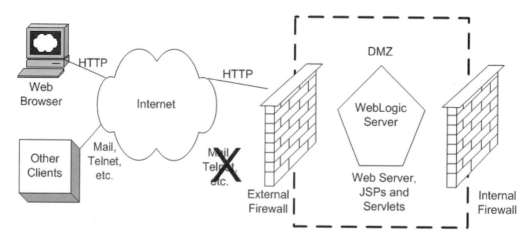

Figure 14–7
Firewalls protecting a DMZ and internal network with WebLogic Server.

Integrating Web Deployments with Data Stores

Most applications using WebLogic Server will necessarily include a data store, usually a Relational Database Management System (DBMS) such as those from Oracle, IBM, Sybase, or Informix. Using JDBC, these data stores provide deployments with the capability to execute transactions and persistently store data in a highly scalable and reliable manner. More information on how to configure WebLogic Server to use a database is included in the WebLogic Server documentation.

In a Web deployment, it is important not to expose your data store directly to the public Internet. However, this need to protect the data must be balanced with offering customers and users more convenient, more dynamic access to the data stored there. Accessing DBMS data from the Internet is typically accomplished by placing the database server on the network behind the internal firewall. Figure 14–8 shows a WebLogic Server deployment that includes a relational data store.

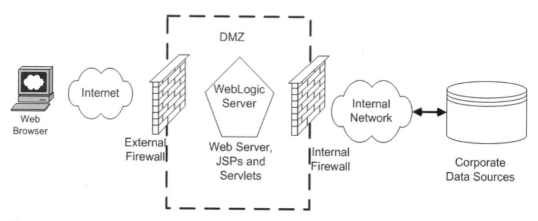

Figure 14–8
Deploying your data store with WebLogic Server in a Web deployment.

Requests from the Internet are routed to WebLogic Server. WebLogic Server relies on the data store that is located behind the internal firewall for transactional support and data storage.

> **Best Practice:** Protect your database server as much as possible by placing it behind an inner firewall.

Using WebLogic Server Clustering

For WebLogic Server's most common deployments—enterprise-scale applications deployed within an intranet or to the Internet—you must build for scalability, availability, and performance from the outset. WebLogic Server's software clustering functionality is a critical success factor in an enterprise-scale deployment of an e-commerce application. A WebLogic Server *cluster* features multiple instances of WebLogic Server pooled to provide redundant, replicated application components that are connected to one another by a local area network (LAN). Software clustering lets a number of WebLogic Servers share a network name so they can function cooperatively. Clustering is the mechanism that supports production services, including:

- *Load balancing*—Distributing work among WebLogic Servers in a cluster to most efficiently utilize available server resources.
- *Scalability*—Adding WebLogic Server instances dynamically to a cluster to increase processing capacity without interrupting service.
- *Failover and application fault-tolerance*—Transparently switching to the next WebLogic Server in a cluster when a server becomes unavailable.

The next sections provide background on the need for clustering in a distributed environment, an overview of the WebLogic Server 8.1 clustering architecture, and recommendations for utilizing clustering in an enterprise deployment. For more detailed information on WebLogic clustering, please see the WebLogic Server documentation at *http://e-docs.bea.com/wls/docs81/cluster/index.html*.

Why WebLogic Clustering?

There are a variety of benefits to distributing applications across server resources networked into a single processing unit. Distributed servers are typically less expensive and can be more flexibly deployed than "the big iron." Emerging technologies such as GRID computing provide more flexible options to most efficiently utilize the available hardware resources. As long as the application is designed properly, scalability is achieved easily by adding new servers into the pool of resources. In addition, single points of failure can be minimized or even eliminated in many environments, providing reliability to match traditional mainframe platforms.

The primary way to deliver on the reliability and scalability advantages of a distributed architecture is through pooling or grouping servers and replicating application components across these pools. Traditionally, this pooling has been implemented either (1) using software replication service, such as a transaction processing monitor like Tuxedo or an object transaction monitor in CORBA architectures, or (2) using a hardware clustering solution. Although hardware clustering delivers "hardware redundancy," it is not designed to address the unique needs of the application, such as session management, persistence, transactions, or security. With software clustering, individual servers may fail or be taken offline for maintenance, but the outage can be isolated and application traffic routed to another instance without the client or user experiencing any sort of failure.

In WebLogic Server, this pooling of resources is known as *clustering*. WebLogic clustering delivers these benefits to the J2EE application. The client views the WebLogic cluster as a single processing unit, even though the cluster is made up of multiple server machines as well as multiple instances per server machines. The client binds to an application component name, retrieved from a name service such as JNDI, and doesn't really care where the request actually executes within the cluster. In the WebLogic model, the JNDI name service offers location transparency for the application components, mapping the object's name to the explicit addresses of the clustered servers hosting the object.

Best Practice: Although hardware clustering provides failover and redundancy of hardware servers, software clustering is also required for enterprise deployments. While hardware clustering may address the fault tolerance of the hardware servers, WebLogic clustering takes into account the application's needs, such as session management, shared naming, transactions, security, and application redundancy. A best practice is to always use WebLogic clustering even when leveraging hardware clustering solutions.

WebLogic Clustering Architecture

Within the WebLogic clustering model, there are different models to cluster Web components, application components, and server resources. The reason is that each of these services is invoked differently. An HTTP request to a servlet or JSP is invoked from a browser, whereas an EJB is called from a richer, more robust client that allows more clustering functionality. We briefly review each of the mechanisms for utilizing WebLogic clustering.

Web Applications

Since Web applications—servlets and JSPs—are invoked by loading a URL into a browser, any sort of clustering must be implemented on the Web container. For stateless applications, any copy of the servlet or JSP in the pool can respond to the client's request; however, stateful Web applications require a session persistence mechanism. The session information can be maintained in a browser's cookie, but this approach won't work if the user chooses to disable support for cookies within the browser.

To address this need in J2EE, the servlet specification defines the HTTP *Session Object* to maintain state on the server. WebLogic Server provides three mechanisms for storing the HTTP Session Object:

1. Persist to a relational database accessible from all servers in the cluster.
2. Persist to a file accessible from all servers in the cluster.
3. Persist to memory.

The advantage of the memory persistence model is that it greatly reduces the I/O overhead of access to the session object; the challenge is how to prevent the session object from being lost should a problem occur on the WebLogic server instance.

In a clustered Web application, requests for a URL are directed to the Web server(s). These can be a front-line of WebLogic servers or third party Web servers. If WebLogic is the Web server, then the server uses WebLogic Server's `HttpClusterServlet` to distribute requests among all the nodes in the cluster. For information on how to configure `HttpClusterServlet`, see the WebLogic Server documentation at *http://edocs.bea.com/wls/docs81/cluster/failover.html*. If you are using a third-party Web server, such as Apache, SunOne/iPlanet Enterprise Server, or Microsoft IIS, then the WebLogic HTTP proxy plug-in will distribute requests among all the nodes in the cluster.

WebLogic clustering handles session persistence in the in-memory model by implementing a process-pair. The initial server instance hosting the session object is the primary, and a secondary instance is chosen from within the cluster. The session object is then copied from the primary to the secondary. Changes made to the session object are propagated automatically to the secondary. However, whether there are two instances or 200 in the cluster, only the primary and secondary are aware of this particular session object. In the event the primary instance fails, subsequent requests are directed to the secondary instance, which becomes the primary, and a new secondary is nominated. Likewise, if there is a failure on the secondary, a new secondary is nominated. In this way, sessions are highly available while still providing good performance and without imposing architectural constraints on how large the cluster can be.

Application Components

Whereas in the Web component model, no assumptions can be made about the client, in the application component model (e.g., EJBs or RMI objects), the client invoking the EJB is leveraging RMI for communications. When clustered, WebLogic utilizes a *replica-aware stub* for balancing load and failover. This special stub is aware of all the clustered replicas of an application object. Replica-aware stubs are created when the application is compiled and do not require any cluster-specific application coding.

A key advantage of the replica-aware stub is the ability to support more robust load-balancing models. Clustered EJBs and RMI objects can be distributed using round robin, weight-based, random, round-robin affinity, weight-based affinity, and random affinity algorithms. The affinity models are new in WebLogic Server 8.1 and consider existing connections between the client and requested object for balancing load. The advantage is less network latency by reusing an existing connection when one exists rather than opening a new connection; if a connection does not exist, a new connection will be opened.

When a client invokes a method on a clustered EJB or RMI object and the server hosting the object is unavailable, the replica-aware stub catches the exception and automatically routes the request to an available replica. Load-distribution algorithms are selected for a clustered EJB or RMI object via settings in the Administration Console; the replica-aware stubs then implement the selected algorithm.

Other WebLogic Resources

WebLogic also provides ways to cluster resources provided by the server, such as JDBC connection pools and JMS destinations. For JDBC, WebLogic allows you to cluster JDBC resources, including data sources, connection pools, and multipools. When clustered, the JDBC resource must exist on each managed server within the cluster. This can be accomplished by targeting the JDBC resource to the entire cluster. JDBC data sources and connection pools allow a client making the request to retry another connection if the initial connection is not available. JDBC multipools—a pool of connection pools—deliver failover for DBMS connections across a cluster. The key in utilizing clustered access to JDBC resources is to obtain the connection to the resource from the WebLogic JNDI tree. More information about JDBC data sources, connection pools, and multipools can be found in Chapter 5. More information on clustering these resources can be found in the BEA WLS documentation at *http://e-docs.bea.com/wls/docs81/ConsoleHelp/jdbc.html#jdbc012*.

While not explicitly clustering JMS queues or topics, WebLogic does allow you to cluster JMS destinations. Clustering of multiple JMS servers is supported through transparent access to JMS destinations by any WebLogic instance across the cluster. Although WebLogic supports distributing JMS destinations and connection factories throughout a cluster, each JMS topic or queue is managed separately by the WebLogic instance on which it is deployed. Automatic failover of messages in a queue is not supported in WebLogic Server 8.1, but steps are documented for manually migrating messages to a new queue as long as these messages are kept in a persistent store such as a relational database or the filesystem.

Configuring the Network for WebLogic Clustering

Within a WebLogic Server cluster, instances communicate with each other to share information about client data and enable load balancing and redundancy. WebLogic Server nodes in a cluster communicate via *multicast*, which is a style of network communication that's like a radio broadcast—everyone tuned in to the right frequency can hear what you have to say. Each instance within the cluster is tuned to the cluster frequency and receives your message. This highly efficient protocol enables nodes in the WebLogic Server cluster to send messages addressed to all of the other nodes with updates on recent events.

Multicast uses IP (the Internet Protocol that is the part of TCP/IP) on a LAN to efficiently communicate between nodes of the cluster. Multicast does not incur the overhead that is required by TCP. TCP employs a *point-to-point* model; to use TCP in a cluster of *n* servers, each server would have to make *n* − 1 connections to the other servers, one connection for each other server in the cluster. As you can imagine, this architecture does not scale because every request causes dozens or hundreds of connections to be created and removed. This is the reason multicast is used for intercluster communications in WebLogic.

A key point is that application-to-application communication does not use multicast. When your clients go from client to server or from server to server to invoke RMI objects, access EJBs, or use WebLogic resources such as JDBC or JMS, their traffic always flows over TCP/IP and not multicast. The one exception to this rule is in the case of the Java Message Service (JMS) multicast transport, as described in Chapter 7.

Multicast Security

Because intracluster messages are circulated on a LAN via multicast, routers and bridges typically do not forward them. This makes a WebLogic Server cluster something that can exist securely inside of the DMZ (see Figure 14–9).

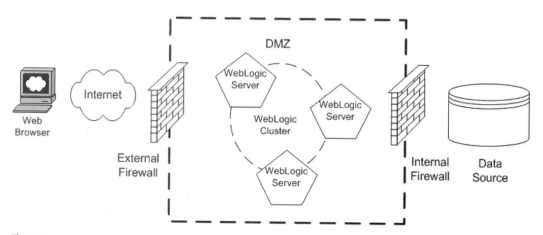

Figure 14–9
Cluster traffic within the DMZ.

Choosing the Right Network Architecture

The LAN connecting the hardware servers for the WebLogic Server cluster typically supports TCP/IP. WebLogic Server clustering relies on Internet-style addressing, including IP addresses. You should follow the instructions included in the WebLogic Server documentation for the specifics on configuring your LAN for a WebLogic Server cluster.

It is strongly recommended that you employ a high-speed network of at least 100Mbps or greater to connect the nodes in your WebLogic Server cluster. This will improve response time and minimize network latency and other problems in maintaining a stable cluster environment.

Best Practice: A higher speed network for the cluster helps to improve response times.

WebLogic Clustering with Multi-CPU Servers

You can place multiple instances of WebLogic Server on a single hardware server if you are deploying WebLogic Server on a large multi-CPU server. This optimizes communication and management of WebLogic Servers. Each instance of WebLogic Server will be treated as a unique instance, even if it is deployed on a shared server. For example, if you are deploying WebLogic Server on a four-CPU server, you can have one instance of WebLogic Server on each CPU or one instance for every two CPUs.

Clustering several WebLogic Server instances on a single machine more efficiently utilizes the underlying hardware, for example, improving the performance of the JVM. Java's automatic garbage collection, or the restoration of unused memory to the free memory space for the applications, can affect processing of application code, even in virtual machines supporting asynchronous garbage collection. The memory allocated to a JVM—called the *heap*—should be adjusted according to the application's needs. A larger heap will allow the JVM to garbage-collect less frequently, but each collection will take more time to harvest the memory.

Based on the cost of larger heaps, an efficient deployment design is to have multiple instances of WebLogic Server on a single hardware server, using the smallest heap size that you can. A minimum heap size of 256MB is a good starting point. Particularly when an application is not persisting much application state, this model maximizes the power of the underlying server resources. However, there are also cases in which a larger heap size is desirable. For example, if you have a large amount of user data that you are handling at a given time, you want to ensure that you have more memory in the typical deployment. In these cases, it can be valuable to expand the initial heap size to 384MB or even 512MB. Refer to the BEA documentation at *http://e-docs.bea.com/wls/docs81/perform/ JVMTuning.html* for more information on tuning the JVM for optimal performance.

Placing clustered instances on a single piece of hardware also reduces network overhead. If you put a 10-node cluster on 10 individual machines connected by a network, each cluster operation would require WebLogic Server to access the network. Collocated WebLogic Server instances can communicate directly without incurring the overhead of traveling across the wire to other boxes.

A good general rule is that you should have one instance of WebLogic Server for every one to two CPUs, and cluster even if deployed on a single server (see Figure 14–10).

Best Practice: For most efficient utilization of the underlying hardware, it is a best practice to cluster WebLogic Servers when deploying on multi-CPU servers.

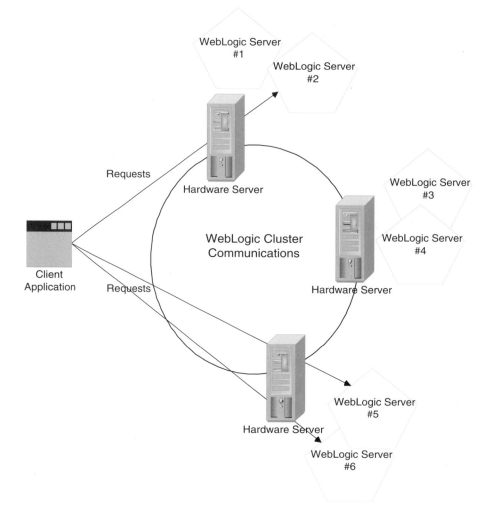

Figure 14-10
A cluster of six WebLogic Servers on three two-CPU servers

Hardware Specifics for Clustering

So far, this chapter has not discussed how other components of the network fit together with WebLogic Server in the hardware environment. Selecting these components is an important area, and one in which mistakes often are made. However, the good news is that choosing hardware for a WebLogic Server deployment and configuring it correctly is not difficult once all of the components are identified.

There are a number of components that fit together in a complete WebLogic Server deployment for the Internet:

- Internet connectivity via an Internet router

- Firewall software or hardware
- A Web router or internal Domain Name Service (DNS)
- Internal LAN infrastructure

The following sections discuss these components in detail.

Securing Internet Traffic

Firewalls are used to filter out inappropriate traffic based on a set of rules. In a WebLogic Server deployment, the first line of firewalls protects the Web servers and the load-balancing mechanisms against unwanted requests. In a typical deployment, these firewalls act as gateways to the Internet and accept Web requests only on designated ports. The methods for configuring firewalls are specific to each vendor who supplies firewalls.

In Figure 14–7, the firewalls had IP addresses that were visible to the Internet. The firewalls are then intelligent enough to route requests and distribute them among the load-balancing mechanisms. Whether this is possible or not depends upon the firewall that you choose. Whatever your architecture, the firewalls should filter out unwanted traffic and then hand off those requests to your load-balancing mechanism.

Most deployments also take advantage of another set of firewalls to protect the enterprise network. If this is an onsite deployment, the second set of firewalls typically protects traffic going from the WebLogic Server deployments to back-end resources such as the DBMS or another legacy system. In the case of a collocated deployment, this firewall may be used to access a virtual private network (VPN) that connects back to the corporate network and its legacy systems for a shared database system.

Distributing Web Traffic

After traffic passes through the firewall, the *load-balancing mechanism* for Web requests handles the distribution of Web traffic. There are four common ways to distribute load:

- *Load-balancing software integrated into the firewall.* Many firewall vendors offer software solutions that can be used with their firewalls to load-balance traffic to WebLogic Server Web servers. In most cases, this type of load balancing is only suitable for small deployments because it does not contain the advanced functionality provided by other load-balancing solutions. If you are making a small deployment of WebLogic Server, using an integrated load-balancing solution may be appropriate.
- *Hardware load balancing.* This solution is the one most commonly used by large-scale Web deployments. Vendors such as Alteon Websystems (*http://www.alteonwebsystems.com*), Cisco (*http://www.cisco.com*), and others offer hardware devices that receive Web requests and distribute those among a cluster of Web servers. These boxes typically work by having a link directly to the Internet gateway and maintain multiple links to the Web servers in the back end. With WebLogic Server 8.1, functionality such as automatic failover and load balancing is integrated directly with these machines.
- *Software load balancing not integrated in the firewall.* This solution takes advantage of TCP/IP manipulation in order to create automated load balancing and failover. It provides the same functionality as hardware load balancing, but in a software-only package. One vendor in this space is Resonate Software (*http://www.resonate.com*).
- DNS *round robin.* This is the oldest of all load-balancing techniques. A local DNS server contains a list of Web servers. Every time a request is made, the DNS server is configured to get a Web server at a different IP address. Unfortunately, there are a number of limitations to DNS round robin; therefore, it is typically not used for serious e-commerce sites. These limitations include the following:

- The load balancing is quite simple. There is no random or parameterized load-balancing algorithms possible.
- DNS is difficult to administer.
- You do not really get failover. If you look up www.foo.com and get w.x.y.z and that server goes down, then the client code will not necessarily re-look it up to failover.

The configuration of the WebLogic Server deployment depends upon which load-balancing solution is used. Because every load-balancing solution is slightly different, configuration details depend on the features of the solution that you choose.

Web Application Deployment Details

Web application deployments are the most common types of deployments for WebLogic Server. For your consideration, we present three patterns that we recommend for Web application deployments.

- The first collocates the WebLogic Server servlet and JSP services with the WebLogic Server EJB services.
- The second groups together the servlet and JSP services with the Web server tier.
- The third uses WebLogic Server as the Web server.

Collocated Front-End and Back-End Services

In this architecture, Web browsers communicate across the firewall to a Web server proxy that includes the WebLogic Server Web server plug-in. This plug-in then redirects requests to WebLogic Server instances in a cluster, which in turn rely upon the database (see Figure 14–11).

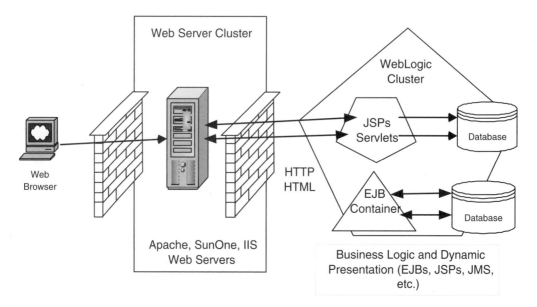

Figure 14–11
Collocated front-end and back-end services.

Web Services in the DMZ; EJB Outside

In this architecture, the Web Services in WebLogic Server are placed inside of the DMZ, with the Web servers. When a request requires that the Web Services rely upon EJB services, RMI calls are made through the firewall to the EJB container, which in turn relies upon the database (see Figure 14–12).

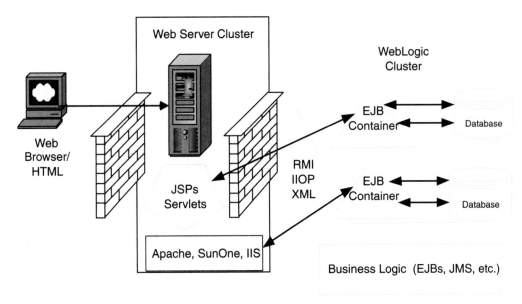

Figure 14–12
Scenario with Web Services in the DMZ and EJB outside.

Using WebLogic Server as the Web Server

In this architecture, the Web Services in WebLogic Server function as the Web server and are placed inside of the DMZ. When a request for an HTML page or a static resource such as an image or multi-media document is made, WebLogic Server responds. When a request requires that the Web Services (JSP, servlet) rely upon EJB services, RMI calls are made through the firewall to the EJB container, which in turn relies upon the database (see Figure 14–13).

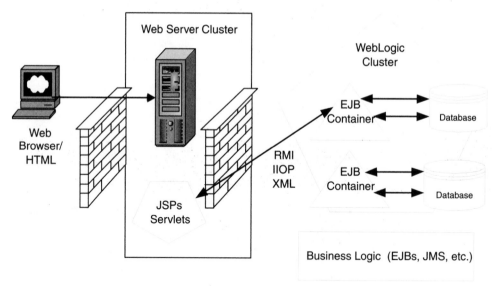

Figure 14–13
Using WebLogic Server as the Web server.

Application Deployments

Application deployments are the simplest to architect for WebLogic Server. In application deployments, the only clients that access WebLogic Server are applications. These communicate via the Java standards for RMI.

Typical Application Deployment Architecture

The typical deployment architecture for an application deployment involves two types of components: client-side applications and WebLogic Server instances. The clients communicate over a network to make requests to the WebLogic Server instances (see Figure 14–14).

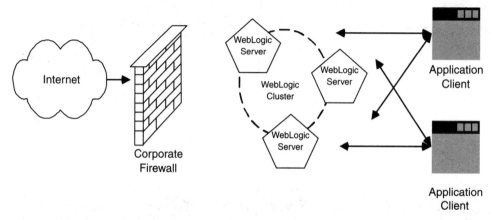

Figure 14–14
Application clients connect directly to WebLogic Server.

Security Considerations in an Application Deployment

Security is important for application deployments. Fortunately, most application deployments exist behind the corporate firewall. This means that the communication between WebLogic Server and the clients travels over a relatively secure network. Figure 14–15 shows a WebLogic Server deployment behind the corporate firewall.

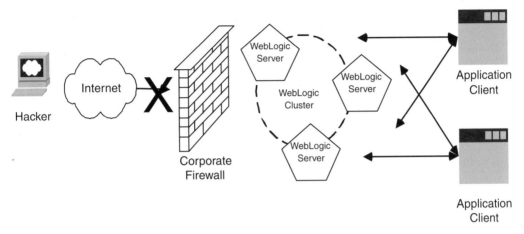

Figure 14–15
A WebLogic Server application deployment behind a corporate firewall.

If WebLogic Server network traffic will pass over an insecure network or the corporate network is not secured, you can secure the application with SSL technology.

Security does not come without a cost, because the server and client must perform resource-intensive encryption operations. WebLogic Server includes optimizations that make this SSL support have less of an impact. In most cases, a server that is not using SSL can serve 25 to 35 percent more clients than a server that is using SSL. However, this depends completely on application details, such as how often clients create new sessions with a server and similar factors.

Best Practice: Always enable SSL for WebLogic Server application clients if there is any risk of prying eyes seeing your data in transit.

Mixed Deployments

Mixed deployments are the most complex WebLogic Server configurations. These are deployments that serve both application clients and Web clients. Care must be taken to ensure security and scalability of the deployment.

Simple Mixed Deployment Architectures

The simple mixed deployment architecture consists of WebLogic Server existing inside of the corporate firewall. External clients typically access WebLogic Server via the Web interfaces across the Internet or another network. Application clients typically exist on the corporate intranet to access WebLogic Server services. Figure 14–16 shows the simple mixed deployment architecture.

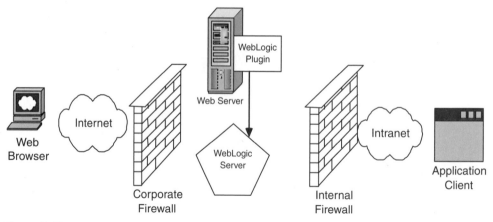

Figure 14-16
Simple mixed deployment architecture.

Note that the application clients access WebLogic Server via the corporate intranet, while external clients access WebLogic Server from the Internet. Internet clients access a Web server such as WebLogic Server, Apache, or Microsoft IIS in the DMZ. This Web server then forwards Web requests to WebLogic Server behind the internal firewall.

Using WebLogic Server Clustering in a Mixed Deployment

As in the application and Web deployments, WebLogic Server clustering is key for any scalable and reliable mixed deployment. WebLogic Server offers both Web and application services clustering with similar architecture.

Integrating with Web Services

As mentioned previously, in the simple deployment architecture, integrating Web Services is key to any mixed deployments of WebLogic Server. Because it is desirable to have WebLogic Server behind the corporate firewall, a Web Service should be enabled to forward requests that enter the Web DMZ.

Security Considerations in a Mixed Deployment

Security considerations for a mixed deployment should be a composite of the considerations used for application deployments and Web deployments. You should protect your information using SSL. You also should protect your information from access using restrictive firewalls.

Best Practice: Security for a WebLogic Server mixed deployment should include all of the security measures used for both Web and application deployments.

Recommended Mixed Deployment Architecture

The recommended mixed deployment architecture is the combination of the recommended WebLogic Server application deployment with the recommended WebLogic Server Web deployment. All of the components that make a recommended Web component, including a DMZ, fire-walls, and integration with Web services, should combine with the components for the application deployment. Figure 14–17 shows these two architectures combined to create a recommended mixed deployment.

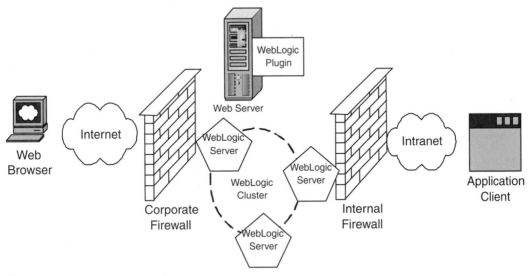

Figure 14–17
A recommended mixed deployment architecture.

Clients from the Internet access the Web Services existing in the DMZ. The firewalls protect the resources existing in the DMZ. Valid Web requests are sent through the internal firewall to the cluster of WebLogic Server servers deployed there.

Application clients access the WebLogic Server cluster directly over the corporate intranet. The WebLogic Server cluster handles those requests in response directly to the client applications. No special configuration is required to enable this mixed deployment.

Application Deployment Process

This section discusses the infrastructure and process that enterprise developers should use in deploying WebLogic Server applications to the production environment.

Infrastructure Components in Application Deployment

Application developers need a few important infrastructure tools—a versioning system, load testing, and quality assurance tools—that ensure the success of WebLogic Server deployments.

Versioning Systems

Versioning systems enable an enterprise to manage multiple versions of application components. The systems are built to accommodate any file type, such as images, source code, compiled application code, and so forth. These files are kept in a single, centralized repository. Typically, this repository resides on a server that acts as the master for the entire repository.

To use the system, WebLogic Server developers check-in and check-out components. Because the versioning system also tracks changes to those files and components, developers can revert to earlier versions. This enables a development group to quickly revert back to the last known version of an application that performed correctly.

Versioning systems also allow for the storage of multiple versions under different names, for example, "version100" for the first version of your system and "version200" for the second. In many WebLogic Server deployments, a production version of the application is frozen, and forward development proceeds on the next generation of the application. Maintenance work can be performed on the production version while forward development is done on the development version.

Choosing a Versioning System

A number of versioning systems are available in the marketplace today. Each of these products offers it's own strengths and weaknesses. Some are free, and some are commercially available:

- Perforce (*http://www.perforce.com*)—The versioning system used by BEA engineers to develop WebLogic Server. It is supported on many platforms and has numerous features that help manage multiple concurrent releases.

- Microsoft Visual SourceSafe (*http://www.Microsoft.com*)—A Windows-based versioning system used by many organizations focused on Windows development.

- Concurrent Versions System (*http://www.cvshome.org*)—An open source versioning system that is widely used.

A number of other versioning systems are available, many of which will suit the needs of a WebLogic Server application deployment. WebLogic Workshop, the development tool provided with WebLogic Server, supports both Perforce and CVS out-of-the-box.

Load Testing and Quality Assurance Tools

WebLogic Server does not include tools for load testing and quality assurance as part of its product suite. You need to use third-party tools to test for capacity and to ensure quality.

Load-testing tools test the application under stress. These tools typically fire up simultaneous sessions to simulate many concurrent users accessing the WebLogic Server application. These tools are programmed to follow a typical user's path through the application. For example, a banking application built on WebLogic Server might use a load-testing tool to simulate 10,000 users checking their balance at the same time.

Quality assurance tools for WebLogic Server applications are often used in conjunction with or as part of the load-testing tool. Quality assurance tools are similar to load-testing tools because they simulate users' paths through the application. However, unlike load-testing tools, quality assurance tools enable the developer to verify the responses from the application to ensure that they are correct.

These tools typically work by coordinating one or more machines to simulate virtual clients. These virtual clients follow scripted interactions with the WebLogic Server application. A quality assurance tool also can check the response coming from the WebLogic Server application to ensure that it is correct.

Choosing Load-Testing and Quality Assurance Tools

A number of solutions for testing and quality assurance for applications are available:

- Mercury Interactive (*http://www.mercuryinteractive.com/*) offers a number of products that incorporate both load testing and quality assurance into a single suite of tools. They also offer services to load test your real application remotely from machines that they operate.
- Segue Software (*http://www.segue.com*) offers a suite of products similar to Mercury Interactive. Their products are similarly targeted at high-end deployments.
- Apache JMeter (*http://java.apache.org/*) is a simple Java-based tool that can be used to generate loads for Web applications. It is available for free and suitable for low-end applications. It offers no coordination between the testing client machines·and no support for quality assurance.
- Microsoft Web Application Stress Tool (*http:/www.Microsoft.com/technet/itsolutions/intranet/downloads/webtutor.asp/*), which is the testing tool we use in Chapter 15 with the WebAuction application. This is a free and easy-to-use tool available for Microsoft Windows.

Stages in Application Deployment

Before we consider deployment scenarios, we need to review the objectives of a successful deployment. These characteristics will ensure you have a reliable deployment process, moving applications from development into test, from test into production. With each phase should be clearly defined goals and strategies; until an application or components achieves the goals for that phase of deployment, it cannot progress to the next level. We recommend following a four-step model to ensure smooth production rollouts. Figure 14–18 represents the stages in application development and deployment.

While there are distinct stages during the application development and deployment process, note that each stage results in feedback that is redirected to the process itself. At all times, information from the production operation, test development, test execution, and staging processes is funneled back to the development and architecture process. In this way, you create a process that results in continual improvement.

Stage 1: Architecture Development and Process Planning

In this stage, the architecture is developed or modified for a WebLogic Server application. Code is then developed to implement that architecture. The application can be a first version developed from scratch or a new release that modifies the original application source code.

The code is kept in the central versioning system. The versioning system includes the notion of multiple *versioning lines*. It is useful to create new code lines for new development and maintain older lines going forward, especially if those older lines are currently deployed in production.

In the typical WebLogic Server application development process, each developer has a development workstation. This workstation has a client to the versioning system and each developer uses that client to synchronize the local copy of the source code. The developer makes changes to the relevant source files.

Before submitting those changes, the developer typically deploys the changes on a local copy of WebLogic Server and executes tests against those changes. Once the developer is satisfied with the changes, he or she changes the source code as necessary and submits those changes into the versioning system.

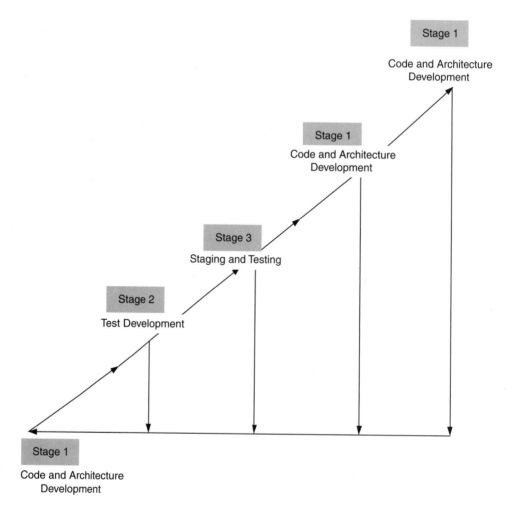

Figure 14–18
Stages in application development.

In addition, it is at this first stage that the entire process for rolling out the WebLogic Server application is developed. This is where plans should be developed around testing and staging any eventual production of the application. If this is not the initial generation of the application, it is likely that feedback from previous steps through the process will be used to improve both the functional aspects of the application as well as the rollout process itself.

Stage 2: Test Development

Complex applications require quality assurance tests. The exact methodology to develop these tests is beyond the scope of this book. Many tests simulate the user experience. For example, a bank application should test the creation of new accounts and the subsequent viewing of balances. Tests should be developed for all new functionality developed for a release.

The tests themselves are also checked into the versioning system because they are specific to the application version. More advanced enterprises should create automated testing based on the application code and include tests for each version of the application. Many enterprises deploy and test the application on a nightly basis, providing constant feedback for developers.

> **Best Practice:** Develop and execute tests for your WebLogic Server application to streamline the quality process and to ensure the expected execution.

Stage 3: Staging and Testing

Before any WebLogic Server application is deployed in production, it should be *staged*. A staged application is one that is deployed in a separate environment that is nearly identical to the production environment. The staging environment should reflect the production environment, down to every detail, including

- Operating system version and patches
- Operating system configuration and parameters
- JVM version and patches
- JVM configuration and parameters
- WebLogic Server version with appropriate service packs
- WebLogic Server configuration
- Application version (the exact code to be deployed in production—no different)
- Network configuration (DNS configuration, TCP/IP configuration, and so on)
- Hardware configuration

Most successful WebLogic Server deployments configure the staging area as a scale model representation of the production area. Ideally, an exact replica of the production environments can be used as a staging environment. If the budget is available, this is definitely preferred. At minimum, a general guideline is that the staging area should be one-third to one-half scale to the production area for small deployments, using eight to 12 CPUs. Larger configurations, such as those of 15 or more CPUs, often can successfully use a staging area that is one-quarter the production configuration size.

Under the staging area environment, tests are executed to ensure that the application will perform properly. In the staging area, two types of tests should be executed:

- *Functional testing*—These tests usually are run using either manual or automatic quality assurance tools. They ensure that the application functionality is complete and performs as expected.
- *Stress testing*—These tests are run using the stress-testing tools in order to ensure that the application scales appropriately to handle the load for which it is designed.

Both functional and stress testing should be completed before deploying the application. Chapter 17 on capacity planning contains substantial information on the testing process for WebLogic Server applications, including functional and stress testing.

> **Best Practice:** Never deploy an application in production without stress and functional testing it first.

Stage 4: Production

After the application has successfully completed functional testing and stress testing in the staging area, it is ready for production. The application code and configuration used in the staging area should be migrated exactly into the production area for deployment. This is most often accomplished by copying both the application code and configuration. They are then placed directly onto the production machines.

Best Practices for Deploying WebLogic Server

Over the history of WebLogic Server, customer experience has revealed a number of best practices for deployment. This section covers some of the best practices that you should keep in mind when designing your own WebLogic Server deployment.

Design for Security

It is important that the architecture of a WebLogic Server deployment be designed with security in mind. Firewalls and other components mentioned in this chapter are all essential to secure WebLogic Server or any other server. In addition, definitely make use of a Web DMZ to isolate any breaches that might occur in your system.

Securing Your Platform

While many architects for WebLogic Server design their deployment for security, they often forget to secure their deployment platform. Remember to review the available documentation for your deployment platform OS for techniques to secure the operating system and hardware platform on which you will run WebLogic Server.

Also, do not forget to follow all of the steps in the WebLogic Server documentation regarding securing your WebLogic Server deployment. A bad configuration can result in open security holes that attackers can exploit.

> **Best Practice:** Do not deploy your WebLogic Server without securing the underlying operating system and hardware environment.

Test and Stage Your Application

In today's Web world, fast and easy development should not be taken as an excuse for not thoroughly testing your WebLogic Server application. One of the biggest mistakes that WebLogic Server developers make is rushing too quickly to deployment.

It is a best practice to develop a test plan that covers testing and quality assurance for your WebLogic Server application. In addition, consider creating a staging environment for your application. If possible, this environment should be identical to your real production environment. Test your application in a staging area to be sure that you will see the performance and quality that you desire.

Deploy your WebLogic Server application only after thoroughly assuring its quality through testing. If possible, write your tests before you write your code. It will assist in locating bugs and also help in solidifying requirements.

Load Testing Your Application

Capacity planning information for WebLogic Server is included in Chapter 17 in this book. We strongly recommend that you work with this guide to develop the appropriate hardware for your system. But, even with the best capacity planning efforts, you cannot be sure that you will have enough hardware and the proper configuration to support the client load that you expect.

One of the greatest mistakes made in application deployment is the failure to test against high loads. Therefore, you should estimate how many clients you want to service as a maximum. Use one of the available load-testing tools such as WebBench (*http://www.veritest.com/benchmarks/webbench/webbench.asp*), Mercury Interactive LoadRunner (*http://www.mercuryinteractive.com/*), or any of the other available Web load-testing tools to test the Web components in your application. For application clients, you probably will need to create your own load-testing applications.

Absolutely do not deploy your application without testing it for handling high loads!

Don't Get Too Creative

This best practice applies to any enterprise software purchase: Do not get creative. Ask your software vendors what configurations they test. How often do they test those configurations? What is their hardware configuration? What type of network do they use? What type of JVM do they use? Get that information and replicate one of the regularly tested configurations in your own deployment.

WebLogic Server is certified to work under a given set of configurations and platforms. It is a best practice to review the documentation for WebLogic Server as to what configurations are tested. Do not stray from those configurations in order to prevent the risk of failure. Similarly, WebLogic Server is tested in the recommended configurations described in this chapter. Plan these configurations in order to minimize the possibility of malfunction or poor performance due to configuration or architecture issues.

Avoid creative architectures in your WebLogic Server deployment. With so many moving parts, go with the herd to ensure your success.

Minimize the Number of Moving Parts

There is a well-known principle that can be applied to the design and deployment of distributed systems—Keep It Simple, Stupid (KISS). Distributed systems are inherently complex due to their very nature—networking latency, multiple machines, and the potential for heterogeneous resources. WebLogic Server can manage much of this complexity for you. However, common sense can go a long way to ensuring production systems that are stable and reliable.

A number of options exist for WebLogic Server deployments. The simplest of these involves WebLogic Server being placed behind a Web routing solution. Currently, a number of these products, both hardware and software, integrate directly with WebLogic Server out-of-the-box. An off-the-shelf configuration should be considered strongly because it minimizes the number of moving parts in a deployment. In addition, although WebLogic clustering can be deployed while mixing hardware machines, it is much easier and simpler to limit yourself to homogeneous hardware for your deployment. Minimizing the number of moving parts means that there are fewer things that can break. As a wise man once told me, "Complex solutions can fail in complex ways."

Putting it all together

In this chapter, we reviewed many of the steps required to prepare an environment for a production deployment, how to take advantage of WebLogic clustering, and some of the tools and techniques for ensuring a successful application in production. This chapter is by no means an exhaustive review on these topics. You should review BEA documentation on administration, production planning, and tuning; read articles in periodicals such as *WebLogic Developer's Journal* or *Java Developer's Journal*; and frequently visit BEA's Developer site (*http://dev2dev.bea.com*) for more information.

chapter 15

Web Auction Design Goals

Chapters 2 through 14 cover the technologies included in WebLogic Server Java 2 Enterprise Edition (J2EE) and suggested best practices for developing to those services. These earlier chapters outline the J2EE technologies and illustrate each technology with simple examples.

You are now ready to review and deploy a more complex application. This chapter includes step-by-step instructions for packaging and deploying the WebAuction application. The example of the WebAuction application should aid you with your own application development and deployment.

Application Architecture

The WebAuction application is a Web-based auction system built with the WebLogic Server and J2EE. Like a real auction, it includes auctioned items organized in categories, bidding, and user accounts. The source code for WebAuction is included on the accompanying CD-ROM. You can also access the application and its source code online at *http://www.learnWebLogic.com*.

Design Goals

The WebAuction application is an e-commerce application that uses nearly all of the J2EE APIs, including these:

- Java ServerPages (JSP)
- Java Database Connectivity (JDBC)
- Java Message Service (JMS)
- Java Naming and Directory Interface (JNDI)
- Enterprise JavaBeans (EJB)
- JavaMail

This application demonstrates how you might use these technologies together to create a full-fledged application.

For many Web applications, the number of potential users can be quite large, and the number of active users could grow dramatically at any time. As a result, Web applications should be written to handle large numbers of users and continue to service requests. The WebAuction application achieves the scalability required of e-commerce applications by taking advantage of J2EE technologies and the enhanced performance and scalability characteristics available in WebLogic Server.

While the WebAuction application demonstrates the design and components found in a production application, there are several simplifications in the application that would not occur in the real world. Since this is a sample application, we include elements to demonstrate important techniques and J2EE features without creating an overly complex application.

Subsystems

Like many e-commerce applications, the WebAuction has two layers: a presentation layer and a business layer (see Figure 15–1). Clients use Web browsers to interact with the presentation layer. The presentation layer (also the Web tier in this example) is responsible for relaying client requests to the business logic layer and rendering the business logic's responses into HTML. As you would expect, the presentation layer is implemented using presentation technologies such as servlets and JSPs.

The business logic layer handles application logic and communication with back-end systems such as the database. The database, which often resides on a separate server, provides a persistent repository for the application's data. The business logic layer uses components including EJB components, JMS, JavaMail, and JDBC. The WebAuction application uses container-managed persistence (CMP), so WebLogic server generates data access code for entity beans in the business tier.

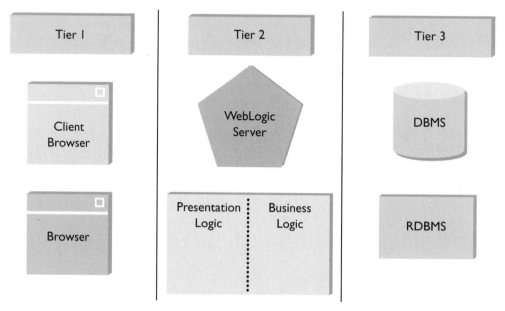

Figure 15–1
Multitier architecture.

Separating the Web and Business Logic Tiers

One design goal for the WebAuction application is to clearly separate the business and presentation layers. This design goal is important because a clear separation helps to keep each component focused and easy to manage. The presentation layer is responsible for generating Web pages, handling user requests, supporting internationalization and tracking a user's identity between Web pages. In the case of the WebAuction, the presentation layer also handles security. In other situations, user authentication may be applied within the business layer.

The separation of presentation and business logic also allows for parallel development. In many environments, separate groups or even separate companies develop each application tier. The presentation layer team designs Java Server Pages and writes servlets. The business logic developers mainly deal with database, messaging, and transaction issues.

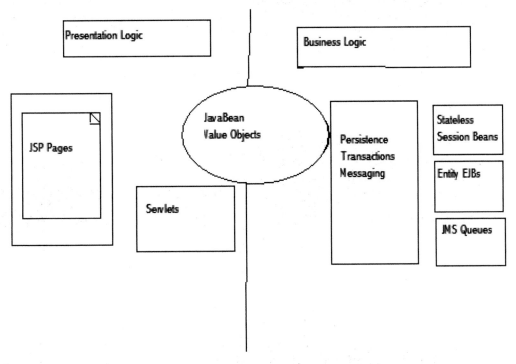

Figure 15–2
Separating presentation logic and business logic.

Presentation Layer

Servlets

The WebAuction application uses servlets to handle user requests. Each servlet represents a single action or a link a user might click. The servlet calls the appropriate methods in the business logic tier and then selects the appropriate view. In this way, the servlets connect the various application components.

Consider the service method of the `CreateItem` servlet. The servlet assembles the input from the user request (in the `itemBean` object) to create an item. If the request succeeds, the servlet forwards the request to the itemaccepted view. If the servlet catches an exception, it forwards the request to an error page.

```
public void service(HttpServletRequest req, HttpServletResponse res)
    throws ServletException, IOException {

    ServletContext sc = getServletContext();

    WebAuction webauction = (WebAuction)
sc.getAttribute(WebConstants.SC_ATTRIB_WEBAUCTION);
    NewItemBean itemBean = (NewItemBean) req.getAttribute("itembean");
    try {
        Calendar cal = Calendar.getInstance();
        webauction.createItem(
            req.getRemoteUser(),
            itemBean.getDescription(),
            itemBean.getCategory(),
            cal.getTime().getTime());
        RequestDispatcher rd = sc.getNamedDispatcher("itemaccepted");
        rd.forward(req, res);
    } catch (RemoteException e) {
        req.setAttribute("javax.servlet.jsp.jspException", e);
        RequestDispatcher rd = sc.getNamedDispatcher("error");
        rd.forward(req, res);
    }
    return;
}
```

JSPs

The WebAuction application uses JSPs to render HTML. The application uses a modular approach to page layout. In most cases, the servlet forwards requests to a template JSP; the template includes common headers, navigation, and footers. The template also includes the body of the page as specified by the servlet. This way, you can modify common page elements throughout the application with a single change. Also, by keeping common elements in the template, JSP body pages can be much simpler. See the following listings as a demonstration that shows the contents of *template.jsp*:

```
<jsp:root>
  <jsp:directive.page session="false" errorPage="error.jsp"/>

  <jsp:useBean id="pageBean"
               scope="request"
               class="webauction.web.javabean.PageBean"/>
  <html>
    <head>
      <title><jsp:getProperty name="pageBean" property="title"/></title>
    </head>
    <body>

      <jsp:directive.include file="../jspf/header.jsp" />
      <jsp:directive.include file="../jspf/header2.jsp" />
      <table width="85%" cellspacing="0">
        <tr>
          <td valign="top"><jsp:include page="navigation.jsp"/></td>
          <td valign="TOP">
            <!-- start application body -->
              <jsp:include page="%=pageBean.getBody()%"/>
            <!-- end application body -->
          </td>
        </tr>
      </table>
      <jsp:directive.include file="../jspf/footer.jsp" />
    </body>
  </html>
</jsp:root>
```

The *main.jsp* page generates the application body portion of the resulting HTML. The following listing shows the contents of *main.jsp*:

```
<jsp:root>
  <jsp:directive.page session="false" errorPage="error.jsp"/>

  <br/>
  <br/>
  <p>Welcome to the WebLogic WebAuction sample application. </p>

  <p>This is the sample application used as a learning tool and
     application development template throughout the book.</p>

  <p>This application is a complete peer-to-peer on-line auction.
     You can register as a user and create your account. You can
     view the items that other users have placed up for bid, place
     your own items up for bid, and place bids on other's items.</p>

  <p>You should see a navigation bar to the left. The navigation
     bar is always available to take you through the auction.</p>

  <p>The source code and instructions for deploying this application
     are available on the CD accompanying the book. </p>
</jsp:root>
```

The resulting page demonstrates how these two components come together. See Figure 15–3 for a screenshot of the generated page.

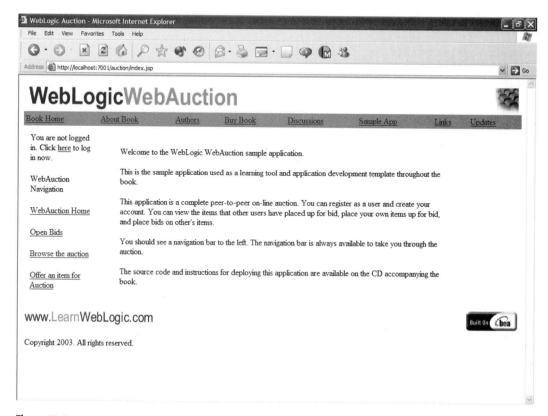

Figure 15–3
WebAuction main page.

Tag Libraries

The WebAuction JSPs include little Java code. Rather than use Java, the WebAuction pages use tag libraries to perform processing during JSP execution. The WebAuction application uses the following tag libraries:

- WebLogic processing tags to selectively render page components and repeat components for each element in a list (e.g., multiple items).
- WebLogic validation tags to validate user input in HTML forms.
- Jakarta TagLibs input tags to redisplay user input in HTML fields.
- JSTL core tags to selectively display page components and repeat components for each element in a list (e.g., multiple items).
- A custom tag library to support sessions by rewriting URLs.

In the following example, the WebAuction *browseitems.jsp* page displays a bid link. The link includes a reference to the bid action and the ID of the specified item, and it uses URL rewriting to ensure that the application will maintain sessions:

```
<jsp:root
    xmlns:a="http://www.learnweblogic.com/webauction/urlrewriting-1.0">
        ...
        <a:link href='%="Bid?id=" + item.getId()%'>
          <jsp:text>Click here</jsp:text>
        </a:link>
        ...
```

Business Layer

WebAuction Stateless Session Bean

The WebAuction stateless session bean is a synchronous interface into the business logic layer. It provides a single, simple interface for interacting with business entities and also provides methods that look up, test for, or create entities within the business layer of the application. The use of a stateless session bean as an intermediary has several effects. First, access logic is simplified because servlets need to configure access to only a single EJB. Further, a single interface hides implementation details of the business entities. As a result, you can modify the implementation of the back end without making changes to the presentation layer.

Below is an excerpt from the WebAuction bean. The getItemWithId() method uses an item ID to look up and returns an object representing the item:

```
public ItemValueHolder getItemWithId(int id) throws NoSuchItemException {
    try {
        Item item = itemHome.findByPrimaryKey(new Integer(id));
        ItemValueHolder ivh = new ItemValueHolder();
        ivh.setItemDescription(item.getDescription());
        ivh.setTopBidAmount(item.getTopBidAmount());
        ivh.setId(id);
        return ivh;

    } catch (FinderException fe) {
        ctx.setRollbackOnly();
        throw new NoSuchItemException(
            "Item with id: "
                + id
                + " does not exist or could not be loaded.");
    } catch (RemoteException re) {
        re.printStackTrace();
        throw new EJBException(
            "Error getting item with id:" + id + ".  The error was: " + re);
    }
}
```

Message-Driven Beans

Message-driven beans provide an alternative interface to the business logic tier. Unlike the synchronous method calls available in session beans, message-driven beans provide asynchronous messaging. The WebAuction application uses the message-driven bean `BidReceiverBean` to accept bids from users. The SubmitBid servlet action can send a bid bean and return to the user without waiting for the bid to be processed. By splitting the bid into two parts, initiation and processing, the application can scale to handle a large number of bids while maintaining fast response times.

Entity Beans

The WebAuction application stores data in the entity beans `BidBean`, `ItemBean`, and `UserBean`. In each case, the bean represents a persistent entity: a bid, item or user within the WebAuction system. In this application, entity beans use CMP to store entity information in a database.

The WebAuction application also maintains relationships between entities in the system. Each entity includes data about the entity and relationships to other entities. An item has a description and is owned by a user; a user includes a name and places bids on items. These relationships between entities are as important as the entities themselves. Figure 15–4 represents the relationships between these entities.

The WebAuction application takes advantage of WebLogic Server's support for relationships within CMP beans. Relationships are a natural and powerful addition to the persistence layer. With relationship support, the application can access entity beans using relationships between the entities. For example, you can access all the bids for a particular user. Or, in more complex scenario, the application can access a user's items and then the related bids for each item. EJB support for relationships means that the application can support relationships with minimal effort. The WebAuction application creates relationships between entities in the entities' `postCreate()` methods and defines these relationships in the ejb-jar.xml deployment descriptor.

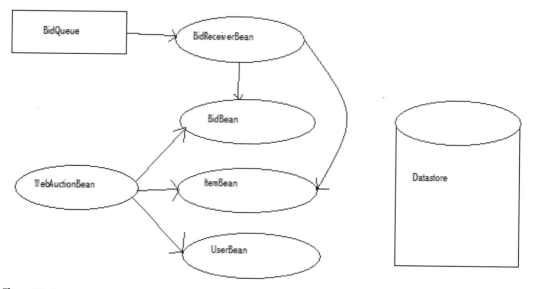

Figure 15–4

Entity bean relationships.

Interfaces

Good interfaces between components are an important but challenging part of software development. When you properly decouple software into modules, implementation becomes easier and cleaner. Interfaces promote information hiding. When you use interfaces to hide information, you minimize the exposure of internal information to other areas of the system. System designs that utilize such interfaces can minimize the dependencies between components and allow architects to redesign, reimplement, or even replace components without impacting other parts of the system.

For instance, you might decide to move business logic from EJBs into stored procedures. You should be able to make this change without changing presentation logic. Without good, clean interfaces, design assumptions and cross-component dependencies creep into application code. These dependencies can make changes to any component devilishly difficult.

Unfortunately, good interface design is hard. Often, a prototype implementation can reveal design flaws or false assumptions. The WebAuction implementation should help serve as a demonstration of design patterns for your own applications.

Consider the following interfaces:

- Browser-Servlet—Servlets represent actions available to users. The `web.xml` deployment descriptor links a URL to a servlet. Thus, to make an action available, include a link to the action the HTML page. The links defined in the *web.xml* file define the range of actions available to a user and represent the first-line interface of the WebAuction application.
- Servlets-JSPs—Servlets pass requests to JSP pages using the `RequestDispatcher`. In addition, the servlets pass information to the JSPs by attaching JavaBean objects to the HTTP request.
- JSP-Tag Libraries—JSPs are a bad place for Java code. Use tag libraries to extract Java code from JSPs. The *.tld* files in the WebAuction WAR file define the interface to the tag libraries.
- Servlet-Stateless Session Bean—The WebAuction servlets use the `WebAuction` stateless session bean for synchronous access to business logic. The WebAuction interface defines the methods available to your servlets, and the ejb-jar.xml deployment descriptor ties this interface to objects that implement the interface.
- Servlet-Message-Driven Bean—The WebAuction servlets use the `BidReceiverBean` for asynchronous access to business logic. Servlets send messages to the `Bid` queue for later processing by the `BidReceiverBean`. The application uses JMS to deliver the messages.

We discuss two of these interfaces in further detail.

JavaBeans in the Presentation Layer

Servlet actions process user requests and pass information to JSP pages in JavaBeans. JavaBeans are simple objects with getter and setter methods for each field in the bean. Either the business logic or the servlets generate these value objects. The servlets attach the objects to the HTTP request. JSP pages access the beans using the `jsp:useBean` and `jsp:getProperty` actions.

Sometimes, either the business layer or the servlet converts one kind of object into JavaBeans for use by JSPs. This approach creates objects you can conveniently access from within a JSP. The disadvantage of this approach is that you must create extra objects to encapsulate information that already exists within the business object. For instance, when the application needs to display bids for a particular user, the WebAuction stateless session EJB creates a value bean for each bid. While the EJB creates additional objects, these objects are more convenient to access within the JSP. Further, by encapsulating information for each bid in an object, you are free to modify the persistence layer without modifying the JSP pages (see Figure 15–2).

Accessing Business Logic from Servlets

The `WebAuction` stateless session bean is responsible for reading information from entity beans and passing results back to the servlet client. Rather than passing back the entity objects themselves, the `WebAuction` bean populates data-transfer objects and returns these. You could pass the entity beans directly to the presentation layer, but this choice limits future flexibility. If you use the entity beans directly within the presentation layer, changes to the system become more difficult as the system grows. Value objects provide an interface that can remain constant even as you update the back-end design.

If you do decide to use entity beans in the presentation layer, make sure your entity beans implement the local interface. Entity beans using the local interface cache data on the client side and calls to getter methods are handled locally and efficiently. If the entity bean implements the remote interface, each call to a getter method call triggers a database query. Worse yet, each request could initiate a new transaction.

Transaction Design

The business logic layer implements the application logic, maintains transactional integrity, and stores the application data.

Within the WebAuction application, the presentation layer calls the business logic layer using JMS messages and calls to the `WebAuction` stateless session bean to access information in the system. These calls are synchronous, so the call waits for a response from the business logic layer.

Transactions within synchronous calls are an important component of many e-commerce applications, but the overall performance of the system can bog down when the number of transactions grows too large or the transactions are not kept short and focused. We can maintain tight control over transaction begin and commit events by managing these events solely in the business logic layer.

Because synchronous calls are not always necessary and can slow overall system performance, the WebAuction application uses asynchronous messages to place bids. When a user bids on an item, the presentation layer sends a `Bid` message to the `Bids` JMS queue and returns to the user. The `BidReceiverBean` is a message-driven bean that handles messages delivered to the queue. When a new bid arrives, the `BidReceiverBean` updates the database and notifies the user of the update by e-mail. Use asynchronous calls in your application to handle larger transactions and to ensure that you can maintain good response times even under heavy loads.

Transaction Flow

Designers often use transactions to ensure that updates to application state are reliable. In the case of the Web auction application, users update application state when they create new users, offer items, or bid on items. In the case of adding users or items, the transaction consists of inserting a record into the appropriate table. Bids are more complicated.

The `BidReceiver` message-driven bean treats the processing of each message from the `Bids` queue as a transaction. The `ejb-jar.xml` deployment descriptor defines the methods of the `BidReceiverBean` with the `Required` transaction attribute (see the assembly descriptor for the `BidReceiverBean`). The transaction begins when the `BidReceiverBean` starts to process the message and continues into the creation of a new entity, a bid. If the transaction aborts, the transaction rolls back any entity bean updates, and the message returns to the JMS queue for processing. The transaction definition ensures that the `BidReceiver` ultimately processes each JMS message at most once, and that even if the server dies while processing a request, WebLogic Server does not lose the `Bid` message.

WebAuction Security

As is common with many e-commerce applications, the WebAuction application requires some degree of security. The WebAuction security model defines user accounts. Users register with the WebAuction site and create user accounts with passwords and an associated e-mail address. In future sessions, the user must log into the system using appropriate user ID and password. This security model has become commonplace and is familiar to most readers.

Not every page in the WebAuction needs to, or should be, protected. In particular, visitors should be allowed to browse the auction without creating a user account. This access allows new users to visit the site without making the commitment of providing user information. Further, by not logging in all users, the application uses fewer resources on the server because the application does not store session data until the user signs in. A user must log into the WebAuction before performing certain tasks, such as bidding on items or placing items in the auction.

The WebAuction application's business layer does not check users. The business logic layer relies on the presentation layer to ensure that the user has met all security requirements. This solution is acceptable for most Web-based designs, and it simplifies the business logic layer. In addition, security checks can slow performance, so avoiding unnecessary access constraints helps improve scalability. However, more stringent requirements might require that every level of an application confirm that each request meets security requirements.

Authenticating Users

The `web.xml` deployment descriptor specifies the security constraints that restrict access to a protected page or action. If a user has not already logged into the system, the WebLogic Server redirects the browser to the login page before accepting the request. For example, this security constraint restricts access to a number of protected actions:

```
<security-constraint>
  <web-resource-collection>
    <web-resource-name>New Item</web-resource-name>
    <url-pattern>/Bid</url-pattern>
    <url-pattern>/GetBids</url-pattern>
    <url-pattern>/Login</url-pattern>
    <url-pattern>/OfferItem</url-pattern>
    <http-method>GET</http-method>
    <http-method>POST</http-method>
  </web-resource-collection>
  <auth-constraint>
    <role-name>user</role-name>
  </auth-constraint>
</security-constraint>
```

The `web.xml` file also declares the abstract role auction:

```
<security-role>
  <role-name> user</role-name>
</security-role>
```

Finally, the weblogic.xml deployment descriptor maps the user role to the auction_user principal.

```
<security-role-assignment>
  <role-name>user</role-name>
  <principal-name>auction_user</principal-name>
</security-role-assignment>
```

Every WebAuction user is a member of the group named auction_user and can access the OfferItem action or any of the other protected actions.

When a user who has not logged in tries to access the OfferItem action, WebLogic Server identifies that the user has not met security requirements and redirects the user to a login screen. The *web.xml* file configures login processing using the login-config element.

```
<login-config>
  <auth-method>FORM</auth-method>
  <realm-name>default</realm-name>
  <form-login-config>
    <form-login-page>/DisplayLogin</form-login-page>
    <form-error-page>/DisplayLogin?failed=true</form-error-page>
  </form-login-config>
</login-config>
```

The WebAuction application uses Form-based authentication, defined in the servlet specification, to verify usernames and passwords. The DisplayLogin action maps to a servlet that specifies the *login.jsp*. This page includes an HTML form and sets the action of the form to the relative URL j_security_check. The *login.jsp* page defines the username using the j_username field-name and the password using j_password. The password field uses the input type of password to keep the browser from displaying the password on the screen. The following excerpt from the *login.jsp* page shows the HTML coding needed for Form-based authentication.

```
<form method="post" name="Login" action="j_security_check">
  <table>
    <tr>
      <td width="30%">Username :</td>
      <td><input type="text" name="j_username" size="15"/></td>
    </tr>

    <tr>
      <td width="30%">Password :</td>
      <td><input type="password" name="j_password" size="15"/></td>
    </tr>
```

```
    <tr>
      <td colspan="2"><input type="submit" value="Login" name="Submit"/></td>
    </tr>
  </table>
</form>
```

The application serves the *login.jsp* page over HTTPS to ensure that the user ID and password are encrypted when passed across the network. The transport-guarantee entry in the *web.xml* file ensures that the application uses a secure transport protocol. See the full `security-constraint` element below:

```
<security-constraint>
  <web-resource-collection>
    <web-resource-name>Login page</web-resource-name>
    <url-pattern>/DisplayLogin</url-pattern>
    <http-method>GET</http-method>
    <http-method>POST</http-method>
  </web-resource-collection>
  <user-data-constraint>
    <transport-guarantee>CONFIDENTIAL</transport-guarantee>
  </user-data-constraint>
</security-constraint>
```

Creating New User Accounts

New users are required to register with the system prior to logging in. During the registration process, users provide information such as a username and password and personal information like first and last names, address, and e-mail address. The user enters this information into a form defined in the *newuser.jsp* page.

The JSP page validates each field of user input using the WebLogic validation tags. If one of the validation rules fails, the tag library redisplays the input page with the appropriate errors. One of the validation rules specifies that the username does not already exist within the system. To confirm that this is the case, the WebAuction application includes a custom validation class, `ValidateUniqueUser.java`. (in the package `webauction.web.helpers`) This validation class calls the WebAuction stateless session bean to check for an existing user with the username.

If user input passes all the validation rules, the validation tag forwards the request to the `CreateUser` action. This action calls yet another method within the WebAuction bean. This time, the method creates the specified user both as an entity within the WebAuction application and as a principal within the WebLogic Server embedded LDAP server, the default authentication provider. Finally, the `CreateUser` logs the user into the system. The following lines from *CreateUser.java* show how:

```
import weblogic.servlet.security.ServletAuthentication;
...
// log the user in
int ret = ServletAuthentication.weak(
                    userBean.getUserName(),
```

```
                              userBean.getPassword(),
                              req);
if (ret == ServletAuthentication.AUTHENTICATED) {
    rd = sc.getNamedDispatcher("usercreated");
} else {
    rd = sc.getNamedDispatcher("error");
}
```

Stateless Session Bean Security

By default, EJBs run as a guest within WebLogic Server. However, there are occasions when an EJB requires special privileges. For instance, only administrators can manage users within the WebLogic Server.

For a user of the WebAuction application to create a new account, the code that creates the user account must run with special privileges. The WebAuction application uses the EJB deployment descriptors to assign special privileges to the WebAuction stateless session bean, specifically so that it can create user accounts. The following configuration elements provide this special status.

First, declare an abstract role in the assembly-descriptor of the *ejb-jar.xml* file:

```
  <security-role>
    <role-name>runAs_role_admin</role-name>
  </security-role>
```

Next, in the same file, specify that the WebAuction stateless session bean should run as this abstract role:

```
  <session>
    <ejb-name>WebAuctionEJB</ejb-name>
    ...
    <security-identity>
      <run-as>
        <role-name>runAs_role_admin</role-name>
      </run-as>
    </security-identity>
    ...
  </session>
```

Finally, tie the role to a principal within the weblogic-ejb-jar.xml deployment descriptor:

```
<security-role-assignment>
  <role-name>runAs_role_admin</role-name>
  <principal-name>weblogic</principal-name>
</security-role-assignment>
```

WebLogic Server creates the weblogic user in the Administrators group by default. If your installation does not include the weblogic account, change the principal to match your environment.

Changes Required for a Production Application

The WebAuction application is only a sample. While the application possesses the main components of a real-world production environment, it includes some simplifications. In your applications, you will want to consider these additional issues.

Limiting Query Results

The WebAuction application uses simple entity bean `finder()` methods to query the database. While these simple finders are acceptable in a prototype, real applications must employ a more sophisticated approach. For instance, the `ItemBean` includes a `finder()` method that returns all the items in a given category. On a real auction site, this query could return thousands of rows. Obviously, a thousand items is too many to display on a single Web page. Further, the process of returning these items can take significant time and computing resources. Use alternative finder methods to return manageable subsets of the full result.

Unique ID Generation

Many common business objects, including the WebAuction application's `Items` and `Bids`, have no natural primary key. When none of the entities' natural attributes uniquely identifies the record within the WebAuction system, the system must generate an identifying value for every new entity. The only requirement for this primary key is that they be unique within the population of `Items` or `Bids`. WebAuction uses a separate stateless session bean to produce these unique IDs. Before the WebAuction creates a new `Item` or `Bid`, the system calls the `IDGenerator`'s `getNextValue()` method to generate a new ID. The item or bid uses this unique ID to create the `Item` or `Bid`.

Use a stateless session bean to hide your technique for generating unique IDs. Within your bean, you can modify your algorithm for creating IDs without impacting other code. The WebAuction uses a sequence or special table to store the latest unique ID in a central location. Unfortunately, this approach requires that the system access the database return to the database an extra time during each entity creation. This approach is acceptable only if the application creates items infrequently.

Use one of several approaches to eliminate multiple database requests; many approaches are available. One approach limits trips to the database by requesting groups of IDs at once and then doling them out as requested. The `IDGeneratorBean` could read the database sequence and increment the counter not by one, but by 1,000. The bean might read the value 3,000, increment the value to 4,000, and then own IDs 3,000 to 3,999. The bean only has to go back to the database after it runs out of IDs. This approach improves performance because it limits extra database requests to one for 1,000 create actions.

Internationalization

Often, real-world Web applications must support multiple languages. While the WebAuction includes only English language output, the application is designed to easily add support for other languages. Move text from JSP pages into an external message catalog. Then create a version of the catalog for each language you want to support. You can extend the application to give the user the option to select a language, and store the user's selection in a session. Modify your JSP pages to check the user's language selection and select the appropriate message catalog.

Database Tuning

Nearly every e-commerce application uses a database for persistent data storage. One important tool for improving e-commerce applications is database tuning. The WebAuction application uses a simple database schema and queries. The database schema uses simple and portable data types, and tables are simple enough to not require sophisticated database skills to understand.

However, production applications require the performance improvements that often result from database tuning. Tune the database's physical schema to improve performance; for example, create indices to speed queries. Also, take advantage of query optimization available in many databases and check execution plans for the application's most frequent operations. Sometimes, a database administrator can change a schema or query slightly and achieve significant performance improvements. Database tuning is a big topic and is highly dependant on the underlying database. While we don't delve into database tuning in this book, you should remember to include this step while developing your application.

Assembling the Application Components: WebAuction

The WebAuction application includes both Enterprise JavaBeans and a Web application. Use an enterprise archive or *.ear* file to package these various components into a single distribution file. Enterprise archives are the J2EE standard for packaging application components and deployment information into a single package. You can then deploy this archive file on WebLogic Server or any other application server supporting J2EE standards.

About Enterprise Archives

Enterprise archives make it easier to archive, package, and distribute your application code because everything is in a single file. An enterprise archive includes everything required to deploy the application code on an application server. You can recognize Enterprise archive filenames using the *.ear* extension of the filename.

Like a Web archive, an enterprise archive is a *jar* file with an alternative extension, but the enterprise archive may contain both Web archive and Java archive files. The enterprise archive includes all the components required for an application including Web applications, Enterprise JavaBeans, and other J2EE components. In addition, the enterprise archive must include an application deployment descriptor (`application.xml`) and may include a WebLogic-specific deployment descriptor (`weblogic-application.xml`). The J2EE application deployment descriptor describes the contents of the archive and includes instructions for how the components should be deployed. An enterprise archive may also include libraries referenced by J2EE modules, help files, and documentation. Use the `jar` utility to create enterprise archives.

The XML-formatted package deployment descriptor (`application.xml`) represents the top-level view of an enterprise archive's contents. The J2EE application deployment descriptor uses the special XML document type definition (DTD) specified by the J2EE standards.

Enterprise Archive Deployment Descriptors

The enterprise archive is a loosely organized collection of resources. As a result, the packager of the archive must describe the contents of the archive. Use the proprietary deployment descriptor `weblogic-application.xml` to customize the deployment within WebLogic Server.

application.xml

An enterprise archive requires an `application.xml` deployment descriptor. The descriptor uses the following descriptor:

```
<!DOCTYPE application PUBLIC
    "-//Sun Microsystems, Inc.//DTD J2EE Application 1.3//EN"
"http://java.sun.com/dtd/application_1_3.dtd">
```

The following is the `application.xml` deployment descriptor for the WebAuction application:

```
<application>
  <display-name>WebAuction</display-name>
  <description>WebLogic WebAuction</description>
  <module>
    <ejb>auction_ejb.jar</ejb>
  </module>
  <module>
    <web>
      <web-uri>auction_web.war</web-uri>
      <context-root>auction</context-root>
    </web>
  </module>
</application>
```

The `application.xml` deployment descriptor includes a number of attributes of the enterprise archive, including a display name for the archive, a description of the archive, and two modules. The first module references a *.jar* file of EJBs used within the application. The second module identifies a Web application and defines that application's `context-root`.

The `root-element` may contain the following elements:

- `icon`—The option `icon` element may contain both a `small-icon` and a `large-icon` element. The body of the icon elements should reference gif files (16 × 16 and 32 × 32) within the enterprise archive, relative to the root of the archive.
- `display-name`—The `application.xml` file requires a display-name element. This name is intended for use by graphic tools but is not currently used by WebLogic Server.
- `description`—Use the optional `description` field to provide a description of the application.
- `module`—Include a `module` element for each J2EE component within your Web application. Components include EJBs, Web applications, client-side Java applications, and resource adaptors (connector). The `module` element contains one of the following child elements: `ejb`, `web`, `java`, or `connector`. The `ejb`, `java`, and `connector` elements simply refer to the corresponding component within the enterprise archive. The web element includes additional elements. Finally, the `module` element may contain an `alt-dd` element. Use the `alt-dd` to override the deployment descriptor in the specified component. Note that the `alt-dd` element only overrides the standard deployment descriptor (e.g., `web.xml`, `ejb-jar.xml`).

- security-role—Define roles used within your application using the security-role element. Each security-role can contain two elements: a description and a role-name to identify the role. You must map these application-defined roles to users and groups within your system. Use the weblogic-application.xml deployment descriptor to make this mapping.

Web module elements contain more structure than other module types. Rather than provide a simple reference to the component within the enterprise archive, the web module contains a web-uri and context-root. The web-uri provides a reference to the Web archive. The context-root overrides the default context-root of the Web application. If the web module does not provide a context-root, WebLogic Server uses the base name of the *.war* file. Note: This context-root must be unique within the WebLogic Server instance.

The WebAuction application includes both a JAR file and a WAR file containing the EJBs and Web application. The application.xml descriptor ties the two together into a single enterprise archive. See the content of the *application.xml* file below:

```
<!DOCTYPE application PUBLIC '-//Sun Microsystems, Inc.//DTD J2EE
Application 1.2//EN' 'http://java.sun.com/j2ee/dtds/
application_1_2.dtd'>

<application>
  <display-name>WebAuction</display-name>
  <description>WebLogic WebAuction</description>
  <module>
    <ejb>auction_ejb.jar</ejb>
  </module>
  <module>
    <web>
      <web-uri>auction_web.war</web-uri>
      <context-root>auction</context-root>
    </web>
  </module>
</application>
```

weblogic-application.xml

The weblogic-application.xml deployment descriptor provides a number of configuration options. This section provides an overview of the options you may select within the weblogic-application.xml deployment descriptor. For more information, refer to the WebLogic Server online documentation at *http://edocs.bea.com/wls/docs81/programming/app_xml.html*. The following list provides an overview of weblogic-application.xml:

- ejb—Defines application-level caching of entity and the startup sequence for message-driven beans.
- xml—Overrides parsers (SAX, DOM, and XSL-T) and defines application-specific entity mappings.
- jdbc-connection-pool—Defines a connection pool and data sources. This pool is available only within the current application.

- `security`—Allows you to map users and groups to roles defined in the `application.xml` deployment descriptor. Note: WebLogic documentation suggests that you can override the default or active security realm using the `realm-name` tag. It is not true. WebLogic Server can only support one active domain at a time. Try as you may, this setting does nothing to change which realm your application will access.
- `application-param`—Sets WebLogic Server parameters. See WebLogic Server documentation for details on specific attributes you may set.
- `classloader-structure`—Customizes how the classloaders for each component relate to one another.
- `listener`—Registers application listeners using the listener tag. Application listeners should implement `weblogic.application.ApplicationLifecycleListener`.
- `startup/shutdown`—Defines startup and shutdown classes for your application. WebLogic Server runs these classes as startup (or shutdown) by calling the classes' `public static main(String[] args)` method.

Enterprise Archive Organization

The enterprise archive is loosely structured. The J2EE standard requires only that `application.xml` deployment descriptor be at the /META-INF directory of the archive. If you include a `weblogic-application.xml` descriptor, it must be in the same directory. The WebAuction application looks like this:

```
auction_ejb.jar
auction_web.war
input-examples.war
WebAuction.war
META-INF/application.xml
META-INF/MANIFEST.MF
```

The `jar` utility creates the manifest file automatically. The manifest lists all the components in the *.jar* file for future reference.

Packaging the Enterprise Archive (.ear)

In this section, we cover how to create an *.ear* file. If you want to practice creating an archive, use the following steps. Otherwise, skip to the next section, *"Deploying the WebAuction Application."*

Before building the *.ear* file, extract the *WebAuction.jar* file to a working directory. In this case, we use *c:\working\WebAuction*. Also, the process in this section uses the command shell. Open a command shell and ensure that the environment is properly set. If WebLogic Server is installed in *c:\bea\weblogic81*, then call *setWLSEnv.cmd* to set your environment:

```
\bea\weblogic81\server\bin\setWLSEnv.cmd
```

To build an enterprise archive, first create a directory and copy application components *auction-ejb.jar* and *auction-web.war* into this directory.

```
cd c:\working
mkdir auction-ear
copy WebAuction\ejb\auction-ejb.jar auction-ear
copy WebAuction\web\auction-web.war auction-ear
```

Create a META-INF directory within the *auction-ear* directory and copy *application.xml* and *weblogic-application.xml* files:

```
mkdir webauction-ear\META-INF
copy WebAuction\application.xml webauction-ear\META-INF
copy WebAuction\weblogic.xml webauction-ear\META-INF
```

Finally, use the `jar` command to create the *.ear* file.

```
cd auction-ear
jar cvf ../auction.ear *
```

The build script provided with the WebAuction example builds the same *.ear* file, but uses an `ant` script. Either way you create the build script, you will need to complete several steps to configure WebLogic Server and deploy the WebAuction application.

Deploying the WebAuction Application

In the previous section, you manually created an *.ear* file. This section describes the steps to deploy this enterprise archive file. Again, these instructions assume you have created a working directory and extracted the *WebAuction.jar* file into that directory. To configure your environment, open a Windows command shell and execute `setWLSEnv.cmd`:

```
> mkdir c:\working\webauction
> cd c:\working\webauction
> jar xf d:\examples\ch15\webauction.jar
> c:\bea\weblogic81\server\bin\setWLSEnv.cmd
```

You should see something like Figure 15–5.

Figure 15–5
Setting the environment.

Configure PointBase

The WebLogic Server distribution includes an evaluation copy of the PointBase database. This example uses PointBase for the WebAuction example, but most any standard databases will work. The following steps demonstrate how to start and configure a PointBase database.

First, start the PointBase database using the command `startPointBase.cmd`:

```
c:\bea\weblogic81\common\bin\startPointBase.cmd
```

The `startPointBase.cmd` command launches a new window (but may not bring the window to the foreground—you might need to look for it). This window represents the PointBase database server and announces it listening on port 9093. See Figure 15–6.

Next, use the PointBase console to configure the database. Run the `startPointBaseConsole.cmd`:

```
\bea\weblogic81\common\bin\startPointBaseConsole.cmd
```

The above command launches the console application and a *Connect To Database* dialog box. Choose *Create New Database* and specify the URL `jdbc:pointbase:server://localhost:9093/auction`. Fill in the fields as shown in Figure 15–7 to create a new database named *auction*. Use the default password, `PBPUBLIC`.

Next, load the *pointbase.ddl* file to generate and populate the tables required for the WebAuction application. (Note: If you are using Oracle or another database with support for sequences, use the alternative DDLs provided in the example.) This file contains the SQL commands needed to configure the environment. Select *File → Open* to launch the *Open...* dialog box. Modify the pull-down *Files*

Figure 15–6
The PointBase server window.

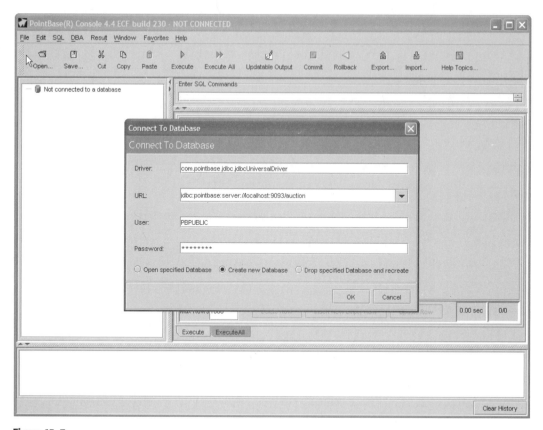

Figure 15–7
Connect to database.

of Type: to include *All Files*, and select the file *tables.ddl* (in our environment, this file is in *c:\work-ing\WebAuction\ddl*).

When you open the *.ddl* file, the PointBase console displays the contents of the file in the *Enter SQL Commands* portion of the console. Run these SQL commands using the *Execute All* button on the console. Figure 15–8 shows the results after running these SQL commands. These SQL commands create the table structure and populate the resulting tables.

The auction database is now configured for the WebAuction application.

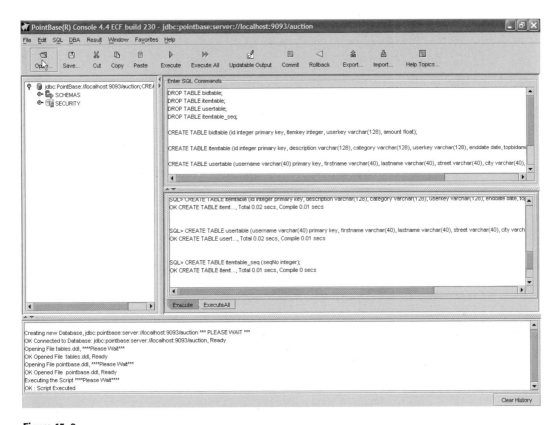

Figure 15–8
Execute DDL in the PointBase Console.

Configure Database Connection Pool

Make sure that the WebLogic Server instance is running and log in. If the WebLogic Server console is running on port 7001, point your browser to *http://localhost:7001/console* and provide user and password values. First, we configure a JDBC connection pool for the WebAuction application. With a connection pool, WebLogic Server manages the creation and reuse of JDBC connections to the auction database. The first step in configuring the JDBC connection pool is to open the WebLogic Server console.

In the left-side navigation tree, open *mydomain* → *Services* → JDBC → *Connection Pools*. Select *Configure a new JDBC Connection Pool...* to create a new connection pool.

On the resulting page, set the Database Type and the Database Driver to use PointBase and the PointBase Type 4 XA driver. Complete this screen as shown in Figure 15–9 and continue to the following screen.

Next, set the name of the JDBC pool and several connection properties. For details, refer to Figure 15–10. Again, the default password for the PointBase database is PBPUBLIC.

The next page lets you confirm that the database connection is properly configured. Click *Test Driver Configuration* to connect to the database. If WebLogic Server can connect to the database, it returns a Connection Successful message. Click the *Create and deploy* button. If WebLogic Server fails to connect, it provides an error message. Go back and check your input, then try again.

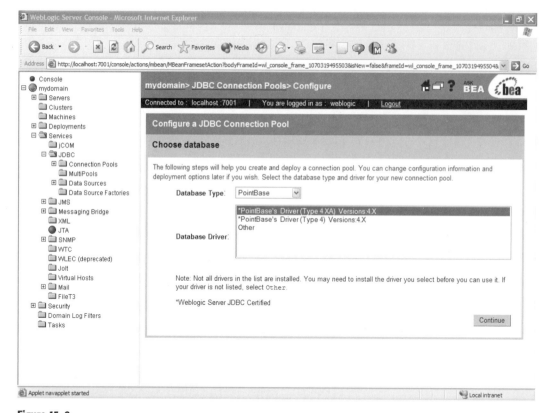

Figure 15–9
Choose a database.

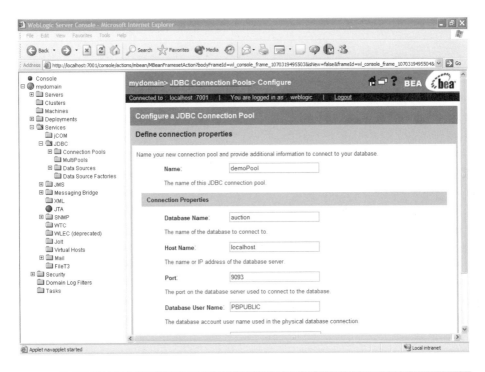

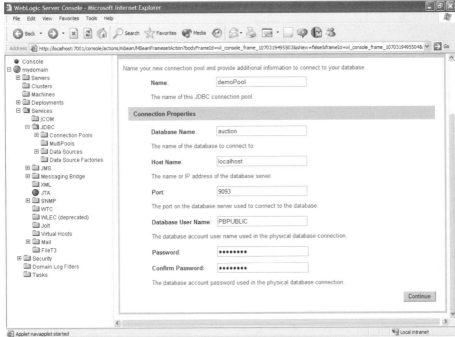

Figure 15-10
Define connection properties.

Configure DataSource

Now that you have created a JDBC connection pool, create a Data Source Name. The WebAuction application uses this name to locate the connection pool. Within the WebLogic Server console, navigate to *mydomain* → *Services* → *JDBC* → *DataSources*. On the resulting page, select the link *Create a new JDBC Data Source....* Complete the resulting screens as shown in figures 15–11, 15–12, and 15–13. These steps configure the data source and target the data source to the server *myserver*. Use `examples-dataSource-auctionPool` for both the Data Source name and JNDI name.

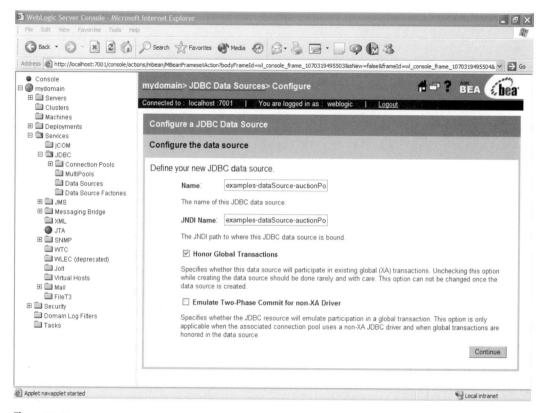

Figure 15–11
Configure the data source.

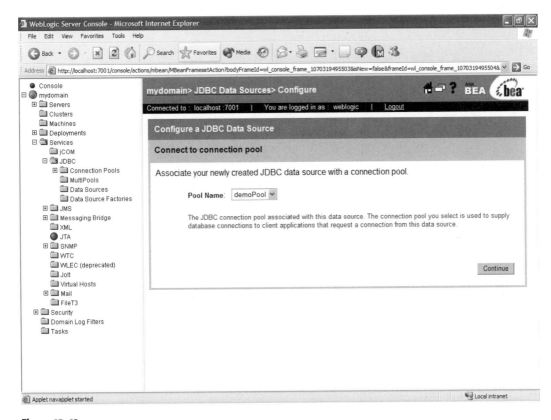

Figure 15–12
Connect to connection pool.

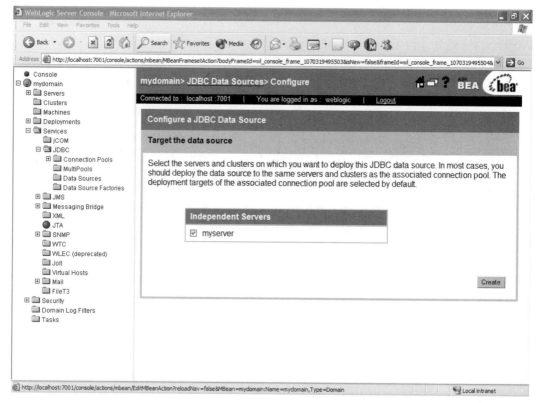

Figure 15–13
Target the data source.

Configure JavaMail

The WebAuction application sends e-mails to auction users to confirm bids processed by the auction system. When the WebAuction application needs to send an e-mail, it locates the appropriate mail session. The mail session defines the host name of your mail server. JavaMail uses this mail server to deliver e-mails sent by the WebAuction application.

Configure mail sessions by navigating to *mydomain* → *Services* → *Mail*. Complete the screens as shown in figures 15–14 and 15–15 to create the mail session and target the session to *myserver*. Replace the value of `mail.host`, listed as `mail.learnweblogic.com`, with the hostname of a local SMTP server.

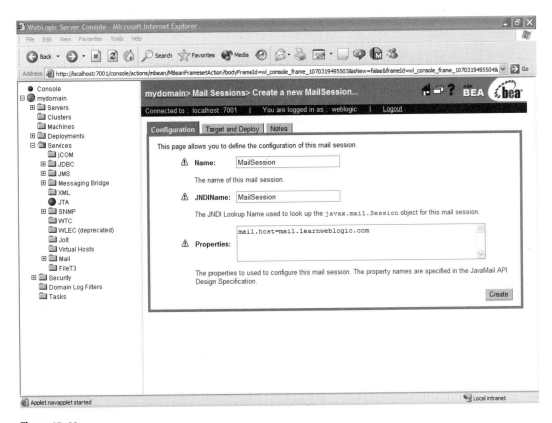

Figure 15–14
Create a new mail session.

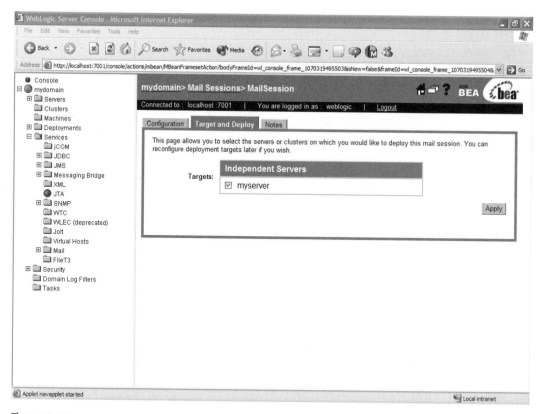

Figure 15–15
Target and deploy.

Configure JMS

The WebAuction application does not process bids directly, but sends a bid message to the
`BidReceiverBean`. In order to use JMS messaging in your WebLogic Server application, you
must set up a JMS server, a place to store messages, and JMS queues for the auction application.

Start by creating a JMS store. You can store messages either to the filesystem or to a database.
For the WebAuction, we use the local filesystem to store messages. First, identify a directory to store
messages; in the example, we use *c:\working\WebAuction\jms-store*. Create this directory or select an
alternative directory. You will use this directory path when you configure your JMS store.

Within the WebLogic Console, navigate to *mydomain* → *Services* → *JMS* → *Stores*, and select the
link *Configure a new JMS File Store...*. Create a new store named `WebAuction File Store`. Complete the screen as shown in Figure 15–16, and click the *Create* button.

Next, create a JMS server to handle JMS messages. Within the WebLogic Console, navigate to
mydomain → *Services* → *JMS* → *Servers* and select the *Create a new JMS Server...* link. You need to name
the JMS server (we use the name `WebAuction JMS Server`) and associate the server with the
JMS store you just created. Complete the screen as shown in Figure 15–17, and click the *Create* button. Then, target the JMS server to the server *myserver*, as shown in Figure 15–18.

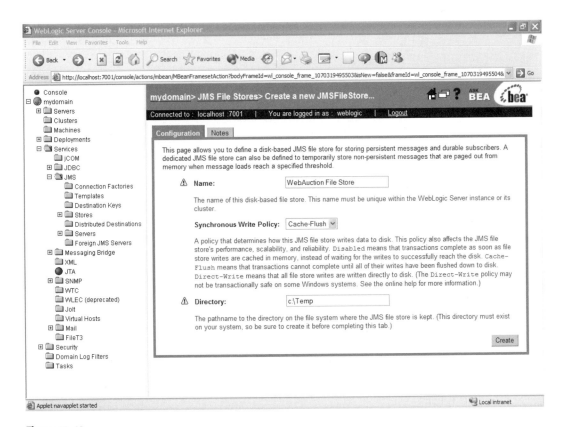

Figure 15–16
Create a new JMSFileStore....

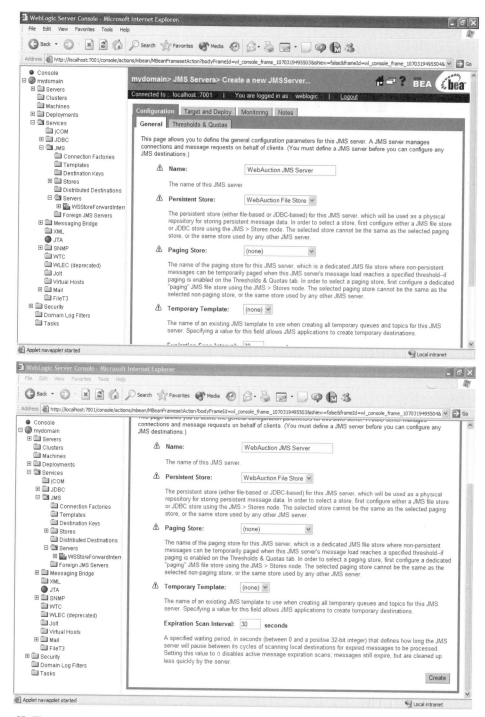

Figure 15–17
Create a new JMS Server....

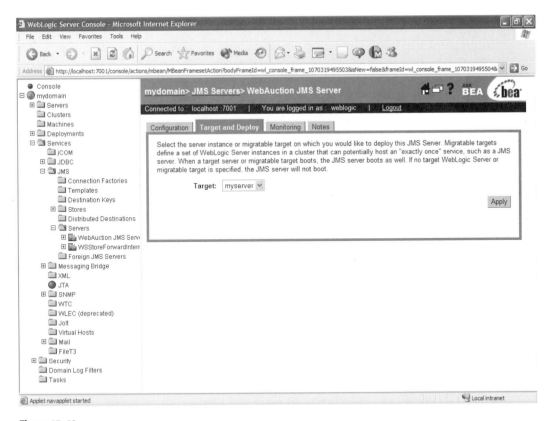

Figure 15–18
Target and deploy.

Now you have created the JMS server. Next, create the queues used by the WebAuction application on this new JMS server. Navigate to *mydomain* → *Services* → *JMS* → *Servers* → *WebAuction* JMS *Server* and select the link *Configure Destinations....* Click *Create a New JMS Queue...*, and complete the resulting screen as shown in Figure 15–19. Create the queue with the *Create* button.

Now, you have created a new JMS Queue for B*ids*. Next, create another JMS queue using the name *OutgoingMailQueue*. The WebAuction application uses both of these queues.

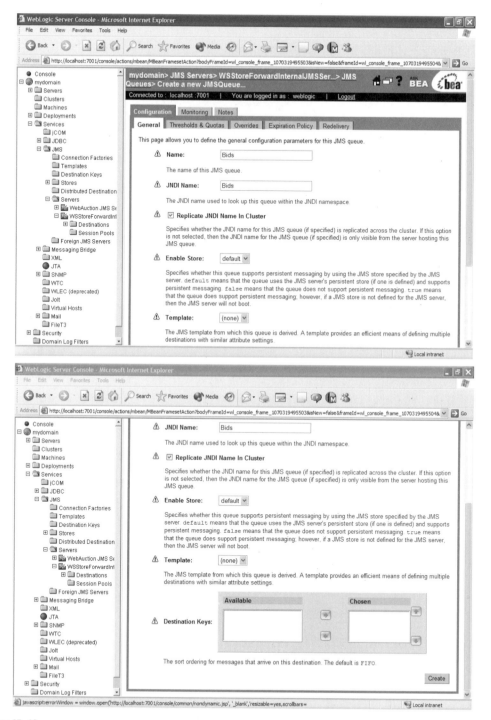

Figure 15–19
Create a new JMS Queue....

Configure Security

The WebAuction application uses the default security configuration. When you configure the domain *mydomain*, WebLogic Server automatically creates the realm *myrealm*. This realm is the default, or active realm, within the domain and defines users and groups within the domain. To configure security for the WebAuction application, add a group for auction users. Navigate to *mydomain* → *Security* → *Realms* → *myrealm* → *Groups* and click the link *Configure a new Group*... Complete the *Name* field with the value `auction_user`, and *Apply* the change. See Figure 15–20.

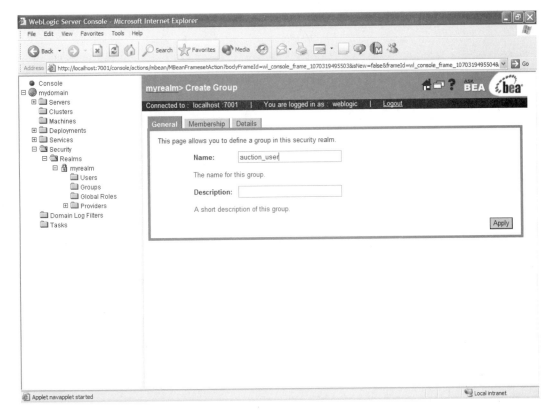

Figure 15–20
Create group.

Build and Deploy the WebAuction Application

The WebAuction application includes `ant` build scripts. These scripts build the Web archive, the Enterprise JavaBeans, and ultimately the enterprise archive. Further, the build script uses the `wldeploy` action to deploy the *.ear* file to an instance of WebLogic Server. Modify properties in the build script (*build.xml*) for your environment. Set properties:

- `weblogic.user`—An administrator username.

- `weblogic.password`—The password for the administrator account.
- `weblogic.adminurl`—The T3 protocol address of the target WebLogic Server instance.

At the command prompt, run the build script using the `ant` command. See Figure 15–21 for typical output.

Any errors in the deployment appear in the output of the build command.

Once you successfully deploy the enterprise archive to WebLogic Server, confirm the deployment by pointing your browser to the auction application at *http://localhost:7001/auction*. The resulting page should appear as in Figure 15–22.

Now that you have built and deployed the WebAuction application, create an account, offer some unused items for sale, and buy some stuff (you can get some real bargains). More importantly, look at the state of the database using the PointBase console; and look at the state of the WebLogic Server using the WebLogic console. Try adding features to the application. By using the WebAuction as a starting point, you can familiarize yourself with the various J2EE technologies.

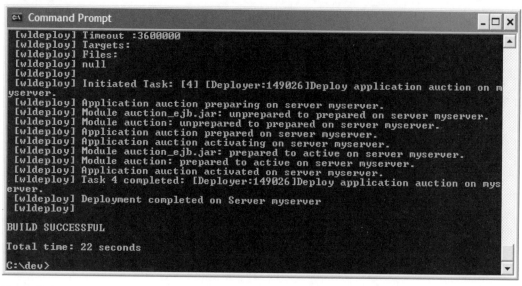

Figure 15–21
Output of the ant build script.

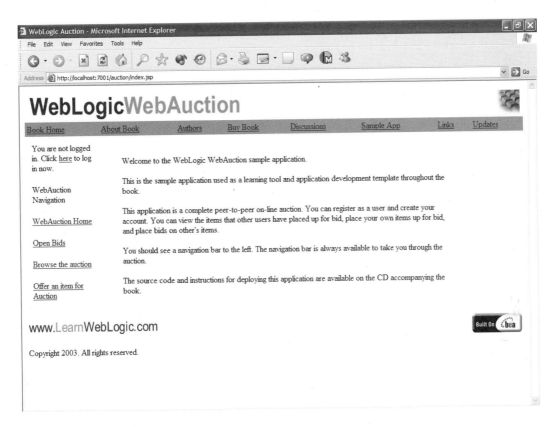

Figure 15–22
WebAuction homepage.

chapter 16

WebLogic Workshop

WebLogic Workshop allows developers to create enterprise-class applications quickly. BEA WebLogic Workshop includes both an IDE for visually authoring Web applications and a runtime framework that sits on top of WebLogic Server and serves as the core for WebLogic Portal Server and WebLogic Integration Server (BEA calls the framework a convergence layer). In WebLogic Platform 7.0, when WebLogic Workshop was first introduced, Workshop supported Web Services only. With WebLogic Platform 8.1, BEA has expanded WebLogic Workshop into a full Web application development tool and incorporated the framework into the Server, Portal, and Integration products.

WebLogic Workshop is made up of an integrated development environment and a runtime framework. Both are designed to help you become more productive regardless of your prior experience with J2EE specification implementations. Because the WebLogic Workshop runtime component is the foundation framework for all WebLogic products, the IDE can be used as the development tool for Portal, page flow construction, Web Services, and other applications and components. The IDE can be used to specify business-process management rules in WebLogic Integration. Thus, there is one tool and one programming model across the WebLogic product stack for development, data access, and deployment, facilitated by WebLogic Workshop's IDE. In addition to facilitating J2EE application development, the new version of WebLogic Workshop shipped with Platform 8.1 provides features that address common Web Services adoption concerns, such as security, reliable messaging, interoperability, and the mismatch between Java and XML. It also provides enhancements to functionality previously supported by the first version of WebLogic Workshop, such as support for extensible Controls (in the Control framework, discussed later in this chapter), support for new WebLogic Platform components such as Liquid Data, integration of Web applications, simplification of development, and streamlined deployment.

WebLogic Workshop IDE

The WebLogic Workshop IDE was created to simplify J2EE application development. J2EE-based systems are particularly flexible and adaptable for e-business applications. Unfortunately, many J2EE development projects are unsuccessful. Few Java developers fully understand the complex J2EE programming model, and this becomes a risk in building J2EE-based applications. If not adequately managed, this risk can cause project overruns. Successful J2EE application development has historically required many highly skilled architects and developers, more time, and more iterations than the standard object-oriented (OO) project. Using the WebLogic Workshop IDE, application developers can build entire applications using components provided by the underlying framework.

This reduces the complexity and risk associated with developing J2EE applications. BEA WebLogic Workshop was designed to position the role of the application developers to complement the roles of the J2EE component builders and architects within the WebLogic environment. WebLogic Workshop allows J2EE developers and architects to concentrate on identifying and building fundamental system components and exposing these EJBs, Web Services, and other components as Controls. Java Controls are reusable components supported by WebLogic's Control framework that encapsulate business logic, commonly used functions, and back-end resource connectivity. Application developers can implement the business logic for an application by incorporating these Controls and using straight Java development to add methods, set properties, and otherwise modify or extend the components. Even non-Java developers can build a simple application using the visually represented components.

One advantage of the WebLogic Workshop programming model and IDE is that it is used across all WebLogic Platform components (WebLogic Portal, WebLogic Integration, WebLogic Server and Web Services, workflows, Controls, and so on). Having a consistent development environment eliminates the learning curve typically associated with building applications for different systems. If you are building a portal-based application, for example, the applications you're presenting to the user might represent EJBs, integration processes to some back-office system, and so on. Because WebLogic Workshop is the common tool used across all of these environments (Portal, Integration, WebLogic Server), development is consistent, predictable, and manageable.

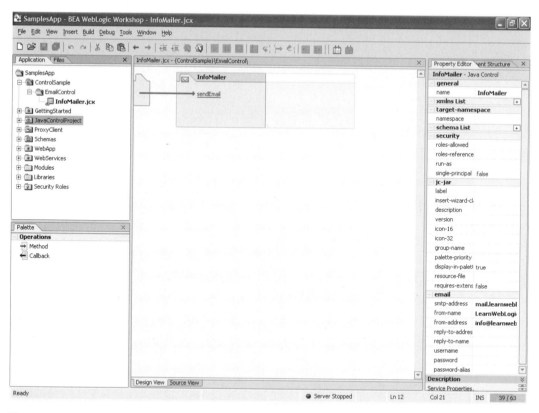

Figure 16–1
WebLogic Workshop Java Controls.

The WebLogic Workshop IDE provides source editing features and can be integrated with source control systems, making development using the IDE very robust. The IDE itself is designed to be extensible so that over time you will be able to build your own IDE extensions if needed.[1]

Launching the WebLogic Workshop IDE

WebLogic Workshop can be invoked on the command line, via a graphical filesystem browser, or from the Start menu using Microsoft Windows. On a Windows machine, *Start* → *Programs* → BEA *WebLogic Platform* 8.1 → *WebLogic Workshop*. Alternatively you could locate the *Workshop.exe* executable file under the *weblogic81\workshop* directory structure and invoke it on the command line or by double-clicking on the file using Windows Explorer. On a Linux or UNIX box, you can run the Bourne shell script called Workshop.sh to start Workshop on the command line, or you can run it by double-clicking on it from a graphical file system browser. The file can be found under your BEA home directory at */bea/weblogic81/workshop/*.

Working with the WebLogic Workshop IDE

If you understand how to work with the WebLogic Workshop IDE, you can build enterprise-class J2EE systems without having to dive into the complexities of the J2EE programming model. This works because of the special notation the IDE uses to communicate with the runtime framework. The WebLogic Workshop runtime framework is designed to interpret annotations embedded in java code. The annotations are javadoc-style comments inserted in the Java code automatically by the WebLogic Workshop IDE that cause to the runtime framework to generate J2EE resources, allowing the user to build enterprise applications without diving into the low-level J2EE inner workings. These annotations are editable explicitly by hand or implicitly via the visual editor. The annotations cause the generation of J2EE infrastructure components by the runtime framework. Since the annotations have special meaning to the WebLogic Workshop runtime framework, be extremely careful if you choose to update them by hand.

Building an application or component with the WebLogic Workshop IDE is meant to be intuitive and straightforward. In this section, we look at the basic elements of the IDE and its features.

Applications

The first thing you must do to use WebLogic Workshop is either open or create an application. Applications can encapsulate many projects in Workshop; everything you build or edit using WebLogic Workshop must be part of an application.

To open an existing application, select *Open* from the File menu of WebLogic Workshop and browse to the existing application (*.work*) file. To create a new application, select *New* → *Application* from the File menu. In the resulting dialog, specify the type of application you'd like to create, the directory in which it should live, the associated WebLogic server instance, and the name of the application. See Figure 16–2.

---

1. See the Workshop Extensibility Development Kit available at http://www.dev2dev.bea.com/extensibility.

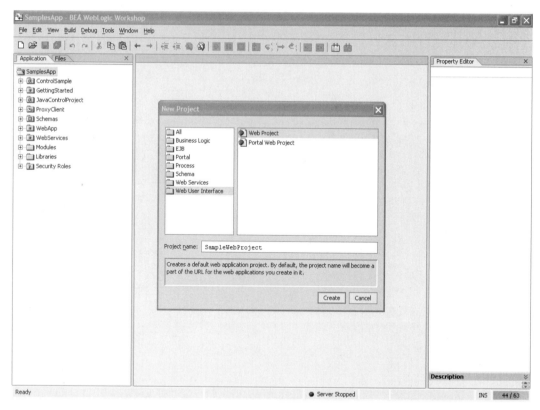

Figure 16–2
Create a new Workshop project.

Projects

Applications are made up of projects. A project might encapsulate a set of Java Controls (reusable components), a set of Web Services, or an entire J2EE-based Web application. When you create a new project using WebLogic Workshop, a corresponding folder is created under the *Application* directory, and files associated with your project, such as JSPs, JWS (Web Services), and so on, are created as part of this folder.

A project can be created by selecting *File* → *New* → *Project*. You will be asked to select the type of project to create (select *All* in the dialog box to see all of your options). When assigning a name to your project, remember that if this is to be part of a Web application, your project name will be part of the URL used to access components of your Web application.

When you create a new project, WebLogic Workshop automatically generates many of the associated files you would normally expect to have to build from scratch. For example, if you create a new Web application project, you'll notice that Workshop creates and populates a default WEB-INF directory (*web.xml*, *weblogic.xml*, etc.), a resources directory containing default cascading style sheets, images, JSPs, and a default page flow (JPF). The remaining project setup tasks become simple configuration tasks as opposed to tedious construction of multiple files.

> **Note:** WebLogic Server supports the APP-INF directory structure.

The WebLogic Workshop Project Model is new with WebLogic Platform 8.1, and we discuss it in more detail later in this chapter.

Components of the IDE

Each file type in WebLogic Workshop has its own Visual Designer (views). There is a core set of Visual Designers supported by WebLogic Server and WebLogic Workshop. Additional extensions are provided for users of other Platform products, like WebLogic Portal and WebLogic Integration.

Design View and Source View

You can find the Design View at the center of the IDE window (see Figure 16–3); it is used for the graphical assembly of parts of a project. In this view, you can construct applications using pictorial representations of components. The Design View is useful for constructing JSPs, HTML files, JPFs, Web Services (JWS), Java Controls (JCX), and the like. Design View is not used for XML configuration files, Java source files, or cascading style sheets.

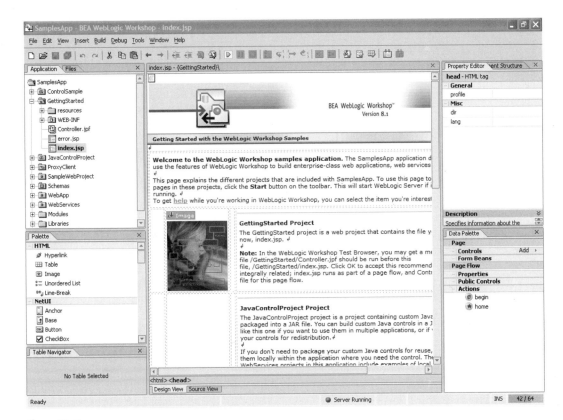

Figure 16–3
WebLogic Workshop Design View.

For example, a Web Service can be represented visually by associating external operations and Java Controls in the Design View. Notice that Controls used to access back-end operations are on the right-hand side of the Design View window.

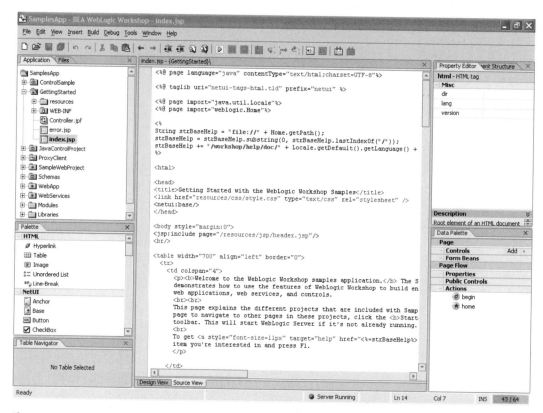

Figure 16–4
WebLogic Workshop Source View.

The Design View shares a tabbed window with the Source View (Figure 16–4). Use the Source View to read or edit the source code associated with the application. The ability to toggle between design and source views allows you to compose the structure of the application or Web service graphically and edit the associated code to extend or customize the application. This two-way editing allows you to work in the most comfortable approach at any time.

Warning: Be careful if you decide to modify the javadoc-style annotations (Figure 16–5) in the Source View; they have special meaning to the WebLogic Workshop runtime component.

```
package async;

/**
 * <p> A web service that uses a TimerControl to delay sending a response b
 * @jc:location http-url="HelloWorldAsync.jws" jms-url="HelloWorldAsync.jws
 * @jc:wsdl file="#HelloWorldAsyncWsdl"
 * @editor-info:link source="HelloWorldAsync.jws" autogen="true"
 */
```

Figure 16–5
WebLogic Workshop annotations.

Flow View

The same window might contain a Flow or Action View tab if the file type in question is a JPF file. Defining JPFs using Action methods instead of relying on HTML links allows for more control over the conditions of page navigation. For example, you can add a new Action method to your JPF by dragging the Action icon from the Palette window into your Flow View (Figure 16–6) , linking that Action method to a resulting JSP, and referencing that Action method using a NetUI anchor tag (more on this later) in the originating JSP (using its Design View). Then, you can customize the Action method to perform appropriate logic, such as role-based decision logic.

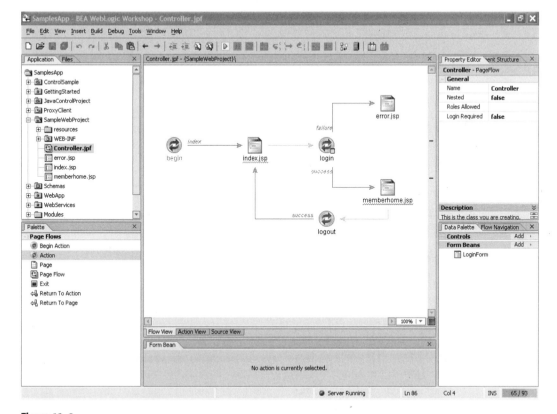

Figure 16–6
WebLogic Workshop Flow View.

Document Structure and Property Editor

The Document Structure and Property Editor share a tabbed space in the IDE. By default, this pane is located to the right of the Design/Source View window, but as with any dockable window or tab, you can move or hide it as appropriate. Using the Document Structure tree, you can navigate through sections of the code in the Source View or display the associated tags in the Design View. The Property Editor (Figure 16–7) allows you to specify attributes of the component selected in the Design View.

Figure 16–7
WebLogic Workshop Property Editor.

Application Window

The names of the projects and their file structures for the application are displayed in the Application window (Figure 16–8), by default on the far left column of the display. You can view any of these files by double-clicking on the filenames in the Application window, and the resulting Visual Designer will be appropriate to the file type.

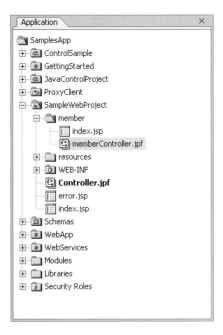

Figure 16–8
WebLogic Workshop Application window.

Palette

The Palette window (Figure 16–9) in the lower left of the WebLogic Workshop screen makes available tools that can be used to build user interfaces, page flows, and so on. The elements displayed in the Palette vary per Visual Designer (file type) and are available for those file types that support views other than Source. HTML elements like forms, tables, and images can be added to a user interface by dragging the appropriate icon to the design view and configuring the element as prompted by the resulting wizard.

Elements corresponding to the WebLogic Workshop data-binding tag library are also displayed in the Palette window. This provides a simple way to add extended HTML elements, such as buttons and checkboxes, to a user interface. It also allows us to insert components that link to specified data, reference controls or page flows, and much more.

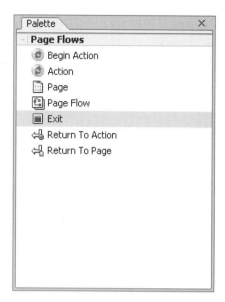

Figure 16–9
WebLogic Workshop Palette window.

Table Navigator

Table Navigator (Figure 16–10) is a table navigation tool that magnifies visual representations of HTML tables and allows for precise drag-and-drop integration from the tag palette.

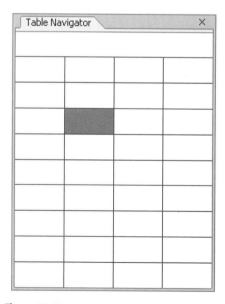

Figure 16–10
WebLogic Workshop Table Navigator.

Data Palette

The Data Palette (Figure 16–11) is available in the lower right-hand part of the default IDE screen layout for certain file types, such as JSPs and JPFs. It facilitates binding data coming from Controls or page flows to visual elements on the screen. It displays the available Controls and methods associated with the Visual Designer for easy incorporation into the Web application.

Figure 16–11
WebLogic Workshop Data Palette.

Web Application Development

Many of the tools listed above are provided as part of the WebLogic Workshop data-binding tag library called NetUI. NetUI encompasses the page-flow programming model and a set of tools. This set of tools provides support for two-way editing, drag-and-drop tags, property sheet consistency (if the sheet changes, the change is reflected in the display), and an extensible tag palette (for reuse of legacy UIs). They also facilitate the identification of field names, types, and validation constraints for form fields. Form validation is handled declaratively through annotations placed in a form class. These tools support many of the wizards we can use to automate the creation of UI over data, business controls, and Web Services controls. For example, a wizard could be run to put a UI over a database Control; the boilerplate would be created for the user to go in and customize later.

> **Note:** As you build your first projects using the WebLogic Workshop IDE, you'll notice *netui:* tags in your files. This tag library provides tags that bind to data sets (repeater, grid, cell repeater, tree control, and so on). They are HTML equivalent data-bound tags (inputs/selects, and so on).

Java Page Flow

JPF is the WebLogic extension of the Struts programming model. Apache's Struts is an implementation of MVC (Model-View-Controller) that provides support for mapping requests (specific URIs) to actions, handling input, flow control, and state management. Working with Struts directly can be complicated. WebLogic Workshop's Struts-based JPF programming model provides tools to help you take advantage of the features of Struts while removing the complexity.

JPF files contain an annotated Java definition of a controller class. The page flow programming model defines the structure of a page flow and includes the JPF controller class, JSPs with associated tags, and related Java Controls that expose logic associated with UI features.

The JPF class is similar in structure to a JWS class, contains special javadoc-style annotations, and exposes Action methods. Action methods contain navigational logic and code to interact with data, business, and service Controls. The pages (JSPs) in the page flow will exist in the same directory as the JPF file and are responsible for presenting data, gathering data, and invoking Action methods. The page-flow controller Actions are invoked via corresponding tags in the JSP files. The page-flow controller instances are kept alive while the user is navigating the page flow, and access is single threaded.

The PageFlowController class (com.bea.wlw.netui.pageflow.PageFlowController) is extended to create new JPF classes. The PageFlowController enables usage of Struts functionality and provides mechanisms for control of navigation and responsiveness to user state.

Since the JPF file acts as a controller for the specified portion of the application (similar to the Struts dispatch action), code specifying flow that is sometimes contained in JSPs should be moved into the JPF file; this allows you to separate the presentation from flow logic. A page flow can be added to a Struts-based application, and vice versa. No Struts-like configuration file is necessary, since what would go into a Struts configuration file is derived from the annotations instead. Page flows compile down to Struts 1.1 subapplications.

Page flow controller instances can be nested for easy reuse. This is useful for instances providing help, login, site evaluation services, and the like. Controller instances stay alive as part of the user session and can put other page flows on the stack, allowing users to navigate through them.

The JPF Visual Designer (Figure 16–12) in WebLogic Workshop provides graphical and source views of a page flow controller class. It also offers a Flow View to facilitate building a page flow with pictorial representations of components.

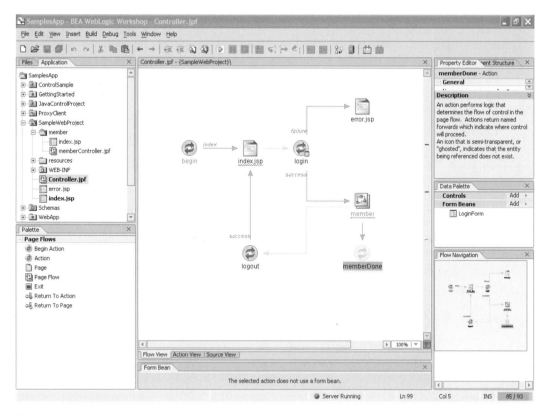

Figure 16–12
WebLogic Workshop Java Page Flow Visual Designer.

Data Binding

WebLogic Workshop 8.1 provides data-binding alternatives to building EJBs, using JDBC and state-less session beans, and building connection pools.

The goal of WebLogic Workshop's data binding mechanisms is twofold. First, data binding supports Web applications that read and update important data sources (such as Web services, data-bases with SQL, business controls, and the like). Second, it allows efficient database access with a snapshot model optimized for read-mostly, while keeping the SQL control with the developer. Additionally, WebLogic Workshop's data binding is designed to lower the boundaries between XML and SQL. It is designed to scale well from simple defaults to custom code at every layer.

The components of data binding include database controls, WebLogic Server RowSets, and the NetUI Tag Library.

Database Controls

Database controls (Figure 16–13) can be used to access a JDBC data source specified in the WebLogic Server configuration. The methods of the database control pass SQL statements to the database, and the connection to the database is handled by the control. This allows a developer to interact with a specified database via SQL without handling any connection-specific tasks.

To add a database control to your application, make sure you're in the Design View; then, use the Insert → Controls → Database menu option. Once the control is created, you can select the visual representation and use the Insert → Method menu options to add methods to the Control. Toggling to the Source View allows you to define parameters for the method.

You can associate a SQL query with the method by double-clicking the arrow next to the method in the Design View and following the resulting dialog.

Once you've added the database control, the code must be edited to take advantage of the control's methods.

Database controls can be configured to execute stored procedures in a back-end-neutral way. They also handle dynamic SQL generation where SQL is generated in response to user actions, page flow grid-details-edit-insert cycle support, and integration with WLS RowSets.

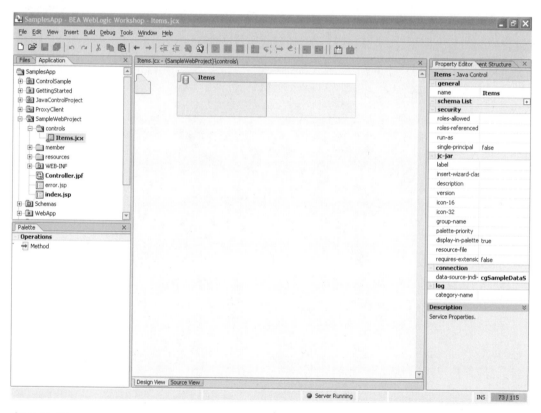

Figure 16–13
WebLogic Workshop Database Control.

WLS RowSets

A WLS RowSet is a cached result set that can be disconnected. It is updateable via a built-in SQL generator driven by the result set plus supplemental metadata. It is convertible to and from XML schema and instance documents. It's built on standard drivers and implements the JDBC optional standard and supports database operations using `javax.sql.RowSet`.

Creating a RowSet Control is best handled by using the Rowset Control Wizard. This wizard facilitates the tricky coordination between the metadata in the Control's JCX file and the annotations in the methods defined in the source file.

NetUI Tag Library

The NetUI tag library includes a set of data-binding tags that allow you to represent data sets on a Web page. The data-binding tags are part of the tag library `netui-tag-databinding.tld`. You can import this library into your JSP (if it's not handled by default) by including it like so:

```
<%@ taglib uri="netui-tags-databinding.tld" prefix="netui-data"%>
```

The data-binding tags are used in one of three ways: first, to invoke a method in a Control and have the resulting data displayed on the page; second, to display RowSet data on the page; and third, to render data sets on a page either in table form or not. Some tags in the latter category facilitate data updates by a user. Let's go through the types of NetUI data binding tags one at a time.

Method invocation tags are used to call methods on Controls or page-flow controllers (note: not Actions). The tags are `netui-data:callControl` and `netui-data:callPageFlow`. Using these tags allows you to call the methods specified by the tags, like so:

```
<netui-data:callControl controlID="testControl" method="runTest"/>
```

In this example, the method called `runTest` from the Control identified as `testControl` in the attribute map. You can specify parameters to the method by adding the `netui-data:methodParameter` tag to the entry.

```
<netui-data:methodParameter value="xyz"/>
```

Repeater tags are used to display data sets in your JSP. The simplest usage of a repeater tag is one in which the elements in your data set are rendered without iteration boundaries, and the entire body of the tag is repeated for each element. An example of this type of usage is as follows:

```
<netui-data:repeater dataSource="{pageFlow.clientlist}">
<netui-html:label value="{container.item.customerNo},
{container.item.customerName}"/>
</netui-data:repeater>
```

You can apply more structure to the display by using certain tags to mark transaction boundaries, as mentioned above. You can also set default text to be displayed in the case where the data set element is empty, or you can allow users to alter the value of the element.

Grid tags can be used to render data from a `RowSet` object. `RowSets` hold data retrieved from a relational database. You can sort and filter this data and display the results using the grid tags.

To see a full listing of the data binding tags, refer to the WebLogic Workshop JSP Tag Reference included in the CD-ROM with this book.

Changing IDE Properties

The IDE layout (Figure 16–14) can be changed by simply selecting a window and dragging it to the part of the screen in which you would like it to appear. You may also choose to have two components share a tabbed window, or you can separate the tabbed items into separate smaller windows.

The Tools menu option allows you to specify IDE properties. You can configure everything from default tab stops in the Source View to the size of the font in the IDE display.

If you are using WebLogic Workshop in an environment that requires all outbound requests go through a proxy server, you will want to specify your proxy server settings in the IDE Properties window. The settings are similar to what you see in a Web browser; you can specify the proxy server hostname and port, and hostnames that do not require proxy server routing.

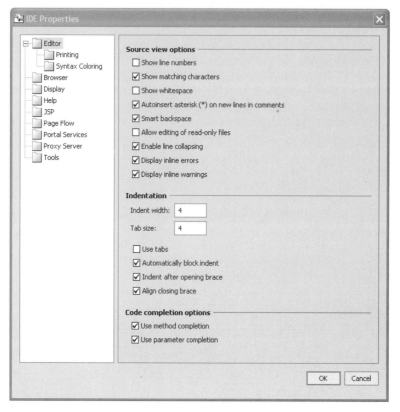

Figure 16–14
WebLogic Workshop IDE properties.

WebLogic Workshop Project Model

The WebLogic Workshop Project Model is designed to support rapid application development (RAD). Support for quick code changes and redeployments is central to this functionality. WebLogic Workshop is designed to support this RAD approach for development for WebLogic Integration, Portal, and general-purpose J2EE. Resources and roles needed for application deployment (like database connectivity) can be defined as part of the application. Performance enhancements come with help from WLS—WLS deploys pieces of an EAR, enabling RAD, while leveraging all security, resource management and deployment models of the J2EE server.

The WebLogic Workshop 8.1 project model defines applications as being composed of projects, libraries, roles, and resources, and it allows for EAR deployment in multiple environments, reflecting the J2EE model. J2EE specifications do not include a set of best practices for build and deployment, but the WebLogic Workshop project model makes it easy to organize source files and assemble applications from components. This facilitates the code-build-debug cycle and allows for generic packaging for deployment to many environments.

Projects

A project can be defined as a unit of development—a set of source files meant to be compiled together—with a dependency structure appropriate for a Web application archive. Possible project types include Web application, Control project (produces a Control JAR file with extra metadata to allow the IDE to display the information for the property sheet), EJB project (from WLS), and JAR project (anything else). The project type impacts the file types for the project, the compile and build process (if it's a Web application, we understand the classloader rules, for example), the development time deployment, and the steps needed to package the project, set up deployment descriptors, and so on.

Libraries

A library is any reusable, prepackaged JAR, including Java Controls, EJBs, Java classes, and more. You can scope a library to the Web application or WAR file (WEB-INF/*lib*) or to the entire application or EAR file (APP-INF/lib). Or, you can put it in the system CLASSPATH. Putting the JAR file in the top-level libraries project will scope it to the application.

Resources and Roles

WebLogic Workshop supports both developer- and administration-level role bindings. A developer can populate project-level lists of role names, declare security settings at the class or method level, and implement security programmatically. An administrator can establish accepted authentication credentials, map those credentials to users, assign users to groups, and map users and groups to roles. In other words, the developer controls development-time bindings, while the administrator controls test, staging and production bindings. Security roles are held in the deployment descriptor for the EAR.

Build and Deployment

Several types of builds are defined as part of WebLogic Workshop: On-demand request-handling builds (similar to JSP compilation), project-level builds, full builds, and packing for deployment.

WebLogic Workshop's internal build system is based on Ant; all internal build and compile tools have an Ant interface. Developers can use their own scripts and expose their internal scripts for further modification (or modify *build.xml*). Ant can also be used to incorporate JUnit or the like for testing.

> **Note:** Apache Ant is a build tool created to facilitate builds targeting multiple platforms. You can customize the tool by extended Java classes, and the configuration files are XML-based. See *http://ant.apache.org/* for more information.

Deployments are optimized differently based on the type of environment in question. Development-time deployment must be rapid, whereas test-time deployment must be controlled and repeatable, and should model the production environment as closely as possible. The application should not have to change per environment, and WebLogic Workshop allows us to change the bindings for the application. Location information, server and port information, resources (queues, databases), and roles can be bound to the execution environment and can be kept outside the application EAR.

The Settings model in WebLogic Workshop keeps the settings at application and project levels (including debug settings, JDK settings, and the like), allows settings to be personal (per open files) or shared (by everyone checked into project), and are source-control friendly.

WebLogic Workshop Support For Web Services

The WebLogic Workshop runtime framework supports Web services by handling Web Service Definition Language (WSDL) mapping and SOAP protocol services. This is bundled with WebLogic Server. It also manages JWS files and their deployment as J2EE applications.

JWS

JWS files are Java files with javadoc-style annotations that allow declarative access to Web service functionality. When compiled, these standard Java methods with annotations will expose SOAP-based Web Services. WebLogic Workshop makes this easy because it handles the mapping of XML elements in SOAP messages to method parameters for you. This means that the methods you've exposed as Web Services need not change as the underlying implementation changes. This helps to preserve loose-coupling, an important design consideration for service-oriented architectures.

JWS files can be created two ways. You can use the WebLogic Workshop IDE and create JWS files using pictorial representations of the Web service components, or you can create them with a text editor by adding the appropriate annotations.

Using the WebLogic Workshop IDE to create a JWS file is as simple as right-clicking on the project folder in which you want to add the Web Service and selecting *New → Web Service*. The name you select for your Web Service will be the Java classname for the JWS file and part of the URL used to access your Web Service.

Once the new Web Service file (JWS) is created, you can select it and toggle to the Design View in the IDE (Figure 16–15). Web Services expose functionality via methods; to create a new method, select *Insert → Method* from the menu bar. A visual representation of the method will appear in the display.

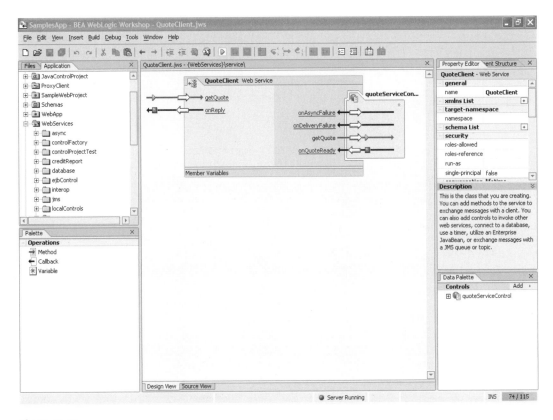

Figure 16–15
WebLogic Workshop JWS Design View.

You can click on the method name to toggle to the Source View of that method (Figure 16–16). From there you can edit the method declaration to accept and return parameters, and add the appropriate code to the method.

Any changes to the method declaration will be reflected in the Design View.

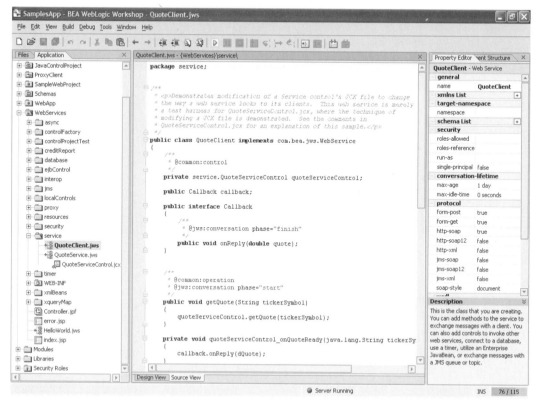

Figure 16–16
WebLogic Workshop JWS Source View.

Asynchronous Conversations

One of the problems with Web Services historically (and as described above) is their reliance on synchronous communication. The consumer of a Web Service must wait for a response from the service before continuing with its own processing. This is not always a realistic model. Web Services may access a variety of data sources, invoke complex processing, even call another Web Service; it is not always reasonable to expect a client to halt its processing while waiting for a Web Service to compute and return a response.

WebLogic Workshop provides support for handling asynchronous conversations; a Web Service can provide immediate acknowledgment to the client, allowing the client to continue its processing, then can provide a subsequent response with the requested information in full.

Providing support for asynchronous communication in your Web Service requires a few steps. First, you need to add a callback method to your Web Service. Generically, a callback is an event-notification mechanism used to inform the client of an occurrence. This method should return the requested data to the client. Second, you should edit the Web Service method invoked by the client to use the new callback method using the following notation:

```
callback.callbackMethodName(inputParam);
```

Third, you need to add a buffer to your Web Service if you want to call back directly from the incoming method invocation. This buffer will handle the immediate response to the client and manage the client requests in a message queue. A unique identifier is associated with each interaction between the client and your Web Service. This allows the client to keep track of which asynchronous response corresponds to which Web Service request.

To enable buffering and management of identifiers, you can use the Properties Editor pane of the IDE. In the Design View, select the arrow next to the method name of your Web Service. In the Properties Editor pane to the right, edit the conversation phase section to indicate *start*. You can do the same thing for the callback method, indicating *finish*. Then you can edit the message-buffer section to enable buffering for both methods. See Figure 16–17.

The Design View for your Web Service will look different following these steps, as shown in Figure 16–18.

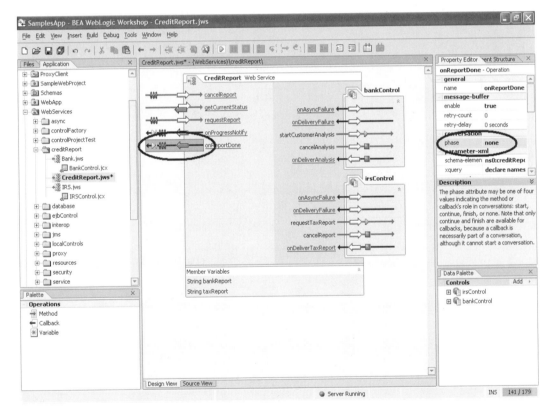

Figure 16–17
Enabling asynchronous Web Services in WebLogic Workshop.

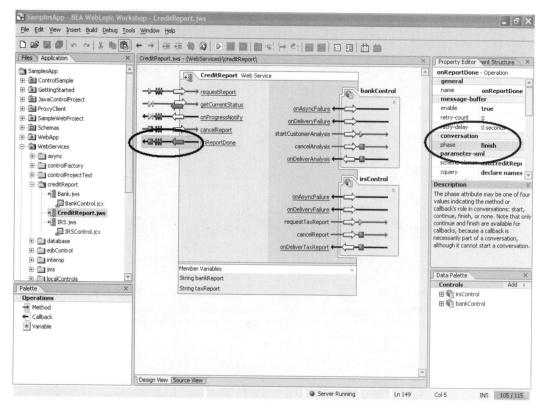

Figure 16–18
WebLogic Workshop Design View of asynchronous Web Services.

Test View

Testing your Web Services requires a build of the project containing your JWS file, starting the server, and invoking your Web Service methods. WebLogic Workshop enables this with one click of the *Start* button on the IDE's tool bar. Assuming there are no errors in your code, a browser window will be launched to expose the Test View. It should be noted that this automated deployment model and integrated testing harness help cut down on the cycle times you would face while doing iterative development.

The Test View screen (Figure 16–19) in the browser window makes available the methods in your Web Service for testing. Clicking the *Test Form* tab will display forms corresponding to the inputs expected by your Web Service methods; this is the quickest way to perform basic tests.

The resulting screen outlines request and response details, including the response payload. When testing asynchronous conversations, it's important to remember to refresh the browser screen to see the callback response and the resulting payload.

The Test XML tab also allows you to invoke the Web Service methods. You can reference the Console, Overview, and Warning screens by clicking their corresponding tabs to get details about what a service is doing and to get useful debugging information.

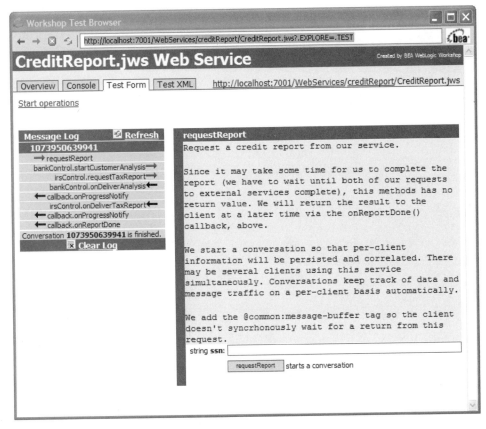

Figure 16–19
WebLogic Workshop Test View.

XMLBeans

Loose coupling is a common goal of integration strategies in enterprise architectures. One problem with many integration solutions is that the method by which disparate systems communicate (the "glue") is not resilient to change. Making this method simple, universal, and easy to debug will help achieve true loose coupling in integration solutions.

XML is often used to format communications between disparate systems, but accessing elements within the XML documents often requires custom code that is system-specific. In order for messages to outlast systems, two categories of tools have traditionally been needed: a message definition (such as an XML schema) and a standardized language for providing the views (XML Query or XSLT).

XMLBeans is a tool library and a compiler that can be incorporated into your development environment. Although it's available with WebLogic Workshop 8.1, it can be downloaded freely and used with any J2EE container.

The goal of XMLBeans in WebLogic Workshop 8.1 is to offer full support for XML Schemas in Java. It's important to understand the significance of XML Schema as a definition format; XML

Schema provides the most explicit description of the messages that must outlast the connected systems. Although the tool library is available for use with any XML document, the Java type generation is available for use only with XML Schema.

One of the classic XML-to-Java conversion issues is that all data associated with an XML document is not retained. For example, in the marshaling from XML to Java, ordering information gets thrown away. In Java, getA() and getB() methods don't require, or care about, ordering. In XML, the point of model groups is to model ordering constraints. XMLBeans strives to retain all XML data, including ordering information. When order is important but not exposed in strongly typed messages, XMLBeans makes a cursor available. You can use the cursor to get ordering information, or you can place the cursor at a particular position and traverse the DOM-like object model by using methods specifying after/before, relative positioning requests, and the like.

When using the XMLBeans compiler, you must have your XML Schemas in a special Schemas project. Create the Schemas project just as you would any project within WebLogic Workshop. After creating a Schema project, drag your XSD files to it or select it through the Import dialog. Using the XMLBeans compiler, the XML Schema files are compiled like Java files, and the resulting CLASS files are placed in an XMLBeans folder. The compiler builds the appropriate Java interfaces and classes and populate associated metadata. You can specify that you would like the files to be compiled as they change on the Project Properties dialog under Build. There is one XSD type for every one Java type. There is one XSD type system per compiled JAR (this allows for segregation of XML-type system versions). The compiled JAR file will be named the same as your Schema project. The JAR file will be placed in the Libraries folder (in the Application pane) of your Schema project.

These XML types can be used on Web Service or workflow methods where the exactly specified XML message shape must be processed. The XSD file can be dropped into a project via the WebLogic Workshop IDE and will look just like a Java Bean. Without any further mapping, it can be used in Java. It looks and acts like a Java type that actually maps perfectly to an XML schema that came in a WSDL. See Figure 16–20.

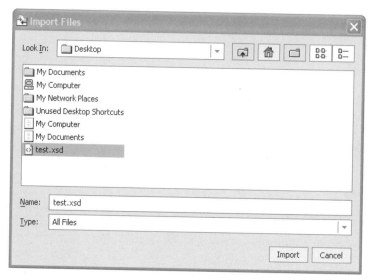

Figure 16–20
An XSD file added to a Workshop.

The idea behind XMLBeans is that any XSD or WSDL will "just work" when picked up, with all data associated with an XML message available. This provides ease of use, robustness, and fast performance.

XQuery Support

XQuery is an XML query language that supports access to and transformation of data to and from XML sources. If you are exposing a Web Service, for example, and would like to support a client who cannot conform to the specifications of your service, you can provide an XQuery mapping in front of your service to map the format of their request to something your service can understand. This type of mechanism removes the need for multiple service implementations to meet needs of various clients. You can have a single service implementation and provide XQuery mappings for those clients unable to conform to your service specifications.

WebLogic Workshop uses XQuery to allow the mapping of XML Schemas and Java objects, completely decoupling the XML from the Java code. You can drive this mapping by using the XQuery mapper in WebLogic Workshop's IDE or by natively entering XQuery code.

Control Framework

Building composite applications out of reusable components and services is gaining popularity in the J2EE community. The concept of assembling component-based applications is supported by a variety of mechanisms across J2EE implementations. One generic mechanism for support of this idea is the Web Service. A finer-grained mechanism, appropriate for use within a single system or environment, is a Java Control.

WebLogic Workshop supports the use and creation of reusable components called Java Controls within its Control framework. Controls encapsulate a single or multiple related functions, such as database queries or interactions with Web Services. Business logic to be reused by many applications or components can be packaged into a Control and exposed via the Control framework.

The Control framework is one of the more powerful components of WebLogic Workshop. Using some combination of Enterprise JavaBeans and message-driven beans, Controls allow us to expose business logic very simply without building custom EJBs to do the job. Any Java resource is a candidate for incorporation by a Control, including EJBs, database connections, and message queues.

Controls can be used by any application using the WebLogic Workshop runtime component (in other words, any application running on WebLogic Platform).

Prepackaged Controls

WebLogic Workshop provides a group of built-in controls representing commonly used access points. Controls available to users out of the box include Database Controls, Web service Controls, Timer Controls, JMS Controls, and EJB Controls.

You can add these Controls to an application via the WebLogic Workshop IDE by selecting the *Control the Palette* window and dragging it into your application design view. See Figure 16–21. This results in either a new Java Control Source (JCS) file or a Java Control Extension (JCX) file being created and associated with your application. If you are creating a new instance of an existing Control definition (a Database Control, for example) a JCX file will be created. Of course, Controls may also be defined manually in code by creating a Control variable and adding the appropriate javadoc notation to a class.

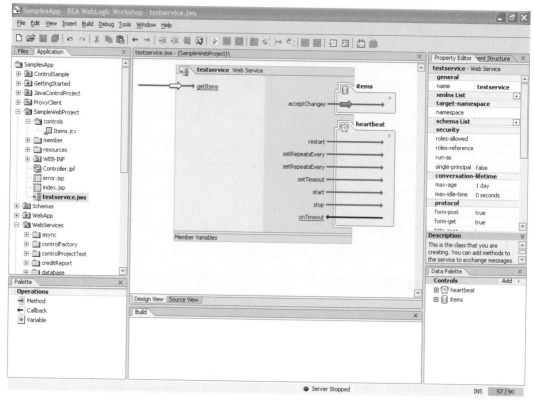

Figure 16–21
Add Controls within WebLogic Workshop.

You can view the resulting Java class in the Source View pane of the IDE. You can edit the Control source code directly if desired.

To access methods defined as part of a Control, use the standard notation for method invocation:

```
controlVariableName.methodName();
```

Control Properties

Control properties are reflected in annotation-style XML in a corresponding properties file. Properties files communicate the attributes that can be set to influence the behavior of the Control. This is useful when leveraging a Control outside of a single project or bundled for reuse. Properties files are typically located in the same folder as the corresponding Control files.

Properties ("tags") are declared at the class or method level of a Control. The attributes of these properties can have default values. If attributes have rules regarding allowable values or types of values, those rules are enforced by WebLogic Workshop in the IDE. The Control can access its property values via a context interface provided at runtime.

Any attributes defined in a Control Properties file can be explicitly retrieved by the Control. This requires two things: a reference to the properties file in the tags annotation in the Control file and a call to the getControlAttribute method for the attributes of interest.

Callbacks

Like asynchronous Web Services, Controls may have callback methods associated with them. Call-back methods can be altered to perform certain functions when fired. A client should create callback handlers to respond to the event notification.

Exposing a callback as part of a Control's public interface mimics the conversational style supported by Web Services. This means that the request to a Control would return nothing, and the expected response would return separately.

This asynchronous flow is useful when you don't want to hold up a transaction waiting for a response from a method. Conversational exchanges can last quite some time, and resources that would otherwise be waiting for a response from a method can instead listen for another request after handing off the method logic to a second thread. This is achieved through a mechanism called message buffering in which method invocations wait on a JMS message queue until resources are available to handle them. Message queuing is configured on the system level and managed automatically by WebLogic Workshop application framework.

A callback handler can be created in client code by clicking on the hyperlink used to display the callback method in the visual representation of the Control. The resulting code can be edited as appropriate. See Figure 16–22.

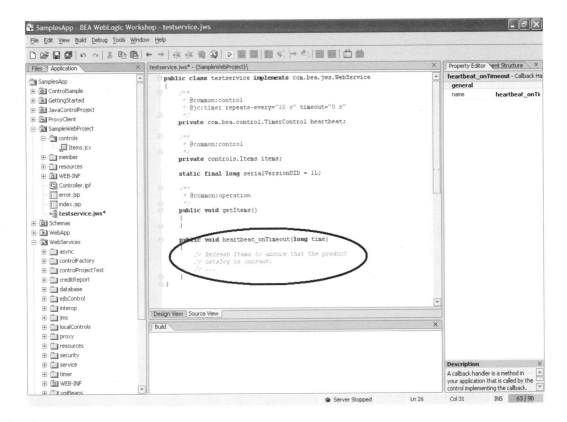

Figure 16–22

Modifying a callback handler in WebLogic Workshop.

Custom Controls

The concept of extensible controls within the Control Framework is new with WebLogic Workshop 8.1. You can leverage the simple, familiar model for tightly coupled business logic to build components for consumption as custom controls. This allows you to take advantage of the Control framework's rich support at runtime, including native support for transactions, security, properties, asynchrony, callbacks, and conversations. You can expose connections to back-end resources and business logic through custom Controls.

It's easy to build a custom control by using the IDE to create a new Control file (JCS) within a project. A user can add a Control file to a folder by right-clicking on the folder and selecting New à Custom Java Control. Once the JCS file is created, the user can use the IDE to add methods, variables, and callbacks to the Control. The source view can be used to add functionality to the Control.

To create the associated properties file, right-click on the folder that contains the Control files using the IDE. The properties file (XML) should exist in the same folder. See Figure 16–23.

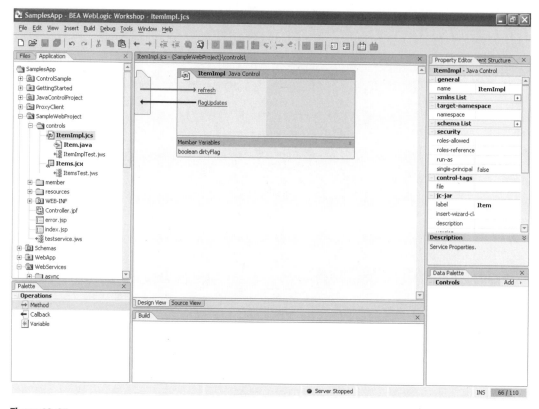

Figure 16–23
Custom Control.

Packaging for Reuse

Custom controls can either be built for use within a particular application or packaged for reuse by multiple applications. To expose a set of Controls for use by other applications, create a new project for your Control files. The resulting JAR file can be used within multiple projects.

Controls Versus Web Services

There are a few things to keep in mind when considering the appropriateness of building or using a Control. If your goal is to expose functionality across organizational boundaries or to applications within your organization using disparate technologies, you should expose that functionality as a Web Service and publish a WSDL for consumption. If you expect that your users are primarily applications within your environment, then you should package your functionality as a Control. Using a Control instead of a Web Service will avoid the overhead associated with marshaling and unmarshaling of Java objects.

It is not always necessary to choose between encapsulating your logic in a Control or in a Web Service. When you build a Control and wish it to be invoked externally, you can simply put a Web Service wrapper on it with a few clicks. Choosing to wrap your business logic in Controls will always work, understanding that Controls can be exposed via Web Services as well.

Controls Versus Adapters

JCA adapters are used to connect to back-end applications and include system-level mechanisms for managing resources like connections, handling transaction propagation, and the like. Adapters shield the application developer from the complexities of back-end connectivity and interactivity. It is possible to use a Java Control to communicate directly with a complex back-end system like SAP or PeopleSoft, but it makes more sense to use the Control to wrap the appropriate adapter. This allows you to take advantage of the JCA functionality while still leveraging the familiar Control framework.

Putting It All Together

BEA's WebLogic Workshop provides support for building applications, components, and Web Services with an intuitive visual editor, removing the complexity associated with building enterprise-class J2EE applications.

In addition to the IDE with robust debugging facilities and a built-in test harness, WebLogic Workshop provides mechanisms for mapping Java code to SOAP messages; wrapping logic in reusable, portable components; building Struts-based page flows with pictorial representations; and placing role-based restrictions on classes and methods, to name a few.

The javadoc-style annotations inserted by the WebLogic Workshop IDE into your Java code has special meaning to the WebLogic Workshop runtime framework. The runtime framework is designed to interpret the embedded annotations and invoke appropriate J2EE resources. This removes the necessity of explicitly controlling these resources in your Java code. Thus, the complexity of the J2EE programming model need not be a consideration when building applications and components.

chapter 17

Capacity Planning for the WebLogic Server

After designing your WebLogic Server deployment and building the application, the next step is to test your deployment to see whether it meets your intended performance criteria. How many registered users should your system support? How many requests per second should it be able to handle? What sort of network and hardware infrastructure is required to meet your deployment goals? This chapter explains both the methodology used in capacity planning and performance information available. We cover the following:

- WebLogic JRockit—We review the optimized, server-side Java Virtual Machine (JVM) packaged with WebLogic Server 8.1 and WebLogic Platform 8.1. JRockit provides a scalable, reliable JVM for Intel-based machines.
- Analysis—We discuss factors to consider for capacity planning.
- Metrics—We set a baseline set of capacity-planning numbers derived from an existing application (we use our sample application, WebAuction) you can use in determining the infrastructure required to meet your deployment requirements.
- Review—We resent capacity planning best practices.

WebLogic JRockit

Note: This section is a review of the JRockit section in Chapter 14. Skip ahead to "Analysis of Capacity Planning" if a review of JRockit is not necessary for you.

The vision behind Java is to provide platform independence for applications. It allows you to write the application once and deploy it on other hardware platforms, without requiring costly code modifications. In its infancy, this platform neutrality came at a price in raw execution speed. However, with time this price has grown smaller and smaller. Products like WebLogic JRockit 8.1 provide a scalable, reliable, high-performing execution engine for deploying enterprise scale applications.

WebLogic JRockit is a Java Virtual Machine (JVM) optimized for server-side applications and for inter-process scalability. BEA designed JRockit specifically for Intel environments running Windows and Linux operating systems. It supports both 32-bit and 64-bit Intel architectures, fully utilizing the additional address space available. Java applications are reliant on the underlying virtual machine and perform based on how well the JVM handles code generation, garbage collection, memory and thread management, and handling of native methods. Originally designed in 1998, WebLogic JRockit delivers an optimized virtual machine designed to exploit the available hardware resources, using adaptive code generation, advanced garbage collection, optimized code execution, and a robust management framework for profiling and tuning.

Compilation Options

JRockit provides two means for optimizing the compiled Java code into native execution. The first mechanism is a Just-In-Time compiler that compiles during server startup. Server-side applications rely on fast execution; however, most JVMs are designed for faster startup and only interpret the Java byte code, waiting to compile into native code until they are requested. JRockit precompiles every class as it loads via the JIT compiler. Although start times are somewhat longer, this cost is amortized over time and the overall result is much faster execution times.

The second area where JRockit provides superior performance is in the optimizing compiler. While compiling all classes with all available optimizations would take too long during server startup, WebLogic JRockit identifies the frequently used methods and runs these through a second, optimizing compiler. By fully optimizing only those functions that will deliver maximum application performance, JRockit provides optimal application performance while still maintaining acceptable server startup times.

How does JRockit recognize what functions warrant the optimized compilation? There is a sampling thread that periodically "wakes up" and checks the status of the various threads executing within the application. The information is recorded and, based on internal heuristics, JRockit determines which threads or functions should be earmarked for optimization. Many functions are never optimized for the life of the server. Typically, these optimizations are done shortly after the server starts, with fewer and fewer optimizations taking place the longer the server runs.

Garbage Collection

A second area of optimization for WebLogic JRockit is in garbage collection. Java applications allocate memory on a heap and when the heap is full it must be harvested, freeing up stale objects and other memory no longer in use. The process of harvesting the heap is known as *garbage collection*. While a server is garbage collecting, the application performance is impacted, since the virtual machine cannot dedicate itself to execution only. You can increase the size of the heap, allowing more objects to be allocated and garbage collection to occur less frequently, but the price you pay is in longer garbage collection times. A tuned garbage collection model will allow optimal heap usage while minimizing the impact of the garbage collection on application performance. Lastly, the application design will have a significant impact on the most optimal garbage collection scheme; garbage collection that performs well for one application may negatively affect performance in another.

To address these needs, WebLogic JRockit supports four different garbage collectors:

- Generational Copying—In this model the memory is separated into two or more areas called *"generations"*. Instead of allocating all objects into a single space and garbage collecting it all at once, objects are allocated into the new generation called the *"nursery"*. This model is best suited to small heap sizes on single CPU machines.

- Single Spaced Concurrent—This collector uses the entire heap and removes pauses completely by executing concurrently with application processing. While the application is executing a background thread is harvesting the heap. This model is best suited for garbage collection without disrupting server execution; however, there is a risk if the garbage collection thread cannot harvest the heap as fast as the application places new objects on it.

- Generational Concurrent—This collector combines the approaches of the first two. New objects are allocated to the new generation, which is garbage collected by "stopping the world" and pausing execution. Active objects in the new generation are moved to a separate generation called the *old generation*. Garbage collection of the old generation follows the concurrent model, with a background thread harvesting concurrently with execution and not causing execution pauses.

- Parallel—In this model all garbage collection are performed in "stop the world" mode, pausing all execution while garbage collection takes place. Multiple threads are used for the harvesting, and although there are execution pauses this model maximizes throughput and memory utilization.

By default, JRockit uses the generational concurrent collection model. The garbage collection model right for your application depends on a number of variables. The ideal model is to minimize the impact of garbage collection, determined by the number of times garbage collection is run and the duration of each run. However, if the application has constraints around response time and cannot tolerate execution pauses, one of the concurrent models may the best choice.

Configuring the garbage collector is done by setting the `–Xgc <collector type>` parameter when starting the JVM. Valid collector types are `gencopy`, `singlecon`, `gencon`, and `parallel`. In addition, you can set the initial and maximum heap sizes using the flags `–Xms <heap size>` and `–Xmx <heap size>` parameters. When using the generational models, you can also control the size of the new generation using the `–Xns <heap size>` parameter. For example, to start JRockit using the generational concurrent collector with an initial and maximum heap size of 512MB and a new generation size of 256MB you would use the following command:

```
java –jrockit –Xgc:gencon –Xms512m –Xmx512m –Xns256m ...
```

Tuning the garbage collection with WebLogic JRockit can deliver optimal performance for your application. However, it is a good idea to consult BEA's documentation before making changes to any of the JVM parameters, as these changes can also result in penalizing your application performance as well. Refer to *http://e-docs.bea.com/wljrockit/docs81/tuning/index.html* for more information on tuning JRockit.

JVM Management and Monitoring

A key capability in tuning your application for optimal performance is identifying the behavior occurring in the underlying JVM. WebLogic JRockit includes useful tools for profiling and tuning the JVM performance. JRockit includes a Management Console for observing real-time information about server and resource utilization. This console can be run stand-alone, or accessed using the WebLogic Server administration console. Through information presented in the console, you can identify bottlenecks to performance and change operating and environment variables to deliver maximum performance. Figure 17-1 illustrates the JRockit graphical console accessed from the WebLogic Server console.

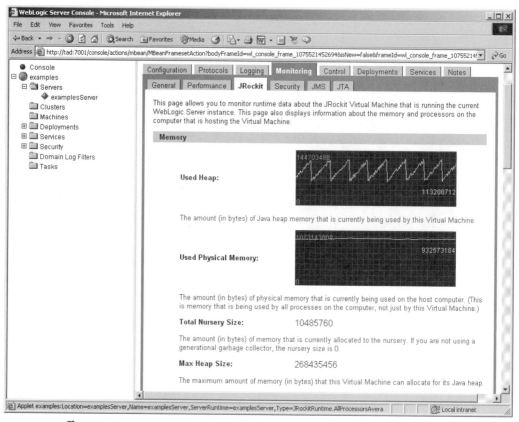

Figure 17-1
JRockit Management Console

JRockit 8.1 also supports the JVM Profiling Interface (JVMPI) and the JVM Debugging Interface (JVMDI), allowing Java applications to interact with the JVM and assist in profiling and debugging activities. This is particularly useful when using third-party tools designed to comply with these standard interfaces.

Analysis of Capacity Planning

Now that we reviewed a powerful component in the WebLogic suite, let's consider how to plan our applications for scalability. The art of determining requirements for a WebLogic Server deployment and planning an infrastructure that will support those requirements is collectively referred to as *capacity planning*. Capacity planning is an attempt to determine the resources, such as CPUs, Internet connection size, and LAN infrastructure, required to support performance. Capacity planning answers the question, What hardware infrastructure and network configuration will enable my WebLogic deployment to fulfill specified performance requirements? Ideally, with an architecture that will scale in a consistent fashion, you can use capacity planning to determine how much of these resources will be required to support the volume of requests as your processing needs grow. A truly scalable infrastructure will not introduce performance bottlenecks as the application scales, putting off the dreaded "point of diminishing returns."

Capacity planning is an inexact science because there are so many factors that influence the capacity of a given application deployment, including the following:

- How database-intensive is the application?
- How large are the pages that Java Server Pages (JSPs) display?
- What is the typical usage pattern for a user?
- How do users access the system?
- How fast is the underlying hardware?

In fact, so many factors influence capacity planning that it borders on being an art form. Nonetheless, it is possible to take some of the guesswork out of the process of capacity planning. In reality, the most influential factor on the hardware capacity necessary to support your application is the application itself. For this reason, this chapter aims only to provide information that will assist your own capacity testing and application design efforts. Creating "a one size fits all" formula to compute the amount of hardware required for a given application is a futile effort.

Factors Affecting Capacity

There are three major areas for focusing capacity-planning efforts for a WebLogic deployment:

- *Server hardware*—Obviously, the capacity of the servers where WebLogic runs directly affects the capacity of the WebLogic deployment. For example, every JSP request from a client requires both memory and CPU time to generate a response from WebLogic. You need to assess the number and power of CPUs, RAM size, JVM efficiency, and other factors relating to the server hardware platform: How much capacity is required from your server platforms?

- LAN *infrastructure*—As noted in previous chapters, a WebLogic cluster relies on a LAN for communication between cluster nodes. Depending upon the application, the requirements for a LAN can vary. For example, a large cluster that is doing *in-memory replication* for either Enterprise JavaBeans (EJBs) or servlet-session replication requires a higher bandwidth network than a small cluster. In addition, the size of session data, the size of a cluster, and the power of the server machines affect the requirements for the LAN infrastructure. You need to assess cluster network hardware performance: How much capacity is required from the LAN between the nodes of the WebLogic cluster?

- *External network connectivity*—The WebLogic deployment communicates to other resources such as databases or legacy systems or communicates externally to systems such as the Internet. You must assess the frequency of connections to external systems and the size of data being transferred: How much capacity is required from the network that connects the WebLogic cluster, the clients, and back-end resources?

This chapter focuses on each of these three areas independently. Capacity planning should be applied across all the components of a WebLogic deployment, not just the servers that run WebLogic. All the components in the deployment affect the capacity of a WebLogic deployment.

Methodology and Metrics for Capacity Planning

Capacity planning is focused on how the WebLogic deployment deals with *maximum performance requirements*. What is the peak load that your deployment will be able to handle? In other words, what is its maximum capacity for handling requests? Capacity-planning methodology focuses on the worst-case scenario, such as when your company's advertisement appears on the Super Bowl and your deployment suddenly receives a flood of millions of new requests. How does an online broker-age service handle the volumes of requests when investors settle their positions at the end of the day? The underlying assumption of planning for the worst case is that your WebLogic Servers and the infrastructure should be able to scale up to that peak load.

In order to quantify the worst cases, set *goals* or *measurable objectives* for capacity: for example, *the WebLogic deployment should be able to handle 10,000 open user sessions at a given time.*

> **Best Practice:** The application deployment should have distinct capacity goals that quantify the maximum capacity required for the deployment. When you have measurable objectives, you can design the WebLogic deployment to meet your needs and better understand the performance characteristics.

Setting Capacity Goals

The first step in capacity planning is *to set goals for the deployment.* These goals should be quantified as maximums:

- **User interactions per second with WebLogic.** This value represents the total number of user interactions that should be handled per second by a WebLogic deployment. User inter-actions are typically accesses to JSP pages or servlets for Web deployments. For application deployments, user interactions are accesses to EJBs.
- **Total number of concurrent user sessions.** This value represents the total number of user sessions that WebLogic should handle at a given time. Concurrent user sessions are mostly an issue for Web deployments when WebLogic is maintaining HTTP session objects around for each user. However, concurrency measures are also important when application deploy-ments access stateful session EJBs. Remember that the number of concurrent user sessions isn't just the users currently accessing the system but also includes the lifetime of current sessions. Long session lifetimes result in a greater number of concurrent user sessions.
- **Storage capacity for user information.** This value represents the capacity required to store user information. In the simplest case, this value is the disk and memory required to store security information for each user. User-related storage is not covered in this chapter because it is either trivial or because it directly depends on external systems such as data-bases. In the trivial case where the WebLogic-based security realm or the database is used for storage of user information, simply multiply the size of each user's information by the total number of users. If each user requires 1MB of storage, then 20 registered users require 20MB; 1,000 users require 1GB, and so on.

To illustrate how capacity planning works for these three basic deployment characteristics, let's come up with some requirements for deploying the WebAuction application. The capacity goal for the WebAuction application is 800 user requests per second, or 69,120,000 requests per day. Note that goals are stated in terms of maximums, the worst-case possibility for capacity.

Server Hardware Capacity Planning

Many usage-related factors affect the capacity of a deployed application:

- Client protocol
- Security profile
- Degree of platform optimization for running Java and WebLogic

This section covers each factor, detailing how each factor affects the overall capacity of the WebLogic deployment.

Client Protocol

The client protocol is directly related to the type of WebLogic deployment. Application deployments and mixed deployments of WebLogic generally rely heavily on the Remote Method Invocation (RMI) programming model to access WebLogic services.

RMI can rely on the native WebLogic T3 protocol or can use HTTP tunneling to allow the RMI calls to pass through a firewall. Performance of RMI tunneled over HTTP is typically worse than that of non-tunneled T3.

Application clients can use HTTP by directly making HTTP POSTs and GETs to access servlets. In these cases, the application client should be treated as a Web browser client generating HTTP requests.

Security Profile

The level of security that is put in place between clients and WebLogic is a factor in determining the capacity of the deployment. WebLogic supports SSL (Secure Sockets Layer) as the security mechanism to ensure privacy and to authenticate users. SSL protects JSP pages for credit card purchases and bank statements, ensuring that attackers cannot view sensitive information.

SSL is a very intensive computing operation. The overhead of SSL cryptography means that WebLogic Server can handle fewer simultaneous connections than in a system without SSL.

You should note the total number of SSL connections required, over time, to determine your average client load. Typically, the server can handle three non-SSL connections for every one SSL connection. Given that users need not use an SSL connection for every request, SSL reduces the capacity of the server substantially. The amount of overhead incurred from SSL is directly related to how many client interactions use it.

Clustering Profile

The clustering profile affects the capacity of the WebLogic deployment. Two factors in clustering affect capacity:

1. Cluster size
2. Usage pattern of in-memory replication

We are assuming that in-memory replication will be used in the cluster architecture because of the scalability advantages it provides. For more information on in-memory replication, refer to the section on clustering in Chapter 12, "WebLogic Administration."

The cluster size directly influences how much network traffic is required to support the cluster. Various categories of traffic flow over the LAN that connects the WebLogic nodes in the cluster. The nodes in the cluster can coordinate some of this traffic, but a larger cluster requires a higher power network to communicate efficiently.

In-memory replication of session information is usually the largest consumer of LAN network bandwidth in a WebLogic cluster. As you recall from previous chapters, both servlets and session EJBs can replicate their session information across the cluster. This provides a hot backup in the case of failure of a given node in the cluster.

To keep the hot backup current with the latest information, the LAN propagates changes to sessions among nodes in the cluster. The use of in-memory replication most directly affects the LAN infrastructure required to support the cluster. See the capacity-planning methodology later in this chapter.

Application Profile

The application profile is a summary of all of the tasks that the WebLogic application must perform in response to client requests. These include serving Web pages, handling client requests, processing forms, dealing with user sessions, opening database connections, managing connection pools, and so forth.

Applications can be simple or they can be quite complex. The WebAuction application is moderately complex, involving a number of different components, including JMS and clustering for its deployment. Clearly, it is possible to create an even more complex application with even more business logic and more complex code paths. Unfortunately, there isn't a good metric for how the application profile can affect capacity. However, the reliance upon back-end systems, such as databases, can help us estimate the complexity of applications using WebLogic.

Dependence on Legacy/Back-End Systems

Most WebLogic deployments rely upon back-end systems such as databases or messaging systems on mainframes. Typically, a WebLogic application uses a database to generate Web content, such as looking up an employee's record. However, as demonstrated in the WebAuction application, requests are made that do not rely upon a back-end system to be served. For example, the welcome page *index.jsp* in the WebAuction application makes no calls to the database or back-end systems.

Obviously, the more reliance there is on back-end systems, the more resources are consumed to meet requests. Each client request for which WebLogic acts as an intermediary to a back-end system consumes hardware and external connectivity resources. In the WebAuction application, the vast majority of requests incur the overhead of accessing the database system.

> **Note:** If your application has a high ratio of legacy system access or accesses more than one legacy system to fill client requests, you should consider your application more complex than the WebAuction application.

Session-Based Information

The amount of session-based information that the WebLogic deployment has to handle also directly affects capacity. The WebLogic deployment must track session objects in memory for each session. This memory is either directly available in RAM or is obtained by swapping out to disk.

> **Best Practice:** The hardware must have enough memory to contain all the current session objects without swapping to disk. As session objects per user become larger or more users' sessions must be held simultaneously, more RAM is required. This RAM is accessible to Java via the Java heap, which is where the Java environment stores all objects and application data. As the system begins swapping, performance is negatively impacted. For optimal performance, the best practice is to make sure there is sufficient memory to hold the current session objects without swapping to disk.

A Baseline Capacity Profile

This section includes baseline numbers for capacity planning using the WebAuction application on standard server hardware in a configuration that simulates a real-world deployment. In this section we use the same testing configuration used in Chapter 14, *"Designing the Production Deployment."* Figure 17–2 presents the test configuration.

Two client machines generate load onto a single server running the WebAuction application. Oracle 8, running on another identical server, acts as the database. The entire configuration is connected by a 100Mb Ethernet. The WebLogic Server uses the WebLogic JRockit Java Development Kit (JDK) 1.4 for Windows 2000 included in the WebLogic distribution with a 256MB heap size, 15 connections in the connection pool to the database, and 15 execute threads.

To generate baseline numbers, a scenario was developed to provide the absolute worst performance possible. By choosing a usage case by a user that demanded the most of the application, we can be sure that any other use will result in better performance, making it a safe bet for capacity planning. Remember, the idea is to measure the amount of hardware required to support your application, and the capacity-planning effort determines the low bar for application performance.

As was determined in Chapter 13, when testing the WebAuction application, updates to the database to add new users were the most expensive operations both in terms of database and application server resources. For this reason, a scenario was created with the following user action flow for one of the client machines:

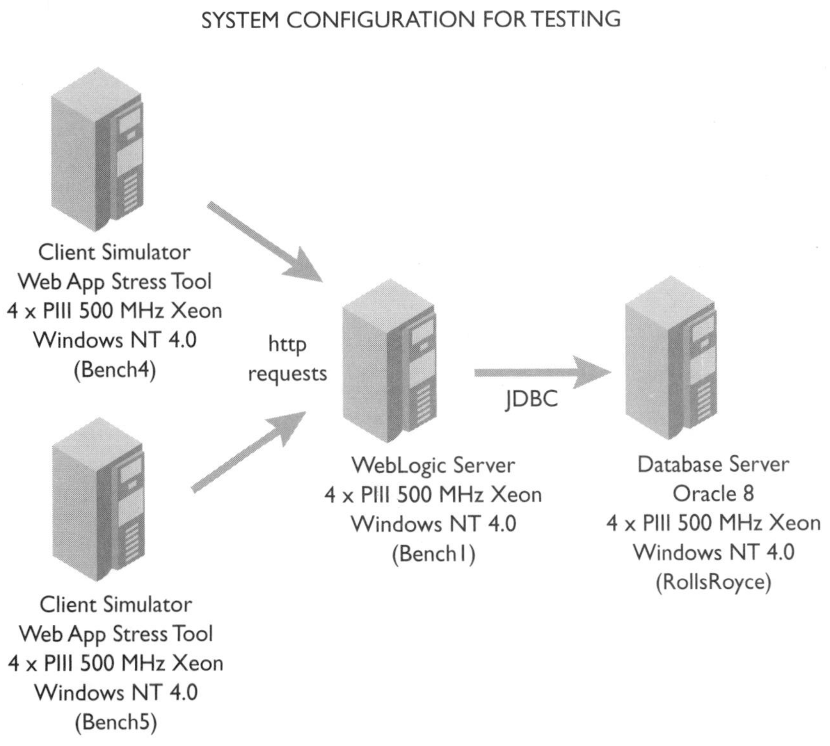

SYSTEM CONFIGURATION FOR TESTING

Client Simulator
Web App Stress Tool
4 x PIII 500 MHz Xeon
Windows NT 4.0
(Bench4)

http
requests

JDBC

WebLogic Server
4 x PIII 500 MHz Xeon
Windows NT 4.0
(Bench1)

Database Server
Oracle 8
4 x PIII 500 MHz Xeon
Windows NT 4.0
(RollsRoyce)

Client Simulator
Web App Stress Tool
4 x PIII 500 MHz Xeon
Windows NT 4.0
(Bench5)

Figure 17–2
Testing configuration.

1. Visit the welcome page (*main.jsp*).
2. Create a new user account (*newuser.jsp*).
3. Browse items in the books category (*browseitems.jsp*).
4. Bid on an item (*bid.jsp*).
5. Browse the user's bids (*currentbid.jsp*).
6. Log out (*logout.jsp*).

Notice that each iteration through the flow results in a new user account being created. The second client machine focuses on doing read operations to simulate what users would be viewing items in the categories:

1. Visit the welcome page (*main.jsp*).
2. Browse items in the books category (*browseitems.jsp*).

Together, these two machines are simultaneously directed at the WebAuction application. The results represent what kind of performance can be expected in a real-world deployment (see Table 17–1):

Table 17-1 Results of Performance Testing With Two Machines

CPUs	New Users per Second	New Users per Day	Http Requests Served per Second	Http Requests Served per Day	Server CPU Utilization
4	3.97	342,720	312	26,956,800	87%
3	2.72	234,720	238	20,563,200	86%
2	2.10	181,440	168	14,515,200	90%
1	1.08	93,600	90	7,776,000	89%

These numbers provide a basis for comparison for other applications. By using clustering and in-memory session replication, you can see that WebLogic scales in a near linear fashion. Thus, by simple multiplication, we can get an idea of what sort of hardware is required to support larger configurations of WebLogic. Next, we need to see how your particular application differs from the WebAuction application.

To illustrate this process of comparing your application to the baseline capacity profile for the WebAuction application, we detail capacity planning for WebAuction in the next section.

LAN Infrastructure Capacity Planning

Now that the server hardware has been determined, we can proceed to plan the capacity of the LAN infrastructure. Fortunately, capacity planning for the LAN infrastructure is simpler than capacity planning for the server hardware. This is mainly because only one factor heavily affects the requirements on the LAN infrastructure: *in-memory replication of session information for servlets and stateful session EJBs*.

In-memory replication of session information is the largest consumer of LAN network bandwidth in a WebLogic cluster. As you recall from previous chapters, both servlets and session EJBs can have their session information replicated across the cluster. This provides a hot backup in the case of failure of a given node in the cluster.

To keep the hot backup current with the latest information, the LAN is used to transmit session changes to nodes in the cluster. Typically, the recommended session size is 5KB to 15KB in size. Larger sessions require higher network bandwidth to support efficient operation.

Table 17–2 summarizes the network requirements for both cluster size and in-memory replication details. Where "switched" is noted, the LAN infrastructure should be based on a switch rather than a hub, which reduces the saturation of the network under load.

Table 17–2 Network Requirements

CPUs Running WebLogic Instances in Cluster	In-Memory Replication Session Size (in KB)	Approximate LAN Capacity Minimum (in MB/s)
2–8	0	100
2–8	<15	100
2–8	>15	Switched 100
8–16	0	Switched 100
8–16	<15	Switched 100
8–16	>15	Switched 1 Gbps
16+	0	Switched 100
16+	<15	Switched 100
16+	>15	Switched 1 Gbps

As you can see, as the cluster size grows, the infrastructure requirements on the network consume more and more bandwidth.

External Connectivity Capacity Planning

Connectivity to external clients and resources is also a factor in capacity planning. The amount of traffic to an external resource such as a database is, of course, application-specific. This section looks at connectivity requirements for clients to WebLogic as well as connectivity requirements to legacy/back-end systems.

Client Connectivity Requirements

A network connection is required to connect WebLogic to its clients on the Web. This network connection may be over the Internet or across the corporate network. In the case of the corporate network, bandwidth is typically very high and capacity planning is not required. However, when connections to WebLogic clients are made over the Internet, it is necessary to make sure that the bandwidth across the Internet is appropriate.

In most cases, simple calculations can be made to estimate the amount of bandwidth required to support Web users. This begins with determining the size of responses that will be sent to clients. To determine the size of these responses, you should look at your application and determine the average size of the responses. Your calculation should include both the HTML code as well as any static images that you're serving, such as JPEG. After determining the average size of the transmission to the requesters, we can create a weighted average based on *how often the various pages are served*.

Let's do this calculation for the WebAuction application. We have the following JSP pages that respond to requests (see Table 17–3).

Table 17–3   Responses per JSP Page

JSP Page	Total Size (with Images) in Kb	Estimated Percent of Total Responses
login.jsp	25	48%
trade.jsp	20	48%
error.jsp	15	4%

The weighted average of these pages is shown in Table 17–4).

Table 17–4   Weighted Average of Responses per Page

JSP Page	Weighted Total Size (with Images) Based on the Percent of the Responses
login.jsp	12Kb (= 25 Kb ∴ 0.48)
trade.jsp	9.6Kb (= 20 Kb ∴ 0.48)
error.jsp	0.6Kb (= 15 Kb ∴ 0.04)
Weighted Average:	22.2Kb (= 12 Kb + 9.6 Kb + 0.6 Kb)

As you can see, only 4 percent of the total requests come from the *error.jsp* JSP page. The *login* and *trade* JSP pages account for 48 percent of the responses. In weighting these responses, we can estimate that the average response to each client request will be 22.2KB.

We can take this average response size of 22.2KB and look at how many requests per second could possibly be handled by different, standard Internet connectivity and network connectivity links (see Table 17–5).

Table 17–5   Theoretical Maximum Number of Responses

Network Connectivity Speed	Theoretical Maximum Responses Served per Second	Theoretical Maximum Responses Served per Day
56.6Kbit modem @ 7.075Kbps*	0.32	27,648
Digital Subscriber Line (DSL) @ 128Kbit/16Kbps	0.72	62,208
T-1/OC-1 Line @ 1.544Mbps/ 193Kbps	8.69	750,816
T3/OC-3 Line @ 44.736Mbps/ 5,592Kbps	251.89	21,763,296
OC-4 Line @ 274.176Mbps/ 34,272Kbps	1543.73	133,378,222

° 56.6k modems are measured in terms of bits per second.

This chart represents only the theoretical maximum because it does not take into account the bandwidth consumed by subsequent requests. Check with your local Internet service providers for more information on the different capacities of digital lines.

In reality, the bandwidth provided by these connections is about 50 to 75 percent of the theoretical maximum. So, a T3 line in practice can transmit 10 to 15 million 22KB pages per day. The numbers here only mean to provide a rough estimate for what one would expect in a WebLogic deployment with a typical response size. It is highly recommended that you consult your Internet service provider for the appropriate level of bandwidth for your application.

Best Practice: There are several resources available regarding Web capacity planning, including *Capacity Planning for Web Performance: Metrics, Models, and Methods*, Almeida and Menasce, Prentice Hall, 1998, ISBN 0-13-693822-1 (*http://www.cs.gmu.edu/~menasce/webbook/index.html*) and *Scaling for E-Business: Technologies, Models, Performance, and Capacity Planning*, Menasce and Almeida, Prentice Hall, 2000, ISBN 0-13-086328-9.

In addition, the following capacity-planning Web portal has a number of useful pieces of information: *http://www.capacityplanning.com/*. This Web site is completely focused on capacity-planning issues for enterprise application deployments.

Best practice is to leverage these resources when determining the optimal configuration for your deployment.

Back-End Resource Connectivity Requirements

Many factors affect connectivity requirements to resources, including how much data is transferred, how often it is transferred, and what the capacity is of the back-end resource. All of these factors vary from application to application. By default, connectivity to back-end resources is viewed in the traditional client/server model in which WebLogic is the client and the back-end resource is the server.

In the case of most legacy resources that connect to WebLogic, such as a database or a mainframe data store, the systems are mature enough to already offer recommendations for capacity planning and connectivity. For example, in the case of Oracle databases, capacity-planning information is available that includes both network connectivity and hardware server requirements. However, much of this capacity-planning information for legacy systems is based on the traditional client/server model, in which application clients connect directly to the database and therefore are not applicable.

Because WebLogic introduces a third tier to the application, in which connections are made from the client to the application server and then translated into requests for the legacy application, you must often use abstractions for capacity planning to back-end resources with WebLogic. In this abstraction, you should view the WebLogic application as a *proxy for the client requests* as it executes work for each individual user. So, if your WebLogic deployment is to service 5,000 requests per second that translate into database access, then you should plan the capacity of your database connectivity and database hardware to be able to handle 5,000 requests per second.

Fortunately, as the three-tier model for applications becomes more common, the database vendors also are beginning to offer capacity-planning information that is tailored to application servers. The requirement that you abstract WebLogic Server as a client to the database is only temporary until the database vendors catch up.

Capacity Planning Best Practices

There exist a number of best practices that should be followed when capacity planning for a WebLogic deployment. The following are a few key items to be aware of.

Be Conservative with Your Capacity-Planning Estimates

The steps detailed in this chapter provide a high-level estimate of the configuration required to meet your deployment goals. Capacity planning with WebLogic is not an exact science. For this reason, it is a best practice to err on the side of caution in terms of estimates. Many successful deployments take server hardware capacity-planning estimates and increase them by 50 percent in order to be absolutely sure that they will have adequate capacity. For deployments where absolute reliability is preferable over cost savings, this is a common practice.

Load-Test Your Application

A great number of things can go wrong in terms of an application's capacity that can never be identified until the application is deployed in practice. For this reason, you should plan to load-test your application either in a prototype form or using the hardware that you plan to deploy upon.

Optimize Your Application

The application built on top of WebLogic is often the most limiting factor to capacity. For this reason, you should plan to optimize your application during the testing process. A number of tools provide insight into hot spots and inefficiencies in your application based on WebLogic:

- jProbe from the KL Group (*http://www.klgroup.com*) and OptimizeIT from Intuitive Systems (*http://www.optimizeit.com*) can be used at development time to find bottlenecks in the code.
- Introscope from Wily Technology (*http://www.wilytech.com*) is a Java product that allows for runtime performance monitoring of any Java component in WebLogic. This tool is designed for monitoring production systems and not for tuning during development.

Plan for Growth

One of the major benefits of WebLogic is the ease in which the infrastructure can be scaled. Growing a cluster is as simple as incrementally adding server machines, even mixing and matching hardware server types within the same cluster. Most WebLogic deployments start small but grow substantially over time as more clients and services come online. For this reason, it is a good practice to plan your WebLogic deployment for growth. You may want to choose a LAN infrastructure that is larger than your current deployment so that it is ready when you want to grow.

In terms of external connectivity to other resources, such as the Internet or legacy systems, the bandwidth and hardware resources should be extensible. Many ISPs offer instant upgrades to Internet connections for higher bandwidth.

chapter 18

Introduction to WebLogic Platform 8.1

Up until now, this book has focused on WebLogic Server. We reviewed the various specifications that are supported, presented WebLogic security, administration and JMX, servlets, JSPs, EJBs, JMS, and reviewed our recommendations for preparing your deployment environment. We included an example application to illustrate many of the best practices and programming models we recommend.

However, there is quite a buzz in the industry around a new product offering from BEA called WebLogic Platform 8.1. The vision of WebLogic Platform, first introduced in 2002, is a complete application infrastructure platform, enabling developers to build and integrate enterprise applications easily and rapidly. In July 2003, BEA introduced WebLogic Platform 8.1, which extends the original vision through a consistent visual development environment and powerful tools to integrate WebLogic applications with an enterprise's existing IT environments. BEA's strategy has been endorsed by many of the industry's pundits and analysts, who predict the convergence away from proprietary point solutions that solve tactical problems and toward single, standards-based solutions designed to address end-to-end problems for the enterprise.

In this chapter, we review the various components in WebLogic Platform 8.1 and how these components can be used to build, test, and deploy J2EE applications, business processes, workflows, messaging applications, enterprise portals, trading partner applications, and more. We show how WebLogic Workshop is the single development and configuration utility for the Platform. Last, we introduce WebLogic JRockit, a highly optimized Java Virtual Machine (JVM) for Intel environments.

It is important to note that one chapter cannot comprehensively present the various components that make up the WebLogic Platform suite of products. The goal of this chapter is to introduce you to WebLogic Platform, its components, and how they relate to one another. You can find a wealth of information on WebLogic Platform 8.1 in BEA's documentation on the Dev2Dev site (*http://dev2dev.bea.com*) and the BEA company site (*http://www.bea.com*).

WebLogic Platform Components

WebLogic Platform 8.1 is a comprehensive suite of products designed to provide a unified, simplified, and extensible environment for building and integrating enterprise applications. Sharing a common infrastructure and common tools, with WebLogic Platform you can develop enterprise portals, leverage existing applications, coordinate business processes, and transform or translate data. For example, an order-processing application could present a personalized user interface, expose Web Services and existing EJB business logic, trigger a business process that interfaces with external inventory and packaged applications, translate XML data into EDI format, and notify the user when her request has been provisioned. The ability to combine these services into a single platform, sharing development tools, administration, and underlying services such as security and transactional context, is changing the industry. Yefim Natis of Gartner Group calls this suite "a milestone, strategic release for BEA Systems."

The WebLogic Platform 8.1 package contains the following components:

- WebLogic Workshop 8.1 Platform Edition—An intuitive visual development environment and runtime framework for WebLogic Server, WebLogic Integration, and WebLogic Portal.
- WebLogic Integration 8.1—An application integration solution for connecting enterprise applications, databases, business processes, and trading partners. WebLogic Integration includes business process management, workflow, data translation and transformation, message brokering, application integration, and support for business-to-business protocols.
- WebLogic Portal 8.1—A complete portal framework, including personalization, commerce, content management, portal administration, user and entitlement management, and delegated portal administration.
- WebLogic Server 8.1—The leading J2EE application server and foundation for WebLogic Platform 8.1.
- WebLogic JRockit 8.1—A high-performance JVM optimized for server-side performance and scalability.

Figure 18–1 illustrates the various components of WebLogic Platform 8.1. It is important to note that each of the modules within the Platform are available separately, allowing you to mix-and-match to meet your needs, adding additional modules within the Platform later to best meet your needs. Let's take a closer look at each of the components in WebLogic Platform.

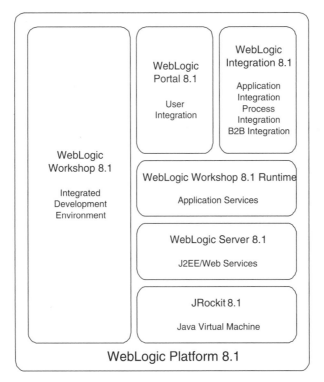

Figure 18–1
WebLogic Platform 8.1 components.

WebLogic Workshop Platform Edition

WebLogic Workshop is both a development tool and a runtime framework that abstracts the underlying complexities of J2EE environment from the application developer. We review WebLogic Workshop's key capabilities in Chapter 16. However, in WebLogic Platform 8.1, WebLogic Workshop not only is used to develop and deploy enterprise applications, but also provides configuration and modeling capabilities for WebLogic Integration and WebLogic Portal. WebLogic Workshop is a single design, development, and configuration tool across the entire suite of WebLogic Platform. For example, using WebLogic Workshop Platform Edition, a developer can change the layout and skin of his portal; create, test, and deploy a Web Service; model a business process complete with work lists for customer service; and transform input data from a binary format into XML.

The goal of WebLogic Workshop 7.0 was specifically to make building Web Services applications easier. Workshop provides a visual, intuitive development environment that even programmers not familiar with J2EE, Web Services, and distributed systems can still use to be productive. The Workshop development environment consists of a number of services, including the following:

- Two-way visual and source editing, allowing changes made in the Visual Design Palette to be reflected in the Source View and changes made directly in the Source View to be seen visually.

- Use of annotated Java code, enforcing patterns such as coarse-grained objects, asynchronous application processes, and loose coupling of interfaces without extensive knowledge of the underlying code constructs.
- A Control architecture in which access to existing, complex services can be wrapped by simple, drag-and-drop Control, insulating the developer from the underlying complexity of the back-office interfaces and APIs and offering a reusable component for future application development.
- Java syntax checking, method completion, and context-sensitive help, saving the developer time by catching syntax errors and providing guidance while developing rather than during the build and package phase.
- Integrated deployment and debugging services, reducing the round-trip time to develop, deploy, test, and modify code through the single development environment.
- XQuery and XMLBeans, enhancing data translation and transformation, and efficiently mapping XML to and from Java objects without many of the inherent constraints.

WebLogic Workshop 8.1 Application Edition extended the Web Services features in the initial release to the complete J2EE environment available in WebLogic Server. With Workshop 8.1, developers can build JSPs, control page flows, create and develop EJBs, and access the underlying services such as JDBC, JMS, JTA, RMI, and JNDI. In addition, this release includes more reliable and more secure Web Services, improved debugging support, and integration with third-party software source-control systems, such as Perforce and CVCS. With WebLogic Workshop 8.1, you have a powerful, yet easy-to-use, development environment for WebLogic Server and J2EE.

WebLogic Workshop 8.1 Platform Edition (see Figure 18–2) extends what was provided in the 8.1 Application Edition to the entire suite of Platform products. The Platform Edition provides the environment for developers who need to create workflows, model business processes, build data transformation, and design and deploy a personalized portal as part of the same visual set of tools. All of the capabilities in the development time are also supported when the application is deployed on the runtime framework.

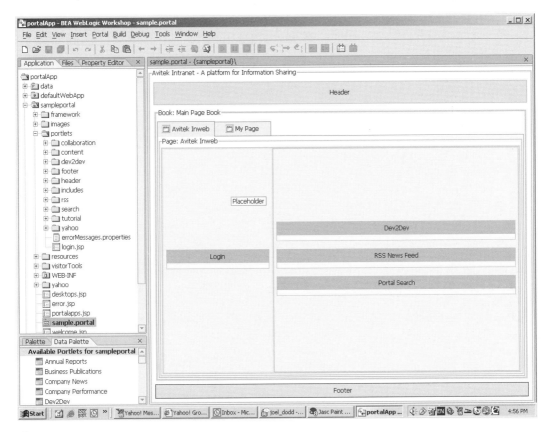

Figure 18–2
WebLogic Workshop Platform Edition.

WebLogic Integration

Integration and *convergence* are two of the factors driving BEA's move to a comprehensive platform of products. In today's dynamic IT environment, almost every application has to tie into third-party application packages, custom applications, messaging systems, mainframe applications, Web Services, content-management systems, trading partners, and on and on. Experience has shown that the vast majority of WebLogic Server deployments include integration with external systems. Through simplified development, a flexible and adaptable set of core services, and easy management and administration, WebLogic Integration (Figure 18–3) is poised to help you solve these problems.

At its core, WebLogic Integration leverages the underlying scalability, reliability, and core functions of WebLogic Server. For example, business processes and workflows are implemented using EJBs and JMS queues and topics, JDBC interfaces to data, and RMI for synchronous communications between objects. WebLogic Integration is designed to leverage advanced features such as WebLogic clustering, and applications can be managed and monitored via JMX and the administration console. Let's consider the features of WebLogic Integration.

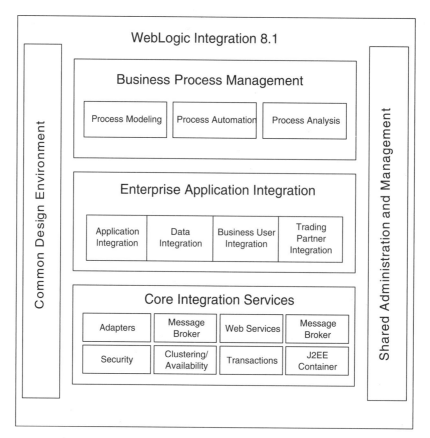

Figure 18–3
WebLogic Integration.

Workflow and Business Process Management

Managing business processes is one of the powerful features of WebLogic Integration. WebLogic Integration delivers functions for process orchestration and management of application flows that span multiple internal systems, external resources, and interaction with users. A business process can be a purely automatic execution, where the output of one step becomes the input of the next step, step-by-step until the complete request is finished. Batch jobs on the mainframe represent a business process, such as order processing or inventory management. Using WebLogic Integration *Business Process Management* (BPM), the enterprise becomes a set of business services, accessed via WebLogic Workshop Controls, which are orchestrated to model business functions and services.

In this section, we review the powerful features delivered in WebLogic Integration BPM. We consider the visual development and design model, using Controls to access external systems, state management, process monitoring and performance tuning, and we discuss how to handle exceptions in a process flow.

BPM Design and Development

Consistent with all the products in WebLogic Platform, you use WebLogic Workshop to design business processes, develop custom functions, and test and deploy the complete modeled process. You deploy your workflows onto one or more instances of WebLogic Server, implementing the WebLogic Integration components. Then, using the administrative tools provided with WebLogic Server and WebLogic Integration, you can monitor the performance of the process flow and make adjustments as necessary.

When designing and implementing a business process in WebLogic Workshop, your primary tool is the *Control*. Controls represent an encapsulation of a complex business function, such as an EJB, database access, or a Web Service. In the context of WebLogic Integration, Controls are an easy way to call services in an external inventory management system, utilize data translation or transformation operations, invoke services on the mainframe, or simply call a Web Service. You will find over a dozen integration Controls packaged with WebLogic Platform, including access to databases, files, HTTP, Web Services, messaging, service broker, and external systems. Controls provide a consistent and simplified way to access existing systems and resources within the business process flow.

Figure 18–4 illustrates how a process designer would model and build a process flow using WebLogic Workshop. Workshop provides a *Business Process Palette* of services and functions; the designer picks the function or Control needed and drags it onto the *Design Palette*. Each step in the business process is represented as a node on the Design Palette. Decision trees allow the process to flow over one or more branches, for example, based on a user's input or some variable. The messages moving from node to node through the process are XML, defined by schema you create or provided as part of some existing system. Custom operations in the business process are coded in Java, and everything deployed rests on the familiar, reliable foundation of WebLogic Server. Switching to the Source View from the Design View, you have access to the underlying Java code that implements the business process.

As you can see from Figure 18–4, modeling business processes in WebLogic Workshop gives you a graphical representation of your process flow. This process flow is stored as a *Java Process Definition* with a *.jpd* file extension, including regions for imports, annotated process language, and process designer–generated code. The definition language is based on the *Process Definition Language for Java* (PD4J) specification, submitted as JSR 207.

WebLogic Integration supports both stateless and stateful business processes, and process flows can be invoked synchronously (poll and wait) and asynchronously (send the request and continue execution). You should note that the invocation model dictates the session model(s) supported. For example, asynchronous invocations are supported with both stateful and stateless process flows, whereas the synchronous invocation model dictates the business process will be stateless. With process flows, WebLogic Integration handles state persistence without requiring additional development and, when compiled, the process flow is optimized—transaction behavior, for example—based on the process design. Session state for stateful workflows is stored in an entity EJB.

Best Practice: You should carefully consider whether to make a process flow stateful or stateless, since there are performance and runtime considerations. Stateful processes must be invoked asynchronously and will have noticeably slower performance due to the additional overhead and state management. There are explicit and implicit transaction boundaries imposed within a workflow. Don't use stateful process flows unless there is an explicit business requirement to do so.

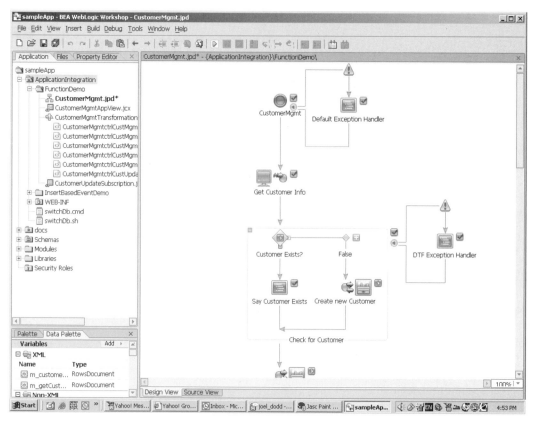

Figure 18–4
WebLogic Workshop and BPM.

Once the business process has been deployed, WebLogic Integration allows the execution of the process to be monitored. Figure 18–5 displays an example of the WebLogic Integration Administration Console. From this console, you can see the number of requests, measure response time, monitor service-level agreements, identify bottlenecks in the process flow, and, new for Integration 8.1, make changes to the flow as warranted. This console will indicate the version of the process flow itself as well. If changes are made, all outstanding requests will complete using the existing version of the workflow, while new requests are routed to the new workflow.

> **Best Practice:** When WebLogic Workshop packages the JPD file for the workflow, it produces an EAR archive file for deployment. However, this EAR file does not include underlying components, such as JDBC connection pools, JMS queues, and other WebLogic resources. If you just deploy the EAR file into the production environment, you will need to ensure the underlying resources are available. A deployment best practice is to stage any process flows before migrating into a production environment and verify the underlying configuration is complete.

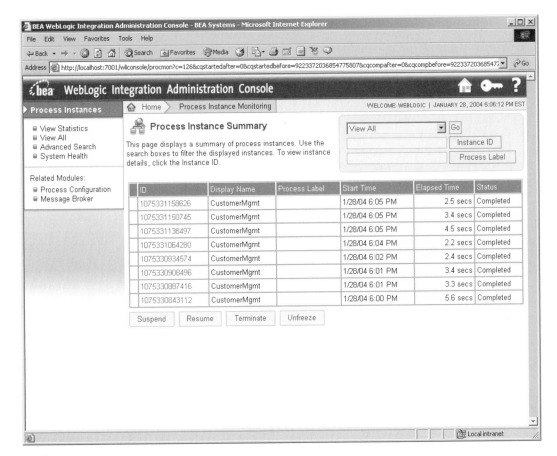

Figure 18–5
Business process monitoring.

Data Translation and Transformation

Within a business process, WebLogic Integration supports services in which data can be trans-
formed from one format to another to based on the needs of the application. For example, one step
in a business process may require EDI data, whereas the next step expects XML data. The customer
could be represented in one step of the process as First Name, Last Name, and in the next step, an
existing back-office system may expect to find Last Name, First Name. WebLogic Integration presents a unified data model, allowing you to translate between typed XML with a known schema,
untyped XML, structured non-XML such as a COBOL copybook, raw unstructured data, and Java
data formats. The transforming features let you rapidly integrate heterogeneous resources and
applications into a single process flow, exactly matching the needs of the business.

WebLogic Integration provides two ways to map data:

- XQuery transformation based on the standard from the World Wide Web Consortium
  (W3C)—A graphical any-to-any mapping tool to associate fields from the source schema

onto a target schema. From the graphical representation, a query is generated and accessed at runtime by the business process. XQuery can be used to translate to and from XML, non-XML, and Java data types.

- eXtensible Stylesheet Language Transformation (XSLT) based on an older standard from the W3C—XSLT is typically used to integrate existing transformations into the business process. XSLT is used to translate from XML in one schema to XML in a different schema.

Transformations are represented as Controls; with Workshop, you create a transformation and package it as a Control. Applications and process flows needing the same transformation simply reference the Control you created. There is built-in support for XSLT transformations when converting from one XML document structure to another. However, a new technology called XQuery can be used to map XML schemas, exposing the completed mappings as transformation Controls, represented as a *.dtf file type*. Figure 18–6 illustrates the XQuery mapping tool.

WebLogic Integration also provides two tools for editing schemas: the Format Builder utility for defining schemas for non-XML documents and XML Spy, a popular tool for working with XML schemas. The schema is represented with an *.xsd file type* for XML documents and *.mfl file type* for non-XML documents. In either case, Workshop automatically compiles these schemas into Java objects, which are then available to be reused to any process flows as XML or non-XML variables. Figure 18–7 represents how data is presented to the application at design time. At runtime, the schemas are con-

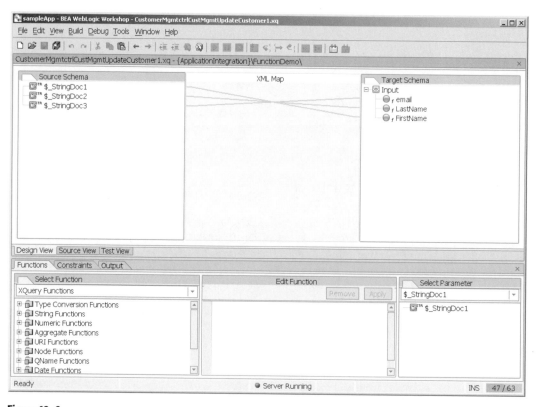

Figure 18–6
XQuery schema mapping.

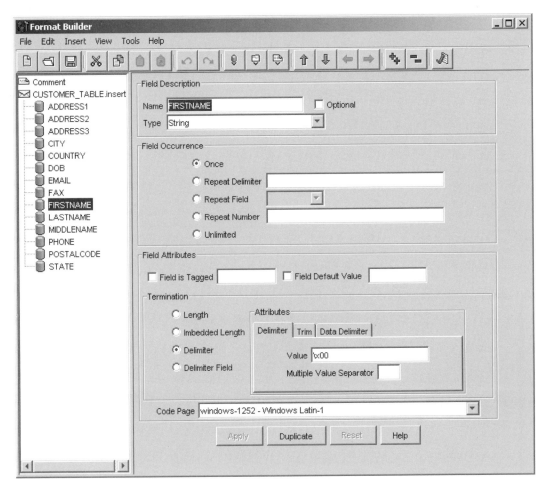

Figure 18–7
Data schemas at design time.

verted into *tokenized datastreams*, which are passed through the XQuery Runtime Engine. The result is a consistent interpretation of the various types of schemas used in WebLogic Integration.

WebLogic Integration Worklists

Business processes represent some business function or operation. One of the challenges is that these functions often require human intervention during the process flow. Requests often must be routed to a specific person or group, with logging and auditing of the activity, and often the complete process is still subject to an existing service-level agreement. In addition, once the human interaction has been completed, the task should be returned into the workflow at the point of the interruption, not back at the beginning of the workflow. For example, a delinquent account may require customer and account information to be gathered, assigned to a collections agent, and processed within a three-day window, or the account will become overdue. WebLogic Integration handles this type of requirement through *worklists*.

WebLogic Workshop exposes worklists as Controls. There are two types of Controls specific to worklists: *task Controls* and *task worker Controls*. The task Control creates an instance of a task and manages its state and data, and the task worker Control allows a task to be claimed, completed, and managed. A BPM process models the actual flow of the action request, and worklist Controls represent specific steps in the flow where human collaboration is required. The assigned tasks can then be viewed from a JSP or a portlet when using WebLogic Portal. In addition, the WebLogic Integration Administration Console allows unassigned tasks to be placed on an assigned work queue. The administrator can track the relationships between processes and tasks; correct errors in an individual task; suspend, resume, and abort tasks; and identify when a task is holding up a process.

J2EE Connector Architecture

Before we dig into the specifics of the WebLogic Integration adapter architecture, it will be helpful to review the J2EE standard on which they are based. WebLogic adapters are based on the J2EE Connector Architecture (J2CA) version 1.0 specification from Sun Microsystems. J2CA is used to tie applications developed with J2EE into the world of *Enterprise Information Systems* (EIS), a term used to describe existing systems, packaged applications, and applications not written in the Java programming language. The specification defines two components—an EIS-specific resource adapter such as those described above and an application server hosting the resource adapter. For WebLogic Integration, WebLogic Server is the container for hosting the resource adapters. Figure 18–8 illustrates the J2CA architecture.

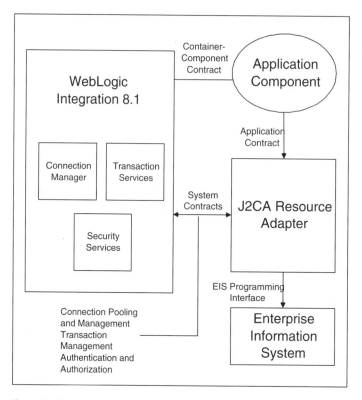

Figure 18–8
J2CA architecture.

Let's dig a little deeper into the J2CA specification. Consistent with other J2EE technologies, J2CA leverages a container model into which the resource adapters are deployed. The application server hosts the resource adapter container and provides transaction, security, and connection management. Within the resource adapter are all the EIS-specific interfaces, APIs, connections, and data structures. The advantage is that these specific interfaces are isolated from the application server and other J2EE applications accessing them.

System contracts Control the interface between the application server and the resource adapter, defining how the application server is to interact with the resource adapter. The following system contracts are specified:

- A Connection Management contract that allows the application server to connect to the EIS and provide advanced features such as pooling connections for scalability.
- A Transaction Management contract to coordinate transactional access between the application server's transaction functions and the EIS, defining transactional boundaries, participants, and span of control.
- A Security contract to enforce secure access to the EIS, protecting the valuable information and reducing security threats.

With these well-defined contracts, the resource adapter can easily be plugged into the application server. This is just a brief introduction to the J2CA specification. For more information on J2CA refer to the Sun J2CA page at *http://java.sun.com/j2ee/connector.*

WebLogic Integration Adapters

One of the primary functions of any integration tool is the ability to interface with existing systems. As we learned in the previous section, WebLogic Integration provides a complete set of adapters based on the J2CA. These adapters provide a clean, standards-based way for applications to access existing systems and packaged applications. Through BEA and technology partners, there are *application integration* (AI) adapters for most popular packaged applications and existing legacy systems, including Siebel, PeopleSoft, SAP, Oracle packaged applications, MQ Series, CICS and IMS, file, HTTP, e-mail, CORBA, Swift, and many others. In addition, a developer kit provides the support for developing custom J2CA adapters when required.

Exposed as *Application View Controls,* WebLogic Workshop makes it easy to develop and integrate with these systems either in building custom applications or as part of a business process flow. The Application View Control calls services synchronously or asynchronously and can be configured to trigger a process flow when an event is received from the back-office system. In both the service and event models, the developer uses XML and mapping tools to interact with the Application View Control, freeing the developer from in-depth knowledge of the protocol, API, or architecture of the enterprise application. For more information on the application integration services, refer to the BEA documentation online at *http://e-docs.bea.com/wli/docs81/aiover/index.html.*

Business-to-Business Integration

WebLogic Integration 8.1 supports the framework for enabling business communications between enterprises and trading partners, both inter-enterprise and intra-enterprise. These applications have special requirements, such as long-running stateful business processes following a conversational paradigm, and adhere to a number of commercially available protocols over which these communications and processes flow.

Provided in WebLogic Integration is a Trading Partner Management service within the WebLogic Integration administrator's console. From this page, you can manage trading partner profiles, security certificates, protocol bindings, services, message tracking and auditing, trading partner activity, and system defaults. As with the other components in WebLogic Platform, the underlying deployment platform is WebLogic Server, such as clustered configuration, message persistence and state management, low-level message acknowledgements and receipts, and transactional guarantees. WebLogic Integration 8.1 supports a wide range of trading partner protocols, including ebXML 1.0 and 2.0, RosettaNet 1.1 and 2.0, and using Web Services. Controls are available for RosettaNet, ebXML, and trading partner management. As Web Services mature and encompass more of the functions necessary to enable B2B transactions and messages, WebLogic Integration will continue to leverage these advancements.

WebLogic Integration Message Broker

A key component to consider when integrating with enterprise systems is the ability to efficiently handle messages via a routing or brokering service. WebLogic Integration includes a robust publish-and-subscribe component called the *Message and Event Broker*. Events are generated, or *published*, onto a topic, and *subscribers* to that topic receive the corresponding messages. For example, in an order-processing application, a business process can subscribe to the NewOrder channel; when a new order is entered into the system, the subscriber can invoke the corresponding flow and complete the processing on the order. The message broker allows applications to communicate in a loosely coupled, anonymous manner that is well-suited to flexible, adaptable architecture.

As part of the BPM services in WebLogic Integration, a business process can specify the channels to which it publishes and subscribes. Publishers broadcast messages without knowing who will receive them, and the message consumers don't need to know anything about the publisher. Subscriptions can start a new process flow or participate and block as part of an existing process flow. Messages can be routed using the *Service Broker* based on a selected parameter extracted from the message, such as high-priority requests and regular priority requests.

Events can also be used to trigger process flows, and there are a variety of *Event Generators* supported in WebLogic Integration, including the following:

- File—Polls a directory for files and publishes them.
- JMS—Dequeues messages from a queue or topic and publishes them.
- Email—Polls POP or IMAP e-mail servers for mail messages and publishes them.
- Timer—Publishes messages at configured times and can be integrated with business calendars.
- Application Views—Publishes messages from a WebLogic Integration AI adapter.

Each of these event generators publishes to one of the *Message Broker channels*. Following the consistent design and development model, you subscribe to the channel using a *channel Control* in the Workshop IDE. Channel files have a *.channel file type* and reside in a Workshop Schema project. You can statically bind to a channel, where an event will trigger a new process flow, or you can dynamically bind to a channel. The structure of the message received or sent is based on the type or format of the channel.

WebLogic Integration Summary

In summary, WebLogic Integration provides a comprehensive environment for developing, deploying, and managing enterprise applications. It provides services for business process management, data transformation, trading partner integration, connectivity, message brokering, application monitoring, and user intervention, all in a unified framework and with simplified, easy-to-use development and administrative tools. The purpose of this section was to introduce you to WebLogic Integration and its various components, but there is a wealth of additional information available on this powerful product and all its capabilities. A good starting point for more information is the BEA documentation at *http://edocs.bea.com/wli/docs81/index.html.*

WebLogic Portal

WebLogic Portal represents the user interface of applications deployed onto WebLogic Platform. The Portal framework provides an aggregation point for access to the user interfaces of the underlying business applications, Web Services, JSPs and servlets, and existing EIS applications. WebLogic Portal includes services for content management, Web-based commerce components, entitlements, the ability to delegate administrative authority, and the tools to manage deployed Internet, intranet, and extranet portals. In addition, WebLogic Portal supports the latest industry standards, such as JSR-168 for portlets. The following sections introduce each of the Portal services, including the Portal framework, content management, and delegated administration. Figure 18–9 presents the WebLogic Portal architecture.

As in other sections in this chapter, the goal here is not to provide you with a detailed description of the components that make up WebLogic Portal, but rather to introduce you to the various

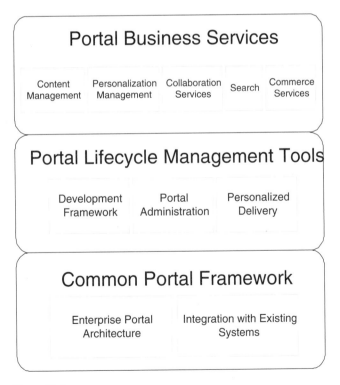

Figure 18–9
WebLogic Portal architecture.

features and their value. More information can be found on the BEA developer's site at *http://dev2dev.bea.com*, the BEA documentation for WebLogic Portal, and articles in current periodicals such as the *WebLogic Developer's Journal*.

What Is a Portal?

Before we jump into WebLogic Portal, it is useful to understand why organizations need a portal. Since the early days of the World Wide Web, organizations have struggled with how to use the Internet to provide their customers with access to valuable information, to improve their relationships with business partners, to lower costs, and to efficiently provide information and application access internally, whether the employees work at corporate headquarters or are distributed around the globe.

The first generation of Web sites served up static Web pages, one page at a time. As customers and users began to demand more information, the second generation of Web sites opened the door to applications, allowing users to access their bank accounts online, order products, and track shipments. As more applications and information became available, organizations realized that support and customer service costs could be reduced through customer and user self-help. However, one challenge became how to offer these services without compromising the integrity of the underlying systems.

Today, many organizations are evolving into the third generation of Web applications. They need to be able to expose their legacy applications, processes, and data in a Web interface, but they also need to serve up more than a single page of information at a time. Portals are designed to meet this requirement. Once defined as the "dial tone" for the Internet, a *portal* is a single point of access to an aggregation of applications and data. For the employee, this may mean a single page with windows to HR applications, investment and 401K data, a worklist of documents for approval, and access to e-mail, calendars, and collaborative discussions with team members. For the consumer, this may mean a personalized presentation of information from several accounts, order history, commerce services, and specific content targeted to personal interests. From the organization's perspective, the problem is how to offer these services while lowering costs, sharing reusable components, and securing access to protect existing assets.

WebLogic Portal Framework

WebLogic Portal provides the services and infrastructure to create and deploy portals. WebLogic Portal includes the tools and services to let you quickly build and assemble portals that provide customers, employees, and partners with audience-specific, integrated windows to EIS applications, information, and business processes, while enforcing business policies, procedures, and security. In addition, WebLogic Portal collects information about how the Portal is used so that services and functions can be refined and tailored to maximize the potential of the Web channels. As with the other products in WebLogic Platform, WebLogic Portal leverages the consistent, powerful WebLogic Workshop development environment.

Portlets

WebLogic Portal starts out with the concept of portlets. *Portlets* represent a unique application or data in its own window. The portal is made up of multiple portlets (see Figure 18–10), such as entering your username and password, checking e-mail, reviewing your calendar, looking up stock quotes, and a worklist of items that require your attention. Portlets are arranged or grouped on pages of the portal, and users can navigate among the pages of the portal using page tabs, drop-down menus, links, or a combination of some or all of the above. Sun specification JSR 168 defines how a portlet is rendered within the portal. WebLogic Portal 8.1 supports this JSR.

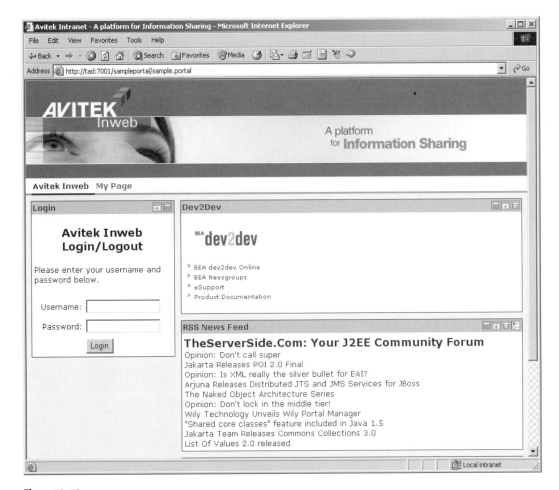

Figure 18–10
Portal page and portlets.

WebLogic Portal is delivered with a wide range of portlets. There are portlets for user authentication, enterprise search, e-mail, collaboration and discussion groups, content management, calendar, contact and to-do lists, Web-clipping, news, stock quotes, and many others. All the bundled portlets are found in the directory <BEA_HOME>\<WEBLOGIC_HOME>\samples\portal\portalApp\sampleportal\portlets.

WebLogic Portal provides access to the MyYahoo! Enterprise Edition suite, a bundle of 100+ modules. This package leverages the broad content providers for Yahoo!, such as Headline News, Company News, Stock Portfolios, Market Summary, Weather, Sports, Maps, Travel, Notepad, Calendar, Package Tracker, and much more. In addition, BEA offers an extensive selection of portlets, third-party integrations, and portal solutions through the Dev2Dev program. You can find a complete list at *http://dev2dev.bea.com/products/wlportal/psc/index.jsp.*

Desktops and Look-and-Feel

The portal page itself also has a certain look-and-feel, including headers, footers, page layouts, navigation Controls, and underlying access Control. The view you see when accessing a portal is called a *desktop*, representing the collection of resources that make up the portal pages, including look-and-feel, portlets, layouts, shells, pages, and books. The desktop is the top-level container for the portal components, or *elements*, included in that specific view of the portal. You would target a desktop at a specific group or subset of users. For example, you could have separate desktops for employees, customers, management, and partners. As such, a portal can have multiple desktops tailored to meet individual needs. As it relates to the lifecycle of portal development and deployment, a desktop represents a specific instance of a *streaming portal*, where portal information is streamed from the underlying database. We review single-file and streaming portals in the section on portal lifecycle.

A desktop contains a *look-and-feel* component that defines the physical appearance of the portal. The look-and-feel component is stored in an XML file with a *.laf* extension and is made up of *skins*—graphics, styles, and JavaScript to determine what the page looks like—and *skeletons*, which define the physical boundaries rendering all of the components. The text, fonts, colors, and spacing are all part of the portal skin, whereas the skeleton includes what the borders look like, how a button is rendered, and the physical aspects of the HTML itself. You can group subsets of look-and-feel elements into a *theme*, allowing you to give individual books, pages, or portlets their own look-and-feel. A desktop also includes a *shell* to control the area around the books and pages of a portal, such as the header and footer for the page. The shell is defined in an XML file with a *.shell* extension, which points to the JSPs and HTML files containing the content to display.

Books and Pages

A *book* in WebLogic Portal 8.1 is a component that defines high-level content organization and page navigation. Books contain pages or other books, offering a model for hierarchical nesting of pages and content. Books are identified in WebLogic Workshop through a Control such as a tab set. A *top-level book* includes all the sub-books, pages, and portlets that make up the desktop. In the top-level book, you also specify the menu navigation style. WebLogic Portal supports three types of navigation menus:

- Single-level menu—Page navigation is controlled by visually layering pages. Sub-books and pages appear as rows below the main book navigation.
- Multilevel menu—Page navigation is handled by a single row of tab-like page links for the top-level pages. Sub-books and pages appear in dropdown lists for each selection.
- No navigation menu—Page navigation is not specified but rather handled on a page-by-page basis.

The menu navigation style is specified in an XML file with a *.menu* extension. The menu file references a menu class that determines the menu behavior, and the menu class references a skeleton JSP file that renders the menu to deliver what you actually see on the page.

Books and pages allow the portal designer to control how the portal pages and portlets are organized on the desktop. *Pages* contain the portlets that display the actual portal content. Different pages of the desktop can have separate books, pages, and portlets. The *layout* is an HTML table definition in which you specify where books and portlets are positioned on a page. You can determine if portlets will be arranged horizontally (side to side) or vertically (with one portlet on top of another), or even a combination of the two. Layouts are defined in an XML file with a *.layout* extension and a corresponding HTML text file, and are rendered via skeleton JSPs. WebLogic Portal includes default layouts for three columns across, two columns with a spanning horizontal row, or multiple columns and rows, among others. Once you have decided on a layout, you set *placeholders* for the individual cells in a layout in which portlets are placed.

Portal Lifecycle Management

Just like the other components within the WebLogic Platform family, WebLogic Portal uses the WebLogic Workshop development environment for creating, designing, and maintaining your portal. Portal components are represented in the Workshop environment via Controls, making it easy for the developer to wire together a portal without detailed knowledge of the underlying portal components. Workshop represents the aggregate concept of a portal in a single XML file with the *.portal* extension. In this section, we review the design, test, and deploy services WebLogic Platform provides for portal applications. Figure 18–11 illustrates the stages in a portal lifecycle.

To get started, you either create a new Portal from within WebLogic Workshop or add Portal services and a Portal Web application to an existing enterprise application, such as a business process or Web services application. You can find the complete steps for creating a new portal or updating an existing application in the BEA documentation at *http://e-docs.bea.com/workshop/doc/en/portal/overview/BuildingPortalAppsOV.html*.

Once the portal is created, you begin by opening the *.portal* file, located in the Portal Web application folder, into the Workshop Design window. From the Workshop designer, you can add and rearrange portlets, change the layouts, modify the look-and-feel, and create campaigns, all without

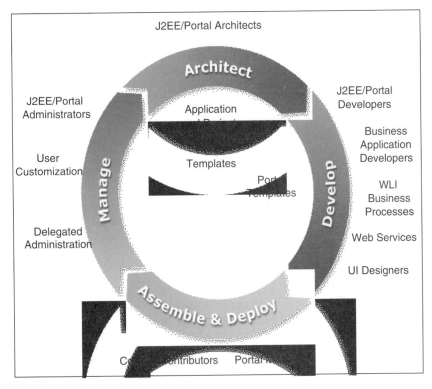

Figure 18–11
WebLogic Portal lifecycle.

complex Java programming. When you're finished, you build the Portal and bring up the Workshop test browser to review what you've done. All the powerful development features, such as two-way editing, property settings, and Controls, are available to the WebLogic Portal designer.

As with the other WebLogic Platform modules, WebLogic Workshop includes *Portal Controls* to ease design and development of portals. Specifically, there are three types of portal Controls you can use:

- Personalization Controls—Here you will find Controls for creating users, establishing user login, and accessing properties in a user's profile. A query Control is included for accessing roles associated with the user. With these Controls, you can access WebLogic Portal *Interaction Management* to personalize a user's portal.
- Event Controls—These portal Controls enable user tracking and personalization based on an event, such as a click within a portlet, a click on some content, a visitor registration, or a generic tracking event. For example, you could trigger sending an e-mail to visitors once they have registered with your site.
- EJB Controls—You use EJB Controls for easy access to the underlying portal framework, such as access to managing property sets, user profiles, and group managers.

These Controls allow you to design and customize your portal, reusing existing components and services, without extensive programming and knowledge of the underlying APIs. More information about Portal Controls can be found by following the Portal Controls Reference link from the WebLogic Portal documentation at *http://e-docs.bea.com/wlp/docs81/index.html*.

While you are designing and refining your portal in Workshop, you are working on a development version of the portal called the *single-file* portal. You can think of the development mode as a portal template. When you're finished designing your portal and have tested it, you are ready for a production deployment. You deploy the portal as a packaged enterprise application with the *.ear* file or an exploded portal application. The information associated with the portal, including portlets, skeletons, skins, and layouts, is stored in the Portal database, creating a *streaming model* in which the portal configuration is streamed from the database. Desktops are specific instances of the streaming portal, targeted based on your configuration.

WebLogic Portal Content Management

One of the primary capabilities of the portal is to present enterprise content to users—customers, employees, and business partners. Content can take many forms, from documents and static HTML to rich media and unstructured data. Content-management systems provide a way to access, version, and manage these various types of content. Many enterprises already have existing content-management systems and need to serve this content through the portal channel. While you can write code to access content and display it, investing development resources to aggregate and personalize content within a portal is inefficient and adds unnecessary costs. WebLogic Portal 8.1 makes it easier to integrate this content within the framework of a portal.

WebLogic Portal 8.1 provides a simple interface for plugging multiple repositories into WebLogic Portal based on the direction of JSR 170 (Content Repository API). This JSR defines a consistent, standards-based way to interface with third-party content-management systems, alleviating the need for one-off implementations. The interface supports the creation, read, update, and deletion of content, content types, and content hierarchies and their associated subelements using the Portal Administration utility. To ease portal development, many third-party content-management providers, such as Documentum (*http://www.documentum.com*) and FatWire (*http://www.fatwire.com*), are developing JSR 170-compliant WebLogic Workshop Controls that make pulling content into a portal a drag-and-drop exercise. Figure 18–12 presents the WebLogic Portal content-management approach.

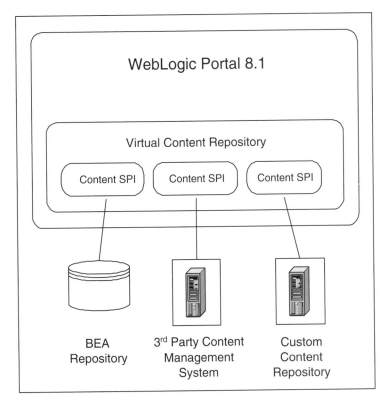

Figure 18–12
WebLogic Portal content management.

In addition, WLP 8.1 ships with an out-of-the-box content repository, the *Content Manager,* which supports the native functions of the content-management interface. This repository is suitable for customers with basic content requirements, such as smaller amounts of content and limited personalization requirements. Using the Content Manager, you can create multiple instances of the BEA repository.

Best Practice: The Content Manager in WebLogic Portal provides a basic set of content-management capabilities tailored to a broad range of applications. If your site contains large amounts of content, you need enhanced control over the publishing and tagging of the content, or you have an existing content-management system, then WebLogic Portal is easily integrated with enterprise-scale content management systems.

Whether using the Content Manager or a third-party content-management system, WebLogic Portal provides a *Virtual Content Repository* (VCR), the top node in a content hierarchy, which maps the portal's content needs onto the defined content repositories. Personalization is accomplished by defining *types* of content and associating rules with how that content is presented to the desired user or group of users. Types, or *content schemas,* define the data necessary to match a target audience to the appropriate content. Types can be string, integer, Boolean, double, calendar, or binary, and include both restricted and unrestricted properties. Refer to the BEA WebLogic Portal documentation at *http://e-docs.bea.com/wlp/docs81/adminportal/help/CM_OV.html* for more information on types and content management.

Security and Tracking Services

WebLogic Portal relies on the underlying security services of WebLogic Server for authentication, authorization, auditing, logging, data privacy, and so on. Users and groups are configured using the WebLogic Security console with the administration environment and WebLogic Portal. Managing and administering portals offer unique challenges, such as tracking users who refuse to identify themselves or delegating some or all of the administrative tasks to a portal management team. WebLogic Portal 8.1 includes the ability to track anonymous users and supports a Delegated Administration framework for efficiently managing portals.

For security, WebLogic Portal has two roles: administrators and sers. *Administrators*, as you might imagine, are responsible for managing the overall portal, including content, users, and visitors, and are also responsible for building portals from the existing portal resources. Just as with WebLogic Server, portal administrators can be grouped. However, WebLogic Portal also permits specific roles to be delegated to all members of the administrator's group or any subgroup. For example, you may need to grant certain management tasks to the team responsible for the employee portal. *Delegated Administration* allows you to hierarchically assign these tasks, which include content management, user management, portal configuration, and the privilege to further delegate administration.

When tracking end users and visitors of the portal, WebLogic Portal utilizes a *Unified User Profile* (UUP). You can leverage existing user data, such as an existing LDAP store, from the UUP as well as specify additional portal-specific properties. Profile information, such as the user's social security number, geography, or job title, is then used to tailor or *personalize* the portal rendering. For example, all the users who reside in Birmingham, Alabama, can access weather, news, and college football information specific to their region. You can also deliver targeted marketing campaigns, e-mails, and discounts to this segment. Users are grouped into *user segments* based on dynamically assigned characteristics such as group membership, browser type, or profile values.

WebLogic Portal 8.1 includes a special type of user profile for the *anonymous user*. Many times, users will visit your site without actually registering. Capturing this information can allow you to encourage the visitor to return to your site and register. There are five profile types for anonymous users.

- Anonymous—If anonymous user tracking is disabled, then visitors to the portal who have not registered are considered *anonymous*.
- Trackable—Once you enable anonymous user tracking, any first-time visitor to your site will be considered a *trackable* user.
- Tracked—A trackable visitor who remains on your site for a specified time and has cookies enabled on his browser becomes a *tracked* user. A specific identifier is assigned and set in the cookie, and the visitor's interaction with your site is recorded and persisted. In addition, when a tracked user returns to your site, this persisted information is available and can be used for campaigns or advertisements.
- Registered—Once a tracked user registers with your site, he becomes a *registered* user, and his activities on your site, even when they were anonymous, are updated in their profile.
- Unknown—If WebLogic Portal cannot determine a user's status, then he is considered an *unknown* user.

You enable anonymous user tracking by configuring the `PortalServletFilter` within the `web.xml` file inside your Web application. The parameter `createAnonymousProfile` is set to `true` when you are tracking anonymous users. The following code segment represents a complete `web.xml` file with the `createAnonymousProfile` enabled:

```
<!-- Portal Servlet Filter, always required for Portal -->
<filter>
<filter-name> PortalServletFilter </filter-name>
<filter-class> com.bea.p13n.servlets.PortalServletFilter </filter-class>
<init-param>
<param-name>fireSessionLoginEvent</param-name>
<param-value>false</param-value>
<description> Option to fire SessionLoginEvent , defaults to false if not
set</description>
</init-param>
<init-param>
<param-name>createAnonymousProfile</param-name>
<param-value>true</param-value>
<description> Filter will create an anonymous profile for every session.
Defaults to true if not set</description>
</init-param>
<init-param>
<param-name>enableTrackedAnonymous</param-name>
<param-value>true</param-value>
<description> Option to track anonymous users , defaults to false if not
set. 'createAnonymousProfile' is ignored if this is true</description>
</init-param>
<init-param>
<param-name>trackedAnonymousVisitDuration</param-name>
<param-value>5</param-value>
<description> Length in seconds visitor must be on site before we start
tracking them . Defaults to 60 seconds if not set</description>
</init-param>
</filter>
```

WebLogic Portal Commerce Services

As part of a comprehensive portal solution, WebLogic Portal 8.1 includes a complete set of commerce services, which include order management, shopping cart, and packaged modules to interface with external shipping, payment, tax, discount, and product catalog. The commerce services in WebLogic Portal are packaged as a set of J2EE components, commerce APIs, and a set of JSP tags to the portal application and portal Web project.

To take advantage of the Portal's commerce capabilities, right-click over the Portal Application folder in WebLogic Workshop and select *Install ‡ Commerce Services*. This command adds commerce components, campaign management, utilities, and supporting files to your portal project. Next, you add the commerce JSP tags to your project by right-clicking over the Portal Web folder in WebLogic Workshop and choosing *Install ‡ Commerce Taglibs*.

WebLogic Portal Review

As with other sections in this chapter, the goal in these sections is to introduce you to WebLogic Portal. There is a great deal more information, and you should refer to the product documentation for more details. WebLogic Portal provides a dynamic, flexible environment for aggregating many applications and services into a single site, ties in enterprise content management, and includes robust management and administration utilities. By sharing the common services throughout WebLogic Platform, you have a consistent framework for delivering enterprise applications.

WebLogic Server 8.1

At the core of WebLogic Platform 8.1 is WebLogic Server. The rest of this book describes the powerful capabilities of WebLogic Server. This section points out how WebLogic Server is leveraged to provide WebLogic Platform enterprise-ready services, such as high availability, reliability, scalability, manageability, and security.

The various products within the Platform suite each utilize the J2EE-based runtime provided by WebLogic Server. For example, WebLogic Portal is made up of a series of J2EE modules, packaged into Web Archives (WAR files) and Enterprise Archives (EAR files). (See Chapter 14 for more information on packaging J2EE applications.) WebLogic Integration leverages Enterprise JavaBeans, the Java Messaging Service, RMI, JDBC, JMX, J2CA, all deployed as needed within running instances of WebLogic Server. In addition, WebLogic Platform depends on WebLogic Server for clustering, security, and management. The common infrastructure offered by the server lowers the cost of deploying and managing enterprise applications, reduces the complexity of distributed applications, and reduces the costs associated with integrating what would otherwise be disparate portal, Enterprise Application Integration (EAI), and application server products.

Configuring a WebLogic Platform, Integration, or Portal domain uses the same WebLogic Server configuration wizard as described in Chapter 12. Instead of selecting a WebLogic Server domain template, you would select a WebLogic Platform, WebLogic Integration, or WebLogic Portal domain. When you select one of these domain templates, WebLogic preloads all the classes, utilities, and application components that correspond to the Platform modules. Securing Platform applications relies on the underlying application server core services, and administering the applications can be done through WebLogic's Administration Console and exposed JMX APIs. Consistent tools, common core services, and a shared infrastructure all contribute to the lower complexity, lower cost of maintenance, and reduced risk delivered with WebLogic Platform.

WebLogic JRockit

WebLogic JRockit is a key component of WebLogic Platform, offering an optimized execution environment for Intel environments running the Windows and Linux operating systems. All the applications bundled in WebLogic Platform are certified and supported on JRockit 8.1. We provided a complete review of WebLogic JRockit in Chapters 14 and 17 and refer you to either section for more details on how JRockit can be leveraged and tuned for optimal performance and scalability.

WebLogic Platform Summary

In this chapter, we presented a brief introduction to the various components of WebLogic Platform 8.1. We included brief overviews of WebLogic Integration and WebLogic Portal, illustrated how WebLogic Workshop provides a consistent design and development tool across the entire platform, and how the components are deployed into WebLogic Server. We reviewed the benefits of a single, integrated platform for implementing enterprise applications, from the user interface to business processes, from the J2EE environment to EIS systems, from designing and modeling process flows to managing and monitoring production applications. As noted in the introduction, the goal of this chapter was to introduce you to WebLogic Platform. Much more information can be found on WebLogic Platform through the BEA developer's site at *http://dev2dev.bea.com*.

Web Services Overview

Web services allow distributed systems to share functionality. Applications have been exposing services for some time, but until recently interfaces and bindings were not described using a common language. Consumers of the services were expected to build their own consumption mechanism on a per-service basis specific to the message exchange mechanism defined by the provider of the service. The definition of Web services by mainstream standards bodies changed this. Now clients can expect to consume Web services using SOAP messaging as per the public contract described by a WSDL document. This allows consumers to define a single Web services consumption strategy for incorporation of functionality hosted by disparate systems.

The idea of exposing services providing logic and/or data to other applications or systems is not new. Historically, interoperability issues between applications have been addressed by the definition of a contract specific to the system exposing the service. Applications needing to leverage this functionality or data had to conform to the protocol (transport, language, platform) specified by the contract. This strategy introduced significant development activity per consumed service, since typically no two services could be consumed the same way. Some efforts were made to standardize this type of contract to ease the interoperability process, but were specific to J2EE or to CORBA or the like. These efforts failed ultimately because the solution still bound the participants to either a particular language, or a particular platform or transport.

Some of the interesting challenges faced by development teams involve requirements for incorporating functionality provided by internal or external systems into their applications. Rather than addressing each instance of this type of requirement with a separate solution, developers can define a single Web services consumption strategy to be applied in every instance.

A.1. Standards

Multiple organizations are involved in the definition of Web services standards. The Web Services Interoperability Organization (WS-I) includes in their listing of non-proprietary Web services specifications SOAP, a transport-independent message exchange format, WSDL, an XML-based description language for public contracts, and UDDI, a directory standard for dynamic discovery of Web services and their providers. A number of emerging standards are on the horizon that address issues like reliability and trust management. WebLogic Server implements a few of these emerging standards, as we see later in this section. This section is an introduction to some of the specifications of interest.

A.1.1. XML

SOAP messages and WSDL documents are built with XML. XML provides a straightforward way to indicate not only values, but also weighting of those values, a meaningful sort order, and other significant attributes.

XML Overview. Extensible Markup Language (XML) is a tag-based, textual representation of data. The nature of its popularity is two-fold: first, as a robust data-representation method, and second, as a language- and system-independent communications format.

XML allows data elements or types to be multi-dimensional; for example, instead of traditional name-value pair definitions, like so:

```
test.name=MyTest
test.type=Load
test.duration=15
othertest.name=BreakIt
othertest.type=Stress
othertest.duration=18
```

The data can be represented by defining a "test" element, and many instances of that element can be used. For example:

```
<?xml version="1.0"?>
<tasks>
     <test>
          <name>MyTest</name>
          <type>Load</type>
          <duration>15</duration>
     </test>
     <test>
          <name>BreakIt</name>
          <type>Stress</type>
          <duration>18</duration>
     </test>
</tasks>
```

XML attributes can be used in conjunction with elements to associate a single data value with that element.

```
<test priority="high"/>
```

versus

```
<test><priority>high</priority></test>
```

Attributes are used to represent simple data. Complex data should always be represented in an element.

DTDs. Document Type Definitions (DTDs) are used to enforce rules regarding data representation in XML documents. Allowable tags and tag nesting, as well as attributes, are specified by the DTD document.

The syntax of a DTD is similar to that of a grammar. Limiting the types of acceptable reasons for return to three specific reasons, for example, might be achieved by a DTD entry like this:

```
<!ELEMENT EndStatus (Passed|Failed|Incomplete)>
```

Associating a DTD with an XML file can be forced by either including or embedding the DTD in the XML file.

XML Schema. XML Schemas are an alternative to DTDs. One advantage of XML Schemas over DTDs is the support for more granular specifications. Since WSDL documents are in the form of XML Schemas, XML Schemas are of more interest to us than DTDs in this section.

Schema syntax is as follows:

```
<?xml version="1.0"?>
<xsd:schema xmlns:xsd=http://www.w3.org/2001/XMLSchema>

<xsd:element name="task" type="TaskType"/>

<xsd:complexType name="TaskType">
        <xsd:sequence>
            <xsd:element name="taskName" type="xsd:string"/>
            <xsd:element name="owner" type="Employee"/>
            <xsd:element name="dueDate" type="xsd:date"/>
            <xsd:element name="priority" type="xsd:string"/>
        </xsd:sequence>
</xsd:complexType>

<xsd:complexType name="Employee">
        <xsd:sequence>
                <xsd:element name="fname" type="xsd:string"/>
                <xsd:element name="lname" type="xsd:string"/>
                <xsd:element name="employeeID" type="xsd:Long"/>
                <xsd:element name="position" type="xsd:string"/>
                <xsd:element name="hireDate" type="xsd:date"/>
            </xsd:sequence>
        </xsd:compexType>
```

In this example, a Task element is defined as having a name, an owner of type Employee, a due date and a priority. An Employee has a name, an employee ID, a position and a hire date.

An XML document corresponding to the schema definition might be as follows:

```xml
<?xml version="1.0"?>
<task>
    <taskName>TestPlan</taskName>
    <owner>
        <Employee>
            <fname>Joseph</fname>
            <lname>Daniel</lname>
            <employeeID>156919</employeeID>
            <position>EngMgr</position>
            <hireDate>2000-01-09</hireDate>
        </Employee>
    </owner>
    <dueDate>2005-01-25</dueDate>
    <priority>high</priority>
</task>
```

XML Schema definitions are of particular interest to WebLogic Workshop users; the new XML-Beans mechanism allows XSD files to be dropped into a project via the Workshop IDE and, without any further mapping, accessed as a Bean in Java. It looks and acts like a Java type that maps perfectly to an XML schema that came in a WSDL.

To read more about XML Schema, see *http://www.w3.org/XML/Schema*.

A.1.1.2. WSDL

Consuming a Web service requires knowledge of what the service provides as well as the format of the data to be sent and received. This is described using the Web Service Description Language (WSDL). The configuration of the data the service expects to receive upon invocation and the data it expects to return in response is defined as part of the Web service's WSDL. The services exposed are indicated in the associated WSDL.

WSDL definitions are XML documents similar in form to an XML Schema. A WSDL document will contain elements that describe the Web service. These elements list the types of data available (**types**), the methods available for use (**messages** and **operations**), groupings of these methods (**port types**), specifications for accessing these method groupings (**binding**), and where the service is made available (**ports**). The types, messages, operations, port types, bindings, and ports are made available at the URI specified in the **service** element of the WSDL.

Although WSDLs can be used with any message exchange format or network protocol, the Web services specifications address WSDLs with SOAP messages over HTTP(S). Components of a WSDL can be mapped to UDDI entities, facilitating the exposure of service descriptions via UDDI lookup.

Building a WSDL is one of the more esoteric tasks related to Web services. Fortunately, WebLogic Workshop and other available tools read and write WSDL files, so most Web services creators will not have to build WSDL documents from scratch. For a simple example, consider a Web service called Example.jws (a WLS Web service class) with a single method that when invoked sets a global variable, like so:

```java
public void SetVar() {
    toggleIt = "True";
}
```

The associated WSDL generated by Workshop would look like this:

```xml
<?xml version="1.0" encoding="utf-8"?>
<!-- @editor-info:link autogen="true" source="Example.jws" -->
<definitions xmlns="http://schemas.xmlsoap.org/wsdl/" xmlns:conv="http://
www.openuri.org/2002/04/soap/conversation/" xmlns:cw="http://www.openuri.org/
2002/04/wsdl/conversation/" xmlns:http="http://schemas.xmlsoap.org/wsdl/http/
" xmlns:jms="http://www.openuri.org/2002/04/wsdl/jms/" xmlns:mime="http://
schemas.xmlsoap.org/wsdl/mime/" xmlns:s="http://www.w3.org/2001/XMLSchema"
xmlns:s0="http://www.openuri.org/" xmlns:soap="http://schemas.xmlsoap.org/
wsdl/soap/" xmlns:soapenc="http://schemas.xmlsoap.org/soap/encoding/"
targetNamespace="http://www.openuri.org/">
  <types>
    <s:schema elementFormDefault="qualified" targetNamespace="http://
www.openuri.org/" xmlns:s="http://www.w3.org/2001/XMLSchema">
      <s:element name="SetVar">
        <s:complexType>
          <s:sequence/>
        </s:complexType>
      </s:element>
      <s:element name="SetVarResponse">
        <s:complexType>
          <s:sequence/>
        </s:complexType>
      </s:element>
    </s:schema>

  </types>
  <message name="SetVarSoapIn">
    <part name="parameters" element="s0:SetVar"/>
  </message>
  <message name="SetVarSoapOut">
    <part name="parameters" element="s0:SetVarResponse"/>
  </message>
  <message name="SetVarHttpGetIn"/>
  <message name="SetVarHttpGetOut"/>
  <message name="SetVarHttpPostIn"/>
  <message name="SetVarHttpPostOut"/>
  <portType name="ExampleSoap">
    <operation name="SetVar">
      <input message="s0:SetVarSoapIn"/>
      <output message="s0:SetVarSoapOut"/>
    </operation>
  </portType>
  <portType name="ExampleHttpGet">
    <operation name="SetVar">
      <input message="s0:SetVarHttpGetIn"/>
      <output message="s0:SetVarHttpGetOut"/>
    </operation>
  </portType>
```

```
  <portType name="ExampleHttpPost">
    <operation name="SetVar">
      <input message="s0:SetVarHttpPostIn"/>
      <output message="s0:SetVarHttpPostOut"/>
    </operation>
  </portType>
  <binding name="ExampleSoap" type="s0:ExampleSoap">
    <soap:binding transport="http://schemas.xmlsoap.org/soap/http"
style="document"/>
    <operation name="SetVar">
      <soap:operation soapAction="http://www.openuri.org/SetVar" style="document"/>
      <input>
        <soap:body use="literal"/>
      </input>
      <output>
        <soap:body use="literal"/>
      </output>
    </operation>
  </binding>
  <binding name="ExampleHttpGet" type="s0:ExampleHttpGet">
    <http:binding verb="GET"/>
    <operation name="SetVar">
      <http:operation location="/SetVar"/>
      <input>
        <http:urlEncoded/>
      </input>
      <output/>
    </operation>
  </binding>
  <binding name="ExampleHttpPost" type="s0:ExampleHttpPost">
    <http:binding verb="POST"/>
    <operation name="SetVar">
      <http:operation location="/SetVar"/>
      <input>
        <mime:content type="application/x-www-form-urlencoded"/>
      </input>
      <output/>
    </operation>
  </binding>
  <service name="Example">
    <port name="ExampleSoap" binding="s0:ExampleSoap">
      <soap:address location="http://localhost:7001/TestWebSvc/Example.jws"/>
    </port>
    <port name="ExampleHttpGet" binding="s0:ExampleHttpGet">
      <http:address location="http://localhost:7001/TestWebSvc/Example.jws"/>
    </port>
    <port name="ExampleHttpPost" binding="s0:ExampleHttpPost">
      <http:address location="http://localhost:7001/TestWebSvc/Example.jws"/>
    </port>
  </service>
</definitions>
```

Notice the outermost `<definitions>` element that defines a grouping of related services. Message contents are specified within `<types>` elements. Contents can be defined as low-level data types, such as float, double, string, int, date, and so on. The format of the data in the messages is specified in the `<message>` element. The messages defined above are grouped into a one logical procedure in the `<portType>` element. Notice the namespace prefix in front of the elements. This explicitly makes the relationship to messages. The `<binding>` element describes how the procedure described in the `<portType>` will be conveyed using SOAP. The transport protocol is specified here as HTTP. SOAP over HTTP requires the definition of a SoapAction for use in HTTP headers. Thus mechanisms examining the HTTP message headers will be able to handle messages with SOAP payloads appropriately. The `<service>` element specifies the URI for invoking the service.

WebLogic Workshop allows you to generate a WSDL document from an associated JWS file (the Java class providing the service you are exposing). Generating a WSDL using Workshop is as simple as right-clicking on the JWS file in the Application pane and selecting the "Generate WSDL File" option from the drop-down menu. You will see a corresponding WSDL file name appear in the Application pane linked to your JWS file.

WSDL files generated by Workshop specify `localhost` as the service location, so you will want to edit the WSDL file to reflect the appropriate exposure information.

The WSDL defines XML data types that must correspond to Java types. The XMLBeans mechanism included with Workshop facilitates the creation of the Java code. After dropping XSD files into a project using Workshop, Java beans that look like the Java types mapping to the XML data types in a WSDL are generated and can be accessed directly.

A.1.1.3. UDDI

Users can be explicitly made aware of a Web service and provided with the associated WSDL document, or alternately, users can lookup available Web services via the Universal Description, Discovery and Integration (UDDI) protocol. UDDI is a mechanism for finding Web services via queries against a published set of metadata.

The UDDI specification facilitates the mapping of service providers and WSDLs to UDDI structures. This will allow for dynamic discovery of Web services as industries standardize service types. Currently, UDDI directories are used by human users rather than applications until enough industry support makes usage more realistic.

It is anticipated that UDDI will become quite popular and widely-used in the future. For more information about UDDI, visit `http://www.uddi.org`.

A.1.1.4. SOAP

The Simple Object Access Protocol (SOAP) defines how XML messages are sent between heterogeneous environments, travel over multiple protocols, and pass unchanged through proxies and routers. This procedure is at the core of Web services.

A SOAP message is simply an XML document (you can think of a SOAP message as an XML version of a remote procedure call). The body of the message contains an element used for data exchanged between sender and receiver. The SOAP message may also contain a header element, although it is not required. A simple SOAP message example is as follows:

```
<SOAP:Envelope
  xmlns:SOAP=http://schemas.xmlsoap.org/soap/envelope/
    <SOAP:Body>
```

```
    <GetNewAmount xmlns="http://namespaces.example-currency-
rates.com">

        <amount>5.1234</amount>

        <currency>Dollar</currency>

    </GetNewAmount>

  </SOAP:Body>

</SOAP:Envelope>
```

In this example, notice that a currency conversion is being requested—from 5.1234 of some unit to the US Dollar. This message would have been the payload associated with an HTTP (or other) request or response.

In addition to the SOAP body, the envelope can also contain a Header section. A SOAP header can pass unchanged through logical and physical route stops, making it the ideal place to store information like conversation IDs and callback locations, security-related information like digital signatures, or even route-specific information. HTTP intermediaries will not look at or alter the SOAP header, since it's all just part of the payload. This makes the SOAP Header the logical place for any extensions to SOAP. Emerging standards like WS-Security, WS-Reliability and WS-Policy are extensions to SOAP that leverage the Header.

SOAP exchanges are typically request-response format, although more complex interactions are supported by the specification. A SOAP request is sent to invoke a specific procedure in anticipation of a precise response. Emerging standards allow support for asynchronous exchange of SOAP messages, and that mean the response you get might be a simple acknowledgement of your request to be followed later by the requested data.

The expected usage of SOAP is much like that of RPC-type requests. Supporting requests in RPC-style introduces some data format restrictions not typically found in XML documents. Any such restrictions would be reflected in the XML schema associated with the SOAP message.

For accessibility reasons, SOAP messages are typically sent over HTTP in a MIME encoded package, although SOAP is not tied to a specific protocol. WebLogic Workshop can generate SOAP messages to be sent over JMS as well as over HTTP, for example. SOAP over SMTP is supported by some distributions; for example, Apache's SOAP distribution supports SOAP over the SMTP transport. The thing to remember is that SOAP is not bound to any transport, making it a flexible and portable component of your interoperability strategy.

A.2.   Workshop's Security Features for Web Services

The general security concerns relating to Web services are the same as for any distributed functionality. How will you determine who is using your service? How will you verify the appropriateness of this use? What measures will you take to ensure message integrity and privacy?

Web services have traditionally relied on transport-based security (like SSL) to alleviate privacy concerns. Web service implementers use J2EE-based security, requiring users to have roles defined in a profiling system, or a physical layer of security (firewalls, and so on), or some combination of both. The security mechanisms based on emerging standards outlined in this section simplify the process of securing Web services.

A.2.1. Role-based Security

Workshop's conceptual security model allows tasks to be defined on both developer and administrator levels. A developer can populate project-level lists of role names, declare security settings at the class or method level, implement security programmatically, and so on. An administrator would establish accepted authentication credentials, map those credentials to users, assign users to groups, and map users and groups to roles.

These roles can be applied to users of Web services. By requiring the consumer to pass an encrypted username as part of the SOAP message in the request, your Web services can leverage these role bindings just as any application would.

You can specify class or method level role-based settings in the source view of your Web service. Adding the @common:security roles-allowed annotation allows you to specify authorized user roles for that class or method. The roles you specify using this annotation are automatically included in the appropriate deployment descriptors for the EJB created when Workshop compiles your Web service (JWS) file.

You can specify a role-based restriction on all the methods in a class by using a class level annotation, like so:

```
/**
 * Allow users of type QA to access all methods in this class
 *
 * @common:security roles-allowed="QA"
 */
public class LaunchTests implements com.bea.jws.WebService
{
     public String testScript()
     {
         // execute tests
         return "Tests Initiated";
     }
}
....
```

You can also place a role restriction on the method level by including the annotation in the comment preceding the method.

A.2.2. WS-Security

WS-Security is an emerging OASIS standard for message-based security. By using SOAP headers to carry security information rather than using transport-level security, WS-Security addresses authentication, message integrity (ensuring that the message hasn't been altered in route—it incorporates an XML digital signature specification), and message privacy (with XML encryption). Messages can travel over multiple protocols and can pass unchanged through proxies and routers. The version of Workshop introduced with Platform 8.1 supports this.

Workshop uses underlying WLS mechanisms to read and write SOAP headers and message certificates and map to user accounts. Signed and/or encrypted messages are supported.

Using WS-Security in WebLogic Workshop requires a couple of things. First, a WS-Security policy file (WSSE file) must be created and associated with the corresponding JWS file. The policy file will have a .wsse extension. You can create this file by creating a new file of type "WS-Security Policy File" using Workshop. The name of this policy file must be added to the JWS file in annotations like this:

```
/**
 * @jws:ws-security-service file="NewPolicyFile.wsse"
 * @jws:ws-security-callback file="NewPolicyFile.wsse"
 */
```

The policy file itself will specify what security requirements apply to incoming SOAP messages and any special additions to be made to outgoing SOAP messages (to comply with any security requirements of the requestor). The policy file is an XML document containing tags corresponding to the requirements. For example, to specify that incoming SOAP messages must include a user-name, the <token> element would be used:

```
<?xml version="1.0" ?>
<wsSecurityPolicy xsi:schemaLocation="WSSecurity-policy.xsd"
    xmlns="http://www.bea.com/2003/03/wsse/config"
    xmlns:xsi="http://www.w3.org/2001/XMLSchema-instance">

    <wsSecurityIn>
        <token tokenType="username"/>
    </wsSecurityIn>
</wsSecurityPolicy>
```

In this case, you would want to specify that the username be encrypted by using the <encryptionRequired> element as well. The Workshop Help pages provide a full listing of tags available for use in WSSE policy files.

A.3. Synchronous Versus Asynchronous Conversations

Synchronous conversation is the customary method of interaction between systems. In synchronous conversations, a request is sent to an application or system and the process blocks until the response is received. In many cases, this approach is fitting. In cases where the action requested is complex or dependent on yet another system, or in cases where the action requested is to be performed at some time in the future, asynchronous conversations should be considered.

A.3.1 Characteristics

Asynchronous Web services allow the consumer to get an immediate acknowledgement from the service. The consumer will get a corresponding full response at some time in the future, either as a result of a subsequent request or dynamically from the service. This means that some method of identifying subsequent communications as being part of the same conversation must be defined. The other issue to be considered is how to maintain state during the activity associated with a single conversation. You don't want to have to pass all data of interest back and forth in each request or response within a conversation. The good news is that setting up your Web service to support asynchrony is fairly straightforward using Workshop.

Workshop handles conversation management for you. It allows you to specify that methods and callbacks are part of a particular conversation. To assign methods in your Web service to a conversation, toggle to the Design view and select the method that will start the conversation. Go to the Properties window and select the 'start' phase attribute from the conversation property.

Do the same for each subsequent method or callback in the conversation, selecting 'continue' as the phase attribute. For the final method in the conversation, set the phase attribute to 'finish'. If no conversation phase is assigned to a method in your Web service, the default value of 'none' will be applied. This indicates that the method is not within the scope of the conversation.

The client request for each phase of the conversation will a corresponding header element in the SOAP header. For example, the <StartHeader> would be included in the SOAP request for a method you've set to "start" the conversation. This header includes <conversationID> and <callbackLocation> elements. The <ContinueHeader> and <CallbackHeader> elements would contain just the conversation ID, since the callback location was sent with the initial request.

Once you have identified the methods in a conversation, Workshop will maintain state data by serializing the member variables of your Web service and persisting the serialized object. This means that your member variables will need to be serializable, if they are not by default (as with primitives and corresponding objects).

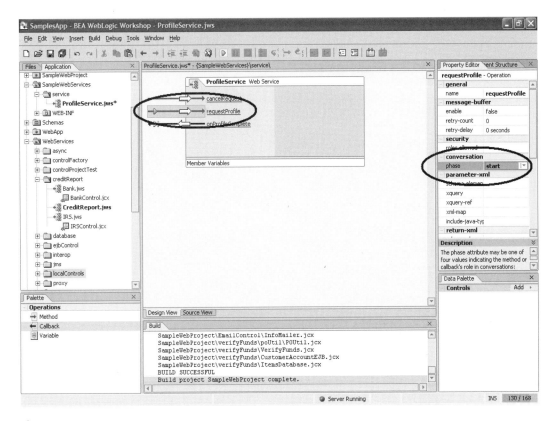

Figure A–1
Define a method as the start of a conversation in WebLogic Workshop

The nature of the methods included in your conversation will vary depending upon the service you are providing. Defining a callback method in your service allows your service to respond to the consumer via this method once your processing is complete and the full response is ready. The consumer would indicate the callback location in the header of the SOAP request sent to invoke the conversation, so your callback method will know where to send its response. If a client is unable to receive callbacks, you can define a polling interface as part of your service. This could be a set of methods for the consumer to invoke to check the readiness of the final response from your service.

It is important to include exception handling in your Web service design. If you are planning to use asynchrony and expect WebLogic Workshop to maintain state, understand that the serialization and storage of your member variables will not take place if an exception is thrown from a method. If an exception is thrown, you should end the conversation and notify the consumer of the status. The onException callback handler is available for handling exceptions thrown from callbacks.

The conversation ID convention described above is WebLogic-specific, so if the consumer of your Web service is not WebLogic-based, special considerations must be made for conversations.

A.3.2 Buffering

The asynchronous conversational activity described above is enabled through the use of message buffers. Message buffers can be added to the methods or callbacks of your service, as long as the return type is void and the member variables are serializable. When you buffer a message, WebLogic will return an immediate acknowledgement to a client before invoking the associated method. Meanwhile, the message is buffered on the server (locally). This allows the client to continue processing while the Web service performs the requested action. Message buffers can also be added to callbacks. This allows you to continue to process without waiting on a response from a client receiving the callback.

Methods or callbacks with message buffers must return `void`. No other value can be returned since WebLogic does not process the method before returning the acknowledgement.

Adding a message buffer to a particular method is as simple as selecting the method in Workshop's Design view, then setting the message-buffer property to 'enabled' in the Properties pane. You can also specify a maximum retry count as well as the delay between retries.

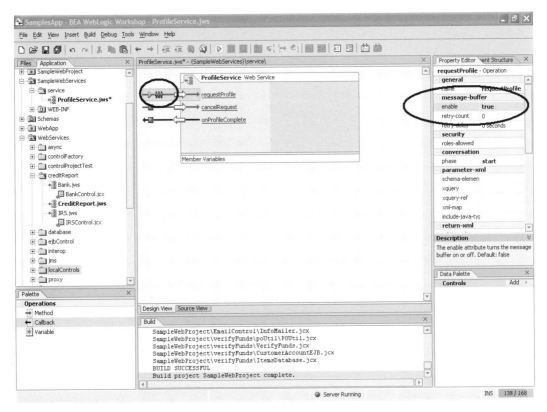

Figure A-2
Enable conversations in WebLogic Workshop

A.3.3 Callbacks

When designing an asynchronous Web service, you must decide how to handle the post-acknowledgement communication with the consumer. One approach is to define a set of methods to be used for polling. In this scenario, the consumer would periodically invoke these methods to request the full response from your service. When your service was ready, it could return the requested data in response to one of these methods. A more elegant approach is to define a callback method if potential clients will support it.

A callback method initiates a request to the consumer of your service with a message containing the results of your processing. The callback is explicitly invoked from within the method associated with the service. At a high level, the steps leading up to a callback being made to the client include the consumer sending a request for a service, the corresponding method (with message buffering) being invoked and an acknowledgement being sent in response to the client's request, and the method invoking the callback once processing is complete. This scenario assumes that the <StartHeader> included in the original SOAP message contained a <callbackLocation> element defining the destination for the callback. Subsequent messages from the consumer might be part of the same conversation; a callback does not necessarily correspond to the end of a conversation.

To add a callback using Workshop, toggle to the Design view of your JWS file. In the Palette pane under Operations, find the Callback icon and drag it into the Web service pane and rename it.

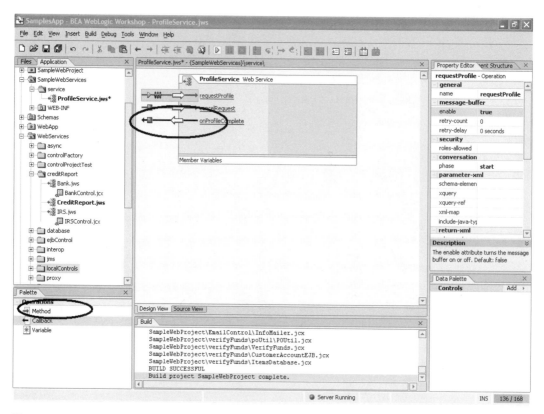

Figure A-3
Create Web Service callback in WebLogic Workshop

To customize the callback, click on the callback name to get to the source code. Then you can change the return type and specify parameters to the callback method.

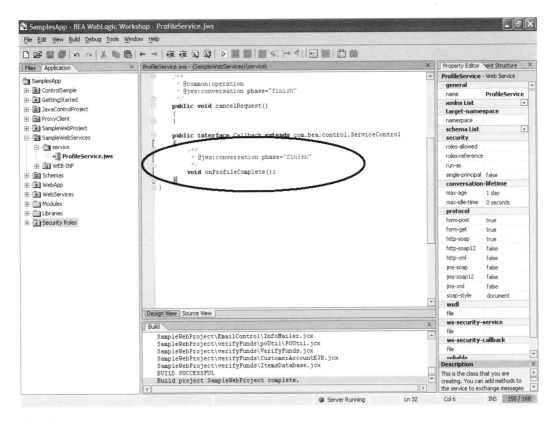

Figure A–4
Customize the parameters and types of callbacks

You will want to add the callback to the same conversation to which the calling method belongs. To do this, select the callback method in the Design view, go to the Properties pane and assign a Conversation phase (either 'continue' or 'finish').

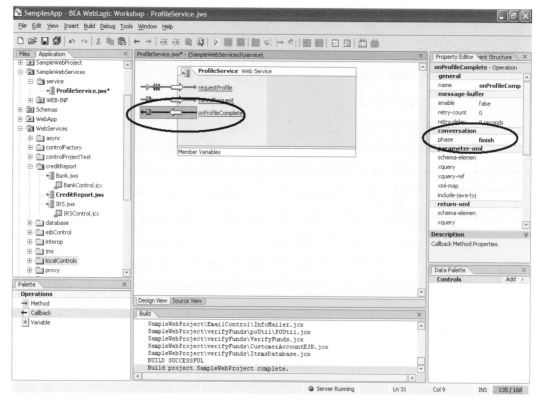

Figure A–5
Set Callback method to finish conversation in WebLogic Workshop

A.4 Web Services and J2EE

J2EE implementations like WLS 8.1 facilitate enterprise-level integration between applications and data sources. With the specifications defined as part of J2EE 1.4, they are also positioned to support Web services offerings.

The J2EE 1.4 specification defines robust support for Web services. It defines the JAX-RPC 1.1 API to facilitate Web service development, and the Web Services for J2EE specification including requirements for deployment. Until J2EE 1.4 is formally released, the JAX-RPC API is available for use in J2EE 1.3 environments with the downloadable Java Web Services Developer Pack.

JAX-RPC (Java API for XML-based RPC) allows developers to use an RPC-like programming model to define servlet-based endpoints (services) or EJB endpoints. It also provides mapping mechanisms between Java and WSDLs. From one Java interface, you can generate a corresponding WSDL descriptor and the associated SOAP serialization. On the other hand, you could start with a WSDL descriptor and generate skeleton code using this mapping. JAX-RPC leverages SAAJ (SOAP with Attachements API for Java) to manage SOAP message content through a simple object model.

Implementing JAX-RPC based Web services from scratch requires some J2EE expertise.   The WebLogic Server 8.1 Web service features shield the developer from the specifics of JAX-RPC while leveraging its component-based Web service development support.   WLS 8.1 supports the HTTP transport for Web services through java.net.   XML parsing and transformation is handled through JAXP, SOAP and WSDL processing is managed through a fairly complete implementation of JAX-RPC and SAAJ, and a proprietary UDDI mechanism is in place for support of dynamic discovery.

In WebLogic 8.1, you can define a Web service endpoint as a Java Web Service (JWS) class.   This is basically a servlet that processes Web service requests and produces an HTTP response with a SOAP payload, as described in the WebLogic Workshop chapter of this book.   Other endpoints might include a Web service EJB or other backend component.   Building Web service components with WebLogic Workshop using the underlying WebLogic Server JAX-RPC implementation leverages one of the most powerful Web service offerings in this space.

A.5   Using WebLogic Workshop to Build a Web Service

Creating a Web service using WebLogic Workshop usually starts in the Design View pane.   You can start by creating a servlet endpoint in the form of a Java Web Service (JWS) file in a folder within your project.

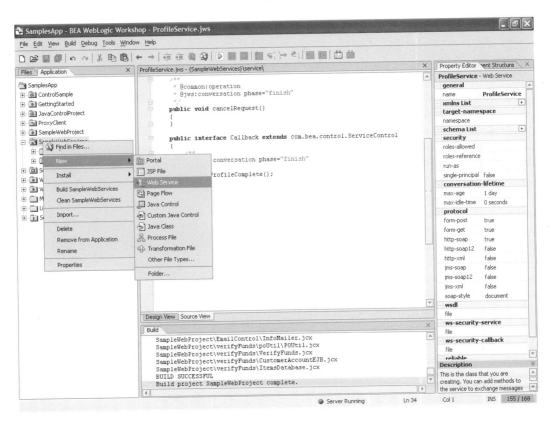

Figure A–6
Create a new Java Web Service in WebLogic Workshop

You can add methods to the JWS file and specify their parameters while still in the Design View of the IDE. You can also add Controls to your service at this time (make sure to handle callbacks from these Controls if they are asynchronous).

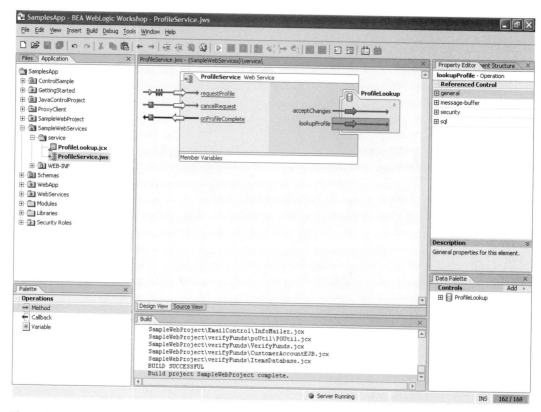

Figure A–7
Add control to Java Web Service in WebLogic Workshop

If your Web service will support asynchrony, you can add callbacks to the service.

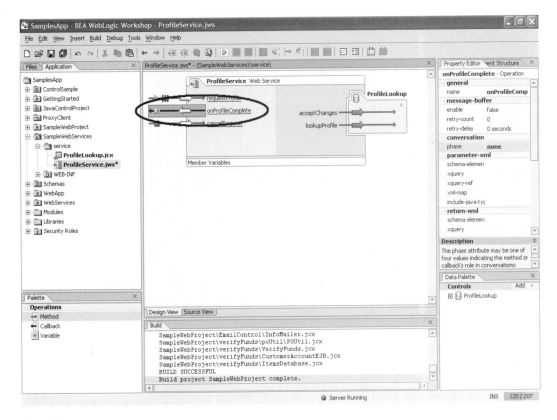

Figure A–8
Add callback to Java Web Service

If your Web service is conversational, note that in the Design View.

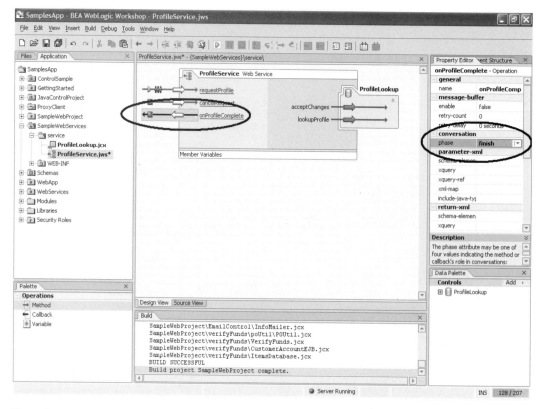

Figure A–9
Set conversational state in Java Web Service Callback

We have now defined the public contract for our Web service without writing Java or XML code. Toggling to Source View, you can fill in the method outlines with Java code.

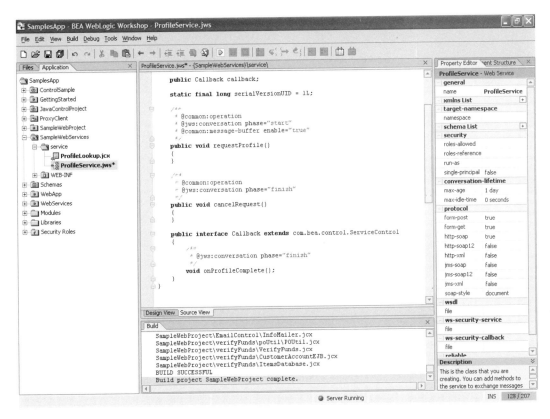

Figure A–10
Provide code to define Web Services

WebLogic Workshop also provides a test harness for your Web service called the Test View, which runs in a browser. Using Test View, you can look at the XML your service returns to a consumer.

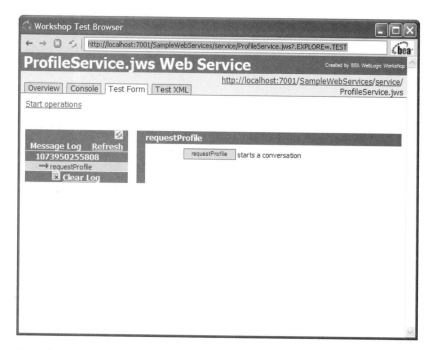

Figure A-11
WebLogic Workshop Test View for Java Web Services

Deploying a Web service is just like deploying any other application on WLS 8.1. You package the application as an EAR file and deploy it to a WLS 8.1 environment. Deployment complexity will depend on the nature of your production environment. The good news is that you can follow the deployment strategy of any other application in your environment.

A.6   Putting It All Together

Web services provide standards-based access to functionality or data, and are typically accessed programmatically by other applications. WebLogic Server 8.1 supports the WS-I Web service stack, including SOAP 1.1, WSDL 1.1, UDDI 2.0, and XML Schema 1.0. The complexity of the standard Java APIs for Web services (JAX-RPC, SAAJ, JAXP) is hidden from developers by the WebLogic Workshop programming model.

A.7   References

The SOAP and WSDL standards are defined by the World Wide Web Consortium or W3C. The W3C homepage is: http://www.w3c.org.

The working body that defines the UDDI standard is OASIS. The OASIS homepage is http://www.oasis-open.org/home/index.php.

The specification for HTTP is available as an RFC. HTTP 1.1 is available at: ftp://ftp.isi.edu/in-notes/rfc2616.txt

The content-types used by HTTP are defined in the RFC Multipurpose Internet Mail Extensions (MIME) Part Two: Media Types. This document is available at: ftp://ftp.isi.edu/in-notes/rfc2046.txt

The BEA WebLogic Server 8.1 documentation on Building Web Services can be found at: http://e-docs.bea.com/workshop/docs81/doc/en/core/index.html.

index

A

Actions:
    JavaBeans, 130–136
    JSPs, 127–130
        `jsp:forward` action, 128–129
        `jsp:include` action, 128
        `jsp:plugin` action, 129–130
        `jsp:text` action, 130

`addDateHeader()`, 31

`addHeader()`, 31

`addIntHeader()`, 31

Adjudication provider, 408

Administration, WebLogic Server 8.1, 374–380
    monitoring via JMX MBeans, 378–380
    overview, 375–378
    security, 420–430

Administration Console, 380

Administrative APIs, 381

Administrative tools, WebLogic Server 8.1:
    Administration Console, 380
    administrative APIs, 381
    command-line scripts, 380
    WLShell scripting tool, 381–383

Administrators, 568

Agents, JMX, 374

Application deployment, 454–455
    infrastructure components in, 457–459
    load testing/quality assurance tools, 458–459
    process, 457–462
    security considerations in, 455
    stages in, 459–462
        architecture development/process planning, 459–460
        production, 461
        staging/testing, 461
        test development, 460–461
    typical architecture, 454–455

versioning systems, 457–458

Application integration (AI) adapters, 559

`application` scope, 116

Application security, 397–431
    Secure Sockets Layer (SSL), 400–402
        certificate authorities, 401
        commercial certificate authorities, 401
        digital certificates, 401
        encryption, 402
        public key encryption, 400–401
        symmetric key encryption, 400
    security technology overview, 397–402
        auditing, 399
        authentication, 398
        authorization, 398
        firewalls, 399
        logging, 399
        policies, 399
        roles, 399
        users and groups, 398

Application View Controls, 559

`application.xml`, 481–482

Architecture development/process planning, 459–460

Asynchronous conversations, 522–524

Attribute change events, 60–61

`attributeAdded()`, 61
    `HttpSessionAttributeListener`, 78

`attributeRemoved()`, 61
    `HttpSessionAttributeListener`, 78

`attributeReplaced()`, 61
    `HttpSessionAttributeListener`, 78

Auditing, 399

Auditing provider, 407

Authentication, 398
    HTTP authentication types, 415–416

Authentication provider, 407

Authorization, 398

597

Company's only obligation under these limited warranties is, at the Company's option, return of the warranted item for a refund of any amounts paid by you or replacement of the item. Any replacement of SOFTWARE or media under the warranties shall not extend the original warranty period. The limited warranty set forth above shall not apply to any SOFTWARE which the Company determines in good faith has been subject to misuse, neglect, improper installation, repair, alteration, or damage by you. EXCEPT FOR THE EXPRESSED WARRANTIES SET FORTH ABOVE, THE COMPANY DISCLAIMS ALL WARRANTIES, EXPRESS OR IMPLIED, INCLUDING WITHOUT LIMITATION, THE IMPLIED WARRANTIES OF MERCHANTABILITY AND FITNESS FOR A PARTICULAR PURPOSE. EXCEPT FOR THE EXPRESS WARRANTY SET FORTH ABOVE, THE COMPANY DOES NOT WARRANT, GUARANTEE, OR MAKE ANY REPRESENTATION REGARDING THE USE OR THE RESULTS OF THE USE OF THE SOFTWARE IN TERMS OF ITS CORRECTNESS, ACCURACY, RELIABILITY, CURRENTNESS, OR OTHERWISE.

IN NO EVENT, SHALL THE COMPANY OR ITS EMPLOYEES, AGENTS, SUPPLIERS, OR CONTRACTORS BE LIABLE FOR ANY INCIDENTAL, INDIRECT, SPECIAL, OR CONSEQUENTIAL DAMAGES ARISING OUT OF OR IN CONNECTION WITH THE LICENSE GRANTED UNDER THIS AGREEMENT, OR FOR LOSS OF USE, LOSS OF DATA, LOSS OF INCOME OR PROFIT, OR OTHER LOSSES, SUSTAINED AS A RESULT OF INJURY TO ANY PERSON, OR LOSS OF OR DAMAGE TO PROPERTY, OR CLAIMS OF THIRD PARTIES, EVEN IF THE COMPANY OR AN AUTHORIZED REPRESENTATIVE OF THE COMPANY HAS BEEN ADVISED OF THE POSSIBILITY OF SUCH DAMAGES. IN NO EVENT SHALL LIABILITY OF THE COMPANY FOR DAMAGES WITH RESPECT TO THE SOFTWARE EXCEED THE AMOUNTS ACTUALLY PAID BY YOU, IF ANY, FOR THE SOFTWARE.

SOME JURISDICTIONS DO NOT ALLOW THE LIMITATION OF IMPLIED WARRANTIES OR LIABILITY FOR INCIDENTAL, INDIRECT, SPECIAL, OR CONSEQUENTIAL DAMAGES, SO THE ABOVE LIMITATIONS MAY NOT ALWAYS APPLY. THE WARRANTIES IN THIS AGREEMENT GIVE YOU SPECIFIC LEGAL RIGHTS AND YOU MAY ALSO HAVE OTHER RIGHTS WHICH VARY IN ACCORDANCE WITH LOCAL LAW.

ACKNOWLEDGMENT

YOU ACKNOWLEDGE THAT YOU HAVE READ THIS AGREEMENT, UNDERSTAND IT, AND AGREE TO BE BOUND BY ITS TERMS AND CONDITIONS. YOU ALSO AGREE THAT THIS AGREEMENT IS THE COMPLETE AND EXCLUSIVE STATEMENT OF THE AGREEMENT BETWEEN YOU AND THE COMPANY AND SUPERSEDES ALL PROPOSALS OR PRIOR AGREEMENTS, ORAL, OR WRITTEN, AND ANY OTHER COMMUNICATIONS BETWEEN YOU AND THE COMPANY OR ANY REPRESENTATIVE OF THE COMPANY RELATING TO THE SUBJECT MATTER OF THIS AGREEMENT.

Should you have any questions concerning this Agreement or if you wish to contact the Company for any reason, please contact in writing at the address below.

Robin Short
Prentice Hall PTR
One Lake Street
Upper Saddle River, New Jersey 07458